sixth edition

Assessment
in Counseling
Procedures and Practices

Danica G. Hays

AMERICAN COUNSELING
ASSOCIATION
6101 Stevenson Avenue, Suite 600
Alexandria, VA 22304
www.counseling.org

sixth edition

Assessment in Counseling
Procedures and Practices

American Counseling Association
6101 Stevenson Avenue, Suite 600 • Alexandria, VA 22304

Associate Publisher	Carolyn C. Baker
Digital and Print Development Editor	Nancy Driver
Senior Production Manager	Bonny E. Gaston
Production Coordinator	Karen Thompson
Copy Editor	Beth Ciha

Cover and text design by Bonny E. Gaston

Library of Congress Cataloging-in-Publication Data
Names: Hays, Danica G., author.
Title: Assessment in counseling : Procedures and practices / Danica G. Hays.
Description: Sixth edition. | Alexandria, VA : American Counseling Association, [2017] | Includes bibliographical references and index.
Identifiers: LCCN 2016048742 | ISBN 9781556203688 (pbk. : alk. paper)
Subjects: LCSH: Psychological tests. | Counseling.
Classification: LCC BF176 .H66 2017 | DDC 150.28/7—dc23 LC record available at https://lccn.loc.gov/2016048742

For Chris—my partner, best friend, and colleague.

For Charlotte and Gracie—my independent, smart, and funny daughters.

Thank you for making everything more meaningful.

Table of Contents

Preface   xi

Council for Accreditation of Counseling
and Related Educational Programs 2016 Standards
and Corresponding Chapters   xiii

Acknowledgments   xv

About the Author   xvii

Section I
Foundations of Assessment in Counseling

Chapter 1

Use of Assessment in Counseling   3

   Introduction to Assessment   3

   Key Assessment Terms   4

   Purpose of Assessment in Counseling   6

   History of Assessment   9

   Assessment Usage in Counseling Settings   15

   Key Questions for Selecting Assessments   21

   Chapter Summary   23

   Review Questions   25

   Resources for Further Learning   25

Chapter 2

The Assessment Process   27

   Types of Assessment Methods   27

   An Overview of the Assessment Process   31

   Monitoring Client Progress and Evaluating Counseling Outcomes   39

   Chapter Summary   45

   Review Questions   45

   Resources for Further Learning   45

Chapter 3

Ethical, Legal, and Professional Considerations in Assessment 47
Standards and Guidelines for Evaluating Tests and Test Usage 48
Key Ethical and Legal Considerations in Assessment 54
Professional Issues in Assessment 60
Chapter Summary 64
Review Questions 64
Resources for Further Learning 65

Chapter 4

Multicultural Considerations in Assessment 67
Multicultural Counseling Competency and Assessment 68
Fairness and Cultural Bias in Assessment 69
Cultural Factors in Assessment 71
Assessment and Gender 78
Assessment and Race, Ethnicity, and Socioeconomic Variables 81
Culture-Fair Tests 84
Dynamic Testing 87
Disability and Assessment 89
Assessment of Older Adults 92
Chapter Summary 95
Review Questions 96
Resources for Further Learning 96

Section II

Basic Statistical and Measurement Considerations

Chapter 5

Measurement Concepts 99
Scales of Measurement 99
Reliability 101
Validity 108
Assessment Development 114
Chapter Summary 116
Review Questions 116
Resources for Further Learning 117

Chapter 6

Understanding and Transforming Raw Scores 119
Raw Scores 120
Measures of Central Tendency 122
Measures of Variability 123
Characteristics of Data Distributions 124
Norms and Ranks 126
Standard Scores 128
Standard Error of Measurement 131
Chapter Summary 133
Review Questions 133
Resources for Further Learning 133

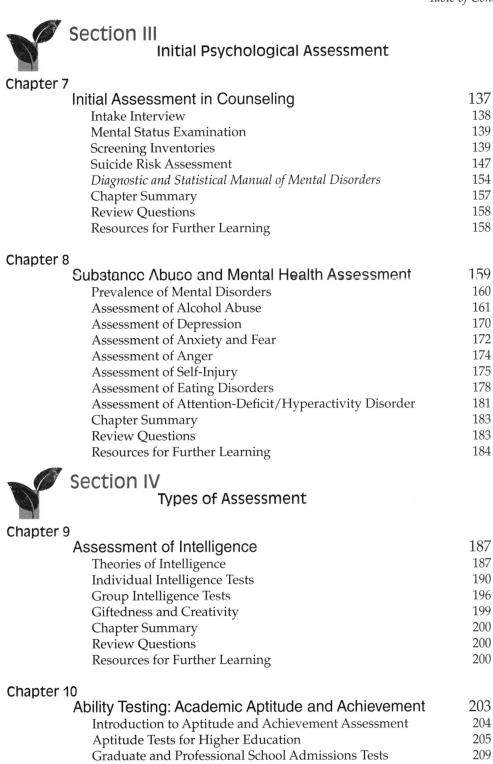

Section III
Initial Psychological Assessment

Chapter 7

Initial Assessment in Counseling 137
Intake Interview 138
Mental Status Examination 139
Screening Inventories 139
Suicide Risk Assessment 147
Diagnostic and Statistical Manual of Mental Disorders 154
Chapter Summary 157
Review Questions 158
Resources for Further Learning 158

Chapter 8

Substance Abuse and Mental Health Assessment 159
Prevalence of Mental Disorders 160
Assessment of Alcohol Abuse 161
Assessment of Depression 170
Assessment of Anxiety and Fear 172
Assessment of Anger 174
Assessment of Self-Injury 175
Assessment of Eating Disorders 178
Assessment of Attention-Deficit/Hyperactivity Disorder 181
Chapter Summary 183
Review Questions 183
Resources for Further Learning 184

Section IV
Types of Assessment

Chapter 9

Assessment of Intelligence 187
Theories of Intelligence 187
Individual Intelligence Tests 190
Group Intelligence Tests 196
Giftedness and Creativity 199
Chapter Summary 200
Review Questions 200
Resources for Further Learning 200

Chapter 10

Ability Testing: Academic Aptitude and Achievement 203
Introduction to Aptitude and Achievement Assessment 204
Aptitude Tests for Higher Education 205
Graduate and Professional School Admissions Tests 209
Academic Achievement Tests 211
High-Stakes Testing 215
Study Habits Inventories 217
Chapter Summary 218
Review Questions 219
Resources for Further Learning 219

Chapter 11

Career and Life-Planning Assessment   221

Introduction to Career and Life-Planning Assessment   222
Measures of Career Readiness   224
Introduction to Comprehensive Assessment Programs   233
Standardized Assessment Programs   234
Chapter Summary   241
Review Questions   241
Resources for Further Learning   242

Chapter 12

Measures of Interests and Values   245

Introduction to Interest Inventories   246
Popular Interest Inventories   248
Values Inventories   263
Chapter Summary   272
Review Questions   273
Resources for Further Learning   273

Chapter 13

Assessment of Personality   275

Introduction to Personality Assessment   276
Popular Structured Personality Assessments   277
Popular Unstructured Personality Assessments   294
Health and Lifestyle Inventories   298
Chapter Summary   299
Review Questions   299
Resources for Further Learning   300

Chapter 14

Assessment of Interpersonal Relationships   303

Inventories for Couples and Family Counseling   304
Assessment of Intimate Partner Violence   308
Assessment of Child Abuse   312
Genograms   313
Additional Interpersonal Assessment Inventories   317
Chapter Summary   318
Review Questions   319
Resources for Further Learning   319

Section V
The Assessment Report and Future Trends

Chapter 15

Communication of Assessment Results   323

Communication of Findings   323
The Assessment Interpretation Interview   325
The Case Conference   328
The Assessment Report   329
Chapter Summary   333
Review Questions   333
Resources for Further Learning   334

Chapter 16

Future Trends in Counseling Assessment   335

The Assessment Process: Looking Back to Look Ahead   336

Changing Client Demographics and Assessment Practice   337

Globalization and Problematizing Counseling and Assessment   338

Technological Advances   339

Increased Sophistication of the Assessment Process   340

The Continuation and Adaptability of Educational Accountability   341

Assessment and Managed Care   343

Building Assessment Systems   343

Building Partnerships With Health Professions   344

Assessment as Relevant and Actionable   345

The Next Frontier in Counseling and Assessment Research   345

Chapter Summary   347

Review Questions   348

Resources for Further Learning   348

Appendix A

Statistical Formulas   349

Appendix B

Sample Assessment Report   351

Appendix C

Test Your Knowledge Answer Key   357

References   359

Subject Index   403

Name Index   421

Preface

The purpose of this book is to provide information about the various assessment procedures that are specifically relevant for practicing counselors. The book deals with the use of these assessment procedures in the counseling process; emphasizes the selection, interpretation, and communication of psychological test results; and highlights the basic principles of psychological assessment. It stresses the importance of integrating assessment results with other information about the client. One primary assumption undergirds this text: Counselors engage in assessment practices *every day*, and these practices affect relationships, treatment decisions, and culturally responsive counseling. Furthermore, assessment involves both quantitative and qualitative indicators.

This book is not designed to be a comprehensive textbook or desk manual on the various assessment tools themselves. A number of excellent books describe psychological tests and other assessment procedures in detail. It is expected that counselors will make use of such publications along with other resources as they evaluate assessment tools. As with the previous editions of this book, the latest developments regarding those assessments commonly used by counselors and other mental health professionals are included. New to this edition are some innovative ways to integrate assessment into the counseling profession. Core areas identified by the Council for Accreditation of Counseling and Related Educational Programs (CACREP) are also included to help ensure that counselors and counselor trainees are prepared adequately to engage in testing and assessment practices within the field.

Some of the key features of the sixth edition of this text include the following:

- Bolded key terms to facilitate comprehension of major concepts
- Chapter pretests ("Test Your Knowledge") to gauge previous learning
- Self-development activities, such as reflective exercises and class and field activities
- "Tip Sheets," or practical, user-friendly information about major assessment concepts, issues, and practices
- The inclusion of practitioner voices on various assessment topics ("Assessment in Action")
- Case examples that highlight assessment issues and score reports
- Sample assessment items with an expanded list of common assessment tools
- Coverage of the history of assessment, test-access issues, cultural bias in assessment, high-stakes testing, qualitative assessment, and specialty areas of assessment and related standards

- Review questions and chapter summaries
- Resources for further learning
- A sample assessment report
- Common statistical formulas used in assessment

The sixth edition of this text builds on some of the key additions of the fifth edition in several ways. First, this edition includes updated references for assessment tools and scholarship in assessment-related procedures and practices. Second, this edition has an increased focus on multicultural counseling competency and social justice as it pertains to the counseling and assessment process. Third, the text includes at the end of each chapter resources for further learning. Finally, supplemental materials for instructors have been developed and are available through the American Counseling Association; these materials include chapter outlines, chapter PowerPoints, a test bank of multiple-choice and true/false items, and a sample syllabus.

The text is organized into five sections. Section I, "Foundations of Assessment in Counseling," includes introductory concepts of assessment that are useful for conceptualizing measurement and statistical concepts and working with various types of assessment. The four chapters in this section include a discussion of basic assessment terms; the history of assessment; the purpose and use of assessment; the assessment process related to selection, administration, interpretation, and communication; ethical, legal, and professional issues in assessment and related assessment standards; and multicultural assessment practices. Section II, "Basic Statistical and Measurement Considerations," includes two chapters that address foundational knowledge in statistics and measurement. Specifically, the following concepts are discussed: scales of measurement; reliability, validity, and correlation; test development; measures of central tendency and variability; and raw score transformation. Section III, "Initial Psychological Assessment," includes two chapters related to common assessment tasks typically found at the beginning of the counseling relationship to gauge mental health and substance abuse symptoms. This section addresses the intake interview; mental status examination; several general screening inventories; specialized assessment of suicide risk, substance abuse, depression, anxiety, anger, self-injury, eating disorders, and attention-deficit/hyperactivity disorder; and use of the *Diagnostic and Statistical Manual of Mental Disorders*.

Section IV, "Types of Assessment," is the largest section and includes six chapters. The section is devoted to specific classes of assessment, including intelligence, ability, career development, and personality. In this edition, you will find expanded coverage in areas such as high-stakes testing, projective assessments, and interpersonal assessment involving intimate partner violence and child abuse. Furthermore, recent revisions in intelligence and ability assessment are discussed. Section V, "The Assessment Report and Future Trends," first provides a chapter that outlines general guidelines for communicating assessment findings to a client and other stakeholders as well as developing a research report. The second chapter in this section, new to this edition, focuses on future trends in assessment—in particular ways that counselors can expect to respond to issues such as a changing cultural landscape, globalization, and technology. The text also includes several appendices: common statistical formulas (Appendix A), a sample assessment report (Appendix B), and an answer key for "Test Your Knowledge" items (Appendix C). Throughout the text, greater attention has been paid to multicultural and social justice considerations in assessment.

In graduate courses that cover the use of tests and other assessment procedures in counseling, information about various tools is typically covered, but the actual use of psychological assessment procedures in counseling often must be learned through trial and error. This text should help remedy this situation by providing information to assist the counselor in choosing, administering, and interpreting assessment procedures as part of the counseling process.

Council for Accreditation of Counseling and Related Educational Programs 2016 Standards and Corresponding Chapters

Assessment and Testing Section

Standard	Chapter
a. Historical perspectives concerning the nature and meaning of assessment and testing in counseling	**1, 16**
b. Methods of effectively preparing for and conducting initial assessment meetings	**7**
c. Procedures for assessing risk of aggression or danger to others, self-inflicted harm, or suicide	**7, 8**
d. Procedures for identifying trauma and abuse and for reporting abuse	**14**
e. Use of assessments for diagnostic and intervention planning purposes	**2**
f. Basic concepts of standardized and non-standardized testing, norm-referenced and criterion-referenced assessments, and group and individual assessments	**2, 6**
g. Statistical concepts, including scales of measurement, measures of central tendency, indices of variability, shapes and types of distributions, and correlations	**6**
h. Reliability and validity in the use of assessments	**5**
i. Use of assessments relevant to academic/educational, career, personal, and social development	**9–14**

(Continued)

Assessment and Testing Section

Standard	Chapter
j. Use of environmental assessments and systematic behavioral observations	**2, 4, 16**
k. Use of symptom checklists, and personality and psychological testing	**2, 13**
l. Use of assessment results to diagnose developmental, behavioral, and mental disorders	**7, 8, 9**
m. Ethical and culturally relevant strategies for selecting, administering, and interpreting assessment and test results	**3, 4**

Acknowledgments

I thank Carolyn Baker, American Counseling Association (ACA) associate publisher, for her support and responsiveness throughout the writing and production process. I am also grateful for the work of Bonny Gaston, senior production manager, and the other ACA staff members who made this edition possible.

I appreciate the contributions of Albert B. Hood and Richard W. Johnson to the practice of psychological assessment in general and as authors of the first four editions of this text. The counseling profession has certainly been influenced by their countless achievements in research and practice, and I am humbled to build on their work in this sixth edition.

Finally, I am thankful for my students and mentors in the assessment world who remind me every day of the important role of assessment.

About the Author

Danica G. Hays, PhD, is a professor of counselor education and executive associate dean in the College of Education at the University of Nevada, Las Vegas. She earned a PhD in counselor education and supervision, with an emphasis in multicultural research, from Georgia State University. Her research interests include qualitative methodology, assessment and diagnosis, trauma and gender issues, and multicultural and social justice concerns in counselor preparation and community mental health. She has published numerous articles and book chapters in these areas as well as these books in addition to this text: *Developing Multicultural Counseling Competence: A Systems Approach, Qualitative Inquiry in Clinical and Educational Settings, Mastering the National Counselor Exam and the Counselor Preparation Comprehensive Exam, The ACA Encyclopedia of Counseling,* and *A Counselor's Guide to Career Assessment Instruments.* She has extensive leadership history in the Association for Assessment and Research in Counseling (AARC) and the Association for Counselor Education and Supervision (ACES), including serving as AARC president, AARC founding journal editor for *Counseling Outcome Research and Evaluation,* ACES journal editor for *Counselor Education and Supervision,* and president of an ACES region. She is a recipient of the Outstanding Research Award, Outstanding Counselor Educator Advocacy Award, and Glen E. Hubele National Graduate Student Award from the American Counseling Association as well as the recipient of the Patricia B. Elmore Excellence in Measurement and Evaluation Award and President's Special Merit Award from the AARC.

Section I

Foundations of Assessment in Counseling

Use of Assessment in Counseling

What is assessment? What are the different ways counselors use assessment in the work they do? How did assessment become such an important part of counseling? In this chapter, several key assessment terms are defined, and the purpose and uses of assessment are described. Then, a brief history of assessment is provided followed by a discussion of current attitudes toward assessment use. Finally, the chapter concludes with key questions and guiding principles of assessment in counseling.

Test Your Knowledge

Respond to the following items by selecting T *for "True" or* F *for "False":*

❏ T ❏ F 1. Assessment aids counseling by providing information for the client alone.

❏ T ❏ F 2. *Assessment* and *test* are synonymous terms.

❏ T ❏ F 3. Early group tests were used to assess intelligence and ability among World War I recruits.

❏ T ❏ F 4. A problem-solving model is a useful method for conceptualizing the purpose of assessment.

❏ T ❏ F 5. Personality assessment is the most significant area counselors are known for in assessment development.

Introduction to Assessment

Assessment is a part of everyone's daily lives. In any instance where someone has to make a judgment or solve a problem based on an outcome or information gained, assessment is occurring. Individuals are recipients and participants of assessment data. Think back to your early memories of being assessed, tested, or evaluated in some way. Did it relate to a spelling or history test in school? Did it involve a report card you brought home? Were you being assessed for a disability or placed in a gifted program? Did you feel sad or anxious about something? Now, think of maybe more recent memories: taking a college or graduate entrance exam, discussing with a physician or counselor some symptom or issue you are experiencing, selecting a career path, interviewing for a job, even trying out a new recipe or working on a home improvement project, to name a few. No matter the memories—positive or negative—assessment occurs in various settings: schools, colleges, and universities; homes; health care settings; agencies; neighborhoods; communities; and so on.

It is not surprising, then, that assessment has always played an important part in counseling. From its inception, the field of counseling typically involved helping students with academic and career planning on the basis of test results. In recent years, the role of counseling (and the nature of assessment) has broadened to address a variety of concerns, such as self-esteem, shyness, personal growth, family and couple relationships, sexual identity, sexual abuse, cross-cultural communication, substance abuse, eating disorders, depression, anxiety, and suicidal ideation. Counselors also rely on assessment data for program planning and evaluation. Clients use assessment results to understand themselves better and to make plans for the future. The assessment process can be therapeutic in itself by helping clients to clarify goals and gain a sense of perspective and support.

Key Assessment Terms

There are many terms associated with assessment in counseling. In this section, five key terms (i.e., *assessment*, *tests*, *measurement*, *variable*, and *psychometrics*) are presented. Throughout the text, information on terms associated with these are outlined. Before defining these terms, it is important to define what the term *client* means throughout the text. A **client** may be an individual or group of individuals being assessed in various settings, such as counseling agencies, private practice settings, schools, colleges and universities, and career centers. A client can also refer to places or settings in general, such as in cases of program evaluation (e.g., a character education program). Finally, a client may be associated with objects or things such as dropout rates, divorce rates, violence, trauma, or neighborhoods. In essence, clients are people, places, or things.

Assessment

Assessment is an umbrella term for the evaluation methods counselors use to better understand characteristics of people, places, and things. Other terms used interchangeably in counseling to describe assessment are *appraisal* and *evaluation*. For most purposes, assessment can be conceptualized in terms of problem solving (Greiff, Holt, & Funke, 2013; Suhr, 2015). The *Standards for Educational and Psychological Testing* (American Educational Research Association [AERA], American Psychological Association [APA], & National Council on Measurement in Education [NCME], 2014) defines assessment as "any systematic method of obtaining information from tests and other sources, used to draw inferences about characteristics of people, objects, or programs" (p. 216). The first part of the definition ("any systematic method of obtaining information from tests and other sources") indicates that a broad range of evaluation methods—such as standardized tests, rating scales and observations, interviews, classification techniques, and records—may be used as a means of obtaining data about clients. The second part of the definition ("used to draw inferences about characteristics of people, objects, or programs") emphasizes the use of assessment data to help counselors understand their clients and the situations in which clients find themselves. Collectively, these two definition parts refer to a broad process of tool selection, administration and interpretation of data to provide a basis for forming and testing hypotheses regarding the nature of a client's issues, and possible treatment approaches. The assessment process is discussed in more depth in Chapters 2, 6, and 15.

Some of the common assessment categories discussed in this text are intelligence (Chapter 9), ability (Chapter 10), career (Chapters 11 and 12), and personality (Chapter 13). These categories include both formal and informal assessment methods (see Chapter 2). Following are brief definitions of each category:

- **Intelligence assessment:** evaluation of cognitive abilities such as communication, reasoning, abstract thought, learning, and problem solving. Intelligence has been defined in many ways, although intelligence assessment is primarily measured through tests geared toward more traditional definitions.
- **Ability assessment:** assessment of acquired information (achievement) or an ability to acquire information (aptitude) about a particular subject matter or domain. Ability assessments are typically used for educational purposes, although some career and intelligence assessments may also be categorized as ability measures.
- **Career assessment:** measure of a client's career development process as well as the content domains of that process. Process-oriented variables include career readiness, concerns, planning, and maturity. Content domains involve career values and interests inventories. Career assessment can involve individual tools or more comprehensive assessment programs.
- **Personality assessment:** examination of individual attributes, types, and traits related to cognitions, emotions, actions, and attitudes. Personality assessment can be classified as structured (objective) or unstructured (projective).

As you can see from these descriptions, assessment categories are not fixed and can overlap one another.

Tests

A **test** is a systematic and often standardized process for sampling and describing a behavior of interest for individuals or groups. Tests can measure past, present, and/or future behavior or some reflection or feeling toward a behavior of interest. Tests can be interpreted in reference to a test taker's previous performance (**self-referenced**), some objective or criterion, or that of a standardization sample. Standardization and test norms are discussed in more depth in Chapter 6.

Questionnaires and inventories, such as personality and interest inventories, elicit self-reports of opinions, preferences, and typical reactions to everyday situations. In practice, questionnaires and inventories also are often referred to as tests if they meet certain standardization criteria.

Tests are only one aspect of assessment. Assessment is a more comprehensive activity than testing by itself because it includes the integration and interpretation of test results and other evaluation methods. In sum, assessment involves judgments based on quantitative and qualitative descriptions of client data from a variety of sources.

Measurement

Measurement is a description of the degree to which a client possesses some characteristic. Traditionally, measurement deals with quantitative units, such as those associated with length (e.g., meter, inch), time (e.g., second, minute), mass (e.g., kilogram, pound), and temperature (e.g., Kelvin, Fahrenheit). In the physical sciences, measurement has been described as the actual or estimated magnitude of quantity relative to another (see International Bureau of Weights and Measures, 2012; Michell, 1997). The measurement concept has long been applied to the social sciences, such as when S. S. Stevens (1946) defined measurement as the assignment of numerals to objects or events according to some rule. These "rules" refer to scales of measurement (i.e., nominal, ordinal, interval, and ratio; see Chapter 5). In addition, measurement in social sciences relates to providing data that meet some criteria, and thus tests are administered to assess the degree to which criteria are met.

Variable

Another key term is **variable**, which gets assigned a label through measurement. A variable refers to a construct or concept that can take on more than one value. Values can be qualitative or quantitative. For example, qualitative variables can include groupings such as gender, ethnicity, sports team, and hair color; they tend to involve **categorical variables**. Quantitative variables might include **continuous variables** (i.e., variables measured on some continuum), such as test scores, age, and rank. In assessment, you will encounter several types of variables: **independent variables** (preexisting variable or variable able to be manipulated that is assumed to influence some outcome), **dependent variables** (construct affected by the independent variable; also known as an outcome or response variable), and **extraneous variables** (a "noise" variable that impacts a dependent variable yet is unrelated to the assessment process—also known as a confounding variable).

Psychometrics

Psychometrics is the study of measurement technique and theory. Although a lengthy discussion is beyond the scope of this text, psychometricians have proposed common theories and techniques such as classical test theory, item response theory, Rasch modeling, factor analysis, and structural equation modeling. Classical test theory and its common concepts of measurement error, reliability, and validity are discussed in Chapter 5.

Purpose of Assessment in Counseling

Now that you have a basic understanding of the general terminology, let's take a look at how and why assessment is used in counseling. Assessment is beneficial in counseling because it provides information for both counselors and clients so they can understand and respond to client concerns as well as plan and evaluate programs. In addition, it can be therapeutic and can help clients understand both their past and present attitudes and actions as well as their plans for the future. Thus, assessments serve a diagnostic use, help to evaluate client progress, and are useful to improve or promote client awareness, knowledge, and skills. Gregory (2013) further cited several test uses: classification (i.e., program placement, screening, and certification), diagnosis and treatment planning, client self-knowledge, program evaluation, and research to guide counseling theory and technique development. Whichever purpose(s) counselors cite as the reason for assessment, it is important to convey this purpose to the client throughout the assessment process. That is, assessment should be part of the learning process for a client rather than something that is tacked on to counseling sessions.

Because performing an assessment is similar to engaging in problem solving, the five steps in a problem-solving model can be used to describe a psychological assessment model (Chang, D'Zurilla, & Sanna, 2004; Nezu, Nezu, & D'Zurilla, 2012). Depending on a client's problem-solving style, he or she will have varying levels of success in resolving a problem (Nezu et al., 2012). Following is a brief description of the five steps involved (see Table 1.1 for specific ways the model relates to the assessment process):

Table 1.1
Assessment and Problem-Solving Steps

Problem-Solving Step	Assessment Purpose	Counseling Examples
Problem Orientation: stimulate counselors and clients to consider various issues	Almost any assessment procedure can be used to increase sensitivity to potential problems. Instruments that promote self-awareness and self-exploration can stimulate clients to cope with developmental issues before they become actual problems. Surveys of groups or classes can help counselors identify common problems or concerns that can be taken into account in planning programs for clients.	A counselor conducts a needs assessment, such as an alcohol screening inventory, to identify areas of focus.
Problem Identification: clarify the nature of a problem or issue	Assessment procedures can help clarify the nature of the client's problem and ultimately strengthen communication and the overall counseling relationship as well as clarify goals. For example, screening inventories or problem checklists can be used to assess the type and extent of a client's concerns. Personal diaries or logs can be used to identify situations in which the problem occurs. Personality inventories can help counselors and clients understand personality dynamics underlying certain situations.	A counselor can provide a diagnosis to classify a set of concerns or symptoms, such as the case of a relationship difficulty or an anxiety disorder.
Generation of Alternatives: suggest alternative solutions	Assessment procedures enable counselors and clients to identify alternative solutions for client problems, view problems from different angles, and stimulate new learning. For example, an assessment interview can be used to determine what techniques have worked for the client in the past when faced with a similar problem. Checklists or inventories (such as a study skills inventory or work skills survey) yield data that can be used to generate alternatives.	A counselor uses an interest inventory to suggest alternative career choices for a client. A counselor helps a client identify positive self-statements to create alternatives.
Decision Making: determine appropriate treatment for the client	Counselors use assessment materials to help clients weigh the attractiveness of each alternative and the likelihood of achieving each alternative. The likelihood of achieving different alternatives can be evaluated by expectancy (or experience) tables that show the success rate for people with different types of test scores or characteristics (Guion, 2011). Balance sheets or decision-making grids enable clients to compare the desirability and feasibility of various alternatives (Dollaghan, 2013; Howard, 2001).	A counselor uses a values clarification exercise to assess the attractiveness of various alternatives. A counselor uses a personality inventory to help select a client's intervention.
Verification: evaluate the effectiveness of a particular solution	Assessment procedures to verify success may include goal attainment scaling (Kiresuk et al., 2014), self-monitoring techniques (Korotitsch & Nelson-Gray, 1999), the re-administration of tests that the client completed earlier in counseling, client satisfaction surveys, and the use of outcome questionnaires (Boswell et al., 2013). In addition to serving as a guide for the counseling process, verification efforts also provide a means of accountability for the counseling agency.	Client feedback can be used to make changes to an intervention. A counselor can request a client self-monitoring exercise to assess maintenance of change.

1. **Problem Orientation.** This first step assesses how a problem is viewed (can be positive or negative) and requires the client to recognize and accept the problem. With completion of this step, the client and counselor can begin to approach it in a systematic fashion as indicated by the problem-solving model.
2. **Problem Identification.** This step involves the counselor and the client attempting to identify the problem in as much detail as possible. A client is more likely to continue in counseling and to achieve positive outcomes if the counselor and client agree on the nature of the problem (Tryon & Winograd, 2011). Identification of the problem also aids in communication with others, such as referral sources, family, and friends.
3. **Generation of Alternatives.** In the third step, the counselor and client generate alternatives to help resolve the problem. Counselors use assessment procedures to assist clients in discovering strengths on which they can build to overcome difficulties or enhance development.
4. **Decision Making.** In this step, clients anticipate the consequences of the various alternatives. According to classical decision theory, choice is a function of the probability of success and the desirability of the outcome (Kohar, 2016). This equation emphasizes the importance of assessing both the likelihood of success of various alternatives and the attractiveness of those alternatives for the client. Clients will usually want to consider those alternatives that maximize the likelihood of a favorable outcome.
5. **Verification.** The counselor in this final step should discuss with the client how the client will know when the problem has been solved. This step requires that goals be clearly specified, that they be translated into specific behavioral objectives, and that the possibility for progress in accomplishing these goals be realistically viewed. Counselors are to verify the effectiveness of their interventions.

In understanding the purpose of assessments in counseling, it is also important to understand what purposes *do not* characterize assessments—particularly tests. Tyler (1984) highlighted several things tests do not measure:

- Tests cannot measure unique characteristics, only attributes common to many people.
- Individual assessment cannot be used to make group comparisons; counselors can only estimate how well an individual will function in a culture for which the assessment is appropriate. Tests are not suitable for comparing groups that are not identical.
- Because test scores are plotted on a distribution of scores, we tend to infer scores on the distribution ends as "good versus poor" (p. 48). To this end, counselors often evaluate scores without examining the appropriate norms and without considering that highness or lowness of scores do not measure a client's worth.
- On a related note, a "good score" may measure some absence of pathology (such as in personality assessment) rather than universal attributes to which humans aspire.
- Tests cannot measure innate characteristics. Although there are biological components to some attributes (such as intelligence), beginning at birth these components interact with various environmental factors that further shape responses. Thus, even if counselors can assume that intelligence tests are free from cultural bias (which they are not), responses on intelligence tests are a combination of hereditary tendencies and individual responses to particular environments.
- Test scores are not final measurements of anything but outlets—in conjunction with multiple assessment sources—for facilitating client growth. Clients' high-stakes decisions should not be based solely on test scores.

To this list, I add the following:

- Tests cannot measure all things equally. Some things, such as reaction time, may be easier to assess than others, such as intelligence or disability.

- Tests are not necessarily indicative of the totality of behaviors, attitudes, or skills. Tests are only one sampling of these areas and thus should be evaluated as such.
- Test results are not always useful. In fact, they are often misused in decision making and applied to individuals inappropriately. Concerns include the following: (a) misuse with minority groups, who may differ significantly from the population for whom the test was developed; (b) use of tests to label or stereotype a person based on the test results; and (c) the disproportionate influence of tests in so-called high-stakes decisions, such as selection for college or employment. In some situations, too much emphasis may be placed on test results, often because of their quantitative or scientific nature; in other situations, pertinent test information may be disregarded, especially if it conflicts with an individual's personal beliefs or desires.

Please see the Tip Sheet at the end of the chapter for sound assessment procedures.

History of Assessment

Let's step back from how assessment is used (and should not be used) today and reflect on how counselors began using assessment in the first place. This section presents early key developments in intelligence, ability, interest, and personality assessment; most of these developments occurred from the late-19th to mid-20th century. After reviewing this brief history of assessment, perhaps you can understand why current assessment practices across various settings exist, how beneficial assessment can be to counselors and clients, what mistakes those who have administered tests have made, and why certain practices should be continually challenged and scrutinized. Table 1.2 provides a timeline of major assessment developments.

The discussion focuses primarily on historical events from the mid-1800s until present day. The earliest form of testing dates back to Ancient China, where in 2200 BC (more than 4,400 years ago!) the Chinese used a civil service testing program to assess, evaluate, place, and promote its employees. Every 3 years officials tested employees on five topics: civil law, military affairs, geography, agriculture, and revenue. The testing program was abolished in 1906 after several complaints and questions about its administration and utility, although the program influenced American and European civil service program placements in the 1800s. Let's jump 4,000 years later, when individuals began recording formal assessment procedures in the social sciences.

Developments in Individual Intelligence Assessment

In the mid- to late 1800s, there was an increasing interest in studying individual human differences, particularly concerning intelligence. Charles Darwin's *Origin of Species,* with its focus on genetic variation and evolution and thus individual differences, was used as a case for testing human differences. The study of intelligence increased, given its links to discussions of evolution at the time. In the late 1800s, experimental psychologists—primarily Wilhelm Wundt (1832–1920), Sir Francis Galton (1822–1911), and James Cattell (1860–1944)—revolutionized the way intelligence and ability were measured. They focused on quantifiable measures of sensory processes (e.g., visual and auditory processes, reaction time) using brass instruments in human laboratories to indicate intelligence. Wundt, one of the founders of modern psychology, studied mental processes and was able to highlight that individual differences do exist (even though his interests were more in understanding general features of the psyche). Galton, Charles Darwin's half-cousin, was considered a prolific scholar and creator of several significant mathematical and scientific concepts, such as correlation, regression, and central tendency statistics; meteorology; fingerprinting; hearing loss; and heredity. He is considered the founder of eugenics, claiming genetics was the determinant of genius and mental competence differences. Galton is also referred to as the founder of mental tests; he demonstrated that

Table 1.2
Key Historical Events in Assessment

Year	Event
2200 BC	The Chinese test aspiring public officials for work evaluations and promotion decisions
1879	Wundt founds the first psychological laboratory, conducting several experiments with brass instruments
1880s	Galton initiates the social science testing movement, measuring individual differences in sensory processes
1890	James Cattell coins the term *mental test*
1900	Esquirol and Seguin perform formalized intelligence assessment in medical communities
	College Entrance Examination Board (CEEB; now known as the College Board) created
1905	Binet–Simon scale developed; revised in 1908 and 1911
	Goddard misuses test at Vineland Training School and Ellis Island
1916	Stanford–Binet Scale created
1917	Army Alpha and Beta tests, Woodworth Personal Data Sheet developed
1921	Rorschach Inkblot Test published
1923	Terman and colleagues develop the Stanford Achievement Test
1926	Scholastic Aptitude Test published by CEEB
	Strong Vocational Interest Blank created
1938	Buros Center for Testing develops the *Mental Measurements Yearbook*
	Thematic Apperception Test (TAT) created
1939–1950s	Wechsler Scales of Intelligence developed
1940s	Myers–Briggs Type Indicator published
1942	Minnesota Multiphasic Personality Inventory (MMPI) created
1947	Educational Testing Service created
1964	Civil Rights Act
1965	Elementary and Secondary Education Act (ESEA) (Pub. L. No. 89-110)
1974	Family Educational Rights and Privacy Act
1975	Education of All Handicapped Children Act (Pub. L. No. 94-142)
1990	Americans with Disabilities Act (Pub. L. No. 101-336)
1994	Improving America's Schools Act (ESEA Reauthorization)
1995	Individuals with Disabilities Education Act Amendments
1996	Health Insurance Portability and Accountability Act (HIPAA)
2001, 2007	No Child Left Behind Act (Pub. L. No. 107-110)[a]
2015	Every Student Succeeds Act (ESEA Reauthorization)

Note. Pub. L. = Public Law.
[a]Additional legislation concerning assessment is presented in Chapter 3.

individual cognitive differences do exist and can be measured. Although Galton's tests are now considered simplistic, in the 1880s and 1890s he tested more than 17,000 individuals on physical (e.g., height, weight, head size, length of middle finger) and behavioral (e.g., hand-squeeze tests, lung capacity, visual acuity, reaction time) domains to indicate intelligence (Nickerson, Perkins, & Smith, 2014). Cattell, who studied with both Wundt and Galton, coined the term **mental test** and articulated 10 mental tests (presence of each indicates intelligence) similar to Galton's. Examples include strength of hand squeeze, rate of hand movement, degree of rubber tip on forehead pressure needed to cause pain, weight differentiation of identical-appearing boxes, reaction time for sound, and number of letters repeated upon hearing them.

Thus, in the early 20th century, there was increased interest in what was called mental testing—now referred to as intelligence testing. Work in the medical community, where there was an increasing distinction between emotional problems and intellectual disabilities (i.e., mental retardation), set the stage for more formalized intelligence assessment. In Paris, France, two physicians—Jean Esquirol (1772–1840) and Edouard Sequin (1812–1880)—studied language use, identified various levels of verbal intelligence, and examined motor function in patients to initially conceptualize performance intelligence. Sequin was particularly instrumental in performance tests, with the development of the **Sequin**

form board. This board is still used today in neuropsychological tests and involves fitting 10 blocks within designated slots on an upright board.

The first intelligence test was developed by Alfred Binet (1857–1911), who as minister of public instruction in Paris introduced the 1905 **Binet–Simon scale** in collaboration with his Sorbonne colleague Theodore Simon (1972–1961). They were commissioned by the French government to assess children with intellectual disabilities. They developed a scale that contained 30 tasks and was designed to assist in educational placement; the scale relied on a general factor of intelligence, versus lower level sensory processes, and it relied heavily on verbal ability (Carson, 2014; Richardson, 2011). Sample tasks included following a movement with eyes, repeating three spoken digits, repeating a sentence of 15 words, putting three nouns (e.g., *Paris, river, fortune*) in a sentence, reversing the hands of a clock, and defining abstract words by distinguishing between them (e.g., *boredom* and *weariness*).

In 1908, Binet and Simon revised the scale and dropped many of the simpler tasks (used previously to classify those with severe intellectual disabilities) and added higher level tasks. The revised scale contained 58 tasks. The concept of *mental level* was developed for this scale, later referred to as *mental age*. Using a standardization sample of 300 children ages 3 to 13, Binet and Simon were able to calculate the number of items passed by the majority of children of a certain age. In the 1911 scale revision, mental level was further refined, whereas each age level had five associated tasks. Ultimately, mental age was compared against chronological age, and others suggested that an **intelligence quotient (IQ)** be developed.

The 1908 Binet–Simon scale was significantly misused, particularly in the United States at the Vineland Training School in New Jersey—a school for "feebleminded" children. Henry Goddard, the first American psychologist to translate the Binet–Simon scale, tested 378 school residents, classifying 73 as "idiots," 205 as "imbeciles," and 100 as "feebleminded." He then tested 1,547 "normal" children and noted that 3% of the sample could be classified as feebleminded. Goddard was invited in 1910 to Ellis Island to assess intelligence among immigrants. Through his assessments he increasingly emphasized that the rate of feeblemindedness was much higher among immigrant populations (Carson, 2014). Specifically, he found feeblemindedness for his small immigrant samples at the following rates: 83% of Jews, 80% of Hungarians, 79% of Italians, and 87% of Russians (see Goddard, 1917). These findings were used to make the case that feebleminded individuals were a threat to social order, and thus low-IQ immigrants should be deported. Unfortunately, Goddard's writings heavily influenced immigration restrictions (Carson, 2014). Fortunately, Howard Knox developed several performance tests to be used with immigrants and was able to debunk some of Goddard's conclusions (see Figure 1.1). Knox's work highlighted the necessity of future intelligence tests containing performance or nonverbal parts (Richardson, 2003, 2011).

In 1916, Lewis Terman (1857–1956) and colleagues at Stanford University revised the scale (i.e., **Stanford Binet Scale**) and suggested that IQ be calculated by dividing an individual's mental age by his or her chronological (actual) age and multiplying that fraction times 100. For example, if a 10-year-old child performs at the level of an 11-year-old (mental age), his IQ would equal 110. The Stanford Binet Scale was the gold standard in intelligence testing for several decades and is now in its fifth edition. In 1927, Charles Spearman (1863–1945) conceptualized a general and specific factor theory of intelligence, and in 1941, Raymond Cattell (1905–1998) coined the terms *fluid* and *crystallized intelligence*, influencing how future assessments were constructed and interpreted. Other developments, including the Wechsler scales (Wechsler, 1949, 1955, 1991, 1999, 2003, 2008, 2009), are discussed in Chapter 9.

Developments in Group Intelligence Assessment

Although individual intelligence tests had made significant contributions in a short time—including a beginning understanding of the misuse of testing—test administrators learned quite quickly that group testing was more time efficient. The use of group tests became

Figure 1.1
Knox Administering Performance Tests to Ellis Island Immigrants, 1912–1916

Note. From "Howard Andrew Knox and the Origins of Performance Testing on Ellis Island, 1912–1916," by J. T. E. Richardson, 2003, *History of Psychology, 6,* p. 153. Copyright 2012 by the American Psychological Association (APA). Reprinted with permission. The use of APA information does not imply endorsement by APA.

increasingly warranted when during World War I there was a need to screen new recruits. Robert Yerkes (1876–1956), while president of the American Psychological Association (APA), developed the first two group tests: the Army Alpha and Army Beta intelligence tests. The **Army Alpha** measured verbal ability, numerical ability, ability to follow directions, and knowledge of information. The **Army Beta** was a nonverbal counterpart to the Army Alpha and was used to evaluate illiterate or non-English-speaking recruits. During World War I, more than 1.5 million recruits were administered these tests for placement purposes. Figure 1.2 provides sample items from these tests.

Developments in Ability Assessment

Eventually, group tests were used to assess more than just intelligence. Group aptitude tests were developed after World War II, as more specialized careers (e.g., flight engineers, pilots, navigators) required more stringent selection for flight schools, and previous intelligence tests (i.e., Army Alpha, Army Beta) were not sufficient (Gregory, 2013). In essence, it was clear that previously developed intelligence tests were limited because not all important job functions were covered.

With greater attention paid to education after World War I, ability testing flourished in public schools and higher education. The Army Alpha and Beta tests were released for public use and became the model for future ability tests. Edward Thorndike (1874–1949) spearheaded the development of several standardized achievement tests in public schools, including rating scales, spelling tests, arithmetic reasoning, and handwriting assessments, to name a few. These tests were distinguished from earlier ones by a more reliable administration format. The **College Entrance Examination Board** (CEEB) was established in 1900 to regulate group test use in colleges and universities. In 1926, the CEEB developed the first aptitude test for college admissions, the **Scholastic Aptitude Test** (SAT; Goslin, 1963). Functions of the CEEB were subsumed under the Educational Testing Service (ETS) in 1948, creator of modern-day assessments such as the **Graduate Record Examination** (GRE), **Law School Admissions Test** (LSAT), **Praxis**, and **Test of English as a Foreign Language** (ToEFL). In addition, Terman and his colleagues in 1923 developed a standardized achievement test, the **Stanford Achievement Test** (SAchT). So, as a student in the 1930s and 1940s, you certainly would have had significant exposure to testing!

Army Alpha

1. A company advanced 6 miles and retreated 2 miles. How far was it then from its first position?
2. A dealer bought some mules for $1,200. He sold them for $1,500, making $50 on each mule. How many mules were there?
3. Thermometers are useful because
   a. They regulate temperature
   b. They tell us how warm it is
   c. They contain mercury
4. A machine gun is more deadly than a rifle because it
   a. Was invented more recently
   b. Fires more rapidly
   c. Can be used with less training

For these next two items, examinees first had to unscramble the words to form a sentence, and then indicate if the sentence was true or false.

5. happy is man sick always a
6. day it snow does every not

The next two items required examinees to determine the next two numbers in each sequence.

7. 3   4   5   6   7   8   ___   ___
8. 18   14   17   13   16   12   ___   ___

A portion of the Army Alpha required examinees to solve analogies.

9. shoe—foot. hat—kitten, head, knife, penny
10. eye—head. window—key, floor, room, door

In these next two examples, examinees were required to complete the sentence by selecting one of the four possible answers.

11. The apple grows on a shrub, vine, bush, tree
12. Denim is a dance, food, fabric, drink

Other portions of the test required examinees to follow instructions in performing paper-and-pencil tasks.

Answers: 1. 4 miles;   2. 6 mules;   3. B;   4. B;   5. False (A sick man is always happy);   6. True (It does not snow every day);   7. 9, 10;   8. 15, 11;   9. Head;   10. Room;   11. Tree;   12. Fabric

Army Beta

In the items below, examinees were asked to identify what was missing from each picture.

Answers: 1. Mouth;   2. Eye;   3. Nose;   4. Hand;   5. Chimney;   6. Ear;   7. Filament;   8. Return address;   9. Strings;   10. Corkscrew;   11. Trigger;   12. Tail;   13. Claw;   14. Shadow;   15. Ball; 16. Net;   17. Arm;   18. Speaker;   19. Arm in mirror;   20. Diamond

Figure 1.2
Sample Army Alpha and Army Beta Items

Note. Retrieved from http://official-asvab.com/armysamples_coun.htm. Available in the public domain.

Developments in Career Assessment

Upon reading about major developments in intelligence and ability testing, it may be evident to you that there was some focus on vocational assessment at the same time. Similar to how intelligence and ability assessments developed from societal needs (e.g., educational reform and placement, military screening), career assessment developed in response to societal changes of the Industrial Revolution, beginning in the late 1800s. With economic development came both positive and negative social conditions with major vocational implications. Frank Parsons developed in 1908 the **Boston Vocational Bureau** to address social conditions through vocational guidance. Specifically, the bureau assisted schoolchildren with career selection, a process involving career assessment. Parsons's work evolved to create more than 900 programs in high schools across the United States by 1918.

In addition to Parsons's trait and factor assessments, some of the earlier vocational assessments were interest inventories. Miner (1922) is credited with the first formal interest inventory to assist high school students with career selection. E. L. Thorndike (1912/1923) studied the interests of 100 college students, leading to the development of several interest inventories, such as the Carnegie Interest Inventory, the **Strong Vocational Interest Blank** (Strong, 1927), and the **Kuder Preference Record** and its revisions (see Kuder, 1934, 1966; Kuder & Diamond, 1979; Zytowski, 1985), to name a few. Special aptitude tests were developed for use in vocational counseling to test things such as mechanical, clerical, and artistic aptitudes. As aptitude tests evolved in vocational counseling, the need for multiple aptitude tests became more evident. For example, the **Armed Services Vocational Aptitude Battery** (ASVAB) is the most widely used multiple aptitude assessment in the world; it is used for military service qualification (discussed further in Chapter 11).

Developments in career assessment highlight the specific role counselors have played in the assessment world. That is, during the early days of the profession, counseling and testing were virtually synonymous. In fact, many of the counseling centers established during the 1930s and 1940s were called counseling and testing centers.

Developments in Personality Assessment

After World War I, society saw an increased interest in personality assessment as well. Personality assessment has its roots with Galton (1883), Kraepelin (1892), and Jung's (1910) use of free association tasks for psychiatric patients and normal populations to assess personality. Essentially, individuals would respond with the first word (or several words, depending on the assessment) that came to mind for a stimulus word. Personality assessment began to flourish in the early 1900s.

World War I saw the development of the first personality questionnaire to screen recruits, the **Woodworth Personal Data Sheet** (Nickerson et al., 2014). The Personal Data Sheet contained 116 yes/no items to detect mental health problems. Sample items include "Do you have a strong desire to commit suicide?" "Do ideas run through your head so that you cannot sleep?" and "Are you bothered by a feeling that things are not real?" (Gregory, 2013). Building from the Personal Data Sheet, other psychometricians (e.g., Allport & Vernon, 1931; Thurstone & Thurstone, 1930) developed personality assessments with multiple dimensions or scales to understand personality. One of the most famous personality assessments—the **Minnesota Multiphasic Personality Inventory** (MMPI), which is now in its second edition—includes methodology similar to that of its predecessors, comparing responses from normal and mentally disturbed individuals across various scales. In addition, it includes several validity scales to assess for "faking good" and "faking bad." The MMPI-2 is discussed further in Chapter 13.

With the increased attention on objective personality assessment, several test developers were interested in different methods for assessing personality. Projective techniques of assessment were developed as a means for understanding associations and responses to stimuli; for example, Hermann Rorschach (1884–1922) developed a tool using 10 inkblots (**Rorschach Inkblot Test**). Influenced by the works of Jung and other psychoanalytics, Rorschach believed these stimuli could reveal something about an individual's unconscious. Other projective techniques were developed during the early 1900s, including the **Thematic Apperception Test** (TAT) and the **House–Tree–Person** (Buck, 1992). Projective tests clinical interview, became more evident with the advent of the *Diagnostic and Statistical Manual of Mental Disorders* (*DSM*) in 1952. The *DSM* is discussed in more detail in Chapter 7.

Assessment Today and Beyond

Today, there are tests or other assessment tools for *everything*. Counselors' roots in vocational guidance certainly highlight their influence on career assessment. Today, counselors interact with intelligence and ability test results as they work with clients and also administer, interpret, and apply data from vocational and personality assessments to help clients make important decisions and gain self-awareness. Such test results also help counselors screen and classify clients as well as identify or refine programs and interventions. Increasingly, counselors are engaged in all categories of assessment.

Given the synergistic ways that counselors use multiple types of assessment today, the future holds endless possibilities for infusing assessment into clients' lives. The increased use and development of technology across clinical and educational settings will extend knowledge of current assessment theory and of the sociocultural and political contexts in which clients live. This in turn is likely to drive innovative, dynamic, and more advocacy-oriented assessment practices well integrated into clients' everyday experiences. Chapter 16 discusses more about future trends in assessment.

Assessment Usage in Counseling Settings

With counselors interacting with assessment data from a variety of assessment tools, there are various types of and ways assessments are used. Researchers have examined testing practices over the past several decades for helping professionals in counseling (Bubenzer, Zimpfer, & Mahrle, 1990; Frauenhoffer, Ross, Gfeller, Searight, & Piotrowski, 1998; C. H. Peterson, Lomas, Neukrug, & Bonner, 2014), psychology in general (Hogan, 2005; Piotrowski, 2015a, 2015b), vocational rehabilitation (Donoso, Hernandez, & Horin, 2010), clinical psychology (Camara, Nathan, & Puente, 2000; Watkins, Campbell, Nieberding, & Hallmark, 1995), neuropsychology (Camara et al., 2000), and school psychology (Hutton, Dubes, & Muir, 1992; Kennedy, Faust, Willis, & Piotrowski, 1994; Wilson & Reschly, 1996). Some tests have remained popular across disciplines and decades, with the Wechsler Adult Intelligence Scale (WAIS) and MMPI-2 remaining the top choices. C. H. Peterson et al. (2014) investigated the frequency with which 926 counselors used 98 assessment instruments (see Table 1.3 for the 16 most frequently used tools as reported by this sample).

Since 1969, the top five projective tests across disciplines have been stable and include the following: Rorschach Inkblot Test, TAT, Sentence Completion Test, House–Tree–Person, and Draw-A-Person Test (Donoso et al., 2010). Furthermore, Piotrowski (2015b) conducted a 15-year review of the usage of projective techniques worldwide; for 14 of 28 studies, at least one projective technique has ranked in the top five assessment instruments used across all categories. Human figure drawings, sentence completion exercises, and the TAT were among the 15 most frequently used among practitioners for 25 of the 28 studies reviewed.

However, there are several variations in assessment usage. There are many reasons why helping professionals select the instruments they do: professional discipline, type of cli-

Table 1.3
Frequency of Assessment Use Among Counselors

Test	All			SCs			CMHCs			OCs		
	Rank	M	%	Rank	M	%	Rank	M	%	Rank	M	%	Rank
Beck Depression Inventory[a]	1	1.95	43	8	3.17	73	1	2.48	60	4
Myers–Briggs Type Indicator[b]	2	1.95	41	8	2.20	52	5	3.18	78	1
Strong Interest Inventory[c]	3	2.10	47	7	1.86	39	9	3.14	73	2
ACT[d]	4	2.85	55	1	1.32	15	48	2.04	39	6
SAT/PSAT[d]	5	2.85	56	1	1.37	18	42	1.96	39	7
Self-Directed Search[c]	6	1.92	38	11	1.62	29	20	2.63	57	3
Wechsler Intelligence Scale for Children[e]	7	2.44	49	4	1.80	33	13	1.81	34	13
Conners' Rating Scales[a]	8	2.52	50	3	1.85	32	10	1.61	27	20
Beck Anxiety Inventory[a]	9	1.55	26	24	2.46	54	2	1.92	39	10
Substance Abuse Subtle Screening Inventory[a]	10	1.36	17	38	2.28	48	3	1.86	33	11
Wechsler Adult Intelligence Scale[e]	11	1.67	28	19	1.83	35	11	1.95	40	9
Woodcock–Johnson Tests of Cognitive Abilities[e]	12	2.23	44	5	1.45	22	36	1.61	25	20
O*NET System and Career Exploration Tools[c]	13	1.74	30	17	1.26	13	59	2.26	46	5
Wide Range Achievement Test[d]	14	1.89	36	13	1.56	22	22	1.76	30	16
Minnesota Multiphasic Personality Inventory[b]	15	1.35	18	41	1.93	43	6	1.86	41	11
Woodcock–Johnson Tests of Achievement[d]	15	2.18	44	6	1.38	18	41	1.58	24	23

Note. From "Assessment Use by Counselors in the United States: Implications for Policy and Practice," by C. H. Peterson, G. I. Lomas, E. S. Neukrug, and M. W. Bonner, 2014, *Journal of Counseling & Development, 92,* p. 92. All = all counselors combined; SCs = school counselors; CMHCs = clinical mental health counselors; OCs = other counselors; PSAT = Preliminary SAT; O*NET = Occupational Information Network.
[a]Clinical/behavioral test. [b]Personality test. [c]Career test. [d]Educational/achievement test. [e]Intelligence/cognitive test.

ent issue (Piotrowski, 2007), a need to show intervention effectiveness (Marotta & Watts, 2007), referral question, previous testing experiences, a test's psychometric properties, test administrators' graduate training experiences, agency or setting requirements, test availability, and therapists' theoretical orientation (Watkins et al., 1995). Although preferences for particular assessments have changed somewhat over the years, counselors continue to make extensive use of them for a variety of purposes. Counselors identify benefits of assessment for personal and career counseling. In regard to personal counseling, they emphasize the importance of assessing the client's potential for harm to self and others, the client's movement toward counseling goals, the extent of a client's psychological dysfunction, and overall treatment outcomes. In regard to career counseling, counselors stress the importance of test results for client decision making.

In Assessment in Action 1.1 (see pp. 18–19), counselors across settings discuss their use of assessment. Most of the specific tests mentioned are discussed in this book. It is important for counselors to learn about these tests so that they can use them successfully in their own practice and so that they can interpret scores on tests for clients referred to them by other professionals. Some of these instruments require advanced training beyond that obtained in most master's degree counseling programs.

Mental Health Counseling

Counselors often work in mental health agencies with other professionals to assess and treat clients encountering a variety of personal problems. Many of the instruments mental health counselors administer, score, and/or interpret require additional training. According to C. H. Peterson et al. (2014), the five most frequently used assessment instruments among mental health counselors are the Beck Depression Inventory, Beck Anxiety Inventory, WAIS, Mini-Mental State Examination, and the Myers–Briggs Type Indicator.

Career Counseling

Career assessment and counseling are pursued by counselors in a broad range of settings, including employment services, Veterans Affairs hospitals and mental health agencies, rehabilitation centers, and school and college counseling offices. Counselors in these settings benefit from a wide variety of career assessment instruments from which to choose for career counseling purposes. Wood and Hays (2013) described more than 300 instruments used to measure different factors important in career assessment.

Popular instruments designed specifically for career assessment include interest measures such as the Strong Interest Inventory or one of the Kuder interest inventories, aptitude tests such as the Differential Aptitude Tests or the ASVAB, and values measures such as the Work Values Inventory (Watkins, Campbell, & Nieberding, 1994). Because of their widespread use in career counseling over a number of years, these three types of measures (interest, aptitude, and values—sometimes called "the Big Three") have been looked on as the most crucial ones to take into account in career assessment (Swanson & D'Achiardi, 2005). Other measures pertinent to career counseling include measures of career choice and development, such as the Career Maturity Inventory and Career Decision Scale. The different career assessment measures have been used to (a) increase client self-knowledge, (b) help clients make career choices, and (c) encourage client participation in career counseling and subsequent decision making (Herr, Cramer, & Niles, 2004; Watkins et al., 1994).

School Counseling

Counselors in elementary, middle, and high school settings frequently are involved with assessment activities in their work with students, parents, and teachers. A survey of members of the American School Counselor Association found that school counselors frequently performed the assessment activities shown in Table 1.4 (Ekstrom, Elmore, Schafer, Trotter, & Webster, 2004). At least 75% of the counselors in the survey indicated that they performed these 12 activities often or occasionally. School administrators and teachers typically consider school counselors to be "test experts," whom they will consult in test matters such as those listed in Table 1.4 (Impara & Plake, 1995).

In many cases, school counselors do not administer standardized tests, but they are expected to be able to interpret the results from such tests to students, parents, and teachers (Blacher, Murray-Ward, & Uellendahl, 2005). In fact, school counselors are increasingly required to interpret and use assessment findings from standardized tests in high-stakes decisions that impact academic and college placement (American School Counselor Association, 2012). This requirement is evident in what school counselors report frequency using: C. H. Peterson et al. (2014) noted that the most frequently used tools among school counselors were the ACT, SAT/PSAT, Conners' Rating Scales, Wechsler Intelligence Scale for Children (WISC), and the Woodcock–Johnson Tests of Cognitive Abilities.

17

Table 1.4
Frequent Assessment Activities of School Counselors

Assessment Activity	Frequency[a] (%)
Referring students to other professionals, when appropriate, for additional assessment/appraisal	98
Interpreting scores from tests/assessments and using the information in counseling	91
Reading about and being aware of ethical issues in assessment	86
Reading about and being aware of current issues involving multicultural assessment, the assessment of students with disabilities and other special needs, and the assessment of language minorities	84
Synthesizing and integrating test and nontest data to make decisions about individuals	84
Reading a variety of professional literature on topics such as use of testing and assessment in school counseling, school counseling research, and career counseling research	84
Communicating and interpreting test/assessment information to parents	81
Communicating and interpreting test/assessment information to teachers, school administrators, and other professionals	80
Helping teachers use assessments and assessment information	80
Making decisions about the types of assessments to use in counseling groups or for individual students	78
Using assessment information to evaluate student performance	78
Using assessment information to monitor student performance	78

Note. From "A Survey of Assessment and Evaluation Activities of School Counselors," by R. B. Ekstrom, P. B. Elmore, W. D. Schafer, T. V. Trotter, and B. Webster, 2004, *Professional School Counselor, 8,* p. 27. Copyright 2004 by the American School Counselor Association. Reprinted with permission. No further reproduction authorized without written permission of the American School Counselor Association.
[a]Assessment activities that at least 75% of responding school counselors reported performing "often" or "occasionally."

Assessment in Action 1.1
Assessment Across Counseling Settings

For the last ten years in the career-service field, I have strongly advocated for the descriptive versus the prescriptive interpretation of psychometric-measurement instruments. Given the controversy about the validity and reliability of self-reported psychometric data, I believe that the power of these instruments lies in the theories behind them and the opportunity we have to help our students and alumni to estimate and test their results based on engaging or experiential applications of the operational definitions of the constructs. I thus focus on their recall of most meaningful experiences, regardless of their type or proximity, and briefly review with them the theory until they can grasp it reflectively and experientially, generate their preferred result, and apply it to their experiences. The outcome of this exercise is our collaborative ideation of the career or relational-dynamic applications of their estimate and its eventual comparison to their reported result.

—Daniel Pascoe Aguilar, PhD, MDiv
Co-Director of the University of Oregon Career Center

Counseling assessments at the K–12 setting sometimes look different from assessments in other areas of counseling. Informal assessments (particularly at the elementary level) may include procedures as simple as thumbs up, thumbs down, hands up, hands down, interviews, and/or questionnaires to show student understanding of subject matter. While doing classroom guidance lessons, I often ask students to raise their hands to show that they understand certain behaviors. For example, while doing a second-grade classroom guidance lesson on respect, I have had the students raise their hands to show which of the listed behaviors demonstrated respect. While it is very informal, it allows me to do a quick check to gain an understanding of which students actually grasped the concept of the lesson and have learned examples of what respectful behavior looks like. Oftentimes, informal and formal assessments are used to evaluate school needs, classroom needs, and individual needs.

Formal assessments in the K–12 setting are used for various reasons. When working with students to create groups, to determine grade-level placement, and to assist with college preparation, school counselors in Virginia are able to utilize formal assessments such as the Phonological Awareness Literacy Screening (PALS), Standards of Learning (SOL), and Scholastic Aptitude Tests (SAT). Other formal assessments used to assist career education programs are the Virginia Education Wizard's Career Assessment and the Naglieri Assessment Tests, which are used to assess students for Talented and Gifted (TAG) programs.

Because effectiveness in assessment and evaluation is critical to comprehensive school counseling programs, the American School Counselor Association's National Standards state that assessment results be utilized in educational planning (Bowers & Hatch, 2005). Whether the assessment is informal or formal, it is important that school counselors have an understanding of their school's needs and that the data are appropriately used to assist students.

—Brandy K. Richeson, PhD
School Counselor Educator, Hampton University

The University of Central Florida (UCF) Marriage & Family Research Institute (MFRI) is a research institute focused on improving the quality of life for individuals, couples, and families. The MFRI utilizes various assessments to measure the effectiveness of the services provided and to engage in data driven decision making. The current grant funded project, *Project Harmony*, aims to assess the impact of a relationship education intervention between treatment and control groups. Impact will be measured on proximal and distal outcomes of improved family functioning and reduced poverty for individuals and couples. Proximal outcomes are defined as "skills and knowledge of principals," whereas distal outcomes are defined as "indicators of relationship health" (Wadsworth & Markman, 2012). Assessments include (a) the Dyadic Adjustment Scale (DAS; Spanier, 1976), (b) the Dyadic Coping Inventory (DCI; Bodenmann, 2008), (c) the Communication Patterns Questionnaire–Short Form (CPQ-SF; Christensen & Sullaway, 1984), (d) the Parental Alliance Measure (PAM; Konold & Abidin, 2001), and (e) the Parenting Stress Index-4 (PSI-4; Abidin, 2012).

—Sejal M. Barden, PhD
Executive Director, MFRI
Principal Investigator,
Project Harmony

Counseling Research and Counselor Education

As counselors practice and use assessments in their work with clients, it is important that they understand and contribute to current research for a particular assessment tool. Hogan and Rengert (2008) noted 410 assessments used in research, as cited in four journals published in the counseling field for 2002–2005 (*Journal of Counseling & Development*, *Journal of Counseling Psychology*, *Journal of Mental Health Counseling*, and *Professional School Counseling*). Table 1.5 provides a list of the top 30 instruments used in research studies for these journals; each of these instruments was used at least four times during the review period.

Although Table 1.5 may not be comprehensive, given that several counseling journals were omitted from the analysis, the findings do highlight some differences between what tools practitioners say they use with clients versus those with which they conduct and publish research. Hogan and Rengert (2008) noted the following: The Strong Interest Inventory (Harmon, Hansen, Borgen, & Hammer, 1994) was the only instrument to make both the self-report and published research lists; there were no projective techniques included in the research studies; the Sixteen Personality Factor Questionnaire (Conn & Rieke, 1994) and the Bender Visual Motor Gestalt Test (Brannigan & Decker, 2003) did not appear in research studies; and there was only one use each of the WAIS (Wechsler, 1997), WISC

Table 1.5
Top Tests Used in Research Studies in Four Counseling Journals for 2002–2005

Test	Times Used
Beck Depression Inventory	18
Rosenberg Self-Esteem Scale	12
Experiences in Close Relationships	8
Hopkins Symptom Checklist	8
Multigroup Ethnic Identity Measure	8
Brief Symptom Inventory	7
Center for Epidemiologic Studies–Depression scale	7
Outcome Questionnaire–45	7
Perceived Stress Scale	7
Asian Values Scale	6
Career Decisions Scale	6
Marlowe–Crowne Social Desirability Scale	6
Session Evaluation Questionnaire	6
Balanced Inventory of Desirable Responding	5
Differentiation of Self Inventory	5
Eating Disorder Inventory	5
Strong Interest Inventory	5
Adult Attachment Scale–Revised	4
Child Behavior Checklist	4
Clinical Vignettes	4
Dynamic Adjustment Scale	4
Global Assessment of Functioning	4
Multidimensional Perfection Scale	4
National Education Longitudinal Scale of 1998	4
Positive and Negative Affect Schedule	4
Satisfaction With Life Scale	4
Self-Construal Scale	4
Self-Efficacy Scale	4
Social Connectedness Scale	4
Symptom Checklist–90–Revised	4

Note. The four journals were *Journal of Counseling & Development*, *Journal of Counseling Psychology*, *Journal of Mental Health Counseling*, and *Professional School Counseling*. From "Test Usage in Published Research and the Practice of Counseling: A Comparative Review," by T. P. Hogan and C. Rengert, 2008, *Measurement and Evaluation in Counseling and Development, 41*, pp. 51–56.

(Wechsler, 2003), and Wide Range Achievement Test (WRAT; Wilkinson, 1993), with no other use of intelligence or ability tests in the research studies. In sum, counselors need to be aware of the discrepancies in test use across disciplines and settings and among what is used in research.

In addition to areas in which there is limited research on some of the tools used in counseling practice, there seems to be some frequently used tools in practice not frequently addressed in counselor education. Neukrug, Peterson, Bonner, and Lomas (2013) also investigated the assessment instruments taught by counselor educators. Among the 210 counselor educators surveyed, the 15 identified as the most frequently used were as follows: Beck Depression Inventory, Myers–Briggs Type Indicator, Strong Interest Inventory, Self-Directed Search, MMPI, WAIS, WISC, Mini-Mental State Examination, Beck Anxiety Inventory, Sixteen Personality Factor Questionnaire, Substance Abuse Subtle Screening Inventory, TAT, House–Tree–Person, Millon Clinical Multiaxial Inventory, and Stanford–Binet Intelligence Scale.

Key Questions for Selecting Assessments

Psychological assessment procedures differ from each other in a variety of ways. As indicated in the following paragraphs, these differences can be categorized by six basic questions regarding the nature of the assessment method itself.

Who Is Making the Assessment?

Is the person making a self-assessment, or is another person making the assessment? Measurement specialists have differentiated between "S-data" based on self-reports and "O-data" based on the reports of others, such as teachers, supervisors, family members, and friends. Both types of data are needed to obtain a full appraisal of the individual. For example, a process known as 360° (full-circle) feedback is sometimes used in business settings to evaluate employee performance from multiple points of view, including those of managers, peers, subordinates, customers, and self. Although not readily available, reports from others are particularly helpful in assessing conditions when self-reports may be distorted or limited, such as substance abuse, personality disorders, and childhood disorders.

In general, self-reports and other-reports offer different perspectives regarding an individual. Research indicates that the two types of data can complement each other or help to substantiate the existence of less favorable diagnoses not reported for one type of data. For example, Oltmanns, Friedman, Fiedler, and Turkheimer (2004) found that the performance of recruits in the military was more effectively predicted by a combination of S-data (information from a self-report questionnaire) and O-data (ratings made by fellow recruits) than by either type of data by itself. Furthermore, Tandler, Mosch, Wolf, and Borkenau (2015) found that S-data and O-data were mixed in assessments of personality disorder symptoms: Individuals with high personality disorder symptomatology reported themselves more favorably (S-data), whereas peer data (O-data) showed greater symptomatology and thus less favorable findings.

What Is Being Assessed?

"What" here refers to the subject of the assessment procedure. Is the individual or the environment the subject of the assessment? Counselors have usually been interested in individual assessment; however, instruments that evaluate the environment (e.g., classroom atmosphere or residence hall settings) can also provide important information for understanding or treating a problem. The client's behavior depends on both individual and situational characteristics, so counseling can be most effective when psychological assessment includes both the individual and the environment.

If the individual is being appraised, does the content of the assessment deal primarily with affective (feeling), cognitive (thinking), or behavioral (doing) aspects of the individual? Affective characteristics may be subdivided into temperamental and motivational factors (Guilford, 1959). Temperamental factors include the characteristics assessed by most personality inventories, for example, self-sufficiency, stability, and impulsiveness. Motivational factors refer to interests or values. According to Guilford (1959), temperament governs the manner in which an individual performs, whereas motivation determines what activities or goals the individual will choose to pursue.

Cognitive variables may be based on learning that takes place in a specific course or learning that is relatively independent of specific coursework. This distinction describes a basic difference between achievement and aptitude tests. Achievement tests evaluate past or present performance; aptitude tests predict future performance. Behavioral measures include responses that are voluntary or involuntary in nature. Voluntary responses may be assessed either by self-monitoring or by other-monitoring techniques. A systematic record is kept of measurable items, such as calories consumed or hours spent watching television. In the case of involuntary responses (e.g., blood pressure or heart rate), various types of physiological measures are used to assess individual reactivity. Biofeedback devices, often used to teach relaxation methods, are a good example of the latter type of assessment measure.

The question of what is being assessed also pertains to the variables chosen for the assessment process. Individuals can be assessed by common variables that apply to all people or by unique variables that apply only to the individual. In the first case, sometimes referred to as *nomothetic assessment*, emphasis is placed on variables that show lawful or meaningful distinctions among people. The group provides a frame of reference for determining which variables to assess and how to interpret the results. In the second case, sometimes referred to as *idiographic assessment*, emphasis is placed on those variables that can be most helpful in describing the individual. The individual serves as the reference point both to identify relevant variables and to interpret data.

Most psychological tests, such as interest and personality inventories, use the nomothetic approach. These tests use the same scales to describe all clients. Scores are interpreted in regard to a set of norms. In contrast, many of the informal assessment procedures, such as the interview, case study, or card sorts, use an idiographic approach. A different set of variables is used to describe each client. Nomothetic techniques can be more readily interpreted, but they may not be as relevant or as penetrating as idiographic methods, which have been designed to measure variations in individuality (Grice, 2004; Hurley & Murphy, 2015). However, M. Schmidt, Perels, and Schmitz (2010) noted that a combination of these methods may be more useful, as the different methods have varying foci.

Where Is the Assessment Taking Place?

The location where the assessment takes place is important in the sense that it helps to differentiate between test results obtained in laboratory settings and those obtained in natural settings. Many psychological tests must be administered under standardized conditions so that the test results can be interpreted properly. For these tests, a testing room or laboratory is usually used. If the circumstances of test administration differ from person to person, differences in the testing conditions can influence test results. Some measures, such as employee ratings, are obtained in natural settings under conditions that may vary considerably for different individuals. Variations in job circumstances can greatly affect the ratings. Interpretations of the results must take into account the setting in which they were obtained.

When Is the Assessment Occurring?

The question of when an assessment takes place is of value in distinguishing between assessments planned in advance (prospective) and those based on recall (retrospective).

Self-monitoring techniques are usually planned in advance. For example, students may be asked to keep track of the number of hours that they studied or the number of pages that they read during a study period. In contrast, biographical measures such as life history forms are recorded to the best of the individual's recollection after the event has occurred.

Why Is the Assessment Being Undertaken?

The question of "why" pertains to the reason for administering the test rather than to the nature of the test itself. The same test can be used for a variety of purposes, such as counseling, selection, placement, description, and evaluation. When tests are used in counseling, all data obtained must be regarded as confidential. Such private data may be contrasted with public data—data originally obtained for another purpose, such as selection or placement. Examples of public data include academic grades, education level, or occupational status. Counselors use public as well as private data in helping clients to address certain issues, because the public data can provide a great deal of information about the client's past performance under various circumstances.

How Is the Assessment Conducted?

"How" here refers to the manner in which the test material is presented, how the data are analyzed, and how the score for the assessment procedure is obtained. First, is the type of behavior that is being assessed disguised or undisguised? Projective techniques (described in Chapter 13) are designed so that the respondent is typically unaware of the true nature of the test or of any "preferred" answer. Because the intent of the test is disguised, it is more difficult for respondents to fake their answers to produce a particular impression.

Second, is the information obtained in the assessment analyzed in a quantitative or qualitative fashion? Quantitative procedures, which include most psychological tests, yield a specific score on a continuous scale. Qualitative procedures, such as card sorts, work samples, or structured exercises, produce a verbal description of a person's behavior or of a situation that can be placed into one of several categories (e.g., outgoing vs. reserved personality type). By their very nature, quantitative procedures have been more thoroughly studied in terms of reliability and validity. Qualitative procedures, however, are more open-ended and adaptable for use in counseling, especially with a diverse clientele (Brott, 2015; McMahon & Patton, 2015).

Finally, are scores arrived at objectively, free of individual judgment, or subjectively, based on the scorer's best judgment? Tests that can be scored by means of a scoring stencil are objective. That is, different individuals using the same scoring stencil with an answer sheet should obtain the same score if they are careful in counting the number of correct answers. In contrast, rating scales are subjective—the score assigned will often vary depending on the individual rater.

Chapter Summary

Assessment has a long history in counseling and serves several functions that ultimately assist to transform lives and improve interventions. The chapter reviewed foundational information about assessments, including key terminology, assessment use and purpose, and developments in intelligence, ability, vocational, and personality assessments throughout history. The next chapter discusses the assessment process and types of methods used with clients to measure individual and counseling outcomes.

Assessment refers to the process of integrating and interpreting client information from a broad range of evaluation methods. This process can be improved by adhering to the basic principles of psychological assessment outlined in this chapter. Tests have been criticized for both their limitations and their misuse. Counselors need to be aware of test limitations and must obtain appropriate training and supervision in regard to the tests that they plan to use. The process of assessment can be described as both a science and an art. Many of the instruments used in assessment have been developed by means of empirical research and improved over time; however, the process of interpreting the assessment data often depends on the counselor's best judgment. In addition to learning about different evaluation procedures, counselors need to consider how they can improve the judgments they make in the assessment process. Please review the Tip Sheet below to understand guiding principles of assessment in counseling.

Tip Sheet
Principles of Assessment in Counseling

✓ Know the purpose of the assessment to assist you both in selecting and in interpreting assessments.

✓ Include the client as a collaborator in selecting topics for assessment and in interpreting the results.

✓ Be aware of the strengths and limitations of the assessment procedures used in counseling, including information about the psychometric properties of tests and the psychological findings regarding the behavior being assessed.

✓ Understand the theoretical construct or condition being measured by a test, such as attention-deficit/hyperactivity disorder, and recognize whether the test adequately measures this construct.

✓ Be well versed in all aspects of test use, including selection, administration and scoring, interpretation, and the communication of results.

✓ Use several methods of assessment for an overall assessment in order to provide a broader view of an issue and corroborate the results of any one assessment method. Be sure to use both quantitative and qualitative tools.

✓ Assess more than a single variable at a time. A multidimensional approach enriches the assessment process by providing additional information that can be helpful in forming assessments. It presents a "big picture" of the client's situation that can be important in viewing a client's concerns from different angles.

✓ If possible, use instruments that include validity checks, such as "fake good," "fake bad," and "random responding" scales. Make sure that a client's test responses are valid before attempting to interpret the test results.

✓ Consider the possibility of multiple problems, such as depression coupled with substance abuse, anxiety, or physical problems. Clients with mental disorders often meet the criteria for more than one disorder at the same time (Kessler, Chiu, Demler, & Walters, 2005; Rector, 2012).

✓ Assess the situation as well as the client. Avoid attribution bias, which indicates a predisposition to attribute the cause of problems to the individual rather than to the situation. Environmental factors interact with individual characteristics in affecting a person's behavior in a particular situation.

✓ Consider alternative hypotheses. Counselors need to be watchful for confirmatory bias, that is, a tendency to look only for evidence that will support a favorite hypothesis. Seek data that may support an alternative hypothesis as well as data that may prove a pre-established hypothesis. For example, a counselor who believes that a student is failing in school because of lack of ability should also consider other factors, such as health, personal or family problems, and study skills, that may be affecting academic performance.

✓ Treat all assessments as tentative. As additional data become available, the counselor should be ready to revise the assessment.

✓ Keep in mind the regression effect when interpreting very high or very low scores, all of which are influenced to some extent by chance factors. On retesting, a client's scores tend to regress toward the mean of the population that the client represents. That is, clients who obtain unusually high or low scores on a test the first time usually will not score as high or low on an equivalent form of that test the next time they take it. For this reason, it is often helpful to test a client more than once.

✓ Become familiar with the condition or issue being assessed. Make use of base rates (frequency of occurrence of a particular behavior or diagnosis within a given population) in undertaking and forming an assessment. For example, because of the frequency of problem drinking among college students, counselors should routinely assess college clients for alcohol abuse (Levin et al., 2012).

✓ Consider the influence of individual factors, such as age, gender, education level, and ethnicity, on test results. Use separate norms that take such factors into account when they are available.

✓ Be aware of common cultural or personal biases that may influence assessment decisions. Studies show that race bias, social class bias, and gender bias may affect clinical judgment.

✓ Identify, interpret, and incorporate cultural data as part of the assessment process. Use measures of acculturation, such as number of generations in new culture and language preference, to help determine whether a client fits the population on which a test was developed and normed.

✓ Consult with other professionals regarding assessment procedures and outcomes. Continue learning about assessments and the underlying constructs they measure.

✓ Use the assessment results to provide feedback to clients as part of the therapy process. Assessments should include an evaluation of a client's strengths as well as limitations.

Review Questions

1. What are the five functions of assessment, as identified in the problem-solving model?
2. What are some of the ways assessments should not be used?
3. Who are the key players in the development of intelligence, ability, vocational, and personality assessment?
4. How have historical events influenced how tests were developed and used over the past 100 years?
5. What are the primary assessments used in the counseling setting?

Resources for Further Learning

American Educational Research Association, American Psychological Association, & National Council on Measurement in Education. (2014). *Standards for educational and psychological testing.* Washington, DC: American Educational Research Association.

Carson, J. (2014). Mental testing in the early twentieth century: Internationalizing the mental testing story. *History of Psychology, 17,* 249–255.

DuBois, R. (1970). *A history of psychological testing.* Boston, MA: Allyn & Bacon.

Kiresuk, T. J., Smith, A., & Cardillo, J. E. (2014). *Goal attainment scaling: Applications, theory, and measurement.* New York, NY: Taylor & Francis.

Chapter 2

The Assessment Process

Assessment, no matter the setting in which it is used, serves to provide clinical information that assists both counselors and clients. This chapter provides information about the types of assessment methods available to counselors. Then, two types of assessment are discussed: the assessment process with clients and assessment of client progress and counseling outcomes.

Test Your Knowledge

Match the items in the right column with the most appropriate component of the assessment process in the left column:

_____ 1. Test selection	a. A counselor reviews and applies scoring procedures.
_____ 2. Test administration	
_____ 3. Test interpretation	b. A counselor presents a comprehensive picture using several assessment data sources.
_____ 4. Communication of findings	
_____ 5. Outcome assessments	c. A client completes a satisfaction form at the end of a comprehensive session.
	d. A counselor and client consider various assessment methods.
	e. A counselor attends closely to testing conditions.

Types of Assessment Methods

In Chapter 1, four major assessment categories were discussed: intelligence, ability, career, and personality assessment. There are several types of assessment methods that can be found within those categories. This section first outlines three major distinctions in assessments: group versus individual assessment, standardized versus nonstandardized assessment, and speed versus power tests. Then, specific assessment types are described: rating scales, projective techniques, behavioral observations, interviews, biographical measures, and physiological measures. Some assessment categories, such as intelligence and ability, typically involve standardized power tests. Other categories, such as career and personality, are more likely to contain a wider range of assessment methods.

Group Versus Individual Assessment

Some assessments are designed to be administered to one individual at a time by a trained examiner; others can be administered to a group of people. **Group assessments** allow information to be obtained from many people within a short period of time at relatively little cost, whereas **individual assessments** permit counselors to adapt the test administration to the needs of the client. Individual assessments must be used with certain populations, such as young children or people with particular disabilities. Individual assessments permit observational data, such as the client's language proficiency and level of cooperation, to be obtained in addition to test scores.

Standardized Versus Nonstandardized Assessment

As discussed in Chapter 1, standardization is a defining feature of a test; thus, standardized tests must meet certain standards during the testing process. These standards include uniform procedures for test administration, objective scoring, and the use of representative norm groups for test interpretation. Most standardized tests have clear evidence of their reliability and validity (see Chapter 5). **Standardized tests** can include the following assessment procedures, each of which is discussed in this book: intelligence tests, ability tests, personality inventories, interest inventories, and values inventories.

Nonstandardized assessments include rating scales, projective techniques, behavioral observations, and biographical measures, all of which are discussed below. Nonstandardized techniques produce results that are less dependable (i.e., less reliable and valid) compared with standardized techniques; however, they allow counselors to consider aspects of behavior or the environment not covered by traditional psychological tests. Counselors must be concerned not only about the dependability of test results but also about the exhaustiveness of the results (Kane, 2013). Tests that provide highly dependable information often describe only a small part of the information a counselor needs. Nonstandardized assessments provide less dependable information but can nonetheless aid counselors in obtaining information on topics that would be missed by formal testing procedures.

Some researchers have conceptualized nonstandardized techniques in assessment as qualitative assessment. **Qualitative assessment** involves informal and flexible procedures often used in individual and group counseling. This type of assessment focuses largely on increasing client self-awareness within a session. Some examples of qualitative assessments include simulation exercises, projective techniques, and card sorts. Brott (2015) and McMahon and Patton (2015) provide more specific examples of qualitative assessment methods.

Speed Versus Power Tests

Some ability tests place a heavy emphasis on speed of response and are known as **speed tests**. These tests are homogenous in content and often consist of a large number of easy items that a person must complete quickly. Examples of speed tests with relatively short time limits include finger and manual dexterity tests and clerical speed and accuracy tests. In contrast, **power tests** contain items of varying difficulty, most of which the person is expected to complete within the time limits. If 90% of the people for whom the test is designed can complete the test within the time limits, the test can be described as a power test. Although speed can still be a factor for some students on power tests, speed would not have much influence on the total score for most students. Most intelligence tests, scholastic aptitude tests, and achievement tests are basically power tests.

Rating Scales

Rating scales, which provide subjective estimates of various behaviors or characteristics based on the rater's observations, are a common method of assessment. Rating scales include self-ratings, ratings of others, and ratings of the environment. They often provide a series of items and scoring criteria and are frequently useful as pre- and posttest evaluations of some behavior or attitude.

Because of their subjectivity, rating scales have a number of disadvantages. Raters can make several types of errors, especially as the amount of time increases between an observation and the actual rating, if there are changes in the length of the observation period, or if there are changes in how the construct being measured is defined. Common errors associated with rating scales are (a) the halo effect, (b) error of central tendency or range of restriction error, (c) leniency error, (d) drift, and (e) decay. In the case of the **halo effect**, raters show a tendency to generalize from one aspect of the client to all other aspects. For example, if a person is friendly, that person may also be rated highly in unrelated areas such as intelligence, creativity, leadership, and motivation. The **error of central tendency** or **range of restriction error** describes the tendency to rate all people as "average" or near the middle of the rating scale. The **leniency error** refers to the tendency to rate the characteristics of people more favorably than they should be rated. **Drift** refers to systematic changes in how a variable is interpreted or defined over time. For example, a supervisor observing an employee on the criterion of "being a team player" may over time and across situations change how he or she defines "being a team player." The final error, **decay**, refers to decreased reliability in how well an event is observed—usually as a function of an increased observation period. For example, if a school counselor typically observes a third grader for 30-minute increments on a behavior of interest, and then increases the observation period to 60 minutes, fatigue or other factors may influence how well that school counselor is able to note that behavior.

To control for such errors, raters are sometimes asked to rank individuals relative to another on each rating scale. As an alternative, raters may be forced to distribute their ratings across the entire rating scale according to the normal curve or a similar system. When these techniques are applied to a large number of people, they prevent ratings from bunching up in the middle of the distribution or at the top end of the distribution. Kenrick and Funder (1988) offered the following suggestions for improving the validity of ratings: (a) use raters who are thoroughly familiar with the person being rated, (b) require multiple behavioral observations, (c) obtain ratings from more than one observer, (d) use dimensions that are publicly observable, and (e) identify behaviors for observation that are relevant to the dimension in question. These suggestions can help counteract limitations posed by the various sources of invalidity.

Examples of rating techniques include the semantic differential and situational tests. The **semantic differential** technique requires raters to rate concepts (e.g., "my job") by means of a series of bipolar scales, or **rank-order scales**, where raters or clients assign numbers to items by priority level or relevance. **Situational tests** require the person to perform a task in a situation that is similar to the situation for which the person is being evaluated. For example, the in-basket technique requires candidates for an administrative position to respond to the daily tasks of an administrator by means of an in-basket (work assignment basket) that simulates the actual work assignments of administrators. Situational tests can often meet the conditions suggested by Kenrick and Funder (1988). For this reason, they often are beneficial in predicting performance in a situation similar to that of the test. Situational tests are frequently used to assess leadership or management skills.

Projective Assessments

Projective assessments use vague or ambiguous stimuli to which people must respond. Because the stimuli (e.g., inkblots, ambiguous pictures, and incomplete sentences) are vague, people tend to make interpretations of the stimuli that reveal more about themselves than about the stimuli. They "project" their own personality onto the stimuli. Responses are usually scored subjectively. Common projective techniques include the Rorschach Inkblot Test, TAT, and Rotter Incomplete Sentences Blank. The use of projective techniques in counseling is discussed further in Chapter 13.

Behavioral Observations

Behavioral observations refer to behaviors that can be observed and counted. The observations are planned in advance or based on recent events. The behaviors, which usually occur in a natural setting, are monitored by the client, by an observer such as a partner or parent, or both. The observer usually records the frequency of a discrete behavior, for example, the number of "I" statements made in an interview or the number of conversations initiated. Frequently, the duration of the response and the intensity of the behavior (as rated by the observer) are also recorded. Behavioral observations have the advantage of pertaining directly to a behavior that a client is concerned about. The behavior can usually be included as part of a goal. The measure is directly related to the client's treatment.

Interviews

Interviews can be structured, where a more standardized set of questions is used to solicit client data, or unstructured, where there are no preset list of questions and the counselor–client interaction guides future questions and probes. Structured interviews offer some standardization—and thus likely provide stability or reliability in test administration—yet they do not allow the counselor to probe responses for more detail. Unstructured interviews generally allow for greater counseling rapport and further follow-up; however, the counselor may miss key assessment areas or spend more time on an irrelevant topic. Semi-structured interviews combine elements of both structured and unstructured interviews and can therefore address some of the disadvantages of each. Interviews are an important part of clinical assessment and are discussed further in Chapters 8 and 9.

Biographical Measures

Biographical measures refer to accomplishments or experiences as reported by the client or as reflected in historical records. For example, a résumé, college application form, or work portfolio usually provides an extensive amount of biographical information. Biographical measures differ from behavioral measures in that the observations are not planned in advance. They differ from rating scales in that the information is usually a matter of fact rather than a matter of judgment. Biographical data (**biodata**) include information maintained in cumulative records by schools or in personnel records by businesses, such as academic grades, extracurricular achievements, job promotions, hobbies, and volunteer work experiences. Biodata are information regarding a person's prior experiences that can provide a sense of one's current knowledge and skills; this information is often used for the purpose of selection (Beatty, 2013). Biodata are usually collected by means of a written form or during the course of an initial interview with a client. Although this information is most often used in a qualitative manner, it can also be quantified for assessment purposes (Beatty, 2013; Oswald, Schmitt, Kim, Ramsay, & Gillespie, 2004).

The value of biographical measures in assessment is expressed in the well-established psychological maxim: "The best predictor of future performance is past performance." As a rule, the best single predictor of college grades for an individual is usually that person's high school grades. A person who has functioned well in a particular job in the past will probably perform well in related types of activities in the future.

On the one hand, biographical measures are both economical and efficient. They can provide information on topics such as leadership experiences or creative accomplishments that may be difficult to assess by other means. On the other hand, they may be inappropriate or difficult to interpret if the person's experiences have been unusual or severely limited. Biographical measures yield a broad range of information, but the meaning of the information requires additional interaction with the client or others familiar with the situation.

Physiological Measures

Physiological measures can be particularly helpful in understanding and monitoring client behavior because of the unique information that it provides. It enables a client's condition, such as anxiety, to be assessed at a more basic level than that made possible by traditional assessments such as standardized tests and behavioral observations (Norman, Hawkley, Luhmann, Cacioppo, & Berntson, 2012). Measures such as heart rate, breathing rate, muscle contractions, and blood pressure, which are primarily involuntary in nature, can reveal information regarding a client's condition that might otherwise be missed (Brannon, Feist, & Updegraff, 2013; Lawyer & Smitherman, 2004). Advances in instrumentation and procedures (e.g., biofeedback devices, cardiac monitoring systems, and alcohol biomarkers) and collaboration with other professionals in a team approach make it feasible to include such variables in the assessment process.

An Overview of the Assessment Process

With a basic understanding of the assessment methods that can be used in the assessment process, let's discuss the assessment process itself. The assessment process is synonymous with the counseling process (see Figure 2.1). Both processes involve the continual dialogue between counselors and clients about presenting and underlying issues, the use of various tools to understand more fully those issues as well as attributes that may assist clients to address those issues, and the ongoing interpretation, reflection, and communication

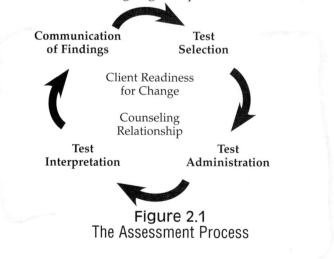

Figure 2.1
The Assessment Process

of changes as new data enter the counseling relationship. To this end, counselors need to begin counseling with the end in mind: How do they see themselves communicating (and intervening) effectively with clients? How do early decisions about the types of tools selected affect the counseling relationship? In sum, assessment should be seen as a part of the counseling process and not as an interruption of it.

Before beginning the process of selecting assessment tools, counselors need to determine a client's readiness for change. Clients differ in their readiness for counseling and in their expectations of counseling. In their work with individuals with addictive behaviors, Prochaska, DiClemente, and Norcross (1992) and Prochaska, Norcross, and DiClemente (2013) noted five stages of change experienced by a client: precontemplation, contemplation, preparation, action, and maintenance. These same stages of change pertain to clients with a wide variety of problems (Prochaska et al., 2013). Furthermore, these stages relate to the overall assessment process.

In the **precontemplation stage**, individuals are not especially aware of their problems and have no plans to change their behavior in the foreseeable future. Thus, they typically seek counseling at the insistence of someone else who is concerned about their problems. Research indicates that such individuals benefit less from counseling and perceive their counseling relationship less favorably than do those in more advanced stages of change (Soberay, Grimsley, Faragher, Barbash, & Berger, 2014). For the **contemplation stage**, individuals are aware of their problems but have not yet made a serious commitment to do anything about them. Individuals in this stage are considering making changes in their behavior sometime within the next 6 months; however, it may be much longer before they actually do make changes.

In the **preparation stage**, individuals have begun to make small changes in their problematic behaviors, with the intention of making more complete changes within 1 month. Individuals reach the **action stage** when they successfully change their behavior for short periods of time. If changes persist for longer than 6 months, the client enters the **maintenance stage**, in which the goal is to maintain the behavioral and attitudinal changes that have occurred.

If a client is in one of the earlier stages of change (i.e., precontemplation or contemplation), the counselor may have difficulty selecting appropriate tools as the client may not discuss problems accurately and may exhibit resistance during test administration, interpretation, and communication. As clients become more aware of their problems and begin making incremental changes, the assessment process becomes richer and increasingly uses multiple assessment methods to communicate data to facilitate treatment planning and intervention. Assessment of the client's stage of change is crucial for determining the most effective treatment technique. As noted by Prochaska et al. (2013), different approaches should be used for clients in different stages.

Most clients recycle through some or all of the stages several times before successfully achieving long-term changes. Although recycling is the norm, most clients learn from their previous attempts so that they make faster progress through the cycle in subsequent attempts to resolve their problems. The University of Rhode Island Change Assessment, a 32-item questionnaire that assesses attitudes and behaviors associated with different stages of change, can be used to help determine a client's readiness for change (P. J. Cohen, Glaser, & Calhoun, 2005).

Test Selection

Test selection refers to the decision-making process counselors use throughout the counseling relationship to aid in client evaluation and treatment planning, using a wide range of assessment methods. If at all possible, clients should actively participate in selecting the tests that will be used in counseling. From a therapeutic point of view, clients should collaborate in deciding what questions they wish to answer by the use of tests or other assessment procedures. If convinced of the tests' usefulness, clients may be more motivated to do their best on ability tests and to be accurate and truthful in responding to items on interest and personality inventories. By having participated in the decisions to use the tests, clients are also more likely to accept the results and interpretations with less defensiveness. They can be more objective in their perception of the test results.

Individuals often approach tests with some anxiety, particularly aptitude and achievement tests where they may fear failure. Anxiety regarding testing can influence the entire counseling process. Even interest and personality inventories can reveal aspects of a person's character that may indicate weaknesses or undesirable features. To reduce the threatening aspects of tests, you should make clear to clients that the purpose of testing is to provide self-understanding, not evaluation or judgment. It is important to convey to clients the feeling that they will be accepted whatever the test results happen to be.

In the case of academic or career counseling, clients often feel dependent on tests. They perceive the counselor as an expert who will select tests that will tell them what to do. Active participation by clients in test selection helps to counteract overreliance on the counselor.

Generally, a client does not select specific assessment tools. That is a technical matter that counselors must decide on the basis of their knowledge of assessments. Instead, the client helps to decide the types of assessments that can provide the information most useful for whatever actions or decisions are going to be made. Clients are not nearly as interested in specific characteristics of assessments as they are in the implications the results will have for them. The types of tests are therefore described in a general fashion. For example, you should describe the Strong Interest Inventory to a client simply as "an interest inventory that enables you to compare your likes and dislikes with those of people in different occupations." You should not overwhelm the client with a detailed description of the instrument itself.

After you and a particular client have agreed on the type of test, you must decide which specific test would be best to use. In particular, you want to consider the test's reliability, validity, normative data, and practicality for its intended purpose. Does the test possess sufficient reliability and validity to answer the questions posed by the client and his or her situation? Does the test provide appropriate normative data for the client? Is the test easy to administer and score? How expensive is it? Is the reading level appropriate? Is this assessment procedure culturally appropriate for the client? Counselors can best answer these questions, which require specialized knowledge regarding the technical quality of different assessments.

When a client states a need for a test, the counselor should not necessarily take that statement at face value. For example, if a client requests a personality inventory, the counselor should explore the meaning of the request, not simply accept it. A particular client may be experiencing a significant problem, such as anxiety or depression, that should be explored before tests are assigned. The client may be asking for help regarding a particular problem but having difficulty revealing the problem or asking for help directly. The request for tests serves as an avenue to get at the major problem.

Tests should not be used unnecessarily. Other sources of data in addition to tests should also be explored. In a college counseling center, little is gained by selecting scholastic aptitude tests when records of college entrance tests, high school grades, and college grades are readily available. Other counseling agencies, of course, often start with no previous information. Nevertheless, counselors can first attempt to explore with clients self-descriptions and previous experiences that may provide relevant information. Clients' recall of previous experiences can provide a great deal of information either to supplement test results or to eliminate the need for particular tests.

At this stage of the assessment process, particularly at the beginning of counseling, tests are not the only assessment method to consider. For example, you may be interested in using an initial clinical interview or preexisting biographical data. It is important to involve clients in this process if possible or at least to explain briefly the purpose for collecting data using these methods. Now, let's discuss how we obtain information about assessments to guide the selection process.

Sources of Information About Assessment Procedures

After you understand a client's orientation toward problem solving and thus assessment purpose, the test selection process now involves selecting the actual assessment tools. This section provides key information sources for locating and obtaining assessments. Your university library will likely have many of these sources in print or online format. After you review this section, complete Activity 2.1.

Mental Measurements Yearbook. The best general source of information about commercial tests is the ***Mental Measurements Yearbook*** (*MMY*) series. The *MMY*, now in its 19th edition (J. F. Carlson, Geisinger, & Jonson, 2014), provides access to information about commercially published tests and test reviews. The *MMY* also provides a reference list for each test. Oscar Buros, its first editor, developed the *MMY* in 1938. The *MMY* is published every few years, and online access is available for *MMY* reviews 1985 to present. A key inclusion criterion for a test to appear in the *MMY* is that the test must be new or revised since the previous *MMY* edition. Critical reviews are not published for each test in each yearbook because each new volume is designed to add to, rather than replace, information found in prior volumes.

There are many ways to search for a test. If you have some information about a specific test, such as the TAT, you can search by its full name (i.e., Thematic Apperception Test), acronym, publisher, or author. If you do not have a specific test in mind, or do not have adequate information, you can search by test purpose, category, or intended population (age, grade level, gender); by individual versus group administration; by publication date; by *MMY* volume number; by number of available reviews; or by many other search fields. There are several indices (e.g., test title, classified subject, publisher, names of authors, publisher directory) as searchable options if you decide you would like to search the print version of the *MMY* (or *Tests in Print*, described next).

Tests in Print. Published initially in 1961 by the Buros Institute of Mental Measurements, *Tests in Print* (*TIP*, 9th ed.; N. Anderson, Schlueter, Carlson, & Geisinger, 2016) is designed to serve as a comprehensive index of all tests in the Buros system (and appearing in previous *MMY*s and other materials). The *TIP* provides descriptions and references of all tests in print, including those for commercial use. Specifically, for any test, *TIP* indicates test purpose, acronym, in-print status, cost, publisher and author information, intended population, administration and scoring information, and publication date. *TIP* also includes a list of tests that have gone out of print since its last edition. However, you will not find test reviews such as in the *MMY*. Searching for a test is done in a manner similar to how you search in *MMY*.

Tests and Test Critiques. There are two other resources you may find useful as you search for tests. *Tests* is a more concise reference to test descriptions for thousands of tests in psychology, education, and business. Tests are arranged alphabetically by category. It is updated annually and contains similar information to the previously discussed references, with the exception of psychometric data and test reviews. *Test Critiques* is designed as a supplement to *Tests* and provides more extensive test descriptions, helpful information about the testing process, and test reviews. These resources are available from PRO-ED Publishers.

Other Test Information Resources. In addition to these four major references, counselors are most likely to find information about assessment procedures pertinent to their work in the following counseling-related journals: *Measurement and Evaluation in Counseling and Development, Counseling Outcome Research and Evaluation, Journal of Counseling & Development, The Career Development Quarterly, Journal of Counseling Psychology, Psychological Assessment, Journal of Personality Assessment, Journal of Career Assessment,* and *Assessment.* For other methods of accessing test information, please see "Resources for Further Learning" at the end of the chapter.

Locating Specific Assessments

Once you have reviewed several of these resources, you will need to contact a test publisher or author to obtain a specific commercially published assessment. Although there are a vast number of tests available in the United States and there is a constant stream of new tests and revisions of old tests on the market, most of the tests are published by a few large publishers, such as Psychological Assessment Resources, Consulting Psychologists Press, and Pearson Assessments. All major publishers list their products through catalogs and update test information regularly, including costs, ancillary materials, and alternate test forms. For a fee, most test publishers will provide qualified test users with a specimen set of a test that includes the test itself, answer sheets, scoring keys, and a test manual. For unpublished tests and other assessment methods, you will likely need to contact directly an author in a journal or book.

Activity 2.1
Locating Assessments

Select a topic of interest and testing purpose and use at least two of the sources described earlier to uncover information about assessments for that topic and purpose. What sources did you use? What information did you find in each? How do the sources compare with one another? Discuss in small groups the benefits and challenges of various assessment sources.

Test Administration

Test administration, or administration of assessment tools in general, will vary as a process depending on the audience, purpose, and format. For example, administering an individual test as opposed to a group test assumes a greater degree of familiarity with the test instructions and procedures and increased interaction with a client. With group tests, greater test anxiety may be a factor.

With respect to purpose, standardized tests must be administered in a specified manner under controlled conditions with uniform instructions and materials. Counselors who administer the test must be familiar with the instructions and other aspects of the administration. The knowledge necessary for administering a test differs greatly depending on the test. On the one hand, standardized scholastic aptitude tests can be administered with relatively little training. On the other hand, the knowledge and skill needed to administer individual intelligence tests require extensive coursework and practicum experience.

Furthermore, various test formats (paper-and-pencil vs. computer based) yield unique administration considerations. Computer-based testing allows greater flexibility in test administration, briefer test administration time, and a greater degree of test standardization. However, some individuals may have trouble using the computer. Students have reported difficulty in responding to items presented on the computer where they cannot easily go back to check previous answers or leave an item blank for later consideration. Computer anxiety may interfere with some people's performance on computer-administered tests, especially older people, women, and individuals from a lower socioeconomic background (A. L. Powell, 2013). Counselors should make certain that examinees are familiar and comfortable with using the computer. Clients should be given the opportunity to practice responding to computer-based items prior to testing.

Inexperienced test administrators often do not fully appreciate the importance of the test administrator's role. Irregularities identified in test administrations in school settings include timing the test inaccurately, altering answer sheets, coaching, teaching the test, scoring tests incorrectly, recording test data incorrectly, and cheating by students (National

Council on Measurement in Education, 2012). Most test manuals provide detailed instructions for administering a particular test, and such instructions should be followed exactly. It is the standardization of instructions that makes it possible to compare one person's scores with those of another or with different groups.

In addition, counselors need to be aware of the **expectancy effect** or **Rosenthal effect** during test administration. This effect relates to the notion that data sometimes can be affected by what the administrator expects to find. On a related note, counselors who seek to confirm negative stereotypes, intentionally or unintentionally, during test administration influence test performance. This effect is known as **stereotype threat** and is likely a contributing factor to long-standing racial and gender gaps in academic performance (Spencer, Logel, & Davies, 2016; Steele & Aronson, 1995; Steele, Spencer, & Aronson, 2002). Stereotype threats can be a factor when individuals of a minority status (e.g., women, racial/ethnic minorities) are instructed that a test's purpose is to assess a construct (e.g., math skills, intelligence) they internalize as lacking in themselves, or when those individuals are simply in a testing environment with others who possess positive stereotypes for a particular construct.

Thus, in administering tests, counselors must elicit the interest and cooperation of the test taker. In obtaining rapport, counselors attempt to convince test takers that the results will be useful and that they are not wasting their time in a task that will be of little consequence or value to them. Usually clients are cooperative if they have voluntarily sought counseling. If they are being tested against their will, perhaps because of a court order or because they feel that the test information is not important, good rapport may be difficult to establish.

Individuals should be informed prior to testing about conditions that may improve their performance on aptitude or achievement tests, such as taking a practice test or reviewing certain material (American Counseling Association [ACA], 2014). During the test administration itself, counselors should encourage clients to follow instructions carefully and to perform as well as they can. With small children, tests may be presented as a game. For interest or personality inventories, clients should be encouraged to answer honestly and frankly in order to preclude invalid results. Counselors should be familiar with the test being administered so that clients do not doubt the administrator's competence. Self-confidence, together with a warm and friendly manner, should be exhibited.

The testing environment should be suitable for test administration, with adequate seating, lighting, and ventilation and an appropriate temperature. It should be free from noise, interruptions, and other distractions. Time limits should be followed exactly, and measures should be taken to prevent cheating. Factors, even minor ones, that can alter test performance should be recognized and minimized. These factors contribute to the error variance in test scores. Any problems in administering the test should be noted and taken into account when interpreting the test results.

At times, test administration procedures may need to be altered to take into account such matters as a client's disability or language problems (AERA, APA, & NCME, 2014). Accommodations in test administration, such as additional time or the use of an interpreter, should be made if they can improve the opportunity for the client to demonstrate his or her abilities but not if they provide that client with an advantage over other test takers. Sometimes it is difficult to make this distinction, but the test administrator must make the best decision possible. Any alterations in administration procedures should be noted and included in the report of test results.

Test Interpretation and Communication of Findings

Although test interpretation and communication of findings is discussed in more detail in Chapters 6 and 15, respectively, it is important to mention these components briefly in an overall discussion of the assessment process. **Test interpretation**, which includes evaluation of data from a variety of methods, is much more than simply scoring an assessment tool. The more intentional counselors are about infusing interpretation in the general counseling process, the more therapeutic the assessment process can be. The manner in which tools can aid in self-awareness and decision making can ultimately provide greater insight in counseling and save time and money for clients.

Communication of findings can occur both during and after test interpretation. In fact, when counselors communicate with clients as they interpret assessment data, the process can yield a richer dialogue and better treatment planning. Communication can occur informally, such as during a counseling interaction, or more formally, such as the case with a written report for individual or group settings. During the communication process, it may become apparent that additional assessment is needed. If so, counselors may opt to cycle through the assessment process again.

There are a few general considerations related to test interpretation, specifically related to scoring procedures. Tests can be scored by hand or by computer. Tests that are scored by hand often involve the use of a scoring template that can be placed over the answer sheet to identify incorrect responses. In some cases, clients score their own tests by the use of "self-scorable" answer sheets that reveal the correct answers behind a seal on the reverse side of the answer sheet. Examples of measures for which clients score their own answer sheets include the Myers–Briggs Type Indicator (MBTI) and the Self-Directed Search. If more than a few tests or scales are involved, hand scoring can become time consuming, tedious, and subject to error. If at all possible, hand-scored tests should also be scored by another person to ensure accuracy of results.

Compared with hand scoring, computer scoring is more rapid, accurate, and thorough. The computer makes it possible to undertake elaborate test-scoring programs such as those required for the Strong Interest Inventory and the Campbell Interest and Skill Survey that would be virtually impossible to do by hand. For the most part, the computer is an exceedingly efficient scoring machine and at times may appear to be infallible; however, it is important to remember that scoring errors can and do occur, especially at the programming level.

If test results appear questionable, they should be rechecked. In addition to specific scores, computers can also generate test interpretations by means of scoring rules, or algorithms, stored in the computer's memory. Computer-based test interpretations (CBTIs), such as those that have been developed for the Minnesota Multiphasic Personality Inventory, provide a second opinion that counselors can use both to create and to test hypotheses about clients. Compared with counselor interpretations, CBTIs that have been derived from extensive databases by test experts can be more comprehensive, objective, consistent, and reliable (Sampson & Makela, 2014). Despite their apparent advantages, CBTIs can also pose a number of problems. In some cases, the developers of CBTIs lack appropriate qualifications. In other cases, the interpretations can be too general (e.g., they may be statements that are true for just about everybody) or they may contradict one another. Frequently, they are accorded "unrealistic credibility" because of their computer origin. To prevent misuse of CBTIs, a counselor should not rely on them unless he or she possesses sufficient knowledge about the assessment instrument itself to be able to evaluate independently the accuracy of the interpretations. In addition, clients should not be expected to be able to use CBTI reports without the aid of a counselor unless the reports have been specifically validated as "self-interpreting" (Osborn, Kronholz, Finklea, & Cantonis, 2014; Sampson & Makela, 2014).

A test can have well-established validity for various uses, but that does not necessarily ensure the validity of a CBTI derived for that test. The scoring rules on which the CBTIs are based are often a trade secret so that it is difficult to evaluate how adequately they have been developed. Counselors must examine CBTIs in light of other information that they have been able to collect about the client. They should use their best professional judgment to take into account any individual or situational factors that could alter the CBTI for a particular client. As with any test data, the results should be viewed as hypotheses that need to be confirmed or revised on the basis of other information that is collected regarding the particular client.

In addition to these general considerations, counselors are encouraged to review guidelines provided by the International Test Commission (ITC) to minimize errors in test scoring and reporting (see ITC, 2014). Now that you have reviewed the assessment process components, it's time to consider how you might approach a hypothetical client at each phase. Review Case Example 2.1, the Case of Jeffrey, and respond to the accompanying questions. First, consider some tips in the assessment process.

Tip Sheet
The Assessment Process

✓ Successful testing is being prepared. Have a script (written or memorized) for every part of the assessment process to minimize any negative effects assessment may have on the counseling process.

✓ Involve clients in the test selection process as much as possible.

✓ Explore with clients ways that assessment data can be useful to increase intrinsic motivation. Remind them that the primary purpose of assessment is not evaluation and judgment but, rather, a tool for client exploration to assist in making decisions.

✓ Review several sources of information before selecting an assessment tool. Ensure that the tool serves an appropriate function, possesses relevant support, and is suitable for your clientele.

✓ Gain knowledge about an assessment tool, including familiarity with test content, purpose, psychometric properties, and test administration and scoring procedures.

✓ Use multiple assessment methods to create a more comprehensive picture for the client.

✓ Present to clients the assessment purpose and description in the most clear, concise, and interesting manner.

✓ For administration of individual tests, memorize the exact verbal instructions if possible. Have materials ready for use and easy to reach.

✓ Maintain the security of testing materials before and after test administration.

✓ In group testing, double-check that you have all materials (e.g., answer sheets, pencils, test booklets) available for the testing day.

✓ Administer and interpret an assessment tool exactly as stated in the manual unless there is an empirically supported reason for altering (e.g., test bias, accommodations for disability).

✓ Consider testing conditions that may influence test scores before administering the test. Conditions may include location of room, noise level, seating arrangement, lighting, work space, quality of instructions, rapport between counselor and client, and amount of time needed to complete assessment.

✓ Reflect on how cultural and other demographic differences impact the assessment relationship. Such issues may include how familiar individuals are with a test administrator, differences among test takers, stereotype or expectancy effects, presence of a disability, or experience with different testing formats.

✓ When introducing an assessment, show enthusiasm and interest in the process and motivate clients to respond as best as they can. Reiterate the value and purpose of assessment in general as well as the particular tool being used.

✓ Evaluate scoring procedures carefully and assess for strengths and limitations.

✓ Communicate assessment data in an empowering way, discussing assessment strengths and limitations for aiding a particular client.

✓ Present assessment data in the context of other available information about a particular client, highlighting that data are just one type of client data to consider.

✓ In addition to communicating overall findings to clients, process clients' reactions to the assessment data.

<h1 style="text-align:center">Case Example 2.1</h1>

Jeffrey

Jeffrey is a 16-year-old White male in 11th grade. He lives with his father James (age 49), his mother Linda (age 48), an older brother Keith (age 18), and a younger brother Max (age 14). His parents are both teachers in the same high school as Jeffrey.

Jeffrey's parents made the appointment with you, a professional school counselor at the same school as Jeffrey and his parents. Jeffrey is currently in danger of failing 11th grade, with grades of mostly Ds and Fs, except for a B in computer class. His parents are frustrated because they do not know how to motivate him.

In addition, a teacher found a notebook with written song lyrics with references to guns and dying. Asked for an explanation, Jeffrey just shrugged and said he was bored in class.

Jeffrey previously saw a counselor during elementary school after he seemed to be having trouble fitting in socially in class.

Reflect on the following:

- How might you begin the assessment process? Who would you involve, and how would you involve them?
- What are assessment methods you might consider during the test selection phase?
- How and when might test administration occur?
- What factors may be salient for communication of findings?
- How do you think the assessment process in general might benefit Jeffrey?

• • •

Monitoring Client Progress and Evaluating Counseling Outcomes

How do counselors know whether their selected interventions are effective with clients? At the conclusion of counseling, as well as at intervals throughout counseling, it is important to evaluate the effectiveness of counseling. As the last step of the problem-solving model in Chapter 1 indicates, counselors need to determine whether a particular client's problem has been resolved or reduced. This "last step" is not necessarily the last component of the counseling process, as counselors can assess change at any point in the counseling process and then initiate the problem-solving steps outlined in the model again.

Meier (2015) highlighted two types of feedback points that indicate client progress and outcome, respectively: **Progress monitoring** is the use of clinical information to indicate client progress *during* various phases of the counseling process, and **outcome assessment** involves evaluating clinical data to determine what types of and how much change a client has made *at the conclusion* of counseling. Counselors who engage in both types of evaluation will be able to provide time-sensitive feedback and alter counseling interventions, which may ultimately lead to better outcomes when the client terminates counseling. That is, with a focus on progress monitoring and outcome assessment, there is a close link between assessment and intervention, creating a feedback loop for counselors to make important clinical decisions and maximize treatment success.

The impetus for attending to client progress and counseling outcome is largely the increased accountability counselors face in terms of maximizing positive treatment success and thus minimizing what Meier (2015) termed *treatment failure*. **Treatment failure** is documented in the counseling and psychotherapy literature, and Lambert (2012) noted that

30% to 50% of clients who received empirically supported treatments had not improved by the end of therapy. Furthermore, high premature termination rates—particularly among clients who are culturally diverse (D. G. Hays & McLeod, 2018)—indicate an even greater risk for treatment failure for particular clients. Thus, it is imperative that counselors be mindful of what they are doing within and across sessions and how these interventions interface with client progress.

A focus on progress monitoring and outcome assessment is evident in clinical practice across settings. For example, Meier (2015) encouraged mental health practitioners to engage in **feedback-enhanced therapy**, in which the therapeutic process is heavily directed by a feedback loop of clinical data. Furthermore, **response to intervention** (RTI) is an approach increasingly being used in school settings (Brown-Chidsey & Steege, 2010). Beginning with a global screening of all children (Tier 1), RTI serves to identify children who may be especially vulnerable to maladaptive academic and behavioral outcomes and then provide these children with real-time interventions to address and monitor concerns in either small-group instruction (Tier 2) or individualized interventions (Tier 3).

Outcome measures can be helpful at three levels. At the *individual* level, both the client and counselor can benefit. Clients can profit by seeing progress in resolving issues and improvement in well-being. Counselors can use feedback from clients to learn what counseling approaches are most effective with different types of clients. At the *agency* level, information obtained from clients can help in establishing and modifying counseling programs and in gaining support from those who fund the programs. Finally, for the *profession* as a whole, outcome studies can lead to more successful evidence-based treatments and strengthen the viability and credibility of the profession overall.

When outcome studies are undertaken using the combined resources of a professional organization or a counseling agency, it is possible to conduct a much more thorough and comprehensive evaluation of counseling effectiveness than would otherwise be possible. Although it may not be feasible for all counselors to be involved in a comprehensive outcome study, some effort should be undertaken to evaluate the effectiveness of all counseling interventions.

Prior to engaging in progress monitoring or outcome assessment, counselors are encouraged to consider the reflection questions in Table 2.1. Responses to these questions will help to focus the counselor for a more structured assessment process.

Table 2.1
Reflection Questions for Monitoring and Evaluating Client Outcomes

- What variable(s) am I interested in measuring and why?
- When and how often do I want to measure the variable(s)?
- How will I measure the variable(s)? Should I involve the client, family members and peers, and/or others?
- Should I use standardized procedures, qualitative methods, or a combination of both? How do I collect the data?
- For each variable of interest, what score or indicator will show the presence of symptoms? What score or indicator will show a lack of symptoms?
- How will I know if and when the client is improving? How will I know if and when the client is no longer improving or if the client is worsening?
- Do the selected assessment tools:
  - Allow multiple forms of assessment data to provide multiple points of reference for each variable of interest?
  - Have strong psychometric data (e.g., reliability, validity)?
  - Provide time-sensitive data to indicate changes over time, across phases, and across groups as theoretically expected?
  - Allow evaluation to remain brief not to interrupt the counseling process?
  - Provide clients with an opportunity to use the tools as a treatment intervention in itself (e.g., self-monitoring method)?
- How and when will I report the data? To whom will I report the data?

Counselors can monitor client progress in many ways, such as through periodically administering assessments or analyzing and summarizing themes found in session notes, to name just two examples. Figure 2.2 and Figure 2.3 show these two types of progress monitoring. The first example (see Figure 2.2) illustrates how a client's scores on a depression inventory and work performance scale change over the course of eight counseling sessions. The second example (see Figure 2.3) indicates themes discussed across 10 sessions for a client considering leaving an abusive relationship. As evidenced by these examples, visual displays provide a quick snapshot of changes in reported symptoms as well as when those changes occurred to indicate improvement or a failure to improve. These data can be useful for determining when to make changes in counseling or when to terminate counseling altogether.

In terms of outcome assessment, counselors can make judgments about a client's score or some other outcome indicator in several ways. First, counselors can compare a score to a desired score in another group. For example, a counselor working with a college student experiencing clinically significant anxiety might monitor how that individual's score on the Beck Anxiety Inventory (BAI) compares over time to the normal range of BAI scores for a nonclinical sample. Second, a client's outcome measure can be compared to some criterion. For example, a counselor working with an adult struggling with alcohol abuse might review what alcohol abuse threshold is met according to criteria outlined for the Alcohol Use Disorders Identification Test. Furthermore, Meier (2015) recommended that counselors and other practitioners can gauge client success if a score makes a ± 1 *SD* change. For example, a counselor may consider that eating disorder symptoms have decreased substantially if an adolescent's score on the Eating Disorders Inventory–3 (Garner, 2005) has decreased by at least 1 *SD* from the start of counseling.

No matter the measure selected to evaluate client progress and counseling outcome, assessment tools should be (a) brief, easy to administer and score, and cost effective; (b) sensitive to measuring change over time and across phases as theoretically expected; (c)

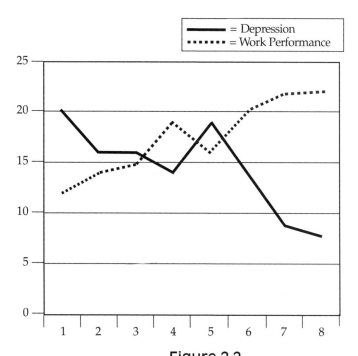

Figure 2.2
Client Monitoring of Depression Symptoms and
Work Performance Across Eight Sessions

Themes	1	2	3	4	5	6	7	8	9	10
Finances			X	X	X				X	
Physical safety	X	X	X				X			
Safety of children	X	X								
Support network—family		X	X	X	X					
Support network—friends						X	X	X	X	X
Career development				X	X		X	X	X	X
Assertiveness training	X					X	X			
Personal wellness	X		X	X	X	X	X	X		
Knowledge of healthy relationships	X	X	X	X						

Figure 2.3
Counseling Session Themes

able to distinguish appropriately between clients possessing different characteristics or belonging to various groups; (d) appropriate for a client's age and presenting concerns; and (e) valid and reliable for the purpose for which they are used (Meier, 2015). When feasible, assessments should use more than one source of feedback (e.g., client, counselor, and observer) and consider more than one outcome variable (e.g., changes in knowledge, understanding, and behavior). Monitoring progress and counseling outcomes should take into account immediate, intermediate, and ultimate goals—such as a more positive attitude toward school, improved grades, and school graduation—and should include evaluations taken at different points in time.

Counselors may use a combination of qualitative and quantitative assessment methods in monitoring for change. Furthermore, the number of assessment tools used will depend on whether counselors are engaged in progress monitoring or outcome assessment. Counselors typically use multiple methods to monitor changes across sessions and counseling phases, whereas they are likely to measure a couple of variables to evaluate change at the end of counseling (Meier, 2015).

Several tools that are considered useful for evaluating client progress and outcome are presented in Table 2.2, such as client satisfaction forms, client self-report scales, client self-monitoring methods, and rating scales. In addition, it is important to remember that any of the assessments presented throughout this text can be included in this process, as appropriate for the counseling situation.

Client satisfaction forms assess the degree to which counseling fulfilled the client's expectations. A number of client satisfaction scales or rating forms have been developed for local use, especially in medical or mental health settings. Client satisfaction forms provide valuable feedback for administrators and professionals; however, they pose difficulties in interpretation because they lack standardization. Client satisfaction can also be inferred by means of therapeutic relationship scales, such as the Working Alliance Inventory (Horvath & Greenberg, 1989). Furthermore, counselors can engage clients in open-ended questions that solicit information from clients regarding what was the most helpful, what was least helpful, and what recommendations they would make for future counseling.

Client self-report scales are used to evaluate changes in a client's status or functioning as perceived by the client. Many of the self-report inventories used in the initial stages of counseling to identify a client's problems (see Chapter 7) can also be used later in counseling to evaluate progress in resolving these problems. In many ways, these instruments are ideal for progress monitoring and outcome assessment because they provide comparable information at different points in time that can be used to show changes that occur during the course of counseling.

Table 2.2
Assessment Tools for Monitoring Progress and Counseling Outcome

Assessment	Type/Purpose	Description
University of California, San Francisco (UCSF), Client Satisfaction Questionnaire–8 (CSQ-8; Attkisson, 2013)	Client satisfaction form	The CSQ-8 provides a global measure of a client's satisfaction with mental health services received.
UCSF Service Satisfaction Scale–30 (SSS-30; Greenfield & Attkisson, 2004)	Client satisfaction form	The SSS-30 provides a more detailed measure of client satisfaction than the CSQ-8. The SSS-30 yields scores on several subscales—such as counselor manner and skill, office procedures, and access to services—as well as an overall satisfaction score. Two additional versions exist: the SSS-16, the short form of the SSS-30; and the SSS-RES, a tool specifically tailored for residential care services.
Outcome Questionnaire 45.2 (OQ-45.2; Lambert et al., 2004)	Client self-report scale	In responding to the OQ-45.2, clients indicate for the previous week the degree to which various symptoms occurred for them. This tool is discussed further in Chapter 7.
Revised Behavior and Symptom Identification Scale (BASIS-R; Eisen et al., 2004)	Client self-report scale	The purpose of the BASIS-R is to yield self-reported clinical data for six domains: depression/functioning, interpersonal relationships, self-harm, emotional lability, psychosis, and substance abuse.
Treatment Outcome Package (TOP; Kraus et al., 2005)	Client self-report scale	Specifically designed for naturalistic settings with three age versions, the TOP assesses multiple client symptoms and degree of functioning.
Session Rating Scale (SRS; Duncan et al., 2003)	Client self-report scale	The SRS is a 4-item scale in which the client provides feedback on aspects of the working alliance, including the relationship, goals and topics addressed, the therapist's approach or method, and the overall quality of the session.
Outcome Rating Scale (ORS; S. D. Miller et al., 2003)	Client self-report scale	The ORS is a 4-item scale that allows clients to rate their sense of personal well-being; family and other close relationships; work, peer, and school relationships; and overall functioning.
Inventory of Common Problems (ICP; Hoffman & Weiss, 1986)	Client self-report scale	The 24-item tool is used in college counseling centers to assess types of problems associated with depression, anxiety, academics, interpersonal relationships, physical health, and substance use. The ICP is discussed further in Chapter 7.
Target Complaints (TC) procedure (Battle et al., 1966)	Client self-report scale/rating scale	The TC procedure requires clients (with the help of a counselor) to identify three specific complaints that they wish to address in counseling and then to rate these complaints according to their severity.
Behavioral Intervention Monitoring Assessment System (BIMAS; McDougal et al., 2012)	Client self-report scale/rating scale	The BIMAS is a rating tool used by teachers, counselors, parents, and clients themselves. The tool is based on the response-to-intervention model and includes five scales: Conduct, Negative Affect, Cognition/Attention, Social Functioning, and Academic Functioning.
Brief Psychiatric Rating Scale for major psychopathology (BPRS; Lachar, Espadas, et al., 2001)	Rating scale	The BPRS is used to rate 16 major symptoms found among psychiatric patients.

(Continued)

Table 2.2 *(Continued)*
Assessment Tools for Monitoring Progress and Counseling Outcome

Assessment	Type/Purpose	Description
Family Life Questionnaire (Last et al., 2012)	Rating scale	The Family Life Questionnaire allows for parent or guardian assessment of four domains of family functioning: Affirmation, Discipline, Special Allowances, and Rules.
Conners' Rating Scales–Revised (Conners, 1997)	Rating scale	This tool is used to assist teachers and parents to evaluate 27 symptoms in children. There are multiple versions of the scales, including the Conners' Parent Rating Scale–Revised, Conners' Parent Rating Scale–Revised Short Form, and the Conners' Teacher Rating Scale.
Global Assessment of Functioning (GAF)	Rating scale	The GAF provides a single score, ranging from 1 to 100, regarding the client's psychological, social, and occupational functioning. The GAF scale is anchored with behavioral descriptions at each 10-point interval; for example, ratings in the "71 to 80" range indicate transient symptoms (such as difficulty concentrating after a family conflict) or slight impairment in functioning (such as falling behind in one's work on a temporary basis).
Goal Attainment Scaling (GAS; Kiresuk et al., 2014)	Rating scale	With the GAS, the counselor or other expert judges establish specific goals for a client based on his or her concerns. The judges then rate on a 5-point scale the client's success in attaining these goals at the end of counseling.

There are some cautions with client self-report scales. Counselors often assume with self-report scales that clients understand what is being asked of them for response or that they can provide the information accurately and comprehensively. Clients—like all individuals—have limited self-awareness and have different abilities to express the self-awareness they do possess. Furthermore, clients may intentionally over- or underreport clinical information in a manner that highlights their characteristics in the most positive light (i.e., social desirability). Finally, repeated self-administration of an assessment tool will likely create unintended reporting errors: Clients can be exposed to a tool too often that they fail to accurately report symptoms or redefine for themselves over time what assessment items are measuring. Thus, they become unaffected by what change the tool is trying to capture because they are tired of being tested.

As a variation on client self-report scales, **client self-monitoring** is commonly used as part of homework that counselors assign; for example, clients can be asked to pay attention to their behaviors, any negative thoughts or impulses, or instances when something positive occurs, to name a few. This process can be a treatment intervention in itself and can foster increased collaboration between counselor and client and improved treatment planning (J. S. Cohen, Edmunds, Brodman, Benjamin, & Kendall, 2013). Because self-monitoring relies on client self-report, it has similar limitations. However, client self-monitoring can be used to supplement traditional self-report scales to help minimize some of these limitations.

In addition to feedback from the client, evaluation of a client's functioning, through the use of **rating scales**, can also be sought from the counselor or others in a position to judge the client's behavior, such as parents, spouses, teachers, supervisors, coworkers, or trained observers. In addition to the measures included in Table 2.2, observer rating forms that highlight domains more specific to a school, agency, or other clinical setting may be useful. Observation of a client's behavior by someone close to the client is important in obtaining information regarding the progress of clients who cannot accurately or consistently report this information themselves. Similar to client self-report scales, rating scales can be problematic as tools for monitoring progress and counseling outcome. As discussed earlier in the chapter, rating scales can yield several errors, such as halo effects, leniency errors, and decay.

Chapter Summary

The assessment process in counseling relates to engaging and collaborating with clients throughout the counseling relationship as well as evaluating the counseling relationship and interventions themselves. In this chapter, several assessment methods were discussed, and their use in the assessment process was presented. These methods include group and individual assessments, standardized and nonstandardized assessments, speed and power tests, rating scales, projective assessments, behavioral observations, interviews, biographical measures, and physiological measures. Then, assessment process components were presented (test selection, test administration, test interpretation, and communication of findings). Clients will be motivated to participate in assessment (and counseling) depending on the stage of change in which they identify as well as the quality of the counseling relationship. In addition, there are several considerations at each phase of the assessment process that affect how clients receive and use assessment data. The chapter concluded with a brief discussion on monitoring client progress and evaluating counseling outcomes and on various assessment methods that may be useful to counselors.

Review Questions

1. How might the various assessment methods presented in this chapter influence the assessment process?
2. How does a client's stage of change benefit and limit each phase of the assessment process?
3. Compare the major sources of information for tests. What do you see as the most useful for you? How do they complement one another?
4. How do paper-and-pencil and computer assessments compare in terms of the assessment process? When might one be more useful than the other?
5. In what ways are outcome assessments helpful for clients? Counselors? The scientific community?

Resources for Further Learning

Publications

Goldman, B. A., & Mitchell, D. F. (2008). *Directory of unpublished experimental mental measures* (Vol. 9). Washington, DC: American Psychological Association.
International Test Commission. (2014). ITC guidelines on quality control in scoring, test analysis, and reporting of test scores. *International Journal of Testing, 14*(3), 195–217. doi: 10.1080/15305058.2014.918040
Meier, S. T. (2015). *Incorporating progress monitoring and outcome assessment into counseling and psychotherapy: A primer.* New York, NY: Oxford University Press.
Wood, C. T., & Hays, D. G. (Eds.). (2013). *A counselor's guide to career assessment instruments* (6th ed.). Broken Arrow, OK: National Career Development Association.

Web Resources

Buros Center for Testing, Test Reviews & Information
  http://buros.org/test-reviews-information
      This site contains test reviews as they appear from the *MMY*, 9th edition, to the present. Thus, this is an online resource for the *MMY* and *TIP*.

ETS, TestLink
> http://www.ets.org/test_link/about
>> This site lists the ETS's collection of 25,000 tests since 1900, with about 1,000 tests available for purchase directly from ETS.

University of Rhode Island Change Assessment Scale (URICA)
> http://pubs.niaaa.nih.gov/publications/Assessingalcohol/InstrumentPDFs/75_URICA.pdf
>> This site provides the complete version of the URICA.

Chapter 3

Ethical, Legal, and Professional Considerations in Assessment

Regardless of the degree to which you think you will use assessment in your practice, it is quite important to understand ethical and legal considerations. Ethical guidelines, assessment standards provided by professional organizations, and legal statutes and key court decisions collectively play a role in how counselors perform various assessment activities. In this chapter, some of the standards and guidelines within professional organizations that are useful for evaluating tests and test usage are discussed. Then, specific ethical and legal considerations related to counselor competence and client welfare—as well as other professional issues in testing—are presented.

Test Your Knowledge

Select the most appropriate choice for each item.

_____ 1. The major responsibility for proper assessment use falls on the _____.
   a. Publisher   b. Test developer
   c. Counselor who uses the test   d. Client

❏ T ❏ F   2. Due to the nature of testing, informed consent is not required for test administration.

❏ T ❏ F   3. The *ACA Code of Ethics* contains a section on assessment ethics.

❏ T ❏ F   4. There are advocacy groups in existence to protect against test restriction lawsuits.

_____ 5. ACA's divisions provide assessment standards for which of the following specialty areas?
   a. School counseling   b. Substance abuse counseling
   c. Career counseling   d. All of the above

Standards and Guidelines for Evaluating Tests and Test Usage

Several sets of standards have been published by professional organizations concerning the development and use of psychological assessment procedures. Counselors should be familiar with each set of standards or guidelines for test usage presented in this section. In this section, several important documents that affect test usage are presented: the *ACA Code of Ethics* (ACA, 2014); the *NBCC Code of Ethics* (National Board for Certified Counselors [NBCC], 2012); *Standards for Educational and Psychological Testing* (AERA, APA, & NCME, 2014); Joint Committee on Testing Practices documents; and ACA general testing standards, such as the *Responsibilities of Users of Standardized Tests* (RUST), *Standards for Qualifications of Test Users*, the *ACA Position Statement on High Stakes Testing*, and the *Association for Assessment and Research in Counseling (AARC) Standards for Multicultural Assessment* (Association for Assessment in Counseling and Education [AACE], 2012; the AARC, one of ACA's divisions, was formerly known as the AACE).

In addition to these general standards and guidelines, AARC has developed several specialty standards in collaboration with other ACA divisions. These specialty standards include *Career Counselor Assessment and Evaluation Competencies* (AACE & National Career Development Association [NCDA], 2010); *Marriage, Couple and Family Counseling Assessment Competencies* (AACE & International Association of Marriage and Family Counselors, 2010); *Standards for Assessment in Mental Health Counseling* (AACE & American Mental Health Counselors Association [AMHCA], 2010); *Standards for Assessment in Substance Abuse Counseling* (AACE & International Association of Addictions and Offender Counselors [IAAOC], 2010); and guidelines for pre-employment testing (AACE & American Rehabilitation Counseling Association [ARCA], 2003).

ACA Code of Ethics

The ***ACA Code of Ethics*** (ACA, 2014) specifies principles of ethical conduct and standards of professional behavior for counselors. Section E of the 2014 Code provides information on evaluation, assessment, and interpretation. Section E components outline the following: general assessment purposes; issues surrounding competence, informed consent, and assessment data reporting; diagnosis; instrument selection; test administration, scoring, and interpretation; diversity in assessment; assessment security; use of outdated assessments and results; assessment construction; and forensic evaluation. Table 3.1 provides more detail about principles specific to assessment.

NBCC Code of Ethics

Section D of the ***NBCC Code of Ethics*** (NBCC, 2012) was developed from the aforementioned *ACA Code of Ethics* as well as the *RUST Statement* (described later), among others. The NBCC codes were initially proposed in 1982 and are now in their eighth revision. Themes of the 95 competencies are as follows: nonmaleficence (counselor do no harm), counselor competence, beneficence (promotion of client welfare), veracity (counselor truthfulness), fidelity to counselor relationship and the counseling profession (facilitating trust and integrity), client autonomy, and counselor accountability to professional standards and practices. Codes specific to testing and assessment address issues of counselor qualifications, informed consent, instrument selection, test administration and interpretation, data reporting, use of obsolete materials and results, test security, technology, and reproduction of test materials and results.

Table 3.1
ACA Code of Ethics and Assessment Practices

Ethical Principle	Description
E.1. General	The purpose of assessment is to guide client decision making, treatment planning, and forensic proceedings using multiple methods. Assessment data should be understood, interpreted, and used properly by all interested parties.
E.2. Competence to Use and Interpret Assessment Instruments	Counselors only engage in assessment practices in which they are competent, including technology-assisted procedures.
E.3. Informed Consent in Assessment	Counselors engage clients in an informed consent process in which they explain the assessment process, how and what tools will be used, and to what extent assessment data will be distributed to others.
E.4. Release of Data to Qualified Personnel	Counselors only release assessment data with the consent of clients or their legal representatives and to those individuals who may be identified as competent to interpret the data.
E.5. Diagnosis of Mental Disorders	Counselors take special care in assessment procedures to provide a proper diagnosis as culturally appropriate. Diagnoses should be provided only when appropriate.
E.6. Instrument Selection	Counselors are careful when selecting assessments and should account for the psychometric properties and/or opportunities for use of multiple assessment sources.
E.7. Conditions of Assessment Administration	Counselors ensure facilitative conditions for clients during assessment administration and should not allow unsupervised administration unless a tool is intended to be self-administered.
E.8. Multicultural Issues/Diversity in Assessment	Throughout the assessment process, counselors are intentional about ensuring that tools are culturally appropriate and that results may be influenced by diversity variables.
E.9. Scoring and Interpretation of Assessments	Counselors are to disclose relevant contextual information regarding the client, the environment, or the test itself when reporting assessment results.
E.10. Assessment Security	Counselors maintain the security of an instrument throughout the assessment process.
E.11. Obsolete Assessment and Outdated Results	Counselors avoid the use of outdated tools or previous results from tools that are no longer valid.
E.12. Assessment Construction	Counselors engage in rigorous steps to ensure the psychometric integrity of a tool when developing an assessment.
E.13. Forensic Evaluation: Evaluation for Legal Proceedings	During legal proceedings, counselors provide objective assessment data based in professional opinion. When counselors are hired for a forensic evaluation, they obtain informed consent, engage in appropriate counseling relationships, and clarify with the individual that the relationship is for evaluation only.

Note. ACA = American Counseling Association.

Standards for Educational and Psychological Testing

The ***Standards for Educational and Psychological Testing*** (AERA, APA, & NCME, 2014) provide criteria for evaluating both the tests themselves and use of the tests. The criteria were prepared by a joint committee of the American Educational Research Association (AERA), the American Psychological Association (APA), and the National Council on Measurement in Education (NCME). When the *Standards for Educational and Psychological*

Testing were published in 1954, this publication emphasized technical standards for test construction and evaluation. As the editions evolved, the joint committee placed increased emphasis on the responsibilities of the test user and the need for fairness in testing. Adherence to the standards by counselors should help to improve testing practices and reduce criticism of tests and test usage.

A portion of the *Standards for Educational and Psychological Testing* deals with the technical quality of tests and test materials and the standards to be followed by test developers and test publishers before distributing the test. Test publishers and authors make money from the sales and royalties on tests that are sold, and there is an obvious temptation to exaggerate the usefulness or the validity of such tests. The committee that developed the standards placed considerable emphasis on the importance of "truth in advertising" in test publishing. Test manuals should provide evidence of both reliability—including information regarding the methods of estimating reliability and the populations on which reliability was measured—and validity, including types of validity studies and validity relevant to the intended use of the test.

Certain standards are designed to prevent the premature sale of tests for general use and to specify when the test is to be released for research purposes only. The *Standards for Educational and Psychological Testing* emphasize that the test manual should not be designed to sell the test but should include adequate information about the administration, scoring, norms, and other technical data to permit the potential user to evaluate the test itself and its potential use as well as to properly interpret its results.

Joint Committee on Testing Practices Documents

The **Joint Committee on Testing Practices** (JCTP) was established in 1985 as a forum for counseling- and education-related associations to collaborate for the common good for fair, accessible, and appropriate use of tests. The overarching goal of JCTP was to improve test use through education, not to limit test access (Naugle, 2009). Throughout its existence, JCTP included representatives from the ACA, AERA, APA, American Speech-Language-Hearing Association, National Association of School Psychologists, National Association of Test Directors, and NCME. Although JCTP disbanded in 2007, their documents are still very useful to counselors. Brief descriptions of some of the major documents (*Responsible Test Use*, *Rights and Responsibilities of Test Takers*, and *Code of Fair Testing Practices in Education*) from its working groups are provided here.

Responsible Test Use

Research conducted under the auspices of JCTP has identified 86 competencies required for the proper use of different instruments (Eyde, Robertson, & Krug, 2010; Moreland, Eyde, Robertson, Primoff, & Most, 1995). Of the 86 competencies, 12 embody minimum proficiencies for all test users, such as avoiding errors in scoring and recording, using settings for testing that allow for optimum performance (e.g., adequate room), and establishing rapport with examinees to obtain accurate answers (see Table 3.2).

Factor-analytic research indicates that the 86 competencies can be reduced to seven broad factors: comprehensive assessment, proper test use, psychometric knowledge, integrity of test results, scoring accuracy, appropriate use of norms, and interpretive feedback. On the basis of research regarding test misuse, the relative significance of the seven factors varies with the particular type of test. For example, competencies in comprehensive assessment are more important in using clinical tests, whereas skills in the appropriate use of norms are more important in vocational tests (Moreland et al., 1995). Examples of appropriate and inappropriate test usage based on the 86 competencies and seven broad factors are provided in the casebook, *Responsible Test Use: Case Studies for Assessing Human Behavior* (Eyde et al., 2010).

Table 3.2
Twelve Minimum Competencies for Proper Use of Tests

Item No.	Competency
1.	Avoiding errors in scoring and recording
2.	Refraining from labeling people with personally derogatory terms like *dishonest* on the basis of a test score that lacks perfect validity
3.	Keeping scoring keys and test materials secure
4.	Seeing that every examinee follows directions so that test scores are accurate
5.	Using settings for testing that allow for optimum performance by test takers (e.g., adequate room)
6.	Refraining from coaching or training individuals or groups on test items, which results in misrepresentation of the person's abilities and competencies
7.	Being willing to give interpretation and guidance to test takers in counseling situations
8.	Not making photocopies of copyrighted materials
9.	Refraining from using homemade answer sheets that do not align properly with scoring keys
10.	Establishing rapport with examinees to obtain accurate scores
11.	Refraining from answering questions from test takers in greater detail than the test manual permits
12.	Not assuming that a norm for one job applies to a different job (and not assuming that norms for one group automatically apply to other groups)

Note. From "Assessment of Test User Qualifications: A Research-Based Measurement Procedure," by K. L. Moreland, L. D. Eyde, G. J. Robertson, E. S. Primoff, and R. B. Most, 1995, *American Psychologist, 50,* p. 16. Copyright 1995 by the American Psychological Association. Reprinted with permission.

Rights and Responsibilities of Test Takers

In one of its efforts to improve testing practices, the JCTP developed a statement that lists the rights and responsibilities of individual test takers: **Rights and Responsibilities of Test Takers Guidelines and Expectations** (JCTP, 1999). For example, test takers have a right to know the purpose of testing, who will have access to their scores, how the tests will be used, and possible consequences of taking or not taking the test. They also have personal responsibilities, such as reading or listening to descriptive test information, informing test administrators of special needs, and asking questions about specific concerns they might have.

This document also provides detailed guidelines for test administrators to ensure that test takers receive their rights and understand their responsibilities. As test administrators, counselors should clarify the rights and responsibilities of test takers and obtain informed consent before proceeding with testing. They should be able to offer reasonable accommodations for test takers with disabilities. Counselors should provide appropriate information to clients concerning the testing process, such as suggestions for test preparation, scoring procedures, opportunities to retake the test, provisions for feedback, availability of interpretive materials, and confidentiality safeguards.

Code of Fair Testing Practices in Education

Whereas the document discussed above outlines the rights and responsibilities of test takers—and the expectations professionals have of them—the **Code of Fair Testing Practices in Education** (JCTP, 2004) outlines the primary obligations of professionals toward test takers. This code, first issued by the JCTP in 1988, has been updated and expanded (JCTP, 2004). The code focuses on the development and use of educational tests from the standpoint of fairness to all test takers regardless of age, gender, disability, race, ethnicity, or other personal characteristics. The revised version of the code lists a total of 31 standards for test developers and test users in four areas: developing and selecting appropriate tests, administering and scoring tests, reporting and interpreting test results, and informing test takers.

These standards, which complement the *Standards for Educational and Psychological Testing,* are not mandatory as such, but they are intended to inspire test developers and test users to consider the importance of fairness in all aspects of testing. For example, test users are encouraged to evaluate test materials for offensive language, to select tests that have been modified appropriately for clients with disabilities, and to consider to what extent test performance for individuals from diverse subgroups may have been affected by factors unrelated to the skill being assessed.

Standards for Qualifications of Test Users

The **Standards for Qualifications of Test Users** (ACA, 2003) was developed by the ACA Standards for Test Use Task Force. This document was based on the *Standards for Educational and Psychological Testing* as well as ACA and ASCA ethical standards, the *RUST Statement*, and JCTP documents. The document includes seven competencies: testing practice and knowledge, knowledge of technical aspects and test construction, knowledge of sampling techniques and norming considerations, test selection and administration to appropriately apply in the counseling context, test administration and interpretation of test scores, diversity considerations, and a general understanding of ethical and legal considerations for appropriate test use and the documents that guide it.

ACA Position Statement on High Stakes Testing

The **ACA Position Statement on High Stakes Testing** (ACA, n.d.) includes 10 recommended principles to consider with use of high-stakes achievement tests, which are increasingly common since the No Child Left Behind (NCLB) Act of 2001 was enacted. Developed using similar documents as the ACA *Standards for Qualifications of Test Users*, the position statement outlines principles related to the following: alignment of assessments with academic and curricular standards; use of multiple measures; awareness of the impact of testing on students; students' equitable access to learning; availability of student remediation; provision of testing resources; technical quality of tests; utility and comprehensiveness of test purpose, findings, and applications for all involved; validity of scores for diverse groups; and policies that allow for a fair and accurate high-stakes testing process.

Responsibilities of Users of Standardized Tests

The AARC developed a policy statement titled **Responsibilities of Users of Standardized Tests** (referred to as the *RUST Statement*). Now undergoing a fourth revision, the *RUST Statement* lists responsibilities of test users in seven categories: qualifications of test users, technical knowledge, test selection, test administration, test scoring, interpretation of test results, and communication of test results. A model developed by the Test User Qualifications working group is included in the third edition of the *RUST Statement.*

AARC Standards for Multicultural Assessment

Originally published in 1992, the **AARC Standards for Multicultural Assessment** is now in its fourth edition (AACE, 2012). The third revision, in 2003, relied on five source documents: the *Code of Fair Testing Practices in Education*, *RUST Statement*, *Standards for Educational and Psychological Testing*, *Multicultural Counseling Competencies and Standards* (Sue, Arredondo, & McDavis, 1992), and the 1996 version of the *ACA Code of Ethics*. The 38 multicultural assessment standards of the latest version are categorized into five major clusters: advocacy, selection of assessments, administration and scoring of assessment, interpretation and application of assessment results, and training in the uses of assessments.

Specialty Assessment Standards

The AARC, in collaboration with several ACA divisions, has developed specialty standards to guide testing practices in more specific counseling specialties such as career, marriage and family, mental health, school, substance abuse, and rehabilitation counseling. Many of these specialty standards will be expanded upon in other parts of the text, so I provide only a general description here.

The *Career Counselor Assessment and Evaluation Competencies*, adopted formally by the AARC and NCDA in 2010, outlines eight general competencies to assist career counselors in assessment and evaluation practices with students, clients, and other stakeholders. Specifically, career counselors are to be skilled in choosing assessment strategies; identifying, accessing, and evaluating instruments; using appropriate administration and scoring techniques; interpreting and reporting results; using results appropriately in decision making; producing, interpreting, and presenting sound statistical information; engaging in responsible assessment and evaluation practices; and using results with other data sources in career programs and interventions.

The *Marriage, Couple and Family Counseling Assessment Competencies*, a collaboration with the American Association for Marriage and Family Therapy in 2009, articulates five competencies for appropriate assessment practices in couples and family counseling. These competencies refer to understanding (a) historical perspectives of systems concepts, theories, and assessment methods; (b) basic technical aspects of assessments; (c) qualitative and quantitative concepts of assessment; (d) strengths and limitations of assessment and diagnosis models; and (e) appropriate test selection, administration, and interpretation for work with couples and families.

The *Standards for Assessment in Mental Health Counseling* was developed by the AARC and AMHCA in 2010 to highlight important knowledge and skill areas related to mental health counseling assessment. The 12 standards refer to such competencies as the use of interview and qualitative assessment procedures; instrument evaluation, selection, and usage; diversity considerations; technical knowledge; appropriate application of assessment results to treatment planning and interventions; communication of test results; use of assessment to determine treatment efficacy; continuing education in assessment; knowledge of and adherence to ethical use of assessments; and pedagogical considerations for appropriate training.

The AARC and IAAOC adopted in 2010 the *Standards for Assessment in Substance Abuse Counseling*, involving 10 standards for appropriate substance abuse assessment. Areas covered in the standards include effective assessment of the effects and withdrawal symptoms of commonly abused drugs; assessment of co-occurring disorders, including process addictions; technical knowledge; use of multiple measures; test selection; test interpretation and appropriate use of findings in substance abuse counseling interventions; continuing education; and pedagogical considerations.

The document titled *Pre-Employment Testing and the ADA*, adopted in 2003 by the AARC and ARCA, provides useful information for counselors working with clients with disabilities under the Americans with Disabilities Act (ADA). Specifically, sections of the document refer to validity considerations; general testing accommodations in terms of test format, time limits, and test content; accommodations for specific disabilities; and resources.

Activity 3.1
Ethical Guidelines and Standards

Select at least two of the above ethical guidelines and testing standards listed in the References list. Review the documents carefully. How are these documents similar to each other? How are they different? Which statements or codes may be particularly challenging for you? How might you refer to these in your counseling practice?

Tip Sheet
Ethical Assessment

✓ Review all pertinent ethical standards, required lists of competencies, and other documents described in the previous section prior to selecting an assessment tool.

✓ Be sure you are well trained and competent in the assessment process overall as well as for specific assessment tools. As discussed in this chapter, competence is usually determined by professional organizations, state credentialing bodies, and test publishers.

✓ Have a basic understanding of key psychometric terms, such as *validity, reliability, standardization, test construction, measurement error,* and *scales of measurement*. Statistical and measurement considerations are discussed in Chapters 5 and 6.

✓ On a related note, review the testing manual or assessment materials for psychometric evidence as well as the history of how, with what sampling frame, and under what circumstances the test was developed. This information will be extremely important as you decide which tools to use and how to interpret findings.

✓ Adopt a philosophy that assessment is a part of counseling to promote client welfare. Collaborate with your clients throughout the counseling process regarding what, when, how, and why various assessments will be used. Engage in ongoing informed consent.

✓ Review limits of confidentiality and process with clients who should receive assessment data about them and why.

✓ Select assessment tools that are culturally appropriate and do not perpetuate client stereotyping. Use multiple assessment methods to provide a comprehensive picture of your client.

✓ Consider under what conditions clinical diagnosis is necessary. Communicate clearly to the client the purpose, strengths, and limitations of diagnosis. Provide a proper diagnosis using multiple assessment methods, considering cultural bias throughout the diagnostic process. Cultural considerations in diagnosis are discussed further in Chapters 4 and 8.

✓ Create appropriate, comfortable, and organized assessment conditions for the client. Administration factors will play an important role in ethically sound test interpretation and may help reduce test anxiety for clients.

✓ Assessment results, when inappropriately interpreted or disclosed, can have very damaging consequences for clients. Avoid using assessment tools that are either outdated or have content or scoring and interpretation methods that are not appropriate for your client.

✓ Be sure to disclose results to relevant individuals, with the consent of clients as ethically required. Continually assess test security and misuse of testing. Involve clients as relevant in the test communication process.

✓ Confirm that clients understand any assessment finding. As you interpret a tool, check in with clients to gauge whether they understand the content of what is presented as well as what the results may mean for them.

Key Ethical and Legal Considerations in Assessment

There are a number of situations in which ethical principles are called into question when psychological tests are used in counseling and placement. Two major interdependent considerations are highlighted in this section: counselor competence and client welfare. In addition, see Table 3.3 for several federal and state laws and regulations—as well as major

Table 3.3
Key Laws, Regulations, and Court Decisions Affecting Assessment in Counseling

Law or Court Decision	Description
Public Laws	
Civil Rights Act, Title VII (1964, 1972, 1978, and 1991)	Assessments used in employment testing must not discriminate against individuals based on age, race, gender, pregnancy, religion, or national origin.
Family Educational Rights and Privacy Act of 1974 (FERPA)	Student test records are to remain secure from unnecessary parties. FERPA advocates for the rights of student and parental view of these records.
Education of All Handicapped Children (Pub. L., 94-142), Individuals with Disabilities Education Improvement Act (IDEIA, Pub. L. 99-457; amendment of Pub. L. 94-142)	Pub. L. 94-142 requires parent-informed consent before assessing students' abilities in order to determine exceptional needs and to develop individualized education programs to maximize educational opportunities. The 2004 amendment (Pub. L., 99-457) extends the right of appropriate education to children 3 years and older, encouraging states to intervene early for children with disabilities. Students have the right to be tested for disabilities at the school system's expense and must subsequently be provided with the "least restrictive environment" for learning.
Vocational Education Act of 1984 (Pub. L. 98-524)	Also referred to as the **Carl D. Perkins Act**, individuals who are disadvantaged (e.g., language barrier, disability, incarceration) are entitled to receive vocational assessment and support.
Education of the Handicapped Act of 1990 (Pub. L. 101-476)	Students with disabilities are entitled to a supportive transition from school to vocational rehabilitation, adult services, employment, or further education.
Americans with Disabilities Act of 1990 (ADA)	Tests used for employment or other selection purposes must accurately measure an individual's ability without being confounded by the disability itself. Also, individuals with disabilities must receive test accommodations as needed.
Health Insurance Portability and Accountability Act of 1996 (HIPAA)	Client records must remain secure, and third parties are to obtain appropriate consent to access those records. Clients have the right to their health records.
No Child Left Behind Act of 2001, Every Student Succeeds Act of 2015	States are to continually assess the mathematics and reading skills of their students to ensure quality in schools. Schools are held accountable for student test scores in these areas.
Selected Court Decisions	
Larry P. v. Riles (1974, 1979, 1984)	Ruled that schools had used intelligence tests that were biased and disadvantaged African American students, placing them inappropriately in special education. Counselors need proper documentation when placing children in special education.
Diana v. California State Board of Education (1973, 1979)	Schools are to provide tests to students both in their first language as well as in English. Counselors are to provide tests in an appropriate language for the client.
Sharif v. New York State Educational Development (1989)	Those working in New York schools (including school counselors) could not use only SAT scores for making scholarship decisions.
Griggs v. Duke Power Company (1971)	A plaintiff must demonstrate job discrimination and an employer must demonstrate that hiring procedures are job related and associated with job performance.
Bakke v. California (1978)	Colleges and universities cannot use a quota system for minority group admissions.
Debra P. v. Turlington (1981)	An achievement test, the Florida State Student Assessment Test, Part II (SSAT II), had been selected within the State of Florida to serve as a literacy examination that all students would take in order to receive a high school diploma. Given a lack of due process and questionable validity of the SSAT II, specifically for Black students who had not been exposed to the covered content in segregated schools, the related state constitutional amendment was challenged. This case prohibited the use of the SSAT II for 4 years, until schools could be fully desegregated and students would have equal access to test preparation.

(Continued)

Table 3.3 *(Continued)*
Key Laws, Regulations, and Court Decisions Affecting Assessment in Counseling

Law or Court Decision	Description
	Selected Court Decisions
Soroka v. Dakota Hudson Corporation (1991)	Applicants for a store security position, posted by the holding company for Target stores, had been asked to complete a psychological screening as part of the application. The California State Superior Court ruled that test items had to be directly related to the job description.

Note. Information is from E. D. Bennett and Hastings (2009) and Erford et al. (2014). Pub. L. = Public Law.

court decisions—that impact assessment in counseling. Review these legal considerations and consider how they might relate to ethical guidelines and assessment standards discussed in the previous section (see Activity 3.1 on p. 53).

Counselor Competence in Testing

An important ethical issue concerns the competence of the counselor to use the various available assessments. The issue is whether those who use various tests have sufficient knowledge and understanding to select tests intelligently and to interpret their results. Because different tests demand different levels of competence for their use, users must recognize the limits of their competence and make use only of instruments for which they have adequate preparation and training. The administration and interpretation of individual intelligence tests, such as the Stanford–Binet or the Wechsler tests; certain personality tests, such as the MMPI-2; or projective personality tests, such as the Rorschach or the TAT, require considerable advanced training and practice to obtain the necessary background and skill for their appropriate use. The question then becomes this: Who determines whether a counselor is competent to use tests? Three sources are discussed in this section. It is important to mention here that even though these sources help dictate who is competent to use tests, the ultimate responsibility falls on the counselor to decide whether he or she is competent to avoid test misuse.

Test Publishers
A number of test publishers set levels of competency to determine who can purchase and use tests; they often require a statement of qualifications from purchasers of psychological tests (Naugle, 2009; C. H. Peterson et al., 2014). Tests are graded by levels in regard to the amount of background and experience required and are sold only to those who meet the standards required for particular tests. These levels of qualifications are usually included in the test publishers' sales catalogs. Psychological Corporation, for example, provides four levels: Level A (no qualifications needed); Level B (master's degree in psychology-related or education-related field, appropriate training, or membership in appropriate professional organizations); Level C (doctorate in psychology-related or education-related field, appropriate training, or license or other credential that requires assessment training/experience); and Level Q (specific background in a specific test, ethical training in assessment). Multi-Health Systems, another publishing company, uses predominantly Level B and C designations. Level B requires appropriate coursework in a program or other training, and Level C includes Level B requirements as well as an advanced degree and training and experience in test use (Naugle, 2009).

Some publishers do not use competency levels. For example, Western Psychological Services only requires you to be a "qualified professional." Test users typically compile a qualification questionnaire, and the publisher determines whether they are qualified (Naugle, 2009). In addition to individual publisher criteria for test user qualification, professionals must also attest to the *Standards for Educational and Psychological Testing* (AERA, APA, & NCME, 2014). It is interesting that the standards themselves do not require counselors to adhere to the level process set by test publishers.

Professional Associations

Counselors are also to review their professional associations' ethical codes and other relevant documents. Fortunately, there is agreement among those who determine competence. For example, counselors graduating from a Council for Accreditation of Counseling and Related Educational Programs (CACREP) or CACREP-equivalent program will have met at least Levels A and B because the qualifications are written in the standards. Naugle (2009) noted that most professional associations accept the following test publisher qualifications and criteria: coursework in tests and measurements; graduate degree in a counseling-related field; supervised experience in testing; appropriate levels of training for specific tests; and appropriate rationale for test use in diagnosis, treatment planning, and interventions. Furthermore, state licensure laws parallel CACREP curricular standards and often require a passing score on the National Counselor Examination as well as supervised experience.

States

As part of their legal statutes, states attend to testing use. State licensure boards also determine test user competence. According to Naugle (2009), all states consider counselors as licensed/certified professionals. Thus, all states recognize assessment as part of the daily practices of counselors. Furthermore, the ACA's 1994 licensure bill influences how state licensure boards determine scope and sometimes practice of assessment. Glosoff, Benshoff, Hosie, and Maki (1995) defined *assessment* in the bill as follows:

> Assessment shall mean selecting, administering, scoring, and interpreting psychological and educational instruments designed to assess an individual's attitudes, abilities, achievements, interests, personal characteristics, disabilities, and mental, emotional, and behavioral disorders and the use of methods and techniques for understanding human behavior in relation to coping with, adapting to, or changing life situations. (p. 211)

This definition of assessment has been instrumental in determining scope of practice for counselors. Naugle (2009) reviewed assessment legislation by the states and noted that the majority specify assessment in the scope of counseling practice and assessment as one core area of curriculum. She noted that only a handful define "acceptable" assessment practices (or restrict specific tests) beyond what is stated in the scope of practice. Many states outline which assessment types can be administered.

Test Competence and Test Access Issues

Although there may be general agreement among professional associations about what test qualifications are, traditionally there has been disagreement about who is qualified—partly because of often vague requirements set forth by test publishers, state statutes, and professional association themselves. In fact, several state psychology boards have sued to restrict nonpsychologists' access to the majority of common psychological assessments. Thus, even though the ACA definition of assessment includes language regarding use of psychological instruments, state psychology boards often argue that those who do not have a psychology license "need not apply."

In a key historical document, Clawson (1997) noted that because professional associations' licensure models offer conflicting definitions of assessment—and these models influence licensure—opposition has occurred regarding test access. For example, there have been unsuccessful attempts at test restriction in Florida, Indiana, South Carolina, Iowa, Louisiana, Arkansas, Kentucky, and California. Interestingly, many of the tests that state psychology boards wanted restricted were developed by nonpsychologists! ACA has responded to test restriction efforts across the past couple of decades.

Fortunately, advocacy from organizations such as the **Fair Access Coalition on Testing** (FACT) has helped to oppose these efforts to restrict test access. FACT's (n.d.) mission is to serve as "protection and support of public access to professionals and organizations who have demonstrated competence in the administration and interpretation of assessment instruments, including psychological tests" (http://www.fairaccess.org). In essence, advocates argue that as long as you have appropriate levels of education, training, and experience, you have the right and capacity to use assessments no matter the profession. They further note that counselors and other professionals should monitor, not restrict, test use as appropriate. FACT members seek to increase public awareness and communicate the rationale for fair access to tests as well as monitor legislation and develop and promote relevant ethical standards.

Why is test access so important? First, there has been a rise in testing needs in various parts of the country as there has been an increased reliance on assessment results in decision making. Second, tests are an important part of counselors' daily practices and activities. As stated in Chapter 1, assessment is synonymous with counseling. If assessment activities are restricted, counselors' professional identity may be restricted. Finally, clients lose when tests are restricted. When counselors' assessment rights are threatened, clients have fewer opportunities to access interventions they may need. In theory, as long as various professionals are not pretending to be other types of professionals—and they have the proper training and experience—they should be able to access tests related to their competence. It is therefore very important for counselors to monitor state legislation and pending lawsuits that may restrict their practices.

Client Welfare Issues

Occasionally, an ethical issue arises regarding the welfare of the client in the assessment process. Is the welfare of the client being taken into consideration in the choice and use of tests? Except in such cases as court referrals, custody determinations, or institutional testing programs, this is seldom an issue in counseling because assessments are usually used to help the client and not for other purposes.

Another client welfare issue deals with the questions of privacy and confidentiality (see ACA, 2014). In counseling situations, clients are typically willing to reveal aspects about themselves to obtain help with their problems; thus, the invasion-of-privacy issue, often a concern in psychological testing elsewhere, is seldom a concern in counseling. Clients obviously would not wish this information to be disclosed to others. Test data, along with other records of the counseling relationship, must be considered professional information for use in counseling and must not be revealed to others without the express consent of the client. Certain types of test results, such as those assessing intelligence or aptitude and those that ask for or reveal emotional or attitudinal traits, often may deal with sensitive aspects of personal lives or personal limitations—most individuals would prefer that such information not be disclosed to others.

Problems of confidentiality often arise when the counselor is employed by an institution or organization, which can result in conflicting loyalties (to the client and to the institution or organization). In these circumstances, counselors should tell clients in advance how the assessment results will be used and make clear the limits of confidentiality. In general, ethical principles state that the test results are confidential unless the client gives his or her consent for the test results to be provided to someone else. The limits of confidentiality and the circumstances under which it can be broken (such as clear and present danger or court subpoena) must be communicated to and understood by the client. These issues are included in various codes of ethics (e.g., ACA, 2014; NBCC, 2012).

In reporting results to others who have a reason and need to make use of the results under the Family Educational Rights and Privacy Act of 1974 (FERPA; see Table 3.3), counselors must ensure that the results of assessments and their interpretations are not misused by others. Is the person receiving the information qualified to understand and interpret the results? It is incumbent on the counselor to interpret the results in a way that they can be intelligently understood by those receiving them, including teachers and parents. In addition, the counselor has an obligation to point out the limitations of the results and any other important information about reliability or validity, as well as a description of the norms used and their appropriateness.

Clients, of course, have the right to know assessment results, with interpretations of the results communicated to them in a language they can clearly understand. The results must be interpreted to clients in such a way that clients understand what the tests mean and also what they do not mean. It is important that clients not reach unwarranted conclusions from the interpretation that they receive.

The manner in which assessment results are communicated to others (when appropriate) should be carefully considered. Results should usually be presented descriptively rather than numerically. The use of labels that can be misinterpreted or damaging should be avoided. Instead, interpretations should be presented in terms of possible ranges of achievement or formulations of interventions to assist the individual in behaving more effectively.

To help ensure confidentiality, counselors should keep assessment results in a place where they are accessible only to authorized individuals. They should be maintained in school or agency files only so long as they serve a useful purpose. With the advent of computerized record keeping, the difficulty of keeping assessment results secure and inaccessible to all but authorized users has increased. Confidentiality must be maintained across a variety of contexts, including postal, telephone, Internet, and other electronic transmissions. This confidentiality includes knowing who receives faxes and who has access to fax machines and answering machines. Effective measures for protecting the security of individual records and reports must be maintained (see HIPAA in Table 3.2).

Counselors are to administer assessments in a standardized manner if possible and appropriate. A potential problem dealing with test administration involves test security (ACA, 2014). It is obvious that test results will not be valid if people can obtain the tests in advance. For high-stakes ability tests, on which important decisions will be based, elaborate procedures are established to ensure that there is adequate security. In addition, tests need to be accurately scored and accurately profiled if the results are to have valid meaning.

Because test publishers have increasingly relied on computers to prepare narrative reports of test results, there are ethical concerns regarding the quality of interpretation. Computer interpretations of such inventories as the Strong Interest Inventory or the MMPI-2 can produce interpretations that run 10–20 pages in length. Such interpretations provide a distillation of the information that has been accumulated in the professional literature and of the pooled experience of a number of experts. Narrative computer printouts are obviously no better than the wisdom and clinical experience on which they are based; however, they protect the client from possible bias or inexperience of an individual counselor while expediting what can be a time-consuming and tedious chore of report writing. These computer interpretations are, of course, based on norms, which are not necessarily appropriate for a particular individual. They should be used only in conjunction with the counselor's professional judgment. The narrative needs to be evaluated by the counselor who knows other facts about the client, the rationale for testing, and the reasons for such evaluation. The misuse of such computer-generated test interpretations has become an issue of increased concern to the counseling and psychological professions.

A final issue deals with the ethical use of psychological tests in research. When tests are given for research purposes, the first principle is that of informed consent: Having had the procedures explained to them, individuals must have the opportunity to choose whether to participate. Minors should also be informed, to the extent of their comprehension, and parental consent is often necessary as well. A particular problem arises in testing research when fully informed consent would provide knowledge regarding the specific objectives of a test that would have a substantial effect on the attitude of the person taking it, therefore yielding invalid research results. In research studies, there are also the ethical issues of privacy and confidentiality.

In general, counselors have had fewer ethical problems in the use of tests than have various other professionals, because counselors typically use tests in their activities on behalf of the client—to assist him or her in regard to decision making or to provide additional information for treatment and self-understanding. They do not usually use tests for "high-stakes" purposes such as selection, promotion, or placement. For school counselors, however, this role is changing because they and other educational administrators are increasingly called on to make crucial decisions regarding student retention, tracking, or graduation based on test results due to increased attention to educational accountability (see Table 3.3). To make appropriate decisions, counselors must have considerable knowledge in assessment, including measurement validity, special accommodations, and unintended consequences.

Case Example 3.1

Charlotte

Charlotte, a 19-year-old female, presents to a college counseling center to seek help for increased anxiety she has had since attending college. She states she is having difficulty understanding the course materials and is failing her courses. Charlotte reports that she seldom finishes class assignments or tests, as she "runs out of time." She notes that she has no previous counseling history or academic problems.

Reflect on the following:

- What additional information do you need about Charlotte?
- How might you counsel her?
- As you consider assessments to use with Charlotte, what are some considerations related to your competence in selecting, administering, and interpreting assessments? What are potential client welfare considerations?
- What ethical guidelines and/or legal standards might you review as you work with her?
- Are there certain legal cases or public laws that might affect your counseling interventions?
- What strengths might you bring to your work with Charlotte? What may be challenges for you?

• • •

Professional Issues in Assessment

There are several professional issues in assessment that need to be considered. This chapter presents issues surrounding testing and technology, counseling process issues, test anxiety, and coaching. In Chapter 4, professional issues related to cultural bias throughout the assessment process are discussed.

Testing and Technology

The increasing automation of psychological assessment will make the administration and scoring of tests, as well as the interpretation of their results, more efficient, more extensive, and more complex. Most of the tests commonly administered by counselors are available for administration, scoring, and interpretation with a computer (e.g., California Psychological Inventory, Differential Aptitude Test, Millon Index of Personality Styles, MMPI-2, Myers–Briggs Type Indicator, 16 Personality Factors Questionnaire, the Strong Inventory, and the Wechsler tests). Standardized interview data can also easily be obtained through use of a computer.

The benefits of testing using the Internet are many, including that it can be cheaper, faster, and more efficient (Butcher, 2013). Large-scale paper-based testing programs include a number of steps that can be eliminated with Internet-based testing. When paper-and-pencil tests are administered, the test answer sheets must be scanned, then collected, checked, counted, bundled, and shipped to a scoring center prior to scoring and profiling, all of which demands considerable time and cost. In contrast, tests administered on the Internet can be scored and interpreted for counselors and clients as fast as the last item is completed. Test publishers, stressing better and cheaper services and worldwide use, have embraced Internet testing. Revising a paper-and-pencil test requires printing and distributing new forms, answer keys, and manuals. Revisions of an Internet test can be downloaded to testing sites anywhere in moments. Internet tests can provide real-world simulations—including multimedia, three-dimensional graphics—and relevant resources, and thus they can assess higher order abilities and types of skills not easily measured by paper-and-pencil tests (e.g., the Test of English as a Foreign Language, which assesses listening and speaking skills over the Internet). Such processes obviously bring new challenges and problems. Various types of security must be maintained to ensure the privacy of client data and test results and to prevent the unauthorized copying of test items or the unauthorized use of testing materials. There are also other security problems, such as receiving spam, transmitting computer viruses, hacking, cheating by examinees, and maintaining copyrights across international borders.

Because Internet-based testing does not involve the use of a test administrator, counselors cannot be sure of the circumstances under which the test was taken (e.g., Did the examinee understand the instructions? Did he or she work independently in answering the items? Was he or she distracted in any way?). Because the counselor is not present at the time of the test interpretation, the counselor is not able to discern how clients react emotionally to the results or how they will integrate the information into their lives. There are also issues in determining appropriate accommodations for examinees with disabilities.

There is a continuing need for the ethical and professional use of these tests supported by reliability and validity (Montalto, 2014). For example, the growth of career resources on the Internet has resulted in many short career interest quizzes and brief personality measures that have no evidence of norms, reliability, or validity (Mallen, Vogel, Rochlen, & Day, 2005). The counseling profession must make it clear that these unproven instruments are no substitute for true standardized assessment instruments.

Counseling Process Issues

Counselors and human development professionals typically use tests for problem-solving purposes to assist the client. In other settings, test results are not necessarily shared directly with clients; in counseling, however, test results are almost always discussed with clients because the goal of counseling is usually to assist clients in making choices and in developing self-awareness. The client is seen as the primary user of test results, with the counselor acting more as a facilitator. Although counselors use the clinical interview and behavioral observation, tests provide an opportunity to obtain standardized information concerning individual differences that can be useful both to plan counseling interventions and to promote clients' understanding of themselves. Counselors help clients explore and identify their abilities, personality characteristics, patterns of interests, and values for the purpose of making choices and changes that can improve their sense of well-being or their lifestyles.

Personality inventories reveal information that can be useful in the counseling process, and interest and aptitude test results can assist in educational and vocational planning. Diagnostic tests in academic areas such as reading or arithmetic skills can help to identify those who need special instruction in particular areas and to plan future educational programs. Because of criticisms leveled against psychological tests when used in selection procedures (and perhaps in part because of some counselors' own experiences with scholastic aptitude tests used for selection purposes), counselors occasionally develop a bias against psychological tests. They refuse to use them even in individual counseling programs, where they can often be valuable.

When using tests in counseling, the counselor must attempt to understand the client's frame of reference. If the counselor is knowledgeable about tests, the counselor can then better help the client understand the information that tests can provide. In interpreting test results, the counselor must help clients understand their implications and their limitations and help clients integrate the test information into their self-perceptions and decision-making strategies.

It has been suggested (and even mandated by legislative action) that tests should not be used because certain disadvantaged groups make poor showings on them. In these situations, the test results often indicate symptoms of a societal ailment. When the tests reveal that the disadvantaged have not had the opportunity to learn certain concepts, there should be an attempt to provide these opportunities, not to dispose of the instruments that reveal such symptoms.

A criticism of using tests in counseling is that validity evidence is based on groups of individuals, and it is not possible to discern the validity of any test score for any one individual. It is in the counseling process that the counselor attempts to help clients determine the validity of that test score for that individual. To use tests properly in counseling, the counselor must know as much about the client and the client's environment as possible. Counselors must also be well informed about tests and have a basic familiarity with them. Although they may not need to have a great deal of understanding regarding the technical aspects of test development and standardization, they do need to have a clear understanding of the general purposes of the particular tests they use, the uses to which they can be put, and the role these tests can play in the counseling process.

In the information age, assessment results will continue to provide important data needed for many decisions. In addition to individual personal and career decisions, there will be increased reliance on assessments to determine minimum skills and competencies for educational institutions, licensing and certification, and personnel selection.

Test Anxiety

Another professional issue involves **test anxiety**, particularly for ability testing (see Chapter 10; von der Embse, Barterian, & Segool, 2013). Small but significant negative relationships have been found between test anxiety and scores on ability tests. This relationship, of course, does not necessarily mean that high levels of anxiety cause lower test scores. Often, those who have done poorly on these types of tests in the past are likely to experience more anxiety. Some studies suggest that a moderate amount of test anxiety can actually benefit test scores, whereas a high level of anxiety may be detrimental. Individuals differ in the amount of anxiety that can be considered to be optimal for best test performance.

These results have been obtained when tests have been given under experimental conditions of high tension and of relaxed situations. For example, in an early study (French, 1962) on this topic, students took the test under normal conditions when the scores were to be reported to the institutions to which they applied and a second time on an equivalent form under instructions that the test results were to be used only for research purposes and not otherwise reported. The results showed essentially equal performance under both the anxious and relaxed conditions. The only difference was that certain students under the anxiety condition attempted more of the mathematical items and therefore achieved slightly higher scores on that subtest than they did under the relaxed condition. Apparently, under the relaxed condition, they gave up a little earlier and therefore achieved slightly lower scores.

When test anxiety involves an excessive amount of worry and fear, clients may have difficulty thinking clearly or organizing their thoughts or may experience mental blanking. Interventions that counselors can use include (a) emphasizing adequate preparation; (b) teaching cognitive–behavioral techniques, such as challenging irrational beliefs and thought stopping; (c) using desensitization techniques; and (d) encouraging relaxation exercises (Sapp, 2013; von der Embse et al., 2013). In general, testing procedures that are well organized, that are smoothly run, and that reassure and encourage should help to reduce the anxiety felt by highly anxious test takers.

Coaching

Coaching refers to test preparation services, provided in many ways such as traditional workshops, online services and software, practice tests, and books with test preparation advice. The effect of coaching or practice on test scores is a controversial one that has received much attention and has been the subject of a number of studies. Obviously, practice or coaching that provides the answers to, for example, an individual IQ test such as the Stanford–Binet or WISC would invalidate the results as an accurate assessment. However, completion of a high school course in mathematics that results in a higher score on a mathematics achievement test probably accurately reflects the student's knowledge of mathematics outside the testing situation. The distinction therefore must be made between broad training and specific training or coaching focused on specific test items.

Coaching has been particularly controversial because of the existence of commercial coaching programs designed to raise scores on admissions tests such as the CEEB's Scholastic Aptitude Test (SAT), the Graduate Record Examination (GRE), or the Medical College Admission Test (MCAT). These coaching programs advertise and almost promise substantially better test performance for those who enroll in their programs. P. R. Sackett, Borneman, and Connelly (2008) noted that some firms claim average score gains of 120–140 points on the SAT, with one firm guaranteeing a 200-point increase. Many of the studies reported have substantial weaknesses that usually include the absence of a noncoached but equally highly motivated control group that is comparable with the coached group in all important ways, including performance on initial tests.

Furthermore, as P. R. Sackett et al. (2008) argued, students typically improve significantly upon retesting even if not participating in a coaching program—a result of a phenomenon known as a practice effect. A **practice effect** refers to familiarity with the types of problems and the problem-solving skills required. As a result, most of the testing programs—the College Board, the American College Testing (ACT) program, and the various professional school testing programs—now provide considerable information about the tests, including booklets with a number of practice test items. Thus, all applicants have the opportunity to take practice tests and to become familiar with the types of items that appear.

In sum, test scores can change, but how much is that change related to coaching specifically? The CEEB has been particularly concerned for two reasons. First, if coaching could help students to improve their scores substantially, then the test results for all students would lose some validity. Second, the commercial coaching programs charge substantial fees and can represent a waste of money if coaching yields little improvement.

Although specific coaching provides little improvement in test performance over and above that achieved by a little familiarization and practice (and this is particularly true on the verbal portions of these tests), additional training in the form of coursework is likely to result in improvement. In addition, a general review of the subject matter covered can substantially increase scores. For example, a student who has not taken any mathematics during the last 2 years in high school can improve scores on the mathematics portion of the SAT by reviewing the courses in algebra and geometry that were taken earlier. A college senior who has not taken any mathematics in college since the freshman year can also improve his or her scores on the quantitative portion of the GRE by reviewing the mathematical and algebraic concepts learned in high school and as a college freshman. A moderate score increase can be gained by reviewing basic skills in the area being tested, taking as many as four or five full-length practice tests with standard time limits, and paying attention to item format, pacing, and priority setting (Rubinstein, 2004). The best results are found when the coaching occurs not just before a major assessment but over longer periods and when incorporated into regular classroom instruction (Crocker, 2005).

Counselors often receive questions from students, parents, and those involved in the selection and interpretation of such scores regarding the efficacy of coaching programs and other review procedures. They need to be cognizant of the effects of different types of training and other activities on test performance.

Chapter Summary

Some of the criticisms of psychological testing and assessment and some of the attacks against their use in educational institutions and employment situations have had constructive effects. Increased awareness of the utility and limitations of testing has resulted in the need for more carefully trained users of test results as the personal and social consequences of testing have become increasingly apparent.

Psychological tests and other types of assessments serve many purposes for various mental health professionals. Counselors use tests primarily to assist individuals in developing their potential. Test results are designed to be used by the clients themselves—and only in the ways that they decide to make use of the test results or not to make use of them. In counseling, tests are not used by others to make decisions for or against a client. By using tests ethically, appropriately, and intelligently, counselors can assist their clients to understand their problems, make use of their potential, function more effectively, make more effective decisions, and live more satisfying lives.

In this chapter, ethical guidelines and assessment standards available to counselors as they engage in their work with clients were presented. These documents are provided by the ACA and its divisions, NBCC, JCTP, and other professional collaborations, including that of the AERA, APA, and NCME. Counselors are encouraged to review both general guidelines as well as those—as available—geared toward their specialty areas. Key public laws and court decisions were also discussed in this chapter. The chapter concludes with several professional issues in assessment: testing and technology, counseling process issues, test anxiety, and coaching.

Review Questions

1. What are the major ethical guidelines and assessment standards available to counselors today?
2. How might your work as a counselor be affected specifically by public law and court decisions outlined in Table 3.3?
3. What are the benefits of using technology in assessing clients? What are the challenges?
4. What are some of the controversies surrounding coaching? How would you approach the discussion with your clients?
5. What are some strategies for engaging in the assessment process ethically?

Resources for Further Learning

Eyde, L. D., Robertson, G. J., & Krug, S. E. (2010). *Responsible test use: Case studies for assessing human behavior* (2nd ed.). Washington, DC: American Psychological Association.

Sapp, M. (2013). *Test anxiety: Applied research, assessment, and treatment interventions.* Lanham, MD: University Press of America.

Chapter 4

Multicultural Considerations in Assessment

As the U.S. population continues to diversify, counselors are increasingly recognizing special considerations and challenges in assessing diverse populations. In assessing a person from another culture, a general rule is that the less the counselor knows of the client's culture, the more errors the counselor is likely to make. It is important for the counselor to be knowledgeable about the culture of the person being assessed and to develop skills for dealing with culture-related behavior patterns. Conversely, it is important not to "over-culturalize." Culture is important in understanding an individual, but it is not the only variable influencing human behavior. Although minimizing cultural bias in assessment is a goal, attempting to remove all cultural differences from an assessment is likely to compromise its validity as a measure of the behavior it was designed to assess. The Tip Sheet at the end of the chapter provides some general guidance for multicultural assessment.

As you will also learn from this text, from assessment courses, and from your own assessment use, assessment practices are far from being fair for all individuals and groups. Fairness in assessment becomes something counselors strive toward yet never fully achieve. Issues of fairness relate to how assessments are constructed; what psychometric evidence is garnered to support them; how and for what purposes they are selected, administered, and scored; and how and what interpreted data are used in developing treatment plans or making decisions with clients. This chapter begins with a discussion of fairness and its counterpart, cultural bias. Cultural considerations (e.g., gender, race, ethnicity, ability status, age) across assessment categories are described with examples and strategies for assessment practices that are more culturally fair.

Test Your Knowledge

Respond to the following items by selecting T *for "True" or* F *for "False":*

❏ T ❏ F 1. A widely accepted view in assessment is that tests are fair if there is equality in overall passing rates, no matter the group membership.

❏ T ❏ F 2. Assessment bias can result in positive results for some cultural groups.

❏ T ❏ F 3. Racial and ethnic minorities tend to display greater psychopathology on standardized personality assessments, such as the MMPI-2.

❏ T ❏ F 4. Most culture-fair tests were created to assess career development.

❏ T ❏ F 5. Even when accommodations are made for clients with disabilities, assessment results should be interpreted with caution.

Multicultural Counseling Competency and Assessment

Dana (2011) argued that multicultural assessment is the "single most omitted step in providing culturally relevant services" (p. 8); **multicultural assessment** can be defined as practices in which counselors attend to the role a multitude of intersecting cultural variables (e.g., race, ethnicity, gender, socioeconomic status, ability status) play in how client concerns are expressed, conceptualized, and treated within counseling. Given the interchangeable nature of assessment and counseling practice, counselors are obligated to possess multicultural competence for working effectively with culturally diverse clients.

The Multicultural and Social Justice Counseling Competencies (MSJCC; Ratts, Singh, Nassar-McMillan, Butler, & McCullough, 2016) is a set of guidelines that calls attention to the awareness, knowledge, skills, and counseling and advocacy interventions required to counsel in a multiculturally competent manner. Counselors and clients bring varying degrees of privilege and oppression experiences to the counseling relationship, and thus culturally based power is an evitable component of counseling—and thus multicultural assessment practices. The complete MSJCC may be found at http://www.counseling.org/docs/default-source/competencies/multicultural-and-social-justice-counseling-competencies.pdf?sfvrsn=20.

The MSJCC includes four developmental domains counselors should attend to as they work with culturally diverse clients: counselor self-awareness, counseling relationship, client worldview, and counseling and advocacy interventions. For the first three domains, the MSJCC includes guidelines in the areas of attitudes and beliefs, knowledge, skills, and action. For example, with regard to the counselor self-awareness domain, counselors are to be cognizant of their own worldview and combination of privileged and oppressed statuses (*awareness*); be familiar with how their cultural identity plays out in their personal and professional experiences (*knowledge*); engage in skill development to communicate, apply, and assess their knowledge (*skills*); and make changes on a personal and professional level through cultural immersion and professional development opportunities (*action*). The fourth developmental domain, counseling and advocacy interventions, specifies that social action should be used in six areas to build multicultural counseling competency: intrapersonal, interpersonal, institutional, community, public policy, and international levels. The developmental domains are depicted by concentric circles that build on one another, beginning with counselor self-awareness to ultimately partake in counseling and advocacy interventions.

Thus, to build multicultural competency for the assessment process, counselors are to reflect on the following questions when entering the counseling relationship:

- What attitudes and beliefs and knowledge do I hold about my privileged and marginalized statuses? What advantages and disadvantages do these statuses provide me for counseling others? What skills do I need to communicate, apply, and evaluate how these statuses impact me personally and professionally during the assessment process? What actions do I seek to increase my self-awareness of my cultural makeup and the degree of power it provides me personally and professionally?
- Before, during, and after engaging in the assessment process with clients, what attitudes and beliefs and knowledge do I hold about a client's worldview and its im-

pact on the process? What culturally responsive skills should I cultivate to foster an affirmative assessment experience for clients—particularly for those with multiple marginalized statuses? What can I do to increase my understanding of factors that shape client worldview and the positive role I can play in advocating for a process that considers the role of client worldview throughout the assessment experience?

- What attitudes and beliefs and knowledge do I possess to foster a strong working alliance for a positive assessment experience? What skills do I need to analyze, apply, and communicate understanding of factors that influence the counseling relationship during the assessment process? What actions can I take to initiate cross-cultural conversations with clients to foster the counseling relationship?
- In order to have a more meaningful assessment experience for clients of various cultural backgrounds and degrees of cultural power, how can I intervene with and on behalf of clients at the intrapersonal, interpersonal, institutional, community, public policy, and international levels?

Fairness and Cultural Bias in Assessment

It is important in the assessment and treatment of all clients for the counselor to display both the sensitivity to be aware of the cultural variables that affect assessment and the competence to translate this awareness into effective assessment. As Malgady (2011) noted, few assessments have been comprehensively vetted for culturally diverse clientele, leading to biased findings that yield ineffective and likely negative treatment outcomes.

Conducting assessments for diverse populations can be challenging in several ways. As these challenges are discussed, an example of each is provided in parentheses. First, there are challenges with the overall assessments themselves. For example, there is difficulty in establishing equivalent assessments across cultures. Also, there may be no appropriate norms against which you can compare your client's assessment data. (*Is this an appropriate way to measure depression for all ethnicities?*) Second, there are concerns about the nature of test items. Do the items represent appropriate content for a particular population? Does item content carry the same meaning across cultures? (*Does the construct of depression overall mean the same thing across groups? Would all groups agree that the items represent the construct fully?*) Finally, there are challenges related to the *people* involved in assessments. For example, clients across cultures hold differing attitudes toward assessment and provide different response sets. Furthermore, test users (e.g., counselors) may have different attitudes toward various assessments than their clients do. (*Are counselors and clients involved in assessment equally familiar and comfortable with the process?*) Even with the challenges of assessment across diverse populations, counselors are often required to use established assessment practices for institutional or reimbursement purposes (Paniagua, 2014). The core issue then becomes fairness in assessment to maximize appropriate assessment use.

Fairness refers to efforts to create equitable experiences for test takers, free from bias. **Bias** then refers to score differences or differences in findings (artificially low or high) that lead to differential ways these data are used for various groups and subgroups. Bias has significant consequences for clients, leading to misdiagnosis or other evaluation errors that affect what counseling interventions or placements clients receive. In this chapter, cultural bias is discussed to better understand how to intervene with clients of various groups and subgroups as well as how to interpret existing assessment data.

Although absolute fairness in assessment is impossible to achieve, it is important to present ways counselors can work toward fairer assessment practices. The *Standards for Educational and Psychological Testing* (AERA, APA, & NCME, 2014) define fairness in four ways. Although these are presented independently, they influence one another. To illustrate the four criteria, consider an example of a 13-year-old Latina, Maya, who is taking a math achievement test.

1. *There is the absence of bias.* With an absence of bias, a construct being measured by a test is interpreted free from factors irrelevant to that construct. For example, a math achievement test is purely measuring learning in math and not some other construct or external factor, such as motivation or the relationship between Maya and her teacher. An assessment free of bias assumes that test takers experience and respond to all aspects of the assessment process similarly, allowing isolated measurement of the test construct. That is, an unbiased assessment would mean that an individual score would have the same meaning, no matter the group membership (P. R. Sackett et al., 2008). Unfortunately, many construct-irrelevant components appear in assessment practice: biased results attributable to imperfect technical qualities of the assessment, different interpretations of test item content, the often impersonal nature of assessment settings, how individuals respond to assessments, and the varying quality of test taker/test user interactions based on perhaps interpersonal or cultural differences. That is, bias can result from the test itself, the test user, the test taker, the testing condition, or some other external factor.

2. *There is equitable treatment of all test takers.* Those involved in assessment should receive the same or comparable assessment procedures in testing, data interpretation, and use of assessment results. Fairness in this way refers to avoiding improper use of assessments, independent of their actual construction. Those being tested have a right, often through standardized procedures, to demonstrate their proficiency on a construct with equitable exposure to become familiar with test format and purpose, appropriate testing conditions, and just and ethically sound reporting of results. With the math achievement example, Maya would have an equitable test administration experience, would have just as much familiarity with the test format itself as others, and could count on having her results appropriately interpreted and reported.

3. *Those with equal standing on a particular test construct should score equally no matter the group membership.* This particular criterion is a contested one in counseling and other disciplines. Suppose Maya scored a 78% while her classmates (predominantly White males) scored, on average, 90% on the same math achievement test. Does this disparity indicate that the test was unfair? According to the *Standards for Educational and Psychological Testing*, maybe, but not likely if the above two criteria are met. P. R. Sackett et al. (2008) argued that "groups may differ in experience, in opportunity, or in interest in a particular domain; absent additional information, one cannot determine whether mean differences reflect true differences in the developed ability being measured or bias in the measurement of the ability" (p. 222). So, the once-ideal notion that passing rates across various groups should be equal is no longer a benchmark of test fairness. Although it seems on the surface that this *should* indicate test fairness, group differences in test results do not in themselves signal possible bias. Now, counselors abiding by the *Standards for Educational and Psychological Testing* would hope those with equal standing would score similarly. So, Maya scoring significantly below her classmates may indicate group differences (e.g., differences by gender and ethnicity) but also may indicate a test was fair if the test were appropriately constructed and administered. (It might be argued that the criterion of equal standing influences the above two fairness criteria, so it is not so easy to assume that test construction and other assessment practices are not influenced by the group differences discussion.)

   The question becomes this: When there are group differences on a construct (e.g., math achievement), are these differences "real" when test construction and testing conditions are fair? If a test in its construction and implementation is fair, then counselors should both examine what factors may be causing group differences and address these factors when assessment data are reported. A counselor will want to use a testing alternative, such as culture-fair tests, if possible, to help minimize group differences. Culture-fair tests are discussed later in this chapter.

4. *Test takers have an equal opportunity to learn.* This fairness criterion is particularly important in ability tests. For example, math achievement tests are supposed to assess comprehension of math concepts and operations that test takers have had the opportunity to learn. When the opportunity to learn material is not present, lower scores may reflect in part this lack of opportunity. When findings are then used for decision making, the test is clearly unfair. Thus, what is included in an assessment should be a result of what is taught. We might assume that if Maya were exposed to the material and allowed to engage with the math curriculum in an equitable manner, then this criterion may be met.

The *Standards for Educational and Psychological Testing* (AERA, APA, & NCME, 2014) categorize bias in two ways: bias associated with test content and bias associated with response processes. Bias associated with test content refers to inappropriate selection of test items, or general content coverage. Bias associated with test responses refer to situations when items elicit responses not intended by the test; this type of bias is also known as a **response set**. Table 4.1 presents several types of assessment bias that can be categorized as content or response bias (or both). Complete Activity 4.1 to identify any bias in existing assessments.

Activity 4.1
Identifying Bias in Assessments

Using the search strategies presented in Chapter 2 (e.g., *MMY*, *TIP*, assessments mentioned in published counseling articles), select a formal or informal assessment tool and identify examples of bias using the list in Table 4.1. How do you think you could minimize bias in the assessment? What MSJCC guidelines (Ratts et al., 2016) might be useful for minimizing bias? Discuss your findings and reactions in small groups.

Cultural Factors in Assessment

There are many cultural factors that influence the assessment process, introducing bias into assessments, as well as into the counseling process and outcomes. Although not an exhaustive list, some of the factors include the culture of counseling, counselor discrimination, mental disorder rates, client motivation and test sophistication, acculturation, and language. After reviewing these factors, please read Case Example 4.1.

The Culture of Counseling

Clients of diverse backgrounds have various levels of understanding and acceptance of counseling in general. *Counselor* and *therapist* have different meanings across racial/ethnic groups, such as physician, folk healer, and medicine man or woman. Furthermore, clients of diverse groups may value relationships with family or community members as instrumental to addressing their concerns. Depending on the racial/ethnic group, salient support systems (or "therapists") might include grandparents, siblings, church leaders, or tribal elders—these supporters may be just as (or more) important than support from a counselor. Counselors should assess the extent to which family and community members play a role in clients' lives and should view these members as part of the counseling process (Paniagua, 2014).

The counseling relationship, because it involves continual assessment practices, also plays an important role in assessment bias. Paniagua (2014) highlighted three relationship levels: (a) *conceptual level*, which involves clients' and counselors' perceptions of honesty, motivation, empathy, and credibility; (b) *behavioral level*, which is the degree of competence

Table 4.1
Types of Assessment Bias

Bias Type	Description	Example
Content	Items are more familiar to one group, thus favoring that group. Items are not relevant to the group being tested.	The word *toboggan* on a verbal analogies test might favor people from northern states over those from southern states.
Semantic	The meaning of test items is not the same for all cultures being tested.	A Latino new to the United States performs poorly on the WAIS Comprehension scale because he is not familiar with basic U.S. customs and situations. A child may perform poorly on the Story Completion subtest of the Kaufman Assessment Battery because the subtest references a scenario unfamiliar to the client.
Conceptual	The assessment does not measure the same construct across cultures.	A depression assessment includes few items that represent somatic complaints, which may be typical of Asian Americans presenting with depression.
Criterion	The interpretation of variables for the group being tested differs when compared with the norm group.	In norming samples of tests, very small numbers of Native Americans are likely to have been included, and even those are likely to represent only a few of the many different cultures from which Native Americans come. A counselor may erroneously compare a Native American client's score to the majority group and make faulty judgments about "normal" behavior or attitudes.
Omission	Items are worded in a way that ignores the possibility of one's membership in a minority group. That is, a group is omitted from reference.	A counselor asks a client what gender the client identifies with, offering only male and female as options. Holmes and Rahe's (1967) Social Adjustment Rating Scale, which assesses major life events, excludes references that relate to LGBT life events (e.g., coming out process, stigmatization, altered family relationships) and includes events experienced predominantly by heterosexual individuals (e.g., divorce, death of a spouse, reproduction).
Connotation	Items with negative connotations reference minority groups.	The inclusion of gender identity disorder in the *DSM-IV-R*, treating those who identify as transgender as potentially having a mental disorder.
Contiguity	Scales intended to evaluate mental disorders appear alongside scales that describe characteristics of minority groups.	Although Scale 5 of the MMPI-2 (the Masculinity–Femininity scale) was designed to measure sex-role identification problems, it includes reference to homosexuality in its interpretation.
Examiner	An examiner's beliefs affect the administration of an assessment.	A counselor assumes an international student cannot speak English well and reads questions in a clinical interview slowly.
Interpretive	An examiner's interpretation of assessment results provides an unfair advantage or disadvantage to a client.	A counselor assumes traditionally feminine characteristics—such as emotionality and interdependence—are pathological and thus assigns a female a personality disorder.
Response	Clients use a response set to answer test items, or a tendency to respond in a particular manner no matter the test content.	Clients from an Asian culture may have been socialized to not disagree with an authority and thus may agree with most or all items on an assessment.

(Continued)

Table 4.1 (*Continued*)
Types of Assessment Bias

Bias Type	Description	Example
Situational	Testing conditions affect individuals differentially.	A student not familiar with timed tests may not understand at what pace to respond to test items on the GRE.
Selection and prediction	Test results are used inappropriately for employment or college admissions. Results lead to differential prediction for any minority group.	The use of a test or other selection procedure results in a substantially higher rejection rate for minority candidates than for nonminority candidates, and the test used in selection is not justified as valid for the job in question.
Technical	The assessment method is not comparable across cultures.	The use of timed tests is not familiar to a particular culture.

Note. Information is from Chernin et al. (1997), Erford et al. (2014), and Paniagua (2014). WAIS = Wechsler Adult Intelligence Scale; LGBT = lesbian, gay, bisexual, and transgender; *DSM–5* = *Diagnostic and Statistical Manual of Mental Disorders, Fifth Edition, Text Revision*; MMPI-2 = Minnesota Multiphasic Personality Inventory–2; GRE = Graduate Record Examination.

for both the counselor (e.g., level of training, specific expertise) and the client (e.g., ability to follow directions and implement skills learned in counseling); and (c) *cultural level*, which is the universalist view that assessment is equally effective across multicultural interactions as long as the counselor displays both cultural sensitivity and cultural competency. With the third relationship level, counselors—no matter their cultural makeup or degree of cultural match with a client—can be beneficial to clients when they display sensitivity and translate multicultural awareness, knowledge, and skills into assessment.

Paniagua (2014) noted that major racial/ethnic groups may interpret counselors who are collecting extensive amounts of data as incompetent for two reasons: First, the counselor may be perceived as technically incompetent for not collecting significant data in the most concise manner; and second, the counselor may be seen as culturally incompetent if he or she appears to be unfamiliar with the particular cultural group. In most cases, clients are more willing to disclose information to a counselor once they believe the counselor is credible and the counselor has identified the key clinical issues and provided some useful directives.

Counselor Discrimination

In discussing the problem of assessment bias or group differences, one must distinguish between test results and innate aptitude. Racism, sexism, and other forms of discrimination (e.g., heterosexism, classism) occur in assessment when counselors use cultural group membership as the explanation for assessment findings. That is, race or other cultural markers are said to cause systemic differences, alluding to minority group membership as deficient in some manner. For example, a counselor may be considered racist if she notes that lower intelligence scores for people of color is an indicator of lower intelligence for these groups. Similarly, an example of sexism in assessment would be if a counselor attributed low scores on a math test to a client being female. The statement that males as a group achieve higher levels of competence in mathematics than females do is a statement regarding past achievement on a given test. This past achievement does not imply that males possess a greater aptitude for mathematics than females—such a statement suggests innateness or biological or genetic determinism.

Counselor discrimination also affects clinical decision making. **Clinical decision making** refers to "the intricate decisions professional counselors make when they assess the degree of severity of a client's symptoms, identify a client's level of functioning, and make decisions about a client's prognosis" (D. G. Hays, Prosek, & McLeod, 2010, p. 114). Arriving at a clinical diagnosis is a significant part of clinical decision making. First, counselors may overdiagnose (i.e., provide more severe diagnoses) when they assess nondominant populations. For example, African American and Latino clients are disproportionately diagnosed with psychotic disorders (R. C. Schwartz & Blankenship, 2014), women are disproportionately diagnosed with personality disorders (Kress, Dixon, & Shannonhouse, in press), clients with sexual minority statuses are almost 5 times more likely to be diagnosed with panic disorder than heterosexual clients (Cochran, Sullivan, & Mays, 2003), and clients with less formal education are diagnosed more often with schizophrenia (Paniagua, 2014). Furthermore, Good, James, Good, and Becker (2003) found that when counselors are unaware of their clients' racial and ethnic identity, they tend to provide less severe diagnoses than when they do know the racial and ethnic identity.

Second, counselors may also underdiagnose (i.e., provide less severe diagnoses or not diagnose at all), particularly when symptoms or presenting concerns do not fit nicely into established (often Western-based) diagnostic criteria or are congruent with how a counselor stereotypes a client of a particular cultural group (D. G. Hays et al., 2010). Examples include African Americans diagnosed with less depression than Whites, or Asian Americans potentially not being diagnosed with depression because they may display only somatic symptoms of depression (Paniagua, 2014). Finally, counselors may misdiagnose entirely. For example, autism has been traditionally misdiagnosed as an intellectual disability in African Americans (Paniagua, 2014). Although it is difficult to determine the degree to which diagnostic differences reflect actual cultural differences, it can be assumed that counselor bias and discrimination play some role.

Rates of Mental Disorders

On a related note, a consideration playing a role in assessment is the disproportionate rates of mental disorders across cultural groups—particularly racial and ethnic minorities. Paniagua (2014) noted that the prevalence and incidence of mental disorders are higher among racial/ethnic minorities. Are mental disorders in general higher for racial/ethnic minorities? Likely not. Paniagua presented some weaknesses in how prevalence and incidence data are collected, which likely depict a grimmer picture for racial/ethnic minorities. First, mental disorders are defined differently across studies because there are no uniform definitions of mental disorders and no agreed-upon assessment tool to measure individual mental disorders. When researchers use different instruments to assess prevalence and incidence, different outcomes arise. When some of those assessments are culturally inappropriate, minority groups are likely rated more severely. Second, assessment reports or studies typically do not discuss thoroughly the sample or the larger population from which the sample was drawn. Also, they typically do not include information about the potential effects of cultural difference, such as language barriers, acculturation level, impact of folk beliefs, effects of oppression, and so on. Thus, when counselors review prevalence and incidence data, they seldom are provided the cultural delimitations of data collection methods.

Mental disorders may, however, be exacerbated by discrimination. Racial discrimination and other oppression experiences are seldom considered a cause of emotional problems. That is, counselors may not reflect whether responses are a result of more generic stressors experienced by the general population (e.g., job loss, death of a loved one) or those resulting from discrimination (Paniagua, 2014). Clients who experience discrimination are more likely to display psychiatric symptoms such as depression, anxiety, paranoia, obsessive–compulsive behaviors, and somatization (Kress et al., 2018).

Client Motivation and Test Sophistication

Some argue that assessment score differences are really differences in test-taking motivation or familiarity with the assessment process. Extreme forms of test anxiety, self-esteem, and achievement motivation have been found to be related to test performance, but there has been little evidence that there are substantial differences in these areas among races, sexes, or social classes. However, clients from minority groups who are not motivated to perform well on a test or who are not sophisticated in regard to the nature of the test items cannot be expected to perform as well on tests as those from the dominant culture, in which these factors have been emphasized.

A classic example of client motivation and test sophistication issues concerns standardized tests. A basic assumption of standardized testing is that the test taker is willing to provide obvious information and to give a performance for a total stranger—the examiner. These basic social assumptions may be in conflict with the interactional rules for individuals in some cultures. For example, it might be hypothesized that Black working-class children or American Indian working-class children are less oriented to public performance for unfamiliar adults than are White middle-class children. It might even be argued that child-rearing practices of many White middle-class parents, which encourage public verbal performance for strangers, program their children for eventual success on standardized tests.

The combination of constriction imposed in most American schools and the competition encouraged there can conflict directly with aspects of African American and Native American cultures. Such conflict may lead to alienation of these students from both the experiences and products of education, of which assessment instruments are a part (Neisser et al., 1996). For example, in testing situations Native Americans may underestimate the seriousness of tests, lack test-taking skills, or lack motivation to perform on tests. For some, tribal beliefs may discourage the type of competitive behavior often present in test-taking situations. They may also have learned English as a second language and learned their first language as a nonwritten language—factors that can easily affect English reading skills. In addition, because they often come from isolated, rural, or impoverished settings, they may lack the type of knowledge and experience expected on certain instruments. The Native American Acculturation Scale (20 items) can be used to estimate the extent of an individual's acculturation to U.S. society (Garrett & Pichette, 2000).

Test sophistication also affects performance for Asian Americans. The later generations of Japanese and Chinese Americans come from backgrounds in which the mean income level equals or surpasses that of Whites, and they hold many attitudes and values similar to the majority culture. There are aspects of their cultures, however, that influence them to place increased emphasis on the results of achievement and aptitude tests and less on other types of performance. In addition, education, especially higher education, is much valued and supported, with particular value placed on attending prestigious institutions of higher education. Thus, there is considerable pressure to attain high enough scores on academic aptitude tests to gain entrance to prominent colleges and universities. Given the within-group variation among Asian Americans, client motivation and test sophistication are quite different for other subgroups, such as Southeast Asians.

Acculturation

D. G. Hays and McLeod (2018) defined **acculturation** as "the degree to which immigrants identify with and conform to a new culture of a host society, or the degree to which they integrate new cultural values into their current value system" (p. 23). Paniagua (2014) noted that acculturation level is defined by the number of years a client has been in the acculturation process, the age at which the client began the process, and the client's country of origin. Although an extensive discussion of acculturation is beyond the scope of this text, following are four acculturation models to consider in terms of how they influence the assessment process: (a) *assimilation model*, when a client identifies only with the dominant or host culture, denying the value systems of their culture of origin; (b) *separation model*, when the client identifies only with values of the culture of origin; (c) *integration model* or *biculturalism*, when the client identifies with values from both the culture of origin and the dominant culture; and the (d) *marginalization model*, when a client rejects behaviors and beliefs from both the culture of origin and the dominant culture (Paniagua, 2014). Though these models provide an initial framework to evaluate client behaviors and values that are presented in counseling, it is important to remember that clients fall under respective models at varying degrees. In addition, in instances of family or group counseling, there may be clients categorized in various models and/or to varying degrees within the same model. For example, a child who grew up in the United States but whose parents immigrated only 10 years ago may have value conflicts that color what problems are presented in counseling as well as overall assessment process and goals.

One useful tool that counselors could integrate into their counseling practice is the Cultural Assessment Interview Protocol (Geiger, 2007). This qualitative assessment tool includes 11 categories of information to inform other clinical information, including assessment data from other tools. These categories include problem conceptualization and attitudes toward helping, cultural identity, level of acculturation, family structure and expectations, level of racial/cultural identity, experiences with bias, immigration issues, existential/spiritual issues, and the client's perception of the provider's cultural identity and behaviors.

Language

Imagine yourself as a non-English speaker, or at least not very proficient in English. The assessment process begins in English, and—assuming you have some English proficiency—you pause to mentally translate to the best of your ability what the counselor says, consider in your own language how to respond, and translate again to the best of your ability to English before responding. The assessment process continues, and your frustration likely escalates as you begin to doubt that you will benefit from counseling. Even though you are communicating with the counselor, you are not likely feeling connected to the counselor or the counseling process. Imagine the difficulties if you cannot read or respond to anything in English. The outcomes are probably worse.

A client's limited English proficiency also potentially serves as a factor of assessment bias, and the counselor must consider individual differences and circumstances in interpreting the test results of clients for whom English is not their native language. A Latino student, for example, who scores low on a standardized test in English may actually have obtained a remarkably good score for someone who has been learning English for only a short period. Furthermore, previous research indicates that clients with limited English proficiency tend to receive more severe clinical diagnoses and are perceived as noncompliant or emotionally withdrawn when they are not interviewed in their native languages (Paniagua, 2014).

With respect to standardized assessment, research does show that administering a test in someone's native language has been linked to higher test scores. For example, Alt, Arizmendi, Beal, and Hurtado (2012) found that administering a math achievement test to Grade 2 English-language learners in their native Spanish language resulted in higher scores.

You may decide to use a translator to aid the assessment process. Should you use a translator, Paniagua (2014, see pp. 23–24) provides the following guidelines:

- Employ a translator who shares the client's racial and ethnic background as well as a similar linguistic expression within that background. Determine what dialect the client speaks before engaging a translator.
- Select an individual who has training in mental health issues and culture-related syndromes.
- Use a sequential mode of translation (i.e., the client speaks, the translator translates the client's words into English, the counselor speaks, the translator translates the counselor's words into the client's language, and so forth).
- Facilitate relationship building between the translator and client prior to the assessment process to strengthen the counseling relationship. Allow time alone to discuss common interests and other cultural similarities.
- Have the translator provide a sentence-by-sentence translation to avoid missing important details.
- Avoid using technical terms with the client, and have the client describe in his or her words the reason he or she is in counseling.
- Anticipate that using a translator during the clinical interview or other assessment procedure will take twice as long as an interview in English.
- Consider the potential effect of the translator when interpreting clinical data.
- Consider the translator's level of acculturation in relation to the client's level of acculturation. Reflect on how differences in acculturation level affect the assessment process.

- Avoid employing a relative or friend of the client as a translator, because a potential lack of objectivity could lead to misinterpretations or other distortions.
- Avoid asking the client's bilingual child to serve as a translator because similar issues of objectivity may arise as may potential family conflicts (which may, in fact, be a source of the presenting problem).

Test adaptation or test translation may be helpful to address language barriers and other factors discussed in this section. **Test adaptation** refers to changing an existing assessment tool to meet the needs of a cultural group not included in the original norm sample. A test is typically adapted through **test translation,** by creating alternate language versions to accommodate the test takers (Zhou & Hansen, 2009). For example, several assessments have been translated to Spanish. Spanish-language editions have been developed for most of the widely used tests, including the Strong Interest Inventory, the Myers–Briggs Type Indicator, the MMPI-2, the Wechsler intelligence scales, the Self-Directed Search, the Sixteen Personality Factor Questionnaire (16 PF), and Cattell's Culture-Fair Intelligence Test.

Case Example 4.1

Paulo

Paulo is a 28-year-old Italian immigrant male who recently arrived in the United States. He is having difficulty managing stress and completing tasks at work. He finds himself more irritable and withdrawn, resulting in increasing problems at work and relationship difficulties with his partner. His employee assistance program (EAP) refers him to you as a mental health counselor. Although Paulo has heard of counseling in his country of origin, he thinks of it as something for "weak" and "crazy" people. The EAP explains to Paulo that you will be able to speak with him about his difficulties and assess him and provide some assistance so he may function better at work and at home. Paulo speaks very limited English.

- What is salient cultural information to consider when working with Paulo?
- How does acculturation level and language affect the counseling relationship and process?
- Based on cultural similarities and differences between you and Paulo, how might he perceive you as his counselor?
- What biases do you hold about Paulo? How might this impact your work with him?
- How might you seek information about rates of mental disorders? What are some things you may consider in reviewing these rates?

• • •

Assessment and Gender

Gender differences in assessment results (with research primarily investigating formalized assessments) may be attributed to gender bias in some manner. It is important to note that instruments tend to reflect only male and female comparisons, and subsequent research provides data for these two categories. Information regarding how assessment findings relate to transgender or intersex populations is nonexistent or at least very limited. Thus, counselors are to use this information tentatively when working with clients who do not identify as traditionally male or female. Furthermore, because sexual orientation overlaps in some ways with gender and because items typically representing a traditional gender characteristic also depict heterosexual characteristics, counselors should cautiously apply these findings.

Aptitude and Cognitive Assessment

Although there are not significant gender differences in scores on intelligence tests (Ball, Cribbie, & Steele, 2013), specific aptitude tests have historically indicated that females tend to score higher on tests of verbal ability, whereas males tend to obtain higher scores on numerical and spatial aptitudes (see Lakin, 2013; Neisser et al., 1996). Females tend to achieve higher grades in elementary school, high school, and college (Fortin, Oreopoulos, & Phipps, 2015; Halpern, 2013; Voyer & Voyer, 2014), although the difference in college tends to diminish when controlled for types of majors and types of courses (Zafar, 2013).

The question regarding lower scores on mathematical ability is a controversial one; some argue that the difference is an innate difference, whereas others argue that it is due to stereotypical attitudes on the part of parents and teachers, which result in students being differentially encouraged to learn mathematics depending on their gender. Most evidence yields at least partial support for the latter explanation because the gap has decreased among adolescents over the past 40 years (Halpern, 2013).

Career Assessment

Gender differences in career assessment also exist. These differences can exist for multiple reasons, such as when items contain various types of assessment bias (see Table 4.1) or as a result of stereotype threat (Spencer et al., 2016; see Chapter 2). It is important to note, however, that gender differences in particular competency areas—such as mathematical performance—are *not* linked to biological superiority of one gender over the other. What seem to be linked to gender differences are cultural beliefs about gender-appropriate career paths, which plays out in career assessment practices.

Gender bias within the career assessment process not only can misguide an individual's career decision-making process but also can have long-standing consequences for how males and females are collectively guided toward particular careers. For example, a male self-administering a career values scale might not prioritize helping others or having flexibility for family because current gender schemas would not consider these acceptable for males; this lack of endorsement could impact career selection and the perception of what careers are suitable for males. As another example, a female may not perceive herself as having mathematical ability, which could lead to a diminished interest in (and ultimately choice for) careers involving mathematics.

Even without the inherent item bias that exists in career assessments, individuals can still have distorted views of their skills, interests, and values that get expressed based on their general experiences surrounding gender within a particular culture. Quite early in an individual's career decision-making process, he or she receives messages from family members, teachers, peers, and other community members regarding what are "appropriate" behaviors for his or her gender; these messages have implications for what skills and interests may be viewed as most suitable for that individual. Thus, cultural beliefs about careers based on gender are expressed and often internalized across the life span, long before an individual engages with a counselor.

As counselors engage in the assessment process, they should be aware of gender messages at both the individual and societal levels: Clients enter the assessment experience with gendered beliefs, and those beliefs can impact perceived competence, interest, and career aspirations. Societal messages about which careers are appropriate for which gender lead to the "gendering" of occupations, which can result in restrictive expression of careers in general. For example, notions about what makes a successful business leader might include being rational, being assertive, and remaining more emotionally distant from employees; these traits can be viewed as traditionally masculine and can limit the expression of what an effective business leader looks like. Furthermore, scholars have noted that "quantitative professions," such as those associated with science, technology, engineering, and mathematics–related fields, are more predominantly linked with males and tend to be rewarded more financially (Correll, 2001); thus, gendered messages can serve to widen gender gaps in wages.

As Correll (2001) noted, "Regardless of whether gender beliefs are personally endorsed or internalized as other people's expectations, they often lead to biased self-assessments" (p. 1698). There are several methods by which publishers have attempted to eliminate, or at least reduce, gender bias on interest inventories. One is by using separate-sex norms. In the case of the Strong Interest Inventory (see Chapter 12), the Occupational Scales are based on separate criterion groups for each sex. The norms for the Basic Interest Scales are based on a combined sample of men and women; however, the profile also indicates how a person's scores compare with others of the same sex as a means of taking into account gender differences. In the case of the earlier forms of the Strong Inventory, many more occupations were shown for men than for women, which had the tendency to limit the number of careers considered by women. In recent years, test authors have developed the same number and type of scales for both men and women. Virtually all inventories have eliminated sexist language, for example, replacing *policeman* with *police officer* and *mailman* with *postal worker*.

Another method by which publishers of interest inventories have attempted to minimize gender bias has been to include only interest items that are equally attractive to all genders. For example, on an interest inventory containing items related to the six Holland themes, males respond more often to a Realistic item such as "repairing an automobile" and females more to a Social item such as "taking care of very small children." Through the elimination of items that are stereotypically masculine or feminine, such differences can be largely avoided. For example, Realistic items such as "refinishing furniture" or "operating a lawn mower" or a Social item such as "teaching in high school" tend to receive approximately equal responses from both men and women (Rayman, 1976). An interest inventory such as the unisex edition of the ACT Interest Inventory, or UNIACT (ACT, Inc., 2016a), increases the probability that males will obtain higher scores on the Social scale and females will score higher on the Realistic scale and thus that every gender will be more likely to give consideration to occupations in a full range of fields. Thus, by providing the same occupational scales for males and females, showing norms for both sexes on interest scales, eliminating stereotypical language, and, for some instruments, developing sex-balanced items, gender bias in interest testing has been greatly reduced. It must be remembered, however, that gender-based restrictions in interest preferences and career choices will continue as long as societal influences limit the experiences that individuals are exposed to or are able to explore.

Earlier and continual career assessment is needed to help minimize sex segregation of careers, increase how careers are defined across genders, and counter the impact of biased traditional assessment tools. Thus, counselors have a responsibility to help modify career-related behaviors and judgments. To consider the influence of gender in the career assessment process as well as career choice overall, counselors can process the following questions with their clients prior to administering and interpreting career assessments:

- What has influenced your career interests and selected career path?
- What have been previous career paths or paths not pursued?
- What have been actual or perceived barriers to various career paths?
- What consequences have you experienced, or do you anticipate experiencing, related to career choice? How much "choice" do you perceive is realistic for career paths in which you are interested?
- How might your previous performance in certain skill areas serve as evidence of your current ability?

Assessment and Race, Ethnicity, and Socioeconomic Variables

Counselors need to recognize the diversity within specific racial and ethnic groups both in regard to acculturation to the U.S. society and in regard to cultural background. For example, Latin Americans, the fastest growing racial/ethnic group, are made up of several major subgroups: the largest group is of Mexican origin, most of whom have settled in the southwestern states. Puerto Ricans are concentrated in the eastern states; Cubans, in Miami, Florida; and Central and South Americans, in Florida and Texas. Although heterogeneous in many ways, their worldview is shaped by several common influences: the Catholic religion (about 85%), some presence of folk beliefs, and a Latino cultural identity (Villalba, 2018).

In counseling Native American individuals, there is a wide range of differences with regard to culture among various American Indian tribes, and because of such large differences, few generalizations are possible. For example, Sioux children are likely to be more integrated into the U.S. society than Navajo children, who more often live on a reservation and speak primarily Navajo (Lichtenberger & Kaufman, 1998). Furthermore, Asian Americans come from more than 20 cultural groups with widely diverse cultural backgrounds and range all the way from fourth- and fifth-generation Asian Americans to the more recent Hmong, Filipino, and Vietnamese immigrants (Luu, Inman, & Alvarez, 2018).

Aptitude and Cognitive Assessment

A frequently offered argument is that intelligence tests and other measures of cognitive aptitude are constructed by and for White middle-class individuals and therefore are biased against lower socioeconomic individuals and others who are not members of the majority culture. Some of this cultural bias could be found in the items on which suburban children might have more familiarity than urban or rural children. Children brought up using a dialect or nonstandard American English might be less able to comprehend the language used on such instruments. Test developers have now become extremely sensitive to this issue and have established panels of experts that include representatives from many cultural groups. Most of this content bias has therefore been eliminated from many of the current forms of these tests, although such changes have been shown to have little if any effect on the scores obtained by many minority individuals (Paniagua, 2014). If the validity of cognitive aptitude test results is different for majority and minority groups, and if counselors encourage or discourage clients about pursuing different levels of education or types of jobs on the basis of these test results, then this type of bias could affect counseling outcomes.

In attempting to understand and competently interpret cognitive assessment results of clients from various backgrounds, counselors must remember that social class is correlated with race and ethnicity and that many cultural differences disappear when socioeconomic status is controlled (Paniagua, 2014). Academic aptitude and achievement test scores are far more related to school academic variables (e.g., grades achieved, types of courses taken, particular school attended) than to race or ethnicity. In a study conducted by the American College Testing Program of students in four racial/ethnic groups (African American, Latino/Native American, Asian American, and White), more than 50% of the variance in ACT scores could be explained by high school academic variables, with an additional 15% explained by student background characteristics and noncognitive, education-related factors. Race/ethnicity or gender explained only 1% to 2% of additional variance in ACT scores over and above the other variables considered in this study (Noble, Davenport, Schiel, & Pommerich, 1999; Sanchez, 2013). Additional research is needed to explore how race, ethnicity, and socioeconomic status affect assessment today.

Some research is available describing the role discrimination against African Americans plays in assessment bias. Because African Americans as a group have experienced great racial discrimination in the past and this discrimination has had an impact on their socio-economic status, their opportunities, and their home environments, it is not surprising that these circumstances would have an effect on test results. Although tests could be biased against any minority group, the most serious controversy exists over the fact that, as a group, African Americans score approximately 1 *SD* below Whites on most standardized tests of cognitive ability (Paniagua, 2014). Much of the controversy centers on the cause of the differences. Some attribute the differences to the disadvantages that African Americans experience in their economic status and their educational and occupational opportunities. Others attribute much of the difference to genetic factors. Neisser and other members of the APA Task Force on Intelligence (Neisser et al., 1996), however, summarized this issue as follows:

> The differential between the mean intelligence scores of Blacks and Whites . . . does not result from any biases in test construction and administration, nor does it simply reflect differences in socioeconomic status. There is certainly no . . . support for a genetic interpretation. At present no one knows what causes this differential. (p. 94)

Numerous studies have been conducted predicting various criteria for both education and job performance for Black and White groups. In general, results have shown that ability tests are equally valid for both minority and majority groups. These studies have used IQ tests to predict school achievement, scholastic aptitude tests to predict college grades, and job-related aptitude tests to predict job success. Both correlations and regression lines tend to be similar for both groups, and in the cases in which minor differences have occurred, there has been a tendency for the test to slightly overpredict the achievement of Black students (G. L. Cohen & Sherman, 2005; P. R. Sackett et al., 2008).

Career Assessment

A major question with regard to the use of career assessments is whether racial/ethnic minorities are sufficiently familiar with the vocabulary, examples, occupational terms, and situations that are used in these tests. Because many of these individuals differ from middle-class Whites in their experiences, orientations, and values, their view of available occupations may be restricted even though their aspirations may equal or exceed those of the middle-class White individuals. Those from disadvantaged backgrounds are likely to be less aware of the great variety of occupations and the skills required for certain occupations. They may also view potential occupations in ways that are quite different from that which is implied in occupational literature. Furthermore, minority students tend to enter narrower ranges of fields of study (Griffith, Cohen, & Ehrenberg, 2015).

Within minority communities, there is often a lack of continuity of values between school and family as well as a lack of diversity in the occupations that exist as models for children from these backgrounds. Family cultures vary considerably among different ethnic groups, which influence career roles and expectations. On various interest inventories, minority students may obtain relatively low scores because such students indicate liking fewer occupational titles or interests than students in the norm group.

Studies have shown that despite these differences, interest measures have similar validities among various minority groups in the United States. Interest inventories can therefore be used with minority clients with the same amount of confidence as with Whites, with the possible exception of those coming from particularly disadvantaged backgrounds. Studies have also shown that interest measures predict college majors similarly for students from various minority backgrounds. Differences have been found on interest measures among different minorities, but these differences have equal predictive value (Fouad & Mohler,

2004). For example, African Americans, who tend to score higher on social interests, are more likely to enter social occupations; whereas Asian American students, who obtain higher scores on biological and physical science interests and lower scores on social and sales interests, are more likely to pursue scientific occupations. Counselors should also be aware that some of the female–male differences found among Whites are similar but more extreme for Latinas.

There is a tendency among Asian Americans to choose vocations in business, science, mathematics, or engineering fields to the exclusion of humanities, social sciences, or law. When interpreting the results of interest inventories in educational and vocational counseling, the counselor should keep in mind this tendency by the minority client to consider a narrow range of possible career goals. Expanding the range of occupations being considered may well be one of the goals of such counseling, although counselors are to be cognizant of the role cultural values play in counseling goals.

Finally, several interest inventories have been translated into a number of other languages. A question that needs to be asked in administering such a version of the inventory is whether the person taking the test is from a culture that has similar expectations and social customs as those for the culture in which the test was devised. Unfamiliarity with the nature and purpose of tests could be a problem, as could different ways of responding. Clients from a culture in which the emphasis is on agreeing with nearly everything (because it is considered impolite to disagree) may obtain test results that lack validity.

Personality Assessment

Although most of the controversy regarding bias in tests has centered on aptitude or intelligence tests, certain tests used in counseling, such as interest and personality measures, have not been entirely free of bias. Returning briefly to gender considerations, most personality measures are scored on norms developed for each sex. Thus, the bias that would result if men and women tended to score differently on a personality characteristic is eliminated. Counselors using particular tests, such as the MMPI-2, should be aware that behavior patterns attributed to certain profile types often differ for men and women.

There is some evidence that various minority groups obtain scores on personality inventories that differ from those typically obtained in a White majority population. For example, Asian American clients are more likely to express psychological problems in terms of somatic complaints. Therefore, an elevation on the Hypochondriasis scale (Scale 1) on the MMPI-2 with Asian clients should be interpreted in light of this cultural phenomenon (Gray-Little & Kaplan, 1998; Paniagua, 2014). A Pacific Islander's deviant scores on the MMPI-2 could easily be accounted for by cultural and language differences from the original sample on which it was normed. In a similar manner, African Americans may also score higher on Scales 8 and 9 because of higher levels of nonconformity, alienation, or impulsivity or because of different types of values and perceptions (Groth-Marnat & Wright, 2016). Differences on personality tests among minority groups and those from other cultures are to be expected, and counselors should take these into consideration in their interpretations of personality test results.

Few consistent differences have been found in comparing Latinos/as and White Americans on the MMPI scales. In most cases when bilingual Latinos/as have been administered both English and Spanish versions, the resulting profiles have been similar. An exception is that those with traditional Mexican Indian spiritual beliefs tend to obtain higher scores on the Schizophrenic Scale, scores that should not be regarded as abnormal or unhealthy (Butcher, Cabiya, Lucio, & Garrido, 2007; Velasquez, Maness, & Anderson, 2002). A number of other variables such as socioeconomic status, education, and intelligence seem to be more important determinants of MMPI performance than ethnic status. Alcohol abuse combined with depression is more often found among Latino clients compared with White male clients. Latinas tend to obtain scores on the Masculinity–Femininity Scale indicating greater femininity. Their expected traditional roles are often in conflict with the greater female role flexibility in U.S. society. Failure to meet these gender-specific roles as wives and mothers can lead to guilt, anger, and depression that may be revealed on personality instruments (Butcher et al., 2007; Prieto, McNeill, Walls, & Gomez, 2001). The only non-trivial difference for Latinos was their scoring lower on the Masculinity–Femininity scale. This is not a pathological scale and suggests a stronger masculine identity in this group.

Native Americans as a group have lost much of their original self-sufficient heritage and now present major challenges for counselors and the entire mental health community because they have the highest rates of poverty, unemployment, alcohol abuse, and suicide (Garrett et al., 2018; Trimble, King, LaFromboise, Bigfoot, & Norman, 2013). For example, members of several different tribes obtained higher scores on numerous scales, such as the MMPI-2 and MacAndrew Alcoholism Scale–Revised. These differences remained when participants were matched on age, gender, and education, which suggests that they indicate real differences in behavior and symptoms—not test bias (Greene, Albaugh, Robin, & Caldwell, 2003). Even with this research, findings should be interpreted with caution and counselors should collaborate with the client on the interpretation.

Asian Americans tend to underuse counseling and mental health services and share experiences and emotions less often with those outside the family (Luu et al., 2018; Meyers, 2006). They are more likely to express concerns in an indirect manner, such as physical symptoms. In general, however, highly acculturated Asian Americans obtain MMPI-2 scores similar to Whites. Differences are found among those less acculturated, with more elevated scores on the majority of the clinical scales. Asian Americans tend to receive lower extraversion scores (indicating more introversion) on the NEO Personality–Revised (Mulder, 2012; Okazaki, Kallivayalil, & Sue, 2002). There have been few studies comparing personality inventory scores of Asian students versus White students.

Culture-Fair Tests

To provide valid tools useful in other cultures or for use with subcultures or minority cultures in the United States, attempts have been made to develop culture-fair assessments that function independently of a specific culture, primarily by eliminating, or at least greatly reducing, language and cultural content. The goal of **culture-free tests** is to provide items that are equally familiar to all groups, with items and procedures that are equitable to all groups. Because this goal is not possible, counselors strive to use **culture-fair tests**, which attempt to minimize cultural bias as much as possible. Culture-fair tests tend to be associated with intelligence tests.

A limitation of most nonverbal tests is that they tend to measure a narrow range of intellectual abilities—primarily visual processing and perhaps short-term memory and processing speed—and thus do not access the full range of intellectual functioning (Ortiz, Ochoa, & Dynda, 2012). In addition, culture-fair tests typically do less well in predicting academic achievement or job performance than do the standard, culturally loaded tests. This finding is not surprising, because academic achievement and job performance often include much culturally important content. Therefore, there are serious questions regarding the use of culture-fair tests for predicting educational or occupational criteria. According to Sternberg (2004), intelligence cannot be meaningfully understood or assessed outside its cultural context. He argued that intelligence can be best assessed by culture-relevant tests instead of by culture-free or culture-fair tests, at least at the present time.

Cattell's Culture-Fair Intelligence Test

The **Culture-Fair Intelligence Test** is a paper-and-pencil test that has no verbal content and is designed to reduce the effects of educational background and cultural influences

(R. B. Cattell, 1973; see Figure 4.1). The test consists of four parts in multiple-choice formats: (a) progressive series completion—a figure must be chosen to complete the series; (b) classification—the object is to choose the figure that is different from the series; (c) matrices—the pattern of change occurring in the figures must be completed; and (d) conditions—the alternative with conditions similar to those of the example figure must be chosen. The test is available in two parallel forms and for three different age or ability levels: (a) children ages 4 through 8 years and adults with mental retardation, (b) children ages 8 through 14 years and average adults, and (c) college students and adults with above-average intelligence. Within particular age levels, the raw scores can be converted to normalized deviation IQ scores that have a mean of 100 and a standard deviation of 16.

Raven's Progressive Matrices

Raven's Progressive Matrices is a widely used culture-fair test that requires the examinee to solve problems involving abstract figures and designs by indicating which of various multiple choice alternatives complete a given matrix (Raven, Court, & Raven, 1993; see Figure 4.2). Progressive changes occur in the vertical dimension, horizontal dimension, or both dimensions in a series of matrices. For each item, the examinee must determine the principle by which the matrices are progressively changing and select the correct alternative from six answers that are provided. It is available in two forms: a black-and-white version for Grade 8 through adulthood and the Colored Progressive Matrices for children

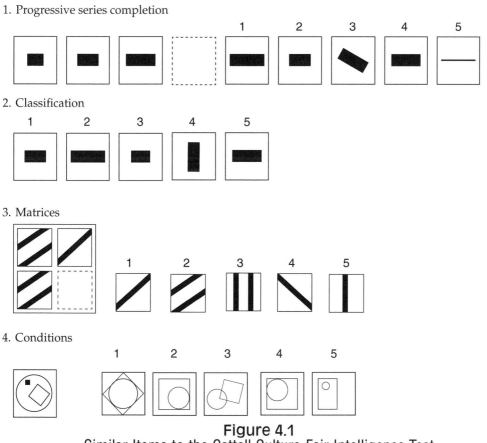

1. Progressive series completion

2. Classification

3. Matrices

4. Conditions

Figure 4.1
Similar Items to the Cattell Culture-Fair Intelligence Test

Note. Items are items similar to those found on the Cattell Culture-Fair Intelligence Test (R. B. Cattell, 1973).

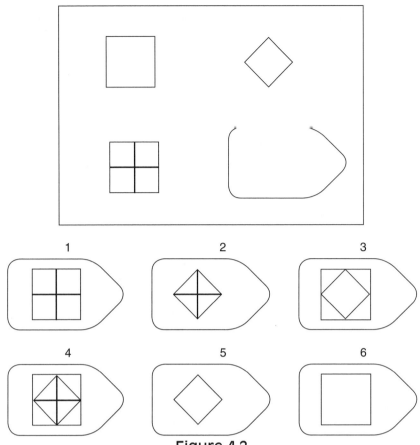

Figure 4.2
Raven's Progressive Matrices–Standard Progressive Matrices Sample Item

Note. Simulated item similar to those in the Raven's Progressive Matrices–Standard Progressive Matrices. "Raven's Progressive Matrices" is a trademark, in the United States, and/or other countries, of Pearson Education, Inc., or its affiliate(s). Copyright 1998 by NCS Pearson, Inc. Reproduced with permission. All rights reserved.

ages 5 to 11 years and for adults with mental retardation. Developed in England, Raven's Progressive Matrices has been used in a large number of cross-cultural studies in many countries. These studies suggest that although this test is one of the best available, it might better be described as culturally reduced rather than culture fair or culture free. Norms are based on samples of English children and adults, and one drawback for its use in the Unites States is its lack of normative U.S. data.

Naglieri Nonverbal Ability Test

The **Naglieri Nonverbal Ability Test** (NNAT) provides a measure of nonverbal reasoning and problem-solving ability based on the use of progressive matrices with shapes and designs that are not unique to any cultural group (Naglieri, 1996; Naglieri & Ford, 2015). This test can be administered at seven different levels for students in kindergarten through Grade 12. Administration time requires about 30 minutes. The test can be used with children who have hearing, motor, or color vision impairments. The NNAT has been standardized for group administration. A second version of this test, the NNAT–Individual Administration form, was created for individual administration for those students who need special attention (Naglieri, 2000). Research indicates that the NNAT produces comparable results for children from different cultural backgrounds and that it can be used to provide a fair assessment of the general intelligence of both White and minority children (Naglieri & Ford, 2015).

Wechsler Nonverbal Scale of Ability

The **Wechsler Nonverbal Scale of Ability** (WNV) is a nonverbal assessment test using the types of nonverbal items found on the other Wechsler instruments (see Chapter 9). It contains six subtests similar to Wechsler measures and has a brief version using only two subtests. It is useful in schools with students from multiple language backgrounds and where traditional intellectual assessment instruments would not be appropriate because of various language-related difficulties.

Goodenough–Harris Drawing Test

Also referred to as the **Draw-A-Person Test**, the **Goodenough–Harris Drawing Test** (Goodenough, 1926; see Chapter 13) is a brief, nonverbal test to assess cognitive development—particularly for minority children and those with a language disability. A counselor instructs the client to draw a whole picture of a woman or man. To evaluate intelligence, the test administrator uses a standardized scoring system of 64 items to rate presence or absence, detail, and proportion of body parts and clothing. Counselors are encouraged to correlate scores on this test with a general measure of intelligence.

TEMAS

TEMAS (Tell-Me-A-Story) was designed for use with dominant and ethnically diverse individuals ages 5 to 18 years. TEMAS is a projective test that uses culturally relevant pictures and offers parallel forms for use with nonminority and minority children; it includes 23 cards with positive or negative narratives, of which 11 are gender specific. TEMAS provides an objective scoring system that assesses a range of functions, including nine personality (e.g., interpersonal, sexual identity, reality testing), 18 cognitive (e.g., reaction time, sequencing, fluency), and seven affective (e.g., happy, sad, angry) functions (Costantino, Dana, & Malgady, 2007). TEMAS was developed by Costantino (1987) and is now available in multiple languages.

Columbia Mental Maturity Scale

The **Columbia Mental Maturity Scale** (CMMS; Burgemeister, Blum, & Lorge, 1972) is an assessment to evaluate reasoning ability for children ages 3–10 who have sensory, motor, or speech deficits. From a group of three to five drawings, a child is asked to select the drawing that does not belong. The CMMS contains 92 cards that test perceptual discrimination by color, size, use, number, classifications, missing parts, and symbolic concepts. The CMMS was originally developed for use with children with cerebral palsy.

Dynamic Testing

One of the criticisms of traditional assessments, particularly those that purport to measure cognitive aptitude, is that these tools may actually be static measures of previous learning. Even with the availability of culture-fair tests that claim to reduce test bias, researchers have shown that a performance gap between dominant and culturally diverse students still exists for these tests (e.g., R. P. Brown & Day, 2006; R. L. Rhodes, 2010), although this gap is more pronounced for younger children (Ortiz et al., 2012). Because many assessment limitations disproportionately impact a culturally diverse and marginalized clientele, and those performance gaps increase the likelihood of higher referrals of ethnic minority students to special education, it is important to continue to seek alternative methods that further minimize these gaps.

Dynamic testing, or the process by which information regarding one's ability is learned from immediate instruction and feedback loops, may help to address some of the limitations of traditional aptitude and intelligence tests (Stevenson, Heiser, & Resing, 2016). Dynamic testing can be conceptualized as follows: (a) A counselor provides minimal instruction on metacognitive skills before each problem solving attempt; (b) based on performance, immediately after the instruction, the counselor is able to gauge further instructional need; and (c) instructional scaffolds are provided depending on instructional needs. Scaffolds, or prompts, that may be provided could include the use of aid cards showing the general problem-solving strategy or more direct cognitive prompts specific to the item (e.g., encoding, inference). It is possible to conduct dynamic testing in a shortened standardized manner (see Resing, Tunteler, De Jong, & Bosma, 2009).

One dynamic tool that may be useful with culturally diverse and marginalized children in the United States is **AnimaLogica.** AnimaLogica is a dynamic assessment of analytical reasoning in children, with analogies presented typically in a 2 × 2 format (Stevenson, Hickendorff, Resing, Heiser, & De Boeck, 2013; see Figure 4.3). Using colored images of animals that occupy three of the quadrants, children have to infer a relationship— between either horizontal or vertical pictures—to identify the missing graphic from a choice of several pictures. Six transformation rules are to be considered when solving the analogy item—(a) animal, (b) color, (c) size, (d) position, (e) orientation, and (f) quantity—and items with more of these rules are considered more difficult to solve. In general, animals are used rather than other types of figures because they tend to be more familiar to young children (Stevenson, Bergwerff, Heiser, & Resing, 2014). Stevenson et al. (2016) conducted research in the Netherlands with 111 young children using the AnimaLogica test. Findings indicated that there were no significant individual differences in working memory between indigenous and ethnic minority children and that the children showed similar indices of cognitive ability.

Figure 4.3
Sample AnimaLogica Matrix

Note. From *Puzzling With Potential: Dynamic Testing of Analogical Reasoning in Children*, by C. E. Stevenson, 2012, doctoral dissertation (p. 140), Leiden University, Leiden, the Netherlands. Retrieved from https://openaccess.leidenuniv.nl/bitstream/handle/1887/19813/07.pdf

Disability and Assessment

Bault (2012) noted that approximately 19% of Americans are living with a disability. Types of disability include deafness, blindness, developmental delays, mental retardation, psychiatric illness, and traumatic brain injury, to name a few (Berens & Erford, 2018). Assessment of clients with physical disabilities in rehabilitation settings may involve three different approaches to vocational evaluation. One approach is psychological testing, a second involves the use of work activities or work samples, and the third is evaluation of actual on-the-job activities.

For some clients with disabilities, psychological testing that provides relatively objective and reliable measures of individual abilities and interests can yield sufficient data to assist in decisions regarding vocational choice, training, and job placement while avoiding the great additional amount of time and expense involved in the other types of evaluation. For others, employability can better be explored through work samples and on-the-job evaluations. Here, the employer becomes directly involved with the problems of the client, client characteristics can be ascertained (particularly in relation to the ultimate objective of more independent living), and a functional appraisal of job-related characteristics can be provided. Disadvantages obviously include dependence on the goodwill of potential employers as well as insurance, wage laws, and regulations that make cooperation by employers difficult. Considerable evaluative information about clients must be obtained in advance if job tryouts are to be successful. The Americans with Disabilities Act of 1990 (see Chapter 3) includes a section that speaks directly to the testing (primarily employment testing) of individuals with disabilities.

Personality measures, interest inventories, general intelligence tests, measures of specific aptitudes, and tests of achievement or current skills have potential for use with various types of special populations. In using such instruments, however, counselors must view results with caution; for example, items related to general health and physical symptoms on a personality test may be answered in a "deviant" direction by people who are physically ill or disabled and therefore yield scores that are difficult to interpret or are easily misinterpreted. Instruments such as the Battery for Health Improvement 2 (discussed in Chapter 13) can assist a counselor in discovering psychological or social factors that may interfere with a rehabilitation client's recovery.

Assessment Accommodations

Section 504 of the Rehabilitation Act of 1973 requires that testing be adapted for students with disabilities so that the test measures what it is designed to measure while allowing for the students' disability. For students with disabilities, academic standards should be maintained while appropriate accommodations in test administration are made. Considerable information regarding the assessment and testing of people with physical disabilities can be found in the professional literature (e.g., Batshaw, Roizen, & Lotrecchiano, 2013; McDaniel, 2013). Included in these publications are lists of assessment instruments appropriate for particular types of disabilities, with recommendations for modifications where necessary.

A cornerstone of the Education of All Handicapped Children Act of 1975 (also called Pub. L. 94-142; see Chapter 3) has been the requirement that an individualized education program (IEP) be written for each eligible student. The team that develops the IEP now must include not only (a) the student's special education teacher, (b) the student's general education teacher, (c) the student's parents, and (d) a local education agency representative, but also (e) a professional educator, such as a counselor or school psychologist who has the knowledge and expertise to interpret the assessment and evaluation results (Batshaw et al., 2013; Yell, Drasgow, & Ford, 2000). An IEP must include (a) a statement of the student's present level of performance and the student's needs, (b) the special educational services that are to be provided to meet these needs, and (c) a valid measure of annual goals and short-term objectives (Rowland, Quinn, & Steiner, 2015). Several test publishers now provide materials to assist in the writing and assessment of IEPs that accompany their educational achievement tests.

The Individuals with Disabilities Education Improvement Act (IDEIA) amendments also include requirements regarding the question of the participation of students with disabilities in statewide and districtwide assessments. Such participation becomes especially controversial when high-stakes testing programs are involved, such as those required by federal legislation such as the Every Student Succeeds Act of 2015 (see Chapters 3 and 10). In the past, many students with disabilities were excluded from such large-scale achievement tests, but with the emphasis on accountability for all students, their participation is now required by law.

School counselors are usually involved in and often responsible for the organization and administration of such testing and must make difficult decisions regarding which accommodations (e.g., extending time limits, providing a reader, using a calculator) are appropriate for particular students (Elliott, McKevitt, & Kettler, 2002; Lai & Berkeley, 2012). If testing, even with accommodations, is not appropriate, reasons must be given along with a statement of how the student will otherwise be assessed. In most states, the student's IEP plan must contain the appropriate accommodations in order for them to be used in the testing situation. Counselors should make it clear to the student's IEP team that this information needs to be included.

National testing programs such as ACT and the College Board (the major achievement test publishers) and statewide testing programs provide special test forms and special testing arrangements for examinees with disabilities who are unable to take the test under standard testing conditions. These options include audio recordings, Braille, large-type editions, magnifiers, use of a reader, use of an amanuensis to mark responses, or extended time for testing. When college admission tests are administered with accommodations, the resulting scores are flagged to indicate nonstandard conditions. This policy is consistent with the *Standards for Educational and Psychological Testing* (AERA, APA, & NCME, 2014), but those with disabilities may see it as a violation of privacy and as a violation of the Americans with Disabilities Act.

Adaptive devices for computers can provide clients with disabilities with options other than paper-and-pencil responses or the traditional computer keyboard. As a result, individuals with disabilities can complete a test with minimal staff assistance. Examples include voice input, simplified keyboards, joysticks, pneumatic controls, head pointers, and Braille keyboards. Without the computer, individuals with disabilities have typically completed tests with the assistance of another person who read or responded to test items for the test taker. The problem with an intermediary is that that person may influence the test taker's response, or the test taker may modify his or her responses because of the presence of another individual.

Visual Disabilities

People who are functionally blind must be assessed through senses other than sight, such as by auditory (readers) or tactile (Braille) means (McDaniel, 2013). Fewer than 25% of those classified as legally blind (corrected visual acuity of less than 20/200, which determines eligibility for government benefits) have no usable vision. Those not functionally blind are described as low vision or partially sighted and can often use large type-print or magnifiers. Extra time must be provided as these accommodations, including reading large type, are slower; for example, reading Braille takes 2.5 times as long. A study of the SAT results of visually impaired students using different accommodations (all with extra time) yielded results comparable with those of sighted students. The only exception was that those using Braille found certain graphics or nonverbal content mathematics items to be more difficult (R. E. Bennett, Rock, Kaplan, & Jirele, 1988). Furthermore, it is important to remember that research shows that individuals with visual disabilities who receive appropriate accommodations show significant differences in mathematics and reading scores compared to those who do not receive accommodations (Kettler et al., 2005).

The verbal scales on the WISC and the WAIS and certain parts of the Stanford–Binet are widely used with blind and partially sighted individuals. Some of the comprehension items need rephrasing to be appropriate, and attention should be paid to the possibility that lower scores on certain subtests may result from experiential deprivation. The performance scales have less validity if visual impairment is more than minimal. Individuals born without sight who have no visual memories may have difficulty with some concepts such as *color*, *canyon*, *skyscraper*, or *elephant*. They may also find it difficult to develop competent social skills because they cannot see others' social behaviors and nonverbal communications. Interest inventories such as the Strong Interest Inventory or the Kuder General Interest Survey are frequently used with visually impaired people by reading items aloud or by tape recording.

Hearing Disabilities

Individuals who are deaf or hard of hearing are also a heterogeneous population with disabilities ranging from mild to severe, to profound. Some have been deaf since birth (congenital), whereas others became deaf later in life because of disease or trauma (Berens & Erford, 2018). Therefore, any assessment should begin with a discussion of communication preference—spoken, written, or signed. Children who are deaf are nearly always delayed in their speech and language skills, and this deficit continues into adulthood (Batshaw et al., 2013). They develop a smaller vocabulary, which affects reading, spelling, and writing scores. Verbal IQ tests are therefore never used, but normal scores can be expected on performance tests. The performance scales on the Wechsler tests are the most commonly used. Other nonverbal IQ tests such as the Raven Progressive Matrices or the Matrix Analogies Test can be administered when appropriate.

Norms for the hearing impaired are available for the WISC and the Metropolitan and Stanford Achievement Tests. Mean ACT assessment scores of students with auditory disabilities fall below the means obtained by students with visual, motor, or learning disabilities (Scarpati, 2013). Certain tests and inventories may be administered to the population with American Sign Language (ASL), and responses can also be communicated through an ASL interpreter. The WAIS-IV and the MMPI-2 are available in ASL translations.

Cognitive Disabilities

Because cognitive disabilities cause problems adjusting to the demands of the environment, the diagnosis of intellectual disability is usually made not only on the basis of individual intelligence tests but also on the basis of an assessment of adaptive behavior. Intelligence and adaptive behavior are obviously closely related, but adaptive behavior is more synonymous with such terms as social maturity, personal competence, and social competence—that is, how effectively individuals cope with and adjust to the natural and social demands of their environment. Can they function and maintain themselves independently, and can they meet the culturally imposed demands of personal and social responsibility? Measures of adaptive behavior generally consist of behavioral rating scales administered in an interview or by observation (Tassé et al., 2012).

Vineland Adaptive Behavior Scales
The **Vineland Adaptive Behavior Scales** (2nd ed.; Vineland II; Sparrow, Cicchetti, & Balla, 2006) is available in survey interview, expanded interview, and parent/caregiver and teacher rating forms. These scales were developed from the original measures designed to

assess social competence by Edgar Doll of the Vineland Training School in Vineland, New Jersey. The interview, which follows a semistructured format, is conducted with the client's parents or caregivers. It is conducted without the client being present. The teacher rating form is designed to be completed by either the general schoolteacher or the special education teacher. It has a questionnaire format that deals primarily with adaptive behavior in the classroom. The parent/caregiver form uses a rating scale format that covers the same content as the interview. The Vineland II taps four domains: daily living skills (self-care, dressing, washing), communication (receptive and expressive language), socialization (interpersonal interactions and play), and motor skills (gross and fine coordination; Floyd et al., 2015). The expanded form also includes the maladaptive behavior index assessing undesirable behaviors that interfere with adaptive behavior.

The standardization sample for the current version of the Vineland scales included 3,000 individuals, 100 in each of 30 age groups stratified to represent the U.S. Census population. Test–retest reliabilities are reported from .80 to more than .90, and interrater reliability ranges from .60 to .75 for the first edition of the Vineland (Floyd et al., 2015; Sattler, 2005). As might be expected, the expanded form was the most reliable of the three forms, and the short classroom form was the least reliable. The scales are designed to assess adaptive behavior from birth to 18 years old and among low-functioning adults. The instrument is used with individuals with mental retardation and those who are emotionally disturbed or are physically, hearing, or visually impaired to develop individually educative treatment programs or vocational rehabilitation programs. Supplementary norms are available for each of these groups.

Supports Intensity Scale

The **Supports Intensity Scale** (SIS; American Association on Intellectual and Developmental Disabilities, 2013) assesses support requirements in 57 life activities and in 28 behavioral and medical areas. The SIS is useful in evaluating the practical supports that people with developmental disabilities need to lead independent lives. It consists of an eight-page interview and profile form in either print or electronic format and has become the standard evaluation instrument for many agencies, including one entire state.

Assessment of Older Adults

The number of older people living in the world has grown dramatically. In the United States, 1 person in 7 is more than 65 years old, and by the year 2025 this figure will be 1 in 5 (Ortman, Velkoff, & Hogan, 2014). Older adults are often divided into two cohorts: the young–old, 65 to 84 years, and the old–old, 85 years and older. The need to assess both their mental health and cognitive functioning has led to the development of instruments specifically designed to assess older clients as well as guidelines for their use.

The **Clinical Assessment Scales for the Elderly** (CASE) provide information for diagnosing *DSM* Axis I disorders (C. R. Reynolds & Bigler, 2000). There are 10 clinical scales—for example, Anxiety, Depression, Psychoticism, and Substance Abuse—along with three validity scales. Two forms are provided: One form has 199 items (CASE-F) and can be completed by the client, and a second form (CASE-R) has 190 items and can be completed by a knowledgeable caregiver, such as a spouse, son or daughter, or health care worker. Norms are based on 2,000 adults ages 55–90 matched to census data. Two brief versions, the 100-item CASE–Short Form (CASE-SF) and the 88-item CASESF–Form R, are also available (DePaola, 2003).

Several standardized methods that involve tasks such as drawing a clock, making change, or answering certain questions have been devised to assess cognitive functioning and cognitive deficits among older people. The most popular of these methods is the **Mini-Mental State Examination** (MMSE; Folstein, Folstein, McHugh, & Fanjiang, 2001).

The MMSE represents a brief standardized method to assess mental status and consists of several items on which the maximum score for each ranges from 1 to 5 for a maximum score of 30 (see Figure 4.4 for sample items).

Adults who are functioning normally usually obtain scores of 27 or higher, and 23 is the most widely accepted cutoff score, indicating some cognitive impairment (although others use cutoffs that range from 22 to 25). Scores of 10 or less indicate severe cognitive deficits. Test–retest reliabilities range from .80 to .95, and the MMSE has shown high validity (87% correct) in predicting clinically diagnosed cognitive impairment (Albanese, 2003). In use since 1975, the MMSE has been criticized for having too many easy items and too many cutoff points and no standard scores (Lopez, Charter, Mostafavi, Nibut, & Smith, 2005; Mitchell, 2013).

Alzheimer's disease is the most common disorder causing cognitive decline in old age; it is a progressive and irreversible disease. Therefore, if the MMSE reveals cognitive impairment, the next step is to conduct a more extensive examination of the deficit and to determine whether it is due to Alzheimer's disease or whether it is a more treatable impairment such as depression, vascular dementia, or substance abuse dementia (American Association for Geriatric Psychiatry, Alzheimer's Association, & American Geriatrics Society, 1997). The further diagnostic screening includes both medical and psychological tests often involving the administration of certain portions of the WAIS-IV or the **Wechsler Memory Scale** (WMS-III).

The WMS-III is receiving considerable use because of the growing importance of assessing memory functions in an increasing aging population of older adults (Groth-Marnat & Wright, 2016). It is an individually administered battery designed to assess a full range of memory functions in line with current theories of memory and to distinguish normal memory loss from the early symptoms of dementia. It is composed of six primary and five optional subtests yielding eight index scores. The index scores allow a comparison between visual and auditory memory and between immediate and delayed memory. It was co-normed with the WAIS-III, which allows a direct comparison between WMS-III scores and WAIS-III IQ scores. For example, an IQ score of 20 points or more higher than the WMS-III can indicate possible brain dysfunction. The WMS-III takes 40 or more minutes to administer (although there is an abbreviated form), and norms are now available for age ranges up to

Orientation to Time
"What is today's date?"

Registration
"I am going to say three words and you repeat them after I stop. Are you ready?
Here they are . . .

BOOK *(pause)*
CHAIR *(pause)*
TREE *(pause)*

Naming
"Can you tell me what this is?" *(Point to a rubber band.)*

Reading
"Please read this and do what it says." *(Show examinee the words on the stimulus form.)*

TAP YOUR NOSE

Figure 4.4
Mini-Mental State Examination Sample Items

Note. Items similar to those on the Mini-Mental State Examination.

89 (Hambleton, 2005). Reliabilities of .74–.93 for the subtest scores and .82 or higher for the indices are reported (A. M. Horton, 1999; Psychological Corporation, 1997; Wechsler, 1997). In assessing functional impairment, both cognitive and health status must be considered. This type of assessment usually includes an appraisal or checklist of Activities of Daily Living (ADLs; e.g., feeding, toileting) and Instrumental Activities of Daily Living (IADLs; e.g., financial management, preparing meals, shopping; Blando, 2011; Scogin & Crowther, 2003).

When assessing older clients, counselors need to be aware of possible fatigue and the influence of medications. After testing, the resulting assessment data can serve as a baseline against which to compare future changes in cognitive functions. Reimbursement for psychological assessment is provided under Medicare and Medicaid, and to receive such compensation it is important to understand and use the Current Procedural Terminology (CPT) coding system.

Tip Sheet
Multicultural Assessment

✓ Collaborate with the client throughout the assessment process. Procedural information as well as specific assessment data are to be shared openly with the client. Discuss implications of "negative" assessment data and solicit additional information from the client to place results in context.

✓ Remember that careful standardization and administration of assessments helps to maximize equitable opportunity for these tools to indicate accurately a construct of interest.

✓ With each client consider how the assessment process is multicultural. Even when working with clients from dominant groups, there are likely minority statuses in some cultural groups.

✓ Explore your biases and assumptions about cultural groups in terms of age, race/ethnicity, gender, ability status, socioeconomic status, and sexual orientation, to name a few. Consider how both positive and negative biases you hold influence how you will assess clients.

✓ Be aware of how racism and other forms of oppression are used to explain assessment data differences.

✓ Collect data gradually over several sessions rather than trying to learn everything in one counseling session.

✓ Understand your client's worldview to determine appropriate assessment methods.

✓ Use the least biased assessment strategies first. Paniagua (2014) identified the least to most biased assessment strategies: physiological assessment, direct behavioral observations, self-monitoring, behavioral self-report rating scales, clinical interviews, trait measures, self-report of psychopathology measures, projective tests with structured stimuli, and projective tests with ambiguous stimuli.

✓ Use a client's native or preferred language when conducting an assessment.

✓ Use inclusive language throughout the assessment process. For example, use terms such as *partner* or *significant other* instead of *spouse*. In addition, avoid unnecessary categorizations. For example, instead of asking a client if he or she is male or female, ask which gender he or she identifies.

✓ Assess for various stressors to better understand how the client's concerns may be potentially caused or maintained by these stressors. Consider how these stressors may be misrepresented in assessment data if not discussed in the assessment report or treatment plan.

✓ Be sure to represent in any assessment report how confounding factors, such as educational opportunity or socioeconomic status, affected assessment results.

✓ Determine the potential impact of acculturation level on the assessment process and findings. Solicit information informally about country of origin, age of immigration, years in the United States, and knowledge of counseling and assessment procedures. Alternatively, you may want to use a standardized acculturation scale.

✓ Collect information from the client about his or her identity development level using various identity development models (e.g., racial identity, sexual identity).

✓ Be aware of changing U.S. demographics as you work with diverse populations.

✓ Report on the limitations of research studies that report assessment data for a particular group as you interpret and apply assessment data for your client. Understand how previous assessment research might distort incidence and prevalence data on mental health disorders for particular groups.

✓ When reviewing available assessment data for particular groups, reflect if the sample is representative of the general population as well as if subsamples are representative of U.S. subgroups.

✓ Consult test manuals and other assessment materials to learn about the norm groups and subgroups as well as specific information about available versions of instruments.

Chapter Summary

For all assessment procedures, it is important to consider multicultural factors. This chapter began with a description of test fairness and its four components: (a) there is an absence of bias, (b) there is an equitable treatment of all test takers, (c) those with equal standing on a particular test construct should score equally no matter the group membership, and (d) test takers have an equal opportunity to learn. Furthermore, this chapter provided types of assessment bias that may compromise test fairness.

Cultural factors that influence the assessment process include the following: the culture of counseling, counselor discrimination, mental disorder rates, client motivation and test sophistication, acculturation, and language. After these cultural factors were discussed, the impact of gender on the assessment process was described, including an outline of how traditional gender differences in aptitude and cognitive and career assessment have been addressed in both item construction and increased exposure to diverse experiences. The impact of race, ethnicity, and socioeconomic variables was also outlined as it relates to aptitude, cognitive, career, and personality assessment. Although historical research has indicated that content bias has been minimized for these variables—particularly when socioeconomic status is controlled—there is no definitive information about why racial and ethnic differences still exist among these types of assessments.

Counselors are to use culture-fair tests whenever possible because bias exists in assessment. This chapter identified several culture-fair tests: Cattell's Culture-Fair Intelligence Test, Raven's Progressive Matrices, Naglieri Nonverbal Ability Test, Wechsler Nonverbal Scale of Ability, Goodenough–Harris Drawing Test, and the Columbia Mental Maturity Scale. However, there are several limitations noted with use of culture-fair tests. Dynamic testing was presented as another alternative to traditional assessments.

The chapter concluded with sections on how assessment practices relate to disability status and older adults. With respect to disability status, various legislation was discussed to provide counselors guidance in accommodating individuals with disabilities. In addition, instruments and assessment strategies useful when working with those who have visual, auditory, and cognitive disabilities were outlined. With respect to assessment of older adults, several assessments for working with this population were discussed.

Review Questions

1. What are the criteria for fairness according to the *Standards for Psychological and Educational Testing?*
2. Provide at least two examples of bias in assessment.
3. What are examples of culture-fair tests? What do they help to achieve?
4. What are some of the multicultural considerations in cognitive, career, and personality assessment?
5. What accommodations can counselors provide for individuals with disabilities?

Resources for Further Learning

Publications

Halpern, D. F. (2013). *Sex differences in cognitive abilities* (4th ed.). New York, NY: Taylor & Francis.

Paniagua, F. A. (2014). *Assessing and treating culturally diverse clients: A practical guide* (4th ed.). Thousand Oaks, CA: Sage.

Resing, W. C. M., Tunteler, E., De Jong, F., & Bosma, T. (2009). Dynamic testing in indigenous and ethnic minority children. *Learning and Individual Differences, 19,* 445–450. doi:10.1016/j.lindif.2009.03.006

Web Resources

Association for Assessment and Research in Counseling
   http://aarc-counseling.org/resources
      The link provides several assessment guidelines, including the Multicultural Assessment Standards.

International Test Commission (ITC), ITC Guidelines for Translating and Adapting Tests
   https://www.intestcom.org/files/guideline_test_adaptation.pdf
      This file contains the most updated guidelines for test adaptation with culturally diverse clientele.

Section II

Basic Statistical
and Measurement
Considerations

Chapter 5

Measurement Concepts

This first chapter (of two) in Section II outlines basic measurement concepts in assessment: scales of measurement, reliability, validity, and test development. Whether counselors are selecting or developing their own assessments or are interpreting assessment findings from multiple sources, they must have a basic understanding of psychometrics.

Test Your Knowledge

Respond to the following items by selecting T *for "True" or* F *for "False":*

☐ T ☐ F   1.   Most psychological assessments use ordinal scale data.

☐ T ☐ F   2.   Nominal scale data refer to variables that can be divided into independent categories.

☐ T ☐ F   3.   Reliability refers to the degree to which one is measuring an underlying construct.

☐ T ☐ F   4.   Validity evidence is also concerned with social consequences and uses of data.

☐ T ☐ F   5.   Reliability evidence yields more evidence about the assessment than a particular sample.

Scales of Measurement

Imagine a toolbox you might have for home improvement projects. In this toolbox, you have a variety of tools, some more specialized than others or more appropriate for certain projects. Selecting scales of measurement is like selecting tools from a toolbox: Counselors measuring assessment variables select the right tool or scale for a particular function. Thus, **scales of measurement** are the different ways we measure constructs in the assessment process. There are four scales of measurement, with the more complex scales (i.e., those that perform more functions) allowing for more precise measurement: nominal, ordinal, interval, and ratio. How you choose to measure a variable in the assessment process directs what scale of measurement you use. The more precise the construct is that the counselor wants to assess, the more "advanced" the selected scales must be. (Of course, this general rule assumes that the assessment variable counselors are measuring is a close-to-perfect depiction of a construct. This topic is discussed in more detail later in the chapter.) Scales of measurement may have any (or none) of the following characteristics: magnitude, equal intervals, and absolute zero. Table 5.1 provides an example of the precision and increasing complexity of each type of scale using football players' heights.

Nominal Scales

A **nominal scale** is the most basic measurement scale in that it is used for naming or classifying only. Examples of nominal scales include gender, race, political affiliation, mode in a data distribution, or presence or absence of a diagnostic criterion. A nominal scale does not possess magnitude, equal internals, or an absolute zero. A variable can be coded with numbers (e.g., 0 = undergraduate student, 1 = graduate student); however, the numbers do not indicate magnitude (i.e., 1 is greater than 0).

Ordinal Scales

An **ordinal scale** refers to order or rank of nominal categories. Because information can be gleaned about an individual having more or less of some variable, ordinal scales are characterized by magnitude. However, the intervals or "spaces" between ranks are not likely equal, and thus the relative size among intervals is difficult to know. Ordinal scales are often used in psychological assessment, such as when Likert scales (e.g., 1 = *strongly disagree* to 6 = *strongly agree*) constitute an assessment, yet the distance between a score of 1 and 2 compared with that between a 5 and a 6 is not likely equal. Examples of ordinal scales include degree of job satisfaction, university national rankings, and median values or percentile ranks of a data distribution. Counselors are warned against averaging (cal-

Table 5.1
Scales of Measurement

Type of Scale	Magnitude	Equal Intervals	Absolute 0	Height Example
Nominal	No	No	No	Football players are grouped into three groups: tall, average height, and short.
Ordinal	Yes	No	No	Football players stand in a line based on their height in descending order; the tallest player is first in the line and the shortest last.
Interval	Yes	Yes	No	Those football players who measure 5', 5'6", 6', and 6'6" are compared to determine which interval (group) has the greater height advantage.
Ratio	Yes	Yes	Yes	Football players' heights are compared in order to compute the precise difference between the players.

culating the mean) of a test score, such as in the case of degree of job satisfaction. If job satisfaction was measured on a Likert scale—or some other assessment scale with unequal intervals—computing a typical score is problematic. Oftentimes, counselors mistakenly treat ordinal scales like interval scales when interpreting and reporting assessment data.

Interval Scales

An **interval scale** possesses magnitude and equal intervals. Examples of interval scales include temperature, checklist of behaviors, and standard deviation. Because there is an equal distance between data points, counselors can assume that the difference between two points is the same as that of another two points (e.g., the difference between 20° and 25° is the same as that between 100° and 105°). Although you can add and subtract values on an interval scale with confidence, you should not multiply or divide values because there is no absolute zero. With the temperature example, you can say that 105° is warmer than 100°, but you cannot say it is 5% warmer, because 0° does not actually mean the absence of temperature. Counselors should be cautioned that more (e.g., higher assessment scores) does not necessarily equate to better. Because variables are not measured perfectly in assessment, it is difficult to know what a score might actually mean.

Ratio Scales

Whereas a nominal scale is the simplest scale, a ratio scale is the most advanced and precise measurement scale. A **ratio scale** possesses magnitude, equal intervals, and an absolute zero. Examples of ratio scales include time and height. Because 0 seconds or 0 inches is possible, for example, you can multiply and divide these values (e.g., one client completed an assessment twice as quickly as another client). Ratio scales are seldom used in counseling assessment.

Activity 5.1
Measuring Constructs

Identify a construct or variable and how you might measure it using the four scales of measurement. What are the advantages and disadvantages of each scale?

Reliability

Reliability as a technical subject is extremely important for those who use psychological tests. Let's say for example that you are interested in measuring substance abuse symptoms to make treatment decisions. You select a substance abuse screening tool (e.g., Substance Abuse Subtle Screening Inventory, or SASSI-4; SASSI Institute, 2016), and you find that the individual likely presents with substance dependence based on the scoring key. Because you are recommending further treatment for this client, you want to be sure that score would be consistent if the SASSI-4 was administered again, and, you want to ensure the client responded in a consistent manner during the single administration. **Reliability** refers to how consistently a test measures and the extent to which it eliminates chance and other extraneous factors in its results. Synonyms for reliability include dependability, reproducibility, stability, and consistency.

In the first part of this section, conceptual information about reliability is presented. This conceptual information refers to the notion of measurement error; reliability is a correlation coefficient of that measurement error. After this foundational information,

information about types of reliability counselors encounter in the assessment process are presented.

Measurement Error

Counselors are interested in measuring much more complicated human characteristics than people's physical aspects, and such complex qualities as anxiety, intelligence, depression, and achievement are difficult both to define precisely and to measure. **Measurement error**, then, is the positive or negative bias within an observed score. That is, a score that a person receives on a test is made up of two elements: the person's true score and an error score that may add to or subtract from the true score. A true score is never known. Because greater error results in more inconsistency in scores, measurement error should be minimized. Following is an illustration of how error impacts scores:

$$X = T + e,$$

where observed score (X) = true score (T) + error score (e).

A test with perfect reliability would equate to no measurement error. This situation is actually impossible, because error originates from the individual, test, and/or testing condition. Let's consider the SASSI-4 example again with a group of clients. *Individual error* might include test anxiety, motivation, interest in responding in a socially desirable manner, heterogeneity of the group tested, and test familiarity. *Test error* might be found if, for example, not all substance abuse symptoms were adequately represented by the instrument or if there was homogeneity of items (items that vary will have greater error) or the test length was not ideal (e.g., shorter tests yield lower reliability estimates for samples). *Testing condition error* might refer to scoring errors or distractions within the testing environment, such as insufficient administration time or a noisy agency.

Attempts to maintain uniform test conditions by controlling the instructions, time limits, and the testing environment are undertaken to reduce error variance and make test scores more reliable. No test produces scores that are perfectly reliable, though, and because psychological measurement is often imprecise, it is important to check the accuracy and consistency of the instrument constantly to ensure that the unreliability is kept within reasonable limits. The *Standards for Educational and Psychological Testing* (AERA, APA, & NCME, 2014) emphasize that test developers should provide test users with substantial amounts of information on test reliability and measurement error. This information should include specific details about populations on which reliability data were obtained, standard errors of measurement for all types of scores reported, and intervals between retests and interrater consistency where appropriate.

Correlation and Reliability

The **correlation** statistic assesses the degree to which two sets of measures are related—for example, how a tested trait or ability is related to a behavior. Each correlation coefficient contains two bits of information: The sign of the correlation tells whether the two variables tend to rank individuals in the same order (+) or in reverse order (−), and the magnitude of the correlation indicates the strength of this relationship (i.e., larger values indicate greater strength). Among the several different types of correlation coefficients that can be computed, the Pearson product-moment correlation coefficient (r) is the most common and can range in value from +1.00, indicating a perfect positive relationship; through .00, no relationship or a chance relationship; to −1.00, a perfect negative, or inverse, relationship. When values are plotted in a scatterplot, you can see that higher values depict more linear relationships between two variables (see Figure 5.1).

What does the value of the correlation coefficient mean? It depends. Although a larger coefficient (the closer it gets to ±1.00) indicates a stronger relationship, the specific mean-

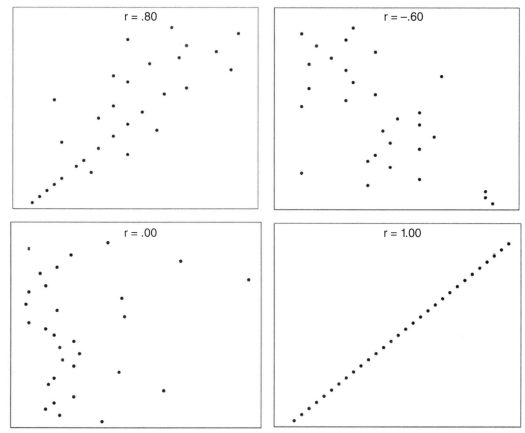

Figure 5.1
Sample Scatterplots

ing of a value depends on what is being correlated. For example, a correlation of .70 for two sets of scores for a sample that was administered a simple assessment tool twice only a week apart may not be considered strong. However, the same value might be considered stronger if one were examining the relationship between an available test and a newly developed one measuring anxiety.

Once counselors have some idea of the strength and direction of a correlation, a **coefficient of determination** can be calculated to provide more information about the shared variance between the two variables. A coefficient of determination is calculated by squaring the correlation coefficient. This value provides counselors with insight into how much shared information is provided by knowing the two data points. With higher correlations (e.g., .80), there is greater shared variance explained (e.g., 64%).

What does correlation have to do with reliability? Recall that an observed score is made up of true and error scores; thus, a reliability estimate expresses the relationship between the true and observed scores:

$$r = \frac{true\ score\ (T)}{observed\ score\ (T + e)}.$$

Thus, each half of the fraction is conceptualized as a variable, and then they are correlated with each other. In essence, reliability is the relationship of one score with another actual or hypothetical test (R. Thorndike, 1985).

Another example of how reliability estimates are correlation coefficients involves test–retest reliability (explained later in this section). Consider the following two sets of scores for a self-esteem inventory for 10 children (higher scores indicate higher self-esteem):

Testing Period 1	Testing Period 2
50	75
45	48
44	50
43	55
30	36
25	22
75	73
60	62
51	49
68	64

The correlation coefficient between these two sets of scores is +0.85. This coefficient indicates a strong positive relationship between the two test administrations, demonstrating consistency for the sample. (See Appendix A for the statistical formula.) A completely unreliable measure (large measurement error) will yield a reliability coefficient close to .00, and a completely reliable test (no measurement error) will approach ±1.00.

Reliability coefficients usually run within the range of .80 to .95, but what is considered to be acceptable reliability varies substantially depending on both the testing circumstances and the type of reliability. For national testing programs, such as the GRE or the Iowa Tests of Educational Development, reliability coefficients are expected to be above .90. For certain other types of psychological tests, reliability may be substantially lower. A score on the Depression scale of the MMPI, for example, is an indication of the person's mood at the time the inventory was administered. Because people's moods change, a very high test–retest reliability would be neither expected nor desired. Thus, for personality measures, interest measures, and attitudinal measures, test–retest reliability coefficients often fall below .90, although if they fall below .70, the consistency of the instrument becomes suspect (Cicchetti, 1994).

There are two final notes about reliability and correlation coefficients. First, although individuals refer to the reliability of a test, reliability is actually the property of the test scores for the particular group on which it was administered—not of the test itself. The size and type of sample also affect the coefficient, as a smaller, more homogenous sample introduces more error. Thus, you can expect to find a range of reliability estimates depending on the sample composition. Second, a substantial correlation between two variables does not imply that either variable causes the other. They both can be under the influence of a third variable. For example, children's heights could show a significant correlation with their scores on a vocabulary test, but both of these variables could be related to the children's ages and maturational growth.

Types of Reliability

Reliability can be measured in several different ways, so there is not a single measure of reliability for a set of test scores but different coefficients depending on how the coefficients are determined. Test scores can vary in their consistency in terms of time, test forms, or test items. Traditionally, there are three basic methods of estimating the reliability based on these variables: test–retest, alternate-forms, and internal consistency (see Table 5.2). The proportion of test error attributable to each of these sources can be calculated by analysis of variance procedures with an approach to reliability measurement known as generalizability theory (AERA, APA, & NCME, 2014).

Test–Retest Reliability
Test–retest reliability measures consistency over time (see Figure 5.2). The correlation coefficient in this case indicates the relationship between scores obtained by individuals

Table 5.2
Types of Reliability

Reliability Type	Description	Source of Error	How to Calculate	Limitations
Test–Retest	Administer a single test twice, with some period of time between administrations.	Time	Correlate the mean individual scores for each administration.	Memory and practice effects, particularly for shortened time between administrations.
Alternate-Forms	Equivalent or parallel forms of a test are administered either at the same time or with time between administrations.	Item content Time, if forms are given at different times	Correlate the mean individual scores for each administration.	Difficult to develop identical items that measure a construct equally.
Split-Half	A single test is divided in half (usually by odd and even numbered items).	Item content	Correlate the mean individual scores of the two test halves. Correct correlation coefficient with Spearman–Brown formula.	Fewer items decrease reliability.
Interitem	A single test is assessed to determine how items on a test are related to one another and to the total score.	Item content	Each item is correlated with a total score for a client and then compared with the overall variability of scores.	Fewer items decrease reliability.
Interrater	Two or more judges rate events or behaviors simultaneously.	Judges	Calculate the ratio between judges' agreements and possible agreements.	A construct not operationalized well, or unclear instructions, may result in greater disagreements.

within the same group on two administrations of the test. Test–retest correlations tend to decrease as the interval between the test administrations lengthens. If the interval is brief, there are potential practice and memory effects, which tend to make the reliability estimation spuriously high. If the time interval is too long, variation can be influenced by events that occur to participants between the two test administrations (e.g., maturation and history effects), and spuriously low estimates of reliability may be obtained.

Alternate-Forms Reliability
Alternate-forms reliability, or **parallel-forms reliability**, is computed by comparing the consistency of scores of individuals within the same group on two alternate but equivalent forms of the same test (see Figure 5.3). Because the test items are different, the effect of memory and other carryover effects are eliminated. The crucial question remains whether in fact the two alternate forms of the test are actually equivalent.

Two tests that measure the same content or variables and that are equivalent in difficulty level can be administered on the same day or very close to each other without

Figure 5.2
Test–Retest Reliability

Figure 5.3
Alternate-Forms Reliability

concern about a practice effect. They can be alternated so that Test A is given to one group first and Test B to the other group first, and the practice effect can thus be controlled. The problem with this type of test reliability is that it is often difficult enough to come up with one good form of a test, much less two good forms. Therefore, unless there is a national testing program with a staff working on developing test forms—as is the case with some of the national testing programs, such as the MCAT or the ACT tests—hope for this form of reliability is unrealistic.

In national testing programs, the problem of developing equivalent forms is met by administering experimental items with each test administration. The people taking the test respond both to items that count and to those that are being tried out for future test versions. The latter items do not count in scoring for that administration but provide data for the construction of future forms of the test. The experimental items do not need to be the same for all those taking the test on a particular date because item information can be collected from random subsamples. This process is how national testing programs are able to produce equivalent forms year after year.

Internal Consistency

Measures of internal consistency provide an estimate of test score reliability that indicates the consistency of responses to the different items or parts of a test during a *single test and administration* (AERA, APA, & NCME, 2014). Two common measures of internal consistency are split-half and interitem consistency (Cronbach's alpha, KR-20).

Split-half reliability is a popular form of establishing reliability because it can be obtained from a single administration by dividing the test into comparable halves and comparing the resulting two scores for each individual (see Figure 5.4). It is administered all at once, so no time-to-time fluctuation occurs. From this point of view, it can be thought of as a special case of alternate-forms reliability. In most tests, the first half and the second half would not be comparable because of differences in the difficulty of the items as well as effects of practice and fatigue that are likely to vary from the beginning to the end of the test. Therefore, most tests are split into odd and even items, except when several items deal with a specific problem, in which case the entire group of items is assigned to one or the other half.

An important weakness in the split-half approach lies in the general principle of sampling—that is, usually the greater the number of items, the more stable will be the concept being measured. All things being equal, the longer the test, the more reliable its scores will be. The split-half procedure cuts the test length in half, thus decreasing the reliability estimate. To correct the computed reliability based on the shorter length, the **Spearman–Brown formula** can be used to yield an estimate of what the reliability would be if it were obtained on the test's full length. For example, if you corrected a split-half reliability estimate (computed as a Pearson correlation coefficient) of .80, the corrected reliability estimate would be .89 (see Appendix A for the statistical formula). However, the Spearman–Brown formula will not correct a reliability estimate substantially for tests with a greater number of items, partly because there is decreasing measurement error with more items.

Interitem consistency is a measure of internal consistency that assesses the extent to which the items on a test are related to each other and to the total score (see Figure 5.5). This measure of test score reliability provides an estimate of the average intercorrelations between all of the items on a test. Depending on the type of response called for on the in-

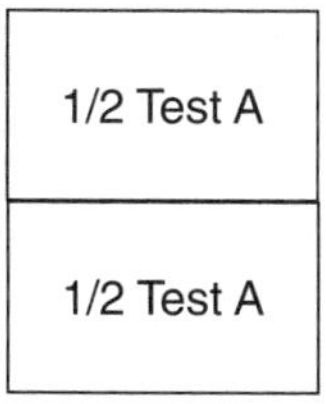

1/2 Test A	
1/2 Test A	

Figure 5.4
Split-Half Reliability

1	2	3	4	5
6	7	8	9	10
11	12	13	14	15
16	17	18	19	20

Figure 5.5
Interitem Reliability

strument, formulas known as the **Kuder–Richardson (KR) formula 20** for two-response answers (e.g., true or false, yes or no) or **Cronbach's alpha** reliability coefficient (i.e., **coefficient alpha**) for more than two alternatives are computed (see Appendix A). All individual item responses for each person in the entire sample are analyzed, and the resulting reliability coefficients indicate the consistency with which the items sample the trait being measured. Figure 5.4 illustrates graphically the intercorrelations for a 20-item assessment (Test A). Each item is correlated with a total score for a client and then compared with the overall variability of scores. Essentially, it is the correlation of all split-half reliabilities.

The interitem reliability coefficient (as well as split-half reliability coefficient) can also be squared to explain variance, in a manner similar to how the coefficient of determination was computed earlier for two sets of scores. For example, let's assume we calculated a reliability estimate of .75. If we square the coefficient, we note that approximately 56% of the variance of that construct (e.g., anxiety) is explained by that assessment.

Activity 5.2
Understanding Reliability

Let's say we are interested in how consistently we measure a domain of interest: distance between a designated classroom door and water fountain. The instructor or a classmate marks approximately equal intervals with masking or duct tape to indicate each interval point. Divide into two groups and select two volunteers per group. Group 1 receives a measuring tape, whereas Group 2 does not receive any measuring device. Group 2 should come to a consensus about how they would like to measure the distance. Have the first volunteer from each group "measure" the distance for each interval as well as the entire distance and record the numbers secretly. Then, have the second volunteer from each group measure the distance and record the data secretly. Reflect on the following questions as a class:

- What were your data at each data collection? How do they compare within your group? How do they compare with the other group?
- How did you provide an example of test–retest reliability? What factors may affect data consistency?
- How did you provide an example of alternate-forms reliability? What factors may affect data consistency?
- If each interval represents an item, and the total distance represents an assessment, how did you provide an example of internal consistency? What are other ways you could have measured internal consistency? What factors affect data consistency?

Interrater Reliability
Interrater reliability refers to the degree of agreement between two or more independent judges. Interrater agreement is calculated by dividing the number of agreements that an

event occurred by the number of possible agreements (i.e., agreements and disagreements). Let's look at an example to see how this is calculated. Two counselors are observing a child on the playground to determine the degree of social interaction (as demonstrated in this example by the child speaking or playing with other children). If the counselors were examining the presence of the behavior in 5-minute intervals for a 45-minute period, they might mark with an X when the behavior occurred for that interval:

Child	5	10	15	20	25	30	35	40	45
Caelum	X	X		X	X	X			X
Gracie	X	X	X		X	X		X	X

For the nine intervals (and thus nine possible agreements), the two counselors agreed five times (56% interrater agreement).

The problem of interrater or interscorer reliability results when subjective judgments are involved in scoring test items. Reliabilities of scored essay tests have always been quite poor, a problem faced by national testing organizations as they have developed writing samples as criteria for college admissions. By giving clear instructions to the examinees regarding length, format, and content and by extensively training the raters, they have attempted to meet this problem. Even so, well-trained raters often vary substantially in the ratings they give to writing samples.

Validity

Whereas reliability is concerned with whether the instrument is a consistent measure, **validity** deals with the extent to which meaningful and appropriate inferences can be made from the instrument (see the *Standards for Educational and Psychological Testing*; AERA, APA, & NCME, 2014). Is there evidence to support the interpretation of test scores for the purpose for which they will be used?

It is possible for test scores to have high reliability with little or no validity for a particular purpose (but in order to have good validity, high reliability is necessary). To better understand the relationship between validity and reliability, imagine a target with a bull's-eye. Let's assume that the bull's-eye is the construct you are trying to measure. The more times you hit the bull's-eye (i.e., consistency), the greater the reliability. However, if the bull's-eye is not the right construct—or is representing the construct insufficiently or inaccurately (i.e., validity)—reliability is meaningless for the test purpose. There is still reliability, yet there is consistent measurement of something other than the domain of interest. If the bull's-eye does represent the construct fully or accurately, consistency in measurement (hitting the target) is very important. Thus, reliability is a precursor to validity but not sufficient in itself.

According to the *Standards for Educational and Psychological Testing* (AERA, APA, & NCME, 2014), test validity should be assessed in terms of the use to which the test is put, such as counseling, selection, or classification. Once the use of the test is clear, the test user should study the evidence of the test's validity for that particular purpose. "Validity is broadly defined as nothing less than the evaluative summary of both evidence for and actual—as well as potential—consequences of score interpretation and use" (Messick, 1995, p. 742). It is therefore important that test manuals contain detailed information regarding both theoretical and empirical evidence of validity for the interpretation and use of test scores.

The question "validity for what?" must always be asked, because the validity of a test varies depending on the purpose and the target population. Similar to reliability, validity is not a characteristic of an assessment but, rather, is the meaning of the findings for a sample (Messick, 1995; Reeves & Marbach-Ad, 2015). For example, scores on the Strong Interest Inventory have considerable test–retest reliability even when the second test is taken many years later. Validity, however, is much more complicated. Because of the large number of scales and the different types of scales, specific definitions must be developed before they can be applied to a criterion to obtain validity. As will be seen later, scores on the Strong Interest Inventory can be used effectively to predict the occupation that a person is likely to enter in the future. However, it is not particularly valid for predicting success in an occupation. People who enter an occupation for which they get a low score may very well not stay in that occupation. People who score high are much more likely to stay in the occupation, but the few low scorers who stay in that field are just as likely to be successful as those who score high. Therefore, a score on a scale of the Strong Interest Inventory may have some validity for predicting whether people will enter an occupation and, if so, how long they will stay in it, but it will have little validity when it comes to predicting success in that occupation.

Validity also asks the question of whether the test scores measure what they purport to measure. Does a test that is supposed to measure arithmetic skills really measure arithmetic skills, or is it composed of word problems of such reading difficulty that it is actually measuring reading ability instead? There are two types of **invalidity**, or threats to validity. First, **construct underrepresentation** refers to failing to include components or dimensions of a construct in an assessment. **Construct irrelevant variance** indicates there is too much "noise," or excess dimensions covered by the assessment tool. Constructs can be deemed irrelevant for a sample when the material is irrelevantly difficult (such as in culturally biased assessments) or irrelevantly easy (Messick, 1995; Reeves & Marbach-Ad, 2015).

The range of validity coefficients runs much lower than that of reliability. Whereas coefficients of .80 to .95 are common for reliability, validity coefficients seldom run above .60 and are more typically in the range of .20 to .40 (Hemphill, 2003; Reeves & Marbach-Ad, 2015). Validity coefficients as low as .10 and .20 can still be useful in predicting future behavior (Rosenthal, 1990). In predicting grades in college from test scores, coefficients are almost never obtained above .60. Even when other measures of high school achievement, personality, and some type of achievement motivation are all combined, validity coefficients above .60 are seldom achieved for college grades.

Types of Validity

Evidence of a test's validity for a particular purpose can be assessed in different ways, as noted in the *Standards for Educational and Psychological Testing* (AERA, APA, & NCME, 2014; F. L. Schmidt & Hunter, 2014). Emphasis is placed on the nature and strength of the evidence for a particular interpretation. Different types of validity evidence are discussed below: content, criterion-related, construct, and treatment. Content and criterion-related can be considered to be subsumed under construct validity (Messick, 1995; Reeves & Marbach-Ad, 2015). **Face validity**, which is really not evidence of validity, is determined if the assessment "looks like" it is measuring what it is supposed to measure. Table 5.3 provides descriptions and examples for each type of validity.

Content Validity

Content validity refers to the representativeness of items from a "population" of items. Items might be questions on a test or questions on a clinical interview, for example. Are items representative of a domain of interest? How well did you sample items? For educational assessment in schools, test items are selected by examining curricula, textbooks, and other materials as well as performance objectives. If the test is designed to measure achievement in high school physics, a number of high school physics teachers, and perhaps some college physics teachers, examine the items on the test to determine whether these items are in fact measuring knowledge of what is typically taught in high school physics. Then, items are weighted in some way to match their relative importance to physics achievement. Content validity, then, involves defining the domain of interest (i.e., physics achievement), identifying items that refer to that domain (i.e., curricula and/or perfor-

Table 5.3
Types of Validity

Type	Description	Example
Content	A sample of items is representative and reflects all major content components of a domain.	A panel of experts evaluates whether a pool of items adequately represents career interest.
Criterion Related	Degree of prediction of a client's performance on a criterion assessed at the same time (concurrent) or sometime in the future (predictive).	A career interest questionnaire score is compared with a selected career.
Construct	Degree to which an assessment is related to a theoretical construct (convergent) or not (discriminant).	A career interest questionnaire is correlated with an established career interest inventory to show the assessments are measuring the same underlying construct.
Treatment	The impact of the assessment findings on the client.	A client is more aware of career interests and is empowered to investigate several career options.

mance objectives), involving judges to ensure that those items correspond to the domain and that items are sampled adequately, and then determining how many items from domain components should be included to represent that domain.

Criterion-Related Validity

Criterion-related validity pertains to validity evidence that is obtained by comparing test scores with performance on a criterion measure. Criteria may include scores on other assessments or may be some external criteria, such as grades, diagnosis, or job satisfaction.

There are two types of criterion-related validity, distinguished by time when a criterion is measured. **Concurrent validity** refers to when test scores and the criterion performance scores are collected at the same time. Correlation coefficients are calculated between the test score and the scores on the criterion variable. For example, a test of mechanical aptitude might be given to a group of working machinists, and then the ratings that they receive by their supervisors might be examined to determine whether the mechanical aptitude scores are related to their current work. Often, measures of concurrent validity are obtained because the test is going to be used in the future to predict some type of behavior—such as the ability to do the work of a machinist.

A second type of criterion-related validity is **predictive validity**. In this case, the client's performance or criterion measure is obtained some time after the test score. For a scholastic aptitude test designed to predict college grades, the grades that students earn in college are examined to determine whether the scholastic aptitude test given in high school has predictive validity. Does it predict what it is supposed to be predicting—in this case, college grades? One of the problems in measuring either concurrent or predictive validity is that the size of the correlation coefficients will be reduced if the range of scores on either the test or the criterion variable is restricted in any way (i.e., **restriction of range**). Because scholastic aptitude test scores are often used to select students for a particular institution, and many students with low scores are eliminated, the group being studied to measure the test's predictive validity will have a narrower range, with a resulting lower validity coefficient. One way of avoiding this issue is to administer the instrument before any selection has taken place and to have the selection take place without regard to the criterion being assessed. For example, in one of the validation studies for the General Aptitude Test Battery (GATB) of the U.S. Employment Service, the entire battery was given to all applicants for jobs in an industrial plant that was being built in a particular town. Workers were then selected without regard to their GATB results. Performance ratings for the workers were obtained at a later date, and these performance ratings were then related to the previously obtained GATB results, which showed substantial predictive validity.

Spuriously high validity coefficients can be obtained from a form of criterion contamination if, for example, the people doing the rating know the test results. University professors' knowledge of graduate students' GRE test results might (but obviously should not) influence the grades they assign, which could result in a higher relationship between test results and graduate GPAs.

An important concept related to the validity of a test concerns the base rates of the characteristic that is being measured in the population. **Base rates** refer to the proportion of people in a population who represent the particular characteristic or behavior that is being predicted. Base rates are important because they have a marked influence on how useful or valid tests are in making predictions. If the base rates are either very low or very high, the predictions made from the tests are not likely to be useful. It almost every student admitted to medical school graduates, then scores on the MCAT are unlikely to differentiate between those who will graduate and those who will not. The best prediction to be obtained would be not to use the test scores but merely to predict that every student admitted will graduate. Suicide rates are examples of low base rates. Although people who obtain high scores on a scale that measures depression are more likely to commit suicide than those with lower scores, most people who obtain high scores on a measure of depression do not commit suicide. Because suicide is relatively rare, the base rate is so low that even with a high score on a depression scale, the most accurate prediction to be made would still be that any individual is not likely to commit suicide.

For many widely used instruments, large numbers of individual predictive studies have been conducted, often with conflicting results. Meta-analyses techniques now allow researchers to collect and synthesize results of many studies. They statistically correct for different sampling and measurement problems and are able to clarify issues and provide considerable evidence for the predictive validity of these instruments (F. L. Schmidt & Hunter, 2014).

The purpose of assessment is, of course, to provide more information than could be obtained by chance or other unreliable means. Validity of assessments is evaluated in terms of how much the assessments contribute to predictions beyond what could be predicted without them. The concept of **incremental validity** refers to the extent to which a particular assessment instrument adds to the accuracy of predictions obtained from other tests or other less extensive methods of assessment. This improvement can result in increased accuracy of prediction, better specificity or sensitivity, or increased efficacy of decision-making judgments beyond that generated on the basis of other data (G. P. Brown & Clark, 2014; Hunsley & Meyer, 2003). The real value of the MCAT would be if the correct prediction rate could be increased beyond that available without the use of the test. Incremental validity should be taken into account in deciding whether to use an additional assessment instrument, and, of course, the financial cost of acquiring more data should be weighed against the importance and the clinical utility of the new information.

The amount of variability in a criterion that a correlation coefficient is considered to account for is determined by the square of the correlation. Thus, a correlation coefficient of .30 means that 9% of the variance is explained. In using a correlation coefficient for prediction, however, Rosnow and Rosenthal (1988) showed that the correlation coefficient can be taken to indicate the improvement in success of prediction over chance alone by the percentage indicated by that correlation. Thus, a correlation of .30 means that using that variable in prediction improves the prediction by approximately 30%. When considered in this way, a moderate correlation can be seen to have considerable usefulness in counseling over that which would have been obtained had that test not been taken into consideration.

When a test is used to make a dichotomous, either/or decision (e.g., acceptable or unacceptable, successful or unsuccessful, positive diagnosis or negative diagnosis), cutoff scores are usually used. The point at which the cutoff score is established is often a matter of relative cost. In some cases, a miss can be very costly; for example, concluding that someone is not suicidal because he or she is below a cutoff score on a suicide potential scale when in fact the person is suicidal. The cost of this type of miss could be that a suicide takes place that might have been preventable. This type of case is called a **false negative**. The person fell below the cutoff score and was therefore predicted not to be suicidal when in fact he or she was suicidal. A **false positive** occurs when a person obtains a score above the cutoff score and, for example, is predicted to be successful on the job but in fact fails and is discharged. Again, the time and money invested in training the person are likely to influence where the cutoff score is placed and, therefore, to influence the proportion of false positives.

The accuracy of classification of individuals into different diagnostic categories or related groups based on a particular cutoff score can be expressed in terms of sensitivity and specificity. **Sensitivity** refers to the accuracy of a cutoff score in detecting those people who belong in a particular category. By definition, testing procedures that are sensitive produce few false negatives. **Specificity** indicates the accuracy of a cutoff score in excluding those without that condition. Testing procedures that possess specificity yield few false positives. Sensitivity and specificity will vary depending on the particular cutoff score used to select individuals considered to be meeting the condition. Generally, if sensitivity is increased, specificity will be reduced and vice versa.

For example, most clients who commit suicide or have seriously considered suicide obtain an elevated score (T score > 65) on the Depression scale of the MMPI-2. However, a large number of individuals who are not suicidal also obtain elevated scores on this scale. When the Depression scale is used in this manner, it can be said to possess sensitivity in identifying potentially suicidal individuals but to lack specificity in ruling out individuals who are not suicidal (Cicchetti, 1994). If a higher cutoff were used (e.g., T score > 75), specificity would be increased, but sensitivity would be lessened (there would be more false negatives because although most people who commit suicide are depressed, their depression scores may not exceed 75).

Table 5.4 provides an example of the relationship among the concepts of sensitivity, specificity, false negative, and false positive. Using an example related to academic achievement, let's consider the decision-making process associated with using the Graduate Record Examination (GRE) in a counselor program admissions decisions. A counseling master's program has selected a 151 Verbal score and 149 Quantitative score as the minimum score for admissions; these cut-off scores were selected as program faculty believe that those scoring at or above these scores are predicted to complete the master's degree in counseling successfully. The degree to which the GRE discriminates well between students who have aptitude for graduate school (i.e., high specificity) is likely to result in accepting those who will successfully complete the program at a high proportion (i.e., few to no false negatives) and rejecting those who would not (i.e., few to no false positives).

Table 5.4
Relationship Among Assessment Sensitivity, Specificity, False Negative, and False Positive Concepts

High Sensitivity	Low risk of false negative	Low risk of false positive
Low Sensitivity	High risk of false negative	High risk of false positive
	Low Specificity	**High Specificity**

Construct Validity

Another type of validity evidence asks the following question: Are the test results related to variables that they ought to be related to and not related to variables that they ought not to be? For example, do results on the test change according to what is known about developmental changes? Do older students do better on the test than younger students; for example, do sixth graders do better on arithmetic tests than third graders?

Evidence that pertains to the theoretical basis of a test is sometimes referred to as **construct validity**—a type of validity that has been used as a means of explaining the psychological meaning of the variable ("construct") measured by the test. In essence, construct validity is synonymous with the term *validity* itself, which focuses on the extent and the nature of the evidence used to support all test interpretations (AERA, APA, & NCME, 2014). As mentioned previously, content validity and criterion-related validity evidence ultimately inform construct validity.

Patterns of relationships to other variables yield validity evidence known as convergent validity and discriminant validity. On the one hand, tests scores should be expected to show a substantial correlation with other tests and assessments that measure similar characteristics (**convergent validity**). Measures of mathematical aptitude ought to be related to grades in mathematics studies. On the other hand, test scores should not be substantially correlated with other tests from which they are supposed to differ; that is, they should show **discriminant validity**. A test of mathematical ability probably should not show a strong correlation with a test of clerical speed and accuracy. A measure of sociability should be negatively related to the score on a schizophrenia scale and positively related to the score on a scale of extraversion. Most validation studies report convergent validity.

If an instrument is related to a particular psychological theory, then the results should fit that theory. **Factor analysis** can determine whether the test items fall together in different factors the way that the theory suggests they should. If a test is constructed along the lines of Jungian theory, such as the Myers–Briggs Type Indicator, the resulting factors from a factor analysis should be related to such Jungian concepts as introversion versus extraversion, sensing versus intuition, and thinking versus feeling.

Treatment Validity

Another type of validity important for counselors and clinicians has been termed *treatment validity*: Do the results obtained from the test make a difference in the treatment? (Chambless & Hollon, 2012). If the test results are useful, if they make a difference in the counseling process, then the test could be said to have treatment validity. For example, Finn and Tonsager (1992) found that clients who had their MMPI-2 scores interpreted to them showed significant improvement on several treatment variables. In a similar fashion, Randahl, Hansen, and Haverkamp (1993) found that clients who had their Strong Interest Inventory profile interpreted to them made significant progress on their career planning. In a more recent study, Essig and Kelly (2015) noted that participants who received therapeutic assessments compared to information only during career assessment feedback showed significant increases in vocational identity scores. Thus, careful attention to interpretation in therapy has benefits for establishing treatment validity.

Postscript: Validity Scales

While counselors strive to ensure that assessments are well designed to accurately represent content, criteria, and appropriate consequences for clients, it is also important to determine the accuracy of a client's responses. That is, patterns in responses that are irrelevant to the actual intention of the assessment (**response sets**) may emerge. **Validity scales** are tools used to determine three types of response distortions: a client pretending to have some problem or disorder (faking bad), a client responding in a socially desirable manner to appear more favorable or less symptomatic (faking good), and a client responding randomly either intentionally or unintentionally (Roivainen, Veijola, & Miettunen, 2015; Van Brunt, 2009b).

Although response sets can be detected at times by examining particular assessment items or globally evaluating assessment results in the context of other client information, some more sophisticated assessments have built-in validity scales. Van Brunt (2009b) identified several validity scales of the 567-item MMPI-2:

- *Cannot Say (?):* number of items left blank;
- *Variable Response Inconsistency (VRIN):* tendency for the client to respond inconsistently;
- *True Response Inconsistency (TRIN):* potential for acquiescence, or tendency to mark all responses as true; TRIN also assesses nonacquiescence, or tendency to mark all responses as false;
- *Lie scale (L):* responses that are deliberately attempting to place the client in a more favorable light;
- *Correction (K):* similar to the L scale yet detects more subtle ways clients may try to hide psychopathology;
- *Infrequency (F):* detects odd and atypical responses and rules out faking good or faking bad motives;
- *Infrequency (Fb):* items found in the last half of the test indicate changes in test-taking strategies;
- *Infrequency Psychopathology (Fp):* items unlikely to be endorsed by respondents regardless of severity of psychopathology;
- *Fake Bad Scale (FBS):* endorsing noncredible symptoms, particularly in the case of personal injury litigants; and
- *Superlative Self-Presentation Scale (S):* responses in which clients create an overly favorable view of themselves.

Assessment Development

Now that you have some background information on scales of measurement, reliability, and validity, let's review general steps in developing assessments and practice some of these steps (see Activity 5.3). To produce a well-designed standardized psychological test or inventory, the test developer generates a large amount of data. First, test items are written, usually by specialists or experts in the field according to the objectives and purpose of the test. The items are then checked for cultural bias, and items that might be unfair or offensive to any group are eliminated.

Activity 5.3
Developing Assessments

To demonstrate principles of reliability, validity, and test construction, you will develop as a large group an assessment. Divide the class into groups of three or four, retaining a few individuals to serve as "judges" of the newly developed assessment.

1. Create an assessment tool to measure depression symptoms. As you think about this tool, consider the following: What is the purpose of the instrument? What is the scaling method? How many items should the group strive to have for the final measure?
   a. In small groups, develop one or two items that seem to be good screening items for depression.
   b. Compile a list of items from each group on the board.
2. Have judges rate each item.
   a. Follow these "rules" for retaining items (or others the judges decide by consensus). All judges must agree on an item that should be clear, un-

biased, and operationally definable. Items should be eliminated if they are too close to another item. If an item is unclear but is still a "good item," provide suggestions for improvement.

3. Revise instrument.
   a. Reflect on how the revised instrument appears to experts and test developers.
   b. Consider how test takers might view the depression measure.

As a class, reflect on the following:

- What are the benefits of relying on experts? Challenges?
- What are some possible concerns with the instrument?
- How have you provided evidence of content validity?
- How could you strengthen content validity? Establish criterion-related and construct validity?
- How would you establish reliability evidence?

Items are then tried out on sample populations similar to the targeted group, and the results are analyzed to determine those items that are of appropriate difficulty and discriminating power. The items must differentiate between people who represent more and less of the behaviors or the domain that is being measured using item response theory models. After the resulting items have been assembled into a test and scored, the scores must be converted into a continuous scale, norms must be developed that are applicable to the groups for which the test is designed, and reliability estimates must be calculated. (Norms are discussed in Chapter 6.) Correlations of the test with other similar variables, with background variables, and with predicted criteria must then be determined. The effectiveness of the test or inventory in accomplishing the objectives for which it was created should continue to be studied on a regular basis after it has been published and put to use.

In the overall construction and development of a test, various validation procedures are applied throughout the developmental stages. All the types of validity can be conceived as contributing to the validity of a test score, which may also include the social value consequences of its use. Measures of internal consistency are built into the early stages of development; criterion-related validation typically occurs in some of the latter stages. Validation continues long after the test has been published and distributed for use.

Tip Sheet
Measurement Concepts

✓ How you choose to measure a variable directs what scale of measurement you use. The more precision you want, the more "advanced" scale you will need to select.

✓ Because a true score can never be known, consider ways in which measurement error within the assessment itself, test taker or client, and assessment condition positively and/or negatively affects the observed score or measurement. Be sure to interpret and present findings with this information.

✓ Be cautious when evaluating correlation coefficients, especially related to validity and reliability evidence. Correlation coefficients should be examined in the context of the type and quality of the assessment as well as the sample composition.

✓ *Reliability* refers to the consistency or generalizability of test scores over time, form, items, and judges.

✓ *Validity* refers to the degree to which accumulated evidence supports the proposed interpretation of test scores for the purpose for which they will be used.

✓ Reliability is a necessary but not sufficient quality of validity. Consistency does not necessarily equate to construct accuracy.

✓ When revising or developing an assessment, select experts who will evaluate how sufficient the content is as well as weight items appropriately.

✓ The quality of the criterion you compare assessment data to matters when establishing criterion-related validity. Reflect on whether there is a clearly established relationship between the criterion and assessment construct.

✓ Evaluate base rates within a population to determine whether an assessment will be useful in distinguishing among individuals.

✓ Critically evaluate cutoff scores to determine level of sensitivity and specificity per item.

✓ Consult test manuals or other assessment materials and review the psychometric properties of an assessment you are administering. Study closely the sample or samples these data originate from to compare with your client or clients.

Chapter Summary

Counselors are to be familiar with several basic statistical and measurement concepts as they approach the testing process. Scales of measurement—nominal, ordinal, interval, and ratio scales—are considered diverse tools counselors can use to measure a variable based on different criteria of precision. Depending on the scale, properties may include magnitude, equal intervals, and absolute zero.

Reliability, a second major assessment concept discussed in this chapter, refers to the consistence of measurement within and across test administrations. There are several types of reliability: test–retest, alternate-forms, split-half, interitem, and interrater reliability. Counselors can use multiple sources of reliability to ascertain the psychometric strength of an instrument. This chapter also outlined several related concepts, including measurement error and correlation.

Reliability is a necessary yet insufficient property of validity for assessments. Validity refers to whether meaningful inferences may be drawn from the assessment score. Content, criterion-related (concurrent, predictive), construct (convergent, discriminant), and treatment validity are major types of validity described in this chapter. The chapter concluded with a section on steps of assessment development.

Review Questions

1. What are the characteristics of the four scales of measurement?
2. What are sources of measurement error? How can measurement error be minimized?
3. How are the reliability coefficient and correlation coefficient similar?
4. What are the types of reliability? What are the benefits and challenges of each?
5. What are the types of validity? Which types most correspond with which types of assessments?

Resources for Further Learning

Allen, M. J., & Yen, W. M. (2002). *Introduction to measurement theory.* Long Grove, IL: Waveland Press.

Chambless, D. L., & Hollon, S. D. (2012). Treatment validity for intervention studies. In H. Cooper, P. M. Camic, D. L. Long, A. T. Panter, D. Rindskopf, & K. J. Sher (Eds.), *APA handbook of research methods in psychology: Vol. 2. Research designs: Quantitative, qualitative, neuropsychological, and biological* (pp. 529–552). Washington, DC: American Psychological Association.

DeVellis, R. F. (2012). *Scale development: Theory and applications* (3rd ed.). Thousand Oaks, CA: Sage.

Meyer, P. (2010). *Understanding reliability.* New York, NY: Oxford University Press.

Taylor, C. S. (2010). *Validity and validation.* New York, NY: Oxford University Press.

Chapter 6

Understanding and Transforming Raw Scores

This second chapter of Section II builds upon basic measurement principles to address how to organize, convert, and interpret raw scores within a data distribution. In this chapter, types of derived scores and measures of central tendency and variability are discussed.

Test Your Knowledge

Select the most appropriate choice for each item.

_____ 1. The middlemost score when all scores are ranked is known as which of the following?
   a. Mean   b. Median
   c. Mode   d. Quartile

_____ 2. What is the range of the following scores: 2, 3, 4, 4, 5, 8, 10?
   a. 7   b. 8
   c. 9   d. 10

_____ 3. What is the mean of the following scores: 2, 3, 4, 4, 5, 8, 10?
   a. 5.00   b. 5.14
   c. 5.25   d. 6.00

_____ 4. A professor gives an exam that is too easy. The distribution of scores is likely to be:
   a. Normally distributed   b. Bimodal
   c. Positively skewed   d. Negatively skewed

_____ 5. The following visual tool is useful for displaying nominal data:
   a. Histogram   b. Frequency polygon
   c. Bar graph   d. Structural equation modeling

Raw Scores

Let's pretend you just received your assessment exam score: an 83. A simple raw score on a test, without any type of comparative information, is a meaningless number. Individuals naturally want to know what scores mean. So in reviewing your exam score, your next question will be about the meaning of that score. To make sense of the score, a score will need to be converted to a **derived score** or compared against some criterion. Scores can be interpreted from three points of view: (a) comparison with scores obtained by other individuals (**norm-referenced**), (b) comparison with an absolute score established by an authority (**criterion-referenced**), and (c) comparison with other scores obtained by the same individual (**self-referenced**). Raw (observed) scores must be organized and then transformed to convey greater meaning.

Table 6.1 presents exam scores for 15 of your classmates, scores we will return to throughout this chapter. If you are comparing your score to theirs, you might search through the scores to see who had the highest and lowest scores and how many individuals scored similarly to you. This norm-referenced interpretation is quite common for interpreting scores on standardized tests. If you knew the cutoff for passing the assessment exam was 80 (criterion-referenced), you might breathe a sigh of relief. However, if you are comparing this score against your previous exam scores (self-referenced), you might be more disappointed if you tend to score 90 and above. Depending on how you choose to interpret your score, you may have a mix of emotions.

Thus, some type of interpretive or comparative information is necessary before any information is conveyed by a score. To say that a client obtained a raw score of 37 out of 60 on an anxiety measure conveys no useful information, nor does the fact that this score of 37 meant that the client answered 62% of the anxiety items. To know that the same client obtained a raw score of 48 on a 60-item measure of tolerance does not indicate that he or she is more tolerant than anxious, nor does it yield any other useful information. Some frame of reference is necessary to give a test result meaning.

Organizing raw score data visually allows counselors to garner information beyond simply scanning a list of raw scores. There are several ways to visually organize raw data: You can use a frequency distribution, histogram, frequency polygon, and bar graph, to name a few.

A **frequency distribution** tabulates the number of observations (or number of individuals) per distinct response for a particular variable. Table 6.2 indicates the frequency distribution of data (exam scores) from Table 6.1. Frequency distributions are presented in a row and column format. To calculate frequencies, you simply count the number of individuals who had each score. Then, you divide the frequency of a particular value by the total number of individuals to calculate the percentage of individuals who had a particular score.

You will notice in Table 6.2 that values (scores) are listed in ascending order in the first column, frequencies are listed in the second column, percentages are in the third column, and cumulative percentages are in the final column (percentage of sample as more data points are added). From this data presentation, we can make some general observations:

- Students scored between 78 and 99 on the assessment exam.
- There were nine different exam scores received for the 15 students.

Table 6.1
Assessment Exam Scores for 15 Students

Student	Score	Student	Score	Student	Score
Katherine	92	Ed	79	Jack	95
Kristina	87	Sheila	79	Karen	87
Shawna	87	Alice	78	Chris	97
Luke	98	Maria	78	Kelsey	99
Mason	99	Maya	83	Doris	92

Table 6.2
Frequency Distribution of Assessment Exam Scores

Score	F	%	Cumulative %
78	2	13.3	13.3
79	2	13.3	26.6
83	1	6.7	33.3
87	3	20.0	53.3
92	2	13.3	66.6
95	1	6.7	73.3
97	1	6.7	80.0
98	1	6.7	86.7
99	2	13.3	100.0

- The frequency column indicates the number of students who received a particular score. For example, only one student received a 97.
- We can estimate students scored mostly in the high 80s or low 90s. For example, three students scored 87, the most frequent score.
- We can add up percentages in the percentage column to figure out how many scored at or below a particular score. For example, 53.3% of the participants scored at 87% or lower.

Thus, a frequency distribution can provide a great deal more information than quickly scanning a set of scores.

A **histogram** is a graph of bars that presents the data from a frequency distribution in a more visual format (see Figure 6.1). Histograms are used with quantitative variables. You will notice that frequency data points are on the y-axis and exam scores are on the x-axis. Both sets of points follow an ascending format, and individual bars cannot be rearranged; empty spaces indicate there were no individuals with that score. Taller bars indicate greater area, or more frequent responses.

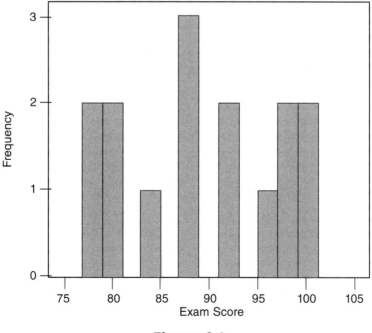

Figure 6.1
Histogram

Note. $M = 88.67$; $SD = 7.96$; $N = 15$.

A **frequency polygon** is a line graph of a frequency distribution (see Figure 6.2). It uses labels similar to the x- and y-axis for the histogram. A frequency polygon can connect points at the peak of values—in this case, exam scores. Higher peaks indicate greater frequency.

Finally, a **bar graph** visually depicts nominal data. Because there are no continuous data involved, bars can be arranged in random order. With bar graphs, there are spaces between data points. Taller bars indicate greater frequency. Figure 6.3 presents the gender of students in the assessment course (in this case, women and men).

Measures of Central Tendency

Now that you understand some ways that data distributions can be visually portrayed, we will talk more in depth about making meaning of an individual score for that data distribution. In a norm-referenced interpretation, individuals' scores are compared with others' scores so various statistics are used for these interpretations. When examining an individual's score, it is often useful to have some indication of the typical or average score and how scores are distributed. **Measures of central tendency** refer to typical score indicators, or the average score for a distribution of scores.

There are three measures of central tendency that are often computed. The **mean**, or arithmetic average, has algebraic properties that make it the most frequently used measure of central tendency. It is equal to the sum of the scores divided by the number of individuals in the group. For the assessment exam scores in Table 6.1, you would sum the scores and divide by 15, the total number of students ($M = 88.67$). The **median** is the middle score below which one half, or 50%, of the scores will fall and above which the other half will fall. To compute the median, line up all the scores in either ascending or descending order and take the middlemost value. If there are two middle values, sum those values and divide by 2. For the assessment exam scores, the median is 87. The

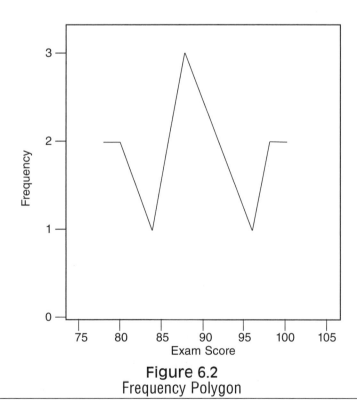

Figure 6.2
Frequency Polygon

Note. M = 88.67; SD = 7.96; N = 15.

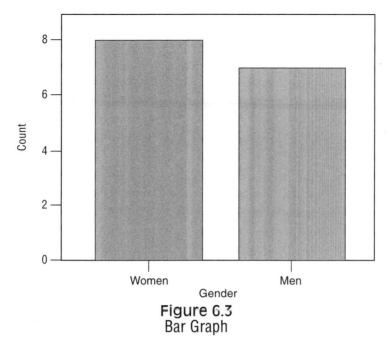

Figure 6.3
Bar Graph

mode is the score that appears the most frequently in a set of scores. The mode for the assessment score distribution is 87.

Measures of Variability

A number of measures of variability have been developed over the years to indicate to what extent scores on a test differ from each other. **Measures of variability** indicate the extent of individual differences around a measure of central tendency. Of the various measures, the range and the standard deviation are the best known and most frequently used. The easiest measure of the variability to understand is the **range**, which simply indicates the distance between the lowest and the highest scores—adding 1. For the sample with assessment exam scores, the range is 22 (99 – 78 + 1 = 22). Although knowing the range can be informative, it does not help very much in interpreting an individual score. An **interquartile range** may be a more useful measure as it removes potential outlying scores (i.e., outliers) and focuses on the range around the median. To calculate the interquartile range, divide scores (arranged in order of magnitude) in four parts, subtract the score that is one quarter from the bottom from the score that is one quarter from the top, and divide by 2. The result shows the range around the median. For the middle half of the sample, the figure is 87 (97 – 79), for the assessment score example.

The **standard deviation** is the most frequently reported measure of variability and represents a standardized number of units from a measure of central tendency. The larger the value, the greater dispersion of scores—that is, the greater the variability. The standard deviation is the most widely accepted measure of variability for test users because (a) it is the basis for standard scores, (b) it yields a method of presenting the reliability of an individual test score (as described in a later section), and (c) it is used in research studies for statistical tests of significance.

Standard deviation is calculated by dividing the sums of squares from the sample size minus 1, and taking the square root of the value (see Appendix A). Sums of squares are calculated by subtracting a score from the mean (deviation score), squaring each deviation score, and summing the squared deviation scores. The standard deviation for data in Table 6.1 is 7.961.

Characteristics of Data Distributions

In a perfect world, data would be distributed perfectly around a measure of central tendency, forming a bell-shaped curve (see Figure 6.4). When data fall perfectly around a measure of central tendency, there is perfect symmetry with both sides of the curve creating a mirror image of the data distribution. This type of curve is referred to as a **normal curve**. For a normal curve, all three measures of central tendency are equal.

In a normal curve, the numerical value of the standard deviation divides the raw score range into approximately six parts, with three above the mean and three below. Scores occurring above or below the distance of 3 *SD* occur only very rarely. In a normal distribution, shown in Figure 6.4, approximately 34% of the sample lies between the median and 1 *SD* above it and another 34% lies within the standard deviation below it. Thus, the distance of 1 *SD* in each direction encompasses approximately

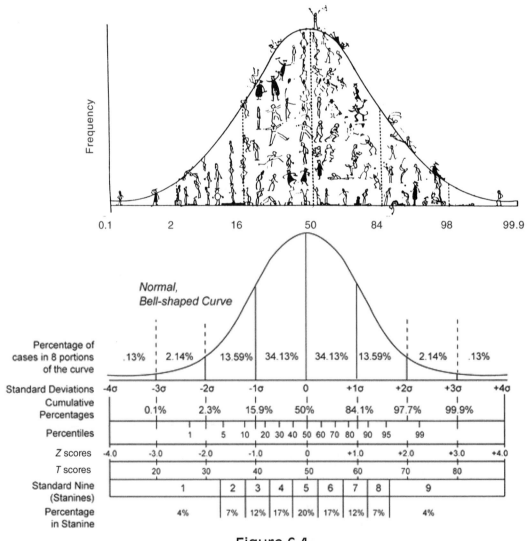

Figure 6.4
Relationships Between Different Types of Standard Scores and Percentiles in a Normal Population

68% of the sample. An additional 14% or so of the sample is found within the second standard deviation above the mean and 14% below the mean, and approximately 2% is found in each of the measurements occurring in the third standard deviation above the mean and below the mean.

A person scoring 2 *SD* below the mean, therefore, falls at the second percentile; at 1 *SD* below, he or she falls at the 16th percentile. A person scoring at the median or mean is at the 50th percentile, a person scoring 1 *SD* above the mean is at the 84th percentile, and a person scoring 2 *SD* above the mean is at the 98th percentile. (Percentiles are discussed later in this chapter.) These percentages and points along the normal curve are shown in Figure 6.4. Because the standard deviation is the basis of standard scores, which are used in reporting the results of most psychological tests used by counselors, these percentages and points along the normal curve should be thoroughly understood and *memorized* by anyone who makes substantial use of psychological test results.

Although data distributions aren't perfect, if a frequency distribution is constructed of a sufficiently large number of measurements, a bell-shaped curve is likely to be produced. Results of most measurements occur close to the average, and relatively few are found at either extreme. If we were to collect assessment exam score data from 1,000 more students, the distribution in Figure 6.1 would become more bell-shaped.

When data are not distributed equally around a measure of central tendency—such as in the case of the assessment exam scores—two characteristics of a score distribution are important to understand. The first characteristic is **skewness**. When larger numbers of individuals score at one of the ends of the distribution, the distribution is not symmetrical and becomes skewed (pulled) in one direction or the other (see Figure 6.5). Differences that result between these measures of central tendency indicate the magnitude and direction of this skewness. If the mean is higher than the median, the distribution is positively skewed; if the mean is lower than the median, the distribution is negatively skewed. One way to remember the direction of skewness is to remember "the tail tells the tale"—that is, the direction of the pulled side of the distribution (tail) reminds us of the type of distribution. The greater the skewness value, the more "lopsided" the distribution is (i.e., more scores fall to the opposite side of the tail). In a skewed distribution, the median becomes the better measure because it is not affected by extreme scores.

Kurtosis is another characteristic of a data distribution. It refers to the "peakedness" or height of a distribution. Given that taller bars in data graphs indicate greater frequency, taller points in a curve indicate greater clustering of data points around the mean; that is, less variation (*leptokurtosis*). In addition, flatter points would indicate greater dispersion (*platykurtosis*). Normal curve distributions are characterized as *mesokurtosis*.

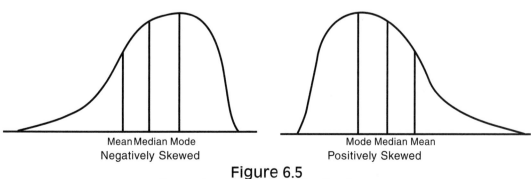

Figure 6.5
Examples of Skewed Distributions

Activity 6.1
Organizing and Computing Measures of Central Tendency and Variability

Use the following scores for a kindergarten readiness test:

5	8	10	7	7
6	9	13	12	3
4	8	3	9	11

- Develop a frequency distribution, histogram, and frequency polygon. What do you notice about the data distribution?
- Compute the following measures of central tendency and variability:

Mean = _____ Median = _____ Mode = _____

Range = _____ Interquartile range = _____ Standard deviation = _____

- Assuming the national mean for the kindergarten readiness test is 8 and the standard deviation is 2, how did this class do compared with the national sample?

Norms and Ranks

Standardized tests by nature are norm referenced. Norms are established by administering the instrument to a standardization group and then referencing an individual's score to the distribution of scores obtained in the standardization sample. Thus, establishing **norms** (group data characteristics) allows us to compare an individual score with a comparison sample. The individual's raw score is converted into some type of derived score, which indicates the individual's relative standing to the normative sample. This derived score, then, provides a comparative measure of the individual's performance on whatever characteristic that instrument is assumed to measure.

It is important to note that the standardization sample should be representative of the population with which the student or client is being compared. For example, if a student is being compared with 10th-grade students, the sample should include a cross-section of students in the 10th grade from his or her city, state, region, or country, depending on the type of comparison one wishes to make. Norm groups should be both systematically assembled and fully described in regard to significant variables such as grade, age, sex, type of school, and location. Separate norms should be developed if certain characteristics, such as ethnicity or socioeconomic background, are to be taken into account in interpreting test results.

Developmental Norms

There are two types of **developmental norms**, or comparison of an individual's score to the individual's grade level or age group. **Grade equivalents** are often used on educational achievement tests to interpret how a student is progressing in terms of grade level. Grade equivalent scores consist of a number representing a grade followed by a decimal representing the 10 months of the school year from September through June. The grades range from K (kindergarten) to 12. Grades above 12 are occasionally used but are not particularly meaningful. The mean raw score obtained by students in each grade is computed, with fractions of a grade determined either by interpolation or by testing students at different times during the school year.

The principal advantage of grade equivalents is the seeming ease of interpretation to those without any understanding of measurement concepts. Actually, grade equivalents are subject to considerable misinterpretation. A sixth grader obtaining a grade equivalent score of 9.3 in arithmetic could easily be assumed by parents and teachers to have a knowledge of mathematics equivalent to the average student in the ninth grade at that time. A more correct interpretation would be that the student obtained a score on the arithmetic test equivalent to the score the average ninth grader would have obtained on that test in the unlikely event that ninth graders might have a sixth-grade arithmetic test administered to them. It would not mean that the sixth grader would have obtained a score equal to the average ninth-grade student on the ninth-grade test, which would undoubtedly have included algebraic and other mathematical concepts unfamiliar to sixth graders. Hence, the score of 9.3 would certainly indicate superior performance by a sixth grader but could not be regarded as equivalent to a ninth-grade performance. In addition, because grade equivalents are computed from mean raw scores, students will vary in a bell-shaped curve above or below the mean. Thus, a teacher might attempt to bring each student up to grade level—all students scoring at or above the mean. If national grade equivalents are used, this goal could perhaps be accomplished in a particular classroom, but if local norms are used, such a feat would obviously be impossible.

Age comparisons, the second type of developmental norms, refer to an individual being compared with others in his or her age group. Age comparisons can be made for various types of assessments, from childhood physical measurements to performance measurements as adults in competitive events such as marathons. Let's examine weight comparisons. If the average weight for a 10-year-old male is 75 pounds (SD = 5 pounds), and a 10-year-old male weighs 85 pounds, the corresponding z score would be 2.00, or a weight at approximately the 97th percentile (more on this later).

Rank

A person's **rank** or standing within a group is the simplest norm-referenced statistic, with its interpretation based on the size and composition of the group. It is used extensively for grades—for example, a high school student who ranks 12th in grade point average (GPA) in a graduating class of 140—but it is seldom used in describing psychological test results.

Percentile Rank

Percentile rank is more often used because it is not dependent on the size of the comparison group. **Percentile scores** are expressed in terms of the percentage of people in the comparison group who fall below them when the scores are placed in rank order. A percentile rank of 65 indicates a score or rank that is as high as or higher than those made by 65% of those in the comparison group. A percentile can be interpreted as a rank out of 100 persons in the comparison group (see Figure 6.4). Higher scores yield higher percentile ranks, and the lower the percentile, the lower the person's standing. The 50th percentile corresponds to the middlemost score, or the median. The 25th percentile is the first quartile point, marking the bottom quarter of the distribution, and the 75th percentile is the third quartile point, above which is found the top one quarter of the scores. The advantage of using percentiles is that they are easily calculated and easily understood by most people (provided it is made clear that a percentile indicates ranking in the comparison group rather than the percentage of correct responses).

Percentiles are computed using the following formula, where B refers to the number of observations with lower values (including the observation point itself) and N refers to the total number of observations:

$$P_R = \frac{B}{N} \times 100.$$

For the frequency distribution in Table 6.2, the percentile rank for a person scoring a 95 would be $11/15 \times 100 = 73.3\%$. You will notice that statistical packages like SPSS provide a "Cumulative Percentage" column that indicates the percentile rank as well.

The principal disadvantage of percentile ranking is that the distribution of most scores resembles the familiar bell-shaped curve (as in Figure 6.4), whereas the distribution of percentiles is always rectangular in shape. Ten percent of the cases fall between the 40th and 50th percentiles, in the same way that 10% fall between the 80th and 90th percentiles. Because of the pile-up of scores near the center of a distribution, a small difference in middle raw scores can yield a large difference in percentile ranks, as can be seen in Figure 6.4. At the extreme high and low ends of the distribution, however, large raw score differences may yield only small differences in percentile ranks. Thus, the difference between an individual increasing his or her percentile rank from the 50th to 55th percentile is not the same increase as from the 90th to 95th percentile. Percentile ranks are generally intended as a means of conveying information concerning a person's relative rank in a group, but because of the nature of percentiles, they are generally not used in additional statistical computations.

Standard Scores

Because there are several problems related to using percentiles and other types of scores, many tests make use of standard scores as the most satisfactory method of reporting test results. Standard scores are based on standard deviations and means. A **standard score** is defined as a score expressed as a distance, in standard deviation units, between a raw score and the mean. There are several common types of standard scores, including z scores, T scores, CEEB scores, Deviation IQs, and stanines.

z Scores

The basic standard score is the **z score**, a score that allows us to estimate where a raw score would fall on a normal curve. That is, if you convert raw scores to z scores, you can compare them across different types of tests easily. A z score results from subtracting the raw score from the mean and dividing by the standard deviation of the distribution. The formula for computing z scores is the following, where X refers to the raw score; M, the group mean; and SD, the standard deviation:

$$z = \frac{X - M}{SD}.$$

Let's practice computing a z score. Recall that previously the assessment exam mean and standard deviation were calculated as 88.67 and 7.961, respectively. If you want to convert your score of 83 to a z score based on this information, your score would represent a z score of –0.712 (83 – 88.67/7.961). This score indicates how many standard deviation units your score was below the mean.

Conceptually, a z score of –1.5 on this scale indicates that the raw score falls 1.5 SD below the mean of the reference group. A z score of 0 means the raw score falls exactly at the mean, and a raw score falling 2 SD above the mean would yield a z score of +2.0. Because z scores directly correspond to points on the normal curve, there is a relationship between z scores and percentile ranks (P_R):

z Score	P_R
−3.0	.0013
−2.5	.0062
−2.0	.0227
−1.5	.0668
−1.0	.1587
−0.5	.3085
0.0	.5000
0.5	.6915
1.0	.8413
1.5	.9332
2.0	.9772
2.5	.9938
3.0	.9987

For a z score of 1.0 (score at 1 SD above the mean), the percentile rank is .8413, or approximately 84%. This result means that someone who scores at 1.0 would score as high or higher than 84% of the group.

T Scores

Because z scores produce both decimals and negative values, they cause difficulties in computations and interpretation. Other types of standard scores have been developed based on a linear transformation of the z score. The most common standard score is the **T score**, which is used on a number of the most widely used educational and psychological tests. By definition, the T score has an arbitrary mean of 50 and standard deviation of 10. The formula for computing a T score is the following:

$$T = 50 + 10z.$$

For our z score of −0.712, the corresponding T score would be 42.88.

The T score is rounded to the nearest whole number, and because most raw scores do not exceed ±3 SD from the mean, T score distributions usually range from 20 to 80. The results of many aptitude, interest, and personality measures are profiled in terms of T scores. To aid in the interpretation of T scores, half standard deviation units along with their comparable percentiles are shown in Table 6.3. The interpretations commonly given to the different ranges of T scores (along with percentile equivalents) are also given in that table (assuming of course that the norms are appropriate to the individual or group being assessed). It can be seen in Table 6.3 that T scores of 45 to 55, the middle 38% of the distribution, are commonly interpreted as *average;* those above 55, as *high;* and those above 65, as *very high.* T scores below 45 can be interpreted to clients as *low,* and those below 35 are interpreted as *very low.*

CEEB Scores

Other test publishers have selected different scales using different means and standard deviations, which can be interpreted the same way as z scores or T scores. The **College Entrance Examination Board (CEEB)/College Board scores** (e.g., SAT, Preliminary Scholastic Aptitude Test/National Merits Scholarship Qualifying Test [PSAT/NMSQT]) are reported in standard scores that use a mean of 500 and a standard deviation of 100. Thus, a raw score falling 1 SD above the mean, which would yield a z score of 1.0, produces a standard score of 600. All scores are reported in increments of 10. The result is a scale that is recognizable

Table 6.3
Interpretation (Assuming Appropriate Norms)
for Given *T* Scores and Percentile Ranks

T Score	Percentile Rank	Interpretation
70	98	Very high
66	94	
65	93	High
60	84	
56	70	
55	69	Average
50	50	
45	31	
44	30	Low
40	16	
35	7	
34	6	Very low
30	2	

for these instruments, although the scores may be thought of simply as *T* scores with an additional zero added:

$$\text{CEEB score} = 500 + 100z.$$

This type of scale can cause a minor problem in that small differences in raw scores may seem to be much larger because of the large-scaled score differences that range through 600 points (200 to 800).

For many years, there was considerable confusion concerning the SAT portions of the CEEB (which is discussed further in Chapter 10). A mean of 500 was established years ago, when a smaller proportion of college-bound students took those tests. The typical college-bound student in more recent years scored well below the supposed mean of 500. In 1995, the scores were "recentered," and 500 again became the college-bound student mean (College Board, 2016c). The total scores of the three parts of the SAT now range from 600 to 2,400. The revised GRE was released in August 2011. Percentiles will be computed from students who have taken them over the past 3 years.

ACT, Inc., uses standard scores similar to those developed for the Iowa Tests of Educational Development ($M = 15$, $SD = 5$). The ACT tests have been standardized with a mean of 21 and a standard deviation of 6, yielding a range of standard scores from 1 to 36.

Standard scores developed for the General Aptitude Test Battery (GATB) used for many years by the U.S. Employment Service yielded a mean of 100 and a standard deviation of 20.

Deviation IQ Scores

When the first intelligence tests were developed, a ratio of mental age to chronological age was developed, and the ratio was multiplied by 100. This ratio was later called the Intelligence Quotient, or IQ. The ratio IQ had a number of problems, including the fact that the ratio became invalid beginning in the adolescent years. **Deviation IQ** standard scores have since been developed to replace ratio IQs. Current results still report the mean at 100, as was the case with ratio IQs, but they report a standard score based on standard deviation units. Therefore, tests such as the Wechsler scales and the Stanford–Binet established a mean of 100 and a standard deviation of 15 or 16, depending on the test. A score of 100 would fall at the mean on the normal curve, a score of 115 (or 116) would fall at 1 *SD* above the mean, and so forth. Again, it is important in interpreting test results with any of these types of standard scores to have firmly in mind the points along the normal curve where these scores fall and the proportions of the population on which the standard scores are based that fall at various points on the normal curve.

Stanines

A **stanine** (based on the term *standard nine*) is a type of standard score that divides a data distribution into nine parts. Each stanine, with the exception of Stanines 1 and 9, divides the standard deviation unit on a normal curve in half (see Figure 6.4). Stanines have a mean of 5 and a standard deviation of 2. The stanines of 1 and 9 at the ends of the distribution contain 4% of the cases, and these increase as in the normal curve so that the center stanine of 5 includes 20% of the cases. Test scores can be converted to stanines by referring to the normal curve percentages in Figure 6.4. Stanines are used infrequently because of the difficulty in explaining their meaning. Their chief advantage lies in the single-digit numbers, which do not imply greater accuracy than most tests can deliver. However, single digits can sometimes suggest a significant difference between two individuals when none exists.

Activity 6.2
Converting Raw Scores

The Hays Happiness Scale has a mean of 25 and a standard deviation of 5. With this information in mind, respond to the following questions:

1. Convert a raw score of 30 into a *T* score and *z* score.
2. Approximately what percentage of the group scored higher than the individual?
3. If this had been an SAT, what would have been the individual's score using the calculated *z* score?
4. If this had been an intelligence test ($M = 100$, $SD = 15$), what would have been the individual's score using the calculated *z* score?

Standard Error of Measurement

This chapter concludes with one additional standardized score, revisiting the concept of reliability. The **standard error of measurement** (*SEM*) yields the same type of information as does the reliability coefficient but is specifically applicable to the interpretation of individual scores. (Recall that *reliability* refers to the consistency of scores for a sample on a particular test.) The most common use of the *SEM* is to construct bands of confidence around an individual's obtained score. It represents the theoretical distribution that would be obtained if an individual were repeatedly tested with a large number of exactly equivalent forms of the same test. Such a cluster of repeated scores would form a curve, with a mean and standard deviation of the distribution, and that standard deviation is called the *SEM*. An individual's single score on a test is assumed to be the mean of repeated scores, and the *SEM* can be interpreted in terms of normal curve frequencies. Thus, if a student's true raw score was 40 on a particular test and the *SEM* was 3, then if the test were repeated many times, 68% of the individual's scores would fall between 37 and 43, and we could be 95% confident that the individual's true score would be between 34 and 46—that is, 2 *SEM* units above or below the obtained score. When the standard deviation and the reliability coefficient of the test are known, the *SEM* is easily computed using the following formula: The *SEM* equals the standard deviation, *SD*, of the test times the square root of the quantity 1 minus the reliability of the test:

$$SEM = SD \times \sqrt{(1 - \text{reliability})}.$$

As an example, the SAT has a standard score mean of 500, a standard deviation of 100, and test–retest reliability of approximately .91 for college applicants. The *SEM* is 30 (100 × $\sqrt{1 - .91}$ = 100 × $\sqrt{.09}$ = 100 × .3 = 30). If Susan, a college applicant, scores 490 on the test, the odds are high (68% of the time) that her true score falls between 460 and 520 (i.e., ±1 *SEM* of the obtained score) and 95% between 430 and 550, which is 2 *SEM*s. Similar estimates can be made of the true scores for individuals on the ACT test, which, with a mean of 18, a standard deviation of approximately 6, and reliability coefficients of about .90, has an *SEM* in the vicinity of 2. In the case of the Wechsler intelligence scales with full-scale score standard deviations of 15 (*M* = 100) and reliability coefficients in the vicinity of .96, the *SEM* equals 3.

Although most test manuals interpret *SEM* according to classical test theory in the manner discussed above, item response theory recognizes that the interpretation of *SEM* varies depending on the degree to which the individual scored above or below the mean. In general, test error is higher for extreme scores because there are fewer items of appropriate difficulty at these levels to measure the variable in question. In addition, extremely high or low scores can be expected to change more on retesting than scores in the average range because of regression toward the mean (Allen & Yen, 2002; Charter & Feldt, 2002).

Tip Sheet
Understanding and Transforming Raw Scores

✓ Individuals naturally want to know what a raw score means. Counselors use various methods to organize the score and provide information about a typical score and how far a particular score falls from that typical score. Visual aids such as a frequency distribution, histogram, and bar graph can show where a score falls in comparison with a data distribution. Measures of central tendency and variability provide additional information about average scores and dispersion of scores, respectively.

✓ Pay attention to the "tails" of data distributions to determine degree of skewness. Tails are pulled by the mean, so the mean statistic will be closest to the tail (unlike the median and mode). If the tail pulls to the left or negative side of the curve, the distribution is negatively skewed. If the tail pulls to the right or positive side of the curve, the distribution is positively skewed.

✓ Do not confuse percentiles with percentages. Percentages can refer to the ratio of the observed score to the possible score (i.e., the number of correct items out of the possible number of correct items). Percentiles refer to the percentage of scores that fall at or below a particular score. So, a 53rd percentile does not mean the individual had 53% correct, but it does mean the individual scored as well as or better than 53% of a sample.

✓ Remember that grade equivalents are comparisons between individual and average scores for a particular grade level. The number, when compared with a grade-level position, tells information about if the individual scored higher or lower than the group mean. So, a score of 3.4 for a grade level of 3.4 indicates the individual scored at the grade level. A score of 5.2 would indicate he or she scored above those at that grade level—not necessarily that he or she scored at a higher grade level.

✓ The z score is the most basic standard score, with a mean of 0 and standard deviation of 1. Counselors can compute any other standard score with knowledge of a z score. Furthermore, raw scores can be compared across assessments if z scores are computed. An advantage of z scores is that they can be compared easily across settings.

✓ Positive *z* scores fall to the right of the normal curve mean, whereas negative scores fall to the left of the distribution.

✓ *SEM* units can be considered standard deviation units for an individual score based on the reliability coefficient. If a counselor knows an individual's score and the *SEM*, he or she can plot the scores at various standard deviation units and estimate the percentage of time a score is likely to fall within a particular interval. Alternatively, the *SEM* can be computed from knowing the reliability of an assessment. Then, the *SEM* can be applied individually to raw scores to create a confidence interval.

Chapter Summary

Understanding and transforming or organizing raw scores is a necessary step for counselors in the test interpretation process. Essentially, raw scores are meaningless and must be converted to some derived score (i.e., norm-referenced, criterion-referenced, or self-referenced). The chapter outlined several graphical options for displaying raw scores or variables in a data set: frequency distribution, histogram, frequency polygon, and bar graph.

To make additional meaning of a raw score, measures of central tendency and variability are calculated. Measures of central tendency refer to an average score and include the mean, median, and mode. Measures of variability refer to indices for scores to ascertain the amount of dispersion of a particular score from the mean. They commonly include range, interquartile range, and standard deviation.

Characteristics of data distributions were also discussed, with the normal curve being the most ideal for a data set. In a normal curve, precise calculations may be made about the percentages of a sample that contain a particular range of scores. Because data aren't usually perfectly distributed, skewness and kurtosis are often calculated to show variability characteristics. A related concept to data distributions concerns norms and ranks. These principles allow counselors to determine where scores fall in relation to a client's peers characterized by the same data distribution.

The chapter concluded with sections on standard scores and *SEM*. Major standard scores include *z* scores, *T* scores, CEEB scores, and stanines. Standard scores are calculated based on a normal curve distribution and allow counselors to compare different types of scores for different types of tests. *SEM*, a concept related to reliability discussed in Chapter 5, refers to the degree of confidence around a client's obtained score. *SEM* is an important concept in interpreting a client's true score from an obtained score.

Review Questions

1. What is the difference between norm-referenced and criterion-referenced assessment? When would you select one instead of the other?
2. What are the measures of central tendency and variability? How do they compare with one another?
3. What is the difference between percentages and percentile ranks?
4. What is the purpose of converting raw scores into derived scores?
5. Discuss the relationship between reliability and *SEM*.

Resources for Further Learning

DeMars, C. (2010). *Item response theory.* New York, NY: Oxford University Press.

Hughes, I. F., & Hase, T. (2010). *Measurements and their uncertainties: A practical guide to modern error analysis.* New York, NY: Oxford University Press.

Weisberg, H. F. (1992). *Central tendency and variability.* Thousand Oaks, CA: Sage.

Section III

Initial
Psychological
Assessment

Chapter 7

Initial Assessment in Counseling

This first chapter of Section III presents some of the key assessment procedures that take place in the beginning of the counseling process. First, the intake interview, mental status examination, and screening inventories are discussed. Second, suicide risk assessment procedures—including suicide risk factors and assessment aids—are presented. Finally, an introduction to clinical diagnosis and decision making is included.

Test Your Knowledge

Select the most appropriate choice for each item.

_____ 1. Which of the following is most often used to collect information about a client's treatment history and current symptoms?
   a. Intake interview
   b. Problem checklist
   c. Mental status examination
   d. Screening inventory

_____ 2. Which of the following is most often used to collect a snapshot of various general mental health symptoms?
   a. Intake interview
   b. Problem checklist
   c. Mental status examination
   d. Screening inventory

_____ 3. Which of the following is most often used to collect information of a client's mood, affect, and thought processes?
   a. Intake interview
   b. Problem checklist
   c. Mental status examination
   d. Screening inventory

_____ 4. Which of the following is not recognized as a suicide risk factor?
   a. Being female
   b. Being male
   c. Living alone
   d. Using substances

_____ 5. Placing too much emphasis on information obtained early in the interview is known as:
   a. Anchoring
   b. Availability
   c. Diagnostic overshadowing
   d. Attribution

137

Intake Interview

The purpose of the **intake interview** is to assess the nature and severity of the client's problems and to determine possible treatment programs. The intake interview process is a critical part of the overall counseling process as clients provide significant information and counselors establish expectations for the general counseling process. To this end, counselors balance their work between gathering information and developing a therapeutic relationship.

The interview, which provides more flexibility than most other assessment procedures, enables the counselor to clarify the client's responses on the intake forms and to explore the client's concerns in some depth. Most intake interviews cover the following topics: (a) general appearance and behavior; (b) presenting problem; (c) history of current problem and related problems; (d) present level of functioning in work, relationships, and leisure activities; (e) use of alcohol or other drugs, including medications; (f) family history of mental illness; (g) history of physical, sexual, or emotional abuse; (h) risk factors, including urge to harm self or others; (i) previous counseling; and (j) attitude of client toward the counseling process. Intake forms vary somewhat, depending on the particular type of services offered within a particular counseling setting.

During the intake process, the counselor should explain the policies of the agency, such as session limits, rules of confidentiality, and referral options. The intake interview should help the counselor to decide the immediacy of the need for counseling, the type of expertise required, and the type of service to be used (e.g., individual counseling, couples counseling, group counseling, or consultation and referral). In general, the intake form should be kept relatively short so that it does not become an imposition in counseling. As counseling progresses, the form can be supplemented with additional questionnaires designed for particular issues, such as career planning, study skills, or relationships. Furthermore, to assess multicultural factors, counselors may want to include a semistructured interview such as the Person-in-Culture Interview (Berg-Cross & Zoppetti, 1991) or the Career-in-Culture Interview (Ponterotto, Rivera, & Sueyoshi, 2000).

Interview Guidelines

Initial interviews usually progress on a continuum from minimal structure to more structure. As the interview proceeds, the client may need help or direction in continuing to respond. Questions that probe or clarify can be used to obtain a clearer understanding of what the client feels or means. Statements like "Can you tell me more about . . . ?" or "Tell me more about how you felt when . . ." or "I don't think I understand what you mean by . . ." solicit relevant information from the client's point of view and help to maintain rapport. Rephrasing of questions can sometimes help to clarify a client's responses if other techniques have not been effective. In general, it is best not to ask "why" questions because they may cause the client to become defensive. It is important to determine what factors led the client to seek help at this particular time. Has the problem recently become worse? Have other people become concerned about the person? Has the problem begun to interfere with the client's functioning at work or home? Answers to such questions can help clarify the nature of the client's problem and assess the client's motivation for participating in counseling.

The counselor should pay attention to the client's nonverbal behavior, such as eye contact, facial expression, and activity level. Observations of the client's nonverbal behavior can be particularly important for clients who may have difficulty communicating with the counselor. It is important as a counselor gauges information from verbal and nonverbal behaviors that cultural differences, as well as any potential power differential between the counselor and client as a result of cultural group memberships, are considered. The information obtained in the initial interview needs to be organized systematically to help identify significant patterns of behavior.

Although interviews can serve as a rich source of information, observations based on interviews are frequently biased or subject to misinterpretation. Common errors of judgment based on interview assessments include the following (D. J. Miller, Spengler, & Spengler, 2015):

- **Anchoring:** placing too much emphasis on information obtained early in the interview;
- **Availability:** relying too much on one's favorite theory or on popular diagnoses such as borderline personality disorder or adult child of dysfunctional family;
- **Diagnostic overshadowing:** ignoring or minimizing problems because they are less noticeable or are of less interest to the counselor; and
- **Attribution:** attributing the problem primarily to the client without giving sufficient consideration to the environment.

These errors can create significant problems for clinical diagnoses, particularly with culturally diverse populations (Alcántara & Gone, 2014; D. G. Hays, McLeod, & Prosek, 2009; D. G. Hays et al., 2010). Counselors may combat these errors by adhering to the principles of assessment (see Chapter 1) and using multiple approaches to assessment.

Mental Status Examination

In some mental health settings, counselors routinely administer a **mental status examination** (MSE) to assess client level of functioning through a series of questions and observations (Polanski & Hinkle, 2000). The MSE should not be used by itself to make a diagnosis, but it can be helpful in suggesting areas in which further assessments should be made. Counselors may perform an MSE as part of the intake interview or at other times if they perceive the client to be disoriented, confused, or out of touch with reality. Chapter 4 discussed the Mini-Mental State Examination (MMSE; Folstein et al., 2001), which is used often in assessment of older adults. There are other published versions of the MSE, including the Mental Status Checklist for children (Dougherty & Schinka, 1989), adolescents (Dougherty & Schinka, 1988), and adults (Schinka, 1988), as well as the Health Dynamics Inventory (Saunders & Wojcik, 2004). Counselors evaluate clients within six MSE categories (see Table 7.1).

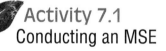

Activity 7.1
Conducting an MSE

Select a popular movie or television show character who would be considered to be experiencing a mental health issue. Rate the "client" based on the six mental status categories described in Table 7.1. Use specific examples.

The MSE is usually administered informally. Interviewers ask questions only in those areas in which they have concerns. Information is picked up naturally during the course of interviewing the client. The results of the MSE can usually be reported in one or two paragraphs.

Screening Inventories

Counselors often use brief, self-report screening instruments to obtain a preliminary, overall view of a client's concerns. Clients are asked to indicate which of a wide range of

Table 7.1
Mental Status Examination Categories

Category	Description and Examples
Appearance, Attitude, and Activity	
Appearance: physical characteristics such as physical disabilities, apparent age, grooming, and dress	Level of consciousness (e.g., normal attentiveness, hyperarousal, drowsy, lethargic, comatose); apparent age; position/posture (e.g., physical location of client, catatonia, use of restraints); attire/grooming (e.g., casually dressed, clean, neat, disheveled, provocative); eye contact (e.g., good, poor); facial expression; and physical characteristics (e.g., tattoos, scars, obesity, marks, sweating)
Attitude: client's approach to counseling or interactions with examiner	Friendly, cooperative, uncooperative, hostile, guarded, resistant, or suspicious
Activity: level and quality of the client's physical movements	Pacing, fidgety, resting tremors, writhing, tardive dyskinesia, lip smacking, blinking, tics, and compulsions
Mood and Affect	
Mood: client's self-reported feeling	Angry/hostile, euphoric/elated, apathetic (bland, dull, flat), dysphoric (despondent, distraught), apprehensive/anxious
Affect: external expression of emotional state; measured objectively by counselor	Counselor compares mood and affect using same mood categories. Appropriateness (congruent, inappropriate, incongruent); intensity (heightened, blunted, flat); and range and mobility (restricted, labile, constructed, fixed)
Speech and Language	
Fluency: initiation and flow of speech	Smoothness of spontaneous speech; use of connectors; grammatical correctness; stuttering
Repetition: repeating words or phrases	"Say 'apple' three times"
Comprehension: understanding of spoken and written commands	Commands to a client such as "open your mouth" and "touch your right leg with your left hand"; client naming objects or listing words
Prosody: attention to tone, rate, rhythm, and musicality of speech in relation to content	Abnormally fast or slow speech; use of inflection; poverty of speech; monotonous speech
Quality of speech: pitch, volume, articulation and amount	Articulation of speech; clients in a manic episode may speak loudly while those in a depressive episode may speak softly with little spontaneity
Thought Process, Thought Content, and Perception	
Thought process: clarity of communication, association or connectedness between topics	Circumstantiality (talking around a subject); tangentiality; flight of ideas (frequent tangentiality); derailment; word salad (severe form of derailment); clanging (word association by sounds); echolalia; neologisms (inventing new words or phrases); perseverations
Thought content: focus on spontaneous, important to assess faulty content	Delusions; overvalued ideas (faulty beliefs deemed by clients as possibly wrong); obsessions; ruminations (persistent focus on negative thought); preoccupation (prominent topic that is not a delusion of obsession); suicidal ideation; homicidal ideation; self-harming behavior; and phobias
Perception: abnormalities related to perception of self or five senses	Hallucinations (auditory, visual, tactile, gustatory, olfactory); illusions; derealization; depersonalization

(Continued)

Table 7.1 *(Continued)*
Mental Status Examination Categories

Category	Description and Examples
Cognition	
Cognition: higher abilities such as intellect, logic, reasoning, and memory	Orientation (oriented to time, place, person); attention (e.g., use of digit span); concentration (e.g., serial 7s, backward reciting of months); registration (repeating a short list of three to five words of new learning); short-term memory (repeating information with a delay of 5 minutes); long-term memory (procedural, declarative, episodic, semantic); constructional ability (vision, motor coordination, tactile sensation); and executive functions (e.g., divergent reasoning)
Insight and Judgment	
Insight: awareness of internal and external realities	Client self-awareness of own behavior and the motives and consequences of that behavior; identification of contributing factors to problem
Judgment: consideration of factors and decision-making process	Decision making (good, risky); impulse control (good, fair, poor)

Note. Information is from R. W. Baker and Trzepacz (2005), Polanski and Hinkle (2000), and Van Brunt (2009a).

symptoms or concerns may have been troubling them during the recent past. The screening inventory can provide an initial measure of both the nature and the intensity of a client's concerns. Because of its scope, it can detect issues of possible importance that might otherwise be overlooked. Once detected, such issues can then be further assessed in the interview and by other means as necessary. Several inventories that have proved to be particularly valuable for use in counseling are described below.

There are several key basic features of screening instruments that affect the precision of screening assessments. Recall that the terms *sensitivity* and *specificity* were discussed in Chapter 5. Sensitivity refers to the probability of a cutoff score on a particular test or measure to accurately detect those who meet the criteria for a certain diagnosis or condition (a true positive result). Specificity, in contrast, refers to the probability of a cutoff score to correctly identify those who do *not* meet these criteria (a true negative result). The **overall accuracy** refers to the combination of sensitivity and specificity (Sacks, 2008):

> If, for example, 100 people have a disorder and the screening instrument correctly identifies 80, the *sensitivity* of the instrument would be 80%. If another 100 people do not have the condition and 60 are accurately identified, the *specificity* of the instrument would be 60%. The *overall accuracy* of the instrument represents the proportion of people correctly identified . . . the overall accuracy is 70% (80 + 60 = 140/200). (p. 10)

Inventory of Common Problems

The **Inventory of Common Problems** (ICP; Hoffman & Weiss, 1986) is used as a screening instrument in college counseling centers. It lists 24 specific problems that college students may confront (see Figure 7.1). These items represent six major types of problems as follows: depression (Items 1–4); anxiety (Items 5–8); academic problems (Items 9–12); interpersonal problems (Items 13–16); physical health problems (Items 17–20); and substance-use problems (Items 21–24).

Clients must indicate to what extent each of the 24 problems has distressed, worried, or bothered them in the past few weeks. Answers range from 1 (*not at all*) to 5 (*very much*). Scores for each scale can range from 4 to 20; total scores can range from 24 to 120. Normative data for a sample of college students collected by Hoffman and Weiss (1986) showed

Instructions: The following items represent common problems of college students. How much has each problem distressed, worried, or bothered you in the past few weeks? Please circle the answer that is most nearly correct for you.

Not at all	*A little bit*	*Moderately*	*Quite a bit*	*Very much*
1	2	3	4	5

1. Feeling depressed, sad, dejected?	1	2	3	4	5
2. Blaming, criticizing, or condemning myself?	1	2	3	4	5
3. Feeling discouraged or like a failure?	1	2	3	4	5
4. Suicidal thoughts or concerns?	1	2	3	4	5
5. Feeling irritable, tense, or nervous?	1	2	3	4	5
6. Feeling fearful?	1	2	3	4	5
7. Spells of terror or panic?	1	2	3	4	5
8. Feeling like I'm "going to pieces"?	1	2	3	4	5
9. Academic problems?	1	2	3	4	5
10. Difficulty caring about or concentrating on studies?	1	2	3	4	5
11. Indecision or concern about choice of career or major?	1	2	3	4	5
12. Feeling like I'm not doing as well in school as I should?	1	2	3	4	5
13. Problems with romantic or sexual relationships?	1	2	3	4	5
14. Family problems?	1	2	3	4	5
15. Difficulty getting along with others?	1	2	3	4	5
16. Feeling lonely or isolated?	1	2	3	4	5
17. Physical health problems?	1	2	3	4	5
18. Headaches, faintness, or dizziness?	1	2	3	4	5
19. Trouble sleeping?	1	2	3	4	5
20. Eating, appetite, or weight problems?	1	2	3	4	5
21. My use of alcohol?	1	2	3	4	5
22. My use of marijuana?	1	2	3	4	5
23. How many psychoactive drugs I use?	1	2	3	4	5
24. How many prescribed drugs I use?	1	2	3	4	5

If so, what? _____

Figure 7.1
Inventory of Common Problems

Note. From "A New System for Conceptualizing College Students' Problems: Types of Crises and the Inventory of Common Problems," by J. A. Hoffman and B. Weiss, 1986, *Journal of American College Health, 34*, p. 262. Copyright 1986 by the Helen Dwight Reid Educational Foundation. Published by Heldref Publications, 4000 Albermarle Street, NW, Washington, DC 20016. Reprinted with permission.

no significant sex differences. Thus, the same set of norms may be used with both male and female clients. The highest mean score (11 points) was obtained on the Academic Problems scale, whereas the lowest mean score (5 points) was recorded for the Substance Use scale. The mean total score for college students was approximately 45 points, with a standard deviation of about 10 (Hoffman & Weiss, 1986).

The ICP possesses sufficient reliability and validity evidence for its use as a screening instrument with most college students, but it should not be regarded as a diagnostic instrument (Hoffman & Weiss, 1986). The results should be used primarily to suggest topics for further exploration in counseling. Counselors can easily readminister the ICP to clients to obtain a rough measure of progress during the course of counseling. If administered to all clients as part of the intake process, it can also be used to provide a comprehensive picture of the types of psychological problems presented at the agency.

From a practical point of view, the ICP offers several advantages for counselors. It can be completed by most clients within 5 to 10 minutes, it represents most of the problems that clients are likely to encounter, and it can be reproduced economically. The ICP has been designed so that it can be used together with the Therapist Rating Form, which asks therapists to classify the type of crisis encountered by the client as psychopathological, developmental, or situational (Hoffman & Weiss, 1986). A case example based on the use of the ICP with a college student is presented in Case Example 7.1.

Case Example 7.1

Linda

Linda came to the university counseling center as a senior because of dissatisfaction with her major. She felt particularly uneasy because most of her peers were participating in job interviews for the next year. She was majoring in finance but was not happy with it. She did not like the competitiveness of the students in her field. According to the intake form that she completed at the same time as the ICP, she wanted help in "choosing a major" and "career planning." She marked all of the items except one in the first three categories (Depression, Anxiety, and Academic Problems) of the ICP as 4 or 5. She was feeling very distressed by her career indecision.

On the Therapist Rating Form, the intake counselor attributed Linda's problems primarily to developmental issues, not psychopathological or situational factors. Short-term counseling was arranged, based on the counselor's judgment. Linda needed help in dealing with developmental tasks, especially in resolving her career choice, not in making fundamental changes in other aspects of her life.

Linda met with a counselor for six sessions for help in acquiring decision-making and assertiveness skills and for assistance in working through conflicted feelings about her career choice. She decided to add human resources management as a second major to that of finance. This combination was supported by the tests (including the Strong Interest Inventory) that she had taken and by the information that she had gained in career exploration.

The ICP was readministered at the conclusion of counseling. Linda marked no 4 or 5 responses the second time she completed the inventory. Her total score, which dropped from 66 to 34, and all of her subscores fell well within the normal range compared with other college students. For Linda, the ICP was helpful both in determining the nature and the severity of her initial complaints and in evaluating the progress that she showed in counseling. Linda's rapid progress in counseling supported the perception of the intake counselor that her problems were developmental, not psychopathological, in nature.

• • •

Symptom Check List–90–Revised

The **Symptom Check List–90–Revised** (SCL-90-R) has been widely used for research and clinical purposes in a variety of medical and mental health settings (Derogatis, 1994; Derogatis & Unger, 2010). As indicated by its name, the SCL-90-R contains a list of 90 symptoms such as "headaches," "feeling critical of others," and "feeling tense or keyed up." Clients respond to items in terms of how much they were distressed by that symptom during the past week. Each item is answered on a 5-point scale ranging from 0 (*not at all*) through 4 (*extremely*). Most clients complete the SCL-90-R within 15 minutes. With practice, it can be easily hand scored.

The SCL-90-R provides scores for the following nine scales: Somatization, Obsessive–Compulsive, Interpersonal Sensitivity, Depression, Anxiety, Hostility, Phobic Anxiety, Paranoid Ideation, and Psychoticism. Scores for each scale show the mean response for the items in that scale. It also yields three total scores: Global Severity Index (GSI), Positive Symptom Total (PST), and Positive Symptom Distress Index (PSDI). The GSI, the best single index of psychological disturbance, shows the mean response to all 90 items. The PST indicates the number of symptoms reported (all items marked 1 or higher). The PSDI, which shows the mean response to all items included in the PST, reflects the severity of the client's symptoms.

Scores on the SCL-90-R vary depending on age and sex. Adolescent nonpatients report more symptomatology than do adult nonpatients. Women acknowledge more symptoms than do men. The SCL-90-R manual provides separate norms for adolescent nonpatients, adult nonpatients, adult psychiatric inpatients, and adult psychiatric outpatients. Each norm is "gender keyed" (Derogatis & Fitzpatrick, 2004, p. 5) to take into account sex differences.

Scores on the different scales show adequate internal consistency and test–retest reliability over short time periods for psychiatric patients. Overall, the SCL-90-R appears to be most valid as a broad measure of psychological disturbance. The test scores have demonstrated sensitivity to many forms of treatment, which indicates that they can be used effectively to monitor the improvement of clients during the course of counseling (Calvert & Kellett, 2014; Gibson, Booth, Davenport, Keogh, & Owens, 2014; Vonk & Thyer, 1999).

The SCL-90-R is particularly valuable as a screening instrument to detect cases that need additional assessment. As a general rule, Derogatis (1994) suggested that counselors should refer clients for psychiatric evaluation if their scores on the GSI or any two of the individual scales equal or exceed the 90th percentile (T score = 63) compared with adult nonpatients.

Brief Symptom Inventory, Derogatis Psychiatric Rating Scale, and SCL-90-Analogue

Several abbreviated versions of the SCL-90-R have been developed. The **Brief Symptom Inventory** (BSI) contains 53 of the 90 items on the SCL-90-R (Derogatis, 1993). Administration time for the BSI is approximately 10 minutes, compared with 15 minutes for the SCL-90-R. Intercorrelations between the two sets of scales range from .92 to .99. According to Derogatis and Fitzpatrick (2004), the BSI is often preferred over the SCL-90-R by clinicians and researchers, even in situations lacking time constraints. The BSI can also be administered as an 18-item form (BSI-18); however, this version of the instrument includes only Somatization, Depression, and Anxiety scales (the three scales most commonly associated with psychological distress and disorder; Derogatis, 2000).

In addition to the self-report forms described above, Derogatis has constructed matching rating scales for use by clinicians familiar with the client. The **Derogatis Psychiatric Rating Scale** and the **SCL-90-Analogue** can be used to obtain clinician ratings on the same symptom constructs included in the SCL-90-R and BSI. Counselors can obtain a more thorough and accurate assessment of a client's status by using both self-rating scales and clinician rating scales. The SCL-90-R and BSI have been used extensively in different cultures throughout the world. The instruments have been translated into more than two dozen languages (Derogatis & Fitzpatrick, 2004).

Outcome Questionnaire 45.2

The **Outcome Questionnaire 45.2** (OQ-45.2; Lambert et al., 2004) is a 45-item self-report instrument used to screen for client affect, interpersonal concerns, and level of functioning in life tasks such as school and work. The OQ-45.2 consists of a total score and three subscale scores, with items rated on a 5-point Likert scale (0 = *never* to 4 = *almost always*). Sample items include "I have thoughts of ending my life" and "After heavy drinking, I need a drink the next morning to get going." Normative data are available for six samples, including college undergraduates, community volunteers, employee assistance program (EAP) clients, counseling center clients, community outpatient clients, and inpatients.

Internal consistency estimates range from .70 to .93, and 3-week test–retest reliability estimates range from .78 to .84. The *SEM* is .93. The OQ-45.2 also demonstrates strong evidence of convergent and criterion-related validity, as there are high correlations with other measures of psychological distress. More recently, Rice, Suh, and Ege (2014) found psychometric support for a shortened measure of two factors. With this new modeling, they cited some of the same psychometric limitations of the original OQ-45.2. The benefits of the instrument include its ease of administration and use in multiple settings. However, given the limited psychometric information available for the subscales and overall factor structure, counselors should only use the total score.

Inventories for Assessing Mental Disorders

Some screening inventories have been designed specifically for use in making psychiatric diagnoses. These include the **Psychiatric Diagnostic Screen Questionnaire** (PDSQ) and the **Patient Health Questionnaire** (PHQ). The PDSQ contains 13 scales, each of which is related to a mental disorder as defined by the *Diagnostic and Statistical Manual of Mental Disorders* (4th ed., text rev.; *DSM-IV-TR;* American Psychiatric Association, 2000; Zimmerman & Mattia, 1999). The PHQ includes scales for eight common mental disorders, such as major depressive disorder and panic disorder (Spitzer, Kroenke, Williams, & the Patient Health Questionnaire Primary Care Study Group, 1999). Both of these inventories are helpful in medical settings in identifying individuals with diagnosable psychiatric disorders unknown to their primary physician.

Brief Psychiatric Rating Scale

The **Brief Psychiatric Rating Scale** (BPRS; Overall & Gorham, 1988) is a tool commonly used to assess therapeutic changes in individuals diagnosed with psychotic disorders. The BPRS is an 18-item tool administered by a clinician; symptoms are rated on a 7-point scale from 1 = *not present* to 7 = *extremely severe.* The BPRS was expanded to 24 items (BPRS Version 4.0; Zanello, Berthoud, Ventura, & Merlo, 2013) to explore the scale's utility for evaluating therapeutic change in major depression symptoms for those receiving crisis counseling.

Tip Sheet
Intake Interviews, MSE, and Screening Forms

✓ Prior to engaging in any initial assessment process in counseling with a particular client, reflect on your level of cultural and social justice awareness, knowledge, and skills as they relate to your and your client's cultural identity. Consider how advocacy interventions can be included throughout the assessment process.

✓ Listen to and observe client information carefully. Use open-ended questions, avoid leading the client, and allow enough time for the client to respond.

✓ Adjust assessment style based on the developmental level and other demographic variables of the client.

✓ Once you have identified the client's problem, be sure to explore the problem from multiple perspectives, gather specific information about the problem, assess problem intensity, assess the degree to which the client believes change is possible, and evaluate previous methods used to resolve problem.

✓ Seek information about behaviors or events that have been helpful in the past or that the client expects might be helpful in the future. For example, when has the problem been least likely to occur in the past? What has kept the problem from getting worse? What is one small step the client could take to improve the situation? Answers to such questions can be useful in considering possible solutions for the client's problem (Dejong & Berg, 2012).

✓ Be aware of the possibility that the client's psychological symptoms may be caused by physical illness, particularly if (a) the client has not responded well to counseling or psychotherapy; (b) the symptoms have not occurred previously, especially for older clients; (c) the onset of symptoms has been relatively abrupt; (d) the client has suffered from recent or multiple medical disorders; (e) the client is disoriented or confused; or (f) psychosocial stressors are absent or minor (Pollak, Levy, & Breitholtz, 1999). If the client is on medications, possible side effects of these medications should be reviewed.

✓ Consider what errors you might be making as part of initial assessment, including anchoring, availability, diagnostic overshadowing, and attribution. Use multiple approaches to assessment to minimize these errors.

✓ Use additional structured and semistructured assessments to garner and triangulate data.

✓ Evaluate the client's mental status as part of the intake interview as possible.

✓ Assess a client's stage of change as part of initial assessment.

✓ Identify critical items on the screening inventory (e.g., items that refer to thoughts of suicide or violent behavior) that can be used to help determine whether the client is in a state of crisis. Be sure to make a suicide risk assessment if the client shows signs of suicidal thinking.

✓ Examine general level of responses. If a client marks a large number of extreme responses, consider the need for immediate counseling and possible psychiatric referral. Ask clients to discuss each of these responses, especially ones that they perceive to be most crucial.

✓ Note the client's responses for substance abuse and health items. These problems may be overlooked in the counseling interview if the counselor does not bring them up with the client.

✓ Readminister an inventory at the conclusion of counseling or after a significant time period has elapsed to evaluate changes that have taken place during the course of counseling. Clients who have shown little improvement may need to be referred.

✓ Use screening inventory scores to consult with supervisors or colleagues regarding the treatment of a case. Screening inventory scores can be used to communicate the nature and severity of the client's issues within a few minutes.

✓ Add items to a screening inventory to assess matters of importance to your agency. For example, one agency added the following items to the ICP to identify potentially dangerous situations: "Urge to harm myself," "Plan to harm myself," "Urge to harm someone else," "Plan to harm someone else," and "Concern that someone else may harm me."

✓ Administer screening inventories for specific topics (e.g., Michigan Alcoholism Screening Test, My Vocational Situation, or Eating Attitudes Tests) when these seem to be appropriate. Ask clients to identify any issues that they might be experiencing that are not represented on the screening inventory.

✓ Consider the possibility that clients could be minimizing or exaggerating their problems. Use both number and intensity of symptoms to help gauge possible distortion. If clients mark most items at a low level of intensity, they could be minimizing their problems. Similarly, if they mark a large number of problems at a high level of intensity, they could be exaggerating their concerns.

✓ Screening inventories should be used in conjunction with other assessment methods. Use individual scales and items primarily as a means of identifying significant subject matter for discussion and further assessment.

✓ Use screening inventories to monitor the caseload in your agency. What types of clients are receiving treatment at the agency? How many of the clients express suicidal ideation? How many of the clients indicate problems with substance abuse? Use these data to develop local norms to help interpret screening inventory responses. The data may also be used to help decide which types of services to emphasize in the agency.

Suicide Risk Assessment

Suicide risk assessment is an important component of initial assessment in counseling. The Centers for Disease Control and Prevention (CDC) reported that in 2013 suicide was the 10th leading cause of death in the United States, with one suicide occurring about every 13 minutes (CDC, 2015b). Worldwide, suicides occur at a rate of one every 40 seconds (Nock, Kessler, & Franklin, 2016). Statistics regarding nonfatal suicidality (e.g., suicidal thoughts, suicide plan, failed suicide attempts) show substantial percentages, with higher rates among high school students compared to adults 18 years and older. For example, about 4% of adults reported having suicidal thoughts, 1% made a suicide plan, and 0.6% attempted suicide; in comparison, about 17% of adolescents had suicidal thoughts, 14% made a plan, and 8% attempted suicide (Kann et al., 2014). It is important to note that there is great heterogeneity within the adult population, with 18- to 25-year-olds having higher rates of nonfatal suicidality than the 26-to-49 and 50-and-older age groups (Substance Abuse and Mental Health Services Administration [SAMHSA], 2014). Data do show, however, that middle-aged adults (45- to 54-year-olds) accounted for the majority of suicides in 2011 (Sullivan, Annest, Luo, Simon, & Dahlberg, 2013). In addition, state-by-state data (CDC, 2015a) indicate a suicide rate range for elderly adults (65 years and older) from 7.7% (South Dakota) to 32.9% (Nevada). Among younger individuals (15 to 24 years old), the range was 6.4% (Massachusetts) to 34.9% (Alaska). Collectively, these percentages concerning successful suicides and nonfatal suicidality provide important context for counselors as they engage in suicide risk assessment.

Clients should be asked directly about their suicidal thoughts if there is any hint of suicidal thinking. The counselor can usually approach this topic with a series of graded questions. For example, the counselor might ask, "How have you been feeling lately?" "How bad does it get?" "Has it ever been so bad that you wished you were dead?" and "Have you had thoughts of suicide?" If the client has had thoughts of suicide, the counselor needs to inquire about the extent of these thoughts. Some counselors are apprehensive about bringing up the topic of suicide with a client for fear that this will encourage the client to think about suicide as an option. In reality, clients who have had suicidal thoughts need the opportunity to talk about these thoughts, and asking about suicide does not encourage suicide.

In essence, suicide risk assessment becomes part of the treatment. The counselor is to establish rapport with each client so that the assessment can be as complete and as accurate as possible. In addition, the assessment process should be a collaborative process that enhances the therapeutic alliance; this is especially salient as clients try to navigate a time of crisis, may be reticent to disclose suicidality, and/or can view counseling as a stressful process in itself.

Talking about suicidal thoughts helps to validate the client's experience. It provides a sense of relief and communicates hope to the client that the problem can be addressed. In contrast, clients who have not had suicidal thoughts will usually reassure the counselor that this is not a concern. In fact, it is sometimes a relief for such clients to see their problems from this perspective: Even though they are struggling with a problem, things are not so bad that they think of suicide. In making a suicide risk assessment, counselors should be both calm and direct. Calmness indicates that it is acceptable for clients to talk about the things they find to be most troubling. Counselors help clients to look at problems in depth and from different points of view. They should make a point of using the words *suicide* or *kill yourself* while conducting the suicide risk assessment. The enormity of the act should be faced directly.

The goal of suicide risk assessment is to identify the level of risk, with increased risk resulting in counselors taking more immediate actions. A. L. Berman and Silverman (2014) noted that traditional levels of risk were *no risk, low risk, moderate risk*, and *high risk* or *imminent risk*. Furthermore, they noted that signs of imminent risk indicate to clinicians a need for hospitalization; some of these signs include the real and present threat of significant harm to self or others, likelihood to injure if not stopped, inability to care for self, and immediacy of suicidal actions. As A. L. Berman and Silverman discussed, however, there is no universal definition of imminent risk, as not all suicide completers display traditional signs of imminent risk. Furthermore, although identifying the level of suicide risk can be useful for selecting interventions, it is of little predictive value for the number of those who will complete suicides after treatment.

Significant Factors in Suicide Risk Assessment

The assessment of suicide risk is basic to the formulation of a treatment or intervention plan. The assessment should involve consideration of the factors discussed below (American Psychiatric Association, 2003; McGlothlin, 2008). Although the literature provides counselors with key suicide correlates and risk factors to be mindful of during suicide risk assessment, these are "broad-stroke" considerations that do not account for the complexity of factors associated with the transition from suicidal ideation to completion (Nock et al., 2016). Thus, counselors are to carefully attend to where clients may be on that continuum and seek very specific information. More specifically, Nock et al. (2016) noted a need

> to better understand how people move along the entire pathway to suicide: from onset of the thought, to developing a plan and intention, to making preparations, to making a decision to act, and actually carrying out the attempt . . . Suicide is an outcome that results from a complex, nonlinear, and time-varying combination of a wide range of factors. (p. 33)

Nevertheless, N. C. Berman, Stark, Cooperman, Wilhelm, and Cohen (2015) identified from the collective literature the following key correlates and risk factors: being White, being an unmarried male with less formal education, the presence of particular psychiatric and substance abuse disorders, encounters with stressful events, and previous suicide attempts. I warn, however, that these are predominant features of successful suicides and do not characterize all completers or those on the transition spectrum from suicidal thought to completion.

Self-Reported Risk

After clients have acknowledged suicidal ideation, they will usually tell the counselor of their perception of their risk level when asked. Questions such as "How likely do you think it is that you will act on your thoughts of suicide?" or "How long can you continue to tolerate the situation as it is?" will often generate responses that will be helpful in the assessment process. A self-report of high risk must always be taken seriously. It is important that counselors ask questions regarding the specific suicidal thoughts and behaviors in which a client has engaged.

Suicide Plan

For those clients with thoughts of suicide, the counselor should ask whether they have considered a plan. If they have a plan, do they intend to act on it? Information about the plan is critical in helping to assess a client's suicide potential. A suicide plan should be evaluated in terms of three factors:

- *Lethality.* Some plans are much more lethal, or likely to succeed, than others. Firearms, jumping from great heights, and hanging are highly lethal. More people kill themselves with firearms than by any other method (National Institute of Mental Health, 2012), and this is the method most commonly used among males (CDC, 2015b). Among females, poison is the most common method (CDC, 2015b). Counselors can assess lethality as low (no suicidal ideation at time of assessment), moderate (suicidal ideation with presence of several risk factors), or high (in process of attempting suicide; McGlothlin, 2008).

- *Availability of means.* Does the client have access to the means of killing himself or herself? For example, is a gun available? Has ammunition been purchased? The counselor needs to obtain clear answers to these specific questions. At times, it may be necessary to interview friends or family members to obtain this information.
- *Specificity.* Finally, how detailed are the client's plans? The risk of suicide increases as plans become more detailed and specific. For example, has the client made plans to give away possessions? Has the client considered what he or she might write in a note? Where would the suicide take place? When would it take place? Even more alarming are clients who have started to act on their plans; for example, those who have written a suicide note or given a pet to a friend.

The best indicators of suicidal risk are ideation, plan, intent, and means (A. L. Berman & Silverman, 2014). If the client is thinking about suicide, has made a plan, intends to carry it out, and has the means, he or she is at extreme risk and immediate intervention is needed. There are a number of steps that should be taken with clients at this point, including validating the emotional pain, exploring the ambivalence felt by the client and connecting to that part of the client that wants to live, developing a crisis management plan, and referring the client for psychiatric consultation and treatment, while maintaining a calm and supportive atmosphere.

Suicide History

A history of suicide attempts, the medical seriousness of previous attempts, and a family history of suicide are all critical factors in assessing suicide risk (McGlothlin, 2008). In fact, the strongest risk factor for predicting suicide is a history of attempts (Fowler, 2012). If a person has attempted or seriously thought about suicide at some earlier time, particularly by lethal means, the risk of suicide for that person is significantly increased (Hawton, Casañas i Comabella, Haw, & Saunders, 2013; Tidemalm, Haglund, Karanti, Landén, & Runeson, 2007). Individuals who have made more than one attempt are especially at risk.

The counselor should check on the history of suicide in the family and among friends. Have family members or friends committed suicide or made suicide threats or attempts? If so, what was the nature of the relationship between that person and the client? Did that person represent a model for the client? How does the client feel about these situations? When did the suicide or suicide attempt take place? Anniversary dates can sometimes provide the impetus for suicide attempts.

Psychological Symptoms

Clients who have mental disorders or psychological distress are much more likely than others to commit suicide (American Psychiatric Association, 2003; Hawton et al., 2013; LeardMann et al., 2013; Tidemalm et al., 2007). More specifically, research indicates increased suicide risk for those with major depression, bipolar disorder, and/or substance use disorders (Hawton et al., 2013; LeardMann et al., 2013); this symptomatology is particularly predictive of suicidality for those with recent inpatient psychiatric care, comorbid disorders, and multiple lifetime depressive and mixed episodes (Tidemalm et al., 2007). Although all client symptoms should be reviewed, critical symptoms include acute suicidal ideation, severe hopelessness, attraction to death, and acute overuse of alcohol (Hawton et al., 2013; McGlothlin, 2008).

Alcohol or other drug abuse significantly increases the risk of suicide for a client (Hawton et al., 2013; Tidemalm et al., 2007). The risk of suicide in individuals who abuse alcohol is 50% to 70% higher than in the general population (American Association of Suicidology, 2017). Counseling programs designed to prevent suicide must also address the related problem of alcohol or other drug abuse.

Medications can also be associated with suicide. The side effects of many medications include depression. The counselor should note whether the client is taking any medications, including any recent change in medications. Medications are also frequently used as a means of suicide. As a safety precaution, someone else should control antidepressant medications prescribed for highly suicidal clients.

Symptoms that suggest severe mental illness such as schizophrenia, bipolar disorder, or other psychotic disorders demand prompt attention. Has the client lost contact with reality? Does the client hear voice commands (auditory hallucinations) telling him or her what to do? All psychotic individuals with thoughts of suicide should be hospitalized immediately to provide protection and relief from their psychosis. Many people who kill themselves are people with severe and persistent mental illness. Psychological autopsy studies indicate that more than 90% of those who commit suicide have a mental disorder (American Association of Suicidology, 2017; Coughlin & Sher, 2013).

Sometimes signs of improvement can increase the risk of suicide. Clients may become more actively suicidal as they begin to come out of a deep depression; that is, when they acquire enough energy to act on their suicidal thoughts. In a similar fashion, clients sometimes will give an appearance of improvement when they have resolved their ambivalence by deciding to commit suicide.

Environmental Stress

Stressful situations are often the precipitating cause of suicidal ideation, especially those involving the loss or threat of loss of interpersonal relationships (Fowler, 2012). What is the nature of the client's environment? Why is the client feeling suicidal at this particular time? What are the precipitating factors? How would the client benefit from suicide? Clients who wish to commit suicide to escape from stressful situations represent a greater risk than clients who see suicide as a means of manipulating the environment.

Has the client encountered significant changes in his or her life, such as divorce, death of a family member, sickness, loss of job, academic failure, or an overwhelming work assignment? Any change, even one that is positive, such as a job promotion or the end of an unhappy relationship, can be perceived as stressful. Change involves loss. Losses that pose the greatest threat include loss of a relationship, loss of a significant role, loss of a dream, or a large financial loss. Sometimes anticipating a loss can be more stressful than the actual loss. Loss can be particularly stressful if the client accepts most of the blame. Client stress can be systematically assessed by means of the Life Experiences Survey (Sarason, Johnson, & Siegel, 1978) or the Life Stressors and Social Resources Inventory–Adult or Youth Form (Moos & Moos, 1994b, 1994c).

Sometimes stress can be associated with an event that happened years earlier if this event has not been addressed. Such events include sexual abuse, physical abuse, the suicide of a parent or sibling, and other traumatic events. Ask clients whether there are things from their past that they find very difficult to discuss. If so, help them to begin to look at these issues in a supportive atmosphere. Recognize the need for long-term treatment for many of these issues.

Available Resources

Counselors need to determine what resources are available for the client. Three levels of resources should be considered: (a) internal; (b) family, close friends, neighbors, coworkers, and others who may have contact with the client; and (c) professionals. First, what are the client's internal resources? In trying to assess these resources, the counselor should ask what has helped the client in the past in similar situations. What is keeping the client from committing suicide? Does the client have plans for the future? To what degree can the client cope with the stress that he or she may be encountering? For example, can the client identify a solvable problem? Can the client distinguish between wanting to die and wanting to be rid of a problem? Can the client see more than one solution to a problem? Can the client identify reasons for living? Some clients experience "tunnel vision" so that they cannot conceive of options other than suicide for dealing with their stress. Does the client benefit from the counselor's attempts to provide assistance? Positive answers to these questions help to reduce the risk of suicide for the client.

Second, find out what type of support system the client has. Fowler (2012) noted the following protective factors: religious affiliation or support, marriage, children in the home, supportive social networks, and therapeutic contacts. If no one seems to be involved with the client at the present time, ask who used to care. Does the client have regular contact with anyone else? Does the client have any confidants? Would the client be willing to share his or her concerns with family members or close friends? In some respects, suicide can be looked on more as a social than as a psychiatric phenomenon. Evaluation of the client's social support system is critical from this point of view. A client's social support system can be evaluated by means of the Multidimensional Scale of Perceived Social Support (Zimet, Dahlem, Zimet, & Farley, 1988) or the Life Stressors and Social Resources Inventory–Adult or Youth Form (Moos & Moos, 1994b, 1994c).

Finally, what professional resources are available for the client? Possibilities include a 24-hour crisis phone line, emergency treatment center, or mental health specialist with whom the client has good rapport. Would the client make use of these resources in case of a crisis? Will the client sign a contract that he or she would contact the counselor or another mental health professional before attempting to commit suicide?

Additional Demographic Factors

In addition to the risk factors discussed earlier, suicide risk is affected by demographic characteristics. Women are more likely than men to have suicidal thoughts (SAMHSA, 2014). Furthermore, they make 3 times as many suicide attempts as men; however, 4 times as many men as women succeed in actually killing themselves (CDC, 2015b; National Institute of Mental Health, 2012). The CDC (2015a) showed that state-by-state rates of completed suicides for both genders combined range from 7.9% (District of Columbia) to 24.5% (Montana). For males, rates range from 12.5% (District of Columbia) to 38.3% (Montana); for females, rates range from 3.6% (Massachusetts) to 10.6% (Montana).

Within the adult population, prevalence rates of suicidal thoughts by race/ethnicity are as follows: 2.9% (Blacks), 3.3% (Asian Americans), 3.6% (Latinos), 4.1% (Whites), 4.6% (Native Hawaiians/Other Pacific Islanders), and 4.8% (Native Americans; SAMHSA, 2014). It is alarming that the CDC (2015b) showed a disproportionate number of completed suicides among Native Americans; suicide is the eighth leading cause of death for this racial/ethnic group in general and the second leading cause of death among Native Americans ages 10 to 34 years. In fact, the suicide rate among Native Americans ages 15 to 34 years is 1.5 times higher than the national average for that age group. It is also important to note that rates of suicidal thoughts, plans, and attempts were significantly higher among Latino adolescents than among White and Black students: 18.9%, 15.7%, and 11.3%, respectively (Brener et al., 2013).

Suicide Risk Assessment Aids

As indicated above, a large number of factors are associated with suicidal thinking and behavior. Assessments can help ensure that the counselor does not overlook crucial factors in making a suicide risk assessment. These aids are designed for use as part of the interview process. All of these aids emphasize the importance of assessing current suicidal symptoms and suicide history. They can provide a guide both for the assessment interview and for the documentation of how comprehensive the assessment is.

It is important to first note key challenges in suicide risk assessment. Even without the challenges noted here, it is difficult to predict suicidality: As Fowler (2012) noted, "Suicide risk is fluid, highly state-dependent, and variable over time" (p. 82). One key challenge in accurate suicide risk assessment is the low base rate of completed suicides in the United States (A. L. Berman & Silverman, 2014; Fowler, 2012). Given the generally low prevalence of completed suicides in the United States, it is more difficult to predict completed suicides. Furthermore, statistics regarding nonfatal suicidality can be underestimated and problematic, complicating accurate assessment even more. Another challenge relates to the notion that available assessment tools tend to measure distal or more static factors (e.g., demographic variables, psychiatric treatment history) or rely on self-reported psychological states; all tend to produce high false-positive rates (Fowler, 2012). And even though the factors presented in the previous section can serve as guidelines for possible risk for suicidality, the majority of those who, for example, identify as male or have psychiatric diagnoses do not attempt or complete suicide. To counter some of these challenges, Fowler recommended that clinicians attend to warning signs or more proximal factors during suicide risk assessment. This includes evaluating details regarding suicidal ideation and plan, stressful life events, and current cognitive/affective states.

SAD PERSONS Scale

The **SAD PERSONS Scale** provides a convenient acronym for 10 factors to keep in mind when assessing a client for suicidal risk (W. M. Patterson, Dohn, Bird, & Patterson, 1983). These 10 factors (arranged in order of the first letter for each factor to spell SAD PERSONS) include *S*ex, *A*ge, *D*epression, *P*revious attempt, *E*thanol abuse, *R*ational thinking loss, *S*ocial support loss, *O*rganized plan, *N*o spouse, and *S*ickness. Specifically, clients receive a point if there is an affirmative response to each of the following risk factors: male sex; under 19 or over 45 years old; presence of depression; previous suicide attempt; excessive ethanol or substance use; rational thinking loss; social supports lacking; organized plan; single, widowed, or divorced; and sickness.

Scores are assessed as follows: 0–4 (low), 5–6 (medium), and 7–10 (high). All clients who receive more than 2 points could be considered for psychiatric referral or hospitalization. The counselor needs to weigh all aspects of the situation in making a decision. Some factors may deserve greater consideration than others, depending on the particular situation. An organized plan is always cause for serious concern. When working with children, counselors may use the Adapted–SAD PERSONS Scale, which takes into account such factors as negligent parenting and school problems (Juhnke, 1996).

Suicide Assessment Checklist

Rogers, Alexander, and Subich (1994) developed the **Suicide Assessment Checklist** (SAC), which includes 12 items based on the client's suicide planning, suicide history, psychiatric history, drug use, and demographic characteristics and nine items based on the counselor's ratings of significant factors (hopelessness, worthlessness, social isolation, depression, impulsivity, hostility, intent to die, environmental stress, and future time perspective). The items are weighted in terms of their criticalness. The authors of this checklist assigned the highest weights to the following factors: having a definite suicide plan, planning to use a highly lethal method (firearm, hanging, car exhaust, drugs/poison, or suffocating), making final plans (such as giving away possessions), writing a suicide note, and being a suicide survivor (having a close friend or relative who has committed suicide). In general, higher scores indicate greater risk; however, counselors also need to take into account other pertinent information, such as third-party reports and their own clinical judgment, in making a final assessment of suicide risk.

Research evidence indicates that the instrument can be used effectively by counselors with a broad range of education and experience (Rogers et al., 1994). High interrater and test–retest reliabilities were obtained for SAC ratings by counselors (both experts and crisis-line volunteers) who judged the suicide risk of individuals role-playing suicidal clients. A large-scale study by Rogers, Lewis, and Subich (2002) found support for the reliability and validity of SAC ratings when used with clients in an emergency crisis center to assess suicide risk.

Suicide Assessment Five-Step Evaluation and Triage

Developed by SAMHSA, the Suicide Assessment Five-Step Evaluation and Triage (**SAFE-T**) method could be a useful tool for evaluating suicide risk factors that help to minimize the risk of false-positive rates and provide for more accurate prediction of suicidality. The steps of SAFE-T are as follows:

> (1) identifying relevant risk factors (noting those are modifiable and therefore targeted for treatment), (2) identifying protective factors, (3) conducting a suicide inquiry including current suicidal thoughts, plans, behavior, and intent, (4) determining level of risk and select interventions to reduce risk, and (5) documenting the assessment of risk, the rationale for the chosen interventions, and follow-up after assessment and interventions. (Fowler, 2012, p. 87)

Fowler (2012) indicated that clinicians should first assess risk factors/warning signs and protective factors. Sample risk factors/warning signs include client and family history of suicide attempts; presenting symptoms of irritability, impulsivity, hopelessness, and so on; triggering events of loss; current family chaos; and increased substance abuse. Sample protective factors identified by Fowler include internal coping resources, external reasons for living (e.g., children, peer support), and religious beliefs. Fowler suggested that after assessing these factors, clinicians inquire about current suicidal ideation, plan, and specific preparatory behaviors. With this collective information, clinicians can use the SAFE-T guidelines to evaluate for relative risk.

Decision-Tree Assessment Strategy

The **decision-tree approach** uses three risk factors—(a) past suicide attempts, (b) suicide plans and preparation, and (c) suicidal desire and ideation—as a basis for assessing suicidality (Chu et al., 2015). All clients with these risk factors are assessed further. Clients who have made more than one previous suicide attempt (multiple attempters) or who have made suicide plans and preparation are classified as at least moderate suicide risks if they possess one other significant risk factor, such as depression, alcohol abuse, or impulsivity. Clients who express suicidal ideas and desires (but who have not made multiple attempts or who have not developed plans and preparations) are regarded as at least moderate risks if they possess two other significant risk factors. Clients with none of the three risk factors listed above are considered to be at low risk.

The decision-tree approach helps the counselor to readily identify clients who need further assessment. It provides a systematic means for determining which clients are at greatest risk for attempting suicide.

The authors of this assessment strategy suggest a range of possible interventions for clients judged to be at least moderate risks for committing suicide. These interventions include an increased frequency and duration of counseling sessions or telephone contacts, a detailed emergency plan (presented in writing to the client), 24-hour availability of emergency or crisis services for the client, professional consultation or referral for psychiatric treatment or hospitalization, active involvement of family and supportive others, and frequent reevaluation of suicide risk and treatment goals.

Safety Planning

Although it is often considered an intervention rather than an assessment aid, safety planning can actually help minimize suicide risk. More specifically, as some clients expressing suicidality will not seek further treatment after initial evaluations—or will experience a delay in receiving treatment—safety planning can serve as a brief, single-session intervention during a suicide crisis (Stanley & Brown, 2012). Although Stanley and Brown (2012) proposed that those working in emergency settings develop the safety plan, their suggested safety plan template can be used in counseling settings during initial assessment.

Sample steps are as follows: (a) identifying warning signs, (b) identifying internal coping strategies, (c) providing examples of social situations and individuals that can help, (d) noting specific individuals or groups that the client can ask for help, and (e) identifying professionals or agencies to contact during a crisis. Furthermore, Stanley and Brown suggested that helping professionals strategize with individuals about how they can keep their environment safe to minimize suicide means.

In summary, counselors should use some form of comprehensive and systematic assessment to determine a client's suicide risk. Each of the interview aids described earlier focuses attention on significant factors that should be included in a suicide risk assessment. By using a systematic approach, the counselor can be sure to assess critical factors relevant to most situations in addition to other factors that may be pertinent in particular situations. Counselors should ask for more detail in those areas in which a problem is detected. Suicide risk factors should be reviewed during each counseling session for clients who may be suicidal. Such a review can serve both as a risk management strategy by assessing and documenting changes in suicidal thinking and behavior over time and as a basis for ongoing treatment planning.

When the counselor makes a suicide risk assessment, it is often important to consult with another mental health professional. Clients who are at risk for suicide may need to be referred for psychiatric evaluation. Psychiatrists can evaluate the client's need for medication, hospitalization, or long-term treatment. The assessment and treatment of suicidal clients frequently requires a team approach.

Case Example 7.2

Nicholas

Nicholas is a 41-year-old African American male presenting to counseling at the request of his neighbor. The neighbor reports to you that Nicholas has mentioned he has been depressed since he lost his job 6 months ago and ended a long-term relationship 4 months ago. Nicholas reports that he has increased his drinking to help him escape and states he "doesn't want to be here anymore." He states that he has considered using a handgun or taking some pills.

Reflect on the following questions:

- What additional information do you need about Nicholas to assess for suicide risk?
- How might you assess for suicide risk?
- How might cultural factors play into your risk assessment?
- Who would you involve to assist Nicholas?

• • •

Diagnostic and Statistical Manual of Mental Disorders

Initial assessment approaches in counseling (intake interviews, MSE, screening inventories, suicide risk assessment), as well as other mental assessment approaches discussed in the next chapter, are useful in clinical decision making and clinical diagnosis. The latest revision of the ***Diagnostic and Statistical Manual of Mental Disorders*** (*DSM*), the *DSM-5*, which was published in 2013, provides a means of classifying psychiatric and psychological disorders for treatment and research purposes. This diagnostic manual, which assumes an atheoretical position, classifies mental disorders based on descriptive, not etiological, factors. The diagnostic categories used by the *DSM-5* serve as the official means of classifying mental disorders in most medical and psychological settings in the United States.

As a diagnostic system, the *DSM* has continued to evolve since its first edition in 1952. The *DSM-5* developers advocated for the use of dimensional assessment in addition to categorical assessment. **Categorical assessment** refers to a clinician noting whether a symptom is present or not and then counting whether a number of symptoms are present to indicate a particular mental disorder. **Dimensional assessment** involves examining the severity of the symptom in the context of the overall disorder. That is, counselors can review mental health symptoms collectively regardless of a particular mental disorder, noting their presence, their severity, and any changes in those symptoms over time. The *DSM-5* contains both categorical and dimensional assessments.

Within each chapter of the *DSM-5*, mental disorders that begin in early childhood are presented first, and disorders that do not appear until later adulthood are presented last in the chapter. The organizational structure of the *DSM-5* includes chapters that follow a life-span perspective:

- Neurodevelopmental Disorders;
- Schizophrenia Spectrum and Other Psychotic Disorders;
- Bipolar and Related Disorders;
- Anxiety Disorders;
- Obsessive-Compulsive and Related Disorders;
- Trauma- and Stressor-Related Disorders;
- Dissociative Disorders;
- Somatic Symptom Disorders;
- Feeding and Eating Disorders;
- Elimination Disorders;
- Sleep–Wake Disorders;
- Sexual Dysfunctions;
- Gender Dysphoria;
- Disruptive, Impulse Control, and Conduct Disorders;
- Substance Use and Addictive Disorders;
- Neurocognitive Disorders;
- Personality Disorders;
- Paraphilias; and
- Other Disorders.

It is important to note that this latest revision of the *DSM* is not without its challenges. First, Wakefield (2016) cited the fact that the revision process itself was concerning to the public, as information regarding the process—during and after the development of the *DSM-5*—was limited and at times secretive. Second, at various points in revising the *DSM* throughout history, there have been discussions about the nuances of distinguishing mental disorder from normal intense distress. As the number of diagnoses has increased and language changes have been made to allow for more individuals to be formally diagnosed, there has been added controversy. More specifically, one camp has argued that more individuals have access to treatment given greater insurance reimbursement opportunities, and another camp has argued that normal distress is increasingly being pathologized (Wakefield, 2016).

The third key challenge relates to how clinicians judge the presence of various symptoms in their diagnostic decision making. The major goal of the *DSM-5* developers was to move away from categorical assessment toward dimensional assessment, with symptom severity scales being accessible on the *DSM-5* website (www.dsm5.org). These scales, however, lack evidence of empirical validation in their construction and do not include empirically guided clinical interpretations. Related to the issue of a lack of validated assessment tools to help in the diagnostic process, another challenge is the high false-positive rates of several disorders (Wakefield, 2016). That is, counselors and other helping professionals are overdiagnosing. This error is partly caused by the lack of an operationalized definition of disorder compared to normal distress, limitedly defined criteria for a symptom and/or disorder, the absence of criteria associated with subthreshold disorders (other specified or unspecified disorders), and the overlap of symptoms among particular disorders (Wakefield, 2016). Furthermore, diagnostic errors are made as a result of clinicians' cultural biases in combination with cultural expressions of symptomatology.

Clinical Diagnosis, Diagnostic Variance, and Culture

Even with revisions to the *DSM*, there are still problems in clinical decision making, specifically when there is limited information about a client or when a diagnostic category does not "fit" a client well. Diagnostic error is a serious concern because it affects treatment planning, the ways in which clients think of themselves, and the ways others perceive clients' level of pathology and functioning (D. G. Hays et al., 2009). With an increasingly diverse clientele, counselors must adapt clinical decision-making procedures to avoid diagnostic error. **Diagnostic variance**, or varying clinical decisions, are common in counseling and other professions. For example, D. G. Hays and colleagues (2009) found for 41 counselors and counselor trainees that, when presented the same case symptoms, participants arrived at 73 different diagnoses with varying levels of severity and specificity.

Research has consistently shown that racial/ethnic minorities and other individuals with minority statuses are disproportionately assigned more severe clinical diagnoses (see D. G. Hays et al., 2010). This finding may be attributable in part to mental health professionals often relying on racial/ethnic (Gushue, 2004) and gender (M. R. Ford & Widiger, 1989) stereotypes in clinical decision making. D. G. Hays et al. (2010) found in a mixed-methodological study examining culture and clinical diagnosis that participants did assign more severe clinical diagnoses to racial/ethnic minorities and females. Even though participants reported that culture did not influence client symptomatology or final diagnostic decisions, ultimately it did. Furthermore, culture was discussed when both the counselor and client were racial/ethnic minorities and the race/ethnicity of the client was significantly related to level of functioning. Clearly, counselors are to carefully arrive at clinical decisions and consider how culture influences the process.

 **Tip Sheet**
Using the *DSM*

✓ Use the *DSM* with clients who appear to have a psychiatric disorder. Use of the *DSM* classification system improves the reliability and validity of the assessment process. Diagnoses of mental disorders made by means of specific criteria such as those listed in the *DSM-IV-TR* are as reliable as diagnoses of general medical disorders (Satcher, 2000).

✓ Become familiar with case study materials and interviewing techniques for determining *DSM* classifications. Appropriate use of the *DSM* requires systematic training and experience in its use.

✓ Consider using a guided interview to assist in the screening and diagnostic process.

✓ Take into account both inclusion and exclusion criteria. A person who meets the inclusion criteria for a mental disorder actually may have a related disorder, a physical illness, or substance abuse, which may not be clear until exclusion criteria are considered. Recent versions of the *DSM* place greater emphasis on exclusion criteria than did earlier versions of this manual.

✓ Assess for the possibility of more than one disorder occurring at the same time. Dual and triple diagnoses of mental disorders for the same person are relatively common (Kessler, Chiu, et al., 2005).

✓ Keep in mind that the presence of risk factors for a disorder does not necessarily indicate the presence of the disorder.

✓ Be careful to use the *DSM* categories to classify a client's condition, not to label the client. For example, a client should be viewed as a person with schizophrenia, not as a schizophrenic. Labeling can lead to stereotyping and self-fulfilling prophecies.

✓ In making *DSM* diagnoses, consider a person's strengths as well as weaknesses, especially as an aid in treatment planning.

✓ Use the *DSM* classification system to enhance communication with medical and mental health referral sources. Most agencies require that clients or patients be assigned a *DSM* code for diagnostic and treatment purposes as well as for third-party payments.

✓ Consult treatment manuals for treatment suggestions for the different types of mental disorders listed in the *DSM.*

✓ In planning treatments, take into account the client's environment and developmental history as well as the *DSM* diagnosis. Psychopathology can often be reframed as a logical response to developmental history.

✓ Be careful not to equate cultural differences with psychological deficits (Kress et al., 2018). The *DSM* is biased toward the North American culture in which it was developed. Counselors need to develop a broad awareness of social and cultural issues to be able to apply the *DSM* effectively with multicultural clients.

✓ Keep in mind the limitations of the *DSM* classification system. Because of its categorical nature, it does not adequately indicate the severity of a particular condition, nor does it sufficiently differentiate among individuals classified within the same broad categories. Furthermore, the categories themselves suffer from artificial boundaries and extensive overlapping.

✓ On a related note, the dimensional assessments of the *DSM* may lack psychometric support or field trials specific to your client.

✓ Consider the *DSM* diagnosis as a hypothesis that is subject to review as circumstances change or as additional data are collected. Determining a *DSM* diagnosis should be looked on as a process, not a static event.

Chapter Summary

The initial phases of counseling require several types of assessment to evaluate overall functioning and plan interventions. The intake interview provides counselors comprehensive data about the presenting problem and relevant historical information to put the presenting problem in context. Furthermore, the MSE—often conducted in conjunction with an intake interview—indicates data related to the client's appearance, attitude, and activity; mood and affect; speech and language; thought process, thought content, and perception; cognition; and insight and judgment.

Screening inventories are brief instruments that are typically used in counseling to gather an overall view of a client's symptoms and the severity of those symptoms. Several screening inventories, such as the ICP, SCL-90-R, Outcome Questionnaire 45.2, PDSQ, PHQ, and BPRS, are available for counselors to use.

Another important initial assessment area involves suicide risk assessment. The chapter provides a discussion of the significant factors associated with suicide risk as well as several suicide risk aids for quantifying these factors, such as the SAD PERSONS Scale, Suicide Assessment Checklist, SAFE-T, and the decision-tree approach.

The chapter concluded with a brief discussion of the *DSM.* In addition, clinical diagnosis factors related to cultural bias were discussed. Counselors are to be familiar with how cultural bias and related stereotypes are associated with misdiagnosis and other forms of diagnostic error.

Review Questions

1. What are the common components of an intake interview?
2. Compare and describe the six major categories of the MSE.
3. What are the benefits of screening inventories? How can they supplement other initial assessment approaches?
4. What are the major suicide risk factors to consider with clients?
5. What are the benefits and challenges of clinical diagnosis using the *DSM?*

Resources for Further Learning

Publications

Alcántara, C., & Gone, J. (2014). Multicultural issues in the clinical interview and diagnostic process. In F. T. L. Leong, L. Comas-Díaz, G. C. Nagayama Hall, V. C. McLoyd, & J. E. Trimble (Eds.), *APA handbook of multicultural psychology: Vol. 2. Applications and training* (pp. 153–163). Washington, DC: American Psychological Association.

Berg-Cross, L., & Zoppetti, L. (1991). Person-in-culture interview. *Journal of College Student Psychotherapy, 5*(4), 5–21. doi:10.1300/J035v05n04_02

Wakefield, J. C. (2016). Diagnostic issues and controversies in *DSM-5:* Return of the false positives problem. *Annual Review of Clinical Psychology, 12,* 105–132. doi:10.1146/annurev-clinpsy-032814-112800

Web Resources

American Association of Suicidology
    http://www.suicidology.org
        This organization offers training resources related to suicide prevention.
American Foundation for Suicide Prevention
    http://www.afsp.org
        This advocacy group provides information and professional development concerning suicide prevention.
American Psychiatric Association, *DSM-5* Development
    http://www.dsm5.org
        This link provides the most updated information and research on the *DSM-5.*
American Psychiatric Association Practice Guidelines
    https://psychiatryonline.org/pb/assets/raw/sitewide/practice_guidelines/guidelines/suicide.pdf
        This link contains the *Practice Guideline for the Assessment and Treatment of Patients With Suicidal Behaviors.*
National Council of Social Service
    https://www.ncss.gov.sg/
        This links to sample intake assessment forms and guidelines.
Substance Abuse and Mental Health Services Administration, Suicide Assessment Five-Step Evaluation and Triage (SAFE-T) Pocket Card for Clinicians
    http://store.samhsa.gov/product/SMA09-4432
        This link provides direct access to ordering the SAFE-T tool.
World Health Organization, Suicide
    http://www.who.int/mediacentre/factsheets/fs398/en/
        This site provides a fact sheet on suicide statistics across the world.

Chapter 8

Substance Abuse and Mental Health Assessment

This second chapter of Section III discusses assessments for specific substance abuse and mental health issues experienced in counseling that may present during the initial assessment and beyond. Special-purpose assessments for screening and evaluating concerns such as substance abuse, depression, anxiety, anger, self-injury, eating disorders, and attention-deficit/hyperactivity disorder (ADHD) are presented. Measures of specific behavioral or psychological disorders can be used to determine to what extent an individual may be suffering from a particular problem.

Test Your Knowledge

Select the most appropriate choice for each item.

_____ 1. Alcohol abuse and alcohol dependence tend to be differentiated by which of the following?
   a. Increased tolerance
   b. More severe withdrawal symptoms and their management
   c. More severe impairment in social, academic, and occupational functioning
   d. All of the above

_____ 2. Which of the following is the most common mood disorder?
   a. Major depressive disorder
   b. Bipolar I
   c. Bipolar II
   d. Dysthymia

_____ 3. Which of the following mental disorders has the highest lifetime prevalence for U.S. individuals?
   a. Mood disorders
   b. Anxiety disorders
   c. Eating disorders
   d. Impulse-control disorders

❑ T ❑ F 4. Self-injury is typically a result of suicidal ideation.

❑ T ❑ F 5. Women are more likely to report symptoms characteristic of mental health disorders than men.

Prevalence of Mental Disorders

No matter the counseling setting, counselors are to consider the impact of mental well-being—or the lack thereof—on clients' daily functioning. Approximately 20% of U.S. adults experience mental illness in a given year, with about 4% of those individuals experiencing symptoms severe enough to disrupt their daily interpersonal, academic, and/or career functioning (National Institute of Mental Health [NIMH], n.d.). Prevalence rates for commonly known mental disorders for adults are as follows: 18% (anxiety disorders), 7% (major depressive disorder), 3% (bipolar disorder), and 1% (schizophrenia; NIMH, n.d.). About 20% of youth ages 13 to 18 live with a mental health condition, with common mental health disorders among this population including mood disorders (11%), impulse control and conduct disorders (10%), and anxiety disorders (8%). Approximately half of all lifetime cases of mental illness begin by age 14, and about 75% begin by age 24 (National Alliance on Mental Illness [NAMI], 2016).

Mental disorders are not only widespread but, for the most part, remain untreated. Although the correlates and consequences of untreated mental illness are wide ranging, it is important to consider that about 51% of U.S. adults have co-occurring mental health and substance abuse disorders (Substance Abuse and Mental Health Services Administration [SAMHSA], 2015a), 26% of individuals who are homeless and live in shelters have a mental illness, and 25% of those incarcerated in state prisons have a recent mental health condition (NAMI, 2016). Although the rate of treatment for those with mental disorders has increased during the past decade, the majority (67%) of those with diagnosable mental disorders have not sought treatment from any sector of the mental health services (Kessler, Demler, et al., 2005). Among those who have received treatment, approximately one half meet the criteria for a mental illness. The typical delay between onset and treatment of a mental illness is nearly a decade (NAMI, 2016).

The lack of treatment is particularly pervasive for racial/ethnic minorities and lesbian, gay, bisexual, transgender, and questioning (LGBTQ) individuals: NAMI (2015) reported that these groups disproportionately have inadequate health insurance and insufficient treatment options. Furthermore, many report experiencing oppression in terms of treatment settings, language barriers, and higher levels of stigma. As an example within the LGBTQ population, approximately 11% of transgender individuals report being denied mental health care (NAMI, 2015). Collectively, when individuals of minority statuses do obtain mental health treatment, the quality of care is poor and perhaps more detrimental than not seeking treatment (D. G. Hays & McLeod, 2018).

These statistics indicate the need for counselors to be familiar with procedures for assessing mental illness and comorbid conditions such as substance abuse. Counselors must be able to recognize the symptoms of mental illness and to provide at least a preliminary assessment of the client's mental state. They must be able to determine when services such as crisis intervention, psychiatric consultation, long-term treatment, and outreach programs may be necessary. Several substance abuse and mental health assessments are discussed throughout the chapter, and selected assessments that are available in the public domain for substance abuse and mental health assessment are presented in Table 8.1.

Although the remainder of the chapter provides information on assessment tools for individual use, it is important to consider performing a community needs assessment—particularly for clients from marginalized backgrounds. SAMHSA (2015b) offers a list of questions counselors and other helping professionals should consider to contextualize clients' mental health and/or substance abuse symptomatology. Specifically, this community-oriented assessment includes questions related to the evaluation of epidemiological data for a particular community and subpopulation, what resources are available and the extent to which those resources are culturally relevant, and community readiness to work with diverse communities and subpopulations concerning various symptomatology. Thus,

Table 8.1
Selected Substance Abuse and Mental Health Assessments in the Public Domain

Mental Health Issue	Assessment Tool
Substance abuse	Addiction Severity Index (ASI)
	Adolescent Alcohol and Drug Involvement Scale (AADIS)
	Adolescent Drug Abuse Diagnosis (ADAD)
	Alcohol Use Disorders Identification Test (including AUDIT-C, short form of AUDIT)
	CAGE Questionnaire
	Michigan Alcoholism Screening Test (available in short form)
	Rapid Alcohol Problems Screen (RAPS4)
	Simple Screening Instrument for Alcohol and Other Drugs (SSI-AOD)
	TWEAK
Depression	Center for Epidemiologic Studies–Depression Scale (CES-D)
	Center for Epidemiologic Studies–Depression Scale for Children
	Depression Anxiety Stress Scales (DASS)
	Mental Health Screening Form III (MHSF-III)
Anxiety	Hamilton Anxiety Rating Scale (HAM-A)
	Modified Mini Screen (MMS)
	PTSD Checklist (PCL)
	Social Interaction Anxiety Scale (SIAS)
Anger	The Ottawa–Georgia Mood Scales
Eating disorders	SCOFF Questionnaire
ADHD	Adult ADHD Self-Report Scale (ASRS-v1.1)
	Learning Needs Screening Tool
	Structured Adult ADHD Self-Test (SAAST)

Note. TWEAK = Tolerance, Worried, Eye-Opener, Amnesia, K/Cut Down; SCOFF = Sick, Control, One, Fat, Food; PTSD = posttraumatic stress disorder; ADHD = attention-deficit/hyperactivity disorder.

counselors should reflect on whether there are different expressions of symptomatology by subpopulation within a particular context, what resources or programs are available and how culturally appropriate those interventions are, and to what degree a particular community views something as a mental health or substance abuse problem and for whom. SAMHSA (2015b) also provides state-by-state data to help inform counseling interventions in a culturally relevant, community-oriented manner.

Assessment of Alcohol Abuse

Given the varying consequences of substance abuse itself for individuals, families, and general society, coupled with the prevalence of comorbidity with mental health issues, counselors are to be knowledgeable about statistical trends in substance use. According to SAMHSA (2015a), about 8% of U.S. individuals ages 12 and older were diagnosed with a substance use disorder in 2014, with common abuses occurring with alcohol, illicit drugs, or a combination of these. Illicit drug use among those ages 12 and older has steadily increased over the past decade, with about 10% of the U.S. population reported in 2014 to have been using illicit drugs in the past 30 days (primarily marijuana at 8.4% and/or nonprescription use of pain relievers at 1.6%). Patterns of alcohol use have remained fairly steady over the past decade. When asked in 2014 about alcohol use within the past 30 days, about 53% of individuals ages 12 and older reported drinking alcohol, 6% described themselves as heavy alcohol users, and about 23% reported binge drinking. Approximately 38% and 11% of college-age individuals (18 to 25 years old) reported for the period that they were heavy alcohol users and engaged in binge drinking, respectively. About 23% of those ages 12 and younger reported using alcohol use, 4% stated they were heavy alcohol users, and 14% described binge alcohol use in any given month.

Most of the substance use disorders involve the use of alcohol; thus, many of the available substance abuse assessments focus primarily on alcohol abuse. Because denial is a central issue in the abuse of alcohol or other drugs, counselors may not learn of the problem if they do not systematically review this matter with clients. Thus, it is important to systematically assess substance abuse symptoms with clients.

Criteria for Alcohol Dependence or Abuse

Although this section focuses on assessment of alcohol disorders, similar diagnostic criteria are used to determine dependence or abuse for all psychoactive substances. Psychoactive drugs include all drugs that alter an individual's mood or thought processes by their effect on the central nervous system. The *DSM* recognizes 10 classes of psychoactive drugs (alcohol, amphetamines, cannabis, nicotine, cocaine, PCP or phencyclidine, inhalants, hallucinogens, opioids, and sedatives) that can lead to dependence. The drugs show some differences in respect to tolerance and withdrawal symptoms.

People with **alcohol abuse** fail to fulfill major role obligations at work or home, repeatedly use in dangerous situations (e.g., driving while intoxicated), and have recurrent legal or social and interpersonal problems. Thus, some examples of excessive drinking include the following: a high level of daily drinking, repeated drinking episodes involving intoxication, drinking that causes physical and mental harm, and drinking resulting in dependence and addiction (Babor, Higgins-Biddle, Saunders, & Monteiro, 2001; CDC, 2015c). **Alcohol dependence** typically involves alcohol abuse symptoms as well as increased tolerance and more severe withdrawal symptoms.

The World Health Organization (WHO) defines alcohol dependence as the presence of

> a strong desire to consume alcohol, impaired control over its use, persistent drinking despite harmful consequences, a higher priority given to drinking than to other activities and obligations, increased alcohol tolerance, and a physical withdrawal reaction when alcohol use is discontinued. (Babor et al., 2001, p. 6)

DSM criteria are congruent with those of the WHO and include substance tolerance; withdrawal symptoms (e.g., "the shakes," transient hallucinations or illusions, anxiety, depressed mood, headache, insomnia, rapid heart rate, or sweating) that affect daily functioning; compulsive and increased substance use; unsuccessful efforts to reduce substance use; use of a great deal of time to obtain, use, or recover from a substance's effects; reduction or cessation of important social and occupational activities; and continued substance use despite physical or psychological problems it is known to produce.

Counselors will often see clients because of the problems produced by drinking, such as deterioration in work performance, conflicts with others, depression, or poor health. The counselor will need to be careful to assess for alcohol (or other substance) abuse that may have caused the problem. In general, counselors should assess clients' ability to control their use of alcohol and the degree to which alcohol usage causes problems in their lives.

To ensure that primary care practitioners take the time to screen patients for alcoholism, the National Institute on Alcohol Abuse and Alcoholism (2005) has recommended using just one basic question for all patients to determine whether further assessment is necessary. Men who drink are asked, "How many times in the past year have you had 5 or more drinks in a day?" For women, the number of drinks is reduced to four. A standard drink is defined as a bottle of beer (330 ml at 5% alcohol), glass of wine (140 ml at 12%), or a shot of 80-proof spirits (40 ml at 40%). People who answer *one time or more* are then asked about heavy weekly drinking (more than 14 drinks for men or seven drinks for women within a 1-week time period). Those who have drunk heavily within 1 week during the past year are then assessed more thoroughly in terms of *DSM* criteria. The assessment tools in the next section can be useful for further evaluation of symptoms.

Popular Alcohol Use Assessments

A variety of assessment procedures may be used to evaluate alcohol use. In most cases, the interview will probably be used to determine the nature and the gravity of drinking problems. Self-monitoring methods and physiological indices such as blood alcohol concentration levels can be used to supplement the interview. Standardized measures may also be used as part of the assessment process. The following screening measures are discussed in this section: CAGE/CAGE-AID Questionnaire, Rapid Alcohol Problems Screen, Michigan Alcoholism Screening Test, Substance Abuse Subtle Screening Inventory–4th edition, and the Alcohol Use Disorders Identification Test. Comprehensive substance abuse assessments are then described, including the Addiction Severity Index, Comprehensive Drinking Profile, Timeline Follow-Back, and Alcohol Use Inventory. Finally, self-monitoring strategies that may be used in substance abuse assessment are presented.

CAGE Questionnaire

The **CAGE** Questionnaire (named for the key words in each of four questions) can be readily used to screen clients for problems related to alcohol use (Ewing, 1984; Kitchens, 1994). The interviewer asks clients if they have ever (a) felt the need to *cut* down their drinking, (b) become *annoyed* when others ask them about their drinking, (c) felt *guilty* about their drinking, or (d) needed to take an *eye opener* to start the day. Each item is scored 1 for "yes" responses; a score of 2 or higher is considered clinically significant (N. Williams, 2014). If clients acknowledge any of these feelings or behaviors, they are likely to have experienced problems with alcohol, and additional inquiry should be undertaken. However, N. Williams (2014) suggested not asking any alcohol use–related questions prior to administering the CAGE given its sensitivity concerns. The **CAGE-AID** is the questionnaire adapted to include drugs, and items are revised by adding "or use (using) drugs" to each item.

Heck (1991) found that the effectiveness of the CAGE Questionnaire in identifying problem drinkers could be significantly improved by asking clients about their social drinking habits, driving habits, and the age at which they began to drink. Problem drinkers rarely or never choose nonalcoholic beverages at social events, frequently drive while under the influence of alcohol, and started drinking on a regular basis while they were still in high school.

Researchers in Copenhagen modified the CAGE by changing the wording in each question from "ever" to "anytime with the past year" (Zierau et al., 2005). They also added two questions that ask about number of days a week that a person drinks and whether drinking occurs outside of mealtime on weekdays. This modified version, known as the **CAGE-C** (for Copenhagen), was particularly effective when used for screening purposes in a population with a large number of at-risk drinkers.

Rapid Alcohol Problems Screen

In several studies, Cherpitel (2000, 2002) found that a shortened version of the **Rapid Alcohol Problems Screen** (RAPS) was more effective than the CAGE and other standard screening instruments in detecting alcohol dependence across gender and ethnic groups. The **RAPS4** contains four items, each of which has shown high sensitivity and specificity in identifying individuals with alcohol dependence. These four items relate to guilt about drinking (*Remorse*), blackouts (*Amnesia*), failing to do what was normally expected (*Perform*), and need for an eye opener or morning drink (*Starter*). Individuals who respond positively to any one of these items should be referred for a more thorough assessment of alcohol problems. The RAPS4 possesses strong specificity and sensitivity (Alcohol Research Group, n.d.).

Michigan Alcoholism Screening Test

The **Michigan Alcoholism Screening Test** (MAST), which has received wide usage over the years, is a brief 24-item instrument that can be answered by the client in fewer than 15 minutes (Evans, 1998; Selzer, 1971). The items describe (a) symptoms of excessive drinking, (b) various problems (e.g., social, family, work, legal, and health) that an individual may have encountered as a result of drinking, (c) concerns expressed by others about an individual's drinking, and (d) efforts that an individual may have made to control drinking or to obtain treatment for excessive drinking. In addition to the original MAST, a 24-item geriatric version (MAST-G) addresses concerns more pertinent to how a retirement status may relate to alcohol abuse. Furthermore, there is a shortened version of the MAST, the 13-item SMAST (Selzer, Vinokur, & van Rooijen, 1975).

The instrument and the scoring weights for each item are shown in Figure 8.1. Scores of 5 or more indicate alcoholism, scores of 4 suggest the possibility of alcoholism, and scores

MICHIGAN ALCOHOLISM SCREENING TEST (MAST)

Instructions: Please answer each question "Yes" or "No" as it pertains to you.

(2) *1. Do you feel you are a normal drinker?
(2) 2. Have you ever awakened in the morning after some drinking the night before and found that you could not remember a part of the evening before?
(1) 3. Does your spouse (or do your parents) ever worry or complain about your drinking?
(2) *4. Can you stop drinking without a struggle after one or two drinks?
(1) 5. Do you ever feel bad about your drinking?
(2) *6. Do friends or relatives think you are a normal drinker?
(0) 7. Do you ever try to limit your drinking to certain times of the day or certain places?
(2) *8. Are you always able to stop drinking when you want to?
(5) 9. Have you ever attended a meeting of Alcoholics Anonymous (AA)?
(1) 10. Have you gotten into fights when drinking?
(2) 11. Has drinking ever created problems with you or your spouse?
(2) 12. Has your spouse (or other family member) ever gone to anyone for help about your drinking?
(2) 13. Have you ever lost friends or girlfriends/boyfriends because of drinking?
(2) 14. Have you ever gotten into trouble at work because of drinking?
(2) 15. Have you ever lost a job because of drinking?
(2) 16. Have you ever neglected your obligations, your family, or your work for two or more days in a row because you were drinking?
(1) 17. Do you ever drink before noon?
(2) 18. Have you ever been told you have liver trouble? Cirrhosis?
(5) 19. Have you ever had delirium tremens (DTs), severe shaking, heard voices, or seen things that weren't there after heavy drinking?
(5) 20. Have you ever gone to anyone for help about your drinking?
(2) 21. Have you ever been in a hospital because of drinking?
(2) 22. Have you ever been a patient in a psychiatric hospital or on a psychiatric ward of a general hospital where drinking was part of the problem?
(2) 23. Have you ever been seen in a psychiatric or mental health clinic, or gone to a doctor, social worker, or clergyperson for help with an emotional problem in which drinking had played a part?
(2) 24. Have you ever been arrested, even for a few hours, because of drunk behavior?
(2) 25. Have you been arrested for drunk driving after drinking?

*Negative responses to these items indicate alcoholism; for all other items, positive responses indicate alcoholism.

Figure 8.1
Items and Scoring Weights (Shown in Parentheses) for the Michigan Alcoholism Screening Test

Note. Adapted from "The Michigan Alcoholism Screening Test: The Quest for a New Diagnostic Instrument," by M. L. Selzer, 1971, *American Journal of Psychiatry, 127,* p. 1655. This instrument is in the public domain.

of 3 or less indicate the absence of alcoholism. Some authorities have suggested using a higher cutoff score (as high as 13) to reduce the number of false positives (Ross, Gavin, & Skinner, 1990; Storgaard, Nielsen, & Gluud, 1994). Nevertheless, the MAST and SMAST demonstrate strong reliability and criterion-related validity (Selzer et al., 1975; Storgaard et al., 1994).

Research indicates that the MAST can effectively identify individuals with alcohol-related diagnoses (Mueller, Schumacher, Wetzlmair, & Pallauf, 2016; Teitelbaum & Mullen, 2000). However, MAST results should be confirmed by means of other assessment procedures. The MAST is limited in that its entire item content is obvious and it does not address substance abuse problems other than alcohol. For clients who may be defensive or who may have problems with drugs other than alcohol, other measures should be considered, such as the Substance Abuse Subtle Screening Inventory (see below).

The MAST and its alternative versions can be used routinely with all clients in a counseling service to detect possible alcohol problems that otherwise might be missed. Case Example 8.1 presents the use of the MAST with one client.

Case Example 8.1

Sally

Sally, a client at a community counseling service, received a score of 16 on the MAST. She answered Items 1, 2, 5, 6, 8, 10, 11, 12, and 23 in the scored direction. Friends had brought Sally to the counseling agency because of problems related to her drinking. Her score of 16 far surpassed the cutoff score of 5 used on the MAST to signal alcoholism.

The MAST contributed to counseling by emphasizing the importance of Sally's drinking problem. Information obtained from the MAST was confirmed by other information related to Sally's drinking habits. Her weekly consumption of alcohol (13 drinks) exceeded that of 97% of American women (see W. R. Miller & Muñoz, 2005; Vogeltanz-Holm, Lilienthal, Kulig, & Wilsnack, 2013). Counseling with Sally revealed that she came from a troubled family and she frequently fought with her mother while she lived at home. Sally reported low self-esteem and a perfectionistic nature. She described herself as demanding and dependent in her relationships. The counselor worked with her on family issues and relationship matters. Sally became more self-sufficient during the course of counseling and more confident in her relationships with others. She began to deal with some of the personal issues represented by her drinking problem. By addressing unresolved problems and using self-monitoring techniques, Sally was able to reduce the amount of her drinking during the course of counseling.

• • •

Substance Abuse Subtle Screening Inventory–4th Edition
The **Substance Abuse Subtle Screening Inventory–4th edition (SASSI-4)** was designed as a screening instrument for detecting adults who may be suffering from substance abuse, especially those who may be defensive or who may deny problems (SASSI Institute, 2016). It is a brief paper-and-pencil instrument that can be completed in 15 minutes and hand scored within a few minutes. It can also be administered by computer or audio recording. According to a survey of 350 addiction counselors, the SASSI is used more often and considered to be more important than any other substance abuse screening instrument (Juhnke, Vacc, & Curtis, 2003).

The SASSI-4 provides scores on 10 scales, including face valid and subtle scales. The face valid scales ask about the frequency of alcohol and other drug usage and problems. The subtle scales contain a number of true/false items about matters that may be indirectly associated with substance abuse. The SASSI effectively identifies individuals with substance abuse problems (Lazowski, Miller, Boye, & Miller, 1998; SASSI Institute, 2016).

Another form of this instrument, known as the **SASSI-A2** (Adolescent version, 2nd ed.), can be used with people ages 12 to 18 years old. Furthermore, a Spanish version of the SASSI exists (**Spanish SASSI**), as does the Substance Abuse Screener in American Sign Language (**SAS-ASL**; SASSI Institute, 2016).

Alcohol Use Disorders Identification Test

The **Alcohol Use Disorders Identification Test (AUDIT)** is a 10-item screening tool used to detect alcohol dependence and its consequences. The AUDIT was developed by the WHO over the course of two decades in six countries. The AUDIT identifies three levels of drinking: hazardous or risky drinking (individual at risk for alcohol-related consequences), harmful drinking (presence of physical or mental consequences), and alcohol dependence. AUDIT items refer to recent alcohol use, alcohol dependence symptoms, and alcohol-related problems; items are strong in distinguishing between low-risk and high-risk drinkers. Items 1–3 detect hazardous drinking, Items 4–6 identify alcohol dependence symptoms, and Items 7–10 screen for harmful drinking (Babor et al., 2001).

The AUDIT can be completed as a self-report format or clinician interview. Items are ranked on a 5-point scale (see Figure 8.2). Authors of the second edition AUDIT manual (Babor et al., 2001) provided interventions based on scoring, with a cutoff score of 8 or higher: Scores of 0–7 warrant alcohol education; 8–15, advice on alcohol use; 16–19, advice and brief counseling and ongoing monitoring; and 20–40, referral to a specialist for evaluation and treatment. The AUDIT demonstrates sensitivity estimates in the mid .90s and specificities in the mid .80s. It is equally useful for males and females (Babor et al., 2001). In addition, it has low sensitivity but high specificity for patients over age 65 (J. E. Powell & McInness, 1994). The instrument correlates strongly with the MAST ($r = .88$; Bohn, Babor, & Kranzler, 1995) and CAGE ($r = .78$; R. D. Hays, Merz, & Nicholas, 1995).

In addition to the AUDIT, two shortened forms of the instrument exist: the **AUDIT-3** and **AUDIT-4**, which contain three and four items, respectively. Gual, Segura, Contel, Healther, and Colom (2002) noted that these versions provided similar results as the original AUDIT.

Addiction Severity Index

The **Addiction Severity Index** (ASI) assesses the impact of the client's use of alcohol or other drugs on the client's medical status, employment or school status, legal status, family and social relationships, and psychiatric status (McLellan et al., 1992). According to Budman (2000), this instrument has become the standard measure of substance abuse in many agencies, with more than 1 million administrations a year in the United States. Now in its sixth version, the ASI yields internally consistent and valid information regarding a client's functioning even when administered in less-than-ideal circumstances, such as inner-city alcohol and drug abuse clinics (Denis, Cacciola, & Alterman, 2013).

There are alternative formats of the ASI. For example, the ASI may also be administered in a multimedia version (called the **ASI-MV**) by virtual interviewers. The ASI-MV provides computer-generated ratings of addiction severity that match (or surpass) those of trained interviewers in terms of reliability and validity (Budman, 2000). Moreover, there is a follow-up version (**ASI-FU**) and an adolescent version (**T-ASI-2**; Brodey et al., 2008). Furthermore, the ASI was recently modified to focus on alcohol, drugs, tobacco, and gambling (**mASI**; Denis et al., 2016). Psychometric data for the mASI support its nine independent domains for addiction screening. Thus, the mASI allows counselors a more comprehensive assessment of addiction than the ASI.

Comprehensive Drinker Profile

The **Comprehensive Drinker Profile** (CDP) is a structured intake interview procedure requiring 1 to 2 hours for completion (Marlatt & Miller, 1984). It provides detailed infor-

Instructions: Place an "X" in one box that best describes your answer to each question.

Question	0	1	2	3	4
1. How often do you have a drink containing alcohol?	*Never*	*Monthly or less*	*2–4 times a week*	*2–3 times a week*	*4 or more times a week*
2. How many drinks containing alcohol do you have on a typical day when you are drinking?	*1 or 2*	*3 or 4*	*5 or 6*	*7 to 9*	*10 or more*
3. How often do you have six or more drinks on one occasion?	*Never*	*Less than monthly*	*Monthly*	*Weekly*	*Daily or almost daily*
4. How often during the last year have you found that you were not able to stop drinking once you had started?	*Never*	*Less than monthly*	*Monthly*	*Weekly*	*Daily or almost daily*
5. How often during the last year have you failed to do what was normally expected of you because of drinking?	*Never*	*Less than monthly*	*Monthly*	*Weekly*	*Daily or almost daily*
6. How often during the last year have you needed a first drink in the morning to get yourself going after a heavy drinking session?	*Never*	*Less than monthly*	*Monthly*	*Weekly*	*Daily or almost daily*
7. How often during the last year have you had a feeling of guilt or remorse after drinking?	*Never*	*Less than monthly*	*Monthly*	*Weekly*	*Daily or almost daily*
8. How often during the last year have you been unable to remember what happened the night before because of your drinking?	*Never*	*Less than monthly*	*Monthly*	*Weekly*	*Daily or almost daily*
9. Have you or someone else been injured because of your drinking?	*No*		*Yes, but not in the last year*		*Yes, during the last year*
10. Has a relative, friend, doctor, or other health care worker been concerned about your drinking or suggested you cut down?	*No*		*Yes, but not in the last year*		*Yes, during the last year*

Figure 8.2
Alcohol Use Disorders Identification Test (Questionnaire Version)

Note. From *The Alcohol Use Disorders Identification Test: Guidelines for Use in Primary Care* (2nd ed.), by T. F. Babor et al., 2001, World Health Organization website: http://whqlibdoc.who.int/hq/2001/who_msd_msb_01.6a.pdf. This test is in the public domain.

mation regarding the history and current status of an individual's drinking problems and related matters. It assesses both consumption and problematic behaviors. Also available are a short form of the CDP, the Brief Drinker Profile; the Follow-Up Drinker Profile, a measure of client progress; and the Collateral Interview Form, an instrument for obtaining information from other people who are close to the client.

Timeline Follow-Back

The **Timeline Follow-Back** (TLFB) enables the client and the counselor to reconstruct the client's drinking or other drug-using behavior for the past year (Sobell & Sobell, 1996). It analyzes the patterns (e.g., daily, weekly, sporadically) and the intensity (light, heavy) of such behavior. Connections between drinking or other drug-use episodes and significant events ("anchor points") in the person's life are studied. Research indicates that the TLFB is reliable and valid when used with adult substance abusers (Wray, Braciszewski, Zywiak, & Stout, 2015), including those from different countries and cultures (Fals-Stewart, O'Farrell, Feitas, McFarlin, & Rutigliano, 2000; Sobell et al., 2001). TLFB reports obtained from clients agree reasonably well with those that are obtained from clients' partners or from urine assays. This procedure yields information that is enlightening to clients as well as to counselors.

Alcohol Use Inventory

The **Alcohol Use Inventory** (AUI) is a comprehensive self-report inventory that assesses patterns of behavior, attitudes, and symptoms pertaining to the use of alcohol for individuals 16 years and older (Horn, Wanberg, & Foster, 1986). Most people complete the AUI, which requires a sixth-grade reading level, within 35 to 60 minutes. It contains 24 scales based on 228 items organized at three levels: 17 primary scales, six second-order scales, and one general alcohol use scale. The scales evaluate alcohol usage in terms of benefits, styles, consequences, and concerns. It is most appropriate for individuals who enter a treatment program as a result of alcohol dependence or abuse. It can be used to establish a treatment plan for a person with alcohol-related issues.

Activity 8.1
Selecting Substance Abuse Assessments

Select one of the substance abuse assessments discussed in this section. Use assessment sources discussed earlier in the text to collect psychometric information on the assessment. Reflect on the following questions:

- What is the psychometric evidence (e.g., reliability, validity, standardization sample, scoring information) for the assessment? How strong is this evidence?
- How would you use this instrument in your practice?
- What are some multicultural and social justice implications of using the tool with diverse populations?

Present the information to the larger group.

Self-Monitoring Methods

Self-monitoring can enhance assessments made by means of interview procedures in a number of ways. Because self-monitoring is based on planned observations, data obtained in this manner should be more accurate and more complete than data based on recall. Self-monitoring has the added advantage of helping clients to see more clearly the relationship between certain events and their drinking behavior. Finally, self-monitoring provides a means of plotting the client's progress in controlling drinking behavior.

Self-monitoring charts typically include the amount of alcohol consumed in a given period of time, the situation in which the alcohol was consumed, and the presence of other people (Krenek, Lyons, & Simpson, 2016). The thoughts or feelings of the person at the time may also be recorded. Temptations to drink, as well as actual drinking behavior, may be tracked.

Self-monitoring assumes that individuals will comply with the instructions to keep a regular record of their drinking. Such recording can be facilitated by use of a log book, handheld computer, or telephone answering service. For example, the use of an interactive voice response system allows clients to record by telephone a log of their drinking. This type of system has proved to increase accuracy of reporting and lead to reduction in drinking by itself without additional interventions (Helzer, Badger, Rose, Mongeon, & Searles, 2002; Krenek et al., 2016; Searles, Helzer, Rose, & Badger, 2002).

Motivational Interviewing

Motivational interviewing (MI), as described by W. R. Miller and Rollnick (2013), can be looked on as a type of guided self-assessment. The counselor, in an empathic, nonjudgmental manner, explores with clients a particular behavior in which change is desired (e.g., excessive drinking or unsafe sex). MI was developed specifically to assist clients who were less ready to change, with support for its use in evaluating and treating substance abuse (Martins & McNeil, 2009). The counselor aids the client in identifying and clarifying ambivalent feelings regarding the problematic behavior, and ambivalence is viewed as a natural part of the change process (Glynn & Moyers, 2010; W. R. Miller & Moyers, 2005).

There are four guiding principles to MI (W. R. Miller & Rollnick, 2013). First, counselors *express empathy*. Empathy is communicated through reflective listening, a technique whereby counselors make a reasonable guess of what the client states to help minimize resistance. Counselors may also want to frequently summarize what the client is saying. Second, counselors *develop discrepancy* for the client. Specifically, counselors help the client recognize discrepancy between behavior and stated values and goals. Third, counselors *roll with resistance*. This principle requires that counselors be patient with the client maintaining a status quo of ambivalence. Counselors avoid pressuring the client and continually look for intrinsic motivation for the client to change. Finally, counselors *support self-efficacy*. This principle involves conveying to clients they are capable of making change.

In one MI study, the interviewer asked college students (all of whom had engaged in excessive drinking) to prepare a written list of pros and cons for drinking alcohol (LaBrie, Pedersen, Earleywine, & Olsen, 2006). The interviewer, while maintaining a neutral position, helped students to make sure that they had evaluated all aspects of their drinking behavior, often by the use of reflections, open-ended questions, and prompts as part of the assessment process. Follow-up research indicated that the students significantly reduced their drinking. The success of this approach was attributed to the careful assessment of pros and cons (called the decisional balance method) within the context of a supportive, nonconfrontational interview. In essence, the assessment also became the treatment.

Tip Sheet
Substance Abuse Assessment Procedures in Counseling

✓ Be sure to ask about the use of alcohol or other drugs as part of the intake procedure. It is important to diagnose and treat a substance use disorder early in counseling when the client is under duress and less guarded.

✓ In addition to individual assessment, assess the environment in which drinking takes place.

✓ Be alert to possible substance abuse problems of individuals with other *DSM* diagnoses. Dual diagnoses involving substance abuse with other mental disorders are relatively common.

✓ Be aware of crucial signs ("red flags") that indicate possible substance abuse. In the case of adolescents, these red flags include such matters as physical or sexual abuse, parental substance abuse, peer involvement in substance abuse or serious delinquency, sudden downturns in school performance or attendance, marked change in physical health, HIV high-risk activities, and severe depression.

✓ Inquire about problems related to drinking. Abusive drinking may be most evident in the problems it produces. Checklists can be helpful for this purpose. For example, "An Inventory of Alcohol-Related Problems" lists 45 drinking-associated problems that can be used by clients to review the outcomes of their drinking behavior (W. R. Miller & Muñoz, 2005; W. R. Miller & Rollnick, 2013).

✓ Ask if other people have been concerned about the client's drinking behavior. Use screening measures such as the CAGE or RAPS4.

✓ Keep the *DSM* criteria in mind in assessing for alcohol dependence or abuse. Determine frequency, duration, and severity of pertinent symptoms. Remember that these same criteria can be used in assessing other types of psychoactive substance dependence or abuse.

✓ If alcohol or other drug problems are detected, use a more thorough assessment procedure to gain a better understanding of the problem or refer the client to specialists for this purpose.

✓ Engage the client in self-assessment. Self-monitoring of drinking behavior can be helpful both in defining the problem and in gauging the success of treatment efforts. MI can help clients assess and resolve ambivalent attitudes toward drinking.

✓ Help clients to become aware of those situations that may trigger drinking for them, such as being with a friend who drinks heavily or drinking late at night.

✓ Teach the use of blood alcohol concentration (BAC) tables to clients with drinking problems so that they can assess the influence of alcohol consumption on their judgment and reaction time (W. R. Miller & Muñoz, 2005). Help them to use these tables to set alcohol consumption limits.

✓ When clients do not accept the fact that they have a problem controlling their drinking (an essential feature of dependency), ask them to try to limit their drinking to a certain amount (e.g., no more than three drinks) on any one occasion for a period of 3 months. This technique has sometimes been referred to as the "acid test" of an individual's ability to control drinking behavior.

✓ If denial appears to be a problem, obtain permission from the client to speak with family members or friends as a means of gaining information about his or her drinking behaviors. Interview these people with the client present in the room.

✓ Use information from all available sources, including work, school, and community records or personnel. Assessment will be more accurate if it is based on multiple sources of information.

✓ Seek supervision to avoid frustration and to improve skills for gathering information from clients who may be in a state of denial.

✓ Refer clients with persistent drinking problems to specialists for assessment and treatment. Assessment should include a physical exam by qualified medical personnel. Inpatient or intensive outpatient treatment in a multidisciplinary setting may be necessary.

Assessment of Depression

As indicated at the beginning of this chapter, mood disorders—including anxiety disorders, major depressive disorder, and bipolar disorder—are the most prevalent mental disorders in the United States (NIMH, n.d.). One of the most common mood disorders is major depressive disorder: In 2014, approximately 6.7% of U.S. adults reported at least one major depressive episode within that year (SAMHSA, 2015a). Women are 70% more likely than men to experience depression during their lifetime, and non-Latino Blacks are 40% less likely to experience depression over their lifetime than non-Latino Whites (although as discussed in Chapter 4 they may be diagnosed with more severe diagnoses; Kessler, Berglund, Demler, Jin, & Walters, 2005). The prevalence of major depressive disorder among U.S. adolescents ages 12 to 17 was 11.4% in 2014 (SAMHSA, 2015a). Given the prevalence of this disorder, as well as the notion that depression is a characteristic of multiple mental health and comorbid disorders, it is important that counselors regularly assess depression.

A large number of self-rating scales have been devised to assess depression. Several of the most popular instruments of this sort are discussed below.

Beck Depression Inventory–II

The **Beck Depression Inventory–II** (BDI-II) replaced the BDI, which was first published in 1961 (Beck, Steer, & Brown, 2003). The current version reflects *DSM-5* criteria for depression more closely than did the earlier version. The BDI-II can be used with clients as young as 13 years of age. The BDI-II includes 21 items that describe symptoms of depression of an affective, cognitive, behavioral, or physiological nature (Beck et al., 2003). Each item uses a 4-point scale of severity ranging from 0 to 3. Clients mark the level of severity for each symptom that best describes how they have been feeling over "the past 2 weeks, including today."

Most clients complete the BDI-II within 5 to 10 minutes. Scoring, which involves tallying answers for 21 items, takes just a minute. For this reason, it can easily be administered, scored, and interpreted as part of a regularly scheduled counseling interview. Scores on the BDI-II are internally consistent for college students and psychiatric outpatients but are subject to change over time (Beck et al., 2003). The BDI-II was designed to be highly sensitive to changes in mood over short time periods. If people experience significant changes in their lives or if they are responding positively to a counseling program, their BDI-II scores should reflect these events. Validity studies indicate that the BDI-II total score effectively differentiates between depressed and nondepressed individuals (Beck et al., 2003). Scores on the BDI-II correlate highly with clinical ratings of depression.

The BDI-II manual (Beck et al., 2003) recommends that scores be interpreted as follows: 0–13 = minimal depression, 14–19 = mild depression, 20–28 = moderate depression, and 29–63 = severe depression. These cutoff scores should be considered general guidelines. The counselor will need to obtain more information to judge the severity of a client's depression. The duration of the symptoms and the possible cause of the symptoms (e.g., loss of a loved one) need to be considered. If the symptoms are of short duration (less than 2 weeks) or if they can be attributed to a grief reaction, they are less likely to indicate psychopathology.

As a general rule, if the score exceeds 28, especially for two administrations of the BDI-II separated by 2 weeks, the counselor should consider referring the client for psychiatric evaluation and possible medication. The item content of the BDI-II can be easily reviewed with clients to obtain more information about a symptom. It usually helps to ask clients which items they are most concerned about. Counselors should pay particular attention to symptoms of hopelessness (Item 2) and suicidal thinking (Item 9). The counselor should be sure to evaluate the risk of suicide for such clients.

BDI-II scores for younger individuals often drop upon retesting, even without treatment. Depression for these individuals may be caused by situational factors, such as impending exams or relationship conflicts, which can change rather quickly. Such factors must be taken into account. For this reason, it is a good idea to readminister the BDI-II periodically during the course of counseling to help monitor changes that may occur. Information obtained from readministrations of the BDI-II can often be helpful in trying to decide if the client should be referred for additional assessment or treatment or if the client has made sufficient progress so that regular sessions are no longer needed. In summary, the BDI-II can be viewed as the test of choice for initially identifying individuals who may be experiencing depression (Stehouwer & Stehouwer, 2005). Additional assessment, especially a clinical interview, must be undertaken to ascertain a diagnosis of depression.

Children's Depression Inventory

The **Children's Depression Inventory 2** (CDI 2) is a self-report measure of depression for children and adolescents ages 7 to 17 years (Kovacs, 2015). This instrument, which is a downward extension of the BDI, consists of 28 self-report items written at a third-grade reading level. For each item, the child or adolescent chooses the one statement from among three listed that most closely describes his or her thoughts, feelings, or behaviors for the past 2 weeks. The CDI 2 has two scales (Emotional Problems and Functional Problems) and four subscales (Negative Mood, Negative Self-Esteem, Ineffectiveness, and Interpersonal Problems). It yields a total score as well as scale and subscale scores. In addition to the CDI 2, Kovacs has created a shortened 12-item version (**CDI 2 Self-Report [Short] Version**) and parent (**CDI-P**) and teacher (**CDI-T**) versions, each with two scales—Emotional Problems and Functional Problems (Kovacs, 2003).

The CDI is one of the most thoroughly researched of all instruments designed to measure depression in children. Although it was developed primarily for research purposes, it has been used increasingly for clinical purposes because of the lack of effective instruments in the field. Kovacs recommended that a *T* score of 65 be used to indicate possible depression in screening situations. If a client obtains a *T* score of 65 or greater on two administrations, he or she should then be evaluated by means of a diagnostic interview.

Atlas (2014) noted that the CDI 2 is a comprehensive assessment tool that can supplement other assessment information to identify and treat early depressive symptoms. The tool may be administered and scores using paper-and-pencil, online, and software methods.

Geriatric Depression Scale

The **Geriatric Depression Scale** (GDS) is a short, self-administered inventory that effectively differentiates between depressed and nondepressed older clients (Yesavage et al., 1983). It consists of 30 yes/no items that focus on affective and cognitive symptoms of depression. Items that assess somatic symptoms have been largely excluded because these items do not detect depression as well in older people as they do in younger populations. Holroyd and Clayton (2000) concluded that the GDS is "the best validated instrument" (p. 6) for measuring depression in geriatric clients who are not cognitively impaired. A shortened form of the GDS exists that includes 15 yes/no items.

Hamilton Depression Inventory

The **Hamilton Depression Inventory** (HDI) is a paper-and-pencil version of the Hamilton Depression Rating Scale, a well-established measure of depression for adults based on a clinical interview (W. M. Reynolds & Kobak, 1995). In contrast to the BDI-II, the HDI measures the frequency as well as the intensity of symptoms. Some of its 23 questions contain subquestions so that 38 items total are included. In addition to the total score, the HDI also provides a relatively pure measure of melancholia (HDI-Mel Scale)—that is, endogenous (originating within the organism) depression—which can be helpful in identifying individuals who may benefit from antidepressant medications (Kobak & Reynolds, 2004). Scores on the HDI have proved to be highly effective in differentiating individuals with varying levels of clinical depression (Zimmerman, Martinez, Young, Chelminski, & Dalrymple, 2013).

Assessment of Anxiety and Fear

About one quarter of the U.S. population can be expected to experience an anxiety disorder sometime during their lifetime (Kessler, Berglund, et al., 2005; Merikangas et al., 2010).

Anxiety disorders, which tend to be chronic, include social phobia, panic disorder, agoraphobia, simple phobia, generalized anxiety disorder, and related ailments. Approximately 18% of the population is likely to have experienced an anxiety disorder during any given year (Kessler, Chiu, et al., 2005). Women are 60% more likely than men to experience an anxiety disorder over their lifetime, and non-Latino Blacks are 20% less likely and Latinos 30% less likely than non-Latino Whites to experience an anxiety disorder (Kessler, Berglund, et al., 2005).

Popular measures of the symptoms of anxiety and fear are discussed below. **Anxiety** can be defined as a significant anticipation of a future threat leading to hypervigilance and cautious or avoidant behaviors (American Psychiatric Association, 2013). The cause of the anxiety is usually unknown or unclear. In contrast, **fear** is an intense emotional response to a known or imminent danger, such as snakes or crowded places.

State–Trait Anxiety Inventory

The **State–Trait Anxiety Inventory** (STAI), the most popular and well researched of all anxiety measures, was first published by Charles Spielberger and his associates in 1970; the current version (Form Y) was published in 1983 (Spielberger, Gorsuch, Lushene, Vagg, & Jacobs, 1983). The STAI consists of two scales: a State–Anxiety scale (S-Anxiety) that measures transitory anxiety and a Trait–Anxiety scale (T-Anxiety) that measures persistent anxiety. Both scales contain 20 items marked on a 4-point scale.

Instructions for the S-Anxiety scale ask clients to indicate how they feel "at this moment"; they indicate to what degree (*not at all, somewhat, moderately so,* or *very much so*) they may be experiencing different feelings, such as tension or calmness. Instructions for the T-Anxiety scale ask clients to rate how they "generally feel"; they indicate how often (*almost never, sometimes, often,* or *almost always*) they experience different feelings, such as restlessness or self-satisfaction. Responses to the S-Anxiety scale show the intensity of an individual's anxious response at the time of measurement; responses to the T-Anxiety scale show the frequency of such responses.

The STAI is untimed but can usually be completed within 10 minutes. The instrument can be easily hand scored; however, the scorer must take into account that approximately one half of the items measure the absence of anxiety, whereas the other half measure the presence of anxiety. For those items that measure the absence of anxiety, the scoring must be reversed.

Reliability studies indicate that scores on the S-Anxiety scale are internally consistent but can change substantially over time depending on the individual's circumstances. For example, scores on this scale can be expected to rise markedly when a person is confronted with a threatening situation, such as an exam or surgery. Individuals who score high on the S-Anxiety scale are usually experiencing a number of symptoms associated with activation of the autonomic nervous system, such as rapid heart rate, perspiration, shortness of breath, shakiness, and hot or cold flashes. Scores on the T-Anxiety scale are both internally consistent and relatively stable over time for most populations. Individuals who score high on the T-Anxiety scale will usually show a larger increase in their S-Anxiety scores in a threatening circumstance, especially in situations that involve social evaluations, than will individuals who score low on this scale. In addition to measuring anxiety proneness, the T-Anxiety scale also taps other psychological problems, especially depression (Bieling, Antony, & Swinson, 1998).

A children's version of the STAI, the **State–Trait Anxiety Inventory for Children** (STAI-C; Spielberger, Edwards, Montuori, & Lushene, 2013), has also been established for counselor use. The STAI-C consists of two 20-item scales (i.e., State and Trait) and provides extensive norms for fourth, fifth, and sixth graders. Internal consistency estimates for the scales are acceptable (total score = .82–.87), and evidence of concurrent and construct validity exists. Because the reading level for the STAI-C is relatively high, the STAI-C should be used only with elementary school students who possess above-average reading ability.

Beck Anxiety Inventory

The **Beck Anxiety Inventory** (BAI) was designed to measure symptoms of anxiety that are relatively independent of depression (Beck & Steer, 1993). The BAI parallels the BDI-II in its manner of construction and interpretation. Similar to the BDI-II, the BAI contains 21 items, each of which is answered on a 4-point scale. Each item measures a separate symptom of anxiety. Raw scores on the BAI are interpreted in terms of four categories (minimal, mild, moderate, or severe anxiety). As with the BDI-II, the BAI can easily be administered as part of the counseling interview to monitor a client's progress over time. The BAI results can be analyzed in terms of four clusters of scores—neurophysiological, subjective, panic, and autonomic—that can be helpful in differentiating among different types of anxiety disorders.

Social Phobia and Anxiety Inventory

The **Social Phobia and Anxiety Inventory** (SPAI; Turner, Beidel, & Dancu, 1996) is a 45-item assessment tool (with filtered items) that measures frequency of social phobia and agoraphobia symptoms: The scale ranges from 0 (*never*) to 6 (*always*). **Social phobia** is defined as having a persistent fear of public scrutiny and expressing anxiety symptoms that will be humiliating or embarrassing; agoraphobia refers to avoiding situations or places where escape might be difficult and having a fear of expressing panic-like symptoms (American Psychiatric Association, 2013). The three SPAI scores are Social Phobia, Agoraphobia, and Difference scores. The SPAI demonstrates strong evidence of various forms of reliability and validity.

Other Measures of Anxiety or Fear

The **Multidimensional Anxiety Questionnaire** (MAQ) provides scores for overall anxiety plus different types of anxiety or fears (physiological-panic, social phobia, worry-fears, and negative affectivity; W. M. Reynolds, 1999). According to Stein (2003), the MAQ is "an excellent choice of a current anxiety assessment tool for clinicians" (p. 601).

Other standardized inventories of anxiety or fear that are of interest to counselors include the **Test Anxiety Scale** (Sarason, 1980), **Mathematics Anxiety Rating Scale–Revised** (Plake & Parker, 1982), **Maudsley Obsessional–Compulsive Inventory** (Hodgson & Rachman, 1977), **Posttraumatic Stress Disorder Symptom Scale** (Foa, Riggs, Dancu, & Rothbaum, 1993), and **Fear Questionnaire** (Marks & Mathews, 1978). These instruments assess specific types of anxieties or fears often encountered by clients.

Several anxiety scales have been developed for special populations (C. R. Reynolds, Richmond, & Lowe, 2003). These include the **Adult Manifest Anxiety Scale for College Students** and the **Adult Manifest Anxiety Scale for the Elderly**, which have been described as "especially welcome instruments" (Kagee, 2005, p. 31) that counselors may find useful in their work with younger and older populations.

Assessment of Anger

Anger is a universal emotion that underlies hostile attitudes and aggressive behaviors. Assessment of anger can aid in crisis intervention and increase understanding of factors related to an individual's anger. An individual's anger can be assessed by means of the **State–Trait Anger Expression Inventory–2** (STAXI-2; Spielberger, 1999). This instrument is designed to measure the experience, expression, and control of anger in individuals who are 16 years of age or older. It consists of 57 items that can be completed in 10 to 15 minutes and scored in about 5 minutes. Norms are available for both adolescents and adults.

The STAXI-2 is analogous to the STAI in that it provides measures of anger both as a state (actual anger at any point in time) and as a trait (potential anger). The Trait–Anger (T-Anger) scale consists of two subscales: Angry Temperament and Angry Reaction. The State–Anger (S-Anger) scale has been subdivided into three subscales: Feeling Angry, Feel Like Expressing Anger Verbally, and Feel Like Expressing Anger Physically. In addition to the T- and S-Anger scales, the STAXI-2 contains several measures of anger expression and anger control. An Anger Expression Index provides an overall measure of total anger expression. Factor-analytic research supports the creation of the separate scales (PAR, Inc., 2012a).

Although initially developed for research purposes, the STAXI-2 can also be helpful in counseling situations by providing a format for considering the different dimensions of anger. The STAXI-2 provides a broad assessment of an individual's anger that can be useful in counseling clients with issues related to anger, hostility, and aggression. Although it provides a foundation for understanding and assessing anger, its scores may be somewhat difficult to interpret because of the unknown composition of the normative sample.

Assessment of Self-Injury

Self-injury is defined as deliberate actions (e.g., cutting, burning, head banging) resulting in physical injury to the self. These actions may or may not relate to suicidality. Self-injury is an increasing mental and public health issue among adolescents and young adults, with symptoms occurring for 4% to 39% of adolescents (Barrocas, Hankin, Young, & Abela, 2012; Craigen, Healey, Walley, Byrd, & Schuster, 2010). Women are 3 to 4 times more likely to report self-injury than men (McAllister, 2003), and there is a dearth of differential data by racial/ethnic membership (Craigen & Milliken, 2010). Self-injury typically gets diagnosed as major depressive disorder, obsessive-compulsive disorder, dissociative identity disorder, schizophrenia, adjustment disorder, or borderline personality disorder, among others (see American Psychiatric Association, 2013). Although these diagnoses may be accurate in some instances, it is likely that self-injury is being misdiagnosed because no official diagnosis of self-injury exists (Craigen & Milliken, 2010).

There are several self-injury assessments available to counselors today, for example, **Self-Injury Trauma Scale** (Iwata, Pace, & Kissel, 1990), **Self-Harm Inventory** (Sansone, Wiederman, & Sansone, 1998), **Self-Injury Questionnaire** (Alexander, 1999), **Deliberate Self-Harm Inventory** (Gratz, 2001), **Self-Injury Implicit Association Test** (Nock & Banjai, 2007), **Suicide Attempt Self-Injury Interview** (Linehan, Comtois, Brown, Heard, & Wagner, 2006), and **Self-Injurious Thoughts and Behaviors Interview** (Nock, Holmber, Photos, & Michel, 2007). Craigen et al. (2010) reviewed these seven self-injury assessments and provided useful psychometric information that can help counselors decide which structured assessment to use in clinical interventions with clients who engage in self-injurious behaviors (see Table 8.2).

Assessment of self-injury involves a comprehensive approach that includes both formal and informal assessment. Formal assessments include those mentioned in Table 8.2 as well as structured assessment protocols to evaluate correlates of self-injury, such as anxiety, trauma history, and depression. Informal assessment involves gathering and integrating information about the client's background, family history, peer and social support, environmental influences, emotional capacity and expression, and coping strategies (Craigen et al., 2010). In Assessment in Action 8.1, Dr. Laurie Craigen discusses her research and clinical work with clients who self-injure. In the discussion of her clinical practice, she provides a client example of a comprehensive assessment approach to evaluating and treating self-injurious behaviors.

Table 8.2
Self-Injury Assessments

Inventory	Author(s)	Year Created	Reliability	Validity	Use/Factors	Predictive Ability	Suicidality
SITS	Iwata et al.	1990	Test–retest		Assessing tissue damage as a result of self-injury	Able to predict current risk	Not evaluated
SHI	Sansone et al.	1998		Predictive; convergent	Identifying self-injury in conjunction with BPD	Predicts presence of borderline personality features	Can differentiate between high and low lethality
SIQ	Alexander	1999	Internal consistency; test–retest	Face; convergent; discriminant	Use with those who have suffered trauma	Measures intent to self-harm	Measures for major suicide concepts
DSHI	Gratz	2001	Internal consistency; test–retest	Construct; convergent; discriminant	Behaviorally based; clinical populations	Able to predict the features of self-injurious behaviors	Suicidal intent assessed
SI-IAT	Nock & Banjai	2007		Predictive	Assessing beliefs and identification with self-injury	Predicts suicidal ideation and behaviors	Evaluated and differentiated
SASII	Linehan et al.	2006	Interrater	Predictive; content	Provides descriptive information on suicidal and self-injurious behaviors	Evaluates past behavior; based on PHI	Suicidal intent and lethality of self-injurious behaviors
SITBI	Nock et al.	2007	Interrater; test–retest	Construct	To assess a wide range of self-injury-related constructs	None stated	Assesses gestures, plan, ideations, and attempts

Note. SITS = Self-Injury Trauma Scale; SHI = Self-Harm Inventory; BPD = borderline personality disorder; SIQ = Self-Injury Questionnaire; DSHI = Deliberate Self-Harm Inventory; SI-IAT = Self-Injury Implicit Association Test; SASII = Suicide Attempt Self-Injury Interview; PHI = Parasuicide History Interview; SITBI = Self-Injurious Thoughts and Behaviors Interview. From "Assessment and Self-Injury: Implications for Counselors," by L. M. Craigen et al., 2010, *Measurement and Evaluation in Counseling and Development, 43*, p. 5. Reprinted with permission from Sage Publications.

Assessment in Action 8.1
Self-Injurious Behavior

Ten years ago, I was introduced to my first client who was cutting herself regularly. At the time, I did not have the knowledge or skills to work effectively with this young woman. However, I was overwhelmed with the amount of emotional pain she was experiencing, and I made a commitment at that point forward to learn as much as I could to help her and other individuals like her struggling with self-injury. Thus, I have conducted qualitative research studies on the experiences that women have with counseling related to their self-injury as well as how they make meaning of their self-injurious behavior. Clinically speaking, I work regularly with individuals who harm themselves, and over the years I have developed a comprehensive assessment approach to evaluating and treating self-injurious behavior.

This comprehensive assessment approach with clients who self-injure can be best illustrated within the following vignette:

> Julia is a 22-year-old woman who self-referred for counseling services. Her presenting problem was anxiety and depression. She recently graduated from college and moved away to start her first professional job. During one of our sessions, I asked her how she typically copes with her anxiety and depression. In a hesitant tone, she revealed, "Some people cry, but I cut myself."

As a clinician, I have two primary responsibilities to Julia. First, I must respond therapeutically, in a supportive, empathic, and nonjudgmental manner. My additional responsibility is to properly assess Julia's self-injurious behavior. When working with clients who self-injure, assessment must occur at both a formal and an informal level.

Formal Assessments

I utilize structured assessment protocols to screen for correlates of self-injury, most commonly, anxiety, depression, and responses to trauma. Thus, in the case of Julia, I would likely have her complete the BDI-II and BAI. I would also select a self-injury assessment for her to complete to evaluate the frequency, lethality, and motivations related to self-injury. In the context of therapy, many clients may not be familiar with and/or comfortable with completing structured assessments. Thus, I think it is important to set the stage early with a client so that assessment protocols may be a regular piece of the counselor's and the client's work together, not only at the beginning of the therapeutic relationship, but also throughout their journey together.

In my experiences, the results of the formal assessments provide me with critical information to guide me in my treatment planning. Also, when clients complete assessments on issues correlated with self-injury—like anxiety, depression, and trauma—it provides me with a multidimensional view of self-injury. In other words, I learn about additional factors that may impact a client's decision to harm him/herself. In a way, these formal assessments allow me to paint a holistic picture of what exists beneath the surface of the wounds.

Informal Assessments

Informal assessments also allow me to create an accurate portrayal of the client's experiences with self-injury. In my experiences, I closely evaluate three main areas: psychological, biological, and environmental factors. The following represents a sample of some of the questions I attempt to explore with the client.

Psychological

- What coping strategies does the client employ to manage his/her emotions?
- Does the client have past experiences with mental illness?
- What role does the self-injury play in the client's life? (Is the self-injury a release, a distraction, a punishment, etc.)?
- Does the client experience any levels of dissociation when harming oneself?

Biological

- Does the client currently take or has he/she taken psychotropic medication?
- How does (did) the client respond to the psychotropic medication?
- Has the client had a recent medical evaluation? (Could there be a medical explanation for the client's self-injury?)

Environmental

- What social supports (peer and family) does the client have?
- Does the client have a family history of mental illness?
- What are the current environmental stressors that the client is experiencing?
- Is the client's experiences with self-injury interfering with his or her ability to sustain relationships, work, etc.?

The results garnered from examining these factors allow me to view my client in a holistic manner. Overall, my dual approach of informal and formal assessment creates a comprehensive approach to examining self-injury in clients. However, it is important that these two approaches are not conducted in isolation. The results of my formal assessments guide my informal assessment approaches as much as the responses I garner from my informal assessments guide my selection of formal assessment tools. Over the years, I have continually used this comprehensive approach to assessing self-injury. However, what continues to amaze me is that just as no client is the same, no assessment approach will be alike!

—Laurie Craigen, PhD
Mental Health Counselor and Assistant Professor,
Boston University School of Medicine

Assessment of Eating Disorders

The *DSM-5* (American Psychiatric Association, 2013) identifies several disorders classified as feeding and eating disorders, including pica, rumination disorder, avoidant/restrictive food intake disorder, anorexia nervosa, bulimia nervosa, and binge-eating disorder; the categories "other specified feeding and eating disorder" or "unspecified feeding or eating disorder" are intended to capture subthreshold disorders that are otherwise aligned with another disorder in the major category. With respect to traditional assessment of eating disorders, prevalence information related to anorexia nervosa, bulimia nervosa, and binge-eating disorder are presented here. It would behoove counselors to be aware of the *DSM-5* criteria for these disorders and compare these criteria to the item content of existing eating disorder assessments that were developed based on previous *DSM* versions.

Anorexia nervosa and bulimia nervosa tend to begin in adolescence or early adulthood. Women tend to make up about 90% of anorexia nervosa and bulimia nervosa cases, although it is important to note that little research has been conducted on eating disorders among other genders. The 12-month prevalence rate in young females is 0.4% and 1% to

1.5% for anorexia nervosa and bulimia nervosa, respectively (American Psychiatric Association, 2013). For binge-eating disorder, the prevalence is less skewed toward women, with 12-month rates of 1.6% (women) and 0.8% (men).

Individuals suspected of meeting *DSM* criteria for an eating disorder should be referred to an eating disorders clinic or health service with a multidisciplinary team that includes a physician, nurse, dietitian, and mental health professional. The person may require a complete medical examination, nutritional assessment, and psychological assessment. Treatment also entails cooperation among the different disciplines to help clients address medical complications, alter eating habits, and alleviate psychological problems by such means as improving social skills and self-image.

Individuals with eating disorders typically wait several years from the onset of the disorder before entering treatment. Early assessment of a person's eating problems can reduce the length of this time period. Counselors can use standardized tests to assess the severity of an individual's eating problems and to help structure a discussion on this topic in counseling. To ensure full and honest reporting, the counselor must establish a trusting relationship with the client before undertaking the assessment.

The Eating Attitudes Test and the Eating Disorders Inventory–3, both discussed below, are two widely used standardized measures available for evaluating eating problems. A third instrument, the Eating Disorder Diagnostic Scale, is a 22-item inventory that seems to be effective in diagnosing anorexia nervosa, bulimia nervosa, and binge-eating disorder in adolescent girls and young women (Stice, Fisher, & Martinez, 2004). In addition to these measures, the Questionnaire for Eating Disorder Diagnoses, which is based on *DSM-IV-TR* criteria, shows promise for use in counseling (Mintz, O'Halloran, Mulholland, & Schneider, 1997).

Eating Attitudes Test

The **Eating Attitudes Test** (EAT-26) is a 26-item screening inventory that measures the symptoms and behaviors associated with anorexia nervosa and other eating problems (Garner & Garfinkel, 1979). Total scores on the EAT-26 have clearly differentiated between individuals with and without eating disorders in research investigations (Mintz & O'Halloran, 2000). The scores are sensitive to treatment so those who have recovered from anorexia nervosa obtain scores similar to individuals without eating disorders.

The EAT-26 can be scored in terms of three subscales—Dieting, Bulimia, and Oral Control—to help determine the nature of the eating problems. The EAT-26 has been used effectively in a number of different cultural settings (e.g., Ahmadi, Moloodi, Zarbaksh, & Ghaderi, 2014; Alvarez-Rayón et al., 2004; Canals, Carbajo, & Fernández-Ballart, 2002; Uehara & Sakakibara, 2015) but may not be useful in evaluating eating disorders in sports (Rodriguez, Salar, Carretero, Gimeno, & Collado, 2015). Case Example 8.2 illustrates the use of the EAT-26 with a client in an intake interview.

Case Example 8.2

Jodie

Jodie's intake counselor asked her to take the EAT-26 as a means of reviewing her eating habits and assessing the need for a referral to an eating disorders clinic. Jodie had come to the community mental health service for assistance with relationship issues, family conflicts, and eating problems. She ate large quantities of bakery goods and sweets about once a week and then used laxatives to purge the extra food.

Jodie obtained a score of 36 on the EAT-26, which placed her almost 2 *SD* above the mean (98th percentile) of adult women. Scores above 30 suggest serious eating concerns. She marked *always* or *very often* to items such as "am terrified about being overweight," "am preoccupied with a desire to be thinner," and "feel that food controls my life." Her EAT-26 score and other intake data indicated that she could probably benefit from a referral to an eating disorders clinic with a multidisciplinary staff for a more thorough assessment of her eating and nutritional habits as well as her physiological and psychological well-being. After discussing the matter with her, the counselor made arrangements for such a referral.

• • •

Eating Disorders Inventory–3

The **Eating Disorders Inventory–3** (EDI-3) consists of 91 items that assess the psychological and behavioral characteristics that underlie eating disorders (Garner, 2005). It differs from the EAT-26 by the inclusion of personality items as well as behavioral and symptomatic items. The EDI-3 provides scores on 12 scales—three that measure attitudes and behaviors specific to eating disorders and nine that measure personality characteristics related to eating disorders. In addition, it yields scores on six composite scales: Eating Disorder Risk, Ineffectiveness, Interpersonal Problems, Affective Problems, Overcontrol, and General Psychological Adjustment.

In addition to the EDI-3 itself, the total EDI-3 assessment package includes two auxiliary forms: the EDI-3 Symptom Checklist and the EDI-3 Referral Form. The EDI-3 Symptom Checklist is used by clients to report frequency of symptoms related to eating disorders (e.g., dieting; exercising; binge eating; purging; using laxatives, diet pills, and diuretics; having a change in menstruation). This information is useful in forming a *DSM* diagnosis. The EDI-3 Referral Form is based on a short form of the EDI-3 and is used for screening and referral purposes in nonclinical settings, such as high schools, colleges, and athletic programs.

The EDI-3 manual provides normative tables for patients with various types of eating disorders (Garner, 2005). Both adolescent and adult clinical norms are provided. The EDI-3 scales produce reliable (internally consistent) results for people with eating disorders, and the EDI-3 has been shown to more correctly identify those at risk for eating disorders than its predecessor (Segura-Garcia et al., 2015). The results are somewhat less reliable for nonpatient samples, presumably because of the restricted range of scores for these samples. Validity studies with the EDI-3 and earlier forms of the EDI show that it differentiates patients with eating disorders from various control groups (general psychiatric patients, recovered patients, and nonpatients) in a variety of settings (Clausen, Rosenvinge, Friborg, & Rokkedal, 2011; Niv, Kaplan, Mitrani, & Shiang, 1998; Podar, Hannus, & Allik, 1999; Schoemaker, Verbraak, Breteler, & vanderStaak, 1997).

Activity 8.2
Selecting Mental Health Assessments

Select one of the mental health assessments discussed in the last half of the chapter. Use assessment sources discussed earlier in the text to collect psychometric information on the assessment. Reflect on the following questions:

- What is the psychometric evidence (e.g., reliability, validity, standardization sample, scoring information) for the assessment? How strong is this evidence?
- How would you use this instrument in your practice?

Present the information to the larger group.

Assessment of Attention-Deficit/Hyperactivity Disorder

Attention-deficit/hyperactivity disorder (ADHD) is a neurodevelopmental disorder characterized by inattention, hyperactivity, or impulsivity—or a combination of these—that impacts children and adults. ADHD is characterized by inattention and/or hyperactivity–impulsivity symptoms that impair social, educational, or occupational functioning (American Psychiatric Association, 2013). Symptoms must be pervasive, maladaptive, and inconsistent with normal developmental expectations in order for a diagnosis of ADHD to be made. Those symptoms must have occurred for at least 6 months, must occur in more than one setting (such as school and home), and must interfere with an individual's functioning. Symptoms must not be attributable to some other disorder, such as a learning disability, anxiety, or depression. For diagnosing ADHD in children and adolescents, counselors should obtain information from parents and guardians as well as teachers. For older adolescents and adults, information from third parties should be obtained whenever possible.

The *DSM-5* indicates that the prevalence of ADHD is about 5% in children and 2.5% in adults. In addition, ADHD tends to be more frequently occurring in males compared to females (i.e., 2:1 in children, 1.6:1 in adults). Furthermore, ADHD occurs in most cultures, although rates differ because of varying diagnostic practices (American Psychiatric Association, 2013). ADHD is not likely increasing in U.S. society over time: In a systematic review of 154 studies between 1985 and 2012 that reported on ADHD prevalence, Polanczyk, Willcutt, Salum, Kieling, and Rohde (2014) found no overall increase in the prevalence of the disorder. The authors contended, however, that increasing rates of ADHD diagnosis are likely related to awareness of the disorder as well as increased health care access among affected individuals and their families.

Because of potential problems with misdiagnosis, a multimodal approach should be used in assessing a client for possible ADHD (de la Cruz et al., 2015). Such an approach should include reports from parents and teachers (or other school professionals) as well as the client. Historical information and observational data may be obtained by interviews, questionnaires, and rating scales. Evidence should be obtained regarding the core symptoms of ADHD, age of onset, duration of symptoms, extent of functional impairment, and associated conditions.

Behavior rating scales, such as the **Behavior Assessment System for Children–Second Edition** (C. R. Reynolds & Kamphaus, 2005) and the **Achenbach System of Empirically Based Assessment** (Achenbach et al., 2003), can be used as screening devices to identify possible ADHD problems among a number of other behavioral problems. These instruments can be helpful in identifying children in need of further evaluation; however, they should not be relied on as a basis for diagnosing ADHD.

More specific scales, such as the **Conners' Rating Scales** (Revised)–ADHD Index and *DSM-IV* **Symptoms Scales** (Conners, 1997), **ADHD Rating Scale–IV** (DuPaul, Power, Anastopoulos, & Reid, 1998), and **Barkley Screening Checklist for ADHD** (Barkley & Murphy, 2006), focus specifically on ADHD symptoms. These instruments are relatively short, able to discriminate between children with and without ADHD, and sensitive to treatment effects (M. B. Brown, 2000). Given recent changes in *DSM* criteria for ADHD, these scales should be used with caution or at least interpreted in the context of *DSM-5* criteria. Studies indicate that ADHD-specific checklists are much more accurate than broadband scales in distinguishing between children with and without ADHD (American Academy of Pediatrics, 2000). The **Adult Attention Deficit Disorders Evaluation Scale** (McCarney & Anderson, 1996), **Conners' Adult ADHD Rating Scales** (Conners, Erhardt, & Sparrow, 1998), and **Brown Adult ADHD Rating Scales** (T. E. Brown, 1996) are instruments that may be used to assess symptoms among adults. Assessment in Action 8.2 provides a clinician's perspective on assessing ADHD symptoms across the life span.

Assessment in Action 8.2
Attention-Deficit/Hyperactivity Disorder

Attention-deficit/hyperactivity disorder (ADHD) is a challenging disorder to persons diagnosed with ADHD and to those who interact with those individuals. The challenge, of course, is how to help persons with ADHD achieve to their highest potential.

As a clinician, I believe the first step in any treatment plan is a careful and appropriate diagnosis. Clients who consult mental health professionals with ADHD-like symptoms present a unique challenge to the clinician. Some clients might have been advised by medical doctors or school officials that they were suffering with ADHD; others might have been prescribed medication as a primary means of treatment. Many clients with a diagnosis of ADHD have comorbid conditions that could complicate and confuse an appropriate diagnosis. Adult ADHD is a relatively new diagnosis for many mental health providers. Since ADHD has no adult onset, in order to make the diagnosis of adult ADHD, the clinician would have to establish a childhood diagnosis or symptomatology during assessment.

Mental health professionals who are familiar with the complexities of ADHD assessment recommend that the following diagnostic tools be used to produce an accurate diagnosis:

- Collect comprehensive medical, social, and academic evaluations of the potential client.
- Consider standardized assessment instruments for client, parent, and teacher(s). (In the case of adult ADHD, consider assessments for significant others.)
- Gather a detailed family history.
- Identify comorbid conditions.

This detailed information will serve the clinician in making an accurate assessment of the client who may have ADHD.

—Bonnie Erb, PhD
Licensed Professional Counselor, Virginia

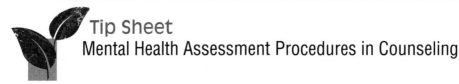

Tip Sheet
Mental Health Assessment Procedures in Counseling

✓ Mental illnesses, particularly anxiety and mood disorders, occur frequently in the United States. Counselors need to be able to detect psychopathology among clients in their caseload.

✓ Include both formal and informal assessment procedures (e.g., interviews, rating scales, structured assessments, questionnaires) when assessing mental health. Although several structured assessments were presented throughout the chapter, mental health symptoms can be assessed as part of the intake interview and/or mental status examination discussed in Chapter 7.

✓ Incorporate clinical data from third parties, including parents, guardians, partners, peers, and teachers. This information may assist you to confirm particular mental health disorders as well as assess degree and severity of impairment to the client's social, academic, or occupational functioning.

✓ Because some structured assessments were developed to mirror *DSM-IV* and *DSM-IV-TR* criteria, interpret results with some caution as you make diagnostic decisions based on the *DSM-5*.

✓ On a related note, interpret psychometric information for particular assessments with caution, as this information may be based on outdated criteria or on inappropriate or inadequate norms.

✓ Although prevalence rates indicate gender, age, and racial/ethnic differences for various mental disorders, carefully evaluate these rates with respect to your specific client. Prevalence rates may be underreported, particularly for males. In addition, as discussed in Chapter 4, racial/ethnic minorities may receive more severe diagnoses and thus may not be treated properly for anxiety and depression.

✓ Consider cutoff scores provided by mental health assessments as guidelines for clinical decision making. For example, other client data and your clinical judgment may indicate a mental health concern (or lack thereof) even if a score does not.

Chapter Summary

Counselors are to continually assess for major substance abuse and mental health issues within the variety of settings in which they work, particularly because substance abuse and mental disorders are prevalent in the United States. The chapter began with a discussion of alcohol abuse assessment tools that have been and can be adapted to assess for other types of substance abuse. Individual assessments include the CAGE Questionnaire, the RAPS, the MAST, the SASSI-4, and the AUDIT. More comprehensive substance abuse assessment tools include the ASI, CDP, TLFB, and AUI, as well as self-monitoring methods and MI techniques.

Assessment of mood disorders, including major depressive disorder and anxiety disorders, was then discussed. Assessments reviewed include the BDI-II, CDI, GDS, HDI, STAI, BAI, SPAI, and MAQ.

Additional mental health concerns such as anger, self-injury, eating disorders, and ADHD were also described. Assessments for these categories include the STAXI-2 as well as several self-injury tools, such as the Self-Injury Trauma Scale, Self-Harm Inventory, Self-Injury Questionnaire, Deliberate Self-Harm Inventory, Self-Injury Implicit Association Test, Suicide Attempt Self-Injury Interview, and Self-Injurious Thoughts and Behaviors Interview. With respect to eating disorders, major measures include the EAT and the EDI-3. ADHD assessments discussed include the Behavior Assessment System for Children–Second Edition, Achenbach System of Empirically Based Assessment, Conners' Rating Scale–Revised, ADHD Rating Scale–IV, Barkley Screening Checklist for ADHD, Adult Attention Deficit Disorders Evaluation Scale, Conners' Adult ADHD Rating Scales, and Brown Adult ADHD Rating Scales.

Although there are several quantitative assessment tools available to address a variety of substance abuse and mental health disorders, counselors may also use more qualitative assessments that evaluate criteria such as those outlined in the *DSM*.

Review Questions

1. What are the criteria for alcohol dependence? How might you assess for these criteria informally and formally?
2. What are the available screening measures for alcohol abuse? How do they compare?
3. How can MI be used when assessing for substance abuse?
4. What are the available assessments for depression and anxiety? How do they compare?

5. How might you conduct a comprehensive approach to assessing self-injury?
6. What are some of the challenges in assessing for ADHD?

Resources for Further Learning

Publications

DuPaul, G. J., & Stoner, G. (2014). *ADHD in the schools: Assessment and intervention strategies* (3rd ed.). New York, NY: Guilford Press.

Feit, M. D., Fisher, C., Cummings, J., & Peery, A. (2015). Substance use and abuse: Screening tools and assessment instruments. In J. S. Wodarski, M. J. Holosko, & M. D. Feit (Eds.), *Evidence-informed assessment and practice in child welfare* (pp. 123–133). New York, NY: Springer.

Miller, W. R., & Rollnick, S. (2013). *Motivational interviewing: Helping people change.* New York, NY: Guilford Press.

National Institute on Alcohol Abuse and Alcoholism. (1995). *Assessing alcohol problems: A guide for clinicians and researchers.* Bethesda, MD: Author.

National Institute on Alcohol Abuse and Alcoholism. (2005). *Helping patients who drink too much.* Retrieved from http://pubs.niaaa.nih.gov/publications/Practitioner/CliniciansGuide2005/clinicians_guide.htm

Web Resources

ADHD Institute, Assessment
> http://www.adhd-institute.com/assessment-diagnosis/assessment/
>> This link provides assessment resources for counselors working with individuals with ADHD.

Anxiety and Depression Association of America
> http://www.adaa.org/
>> The website of this organization provides general information about various mental health disorders, referrals for those seeking help, and advocacy opportunities.

National Eating Disorders Association, Online Eating Disorder Screening
> http://www.nationaleatingdisorders.org/online-eating-disorder-screening
>> This link is an online screening portal for detecting disordered eating symptoms.

National Institute on Drug Abuse, Chart of Evidence-Based Screening Tools for Adults and Adolescents
> https://www.drugabuse.gov/nidamed-medical-health-professionals/tool-resources-your-practice/screening-assessment-drug-testing-resources/chart-evidence-based-screening-tools-adults
>> This link provides a list of evidence-based screening tools for detecting substance abuse.

Section IV

Types of Assessment

Chapter 9

Assessment of Intelligence

Counselors who work in certain settings make use of intelligence test results for educational, vocational, and other types of placements. Some general knowledge of intelligence assessment is important because test results can influence many decisions clients make. This first chapter of Section IV outlines several types of individual and group assessments of intelligence, including a review of major theories of intelligence. The chapter concludes with literature on giftedness and creativity.

Test Your Knowledge

Select the most appropriate choice for each item.

_____ 1. Which of the following is typically *not* considered a traditional definition of intelligence?
    a. Capacity to learn   b. Ability to apply knowledge to new tasks
    c. Having interpersonal   d. Ability to adapt to an environment
       knowledge

_____ 2. All of the following are considered major intelligence theorists *except*:
    a. Binet   b. Wood
    c. Sternberg   d. Cattell

_____ 3. The following intelligence assessment is designed specifically for use with children:
    a. WAIS-IV   b. KABC-II
    c. WPT   d. SB5

❏ T ❏ F 4. IQ remains stable over an individual's lifetime.

❏ T ❏ F 5. Individuals of minority statuses are underrepresented in gifted education.

Theories of Intelligence

What is intelligence? Alfred Binet, in the early 1900s, conceptualized intelligence as a general ability to judge, to comprehend, and to reason well. Charles Spearman described intelligence as the result of understanding from previous experience, noting relationships, and applying knowledge to new tasks. Louis Thurstone (1924/1973) described it as the capacity for abstraction. David Wechsler (1944) explained intelligence as "the aggregate or global capacity of the individual to act purposefully, to think rationally and to deal effectively with his environment" (p. 3). Robert Sternberg (1985) interpreted it as the ability to adapt to one's environment throughout the life span. How do you define intelligence? Complete Activity 9.1.

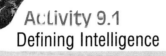

Activity 9.1
Defining Intelligence

How do you define intelligence? When you think of an intelligent person, what characteristics come up for you? What about characteristics of an unintelligent person? How do these compare? Discuss your responses as a large group.

Before presenting the major theories of intelligence, let's review some historical information on intelligence and assessment of intelligence. Recall from Chapter 1 that an interest in intelligence through individual differences began in the mid- to late 1800s, when psychologists (i.e., Wundt, Galton, Cattell) were influenced by Darwin's writings on genetic variation. They were interested in demonstrating individual differences through sensory processes and mental tests. Then, there was increased attention to formalized individual assessments to detect intellectual disabilities and emotional problems in children. These tests attended to both language and performance. With these formal tests of mental processes, psychometricians and other professionals (e.g., Sequin, Esquirol, Binet, Simon) could detect those needing special education programs because mental processes were assumed to increase as a child gets older. Three-year-olds could be expected to be able to point to their nose, eyes, and mouth and repeat two digits. The typical 7-year-old could distinguish right from left and name various colors; the typical 12-year-old could define various abstract words and make sense of a disarranged sentence, and so on.

In 1916, Lewis Terman, with the Stanford–Binet, made use of the concept of mental age developed by Binet and devised the concept of the now-outdated IQ (see Chapter 1). A mental age substantially below a child's chronological age was considered evidence of intellectual disabilities. This type of an IQ score has a number of problems connected with it. In the first place, answering all of the items correctly on the original Stanford–Binet yielded a maximum mental age of less than 20. Thus, anyone 20 or older automatically received an IQ score of less than 100. The usefulness of the ratio score therefore disappears during adolescence. In addition, the concept of a person's IQ has been erroneously viewed by the public as a fixed measure, similar to the color of a person's eyes, rather than as a particular score on a particular test at a particular time. The ratio IQ has therefore been replaced by a derived IQ standard score (known as the deviation IQ) to circumvent some of these problems.

Various definitions of intelligence helped to form theory, and theories helped shape actual assessments. Although the question of what it is that actually makes up intelligence and what it is that intelligence tests actually measure has long been the subject of much controversy, these theories and resulting assessments continue to be used today in academic settings. In the remainder of this section, some of the major theories of intelligence are presented, including Spearman's g factor, Thurstone's primary mental abilities, Cattell–Horn–Carroll theory of cognitive abilities, Sternberg's triarchic theory, and Gardner's multiple intelligences.

Spearman's g Factor

Charles Spearman (1863–1945), applying his work in factor analysis and correlation, asserted that intelligence consisted of a single general (g) factor and several specific ($s_1, s_2, \ldots$) factors.

Specifically, the **g factor** could be surmised from any broad range of cognitive tests, whereas an **s factor** was specific to a test or subtest. Spearman found that individuals who performed well on cognitive tests tended to perform well on others, and he assumed this meant there was an underlying factor of intelligence. He noted that the g factor was more influential to understanding intelligence than s factors; thus, he focused most of his theory description on a general factor of intelligence.

Spearman (1923) noted that some tests could be heavily loaded with a g factor whereas other, more sensory, tests contained primarily s factors. In addition, tests could contain both. He stated that tests with high loadings of g should correlate highly with one another. Figure 9.1 indicates graphically Spearman's g factor theory. The figure depicts the relationship of five intelligence tests or subtests to a general factor. Darker shaded areas represent aspects of a test that measure a general factor of intelligence; lighter shaded areas represent factors specific to a test (e.g., s factor) as well as any measurement error.

Thurstone's Primary Mental Abilities

Whereas Spearman conceptualized a general factor to explain intelligence, Louis Thurstone (1887–1955) argued that several group factors described intelligence better than a single general ability. Seven group or multiple factors have been labeled as **primary mental abilities**: verbal comprehension (e.g., vocabulary, reading comprehension), word fluency (e.g., anagrams, naming words based on some similarity), numerical ability (e.g., speed and accuracy of arithmetic ability), spatial visualization (e.g., mentally "seeing" a three-dimensional object being rotated), associative memory (e.g., pair association), perceptual speed (e.g., comparing visual details of objects), and reasoning (e.g., series completion tests). After conducting research, Thurstone later admitted the primary mental abilities were correlated with one another and thus there appeared to be a general factor with seven second-order factors.

Cattell–Horn–Carroll Theory of Cognitive Ability

One conceptualization by Raymond Cattell (1905–1998) and John Horn (1928–2006) divides general intelligence into two types: fluid and crystallized. **Fluid intelligence** is an individual's ability to be adaptable and flexible in solving new problems, independent of previous knowledge. It is the capacity to learn and behave intelligently. **Crystallized intelligence** deals with an individual's ability to solve problems and make decisions on the basis of acquired knowledge, experiences, and verbal conceptualizations. Essentially, crystallized intelligence is a result of experiential and cultural learning throughout one's lifetime and can be mediated by fluid intelligence. In fact, fluid and crystallized intelligence have been found to be moderately correlated with one another. Most of the tests in the content areas of verbal reasoning and quantitative reasoning would be considered crystallized intelligence, and those in the abstract/visual reasoning area would be considered fluid intelligence. In addition, several major intelligence tests measure both types of intelligence.

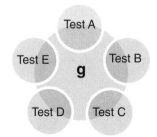

Figure 9.1
Spearman's g Factor Theory

The notion of fluid and crystallized intelligence was expanded by John Carroll (1916–2003). The current model indicates 10 broad abilities that include the following: fluid intelligence, crystallized intelligence, quantitative reasoning, reading and writing ability, short-term memory, long-term storage and retrieval, visual processing, auditory processing, processing speed, and reaction time. The **Cattell–Horn–Carroll theory of cognitive ability** has had a significant impact on many of the tests that have been constructed or revised since 1990 (Flanagan, 2008; Furnham & Mansi, 2014).

Sternberg's Triarchic Theory

Robert Sternberg (born 1949) developed the **triarchic theory of intelligence** that assumes intelligence is based on how well individuals process information. Essentially, there are three types of intelligence that interact with one another: componential intelligence, experiential intelligence, and contextual intelligence. **Componential intelligence** refers to the internal components or mechanisms, which include executive function, performance, and knowledge-acquisition components. These components are necessary to develop intelligent behavior. **Experiential intelligence** results from behaviors and experiences. Thus, past experiences allow one to address new experiences as well as automatize others. **Contextual intelligence** involves one's actions toward the environment, including selecting, adapting to, and influencing one's surroundings (Sternberg, 1994). Collectively, these intelligence types indicate how internal ability is shaped (and shapes) an external environment.

Gardner's Multiple Intelligences

Howard Gardner (born 1943) critiques in his model the traditional view of intelligence and thus intelligence testing. He theorized that intelligence is more than a general factor and noted there are eight types of intelligence, a model he referred to as **multiple intelligences**. These eight types are considered relatively independent from one another and include the following:

- musical intelligence: performance and composition of music;
- bodily–kinesthetic intelligence: control of bodily movements;
- logical–mathematical intelligence: problem-solving ability;
- linguistic intelligence: use of language;
- spatial intelligence: ability to work with 3-dimensional objects;
- interpersonal intelligence: interaction with and understanding of others;
- intrapersonal intelligence: self-awareness; and
- naturalistic intelligence: knowledge and understanding of nature.

Can you think of examples of individuals with one or more of these types of intelligence? How might you measure these? Gardner noted that individuals may possess some degree of all these types, although they probably have some that are more pronounced (Gardner, 2006). Various authorities have further argued that it is time to move beyond the general intelligence model that has dominated counseling and related professions over the past several decades and recognize a much broader view of what makes up intelligence, including such factors as creativity and practical intelligence (Sternberg, Kaufman, & Grigorenko, 2008) or the ability to plan and simultaneously process mental activities (Naglieri, Das, & Goldstein, 2012).

Individual Intelligence Tests

There are several individual intelligence tests that counselors should be aware of when working with clients of all ages. In this section, the most popular individual intelligence tests are described: Stanford–Binet, Wechsler scales, Kaufman batteries, Das Naglieri Cognitive Assessment System, and the Woodcock–Johnson tests.

Stanford–Binet (SB5)

The **Stanford–Binet** became the best-known intelligence test in the world and was used as the gold standard against which all other intelligence tests being developed were validated. The 1916 Stanford–Binet Intelligence Scale had a number of weaknesses and was therefore revised to produce the 1937 scale in two parallel forms (L and M). The ratio IQ score was eliminated, and standard scores were calculated to provide each age with a mean of 100 and a standard deviation of 16. A 1960 revision was developed, and that revision was restandardized in 1972 to provide more adequate norms intended to be representative of the entire U.S. population. A fourth edition was constructed in 1986, in which the authors attempted to provide a continuity with the previous editions by retaining the advantages of the early editions as an individually administered intelligence test and still take advantage of the more recent theoretical developments in cognitive psychology.

The Stanford–Binet Intelligence Scales, in its fifth edition (SB5), follows the Cattell–Horn–Carroll hierarchical model of cognitive abilities; the full-scale battery takes from 45 to 75 minutes to administer. It can be administered to examinees from 2 years to over 85 years of age.

As in the case of the previous editions, individuals are administered a range of tasks suited to their abilities. Testing is begun with two routing subtests (Object Series-Matrices and Vocabulary) to determine the starting point for the remaining subtests. Depending on the performance on these subtests, the examiner begins at one of five developmental levels on each of the other eight tests. Testing then proceeds on each test until at least three out of four items are missed, which determines a ceiling level on that test at which further items can be expected to be answered incorrectly. The routing subtests take only 15 to 20 minutes to administer and can be used by themselves as an abbreviated IQ test.

The battery yields a Full Scale IQ score, Nonverbal and Verbal IQs, and five Factor Indices: Fluid Reasoning, Knowledge, Quantitative Reasoning, Visual–Spatial Processing, and Working Memory. Verbal tests require test takers to read and speak age-appropriate English. Nonverbal tests require fine-motor coordination for manipulating and pointing to objects (Kush, 2005). Standard scores have a mean of 100 but, unlike previous editions, have a standard deviation of 15, as in other major intelligence tests. Individual subtest scores have a mean of 10 and a standard deviation of 3. A standardization sample of 4,800 individuals was stratified by age, gender, race/ethnicity, geographic region, and educational attainment to match U.S. census data.

High reliability of SB5 scores has been reported for all three of the methods used—internal consistency, test–retest, and interscorer agreement. Internal consistency coefficients ranged from .95 to .98 for the IQ scores and from .90 to .92 for each of the Factor Index scores. The 10 subtest reliabilities ranged from .76 to .91. Test–retest reliability coefficients of .89 to .95 for the IQ scores and .83 to .95 for the Factor Index scores were reported. Interscorer agreement was also high (median correlation = .90). Standard errors of measurement are 2.30 for Full Scale, 3.26 for Nonverbal, and 3.05 for Verbal IQs. High correlations with other cognitive tests, including the Wechsler scales and previous editions of the Stanford–Binet, give evidence of convergent validity (Bain & Allin, 2005). A confirmatory factor analysis of the subtests yielded evidence for the five-factor solution. Construction of the SB5 was based on a five-factor hierarchical model of intelligence from overall (Full Scale IQ, or g), to a second level of domains (Five Factors), to a third level of subtests (Kush, 2005).

The SB5 may be hand scored, or counselors can be assisted by a computer program that generates an extended score report. The factor Working Memory was added to the SB5. This factor, which was not in the previous edition, is related to children's learning problems and includes an increased number of nonverbal measures that are useful in working with clients from diverse backgrounds. There are more high-end items to assess gifted performance and more low-end items to better measure children and adults who are functioning at a low level. The colorful toys and materials are especially appealing to children (J. A. Johnson, D'Amato, & Harrison, 2005; Roid, 2003).

Wechsler Scales

The Stanford–Binet was originally developed for children, with some more difficult items added for adults. David Wechsler, working at Bellevue Hospital in New York, believed that there was a need for an intelligence test more suitable for adults, and he therefore developed the Wechsler Bellevue Intelligence Scale in 1939. In addition, believing that the Stanford–Binet placed too much emphasis on language and verbal skills, he developed a totally different performance scale measuring nonverbal intelligence.

Wechsler Adult Intelligence Scale–Fourth Edition

The 1939 scale was revised in 1955 to correct a number of deficiencies that had been found in the earlier form; this revised form became the **Wechsler Adult Intelligence Scale** (WAIS). The WAIS was revised again in 1981 to produce the WAIS-R and was standardized on a sample selected to match the proportions of the U.S. population in regard to race, occupational level, education, and residence (Wechsler, 1981). During the 1990s, a third edition was developed by adding three new optional subtest scores on four factor-analysis-based indices. The fourth revision in 2008 (WAIS-IV), the most recent edition, continues to be a measure of general intelligence through 15 subtests. This revision significantly improves on the previous editions by expanding psychometric properties, developmental appropriateness, and user-friendliness. For example, subtests involving manipulating objects (i.e., Object Assembly, Picture Arrangement) were dropped to leave only one subtest for this purpose (i.e., Block Design). In addition, the Digit Symbol subtest was dropped, and the Verbal and Performance IQ tests are no longer provided (Canivez, 2010).

The 15 subtests of the WAIS-IV are Block Design, Similarities, Digit Span, Matrix Reasoning, Vocabulary, Arithmetic, Symbol Search, Visual Puzzles, Information, Coding, Letter–Number Sequencing, Figure Weights, Comprehension, Cancellation, and Picture Completion. The subtests load on four factors (i.e., Verbal Comprehension, Perceptual Reasoning, Working Memory, and Processing Speed), representing fluid and crystallized forms of intelligence and ultimately a g factor of intelligence (Climie & Rostad, 2011; L. G. Weiss, Keith, Zhu, & Chen, 2013). The Letter–Number Sequencing, Figure Weights, and Cancellation subtests are supplemental subtests to be used only with individuals ages 16 to 69. The entire instrument takes less than 2 hours to complete.

The WAIS-IV was normed on a sample of 2,200 stratified by age, gender, race/ethnicity, geographical region, and education level. There are limitations noted in the manual, which includes disclaimers for language and developmental/ability status considerations.

The WAIS-IV provides a Full Scale IQ (FSIQ), General Ability Index (GAI) and Index scores (i.e., index for each of the four factors), each with a mean of 100 and standard deviation of 15. Ten core subtests are used to generate the FSIQ score, whereas the GAI is calculated from six subtests. Subtest scores have a mean of 10 and standard deviation of 3 for 13 age groups (Canivez, 2010).

The WAIS-IV provides strong evidence for internal consistency, test–retest reliability, and interrater reliability. Spearman–Brown estimates across 13 age groups yield reliability estimate ranges of .97 to .98 (FSIQ), .87 to .98 (Index scores), and .71 to .96 (subtests) for the standardization sample. Test–retest reliabilities for an average of 22 days for four age groups were also strong. Interrater agreement ranged from .98 to .99 for most subtests, although subtests that required greater clinical judgment ranged from .91 to .97 (Canivez, 2010). The manual also provides psychometric evidence of strong content, construct, and criterion-related validity.

Although the WAIS-IV is a significant improvement over its predecessor, Climie and Rostad (2011) noted two weaknesses. First, administration, scoring, and interpretation are labor intensive and thus should only be used in high-stakes testing situations. Second, the test focuses more on "left-brain" intelligences acquired more typically in work or school settings.

Wechsler Intelligence Scale for Children (WISC-V)

The **Wechsler Intelligence Scale for Children** (WISC) was originally developed as a downward extension of the Wechsler Bellevue Intelligence Scale for use with children ages 6 to 16 years, 11 months. It was revised in 1974 (WISC-R) to contain more child-oriented items, to include more African American and female figures, and to provide a normative sample more representative of children in the U.S. population. A revised, updated, and restandardized edition was published in 1991 as the WISC-III, a fourth (WISC-IV) in 2003, and the most recent edition (WISC-V) in 2014. The WISC-V is available in paper-and-pencil or digital formats.

The WISC-V was standardized on 2,200 youth, with the sample stratified by race/ethnicity, parent education level, and geographic region. The developers of the latest revision took additional care to minimize cultural bias by removing potentially problematic items. In addition, special group studies include score ranges for populations such as, for example, those with intellectual disability, individuals with attention-deficit/hyperactivity disorder, people with autism spectrum disorder, English-language learners, and the gifted (Na & Burns, 2016). As Na and Burns (2016) noted, "The increased attention to theory and research and the emphasis on clinical utility (especially with regards to diagnosing learning disabilities) are welcome in the new edition" (p. 159).

The WISC-V framework includes five primary index scales, five ancillary index scales, and three complementary index scales; some of the secondary tests can be used as substitutes to calculate primary index scores as appropriate. Ten primary subtests are used to calculate the primary index scales, with seven of those subtests used to arrive at a full-scale score (FSIQ). The most recent version of the scale features additional measures for visual spatial ability, fluid reasoning, and visual working memory. An FSIQ, in addition to five primary index and three ancillary index scores, is provided. Furthermore, the fifth edition provides ancillary composite scores that may be useful in specific clinical situations.

The five primary index scales (with subtests in parentheses) are Verbal Comprehension (Similarities, Vocabulary, Information, Comprehension), Visual Spatial (Block Design, Visual Puzzles), Fluid Reasoning (Matrix Reasoning, Figure Weights, Picture Concepts, Arithmetic), Working Memory (Digit Span, Picture Span, Letter-Number Sequence), and Processing Speed (Coding, Symbol Search, Cancellation). Ancillary scales are as follows: Quantitative Reasoning, Auditory Working Memory, Nonverbal, General Ability, and Cognitive Proficiency. Complementary scales are Naming Speed, Symbol Translation, and Storage and Retrieval.

Classifications are provided for composite scores: 130 and higher (Extremely High), 120–129 (Very High), 110–119 (High Average), 90–109 (Average), 80–89 (Low Average), 70–79 (Very Low), and 69 and below (Extremely Low).

Wechsler Preschool and Primary Scale of Intelligence (WPPSI-IV)

In 1967, a downward extension of the WISC was developed for use with children 4 to 6.5 years of age called the **Wechsler Preschool and Primary Scale of Intelligence** (WPPSI). The current edition, the WPPSI-IV, was published in 2012 and can be administered to children ages 2.6 to 7.7. The WPPSI-IV was standardized using a sample of approximately 1,700 children in nine age groups stratified by age, gender, race/ethnicity, parent education level, and geographic region.

The WPPSI-IV provides a full-scale score (FSIQ), primary index scores, and ancillary index scores. Primary index scales vary by age subgroup but are as follows: Verbal Comprehension,

Visual Spatial, Working Memory, Fluid Reasoning, and Processing Speed. Ancillary index scales also vary by age subgroup and include Vocabulary Acquisition, Nonverbal, and General Ability.

Sample WPPSI subtests that make up full or index scale scores are as follows:

- Vocabulary: selecting an appropriate picture cited by an examiner from a set of four or providing definitions to words read aloud;
- Picture Naming: naming of pictures;
- Block Design: recreating a model or picture from a stimulus book using blocks;
- Object Assembly: fitting puzzle pieces together to form a meaningful whole within 90 seconds;
- Information: choosing a picture from four options in response to an examiner's informational question or responding to general knowledge topics;
- Word Reasoning: identifying a common concept among specific clues;
- Comprehension: responding to questions based on knowledge of general situations;
- Similarities: completing an incomplete sentence by identifying how concepts mentioned in the sentence are similar;
- Matrix Reasoning: selecting a missing portion of an incomplete matrix from several response options;
- Picture Concepts: choosing one picture per row from two or three rows to form a group;
- Bug Search: scanning a search group (in this case, bugs) and indicating whether a target symbol matches any of the others in the search group; and
- Picture Completion: viewing a picture and identifying the missing part.

Wechsler Abbreviated Scale of Intelligence

There is also a short-form Wechsler instrument, the **Wechsler Abbreviated Scale of Intelligence** (WASI; Wechsler, 1999). Taking only 15 to 30 minutes to administer and appropriate for individuals ages 6 to 89, the WASI is a brief measure tied to both the WISC-III and the WAIS-III. Although the WASI can be a suitable choice when a brief intelligence evaluation is needed, its reduced administration time does impact clinical accuracy compared to other measures, such as the WISC-IV and WAIS-IV. Furthermore, because its results are less stable, it should not be used when a more accurate estimate from a full version is needed (McCrimmon & Smith, 2012).

Kaufman Batteries

More recently, several tests—including the Kaufman tests and the Das Naglieri system—have been developed that make use of Luria's (1980) neuropsychological theory of intelligence. Known as the PASS model, this theory consists of *Planning* (selecting a strategy to efficiently solve a problem), *Attention* (selectively attending to a stimulus and inhibiting competing stimuli), *Simultaneous* (integrating several stimuli into a single whole), and *Successive* (working with things in a specific serial order).

The Kaufmans have developed several intelligence test batteries, including the **Kaufman Assessment Battery for Children** (KABC-II) and the **Kaufman Adolescent and Adult Intelligence Test** (KAIT). The KABC-II is composed of 18 subtests of which up to 10 are administered depending on the age of the child (American Guidance Service, 2005; Kaufman, Lichtenberger, Fletcher-Janzen, & Kaufman, 2005). It is designed for children 3 to 18 years old and yields scores on six different ability indices. It was standardized with the Kaufman Test of Educational Achievement. The KABC-II is considered to be more cross-culturally fair than most comparable tests of intelligence, in part because it separates processing scores from crystallized scores (Scheiber, 2016).

The KAIT consists of six core subtests and four additional subtests in an expanded battery and is normed for ages 11 to 85 years (Kaufman & Kaufman, 1993). It yields scores on both crystallized and fluid intelligence and a composite IQ score, each with reliability coefficients above .90. A short form, the Kaufman Brief Intelligence Test (Kaufman & Kaufman, 2002), which can be administered in 15–30 minutes, consists of a vocabulary (through pictures) portion and a matrices portion using pictures and abstract designs. It is useful when time constraints preclude the use of a longer measure.

Das Naglieri Cognitive Assessment System

Another instrument developed to provide a broader measure of children's cognitive abilities is the **Das Naglieri Cognitive Assessment System** (Naglieri, 2005). It contains 13 subtests (only 12 are used in any administration), yielding four scales labeled *Planning*, *Attention*, *Simultaneous*, and *Successive* (PASS) processing and a full-scale score ($M = 100$, $SD = 15$). Internal consistency and test–retest reliabilities are in the vicinity of .90, and the Planning and Attention scales assess concepts not found on traditional intelligence tests.

Woodcock–Johnson Tests of Cognitive Abilities (WJ IV)

The **Woodcock–Johnson Tests of Cognitive Abilities**, with the fourth edition published in 2014, are a series of 20 intelligence tests first developed in 1977. The scales are based in the Cattell–Horn–Carroll theory of intelligence and produce three composite scores, seven factor scores (i.e., Comprehension-Knowledge, Fluid Reasoning, Short-Term Working Memory, Cognitive Processing Speed, Auditory Processing, Long-Term Retrieval, Visual Processing), and six narrow ability scores or other clinical clusters (Quantitative Reasoning, Auditory Memory Span, Number Facility, Perceptual Speed, Vocabulary, Cognitive Efficiency).

Other Individual Intelligence Tests

There are several individually administered intelligence tests designed to provide brief assessments of cognitive abilities for individuals of widely varying ages (i.e., from age 2.6 to over 90). The **Peabody Picture Vocabulary Test–Fourth Edition** (PPVT-IV; L. M. Dunn & Dunn, 2007) is a brief (10–15 minutes) screening test of listening comprehension and verbal ability. A word is given, and the examinee is told to point to the appropriate one picture out of four on a card. There are two parallel forms, and accommodations for individuals with motor impairments may be made.

The **Wide Range Intelligence Test** is a brief, individually administered test of intellectual ability for ages 4 to 85. It contains four subtests that yield a verbal (crystallized) IQ and a visual (fluid) IQ. The WRIT was standardized on 2,285 U.S. individuals.

Advantages and Disadvantages of Individual Intelligence Tests

Each of these intelligence tests is individually administered and requires a highly trained examiner. Considerable training and practice in administering each test are necessary for a competent administration that produces reliable results without the scoring errors that are an inherent aspect of individual assessment. An experienced examiner has the opportunity to observe and judge a variety of behaviors and aspects of the individual's personality. Thus, for the competent examiner, these tests provide aspects of a clinical interview as well as a standardized test.

Because these individual intelligence tests provide several different types of IQ scores, the counselor has the opportunity to pay particular attention to those clients for whom the difference between the scores is substantial. In such cases, an exploration is warranted to attempt to discern factors that might account for the differences. The different subtest scores also provide an opportunity to examine the pattern of scores that appear as a profile on the report form.

There have been a number of hypotheses advanced regarding emotional, neurological, and pathological problems that yield differential subtest scores. Considerable research has shown differential diagnoses resulting from patterns on such profiles to be questionable. Because the different subtests vary in reliability, difference scores obtained among the subtests can be particularly unreliable. Nevertheless, most sophisticated users of the Stanford–Binet and the Wechsler tests regard differential patterns as suggesting certain types of dysfunction. For example, higher scores on various verbal scales and lower scores on certain performance scales are suggestive of such problems as brain damage; drug abuse; or, in an older person, dementia. Verbal subtest scores falling well below performance scores may suggest poor reading ability or lack of motivation for academic achievement.

The primary disadvantages of individual intelligence tests are their costs, both in terms of time and money, and the extensive training required for them to be properly administered and interpreted. Counselors often lack both the resources and the training to use these instruments themselves. Instead, they refer clients in need of individual testing to competent examiners and receive the results from them. Counselors should encourage such examiners to report their observations and any other information that can assist counselors in interpreting the results, particularly regarding information that can help to explain any discrepancies. In place of individual intelligence tests, counselors are more likely to use group intelligence tests to assess the cognitive abilities of their clients.

Activity 9.2
Selecting Intelligence Assessments

Select one of the individual or group assessments of intelligence discussed in this chapter. Use assessment sources discussed earlier in the text to collect psychometric information on the assessment. Reflect on the following questions:

- What is the psychometric evidence (e.g., reliability, validity, standardization sample, scoring information) for the assessment? How strong is this evidence?
- How would you use this instrument in your practice?
- What are some of the advantages and disadvantages of the assessment?

Present the information to the larger group.

Group Intelligence Tests

Group intelligence tests are considerably more cost-effective than individual tests in terms of the time and expense required for administration and scoring. They require simpler materials—typically only a printed booklet, a multiple-choice answer sheet, a pencil, and a scoring key are needed. They also usually offer more normative information because this type of data is easier to collect for group tests.

As you may recall from Chapter 1, the development of group tests was stimulated by the need to classify almost 2 million U.S. Army recruits during World War I. The Army Alpha and the nonreading companion test, the Army Beta (most current version is the Beta III), were developed for military use. Group intelligence tests designed for educational and personnel uses were developed shortly thereafter, with these two tests as models. Such group-administered tests are now used at every education level from kindergarten through graduate school. They are also used extensively by industry, by the military, and in research studies. The Beta III is widely used when hiring non-English-speaking or illiterate unskilled laborers for whom a verbal test would not be appropriate (Bellah, 2005).

To avoid the term *intelligence test*, because the term *intelligence* is so often misunderstood and misinterpreted, counselors are encouraged to describe these tests, particularly those designed for school use, in terms of mental maturity, cognitive ability, school ability, or academic ability.

Group Intelligence Tests for School Use

Because these tests are administered across a number of grades throughout entire school systems, they are administered in the hundreds of thousands each year. The market for these tests is therefore a profitable one, and a large number are available for use. Four of the most popular and most psychometrically sound instruments are briefly described here. Results are typically reported in a variety of forms: national and local age and grade percentiles, stanines, and normal curve equivalents.

Cognitive Abilities Test

The **Cognitive Abilities Test**, Form 6 (CogAT-6), was published in 2001 and normed in 2000 and 2005. The test has two editions: the Primary Edition, with three levels for kindergarten through Grade 2, and a Multilevel Edition, with levels for use in Grades 3 through 12. The CogAT-6 is composed of three batteries assessing verbal, quantitative, and nonverbal abilities, with each battery consisting of three separate tests with a composite score (Rodgers, 2005). The nonverbal section uses neither language nor numbers but rather uses geometric figures for tasks that require classification, analogies, or figure synthesis. In this portion, the effects of formal schooling, poor reading ability, or non-native English speaker status are minimized. Raw scores on each section can be converted into stanine and percentile scores for both age and grade levels so that the three scores can be compared both with norm groups and within each individual. In addition, the scores can be converted to standard scores that have a mean of 100 and a standard deviation of 16 to produce a deviation standard age score or IQ score. The Cognitive Abilities Tests were standardized along with the Iowa Tests of Basic Skills for kindergarten through Grade 9 and with the Iowa Tests of Educational Development for Grades 9 through 12. They were standardized on a sample of 180,000 students representative of the U.S. census population, with high and stable predictions found at all grade levels between CogAT-6 scores and future scores on the Iowa achievement tests (DiPerna, 2005).

Test of Cognitive Skills

The **Test of Cognitive Skills** is the contemporary version of the long-used California Test of Mental Maturity–Short Form (CTB/Macmillan/McGraw-Hill, 1993). In its original form, the instrument was designed to be the group-test equivalent of the Stanford–Binet and to yield scores similar to those that would be obtained by individually administering the Stanford–Binet. Four test areas are associated with this tool: Sequences, Analogies, Memory, and Verbal Reasoning.

There are six levels, each designed for two grade levels ranging from Grade 2 through Grade 12. The Primary Test of Cognitive Skills is available for kindergarten to Grade 1. Age and grade stanines, percentiles, and standard score norms are available for each subtest. A Combined Cognitive Skills Index provides a deviation IQ score. It was standardized with the Terra Nova and the California Achievement Tests–5.

Otis–Lennon School Ability Test

The **Otis–Lennon School Ability Test**, 8th edition (OLSAT8), has seven levels ranging from kindergarten to Grade 12 (Pearson Assessments, 2012). The test is published in two forms and yields verbal and nonverbal scores based on 36-item subtests and a total IQ score. The test represents a contemporary version of a series of former Otis tests. The OLSAT8 was jointly normed with the Metropolitan Achievement Tests 8 and the Stanford Achievement Tests 10.

Other Group Intelligence Tests

In addition to group intelligence tests used in schools, there are three other group intelligence tests used in a wider range of settings. There are the Shipley Institute of Living Scale, Wonderlic Personnel Test and Scholastic Level Exam, and the Multidimensional Aptitude Battery.

Shipley Institute of Living Scale

The **Shipley Institute of Living Scale–Revised** is a 60-item (40 vocabulary, 20 abstract reasoning) intelligence test that takes approximately 20 minutes to administer. IQ and standard scores are obtained based on age-adjusted norms (Zachary, 1986). Correlations in the vicinity of .8 with Wechsler tests are reported in the manual, along with reliabilities of .8 to .9 for internal consistency and .6 to .7 for test–retest. Originally constructed to assess cognitive impairment, this test is now used as a brief screening device for overall intellectual ability.

Wonderlic Personnel Test

The **Wonderlic Personnel Test** and **Scholastic Level Exam** is a brief 12-minute, 50-item, speeded test of mental ability for adults (Wonderlic, 2005). This test is often used to determine whether individuals have the capacity to learn and solve problems. The Wonderlic Personnel Test has an extensive history of use in business, and the Scholastic Level Exam is often used in educational settings. Ten forms of this paper-and-pencil intelligence test are available, along with Braille and audiotape editions for persons with disabilities. There are extensive norms. It is administered in business and industry to 2.5 million job applicants each year for the selection and placement of employees. It is available in 14 languages and can be administered on a personal computer. Validity data in regard to job success are undoubtedly available locally in many companies but typically are not found in the research literature. The test's validity has been questioned in regard to selection for certain positions when minorities obtaining lower scores on the instrument are screened out of various entry-level positions. Thus, the Wonderlic Personnel Test has been the subject of various court cases in which its use was declared not legitimate when testing procedures resulted in denying fair opportunities to prospective minority employees but acceptable when test results could be shown to be substantially related to the performance on specific jobs.

Multidimensional Aptitude Battery

The **Multidimensional Aptitude Battery–II** (MAB-II) was developed by the late Douglas Jackson as a group-administered paper-and-pencil test to yield the same types of results and scores as the WAIS (Jackson, 1998). This test battery contains five tests on the verbal scale and five tests on the performance scale that involve very similar tasks to the subtests on the WAIS but in a paper-and-pencil format. Scores on the various subtests have a mean of 50 and a standard deviation of 10, and total scores on the verbal, performance, and full scale have a mean of 100 and a standard deviation of 15. It is available in English, French, and Spanish versions.

In the design of the MAB, Jackson made use of the capabilities of modern computers to develop items and scales through item analysis and factor-analysis techniques. The battery can be taken directly on most computers with software that presents instructions and practice items, times the subtests, scores them, and produces four different types of interpretive reports. The advantage of the battery is its ease of administration and scoring; the highly trained examiner necessary to administer the WAIS or the Stanford–Binet is not required. As a group-administered battery, however, it does not provide the examiner with the observational data obtained in using individual instruments. Therefore, it is generally not administered in high-stakes testing situations such as the determination of intellectual disabilities.

Tip Sheet
Interpreting Intelligence Test Results

✓ Use intelligence test results with caution. For many reasons, controversy continues regarding the concept of intelligence, the specific abilities that constitute intelligent behavior, and the magnitude of the roles played by heredity and environment. Incorporate important client data external to testing in your interpretation.

✓ Because most intelligence tests administered in the United States assume a relatively common cultural background with English as the native language, there may be several limitations for clients of diverse backgrounds. Review the test manual and critically evaluate each subtest to select an appropriate intelligence assessment. If assessment results for a client would be significantly biased, consider instead using a culture-fair test as relevant (see Chapter 4).

✓ Be aware of which intelligence tests indicate accommodations for clients with disabilities.

✓ Remember that an IQ score obtained does not represent a fixed characteristic of the individual. Instead, it should be interpreted as a particular score obtained on a particular test at a particular time. This point is especially important for younger clients, for whom test–retest reliabilities are lower, indicating that considerable change and development take place over time. In interpreting the result to a client, rather than say that he or she has an IQ of 112, provide a better interpretation by saying that the client scored in the top quarter of his or her peers on a test that measures an ability useful in learning academic subjects.

✓ Be aware of the **Flynn effect**, a trend in which mean IQ scores have increased over time. In the United States, this has been a 3-point increase per decade (R. L. Williams, 2013).

Giftedness and Creativity

Approximately 3% to 5% of school-age individuals demonstrate high ability, performance, achievement, and/or creativity; these individuals may present with five commonly cited traits of giftedness: creative thinking, excitability or hyperarousal, high sensitivity to others, possession of multiple perceptions or intuition, and motivation or inner strength (Colangelo & Wood, 2015). Children who are identified as gifted may face various academic, interpersonal, and familial challenges. For example, underachievement of gifted students begins in early school years and is a well-developed pattern by high school (Cross & Coleman, 2014). These challenges, coupled with a tendency to overcommit to tasks, often cause emotional distress (Henfield, 2013; J. S. Peterson, 2015). Counselors, especially those in school settings, must be familiar with helping gifted students master a variety of social and academic skills (Colangelo & Wood, 2015; Henfield, 2013).

Giftedness is often not seen as special needs education, and thus counselors may not provide specific attention to gifted individuals (J. S. Peterson, 2015). In fact, Bourdeau and Thomas (2003) found that some counselors may view gifted children as no different than nongifted children. Furthermore, there is an underrepresentation of children of minority statuses in gifted education programs. This underrepresentation may be due to a lack of referral and retention of these students in gifted education programs, negative attitudes toward minority students, issues in standardized testing, lack of minority enrollment in Advanced Placement courses, economic and social factors, or a combination of any of these factors (D. Y. Ford, Grantham, & Whiting, 2008; Henfield, 2013; Henfield, Owens, & Moore, 2008).

There is no single method for identifying children who are gifted; however, the best method available for identifying children with superior cognitive abilities is the standardized, individually administered, multidimensional test of intelligence, such as a Wechsler test or the Stanford–Binet. In some schools, group tests must be substituted for screening purposes when the administration of large numbers of individual tests is not feasible. Other areas of giftedness, such as creativity or talent, are more difficult to assess and must include a combination of procedures including achievements, achievement tests, portfolios, auditions, and teacher and parent nominations (Colangelo & Wood, 2015; McIntosh & Dixon, 2005; J. S. Peterson, 2015; Sattler, 2005).

The **Torrance Tests of Creativity** (Torrance, 1974) are the most widely used tests to assess creativity. They consist of both nonverbal and verbal forms assessing four creative abilities: fluency, flexibility, originality, and elaboration. The nonverbal form uses drawing activities, and the verbal form involves activities such as generating questions or suggesting alternative uses for an object. Each activity is timed and scored on the first three of the creative abilities. The nonverbal activities are also scored for elaboration. Research has shown adequate score reliability. An interesting 22-year longitudinal validity study showed student scores to be related to accomplishments in adulthood (Kerr & Gagliardi, 2003).

Chapter Summary

Although assessment of intelligence may be performed by professionals from other related disciplines, counselors are typically involved in using results for educational and vocational decision making. Several theories of intelligence that aid counselors in conceptualizing intelligence and serve as the basis for the individual and group intelligence tests were discussed in this chapter. These theories include Spearman's g factor, Thurstone's primary mental abilities, the Cattell–Horn–Carroll theory of cognitive ability, Sternberg's triarchic theory of intelligence, and Gardner's multiple intelligences.

This chapter reviewed several individual and group intelligence tests. Individual tests include the Stanford–Binet, Wechsler scales, Kaufman batteries, Das Naglieri Cognitive Assessment System, Woodcock–Johnson, Peabody Picture Vocabulary Test, and the Wide Range Intelligence Test. Group intelligence tests discussed include the Cognitive Abilities Test, Test of Cognitive Skills, Otis–Lennon School Ability Test, Shipley Institute of Living Scale, Wonderlic Personnel Test, and the Multidimensional Aptitude Battery–II. The chapter concluded with a brief discussion of giftedness and creativity.

Review Questions

1. What are the major theories of intelligence?
2. How is intelligence defined according to the major theorists of intelligence? What are the potential limitations of each of these definitions?
3. How do the Wechsler scales compare with the Stanford–Binet?
4. What are some of the advantages of individual intelligence tests? Disadvantages?
5. What are some of the factors affecting gifted students? How might a client's cultural make-up impact the way in which counselors conceptualize and intervene with giftedness?

Resources for Further Learning

Publications

Colangelo, N., & Wood, S. M. (2015). Counseling the gifted: Past, present, and future directions. *Journal of Counseling & Development, 93*, 133–142.

Flanagan, D. P., & Alfonso, V. C. (2016). *Essentials of WISC-V assessment* (2nd ed.). New York, NY: Wiley.

Gardner, H. (2011). *Frames of mind: The theory of multiple intelligences.* New York, NY: Basic Books.

Naglieri, J. A. (2015). Hundred years of intelligence testing: Moving from traditional IQ to second-generation intelligence tests. In S. Goldstein, D. Princiotta, & J. A. Naglieri (Eds.), *Handbook of intelligence* (pp. 295–316). New York, NY: Springer.

Peterson, J. S. (2015). School counselors and gifted kids: Respecting both cognitive and affective. *Journal of Counseling & Development, 93,* 153–162.

Raiford, S. E., & Coalson, D. L. (2014). *Essentials of WPPSI-IV assessment.* New York, NY: Wiley.

Roid, G. H., & Barram, R. A. (2004). *Essentials of Stanford–Binet Intelligence Scales (SB5) assessment.* New York, NY: Wiley.

Schrank, F. A., Decker, S. L., & Garruto, J. M. (2016). *Essentials of WJ IV cognitive abilities assessment.* New York, NY: Wiley.

Web Resources

Peabody Picture Vocabulary Test, Fourth Edition (PPVT™-4)
http://www.pearsonclinical.com/language/products/100000501/peabody-picture-vocabulary-test-fourth-edition-ppvt-4.html#tab-scoring
    This link provides sample reports associated with this assessment.

Stanford–Binet Intelligence Scales, Fifth Edition Detailed Summary Report
http://www.proedinc.com/Downloads/14462%20SB-5_OSRS_SampleDetailedSummaryReport.pdf
    This link provides sample reports associated with this assessment.

Wechsler Adult Intelligence Scale–Fourth Edition (WAIS-IV)
http://www.pearsonclinical.com/psychology/products/100000392/wechsler-adult-intelligence-scalefourth-edition-wais-iv.html
    This link provides sample reports associated with this assessment.

Wechsler Preschool and Primary Scale of Intelligence™–Fourth Edition (WPPSI™-IV)
http://www.pearsonclinical.com/psychology/products/100000102/wechsler-pre-school-and-primary-scale-of-intelligence--fourth-edition-wppsi-iv.html#tab-scoring
    This link provides sample reports associated with this assessment.

WISC-V Interpretive Considerations for Laurie Jones (6/1/2015)
http://images.pearsonclinical.com/images/assets/wisc-v/WISC-VInterpretiveReportSample-1.pdf
    This link provides sample reports associated with this assessment.

WISC-V, Wechsler Intelligence Scale for Children–Fifth Edition
http://images.pearsonclinical.com/images/assets/wisc-v/WISC-V-Score-Report.pdf
    This link provides sample reports associated with this assessment.

Chapter 10

Ability Testing: Academic Aptitude and Achievement

Counselors, particularly those working in academic settings or working with individuals facing academic- and career-related decisions, are to be familiar with ability tests. This chapter discusses several types of ability tests, including tests for higher education, graduate and professional school admissions tests, academic achievement tests, and study habits inventories. In addition, considerations of high-stakes testing and the educational accountability legislation are discussed.

Test Your Knowledge

Select the most appropriate choice for each item.

_____ 1. Generally, _____ refers to previous learning and _____ to learning ability.
a. aptitude; achievement
b. achievement; aptitude
c. aptitude; intelligence
d. intelligence; aptitude

_____ 2. Which of the following is not an aptitude test used in higher education?
a. SAT
b. ACT
c. PACT
d. PSAT

_____ 3. GRE: graduate school admission and _____: school achievement.
a. TerraNova 3
b. LASSI
c. SAMS
d. WAIS

_____ 4. The function of high-stakes testing is to:
a. Ensure state curriculum requirements are met.
b. Provide information for college admissions.
c. Create educational opportunities for students who have experienced educational inequity.
d. Both a and c.

❏ T ❏ F   5. Ability tests typically used for higher education admissions serve both to measure previous learning and to predict learning ability.

Introduction to Aptitude and Achievement Assessment

We have all encountered several forms of ability testing throughout our educational experiences. As school-age children, we were administered various tests to determine placements and graduation or matriculation to higher grade levels. We then experienced several other ability tests to gain admission in college and graduate school. The mention of the SAT or GRE conjures up anxiety for some counselors and counselor trainees! We likely have friends, relatives, or our own children who are being administered ability testing in some form now. Thus, ability testing is a significant part of our lives at various points.

There are two forms of ability tests: aptitude and achievement. Assessment of **aptitude** is generally thought of as an ability to acquire a specific type of skill or knowledge; aptitude tests are typically used for prediction purposes. In the field of aptitude testing, the assessment of scholastic aptitude is particularly important, because academic or scholastic aptitude is significantly related to achievement in various educational programs in high schools, colleges, and professional schools. Because of the importance of higher education as a prerequisite for entering the majority of higher status occupations and professions in today's society, achieving acceptable scores on scholastic aptitude measures is becoming increasingly crucial for those aspiring to such occupations.

Assessment of **achievement** differs from aptitude testing in that it attempts to measure learning that takes place under relatively standardized conditions or as a result of a controlled set of experiences. Achievement tests are designed to measure what has already been learned or knowledge or skills that have been attained, whereas academic aptitude tests attempt to measure learning ability, although such ability is usually related to that which has been developed up to the time of testing.

Thus, achievement tests are usually evaluated on the basis of content validity; that is, the extent to which the test includes content similar to that which the test takers are expected to have experienced. Aptitude tests are usually evaluated in terms of predictive validity; that is, the extent to which success in whatever it is the aptitude test attempts to measure can be predicted from the test results. The distinction between achievement and aptitude tests is not absolute, however. Some aptitude tests are based on a generally standardized prior experience, whereas some achievement tests are designed to measure certain generalized educational experiences that are not especially uniform in nature. For example, the ACT test serves as a scholastic aptitude test to predict success in college; however, its items represent subject matter areas taught in all high school curricula. The new SAT is now similar in this regard, a departure from the previous SAT that was designed to assess aptitude rather than achievement.

Achievement tests vary from the brief achievement test administered by a teacher to evaluate the learning that has taken place during a single lesson to the nationally available achievement test programs produced by the major commercial test publishers. These achievement test batteries are generally designed across a number of grade levels from kindergarten through the 12th grade. The test batteries provide profiles of scores in various academic skill areas. They tend to be based on the "three Rs" in the early grades and to measure information and knowledge in specific academic areas at the secondary school levels. Usually the tests are carefully prepared in regard to content, with items written by teachers and consultants and examined by expert reviewers. The items are then subjected to analyses of item difficulty and item discrimination, with attempts made to eliminate gender and ethnic bias.

Aptitude Tests for Higher Education

Scholastic aptitude tests are used as information sources for selecting and admitting students to institutions of higher education at the undergraduate and graduate or professional levels. They are also used for awarding academic scholarships, in determining athletic eligibility, for awarding financial aid, for placing students in courses, and for academic and vocational counseling and advising. There are two major tests for higher education: the SAT (including the PSAT) and the ACT.

SAT

The SAT has been given since 1926 and is now taken by over a million college-bound high school students each year. Its design, administration, and reporting are carried out by the Educational Testing Service (ETS) in Princeton, New Jersey. Originally called the Scholastic Aptitude Test, it was revised in 1994 and given the redundant name the Scholastic Assessment Test–I (SAT-I). The latest version, available in 2016, is known simply as the **SAT**. It is a 4 hour, primarily multiple-choice test with four major sections: (a) Reading, in which individuals read passages and interpret graphics to show their understanding of the passage and its context; (b) Writing and Language, in which individuals review a passage and identify and fix mistakes or weaknesses in the passage; (c) Math, in which individuals solve algebraic functions, problem-solve and analyze data, and manipulate test item information to solve complex equations; and (d) Essay, in which individuals read a passage and develop an argument to persuade an external audience with ample evidence of that argument. The last major component, Essay, is an optional area that some colleges require.

The first two components, (a) Reading and (b) Writing and Language, are combined as one of the two section scores, and Math is the other section score; each section score ranges on a scale from 200 to 800, with a sum section score ranging from 400 to 1600. There are also three test scores for the first three components ranging from 10 to 40 as well as three SAT Essay scores related to Reading, Analysis, and Writing, with scores ranging from 2 to 8 per area. Furthermore, the SAT provides cross-test scores, based in the first three components listed for the test, that yield scores for analysis in history/social studies as well as analysis in science; these scores range from 10 to 40. Finally, the SAT has seven subscores, which may be considered subscales of the first three components; scores range from 1 to 15.

The College Board also administers the 1-hour SAT-II subject tests in 20 specific subjects (e.g., biology, Spanish), one or more of which is required by some colleges. These subject tests fall within one of five areas: mathematics, science, English, history, and languages.

Preliminary SAT/National Merit Scholarship Qualifying Test

The **Preliminary SAT/National Merit Scholarship Qualifying Test** (PSAT/NMSQT) is typically taken in the 10th or 11th grade (College Board, 2016d). It is considered by some students to be a practice or trial run for the SAT. It is also used to help students choose which colleges to consider in their college decision-making plans. It plays an important role as the initial step in qualifying for National Merit Scholarships.

Similar to the SAT, the PSAT/NMSQT and PSAT 10 include three components: (a) Reading, (b) Writing and Language, and (c) Math. The goals of these components are also similar to those of the SAT. The PSAT/NMSQT and PSAT 10 provide a total score for the two section scores (i.e., Evidence-Based Reading and Writing, Math) that ranges from 320 to 1520; each section score ranges from 160 to 760. There are also three test scores (i.e., Reading, Writing and Language, Math) as well as two cross-test scores similar to the SAT that each range from 8 to 38. Similar to the SAT, the test includes seven subscores across the three components that each range from 1 to 15.

ACT

The ACT, Inc., in Iowa City, Iowa, established in 1959 what was originally known as American College Testing. Now the assessment is known simply as **ACT** to represent myriad tests the company publishes. The ACT tests tend to be used more often by colleges in the Midwest and less often by those on the East Coast, although the majority of institutions in the United States will accept either SAT or ACT scores. The current revision, termed the ACT Assessment, consists of four academic achievement tests, an interest inventory, and a questionnaire regarding student backgrounds and plans. It is administered on six national testing dates. The academic tests take 2 hours and 55 minutes to complete and are designed to assess academic ability in four areas: English, mathematics, reading, and science reasoning. There is also an optional 30-minute ACT Writing Test, an essay that is required by a number of institutions (ACT, Inc., 2016a). In addition to the paper-and-pencil format, the ACT began computer administration in 2015.

The item content of the ACT Assessment is similar to that of the Iowa Tests of Educational Development, on which the ACT tests were originally based. For example, the ACT-Math consists of 60 items from prealgebra, intermediate algebra, geometry, and trigonometry. The Science Reasoning test contains 40 items dealing with concepts from biology, physics, and chemistry. Results are reported on a standard score scale that ranges from 1 to 36 for each of the four academic tests and their seven subscales, along with a total composite score. The mean for college-bound students who take the ACT Assessment is approximately 21 on each of the four academic tests and the composite score. Standard deviations vary from 4.5 to 6.0. The *SEM* is approximately 2 for the academic tests and 1 for the composite score.

Essays as part of the optional Writing section are scored by two readers on a 1–6 scale and added to give a 2–12 score that is reported to the student along with readers' comments. A combined English and writing score is also reported using the 1–36 standard scale.

The 90-item **UNIACT Interest Inventory** is taken along with the ACT Assessment, and it provides scores on six interest areas similar to Holland's (1997) hexagon and a method of plotting interests on the accompanying World-of-Work Map (ACT, Inc., 2009a). Information is sent to colleges, and the ACT reports are also sent to both the high school and the student; such reports contain much information useful in academic and career planning. The reports include student plans, perceived educational needs, interest inventory scores, and rankings of the students' scores at the colleges to which the scores are being sent.

There are two preliminary ACT batteries useful for occupational and, especially, educational planning. The **EXPLORE program** taken by eighth and ninth graders consists of four academic achievement tests along with an interest inventory, educational plans, and background information (ACT, Inc., 2016c). The **PLAN program** for 10th-grade students consists of (a) four academic tests of 20 to 45 minutes each, yielding standard scores of 1 to 32 that are linked to junior/senior-year ACT Assessment scores; (b) the UNIACT Interest Inventory; (c) a student Needs Assessment; (d) a high school grade/course information section; and (e) an educational/occupational plans section (ACT, Inc., 2016d).

ACT's **ASSET Student Success System** is administered in nearly 400 community and technical colleges to assess students' skills with three 25-minute tests: Writing Skills, Numerical Skills, and Reading Skills. The program also collects information about students' educational backgrounds, their plans, and their needs. Additional tests have been constructed to assess skills in certain other academic areas (e.g., chemistry, geometry, and college algebra; ACT, Inc., 2016b).

Validity of Scholastic Aptitude Tests

The ACT and the SAT are approximately equal in their ability to predict college grades. Thousands of studies have been conducted assessing the ability of these tests to predict grades, with the typical correlation ranging in the vicinity of .30 to .50 for freshman grade point averages (GPAs). Correlations tend to be higher at institutions with more heterogeneous freshman classes and lower among homogeneous student bodies, particularly at the very highly selective institutions with restricted ranges of student scores.

Most studies have found that high school grades are the best predictors of college GPAs but that scholastic aptitude tests are able to improve the prediction over high school GPAs or high school ranks alone (College Board, 2016d). That scholastic aptitude test scores would add to the prediction of college success is not surprising. The particular high school GPA that a student obtains depends on a number of factors: the general competitiveness of the high school attended, the grading curve used in that high school, and the types of courses taken, as well as other personal factors. Thus, a high school GPA of 3.2 achieved by a particular student who has taken all college preparatory subjects in a school with a low grading curve and where the majority of classmates are college bound represents a very different level of achievement than that obtained by a student from a less competitive high school who has taken a number of vocational or commercial courses. A national college admissions test represents a common task for all students and therefore can operate as a correction factor for the high school GPA. In addition, for the student with low grades but with substantially higher scholastic aptitude test scores than would be expected from those grades, the scores may suggest hitherto unrecognized academic potential. These scores may represent a "second chance" for such a student.

Test scores tend to be greatly overemphasized by many parents and their college-bound students. Only at the most highly selective institutions are very high scores generally required, and even there, much other information goes into admissions decisions. Students with good high school grades can obtain admission to most colleges unless their test scores are extremely low.

When scholastic aptitude test scores are interpreted to students and their parents, the standard error should be taken into account. On the SAT, the standard error is in the vicinity of 30, suggesting that just over two thirds of the time the student's true score will fall within 30 points in one direction or the other from the obtained score. For the ACT, with a standard error of approximately 2 points, two thirds of the time students' true scores could be expected to fall within 2 points on either side of their obtained ACT standard scores.

Academic Aptitude Test Scores and College Admission

Although the number of U.S. colleges and universities that require very high ACT or SAT scores is not large, almost all 4-year institutions claim to maintain some type of a selective admissions policy. This selectivity varies greatly. Some public institutions will take any student in the top half of his or her high school class or one who obtains a test score at least equivalent to that level. Others take only those in the top quarter, or in the top three quarters, or have other means of selection using formulas with high school rank or high school grades and SAT scores. A few private institutions admit perhaps only one in five applicants from an already very selective applicant pool. There are many other private colleges that, although maintaining that they are selective in their admissions, in fact will admit almost every high school graduate who applies, as will most public community colleges. The result is a great variation in the abilities of the average or typical student on various campuses.

In the United States, a particular GPA earned at one institution is not equivalent to that earned at another institution, and college degrees obtained from different institutions also are not equivalent. Although some differences in levels of competition among colleges are recognized to at least a limited extent by the general public, and perhaps to a greater degree by those in higher education, the actual differences are far greater than all but the most sophisticated observers of American higher education imagine. Levels of competition vary so greatly among institutions that a student obtaining an honors GPA of 3.4 at one institution could easily fail out of a much more competitive institution.

In assisting college-bound students in their decision making about the institutions they might choose, counselors should consider these types of differences. Information regarding the levels of academic competition at particular institutions can be found in certain college guides, such as *Profiles of American Colleges* (Barrons Educational Series, 2015) or *The College Handbook* (College Board, 2017). Anyone involved in college counseling should obtain a guide that contains information regarding high school ranks and test scores of students at different institutions. Armed with the knowledge that the standard deviation on an academic aptitude test at a given institution is likely to be in the vicinity of two thirds or three quarters that of the normative standard deviation of the instrument (4 or 5 points on the ACT Assessment or 60 to 75 points on the SAT) and with the mean score or the range of the middle 50% given in one of the college guides, a counselor can easily calculate a rough estimate of the point at which the student is likely to fall in regard to academic aptitude at that institution.

Combining this information with knowledge of the student's achievement level in high school, it is possible to estimate the general level of competition that a student will find at a given institution. Combined with other information about the student, his or her chances of obtaining admission at that institution can also be estimated. A student might therefore be encouraged to apply to several different institutions, including one or two in which chances for admission and satisfactory performance are favorable. The following case example illustrates how counselors can use academic aptitude test information in their discussions of college choices.

Case Example 10.1

Dylan

Dylan is just beginning his senior year in high school, and he and his parents are having a conference with his guidance counselor. He has a 2.9 GPA in the academic program in his high school and received scores ranging from 18 to 22 for a composite score of 20 on the ACT battery that he took the previous spring. His parents want to talk about colleges and universities that he should investigate and his chances of being admitted to them. Included in their consideration is an Ivy League institution that their nephew attends.

The counselor reports to them that Dylan's score on the ACT is about an average score for college-bound students in the United States. When he takes the SAT a few weeks hence, if he obtains comparable scores, they are likely to be in the 400s. She suggests that unless he were class valedictorian or a star athlete (which he is not), he has little chance of being admitted to a highly competitive institution. She tells them that because the state university admits any high school graduate who is in the top two fifths of his or her graduating class, and because Dylan is at the 65th percentile, he would be admitted to the state university. He would, however, rank toward the bottom at that institution, both in terms of high school record and test scores, and he could find it difficult to achieve more than barely passing grades.

Because Dylan is undecided as to a career or a major, he is planning to enter a general liberal arts program and therefore has a wide range of institutions from which to choose. At some 4-year institutions, he would fall well above the mean and at others well below the mean. At the particular small college he is considering, he would be below the middle but still above the bottom third. His chances of success there would be better than at a number of other institutions that he and his parents have considered.

• • •

The level of competition a student is likely to meet if admitted should also be discussed. Although there are many, including parents, who believe that a student should attend the highest status institution to which he or she can be admitted, some evidence suggests that for many students this is not the wisest move. In a key study, Werts and Watley (1969) indicated that, holding ability constant, those students who attended an institution at which they fell in the bottom portion of the students at that institution were less likely to go on and attend graduate or professional school than those students who had attended an institution at which they were closer to or above the middle of the distribution. Furthermore, Marsh and Hau (2003) found in another popular study that students in highly competitive institutions have reported lower academic self-concepts in a cross-cultural study involving 4,000 students in 26 countries. The phenomenon captured by these two studies, the **Big-Fish-Little-Pond Effect**, refers to the notion that those who attend high-ability colleges or universities will have lower academic self-concepts than similar peers in less competitive colleges or universities (Marsh & Seaton, 2013). In essence, it may not always be desirable for students to pursue the most competitive programs for which they can gain admission.

Graduate and Professional School Admissions Tests

There are two common graduate admissions tests used today: the Graduate Record Examination and the Miller Analogies Test. In addition, professional schools (e.g., law schools, medical schools) often require more specialized admissions tests.

Graduate Record Examination

The **Graduate Record Examination** (GRE) includes both a general test and subject tests, with the general test being the most widely accepted graduate admissions test worldwide (Educational Testing Service, 2016b). There are three portions of the GRE: Verbal Reasoning (GRE-V), Quantitative Reasoning (GRE-Q), and Analytical Writing (GRE-W). The GRE-V measures the ability to analyze, evaluate, and synthesize written material and to analyze relationships among sentence parts or among words or concepts. Specifically, there are reading comprehension, text completion, and sentence equivalence question types. The GRE-Q measures the ability to problem-solve and understand basic mathematical concepts, with attention to mathematical computation and data analysis. There are four types of quantitative reasoning questions that include quantitative comparison, multiple-choice options, and numeric entry and two types of data interpretation questions that are presented as multiple choice or numeric entry. The GRE-W measures critical thinking and analytical writing skills. This section includes tasks related to analyzing issues and arguments (Educational Testing Service, 2016b).

Scores for the revised GRE general test are on a 130–170 scale (GRE-V and GRE-Q sections), and the GRE-W section is reported on a 0–6 score scale. Scores are reported in 1-point and 0.5-point increments for the GRE-V/GRE-Q and GRE-W sections, respectively. The GRE subject tests are reported on a 200–990 scale for the total score (10-point increments), with subtest scores on a 20–99 scale (1-point increments).

For a time, the GRE General Test used an adaptive format in which the examinee was presented with questions of average difficulty, after which the computer selected questions based on the difficulty level of the questions answered correctly and incorrectly. Each correct answer led to a more difficult question, whereas a wrong answer led to an easier one. Scores on the test are based both on the number of questions correctly answered and on the difficulty level of these questions. This procedure resulted in an efficient individualized test; however, item security became a problem because examinees were memorizing questions and answers from previous test takers. Therefore, ETS lengthened the test and returned it to its current format, with the paper-and-pencil version continued only in a few countries where computers are not available.

The GRE is used in selecting students for admission into graduate school and into specific graduate departments. Norms on the tests vary greatly among institutions and among specific departments. A physics department could require substantially higher scores on the quantitative section than on the verbal section, whereas requirements by an English department would be the opposite. An art department might require a portfolio and pay little attention to either. Because of these differences, use of GRE test scores to assist students in selecting institutions and departments in which they are likely to be admitted and are likely to be successful is difficult without knowledge of the norms in specific graduate institutions and departments.

Using GRE scores to predict success in graduate school is particularly difficult for a number of reasons. There is likely to be the problem of restriction in range within particular departments, because GREs and undergraduate GPAs are the major criteria on which students are selected for graduate programs, thus eliminating low scores. In addition, graduate school GPAs may be highly restricted in range because grades of A and B are often the only grades given. For a typical department, however, GRE scores plus undergraduate GPAs still provide a better prediction of academic success than any other readily available variables (Klieger, Cline, Holtzman, Minsky, & Lorenz, 2014).

Miller Analogies Test

The **Miller Analogies Test** (MAT), published by Pearson Assessments, is another test used for the selection of graduate students. The test consists of 120 complex analogy items drawn from the subject matter across a number of academic fields (100 items count, and 20 are experimental). It is available in both paper-and-pencil and computer formats and can be taken in various approved centers around the country. Although the test is administered with a 60-minute time limit, it is largely a power test, not a speed test. It includes items of considerable difficulty so that resulting scores are purported to differentiate reliably among people of superior intellect. It is available in a number of parallel forms, with reliabilities in the general magnitude of .90. In an older meta-analysis study of the MAT (Kuncel, Hezlett, & Ones, 2004), the instrument was shown to be a valid predictor not only of academic variables such as graduate school grades and time taken to finish a graduate degree but also of vocational and career criteria.

Familiarity with the kinds of items on this type of test can significantly affect scores, with substantial improvement resulting from studying practice items or from previous experience with an alternate form. As with the GRE, norms among graduate students in different institutions and different departments vary widely, and knowledge of normative data in relevant comparison groups (provided in the MAT manual) is a necessity if predictive information based on the scores is to have any value. The problems of predictive validity of graduate school success discussed for the GRE are also present for the MAT.

Professional School Tests

A number of aptitude tests have been developed by different professions for selection into their professional schools. In many cases, these tests are universally required for admission to such schools. Such tests include the **Medical College Admission Test** (MCAT; Association of American Medical Colleges, 2016), the **Dental Admission Test** (DAT; American Dental Association, 2016), the **Law School Admission Test** (LSAT; Law School Admission Council, 2016), and the **Graduate Management Admission Test** (GMAT; Graduate Management Admission Council, 2016). These admission tests are typically developed and administered by one of the national testing programs, such as ACT or ETS, and the cost to applicants can be quite expensive.

These tests usually include items similar to those found on scholastic aptitude tests, including measures of verbal and numerical ability. In addition, they usually contain subtests with items relevant to the particular profession. The LSAT includes sections that attempt to assess competence in analytical and logical reasoning. The GMAT, which is administered on demand in a computer-adaptive format only at test centers throughout the world, includes a quantitative and an analytical writing section. The DAT has a perceptual ability portion, and the MCAT includes scores in such areas as the physical and biological sciences as well as a writing sample. Scores on each of the tests are reported in very different types of standard scores with different means and standard deviations. For example, the MCAT yields standard scores ranging from 1 to 15, with a mean of approximately 8 and a standard deviation of approximately 2.5. The LSAT now reports scores ranging from 120 to 180, with a mean of approximately 150 and a standard deviation of approximately 10. For the DAT, scores range from 1 to 30, with a mean of 15 and a standard deviation of 5. The GMAT, used by most graduate schools of business, reports subtest scores ranging from 0 to 60, with a mean of 30, and total scores similar to those of the GRE, with a range of 200 to 800 and a mean of 500. The writing portion receives a score of 1 to 6.

Academic Achievement Tests

Hundreds of thousands of achievement tests are administered each year, primarily in educational institutions ranging from kindergarten through graduate and professional schools. Others are administered for licensure and certification in trades and professions, in medical specialties, or for the selection and promotion of postal workers. This section presents school, college-level, and adult achievement tests. The following major section will discuss high-stakes testing, an issue associated often with school achievement tests.

Although the public often misinterprets the results of these test batteries, considerable pains have been taken to provide the results in understandable language and formats. The test publishers market a wide variety of support and interpretive materials for use with teachers, counselors, parents, and students.

Most students take standardized achievement tests, which are used for a variety of purposes, at regular intervals during their first 12 years of schooling. These tests are used in a diagnostic way to identify the strengths and weaknesses of specific skills and achievements in individual students. As a result of such diagnoses, students can be selected for specific types of instruction, either remedial or advanced in nature. For this reason, the tests are often used as a part of the regular guidance and counseling program in an institution. Counselors thus become involved in interpreting the results to the students themselves, to their parents, and to teachers and other professionals.

School Achievement Tests

The most commonly used national achievement test batteries include (a) the Iowa Assessments, (b) the Stanford Achievement Tests, (c) the Metropolitan Achievement Tests, and (d) the TerraNova Tests. Results are usually reported in a full range of derived scores, including scale scores, national and local percentile ranks, normal curve equivalents such as stanines, and grade equivalents. These four test series are briefly described as examples of such batteries.

Iowa Assessments
The **Iowa Assessments** is a 2012 rebranding of the **Iowa Tests of Basic Skills** (ITBS) and the **Iowa Tests of Educational Development** (ITED); the ITBS and ITED were intended for use with students in kindergarten through Grade 8 and Grades 9–12, respectively. The tests are designed to measure basic educational skills, including vocabulary, reading, language, and mathematics for the early grades, with the addition of social studies, science, and information utilization tests for the upper grades.

In the 2016–2017 school year, the Iowa Assessments unveiled their new tests, the **Next Generation Iowa Assessments**. These assessments are designed for students in kindergarten through Grade 11 and are available in paper-and-pencil or online formats. The assessments are aligned with the Iowa Core and can be used to measure student growth and college readiness as well as gauge instructional outcomes. Items and scales developed for these assessments were piloted and validated with Iowa students through research conducted at the University of Iowa. Score reports can be generated for students as well as school personnel in the school building or at the district level.

The **Iowa Early Learning Inventory** (IELI), also produced from the University of Iowa Testing Program, is a brief observational instrument to be completed by kindergarten or early first-grade teachers to measure six behavioral areas related to school learning. These areas are general knowledge, oral communication, written language, math concepts, work habits, and attentive behavior. The IELI yields an individual learning profile for the student and his or her parents, a class diagnostic report to gauge the comparative developmental level of each student across the six areas, and a group summary of student scores (i.e., the percentage of the group scoring at each developmental level).

Stanford Achievement Test

The **Stanford Achievement Test** Series, 10th edition (Stanford 10), is a series of achievement tests from kindergarten through Grade 12, with separate tests for each of the 13 levels that do not repeat item content except for Grades 11 and 12. Each test battery contains a number of different subtests, with the Stanford Early School Achievement Tests (SESAT) for kindergarten and the first grade and the Tests of Academic Skills (TASK) for Grades 9–12. The typical battery is composed of 8–10 untimed subtests yielding total scores in six or seven subject areas. They contain multiple-choice, open-ended, and writing-prompts items. Easy and difficult items are mixed to prevent students from feeling frustrated and giving up as they reach increasingly difficult items (Carney, 2005). It was standardized in combination with the Otis–Lennon School Ability Test, seventh edition. The Stanford 10 is available in four equivalent forms, along with Spanish (Aprenda 3), Braille, and large-type editions.

Metropolitan Achievement Tests

The Metropolitan test was first published in the 1930s and has undergone a number of revisions since then. Examination of subject-matter textbooks, curricula, and educational objectives and trends has gone into the item development for each revision. The **METROPOLITAN8** (MAT8) is the eighth edition of the Metropolitan Achievement Tests, and it provides 13 overlapping batteries from kindergarten through Grade 12 (Harwell, 2005). The battery consists of a varying number of subtests in basic skills areas beginning with reading, mathematics, and language to which science and social studies are added in the early primary grades and research skills and thinking skills are added in the remaining grades, yielding a total of seven achievement areas. Open-ended versions are available for reading and math, and there is a separate test for writing. Predicted scores for the PSAT in Grades 9 and 10 and ACT and SAT scores for Grades 11 and 12 are available using MAT8 results.

TerraNova Tests

The **TerraNova Tests**, formally known as the California Achievement Test and Comprehensive Test of Basic Skills, assess academic achievement from kindergarten through Grade 12. The test series, now in its third edition, includes assessments of reading, language, mathematics, science, and social studies for all school grades using both multiple-choice and student-constructed response items for four versions. These versions (Survey, Complete Battery, Multiple Assessment, Plus) range from 15 minutes for a subtest to over 4 hours for more extensive versions. In addition to the aforementioned content domains, the Plus version also assesses word analysis, vocabulary, language mechanics, spellings, and mathematics computation.

TerraNova 3 was normed with a U.S. sample of approximately 200,000 students stratified by ethnicity, geographic region, community type, socioeconomic status, and special needs. Statistical procedures indicate no gender or ethnic differences in terms of respondents' scores (J. O. Anderson, 2010). Norm-referenced (e.g., national percentiles, stanines, grade equivalent scores) and criterion-referenced (i.e., five proficiency levels for four age/grade clusters) scoring procedures are provided in the manual. The test series is available in Braille, Spanish, and large-print versions.

All of these national batteries of achievement tests are highly reliable, with interrater reliability typically exceeding .90 per content domain and KR-20 reliabilities yielding adequate reliability for subtests overall. The test series, however, lacks test–retest reliability data. TerraNova 3 also demonstrates strong content, construct, and criterion-related validity. In order to establish local validity, of course, the test content must be examined to determine whether it mirrors the curricula and goals of the particular school or district. J. O. Anderson (2010) noted that, because TerraNova 3 was developed for a U.S. context, there are several items related to areas such as U.S. history and currency and nonmetric units that are inappropriate for use outside the U.S. system.

College-Level Achievement Tests

Several college-level testing programs have been created as a basis for awarding college credit other than by enrolling in college courses. These programs include the **College-Level Examination Program** (CLEP; College Board, 2016b) and the **Advanced Placement program** (AP program; College Board, 2016a) administered by the College Entrance Examination Board (CEEB).

The CLEP contains (a) general examinations that assess college-level achievement in five basic liberal arts areas usually covered during the first 2 undergraduate years and (b) 35 multiple-choice subject examinations, each taking 90 minutes to complete, covering a wide range of popular introductory college-level courses. By achieving a satisfactory score (typically 50 on a 20- to 80-point scale) students can, subject to college policy, receive three to 12 credits toward their degree (College Board, 2016b). The examinations are administered on a computer, and results are immediately available. There is usually a test center charge in addition to the cost of the examination.

The AP program provides materials and examinations for college-level courses to be offered in secondary schools for which high school students may gain college credit or obtain advanced placement in college courses (College Board, 2016a). Once a program for a few select high school students, it now reaches over a million students, and the majority of American high schools now participate. Passing a number of AP examinations can save students substantial tuition fees once they are in college. The examinations, for which there is a fee, are 3 hours in length and contain both multiple-choice and either essay or problem items. The AP provides 35 different examinations in 19 different academic fields. AP examinations are scored on a 1–5 basis, with colleges typically giving credit for a 3 or better but with some of the choosier ones now requiring a 4 or 5.

The ETS's **Test of English as a Foreign Language** (TOEFL; Educational Testing Service, 2016a) has been administered in its paper-and-pencil version since the mid-1960s to international students who have applied for admission to U.S. colleges and universities. The current TOEFL iBT (Internet-based testing) represents the latest advance in computer-administered testing. All four English skills necessary for success in American institutions—reading, writing, listening, and speaking—are assessed over the Internet. The test consists of four sections: Listening, Speaking, Reading, and a Written Essay. For the Listening and Speaking sections, examinees read some text, listen to a brief lecture, and then respond to questions. They wear a headphone and speak into a microphone, and their speech is digitally recorded and transmitted to a scoring network where humans score the responses. The scores on each section are converted to a 0–30 scale, yielding a Total Score of 0–120 (Educational Testing Service, 2016a). It is administered at technology and university centers throughout the world. Tutorials and practice exercises are available on a CD-ROM or can be downloaded from the TOEFL website. Students applying to professional and graduate schools from other countries are usually required to obtain certain minimum scores on the TOEFL.

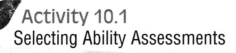

Activity 10.1
Selecting Ability Assessments

Select one of the ability assessments discussed in this chapter. Use assessment sources discussed earlier in the text to collect psychometric information on the assessment. Reflect on the following questions:

- What is the psychometric evidence (e.g., reliability, validity, standardization sample, scoring information) for the assessment? How strong is this evidence?
- How would you use this instrument in your practice?
- What are some of the advantages and disadvantages of the assessment?

Present the information to the larger group.

Adult Achievement Tests

Several test batteries have been created to assess adults' general achievement. These test batteries include the **Tests of Adult Basic Education** (TABE 9/10), the **Adult Basic Learning Examination** (ABLE), and the **Basic Achievement Skills Inventory** (BASI). The tests that comprise the TABE are designed to assess the basic skills that adults need to live and work (Data Recognition Corporation/CTB, 2016). There are five levels, with two parallel forms and a Spanish edition, representing difficulty levels ranging from less than a first-grade level to college level. Reading, mathematics, and language skills are assessed. A locator test of 25 vocabulary words and 25 mathematical items yields scores that indicate the appropriate level to use. Although scores are based on adult norms, grade equivalents to California Achievement Test grade levels are reported along with estimated scores on the Tests of General Education Development, or GED (pre-2002 battery), which are taken by candidates for high school equivalency diplomas.

The ABLE, second edition (Karlsen & Gardner, 1986), provides assessment of adult learning in vocabulary, reading comprehension, spelling, language, number operations, and problem solving. All tests are untimed and may be self-scored. A Spanish edition is available. This battery is often used in adult education programs. The BASI is designed for use with students and adults. It includes six subtests assessing language, reading, and mathematics skills. It is published in two equivalent forms for four age levels (Bardos, 2004).

Other Achievement Tests

There are several academic achievement tests administered on an individual basis to obtain diagnostic information about such skills as reading, mathematics, and spelling. These tests include the **Wide Range Achievement Test**, fourth edition (WRAT4; Wilkinson & Robertson, 2005), the **Kaufman Test of Educational Achievement**–Normative Update (K-TEA-II; Kaufman & Kaufman, 2003), and the **Wechsler Individual Achievement Test**–third edition (WIAT-III; Wechsler, 2009). All provide norms based on national samples from 6-year-olds to adults. The WRAT4 has two equivalent forms and a large-print form. The K-TEA-II has a brief screening form and provides an error analysis form for identifying remediation needs for writing IEPs. The WIAT-III contains 16 achievement subtests (e.g., oral reading, math fluency, listening comprehension) and has been linked with several Wechsler scales.

High-Stakes Testing

Achievement tests are also used (and often misused) in attempts to evaluate the quality of the curricula and instruction within courses, programs, schools, or school systems. **High-stakes testing** is a well-intentioned practice that aims to serve several functions, including ensuring that pertinent content and skills that are embedded within state curricula are learned. Some of these functions include providing teachers and other stakeholders with information about student performance, addressing perceived problems in education, ensuring taxpayer funds are appropriate distributed, and providing information to communities about the qualities of their schools. Scores on high-stakes tests are assumed to serve as a barometer for the quality of instruction, and thus incentives or sanctions could be tied to these scores to impact quality (Madaus & Russell, 2010–2011).

One purpose of high-stakes testing is to create educational opportunities for students that were "left behind" in terms of access and equity. "Testing is viewed as both a system of *monitoring* student performance and a *vehicle of change* driving what is taught and how it is taught, what is learned and how it is learned" (Madaus & Russell, 2010–2011, p. 21).

The use of tests to demonstrate accountability and student learning dates back to fifteenth-century Italy, where tests were used to hold teachers responsible for student learning. Since that time, particular tests have served to hold students and stakeholders accountable, as policymakers have made decisions about often scarce resources (Madaus & Russell, 2010–2011). The **Every Student Succeeds Act** (ESSA) is the legislation guiding high-stakes testing today. Signed into law in 2015, ESSA is a reauthorization of the Elementary and Secondary Education Act of 1965. ESSA replaced the No Child Left Behind (NCLB) Act to allow for greater flexibility in performance indicators as well as the ability of states to design accountability and intervention processes. With this new flexibility to enact their own processes and measures, state departments of education may have opportunities to engage in innovative practices regarding testing accountability. Table 10.1 provides a brief history of high-stakes testing.

The assumption of ESSA is that increased demands on schools and states will increase student and school performance. ESSA requires annual statewide assessments of student learning, with state-driven performance targets and measures. In addition, states provide interventions to improve student learning in the bottom 5% of schools, schools with subgroups that are falling behind, and/or high schools with high dropout rates. ESSA also provides professional development and financial opportunities for principals. Although this can be useful in preparing stronger principals, it could incentivize high-quality teachers to leave the classroom, where direct student intervention is of the utmost importance. Furthermore, now that ESSA allows states to have more control over defining quality teaching, teachers may find that they have more localized voice in determining their place in high-stakes testing and related accountability decisions (G. Robinson, 2015).

Although high-stakes testing may be favorably viewed as focusing instruction, teaching may however become mechanized, ignoring individual student ways of achievement and teacher creativity. What often gets lost is an emphasis on nontested content and skills areas such as the arts, humanities, social studies, and physical education. The result is a limitation on what is taught within a specific discipline, across subject areas, and across grade levels (Madaus & Russell, 2010–2011). In addition, high-stakes testing legislation redirects what teachers must be competent in: Instead of using context-specific learning and instruction to accommodate diverse learners, teachers must ensure that specific content and skills

Table 10.1
A Modern History of High-Stakes Testing

Era	High-Stakes Testing Legislation or Program
1960s–1970s	The **Elementary and Secondary Education Act (ESEA) of 1965** is part of President Lyndon B. Johnson's War on Poverty and Great Society programs, shifting control of educational reform from state and local bodies to the federal government. Title I, a key part of ESEA, provids funding for schools with disadvantaged children. The federal government allocates approximately $1 billion for Title I schools based on child poverty data.
1980s	*A Nation at Risk* (National Commission on Excellence in Education, 1983) is published, highlighting an agenda under President Ronald Reagan's administration of more stringent academic standards and requirements and change in teacher preparation. Federal funding is decreased during this time. Title I is amended in 1988 to mandate that schools demonstrate academic progress through standardized test scores. This mandate shifts funding priorities from poverty data to assessment data.
1990s	President George H. W. Bush works with U.S. governors to develop national educational goals that create several educational reform initiatives, particularly development of academic standards. The **Goals 2000: Educate America Act** is passed in 1994, requiring states to establish academic standards for each grade level and assessments to be administered at least once in Grades 3–5, 6–9, and 10–12 to ensure that those standards are being met. Those districts that failed to meet "adequate yearly progress" (AYP) are required to formally identify solutions to improve their schools.
2000s	President George W. Bush emphasizes that the **No Child Left Behind Act of 2001** (NCLB, 2002) should be developed, because achievement gaps still exists despite the fact that the federal government has appropriated billions of dollars to educational equity. The NCLB provides a timeline for all schools to make AYP, along with consequences for those that do not. In addition, teachers under NCLB have to document their competency (i.e., be "highly qualified"). The NCLB Act is reauthorized in 2007.
2010s	President Barack Obama signs the **Every Student Succeeds Act** into law in 2015, a reauthorization of the ESEA of 1965.

Note. Information related to some of the modern history of high-stakes testing presented in the table is from Duffy et al. (2008).

areas of high-stakes tests are taught (Duffy, Giordano, Farrell, Paneque, & Crump, 2008). However, given that ESSA allows other performance measures beyond test scores to be used to demonstrate success, teachers may be able to focus more on teaching rather than test scores (G. Robinson, 2015).

Recall from Chapter 4 that cultural background influences the way individuals respond to testing. Furthermore, success on achievement tests likely relates to appropriate demonstration of individual accomplishment, something that may not be culturally valued by some test takers (Madaus & Russell, 2010–2011). Thus, test scores may have more to do with the cultural influences than school quality.

School counselors, who typically have the responsibility of coordinating the administration of these test batteries, need to be aware of students' anxiety and stress levels as they approach the tests. Duffy et al. (2008) provided the following strategies for school counselors who work in settings heavily influenced by high-stakes testing legislation: (a) recognize their stakeholder role for responding to the negative impact of mandated assessment; (b) continually evaluate research used to justify teaching methods and school programs, including comprehensive school counseling programs; (c) advocate for students and families when teaching methods and content restrict learning or negatively impact diverse students; and (d) identify the negative impact of assessment and collaborate with others to address consequences.

Activity 10.2
Ability Testing and Multicultural Assessment

Discuss the following in small groups:

- How might ability testing impact diverse individuals negatively? What are specific ability test examples?
- What are ways that you can integrate supplemental information with ability assessment data with your diverse clients?
- How can you advocate for diverse clients with respect to the use of ability testing?

Study Habits Inventories

Counselors in high schools and colleges often work with students who are having difficulties with their coursework or are not achieving academically up to their potential. In working with such students, counselors find that a study habits inventory is often useful for several reasons: first, to allow students to understand how adequate their study habits are compared with those of other students; second, as a teaching tool, because the items on such inventories have useful instructional value; and third, to point out particular weaknesses, which is useful in discussing specific activities for improvement. In addition to their diagnostic purposes, these inventories also act as structured exercises that can help teach good study techniques and point out ineffective attitudes and behaviors. Several of the achievement test batteries used at the high school level, such as the California or Metropolitan achievement batteries, contain subtests that assess study skills.

The **Study Attitudes and Methods Survey** (SAMS) was developed to assess noncognitive factors associated with success in schools (Michael, Michael, & Zimmerman, 1988). The 90-item inventory provides scores for six factor dimensions: Academic Interest—Love of Learning, Academic Drive—Conformity, Study Methods, Study Anxiety, Manipulation, and Alienation Toward Authority. The survey, which takes approximately 20 to 30 minutes to complete, has both high school and college norms available.

The **College Student Inventory** of the Noel-Levitz Retention Management System is designed to identify academic and affective factors related to student attrition (Noel-Levitz, 2016). It contains 17 scales such as Study Habits, Intellectual Interests, Attitude Toward Educators, and Math and Science Confidence. Form A has 194 items, and Form B has 100 items. It is typically administered to entering college students at orientation and yields scores that can alert advisers, instructors, and student service providers to potential problems that a student might face. The tool is available in paper-and-pencil, online, and Spanish versions.

The **Learning and Study Strategies Inventory** (LASSI), in its third edition, is the most widely used learning inventory on college campuses. The 60-item inventory contains 10 scales categorized into three components of strategic learning (i.e., Skill, Will, Self-Regulation). Scales are as follows: (a) Skill (Information Processing, Selecting Main Ideas, Test Strategies), (b) Will (Attitude, Motivation, Anxiety), and (c) Self-Regulation (Concentration, Time Management, Self-Testing, Using Academic Resources). Students administered the LASSI can understand how they compare to other college students in the 10 strategic learning areas. There is a 76-item high school version of the LASSI (LASSI-HS) as well as a web version.

Knowledge that individuals prefer different types of learning styles and, in fact, often learn more effectively when the instructional technique matches their preferred learning style has led to the development of inventories designed to assess such individual learning styles. There are four such inventories, all titled **Learning Style Inventory** (Canfield & Canfield, 1988; R. Dunn, Dunn, & Price, 1987; Kolb, 1985; Renzulli & Smith, 1978). They are designed to help individuals assess their preferred methods of learning and to identify differences among individual learning styles and corresponding learning environments. This information can then be used to provide more individualized instructional methods. These inventories typically yield scores on three or four dimensions of learning styles or modes, such as need for structure, active experimenting, or abstract conceptualizing. Robert Sternberg proposed a theory of 13 thinking styles that he termed *mental self-government*. He constructed the **Thinking Styles Inventory** to assess them (Zhang & Sternberg, 2001). There are significant differences in the types of learning styles assessed by these instruments, thus, the counselor should evaluate the particular purpose for which the inventory is to be administered and select the inventory that best meets that purpose

Tip Sheet
Ability Testing

✓ Almost all counselors can expect to be consulted about ability tests, even if they work in settings where they seldom make use of them. Be familiar with various tests and their benefits and limitations.

✓ Reflect on the function of a specific ability test, as ability tests have functions of either assessing learning, predicting learning, or both.

✓ Present a balanced view of the role of scholastic aptitude tests to students seeking college admission. Although these tests have many criticisms, they can contribute to academic selection and placement by identifying unrecognized academic potential and by acting as a correction factor for high school grades resulting from differing levels of competition.

✓ Interpret college admission test scores with respect to the higher education institution to which the client is seeking admission. There are great differences in the distribution of students in regard to academic aptitude among the different institutions of higher education in the United States. These differences can greatly affect both the chances for admission and the chances for success at specific institutions.

✓ Assist individuals in developing supplemental data evidence to correspond with ability test scores. This evidence is particularly important in situations where the individual may be disadvantaged with the testing process or format.

✓ Critically evaluate teaching and testing practices in light of ESSA and the subsequent emphasis on high-stakes testing. Counselors serve important stakeholder and advocate roles to ensure practices and data are used appropriately.

✓ Convey an interest in research regarding teaching methods and effectiveness, as students' experiences in the classroom—including ability testing—can impact them throughout their academic careers.

✓ Use study habits inventories with students to help them feel more prepared and gauge academic-related difficulties.

Chapter Summary

Individuals encounter a variety of ability tests throughout their formative educational years, and counselors are to be familiar with what scores on aptitude and achievement assessments mean and how they are used in educational decision making. Whereas aptitude assessment reflects one's ability to learn a specific knowledge or skill set, achievement assessment refers to measuring learning of previous content. Academic aptitude tests required for admission to graduate and professional programs typically have similar verbal and quantitative sections but otherwise vary considerably in subjects that are assessed and in the types of standard scores with which they report results. Academic achievement batteries are administered in virtually all primary and secondary schools to provide useful diagnostic information regarding the strengths and weaknesses of students' specific skills and achievements. The results are increasingly used and misused in high-stakes testing and in evaluating the quality of instruction within classes, schools, and school systems.

The two major tests of aptitude in higher education are the SAT and ACT. There are several testing programs that correspond with these tests, including the PSAT, UNIACT Interest Inventory, the EXPLORE and PLAN programs, and the ASSET Student Success System. The chapter addressed several issues related to these tests' predictive validity as well as those issues related to using academic aptitude test scores in college admission decisions. With respect to aptitude assessment in graduate and professional schools, the chapter presented several major assessments: the GRE, MAT, MCAT, DAT, LSAT, and GMAT.

Academic achievement tests involve school-level, college-level, and adult achievement tests. Some of the popular school achievement tests include the Next Generation Iowa Assessments, IELI, Stanford Achievement Test, METROPOLITAN8, and the TerraNova Tests. Those most used at the college level include the CLEP, AP program, COMPASS/ESL, and the TOEFL. Adult achievement tests include the TABE, the ABLE, and the BASI. Achievement tests that may be useful include the WRAT, the K-TEA-II, and the WIAT-II.

The chapter included a discussion of high-stakes testing, a prominent issue in schools today because of ESSA legislation. Counselors, particularly school counselors, are to be familiar with the intended and unintended consequences of high-stakes testing and serve as advocates for change as appropriate. Finally, study habits inventories are presented, including the SAMS, College Student Inventory, and the LASSI.

Review Questions

1. What is the distinction between academic and achievement tests?
2. What are the major tests used for assessing aptitude for higher education? What are the benefits and challenges cited with using these scores?
3. What are some of the criticisms of using GRE scores to predict graduate school success?
4. What was the rationale for the ESSA legislation? What are the benefits and challenges of ESSA and high-stakes testing?
5. How can study habits inventories be used in counseling?

Resources for Further Learning

Publications

Pandya, J. Z. (2013). *Overtested: How high-stakes accountability fails English language learners.* New York, NY: Teachers College Press.

Waugh, C. K., & Greenlund, N. E. (2012). *Assessment of student achievement* (10th ed.). Boston, MA: Pearson.

Web Resources

ACT
http://www.act.org/content/act/en/products-and-services/the-act.html
This website provides information about the ACT, including test preparation materials.

CLEP
https://clep.collegeboard.org
This website contains information on the College Level Examination Program.

College Board

https://collegereadiness.collegeboard.org

This website includes information on the SAT and the PSAT/NMSQT, including sample items.

Educational Testing Service

https://www.ets.org/toefl/ibt/prepare/

This website provides information about the TOEFL, including free test preparation resources.

Every Student Succeeds Act (ESSA)

http://www.ed.gov/essa

This site links to information and updates about ESSA.

LASSI User's Manual

http://www.hhpublishing.com/LASSImanual.pdf

This website contains the manual for the LASSI.

Miller Analogies Test

http://www.pearsonassessments.com/postsecondaryeducation/graduate_admissions/mat.html

This website links to information about the Miller Analogies Test, including sample items and reports.

National Assessment of Educational Progress (NAEP)

http://nces.ed.gov/nationsreportcard/

This website provides updated education statistics across various topics.

Stanford Achievement Test Series, Tenth Edition

http://www.pearsonassessments.com/learningassessments/products/100000415/stanford-achievement-test-series-tenth-edition.html?pid=SAT10C#tab-scoring

This website links to sample score reports for this assessment.

The University of Iowa, Iowa Testing Programs

https://itp.education.uiowa.edu

This website includes information on the various Iowa tests.

Wechsler Individual Achievement Test–Third Edition (WAIT-III)

http://www.pearsonclinical.com/psychology/products/100000463/wechsler-individual-achievement-testthird-edition-wiatiii-wiat-iii.html#tab-scoring

This website includes sample reports for this assessment.

Chapter 11

Career and Life-Planning Assessment

Careers play a predominant role in most people's lives. Career development is a continual process across the life span, and counselors have an important obligation to assess career-related concerns and successes as part (or central) to the counseling process. Counselors help clients with the process of making educational and career choices and adapting to the challenges inherent in career development. Career and life planning involve assessing both the *process* (i.e., attitudinal and cognitive readiness) and *content* (interests, values, and abilities) associated with career development. This chapter focuses primarily on career readiness, which includes measures concerning attitudes toward career planning and career-planning competencies. In addition, comprehensive assessment programs are introduced as a means for identifying academic, career, or social environments that would be compatible with a person's preferences and abilities. The measures of career choice and development discussed in this chapter are important in determining appropriate counseling interventions for clients.

Test Your Knowledge

Select the most appropriate choice for each item.

_____ 1. Which of the following quantitative assessments may be useful in career and life-planning assessment?
   a. Vocational card sort   b. Ability Profiler
   c. Life Career Rainbow   d. Occupational tree

_____ 2. An assessment primarily useful in measuring students' career readiness is:
   a. Development Inventory   b. Career Mastery Inventory
   c. Career Attitudes and   d. Childhood Career Development
      Strategies Inventory   Scale

_____ 3. Which of the following is *not* an example of a comprehensive assessment program?
    a. SIGI-3   b. DISCOVER
    c. O*NET   d. KEYS

_____ 4. Which of the following is a popular assessment program used with military personnel?
    a. ASVAB   b. DAT
    c. DISCOVER   d. O*NET

❑ T ❑ F 5. Career-planning programs that add the use of self-ratings for abilities not assessed with objective tests are more successful in predicting occupational criteria than those that rely on objective tests alone.

Introduction to Career and Life-Planning Assessment

Career counseling is at the heart of the counseling profession, and career assessment has thus been an integral component of counseling and other related fields for more than 100 years (Herr, 2013). Whether it has been used to help place an increasingly diverse workforce during the Industrial Revolution, or to generate data to inform legislative policy, or to administer career assessments or tools to children and adolescents in school settings or adults in diverse settings, career assessment has played and continues to play a major role in understanding and affecting client functioning.

The definition of career counseling, or *vocational guidance* as it is also known, has been articulated over time within various career theories and later applied to and measured using quantitative and qualitative career assessments. In *Choosing a Vocation*, Frank Parsons (1909) described a three-part approach to career counseling:

> (1) a clear understanding of yourself, your attitudes, abilities, interests, ambitions, resources, limitations, and their causes; (2) a knowledge of the requirements and conditions of success, advantages and disadvantages, compensation, opportunities, and prospects in different lines of work; (3) true reasoning on the relations of these two groups of fact. (p. 5)

This approach has been the cornerstone guiding counselors in assessing and intervening in career-related concerns. It is important to note, however, that analyzing how self-knowledge relates to knowledge about the world of work is not simple (McMahon & Watson, 2012). Thus, counselors are to take great care in considering which assessments they use, how they interpret their findings and relate these findings to other client information, and how external factors—including diversity and social justice considerations—matter in career exploration and decision making.

How might career assessment relate specifically to career counseling? Niles and Harris-Bowlsbey (2017) identified seven steps that bridge counseling assessment and practice: (a) becoming aware of the need for career decisions, (b) learning or relearning about vocational self-concept, (c) identifying occupational alternatives, (d) obtaining information about identified alternatives, (e) making tentative choices from among available occupations, (f) making educational choices, and (g) implementing a vocational choice. These steps clearly indicate two key things: Assessment is ongoing throughout the career counseling process, and assessment is expanded beyond a counselor administering tools to the client engaging in activities external to counseling sessions.

Any career assessment process should include attention to multicultural and social justice counseling competencies (Ratts et al., 2016) in the context of career assessment. In addition to the competencies outlined by Ratts et al. (2016) and the Association for Assessment and Research in Counseling (AARC) Multicultural Assessment Standards

(AARC, 2012), a couple of models may be useful during career assessment. Flores et al. (2006) proposed the culturally appropriate career assessment model (CACAM); this model involves the four steps of gathering cultural information, selecting culturally appropriate assessments, administering career assessments, and interpreting career assessment results. In addition, Ridley, Li, and Hill (1998) offered the multicultural assessment process (MAP) model. Similar to the CACAM, the MAP model includes the four phases of identifying cultural data from multiple methods, interpreting these data by developing a hypothesis, incorporating cultural data by using standardized assessments to test the hypothesis, and concluding the assessment process using the results of hypothesis testing.

Counselors may use career assessments for a variety of reasons as they select their interventions, and these uses are closely tied to maximizing client self-exploration and decision making. Herr et al. (2004) identified four uses of career assessment: prediction, discrimination, monitoring, and evaluation. With respect to **prediction**, results from career assessments may be used to predict future career-related performance. Prediction may be clinical or statistical, although statistical prediction (i.e., predictive validity) is preferred. The use of career assessments for **discrimination** refers to continually evaluating an individual's abilities as well as his or her interests. These areas are assessed to determine likelihood of success by discerning which groups the individual is most like. This chapter presents some assessments that measure confidence, barriers, and actual abilities; several interest inventories are discussed in Chapter 12. **Monitoring**, the third use of career assessment, relates to an individual's career progress. In addition to tests that measure readiness, those that monitor can also detect values important to a client (assessment of values is discussed in Chapter 12). In essence, monitoring refers to career maturity and adaptability, with maturity related to readiness in younger populations and adaptability concerned with coping with developmental tasks in adulthood (Hirschi, Herrmann, & Keller, 2015; Hirschi & Valero, 2015; Super, Osborne, Walsh, Brown, & Niles, 1992). The final use, **evaluation**, relates to the use of assessment tools to measure how well individual career goals have been met. In addition, it can refer to how well the career-counseling process relates to client outcomes (Herr et al., 2004).

There is a high demand in career and life-planning assessment for standardized career assessments, particularly with the use of increased technology in counseling. Thus, the majority of this chapter focuses on quantitative assessments that relate to the career development process. As you may recall from Chapter 2, however, **qualitative assessment** techniques may be useful as a stand-alone or supplemental tool when counseling clients. Qualitative assessment involves nonstandardized and often informal approaches to assessment that can include self-estimates of ability, behavioral observations, interviews, biographical measures, projective techniques, and other career-related activities. These techniques may be quite useful to present a client with a holistic picture of values, interests, and abilities that may not be captured by standardized assessments alone (Brott, 2015; McMahon & Patton, 2015).

Counselors may use a vocational **card sort**, which can provide an informal assessment of occupational knowledge. According to a procedure developed by G. W. Peterson (1998), a client sorts occupational titles into separate piles on the basis of the titles' similarity to each other. The client then labels and makes comparisons among the piles. He or she is asked to name the attributes of the occupations in the occupational pile that he or she believes most resembles him or her. Throughout this process, the client verbalizes the reasons for decisions. This process provides helpful insights regarding the maturity of the client's knowledge and understanding of careers. This procedure can serve as a simple means of evaluating a client's career development and as a stimulus for career exploration.

The **Career Style Interview** (Savickas, 1998) may be a useful tool for contextualizing a client's career development by clarifying self-concept through open-ended questions. These questions help to define life roles, strategies, motivations, and desires related to careers (Taber, Hartung, Briddick, Briddick, & Rehfuss, 2011). The interview begins with the opening question, "How can I be useful to you in constructing your career?" Other questions elicit information about leisure activities, interests in various media, favorite subjects, and early recollections (Taber et al., 2011).

Okocha (1998) presented four qualitative career assessment devices that counselors may find useful in the career development process: life career assessment interview, life line, genogram/occupational tree, and Life Career Rainbow. The **life career assessment interview** is a structured assessment containing four components: career assessment (client work, volunteer experiences, education, training, and leisure), typical day (client personality items), strengths and obstacles (barriers in career planning and development), and summary (identification of life themes, interests, and skills). The **life line** tool is a graphical way to measure a client's life history—events that have had a positive and negative significance. This activity is useful to increase a client's self-awareness of values and needs. A **genogram/occupational tree** may be useful in career and life-planning counseling by representing graphically the careers of the client's family across at least three generations (however the client defines family). Several process questions accompany genogram development. Finally, Okocha mentioned the **Life Career Rainbow** (Super et al., 1992) as a qualitative assessment technique. For this tool, a client identifies how nine life roles are salient across the life span. In addition, a client notes possible barriers in attaining ideal roles.

McMahon and Watson (2012) presented a storytelling approach, based in narrative counseling and social constructivism, that can guide counselors to help clients craft future career stories based from quantitative career assessment data. The approach, referred to as the **Integrative Structured Interview** (ISI) process, fosters client self-exploration through several story-crafting questions. Using results from the Self-Directed Search (SDS), McMahon and Watson (2012) present 13 questions related to crafting a story about the code letters, the code order, the code letters in life contexts, personal reflection, and work contexts as well as use of the SDS code in the future based in present and past experiences.

Measures of Career Readiness

Career development involves assessing process and content variables in order to make sound career decisions that are congruent with a client's readiness, knowledge and skill set, interests, and values, among others. This section focuses on measures of career readiness, or the ability to understand and plan careers and other aspects of life across the life span. Career readiness may also be referred to as career maturity and career adaptability (Super et al., 1992). **Career maturity**, which served as the ultimate goal of career development in Super's early work, indicates a client's readiness to accomplish the career developmental tasks appropriate for his or her age. In essence, career readiness indicates how motivated a client may be to engage in career decision making. In later work, Super and others shifted the goal of career development from career maturity to career adaptability (Savickas, 1997; Super et al., 1992). **Career adaptability**, which emphasizes situational factors as well as developmental tasks, refers to a client's readiness to cope with both the predictable and unpredictable aspects of career selection and participation. It broadens the criteria for evaluating career development by acknowledging the client's need to respond to new or novel circumstances. The concept of career adaptability is more appropriate for nontraditional clients, for adults, and for individuals from different cultures (Hirschi et al., 2015; Hirschi & Valero, 2015).

As indicated by the assessments included here, career readiness may entail examining beliefs about careers, level of confidence, and degree of accessibility to information about careers and self. Lack of readiness may create career indecision or blocks to career planning. Table 11.1 presents a snapshot of 15 assessments. This list is not exhaustive, and

Table 11.1
Measures of Career Readiness

Career Assessment	Description	Primary Population	Sample Items
Adult Career Concerns Inventory (ACCI)	Evaluates degree of concern related to development along four stages (exploration, establishment, maintenance, disengagement) and 12 substages. Available free online (Vocopher, n.d.).	Adults	Becoming especially knowledgeable or skillful at work Keeping the respect of people in my field Planning well for retirement
Career Attitudes and Strategies Inventory (CASI)	Assesses agreement with nine aspects of career or work adaptation.	Adults	Family responsibilities limit my career responsibilities. I listen to advice about how I should do my job. I don't like change in my life.
Career Beliefs Inventory (CBI)	Assesses beliefs that may relate to career goals; these assumptions may foster or hinder career planning.	Adolescents Young adults Adults	A career choice is a personal one. There are no jobs that can satisfy me. I am content to maintain my present level of skill.
Career Decision-Making Difficulties Questionnaire (CDDQ)	Assesses ability to cope with difficulties (i.e., lack of readiness, lack of information, inconsistent information) associated with career decisions.	Adolescents Young adults	I know that I have to choose a career, but I don't have the motivation to make the decision now (I don't feel like it).
Career Decision Scale (CDS)	Identifies possible causes of career indecision.	Adolescents Young adults	I am usually afraid of failure. I can't make a career choice right now because I don't know what my abilities are. I need more information about what different occupations are like before I can make a career decision.
Career Decision-Making Self-Efficacy Scale (CDMSE)	Measures ability to make effective career decisions regarding self-appraisal, occupational information, goal selection, planning, and problem solving.	Adolescents Young adults Adults	Use the Internet to find information about occupations that interest you.
Career Development Inventory (CDI)	Assesses readiness to make sound educational and vocational choices. Clients rate the extent to which they have thought about or engaged in planning and explored career-related resources or what information they have to inform career decision making. Available online at no cost (Vocopher, n.d.).	Adolescents Young adults	Getting a part-time or summer job which will help me decide what kind of work I might go into.

(Continued)

Table 11.1 *(Continued)*
Measures of Career Readiness

Career Assessment	Description	Primary Population	Sample Items
Career Factors Inventory (CFI)	Measures need for career information and self-knowledge and difficulty in career decision making.	Adolescents Young adults Adults	Before choosing or entering a particular career area I still need to attempt to answer . . . What things are the most important to me? What are my specific goals in life?
Career Futures Inventory (CFI)	Assesses career optimism, perceived knowledge, and career adaptability.	Young adults Adults	I am good at adapting to new work settings. I get excited when I think about my career. I am good at understanding job market trends.
Career Mastery Inventory (CMAS)	Measures career-planning attitudes and competencies.	Adults	I know who to go to for something I want at work.
Career Maturity Inventory–Revised (CMI-R)	Measures career-planning attitudes and competencies.	Adolescents	I will choose my career without paying attention to the feelings of other people. If you have doubts about what you want to do, ask your parents or friends for advice.
Career Thoughts Inventory (CTI)	Evaluates dysfunctional thinking in career decision making related to self-knowledge, occupational knowledge, and communication.	Adolescents Young adults Adults	No field of study or occupation interests me. I know what job I want, but someone's always putting obstacles in my way. I will never understand myself well enough to make a good career choice.
Childhood Career Development Scale	Measures childhood career progress in terms of interests, planning, curiosity/exploration, and other career development areas.	Children	I wonder about different jobs. I have control over the things I do. I think about where I will work when I'm grown up.
My Vocational Situation (MVS)	Assesses career-related concerns associated with vocational identity, occupational information, and barriers that affect decision making.	Adolescents Young adults Adults	I am not sure that my present occupational choice or job is right for me. No single occupation appeals strongly to me. I am not sure of myself in many areas of life.
Skills Confidence Inventory	Assesses perceived level of confidence in performing six career-related skills.	Adolescents Young adults Adults	Learn to repair electrical wiring Design sets for a play Meet new people

you are encouraged to review other available career readiness measures. Furthermore, only brief descriptions of the assessments are provided here, and additional information may be found using information sources discussed earlier in the text (see Chapter 1). *A Counselor's Guide to Career Assessment Instruments* (C. T. Wood & Hays, 2013) may also be a useful resource. Content variables of career development (e.g., work and personal values, interests) are addressed in the following chapter.

Adult Career Concerns Inventory

The **Adult Career Concerns Inventory** (ACCI) measures the career concerns of adults at different stages in their development (Super, Thompson, & Lindeman, 1988). It contains 61 items, which are scored in terms of four developmental stages (Exploration, Establishment, Maintenance, and Disengagement) and 12 substages. Clients rate each item on a 5-point scale ranging from *no concern* to *great concern* on the basis of their present situation. Although most people obtain their highest score (indicating greatest concern) in the stage that is most common for their age, adults who are in the process of career change can be expected to recycle through some of the early developmental stages.

The ACCI clarifies the nature of the developmental tasks of greatest concern to the client at the present time. It can also be used as a teaching device to alert clients to future career challenges. For situations in which time may be of concern, counselors can use a shortened, 12-item form of the ACCI consisting of one item from each of the 12 substages (Perrone, Gordon, Fitch, & Civiletto, 2003).

Career Attitudes and Strategies Inventory

Like the ACCI, the **Career Attitudes and Strategies Inventory** (CASI) was developed to identify and clarify the career problems confronted by adults ages 17 to 77 years old (Holland & Gottfredson, 1994). The CASI consists of 130 items using a 4-point scale (1 = *false* to 4 = *true*) that survey nine aspects of career or work adaptation, such as work involvement, risk-taking style, and geographical barriers. As indicated by the item content, high scores on this scale indicate the realities and some of the difficulties of dual-role responsibilities. Scores on the scales are correlated with other measures of career concerns according to expectations (Holland & Gottfredson, 1994).

Career Beliefs Inventory

The **Career Beliefs Inventory** (CBI) identifies beliefs that may block career goals (Krumboltz, 1991). It contains 96 items answered on a Likert scale (*strongly agree* to *strongly disagree*) that provide the basis for scores on 25 scales, such as Openness, Control, and Taking Risks. Low scores indicate career beliefs that may be problematic depending on the individual's situation.

The CBI can provide valuable information for discussion purposes, but it should not be used as a basis for decision making because of its limited psychometric properties (see Krumboltz, 1988). Despite its limitations as a measurement tool, the CBI can be useful as an interview or discussion aid. M. E. Hall and Rayman (2002) concluded that the CBI can be used effectively with groups as well as individuals, that it can be used to discuss a client's strengths as well as problems, and that the instrument is accompanied by a large amount of user-friendly materials that can be helpful in understanding the impact of career beliefs on career decision making. Case Example 11.1 is a case discussed in the CBI manual (Krumboltz, 1991, p. 10).

Case Example 11.1

Ted

Ted, a college student, disliked his college major (pre-med) but did not believe that he had any other options. Ted obtained a low score on Scale 12, Approval of Others, which indicated that approval of his career plans from someone else was very important to him. When the counselor asked Ted about the possible meaning of this score, he said that he wanted to please his father, who wanted him to become a physician. The counselor asked him to discuss this matter with his father, which Ted did despite fears that it was a hopeless matter. In so doing, he learned that his father's actual goal was to be supportive, not demanding, at which point Ted felt free to change his major from premed to art. Ted's desire to enter art had been blocked by his belief that his father would "simply die" if he did not fulfill the ambitions he had for him, a belief that was at the root of his difficulties. Use of the CBI helped to expose his thinking on this matter, which was then addressed in counseling by encouraging him to gather further evidence to test the accuracy of his thinking.

• • •

Career Decision-Making Difficulties Questionnaire

The **Career Decision-Making Difficulties Questionnaire** (CDDQ) is a 44-item questionnaire that assesses a student's ability to cope with different types of difficulties in deciding on a career (Gati, Kraus, & Osipow, 1996). Gati and Saka (2001) offered an abridged version with 34 items. The items are derived from a taxonomy of career-decision difficulties that distinguishes between difficulties that occur prior to the decision-making process (lack of readiness) and those that occur during the process (lack of information and inconsistent information). It is scored on three broad categories (lack of readiness, lack of information, and inconsistent information) that are divided into 10 subcategories.

Studies indicate that the CDDQ yields reliable and valid results when used to identify the difficulties experienced by students and young adults in making career decisions (Camp, 2000; Gati et al., 1996). Some cultural, gender, and age differences have been noted. Mau (2001, 2004) found that Asian American students reported more difficulties in career decision making than did students from other cultures. Boys have reported greater difficulties than girls in external conflicts and dysfunctional beliefs (Gati & Saka, 2001). High school students have reported more difficulties than older career deciders (Albion & Fogarty, 2002).

The CDDQ results can be used as a basis for deciding what type of intervention is needed; for example, personal counseling for internal or external conflicts, testing for lack of information regarding an individual's interests or abilities, or referral to an occupational library to address a lack of information about occupations (Gati et al., 1996). Furthermore, an Internet-based career-planning system, Making Better Career Decisions, is available for free (see www.cddq.org).

Career Decision Scale

The **Career Decision Scale** (CDS) was developed by Samuel Osipow and his colleagues to identify the antecedents of career indecision for individuals ages 14 to 23 years old (Osipow, 1987). It includes two scales: a 2-item Certainty scale and a 16-item Indecision scale. The 16 items on the Indecision scale represent 16 reasons for career indecision based on interview experiences with clients. For each item, clients indicate on a 4-point scale to what extent the item accurately describes their situation.

Despite relatively low test–retest reliabilities, results from individual items can be helpful in suggesting hypotheses that can be explored in counseling. The CDS has been widely used as an outcome instrument, often as a pre–post measure in evaluating counseling interventions. It has been used effectively in a wide variety of cultural settings (e.g., Nasab, Abdul Kadir, & Hassan, 2015; Osipow & Winer, 1996; Presti et al., 2013). Although it has some shortcomings, principally in clarifying the meaning of its scores, it has been praised for its ease of use, its applicability in counseling and research, and its extensive research support.

Career Decision Self-Efficacy Scale

The **Career Decision Self-Efficacy Scale**, formally referred to as the Career Decision-Making Self-Efficacy Scale (CDMSE), assesses a client's perceptions of his or her ability to make effective career decisions (Betz & Taylor, 1994). This instrument has been developed as a means of testing and implementing self-efficacy theory and, by extension, social cognitive career theory (Bandura, 1986, 1997; Lent, Brown, & Hackett, 1994). According to these theories, individuals who express confidence in their ability to perform a task (independent of their actual abilities) show greater decisiveness, higher levels of accomplishment, and greater persistence in that activity than do individuals who lack such confidence.

The CDMSE consists of 50 items that represent the critical skills in career decision making suggested by Crites's (1978) model of career maturity. It can be scored on five scales (Self-Appraisal, Occupational Information, Goal Selection, Planning, and Problem-Solving), and scores in these areas can be used to tailor career interventions (Watson, 2013). As predicted by self-efficacy theory, individuals who score low on the CDMSE (indicating lack of confidence in career decision-making ability) are likely to have trouble in deciding on an occupation. CDMSE total scores significantly differentiate among college students with declared majors, tentative majors, and no majors in the expected manner (Betz & Luzzo, 1996). The test authors have developed a shortened, 25-item version of the CDMSE that has produced validity coefficients that are comparable to or higher than those obtained with the full-scale form (Betz, Klein, & Taylor, 1996). Furthermore, Betz, Hammond, and Multon (2005) reported that a 5-point scale is just as psychometrically sound as the 10-point continuum.

Career Development Inventory

The **Career Development Inventory** (CDI) was designed "to assess students' readiness to make sound educational and vocational choices" (A. S. Thompson, Lindeman, Super, Jordaan, & Myers, 1981, p. 7). Although the CDI was constructed some time ago, it "remains the pre-eminent operational definition of career development during adolescence and young adulthood" (Savickas, Briddick, & Watkins, 2002, p. 32).

Part I of the CDI, which includes 80 items, provides two scales each for career-planning attitudes (Career Planning, Career Exploration) and career-planning competencies (Decision Making, World-of-Work Information). A Career Orientation Total score, which serves as a comprehensive measure of career maturity, combines the scores for all four scales. Part II of the CDI, which contains 40 items, evaluates the client's knowledge of the occupational field to which he or she is most attracted. The Knowledge of Preferred Occupational Group scale uses the same 40 multiple-choice items for each occupational group. The correct response for each item (e.g., employment opportunities or educational requirements) varies depending on the occupational field. Part II differs from Part I because of its emphasis on occupational knowledge that pertains to a particular occupational field instead of occupations in general.

Savickas and Hartung (1996) noted that the CDI has been used successfully to predict both career choice perseverance and academic success, and Pietrzak (2013) added that the core scales found in Part I in particular are well developed and well researched. Higher levels of career maturity on the CDI are associated with higher levels of personal and social adjustment (Savickas et al., 2002).

Career Factors Inventory

The **Career Factors Inventory** (CFI) is a 21-item, self-scorable inventory that provides scores on four scales: Need for Career Information, Need for Self-Knowledge, Career Choice Anxiety, and Generalized Indecisiveness (Chartrand, Robbins, & Morrill, 1997).

The scales were designed to measure need for information (first two scales) and difficulty in decision making (last two scales). It provides a relatively broad coverage of the factors underlying career indecision (Kelly, 2002a).

Research supports the structural and discriminant validity of the CFI results when used with college students (D'Costa, 2013; Dickinson & Tokar, 2004). D'Costa (2013) noted that the CFI is somewhat limited both in terms of score reliabilities and available normative data but that it is a useful tool.

Career Futures Inventory

The **Career Futures Inventory** is a brief inventory that provides information about career-planning attitudes and competencies (Rottinghaus, Day, & Borgen, 2005). It includes scales that measure attitudes (Career Optimism, 11 items), competencies (Perceived Knowledge, three items), and overall career maturity or adaptability (Career Adaptability, 11 items). College students with high scores on these scales explore career options more actively and report greater certainty in regard to their career plans than do those with low scores. A short form of the Career Futures Inventory has been developed (see McIlveen, Burton, & Beccaria, 2013).

Career Mastery Inventory

The **Career Mastery Inventory** (abbreviated CMAS to differentiate it from the Career Maturity Inventory [CMI] described below) was constructed by Crites (1993) to assess the career development of adults in the same manner that the CMI assesses the career development of adolescents. Part 1 of the CMAS consists of 90 items with a 7-point Likert scale; this part assesses work attitudes and behavior. Part 2 contains 20 multiple-choice items that measure skill in handling problems in one's work situation.

For Part 1, clients receive a Career Development total score plus scores on six career developmental task scales: Organizational Adaptability, Position Performance, Work Habits and Attitudes, Coworker Relationships, Advancement, and Career Choice and Plans. For Part 2, they receive a Career Adjustment total score together with scores on three adjustment scales: Integrative (reduces anxiety and solves work problems), Adjustive (reduces anxiety only), and Nonadjustive (neither of the above). The test booklet, which has been uniquely designed so that duplicate copies are provided by means of carbon paper, can be both self-scored to provide immediate feedback and machine scored for aggregate data analysis and program evaluation.

The CMAS has been used primarily in business and industrial settings to help design career development programs, to identify common problems among workers within the organizational culture, and to diagnose individual career development task and job adjustment problems. High total scores on the CMAS are correlated with worker satisfaction and job success as measured by performance appraisals and standardized measures (Crites, 1993). Scores on the career development subscales are associated with an individual's age in the manner predicted by Crites's career development model.

Career Maturity Inventory–Revised

The **Career Maturity Inventory–Revised** (CMI-R) is based on Crites's (1978) model of career development. According to his model, career maturity encompasses a hierarchy of factors. He hypothesized a general factor of career maturity similar to the *g* factor in intelligence testing, several group factors, and a large number of specific factors. The group factors pertain to both the process of career planning (attitudes and competencies) and the content of career planning (consistency and realism of career choice). According to McDivitt (2002), the revised version of the CMI "has greatly enhanced" (p. 341) its usefulness for teaching students the process of career decision making and for helping them to gain career maturity.

The CMI-R resembles the CDI in its focus on the career-planning process variables. It yields a career-planning attitude score, a career-planning competency score, and an overall career maturity score in a manner similar to the CDI. It differs from the CDI in its brevity (50 items altogether) and its lack of subscales.

Career Thoughts Inventory

The **Career Thoughts Inventory** (CTI), which is based on cognitive information processing theory, assesses dysfunctional thinking in career problem solving and decision making for adults, college students, and high school students (ages 17 to 83 years old; Sampson, Peterson, Lenz, Reardon, & Saunders, 1996). It includes 48 items designed to measure misperceptions in eight content areas related to career choice and development, such as self-knowledge, occupational knowledge, and communication. It provides a total score and scores on three scales: Decision-Making Confusion, Commitment Anxiety, and External Conflict.

Counselors are urged to discuss high scores on any of the scales or individual items with clients. Counselors help clients to reframe negative thoughts regarding the career process into positive thoughts that are true for them.

Childhood Career Development Scale

The **Childhood Career Development Scale** (CDDS) is a newer measure of career progress based on Super's theory for children (Grades 4 through 6) that shows "excellent promise" (Dagley & Salter, 2004, p. 108; Schultheiss & Stead, 2004). The CDDS is a 52-item measure using a 5-point scale (1 = *strongly agree* to 5 = *strongly disagree*) that provides scores for eight scales: Planning, Self-Concept, Information, Interests, Locus of Control, Curiosity/Exploration, Key Figures, and Time Perspective.

Schultheiss and Stead (2004) designed the CDDS to serve both as a measure of career program effectiveness and as a research tool to examine childhood career development. Although psychometric information is limited on the CDDS, the measure represents an important step in assessing career development for this population (Dykeman, 2013).

My Vocational Situation

My Vocational Situation (MVS) is frequently used as a screening inventory to detect career-planning concerns that need to be addressed in counseling. The authors of this inventory attribute difficulties in decision making to three main factors: (a) problems of vocational identity, (b) lack of information about careers, and (c) environmental or personal obstacles (Holland, Daiger, & Power, 1980). The first scale on the MVS, the Vocational Identity scale, contains 18 items related to career choice uncertainty that must be answered *true* or *false*. *True* responses suggest problems with one's vocational identity. Each of the two remaining scales, Occupational Information (OI) and Barriers (B), consists of one question with four parts. The OI scale provides data concerning the client's need for occupational information (e.g., how to obtain training or employment in an occupation), whereas the B scale points out barriers (e.g., lack of needed abilities or family support) that may be impeding career development. These scales can be used as checklists to suggest specific steps that counselors can take to assist their clients in the career-planning process.

Because of the MVS's brevity, clients can easily complete it before the first counseling interview, in the same manner as other screening inventories described earlier in the text. Research indicates that the meaning of the scores on the MVS may differ somewhat based on gender and race (Toporek & Pope-Davis, 2001). For this reason, MVS results can best be used at the item level as a stimulus for further discussion to determine their significance for the client, rather than as a means of identifying or diagnosing the nature of an individual's vocational problems.

Skills Confidence Inventory

The **Skills Confidence Inventory** (SCI; Betz, Borgen, & Harmon, 1996) was designed to measure a client's level of confidence with skills related to the General Occupation Themes described in the Strong Interest Inventory (described in the next chapter). SCI scores provide a comparison between a client's interests and his or her perceived confidence in carrying out particular abilities. Thus, the SCI is used in conjunction with the Strong Interest Inventory. Jenkins (2013) noted that the SCI is useful for exploring areas where a client has both high interest and yet varying levels of confidence related to career choices

Activity 11.1
Selecting Measures of Career Readiness

Select one of the assessments discussed in this section. Use assessment sources discussed earlier in the text, as well as *A Counselor's Guide to Career Assessment Instruments* (C. T. Wood & Hays, 2013), to collect psychometric information on the assessment. Reflect on the following questions:

- What is the psychometric evidence (e.g., reliability, validity, standardization sample, scoring information) for the assessment? How strong is this evidence?
- How would you use this instrument in your practice?
- What are some of the advantages and disadvantages of the assessment?
- What are some multicultural and social justice considerations in selecting, administering, and interpreting the tool?

Present the information to the larger group.

Tip Sheet
Using Measures of Career Readiness

✓ Determine the type of counseling intervention needed based on the client's level of career-planning readiness. Clients with low levels need individual counseling or long-term group counseling; clients with high levels can benefit from short-term group counseling, workshops, or self-directed activities.

✓ Use items from the career development measures as a checklist to identify problematic issues for further consideration. Counselors can use the items themselves, especially together with supplementary materials or qualitative tools.

✓ Use career development measures to survey the needs of student groups for particular services or resources, such as computer-based career-planning programs, career exploration workshops, or career courses.

✓ Help clients to identify and challenge career myths or distorted beliefs about careers that may be interfering with their career development.

✓ Distinguish between indecision and indecisiveness. Clients who are indecisive will probably need personal counseling in addition to assistance for career planning.

✓ Consider a client's decision-making style when deciding on a counseling intervention. Depending on this style, certain individual and/or group interventions using quantitative or qualitative tools could be useful.

✓ When working with multicultural clients, keep in mind the need to evaluate and to address the institutional and personal challenges they may face both in entering an occupation and in progressing in it. Such challenges include limited educational experiences, low self-confidence, less access to mentors, and lack of political skills and savvy. Consider using local norms for cultures with different approaches to career planning.

✓ In addition to quantitative assessment procedures, counselors should use qualitative techniques, including interviews, observations, and structured career assessment activities, to help evaluate and foster a client's readiness to engage in career planning (Brott, 2015; McMahon & Watson, 2015).

✓ In planning interventions, take into account the complexity of a client's situation (family, social, economic, or organizational factors) as well as the client's capability to make appropriate career choices. External factors include both barriers and supports that can detract from or contribute to a client's readiness to engage in career planning (Leong, 2014).

✓ As counseling or education progresses, ask students or clients to retake career development measures to assess changes in their ability to deal with developmental tasks. Use career development measures as criteria for evaluating the effectiveness of career-counseling programs.

Introduction to Comprehensive Assessment Programs

The first part of this chapter focused on individual measures intended to evaluate various aspects of career readiness. There are also comprehensive assessment programs that can serve as both an assessment tool and counseling intervention to address readiness concerns. Comprehensive assessment programs measure a combination of a person's values, interests, and aptitudes. *Individual* assessments that measure values and interests are discussed in the next chapter; however, comprehensive programs are also popular because of their multipurpose function. Several comprehensive assessment programs adhere to test standardization procedures that include systematic item selection, establishment of representative norms, and ongoing studies of reliability and validity. Only those standardized programs with objective tests of ability are reviewed in this chapter.

There are, however, some nonstandardized assessment programs to mention before reviewing standardized ones. **Nonstandardized programs** use self-ratings to help clients organize their thinking about themselves and various opportunities and include computer-based programs and career education workbooks. They have been validated primarily in terms of their success in encouraging people to explore various occupations and in enabling individuals to make progress in their career decision making.

A number of computer-based career and life-planning programs have been developed in recent years. These programs assist clients in self-assessment, environmental assessment (i.e., educational and occupational information), and decision making. The self-assessment modules usually ask clients to evaluate their interests, values, and skills. On the basis of the self-evaluations, the computer generates a list of appropriate occupations. Examples of these programs include the Career Interests, Preferences, and Strengths Inventory (CIPSI; PRO-ED, 2012), CareerScope Version 10 (Vocational Research Institute, 2011), and the System of Integrated Guidance and Information–third edition (SIGI[3]; Valpar, 2016).

Career and life-planning workbooks, the second type of nonstandardized assessment program, play an important part in comprehensive self-rating programs used by counselors. These workbooks usually include a number of exercises that can be used by clients to assess their interests, values, personality style, and skills. Additional exercises aid clients in exploring the work environment by means of informational interviews and reviews of career literature. The workbooks are well suited to career education classes or career exploration groups. They often use a decision-making or problem-solving model as a framework for presentation of the exercises.

Examples of effective career and life-planning workbooks include *What Color Is Your Parachute?* (Bolles, 2017), *Career Development and Planning: A Comprehensive Approach* (textbook, student manual, and instructor's manual; Reardon, Lenz, Sampson, & Peterson, 2012), and *Making Career Decisions That Count: A Practical Guide* (Luzzo, 2008). Exercises provided in the workbooks are informal or qualitative in nature. They are meant to stimulate interest in career exploration by offering a variety of assessment procedures in a systematic fashion.

Standardized Assessment Programs

Although most standardized assessment programs use self-report inventories to evaluate motivational factors such as interests and values, they vary in their approach to measuring abilities. Assessment programs are likely to use self-reports to evaluate abilities when the results are used for counseling. Many of these programs are best known for their interest inventory, which often serves as the centerpiece of the assessment program.

In contrast with the assessment programs that use self-ratings to measure abilities, a number of programs use objective tests to assess abilities. Objective tests help ensure the validity of test results in those situations in which clients' responses may be biased or distorted, such as may occur when tests are used as a basis for selection. Objective tests can also be used in assessing the abilities of clients who may not have an adequate basis for judging their own abilities.

Each of the assessment batteries discussed in this section includes objective tests of abilities in addition to inventories of interests, values, or experiences. In contrast with self-report ability measures, objective tests assess the client's abilities on the basis of actual performance in a test situation. Six frequently used programs—ACT Career Planning Survey, DAT Career Planning Program, Armed Services Vocational Aptitude Battery, WorkKeys, O*NET System and Career Exploration Tools, and the Career Occupational Preference System—are discussed briefly in this section. Some of these programs supplement the objective aptitude testing with subjective (self-ratings) assessments to expand the number of abilities taken into consideration for career planning. These batteries have been validated most often in terms of their effectiveness in predicting educational or occupational membership and performance.

ACT Career Planning Survey

The **ACT Career Planning Survey** (CPS) is a comprehensive career guidance program designed to aid students in Grades 8–10 in educational and career planning (ACT, Inc., 2009b). It includes two self-report inventories and a pair of objective tests of ability: (a) Inventory of Work-Relevant Abilities, in which students rate their skills in 15 areas that cannot be measured adequately by objective tests; (b) Unisex Edition of the ACT Interest Inventory (UNIACT, discussed in the previous chapter); and (c) Reading and Numerical Skills Ability Tests, which measure basic concepts and skills essential in reading and mathematics.

The CPS differs from the EXPLORE and PLAN assessment programs also offered by ACT (discussed in previous chapter) in that it places more emphasis on career development and less emphasis on academic evaluation and planning. The CPS provides information on a much wider variety of abilities (most of which are self-rated) along with career interests so that it can be used effectively in considering a broad range of occupational opportunities.

ACT provides a *Career Planning Guide* to help students apply their survey results in career exploration. The guide includes a Work-Relevant Experiences Checklist and a Job Characteristics Checklist as additional assessment tools. Students use these instruments to review their work experiences and to consider what characteristics (e.g., recognition, physical activity, or variety) they prefer in their work.

Clients can compare their self-rated abilities and interests with those typically expressed by people in different career areas by means of the World-of-Work Map (see "Resources for

Further Learning" for more information). As indicated on the map, the career areas differ from each other in regard to two basic dimensions: *data versus ideas* and *people versus things*. The CPS report shows the regions on the World-of-Work Map in which a student obtains his or her highest interest and ability scores by means of a color code (abilities = gray, interests = red, both abilities and interests = red–gray mixture). By inspecting this report, students can easily make comparisons among their abilities, their interests, and relevant career areas.

Differential Aptitude Tests

The **Differential Aptitude Tests** (DAT, not to be confused with the Dental Admission Test discussed in the previous chapter) can be used together with the **Career Interest Inventory** (CII) to generate educational and career-planning reports for counselors and students. The DAT, originally published in 1947, was last revised in 1990 as the fifth edition, Forms C and D (G. K. Bennett, Seashore, & Wesman, 1990). The CII measures work and school interests.

Both the DAT and CII include two levels of assessment: Level 1 for Grades 7 through 9 and Level 2 for Grades 10 through 12. Both levels of the DAT and Level 2 of the CII may also be used with adults. When the DAT and the CII are administered together, the results can be integrated by means of a computerized educational and career-planning report.

The DAT contains eight subtests: Verbal Reasoning, Numerical Reasoning, Abstract Reasoning, Perceptual Speed and Accuracy, Mechanical Reasoning, Space Relations, Spelling, and Language Usage. The eight tests require 2.5 to 3 hours to complete. The CII provides scores for 15 occupational groups plus additional information regarding interests in school subjects. The DAT and the CII have been normed jointly with students drawn from different parts of the country, different socioeconomic classes, and different ethnic groups.

Armed Services Vocational Aptitude Battery (ASVAB)

The **Armed Services Vocational Aptitude Battery** (ASVAB) Career Exploration Program consists of a multiple aptitude test battery, a career interest inventory, and career-planning materials and exercises that aid students in identifying and investigating career possibilities. The ASVAB (Forms 23 and 24) is administered and interpreted without charge by representatives of the Armed Services (U.S. Department of Defense, 2005). Test results are used by the military for recruitment, for assessing qualifications of students for different military occupations, and for research. School counselors use the results to help high school students (Grades 10 through 12) and community college students with educational and vocational planning. Testing time, including instructions, is approximately 3 hours. More than one fourth of U.S. high school seniors participate in the ASVAB Career Exploration Program sometime during their high school years (H. E. Baker, 2002).

The ASVAB includes the following eight individual ability scales: General Science (GS), Arithmetic Reasoning (AR), Word Knowledge (WK), Paragraph Comprehension (PC), Mathematics Knowledge (MK), Electronics Information (EI), Auto & Shop Information (AS), and Mechanical Comprehension (MC). (The two scales that emphasized speed of performance—Numerical Operations and Coding Speed—have been dropped in the revised version.) Scores on these scales are added together to form three composite scores, known as Career Exploration Scores, that are used for general counseling purposes, and a fourth composite score, known as the Military Entrance Score (also identified as the Armed Forces Qualification Test), that is used to determine eligibility for military service. These composite scores, which have been derived from factor analyses of the individual scales, are calculated as follows: Verbal Skills = WK + PC; Math Skills = MK + AR; Science and Technical Skills = GS + EI + MC; and Military Entrance Score = Verbal Skills + Math Skills. The Military Entrance Score can be considered a measure of general academic ability similar to the combined Verbal Reasoning plus Numerical Reasoning (VR + NR) score on the DAT. Only the composite scores are used for counseling and selection purposes.

In addition to the ASVAB test scores, the Career Exploration Program includes a new 90-item interest inventory. This inventory, called **Find Your Interests** (FYI), consists of six scales to assess career interests in the same six categories used on many other interest inventories. Work values are assessed informally by means of exercises in *Exploring Careers: The ASVAB Career Exploration Guide.* This guidebook is given to all students who complete the ASVAB, or it can also be accessed on the Internet (U.S. Department of Defense, 2005).

The guidebook also includes OCCU-Find, a chart used to identify occupations that match an individual's abilities and interests. Research indicates that participants in the ASVAB Career Exploration Program show reduced career indecision and increased career exploration knowledge compared with nonparticipants (H. E. Baker, 2002).

According to numerous studies conducted with earlier versions of the ASVAB and the General Aptitude Test Battery (upon which the ASVAB is modeled), the test scores are valid in predicting training and job performance in a wide variety of military and civilian occupations (U.S. Department of Defense, 2005). This research also indicates that the test scores predict equally well for men and women and for different racial and ethnic groups.

WorkKeys

The **WorkKeys** system is a comprehensive work skills assessment program developed by the publishers of the ACT tests (ACT, Inc., 2016e). The program is built around a common scale that measures both the skills of an individual and the skills required for successful job performance. Counselors and educators can use WorkKeys to help students understand their preparedness for specific jobs and careers; employers can use it to establish selection and training programs. WorkKeys may be used with either high school students or adults.

WorkKeys measures foundational skills (i.e., skills needed to learn other skills) in 10 areas related to work on the following scales: Applied Mathematics, Applied Technology, Business Writing, Listening, Locating Information, Observation, Reading for Information, Readiness, Teamwork, and Writing (ACT, Inc., 2016e). The Readiness test, which assesses basic skills in reading and mathematics, can be used as a screening tool to determine whether a person is sufficiently prepared to take the other tests in the WorkKeys system. In addition to measuring foundational skills, the WorkKeys system has been expanded to include two measures (called Performance and Talent) that evaluate attitudes and a third measure (called Fit) that assesses how well an individual's interests and values match those of a specific job.

The skill tests were defined and developed by panels of employers, educators, and ACT staff. All of the test items are based on work situations. They are designed to measure generic work skills that pertain to a variety of work situations, not skills that are specific to a particular job. The tests typically are scored in terms of skill levels ranging from Level 1 (lowest) to Level 7 (highest); however, finer grained scale scores with 40- to 65-point ranges have also been established for use when it is important to detect smaller differences (ACT, Inc., 2016e). Depending on the nature of the test, items are presented in a paper-and-pencil, computer, video, or audio mode with a multiple-choice or constructed-response format. The 10 skill tests vary in testing time from 30 to 64 minutes. Individuals, educational institutions, and employers select the tests most relevant for their particular situation. The tests are usually administered and scored on a selected basis, not as a battery, by service centers certified by ACT, such as a community college.

WorkKeys enables students to assess their qualifications for different occupations by means of eight skill areas (all but Business Writing and Readiness scales). Job analysts have collaborated with subject matter experts (usually workers in the job under study) to judge the appropriate skill levels for different occupations. With these data, ACT has prepared a table of occupational profiles, which shows the median skill level in each of the eight skill areas for nearly 1,400 occupations (ACT, Inc., 2012d). An individual's skill levels are compared with the skill-level requirements for a particular job or occupation by means of this table to determine whether he or she is prepared to enter that job or occupation. For example, the occupational profile for accountants shows that they obtain their highest scores on the Applied Mathematics (Level 6), Locating Information (Level 5), and Reading for Information (Level 5) scales. Individuals who obtain similar or higher scores would appear to be good candidates for further training in this field.

WorkKeys differs from traditional ability tests in that it is criterion referenced, not norm referenced. A test-taker must correctly answer 80% of the items representing any skill level to be qualified at that level. For those cases in which a person does not attain the skill level required for a particular occupation, the test report includes suggestions for improving his or her skills. In addition, organizations endorsed by ACT, such as KeyTrain and WIN Career Solutions, provide interactive instructional materials designed to improve the generic work skills assessed by WorkKeys (ACT, Inc., 2016e).

The WorkKeys system has been extensively validated by ACT, especially in regard to content validity (ACT, Inc., 2016e; Osborn, 2013). Outside consultants reviewed the test items for content accuracy and fairness to minority groups. Statistical analyses were used to identify and eliminate items that functioned differently for various groups of people, such as males versus females or African Americans versus Whites. Subject matter experts confirmed that the eight skill areas adequately represent the type and the range of skills required in the majority of jobs. Ongoing research studies show that scores on the WorkKeys scales correlate significantly with scores on comparable instruments and with job performance ratings in related fields (ACT, Inc., 2016e).

Counselors will find the WorkKeys system to be most valuable in helping clients to appraise their basic work skills compared with those required in various occupations (Osborn, 2013). Case examples illustrating the use of the WorkKeys system in counseling and employment situations can be found on the ACT website (ACT, Inc., 2016e).

O*NET System and Career Exploration Tools

The U.S. Department of Labor created the **Occupational Information Network (O*NET)**, a comprehensive career information system, in the 1990s to replace the *Dictionary of Occupational Titles* (*DOT*). The O*NET system includes (a) the O*NET database, (b) O*NET OnLine, and (c) O*NET Career Exploration Tools. The O*NET database provides extensive information about the primary occupations found in the United States. By combining occupations and eliminating obsolete and obscure occupations, the number of occupations included in O*NET was reduced from the 12,741 occupations defined in the *DOT* to 974.

Each occupation is described in terms of six content areas: (a) worker characteristics (abilities, interests, and work styles), (b) worker requirements (education, knowledge, and skills), (c) experience requirements (training, work experience, and licensing), (d) occupational-specific information (job duties and tasks), (e) occupational requirements (work activities and work context), and (f) occupational characteristics (labor market information). The first three content areas describe individual attributes. The O*NET database indicates the relevance and the importance of each of the variables for the different occupations based on the ratings of experts, employers, and employees (U.S. Department of Labor, Employment and Training Administration [ETA], n.d.). The database is partially updated twice a year, with plans for it to be completely updated in 5-year cycles.

O*NET OnLine enables users to gain easy access to the O*NET database on the Internet. Individuals can readily compare information gained from the Career Exploration Tools and from self-estimates with pertinent information reported in the database for the various occupations (see Activity 11.2).

The Career Exploration Tools have been constructed to measure an individual's abilities, interests, and values; that is, those variables that have been most valid in predicting occupational criteria. The following three instruments have been developed for this purpose: Ability Profiler, Interest Profiler, and Work Importance Profiler. Although these instruments may be used separately, the U.S. Department of Labor, ETA (n.d.) recommends using them together as part of a whole-person approach to counseling. The tools' psychometric properties (e.g., validity, reliability, and fairness analyses) are reported in research reports, which are published along with user's guides on the O*NET Center website (http://www.onetcenter.org/tools.html) as they become available.

Ability Profiler

The **Ability Profiler**, which replaces the General Aptitude Test Battery (GATB) for counseling purposes, includes nine scales that are similar to the nine scales that appeared on the GATB. The nine scales make up three cognitive factors (Verbal Ability, Arithmetic Reasoning, and Computation), three perceptual factors (Spatial Ability, Form Perception, and Clerical Perception), and three psychomotor factors (Motor Coordination, Manual Dexterity, and Finger Dexterity). The GATB General Learning Ability scale has been dropped, and the GATB Numerical Aptitude scale has been divided into Arithmetic Reasoning and Computation scales.

The Ability Profiler differs from the GATB in that it provides new items, revised instructions and scoring procedures, new portions, fewer subtests, and more flexible administration. In addition, time limits were modified to ensure that examinees had sufficient time to complete subtests in which speed of answering questions was not important to test performance. Kinnier and Gorin (2013) noted that the Ability Profiler is an improvement over its predecessor, but counselors should supplement the tool with other career assessments or information.

The examinee's scores on the Ability Profiler are compared with the ability profiles for the different O*NET occupations. Ability profiles for the different O*NET occupations have been estimated by means of GATB validity data and occupational data from the *DOT*. The O*NET system includes five job zones that represent five different levels of experience, education, and training. Within each job zone (which the examinee selects), the computer uses a correlational procedure to determine which occupations have ability patterns that most closely match those of the examinee (U.S. Department of Labor, ETA, n.d.).

Interest Profiler

The **Interest Profiler** measures occupational interests in the same six categories used by most interest inventories: realistic, investigative, artistic, social, enterprising, and conventional (see Holland, 1997). Both paper-and-pencil and computerized versions are available. It is designed to be self-administered and self-interpreted. It requires about 30 minutes to complete.

An individual's highest scores on the Interest Profiler are compared with the interests that are most characteristic for different occupations as means of identifying compatible occupations. Occupational experts designated the predominant interest fields for different occupations. Although the expert raters used the same Holland categories to classify interests as those used by the Strong Interest Inventory and the *Dictionary of Holland Occupational Types*, research has indicated that the agreement among the Holland codes assigned to the same occupations by these three sources is only moderate (Eggerth, Bowles, Tunick, & Andrew, 2005). Counselors should keep in mind that the interpretation of a particular Holland code may vary somewhat from one source to another.

Work Importance Profiler

The third O*NET assessment tool, **Work Importance Profiler**, measures six types of work values: achievement, independence, recognition, relationships, support, and working conditions. Similar to the Interest Profiler, the Work Importance Profiler may be completed in paper-and-pencil form (titled Work Importance Locator) or computer form in about

30 minutes. It is also self-administered and self-interpreted. The relative significance of the different values in various occupations has been determined by job supervisors. This instrument is described in greater detail in the next chapter.

In addition to the individual attributes measured by the Career Planning Tools, the detailed report for any occupation listed in the O*NET database also provides ratings for the importance of other worker requirements (knowledge, skills, work styles, and an expanded list of abilities) and occupational requirements (tasks, work activities, and work context). Many variables or elements are rated in each category. For example, the relevance and importance of 52 abilities for each occupation are rated by a panel of experts.

Activity 11.2
Using O*Net

Visit O*NET OnLine at http://www.onetonline.org/ to become familiar with its uses with clients.

1. Search the online database for occupational information concerning counseling. (You may choose to review a specialty in counseling.) What type of information is provided to you? What are your reactions to this information?
2. Review the career exploration tools such as the Ability Profiler, Interest Profiler, and Work Importance Profiler. What are your thoughts about these resources? How might you use them with clients?

Career Occupational Preference System

The **Career Occupational Preference System** (COPSystem; Knapp-Lee, 2000) provides a comprehensive assessment of interests, values, and abilities designed for use in a wide variety of settings. The COPSystem includes the following measures: (a) the Career Occupational Preference System (COPS) Interest Inventory, which assesses interests in 14 occupational clusters at different education levels; (b) the Career Orientation Placement and Evaluation Survey (COPES), which measures eight bipolar personal values related to the work one does (see Chapter 12); and (c) the Career Ability Placement Survey (CAPS), which measures eight abilities that are important for different types of work (EdITS, n.d.). The complete battery can be administered in less than 2 hours. Answer sheets may be self-scored or machine scored onsite or offsite.

Several versions of the COPS Interest Inventory have been developed to take into account clients' different grade levels and reading abilities. The COPS Interest Inventory itself may be used with Grade 7 students through adults. The COPS-II (Intermediate Inventory)—a highly visual, simplified version of the COPS Interest Inventory based on knowledge of school subjects and activities familiar to younger students—may be used with students in Grades 6 through 12 and with special education populations. The COPS-R (Form R) differs from the COPS Interest Inventory in that it contains sex-balanced items, combined-sex norms, and simplified language (sixth-grade reading level). The COPS-R more closely parallels the COPS Interest Inventory than does the COPS-II. The COPS-P (Professional level) provides an advanced version for college students and adults who may be considering professional occupations. Finally, the COPS-PIC (Picture Inventory) uses only pictures to assess the interests of nonreaders or those with reading difficulties. Spanish versions of the COPS and CAPS are also available (EdITS, n.d.).

The CAPS consists of the following brief, 5-minute tests: Mechanical Reasoning, Spatial Relations, Verbal Reasoning, Numerical Ability, Language Usage, Word Knowledge, Perceptual Speed and Accuracy, and Manual Speed and Dexterity. The COPES, a values measure, takes about 20 to 30 minutes to complete. For each item, the individual selects one of two statements that better reflects his or her values. The eight work values categories of the COPES are as follows: Investigative versus Accepting, Practical versus Carefree, Independence versus Conformity, Leadership versus Supportive, Orderliness versus Flexibility, Recognition versus Privacy, Aesthetic versus Realistic, and Social versus Reserved.

Extensive norms for the COPSystem instruments have been established based on large samples of intermediate, high school, and college students, with the latest normative data provided in 2009 (EdITS, n.d.). Research with earlier versions of the COPSystem indicates that it can be used effectively to predict educational and occupational status. Validation studies indicate that scores on these tests correlate highly with scores for similar tests from other batteries, such as the Differential Aptitude Tests (Bullock-Yowell & Osborne, 2013; Knapp, Knapp, & Knapp-Lee, 1992).

The COPSystem contributes significantly to the counseling process by stimulating clients to explore career fields from different viewpoints (Bullock & Madson, 2009; Bullock-Yowell & Osborne, 2013). The publisher has prepared a *Comprehensive Career Guidebook* and *Leader's Guide* to aid in the interpretation of the COPSystem assessments (EdITS, n.d.).

Tip Sheet
Use of Comprehensive Assessment Programs

✓ Use self-rating career and life-planning programs such as CareerScope, CIPSI, or SIGI[3] to promote self-examination and career exploration.

✓ Use standardized career and life-planning programs to identify educational or career fields that match a client's interests, values, and abilities.

✓ Use objective tests of abilities with clients who may lack an adequate basis for assessing their own abilities or who may be motivated to distort self-assessments.

✓ Supplement objective tests of abilities with informed self-ratings to enlarge the number of abilities considered in career planning. Self-ratings can be helpful in assessing abilities such as interpersonal skills, leadership, organizational skills, and creativity that are difficult to assess with objective tests.

✓ Disregard small differences between test scores on multiple aptitude tests. When feasible, report test results as a band or range of scores (usually spanning 2 standard errors of measurement) instead of reporting them as a precise point on a scale.

✓ Use combined verbal and numerical ability measures to predict school or job success. Not only is this measure more valid than the other test scores in most cases, but it also yields results with smaller differences between males and females.

✓ Develop local norms for interpreting results, especially if the results are used to estimate performance in local courses.

✓ Help students with low ability scores consider how they may improve their scores through appropriate coursework or related experiences.

✓ Interpret aptitude scores as measures of developed abilities. Exposure to the subject matter represented within the test is necessary for the student to perform well on the test.

✓ Use nonlanguage tests, such as the Abstract Reasoning and Spatial Relations tests from the DAT, for students with limited English language skills to determine general ability to learn new material or to perform tasks for which knowledge of English is not required.

✓ Consult supplementary materials provided by most publishers of comprehensive career-planning programs. Use student workbooks to encourage active participation on the part of clients.

Chapter Summary

The career and life-planning assessment process occurs throughout the life span, and counselors can help clients explore both the process and content of career development. This chapter provided key career assessments related to career process, specifically aspects of career readiness. Career readiness, also referred to as career maturity or career adaptability, involves understanding and planning careers while exploring factors that inhibit or foster that process.

Several instruments that assess career readiness were presented in this chapter. These include (in alphabetical order) the following: ACCI, CASI, CBI, CDDQ, CDDS, CDI, CDMSE, CDS, CFI, Career Futures Inventory, CMAS, CMI-R, CTI, MVS, and the SCI. In addition to these quantitative assessments of career readiness, qualitative assessments are available for use by counselors. Some of these include behavioral observations, interviews, genograms, and card sorts.

Comprehensive assessment programs measure a combination of a person's values, interests, and aptitudes. Six standardized assessment programs are discussed in this chapter: ACT Career Planning Survey, DAT Career Planning Program, WorkKeys, ASVAB, O*NET Career Exploration Tools, and COPSystem.

The ACT Career Planning Survey and the DAT Career Planning Program can be used in educational settings to help students choose an academic field or training course based on their interests and abilities. The ASVAB can be used to predict success in both military and civilian occupations for students from a variety of backgrounds. The WorkKeys system enables individuals to compare their basic work skills in eight areas with those required in a broad range of occupations. The O*NET (Occupational Information Network) database provides a means of directly comparing individual characteristics (as measured by the Career Exploration Tools and by self-estimates) with requirements for more than 900 occupations. This system may be easily accessed on the Internet at the O*NET OnLine website. Finally, the COPSystem provides a systematic assessment of interest, values, and ability measures that can be used in a variety of settings to assist individuals or groups in career exploration and planning.

In addition to these standardized programs, computer-based programs such as SIGI[3] and CareerScope as well as career workbooks are useful assessment programs. Comprehensive self-assessments based on computer programs or career and life-planning workbooks can be used to stimulate career exploration and to improve capacity for career planning.

Review Questions

1. What are the four uses of career assessment described in this chapter? How might each relate to issues of career assessment and comprehensive career planning?
2. How would you differentiate the concepts of career maturity and career adaptability? What are ways in counseling you can assess each?
3. What are some of the functions of career readiness assessments presented in this chapter?
4. What are the general components of comprehensive assessment programs?
5. What are the benefits and challenges of career and life-planning assessments discussed in this chapter?

Resources for Further Learning

Publications

Bolles, R. N. (2017). *What color is your parachute? 2017: A practical manual for job-hunters and career-changers.* Berkeley, CA: Ten Speed Press.

Flores, L. Y., Berkel, L. A., Nilsson, J. E., Ojeda, L., Jordan, S. E., Lynn, G. L., & Leal, V. M. (2006). Racial/ethnic minority vocational research: A content and trend analysis across 36 years. *The Career Development Quarterly, 55,* 2–21.

Luzzo, D. A. (2008). *Making career decisions that count: A practical guide* (3rd ed.). Upper Saddle River, NJ: Prentice Hall.

McMahon, M., & Watson, M. (2012). Telling stories of career assessment. *Journal of Career Assessment, 20,* 440–451. doi:10/1177/1069072712448999

McMahon, M., & Watson, M. (Eds.). (2015). *Career assessment: Qualitative approaches.* Rotterdam, The Netherlands: Sense.

Okocha, A. (1998). Using qualitative appraisal strategies in career counseling. *Journal of Employment Counseling, 35,* 151–160.

Reardon, R. C., Lenz, J. G., Sampson, J. P., & Peterson, G. W. (2012). *Career development and planning: A comprehensive approach* (4th ed.). New York, NY: Custom.

Ridley, C. R., Li, L. C., & Hill, C. L. (1998). Multicultural assessment: Reexamination, reconceptualization, and practical application. *The Counseling Psychologist, 26,* 827–910.

Wood, C. T., & Hays, D. G. (Eds.). (2013). *A counselor's guide to career assessment instruments* (6th ed.). Broken Arrow, OK: National Career Development Association.

Web Resources

ASVAB
   http://official-asvab.com/index.htm
      This website links to information and sample items for this assessment.
Career Interests, Preferences, and Strengths Inventory
   http://www.proedinc.com/customer/productView.aspx?ID=8367
      This website links to information and sample items and reports for this assessment.
CareerScope
   http://www.vri.org/products/careerscope-v10/benefits
      This website links to information and sample items and reports for the CareerScope.
COPSystem Career Measurement Package
   http://www.edits.net/products/career-guidance/copsystem-career-measurement.html
      This website links to information and sample items and reports for the COPSystem.
Differential Aptitude Tests for Personnel and Career Assessment (DAT)
   http://www.pearsonclinical.com/talent/products/100000364/differential-aptitude-tests-for-personnel-and-career-assessment-dat-dat.html
      This website links to information and sample items and reports for the Differential Aptitude Tests.
National Career Development Association, Internet Sites for Career Planning
   http://associationdatabase.com/aws/NCDA/pt/sp/resources
      This is a list of Internet sites for career planning.
O*NET OnLine
   http://www.onetonline.org/
      This is the website for the O*NET system.

SIGI[3]

    http://sigi3.org/

        This website links to information and sample items and reports for the SIGI[3].

Vocopher

    http://vocopher.com/

        This website provides free career assessments to qualified professionals.

WorkKeys

    http://www.act.org/workkeys/index.html

        This website links to information and sample items and reports for the WorkKeys assessment.

World-of-Work Map

    http://www.act.org/content/dam/act/unsecured/multimedia/wwmap/world.html

        This website describes the World-of-Work Map.

Chapter 12

Measures of Interests and Values

Factors that pertain to the *content* of career choice and development, such as interests and values, are considered in this chapter. Measures of both interests and values can be helpful in assisting clients to evaluate their motivations in regard to work or other aspects of living. Interests refer to what an individual *likes* to do; values define what a person thinks is *important*. In essence, interests refer to *what* the person chooses to do, whereas values pertain to *why* a person works or undertakes an activity. Several interest and values inventories that counselors use frequently are discussed in this chapter, together with guidelines for their selection and interpretation.

Test Your Knowledge

Select the most appropriate choice for each item.

_____ 1. Which of the following does *not* represent a Holland category?
a. Realistic   b. Mechanical
c. Social   d. Enterprising

_____ 2. The Self-Directed Search is based on:
a. Strong's values typology   b. Holland's hexagonal model
of General Occupational Themes
c. Campbell's theory of   d. All of the above
vocational choice

❏ T ❏ F 3. Interest inventories should be supplemented with ability assessments because they do not measure abilities.

❏ T ❏ F 4. Values can often be searched in career databases to identify occupations that may be most satisfying.

❏ T ❏ F 5. Values clarification exercises tend to be more useful than popular inventories given their psychometric integrity.

Introduction to Interest Inventories

Since at least 1909, when Frank Parsons published his classic book *Choosing a Vocation*, counselors have tried to devise ways to assess career interests. Interest inventories, which ask clients to report their likes and dislikes for various activities, are particularly useful for this purpose. Interest inventories can be classified in a variety of ways, and the most useful distinction pertains to type of scale. Two types of interest scales predominate. The first type, **general** or **basic interest scales**, measures the strength of an individual's interests in broad fields of activity, such as art, mechanical activities, or sports. They are *homogeneous* in nature because they refer to one type of activity. For this reason, they are relatively easy to interpret. In contrast, the second type of scale, **occupational scales**, assesses the similarity of an individual's interest patterns with those of people in specific occupations. These scales are *heterogeneous* in terms of item content and include a variety of items that distinguish between the interests of people in an occupation and those of people in general. Because of the mixed-item content, scores on these scales are more difficult to interpret.

The first type of scale is usually constructed by a rational process. The scale is designed to include items that logically fit together. Examples are the Occupational Theme scales and Basic Interest scales on the Strong Interest Inventory (Strong). Internal validation procedures such as factor analysis are usually undertaken to ensure that the item content of the scale is relatively pure. Scales of this type belong to a "closed system" of scales; that is, the system includes all the scales that are necessary to represent all the different types of interests.

Because scales of the second type are based on those items that differentiate between people, item selection depends on an empirical process (observed differences between groups), not on theoretical or logical considerations. Examples are the Occupational scales on the Strong and the Campbell Interest and Skill Survey. External validation procedures such as discriminant analysis are frequently used to determine the effectiveness of the scales in differentiating among the interests of people employed in different occupations. Empirical scales are usually part of an "open system"; that is, no one set of scales is established to represent the universe of occupational interests. New scales must be constructed as new occupations emerge or as old occupations change.

Both types of scales contribute to the career or life-planning process. Because they are easy to interpret, basic interest scales can be used in a variety of situations in which counseling contact may be limited. These scales can also be helpful in interpreting the scores on the occupational scales when both types of scores are available. The occupational scales, in contrast, provide a means of comparing an individual's interest pattern as a whole with those of people in different occupations. These scales include in a single score the information that is distributed over a number of basic interest scales.

In most cases with students who are high school age or younger, counselors should use interest inventories that provide broad measures of interest. Such scales are not only easier to interpret but they also preclude young students from focusing too early on specific occupations before they have had sufficient opportunity to explore different occupations. Inventories that show scores for specific occupations are more appropriate for college students or other adults.

Interest scores can be used to help clients explore or discover new academic or career possibilities, to decide among various alternatives, or to confirm a previous choice. Interest scores can also be used for considering ways in which a job might be modified to produce greater job satisfaction or for planning leisure-time activities. In addition, interest scores can serve as a starting point for discussing future plans with parents or other significant people in a person's life. Table 12.1 provides a brief history of career interest inventories to serve as a foundational understanding of currently available interest inventories. Furthermore, see the Tip Sheet for guidelines to help you decide when and how to use interest inventories.

Table 12.1
A Foundational History of Career Interest Inventories

Secade	Event
1910s	Davis, a principal, publishes the Student Vocational Self-Analysis for students in Grade 10 (1914); James Miner, a psychologist, uses Davis's scale to explore whether students' interests are related to teacher influence.
1920s	The Carnegie Interest Inventory is developed (1920) and is used by several scholars to distinguish groups by gender preferences (e.g., Moore, Freyd, Crowdery); E. K. Strong, an employee of the Carnegie Institute of Technology, which developed the Carnegie Interest Inventory, develops the first edition of the Strong Interest Inventory—the Strong Vocational Interest Blank (1927). The work of the Carnegie group is foundational to future major interest inventory developments.
1930s	Manson publishes the tool Occupational Interests and Personality Requirements of Women in Business (1931); E. K. Strong develops the Vocational Interest Blank for Women (1933); B. Le Suer developed the Occupations Interest Blank (1937) for high school boys.
1940s	Kuder publishes the Kuder Preference Record (1940) and the Kuder Preference Record, Vocational–Form C (1948); the Cleeton Vocational Interest Inventory is published (1943); Thurstone's An Interest Schedule was disseminated by the University of Chicago (1947); Forer develops the Diagnostic Interest Blank (1948).
1950s	The Kuder Occupational Survey, Form DD was published, along with Lee and Thorpe's Occupational Interest Inventory (1956); the U.S. Department of Labor issues the first edition of the Interest Checklist (1957).
1960s	The Gordon Occupational Checklist is published, along with the Educational Test Service's Interest Index (1961); the Guilford-Zimmerman Interest Inventory becomes available (1963); in 1965, K. E. Clark's Minnesota Interest Inventory and Consulting Psychologists Press' publication of Holland's Vocational Preference Inventory is disseminated; D'Costa, Winefordner, Odgers, and Koons publish the Ohio Vocational Interest Inventory (1968).
1970s	The Strong-Campbell Interest Inventory attempts to remove sex bias by eliminating separate gender test booklets (1974); the California Occupational Preference System—later known as the COPSystem—is initially developed (1974).

Note. Information is from Harrington and Long (2013).

Tip Sheet
Selecting Interest Inventories for Counseling

✓ Keep in mind that interest inventories measure likes and dislikes, not abilities or self-efficacy. Interest inventories identify careers or work situations that clients should find satisfying, but they do not indicate how successful clients would be in those settings or clients' perceptions of their abilities. Hence, interest inventories should be administered along with a measure of abilities and self-efficacy when considering career options (Armstrong & Vogel, 2009; Betz & Rottinghaus, 2006).

✓ Facilitate client motivation to participate in the assessment process because the client will likely benefit more if he or she expresses an interest in the results beforehand. Large changes in interest scores can occur when clients change the manner in which they approach the test. Sometimes clients answer items in terms of what they think other people (especially parents or guardians) would like them to say, or they may respond to the items in regard to their abilities or opportunities instead of their interests.

✓ Remember that general interest inventories are of limited value for people who must make rather fine distinctions, such as choosing between civil and electrical engineering. Search for special purpose inventories as applicable.

✓ Supplement interest inventories with other information about the client and his or her situation, including abilities, values, previous work experiences, and job availability, before a decision is made.

✓ When working with clients with emotional problems, remember that they may make more negative responses and endorse more passive interests than others. Address the emotional difficulties before career planning takes place.

✓ Because scores on interest inventories can show significant changes for clients who are young or after long time periods, consider readministering an interest inventory if it has been longer than 6 months since the client last completed one. Interests are most likely to change for people under age 20 who have experienced large changes in their situation (e.g., new work or school experiences).

✓ Use an interest card sort instead of an interest inventory if you want to understand the underlying reasons for the client's choices. The card sort functions as a structured interview. As originally designed by Leona Tyler, clients sort cards with occupational titles on them into piles of "would choose," "would not choose," and "no opinion." They then subdivide the three piles into smaller piles based on their reasons for placing the cards into those piles. This technique helps counselors to understand the reasons for a client's choice. The counselor and the client together look for themes in the client's preferences that can guide the career exploration process.

Popular Interest Inventories

Six of the most popular interest inventories used for career or life planning are discussed in this section. All of these interest inventories, except for the Jackson Vocational Interest Survey, also include a parallel measure of self-rated competencies, either as part of the inventory itself or as a paired instrument. The two types of measures together can often predict occupational criteria more effectively than either measure by itself.

Strong Interest Inventory

The 2004 **Strong Interest Inventory** (Strong) is the most recent version of a series of interest inventories that began with the publication of the Strong Vocational Interest Blank (SVIB) by E. K. Strong, Jr., in 1927 (Donnay, Morris, Schaubhut, & Thompson, 2005). The SVIB included two forms by gender that were merged when the Strong–Campbell Interest Inventory (SCII) replaced the SVIB in 1974. The SCII was ultimately revised and renamed the Strong Interest Inventory (Strong or SII) in 1994 and was extensively revised in 2004.

The Strong is particularly noteworthy because of its wide usage, its extensive research base, and its innovative role in the field of career assessment (Jenkins, 2013). The Strong has been the subject of extensive research studies in regard to occupational norms, long-term test–retest reliability, concurrent and predictive validity, cross-cultural differences, and counseling applications (e.g., Armstrong, Fouad, Rounds, & Hubert, 2010; Bailey, Larson, Borgen, & Gasser, 2008; Case & Blackwell, 2008; Donnay et al., 2005; Xu & Tracey, 2016). This landmark inventory has led the way for other inventories in the use of criterion-related scale development and in the application of Holland's theory to interest measurement.

The 291 items on the present version of the Strong are divided into six sections (occupations, subject areas, activities, leisure activities, people, and your characteristics). For the first five sections, clients indicate whether they *strongly like, like,* are *indifferent to, dislike,* or *strongly dislike* the activity represented by that particular item. For the last section, they indicate on a 5-point scale to what degree a characteristic is like them. Most people complete the Strong in 25 to 35 minutes. Besides several administrative indices, the Strong produces scores on four sets of scales—the General Occupational Themes (GOTs), Basic Interest Scales (BISs), Occupational Scales (OSs), and Personal Style Scales (PSSs)—each of which is described later. The different parts of the Strong profile are discussed in regard to Michael (see Case Example 12.1) after these sections are presented.

Administrative Indices

The Strong contains three **administrative indices** that provide valuable information for interpreting the rest of the profile. These indices are (a) item response percentages, which show the percentages of *strongly like, like, indifferent to, dislike,* and *strongly dislike* responses for the different sections of the inventory; (b) total responses index, which indicates number of items completed (if this number is lower than 276, the answer sheet is not scored); and (c) typicality index, which reveals the consistency with which a person has responded to the items. The typicality index tallies the number of inconsistent responses to 24 pairs of items that possess similar content (Donnay et al., 2005). For example, if a person marks *like* for accountant as an occupation but *dislike* for accounting as a subject, the responses would be scored as inconsistent for that pair of items. If the number of consistent responses is fewer than 17 (out of 24), the counselor should try to determine the reason for the inconsistency. The client may have a reading problem, may have misunderstood the directions, may have answered the items hurriedly or carelessly, or may, in fact, have an unusual pattern of interests.

General Occupational Themes and Basic Interest Scales

The Strong contains two sets of general or homogeneous scales: the **General Occupational Themes** (GOTs) and the **Basic Interest Scales** (BISs). The GOTs provide a summary or overview of the Strong profile as well as a framework for interpreting the other scales. Each of the six GOTs contains items selected to fit Holland's (1997) descriptions of six types of occupational personalities. Holland found that people (as well as environments) could be broadly classified according to the six types of interests or skills shown in the hexagon in Figure 12.1. This figure shows the nature of the relationship among the six categories,

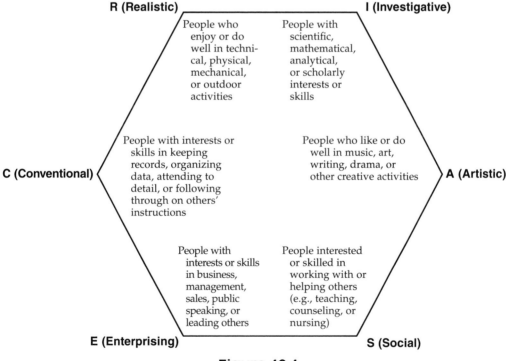

Figure 12.1
Holland's Classification of Personality Types

Note. Reproduced by special permission of the publisher, Psychological Assessment Resources, Inc. (PAR). From *Making Vocational Choices: A Theory of Vocational Personalities and Work Environments,* third edition (p. 35), by J. L. Holland, 1997, Lutz, FL: Psychological Assessment Resources, Inc. Copyright © 1973, 1985, 1992, 1997 by PAR. All rights reserved. Reprinted with permission.

which holds true across gender and all major ethnic and racial groups (Day & Rounds, 1998; Fouad, Harmon, & Borgen, 1997; Leong & Flores, 2013). The closer the categories are to each other on the figure, the more they have in common with each other. For example, people with Social interests are more likely also to possess Artistic or Enterprising interests (interests represented by adjacent categories) than they are the other types of interests. The two dimensions underlying this figure can be described as *people versus things* (Enterprising–Social vs. Realistic–Investigative) and *data versus ideas* (Conventional vs. Artistic).

The 30 BISs function as subscales for the six GOTs. They are grouped into the six GOT categories on the basis of correlations between the two sets of scales. Each of the GOTs subsumes four or more of the BISs. As with the GOTs, the BISs are helpful in understanding the interest patterns associated with different occupations. Compared with the GOTs, the BISs are relatively short, with lengths ranging from 6 to 12 items (Donnay et al., 2005). Thus, scores on these scales can be significantly affected by responses to a few items.

The GOTs and BISs have been standardized so that the combined group of men and women included in the norms will obtain a mean *T* score of 50 and a standard deviation of 10 on each scale. In general, scores above 57 indicate high interest (top 25% of norm group) in that activity, whereas scores below 43 indicate little interest (bottom 25% of norm group); however, interpretation of scores varies somewhat based on the client's gender. The following interpretive comments are used in the Strong reports to indicate the level of one's interest in an activity compared with others of the same sex: "Very High" (91st to 100th percentile), "High" (76th to 90th percentile), "Moderate" (26th to 75th percentile), "Little" (11th to 25th percentile), and "Very Little" (0 to 10th percentile; Donnay et al., 2005). However, a *T* score of 60 on the Mechanics and Construction BIS is interpreted as Moderate for men, but Very High for women.

Gender differences are most notable on scales in the Realistic category. Men in the general representative sample averaged between 5 to 10 points (0.5 to 1 *SD*) higher than women on the Realistic GOT and the Mechanics & Construction, Military, Computer Hardware & Electronics, Athletics, and Protective Services BISs (Donnay et al., 2005). Such differences pertain not only to men and women in general but also to men and women employed in the same occupations, such as engineering (Su & Rounds, 2015). Counselors should take such differences into account when interpreting scores on these scales, particularly for individuals who may be considering nontraditional occupations.

High scores on both the GOTs and BISs are based on *like* responses, whereas low scores are based on *dislike* responses. A large number of *likes* indicate broad interests; a large number of *dislikes* indicate fairly focused interests. In either case, the interest scores should be interpreted in relationship to one another. That is, clients should give careful consideration to their highest scores regardless of their absolute level. Empirical validity studies indicate that both sets of scales effectively discriminate among people employed in different types of occupations (Donnay et al., 2005; Jenkins, 2013). Cross-cultural research with the Strong indicates that the results are equally valid for members of different racial and ethnic groups (Fouad & Mohler, 2004; Leong & Flores, 2013).

As a counseling technique, it is usually helpful to ask clients to look at their four or five highest and lowest scores on the BISs. Do they agree with this description of their interests? Can they think of ways in which they could combine the activities represented by their highest scores in a career or life plan?

Occupational Scales

The Strong profile provides scores for 122 pairs of **Occupational Scales** (OSs) for men and women. The OSs were developed by selecting items that significantly differentiated between the interests of men or women in a particular occupation and men or women in general. The typical scale contains 25 to 30 items selected in this manner. Members of occupational criterion groups used to develop the OSs were screened to ensure they had been employed in the occupation for 3 or more years, were satisfied with their work, and performed typical duties of members of the occupation.

Each of the OSs is coded in terms of the predominant interest pattern of people employed in that occupation based on Holland's classification system (see Figure 12.1). For example, the Biologist scale for men is coded IA (as noted in Table 12.2) because men who are biologists more frequently express Investigative and Artistic interests than do other men. The Holland codes are helpful in organizing the OS scores and in understanding the nature of the interests underlying the scores.

The OSs have been normed so that men or women in the occupation (depending on which sex was used for constructing the scale) obtain a mean T score of 50 with a standard deviation of 10. Men and women in general obtain mean T scores of approximately 20 to 35 for most scales. A score of 40 or above (referred to as "similar interests" on the Strong

Table 12.2
Strong Interest Inventory Scores for Michael, a College Student

Scale	Score	Scale	Score
General Occupational Themes		Military (R)	36
Investigative (I)	64	Taxes & Accounting (C)	36
Artistic (A)	56	Office Management (C)	35
Realistic (R)	51		
Social (S)	46	Occupational Scales[a]	
Enterprising (E)	42	Biologist (IA)	57
Conventional (C)	34	Artist (A)	56
		Graphic Designer (A)	54
		Musician (A)	54
Basic Interest Scales		Geologist (IRA)	53
Science (I)	70	Photographer (ARE)	53
Athletics (R)	57	Technical Writer (AI)	51
Nature & Agriculture (R)	56	Elementary School Teacher (S)	50
Performing Arts (A)	56	Psychologist (IA)	48
Research (I)	56	University Professor (IAS)	48
Visual Arts & Design (A)	56	Librarian (A)	47
Religion & Spirituality (S)	53	Medical Illustrator (AIR)	47
Mechanics & Construction (R)	52	Forester (RI)	43
Medical Science (I)	52	Reporter (A)	43
Social Sciences (S)	52	Social Worker (SA)	43
Teaching & Education (S)	52	Speech Pathologist (SA)	43
Culinary Arts (A)	51	Translator (AI)	43
Writing & Mass Communication (A)	50	Urban & Regional Planner (AI)	43
Entrepreneurship (E)	48	Broadcast Journalist (AE)	42
Marketing & Advertising (E)	46	College Instructor (S)	42
Politics & Public Speaking (E)	45	Editor (AI)	42
Computer Hardware & Electronics (R)	44	Science Teacher (IRS)	41
Counseling & Helping (S)	44	Chiropractor (ISA)	40
Healthcare Services (S)	44	Medical Technologist (IRC)	40
Law (E)	44	Parks & Recreation Manager (SE)	40
Protective Services (R)	40		
Finance & Investing (C)	39	Personal Style Scales	
Human Resources & Training (S)	38	Learning Environment	61
Management (E)	38	Risk Taking	54
Mathematics (I)	38	Leadership Style	45
Sales (E)	38	Team Orientation	41
Programming & Information Systems (C)	37	Work Style	36

Note. Scales in each category are ranked from highest to lowest score. Holland codes for each scale are shown in parentheses. A = Artistic; C = Conventional; E = Enterprising; I = Investigative; R = Realistic; S = Social.

[a]Only the Occupational Scales for which Michael obtained a score of 40 or above (indicating similarity of interests with men employed in the occupation) are listed.

profile) indicates that a client endorses many of the same likes and dislikes as those that differentiate men or women in a particular occupation from men or women in general. A score of 29 or below ("dissimilar interests") indicates a rejection of this interest pattern.

Some clients receive few or no high scores on the OSs. In such cases, scores can still be interpreted in relation to each other. Students with "flat" (undifferentiated) profiles may need additional time and experience to clarify their interests. A 12-year follow-up study indicated that students with flat profiles took longer to get established in their careers; however, at the end of 12 years, they were just as satisfied and successful in their careers as those with differentiated profiles (S. A. Sackett & Hansen, 1995). In fact, the male students with flat profiles in this study showed a higher level of satisfaction with their jobs after 12 years than did those with differentiated profiles, possibly because they may have been more flexible and easier to please.

The same occupations are now represented on both male and female scales. Because most of the mean differences between scores on the male and female scales are relatively small, it is not as important to know the scores of clients on the opposite-sex scales as it once was (Donnay et al., 2005).

In contrast with the GOTs and BISs, high scores on the OSs are based on both *like* and *dislike* responses. People obtain high scores when they share the same likes and dislikes as people in the occupation. In essence, high scores on the OSs point to occupations in which individuals can pursue those activities they enjoy and avoid those they dislike. A few scales, such as Farmer/Rancher and Radiologic Technologist, include a relatively large number of items with positive weights for *dislike* responses. People in these occupations possess rather narrow or focused interests. If clients mark a large number of *dislikes*, they will probably obtain elevated scores on these scales. High scores that are based primarily on dislikes can be misleading. It is important to look at the specific likes and dislikes (as revealed by the BISs) that underlie an OS score.

OS scores are highly reliable, particularly for people 20 years of age and older and over short time periods (less than 1 year). Even over very long time periods (10 to 20 years), the OSs produce similar results for most people based on research conducted with earlier versions of the Strong. Concurrent validation studies show that the OSs significantly differentiate between people in the occupation and people in general (Donnay et al., 2005). A number of longitudinal research studies (ranging in length from 3 to 18 years) have been conducted to examine the predictive validity of the Strong (Low, Yoon, Roberts, & Rounds, 2012). These studies found that from one third to two thirds of the people who took the Strong were later employed in occupations related to their high scores. For example, Hansen and Dik (2005) found that 57% of college students tested as freshmen were employed in an occupation related to their Strong results 12 years later. This figure increased to 73% for a subset of the sample when their scores from the Strong completed in the senior year were compared with their occupation 8 years later. The Strong scores were equally predictive for men and women.

Scores on the OSs show greater validity when they are supported by scores on the BISs that are most relevant; for example, high scores on the Life Insurance Agent OS possess greater predictive validity when they are paired with high scores on the Sales BIS. OS scores are also more valid when clients report that they have had work or volunteer experiences in those fields. Research indicates that the OSs predict occupational membership just as accurately for college students who are undecided about their college major as they do for those who are decided (Bartling & Hood, 1981; Larson, Bonitz, & Pesch, 2013). This finding is important because the Strong is frequently used with students who are having difficulty in making a career decision.

In general, people report greater job satisfaction when their occupation matches the type of occupation suggested by their Strong scores than when it does not; however, the relationship tends to be modest. Presumably, factors other than interests, such as salary, opportunities for advancement, and relationships with supervisors or coworkers, account for much of an individual's satisfaction or dissatisfaction. In addition, some individuals appear to be more flexible in the expression of their interests and can learn to adapt to a wide variety of situations (Darcy & Tracey, 2003; Tracey, Allen, & Robbins, 2012; Tracey & Robbins, 2006).

Personal Style Scales

There are five bipolar **Personal Style Scales** (PSSs) that measure personality factors related to educational and career planning: (a) Work Style: high scorers prefer to work with people; low scorers prefer to work with ideas, data, or things; (b) Learning Environment: high scorers possess academic interests associated with advanced degrees; low scorers possess practical interests associated with technical or trade school attendance; (c) Leadership Style: high scorers prefer to direct others; low scorers prefer to lead by example; (d) Risk Taking/Adventure: high scorers prefer to take chances; low scorers prefer to play it safe; and (e) Team Orientation: high scorers prefer to accomplish tasks as a team; low scorers prefer to accomplish tasks independently. Although these scales have been constructed by different techniques, they are all intended to provide information concerning personality factors associated with career development. Research indicates that the PSSs significantly add to the validity of both the GOTs and BISs in differentiating among occupational groups (Donnay & Borgen, 1996; Donnay et al., 2005).

Case Example 12.1

Michael

Michael, a 20-year-old college junior, completed the Strong to help him in career planning. He believed he had the ability to succeed in "almost anything" but could not decide which career he would find most satisfying. He marked a large number of concerns on the My Vocational Situation checklist (see Chapter 11) that he completed at the same time as the Strong. In particular, he expressed a need to reduce his career uncertainty, to learn more about his career options, and to gain reassurance that he was moving in the right direction. He was considering the possibilities of majoring in chemistry, kinesiology, or some other scientific or technical field at that time. The most pertinent results from his Strong profile are shown in Table 12.2.

Michael's scores on the administrative indices (not shown in Table 12.1) are all within normal response ranges. His total response percentages for the different parts of the inventory were *strongly like* = 10%, *like* = 19%, *indifferent to* = 23%, *dislike* = 27%, and *strongly dislike* = 20%, which is a fairly typical response pattern (Donnay et al., 2005). He answered all of the items on the Strong with no omissions as indicated by his response total of 291. Finally, he obtained a score of 22 (out of 24) on the typicality index, which suggests a high level of consistency. Overall, the administrative indices indicate that he was discriminating, conscientious, and consistent in his approach to the inventory and that the results can be viewed as trustworthy. The administrative indices, which appear at the end of the profile under "Response Summary," should be inspected first before interpreting the rest of the profile to make sure that the results are reliable and to note any unusual pattern of responses.

The GOT scores can be used to arrive at a Holland code to summarize a person's interest. To determine Michael's Holland code, his highest scores on the GOT scales must be identified. As shown in Table 12.2, his highest scores were Investigative (I) and Artistic (A), in that order, which remain the same when gender norms are taken into consideration. Therefore, his Holland code is

IA. With this information, a large number of occupations with similar codes can be identified for the client's consideration by checking resources such as the *Dictionary of Holland Occupational Codes* (Gottfredson & Holland, 1996) or the O*NET database (see Chapter 11). Michael received his highest scores on the Science, Athletics, Nature & Agriculture, Performing Arts, Research, and Visual Arts & Design scales. These scores show a pronounced interest in investigative activities in addition to relatively high interests in athletic, outdoor, and creative endeavors.

As indicated in Table 12.2, Michael obtained high scores (*T* score of 40 or above) on a relatively large number of the OS scales. His interests resembled those of men in 26 of the 122 Occupational Scores on the OSs that can be interpreted by referring to both the GOTs and the BISs. Most of the OSs for which Michael obtained a high score have Investigative or Artistic primary codes in keeping with his highest scores on the GOTs and BISs. His high score on the Biologist OS can be directly related to his high scores on the Investigative GOT and on the Science, Nature & Agriculture, and Research BISs. His Biologist score is also elevated because of his preference for cultural-esthetic activities (indicated by high scores on Artistic GOT and Performing Arts and Visual Arts & Design BISs) and because of his rejection of business activities (as shown by low scores on Conventional and Enterprising scales)—both common features of the interest patterns of scientists and others in similar occupations (Donnay et al., 2005; Harmon et al., 1994). The scores on the GOTs and BISs can be used in a similar manner to clarify the nature of the interest patterns underlying his other OS scores.

With respect to PSSs, low and high *T* scores (scores below 46 or above 54) are said to be "clear" scores that can be interpreted as indicating a preference for one end or the other of the bipolar scales. As indicated in Table 12.1, Michael obtained clear scores on four of the five PSSs. Three of the clear scores fall below 46, namely, Work Style, Team Orientation, and Leadership Style. These scores show a preference to work independently with things or ideas instead of people in situations where he is not expected to lead others. He also obtained a clear score above 55 on the Learning Environment scale, which supports his pursuit of a college degree, especially if he can find a compatible major and career field.

In addition to the profile, he received a copy of an interpretive booklet that provided helpful information for understanding and applying the Strong results in career exploration (see Borgen & Grutter, 2005).

As a means of obtaining some focus, his counselor asked him to select several occupations on the Strong profile that had the most appeal to him. He was asked to look particularly at the scales for which he received scores indicating similarity of interests but not to exclude any occupations. He chose the following occupations: photographer, university professor, librarian, science teacher, and parks and recreation manager. He had obtained scores showing similarity between his interests and those of men employed in each of these occupations. He also expressed an interest in several other occupations with Investigative and Artistic Holland codes as listed in the interpretive booklet that he was provided, including laboratory technician, biochemist, astronomer, chemical engineer, medical research, scientific researcher, and anthropologist.

In addition to the occupations mentioned above, Michael expressed an interest in chemist (IR code) and pharmacist (ICE), occupations in which his OS scores were in the midrange (Chemist = 33; Pharmacist = 36). His Chemist score was lowered because of his very low score (*T* = 38) on the Mathematics BIS. His Pharmacist score is affected by both low math interests and low business interests. If he were to enter pharmacy as a career, he said it probably would be as a hospital or clinical pharmacist, not as a community (business-oriented) pharmacist. He believed that his Mathematics interest score may have increased from what it was when he completed the Strong 2 months earlier. He was failing his calculus course (a course for which he was not well prepared compared with other students) at the time. Since that time, he had re-enrolled in calculus for a second semester, signed up for tutoring, and improved his performance considerably, which helped to increase his liking for the subject. Aside from math, his other grades were very good (primarily As and Bs).

At this point, he thought he would decide to major in chemistry, which would allow him to pursue his interests in science and research. He would like to work for a while as a lab technician after graduating from college and then consider the possibility of returning to graduate school. His counselor discussed with him ways in which he could obtain more information about all of the career possibilities mentioned above, including visiting departmental representatives on campus for each of the academic majors in these fields, interviewing people employed in these fields, using the career research features of O*NET OnLine (the occupational information network sponsored by the U.S. Department of Labor, Employment and Training Administration [ETA]; https://www.onetonline.org), and possibly taking a course in these areas or doing volunteer work in a related field.

He was pleased to obtain information from his Strong profile that supported his interests in science and research. He recognized the potential conflict caused by his low interest in math, which he was attempting to address. He appreciated the information that he received regarding other career possibilities suggested by his interest profile. The Strong enabled him to evaluate systematically his interests in regard to different career fields, which was the type of information that he needed at the time.

• • •

Alternative and Supplemental Strong Assessments

The **Strong Interest Explorer** is a simplified, self-scorable version of the Strong for use with young people beginning in the eighth grade (Morris, Chartrand, & Donnay, 2002). It contains 130 items that can be completed in 10 to 15 minutes. This instrument, which provides scores for 14 basic interest areas, can be used in either individual or group settings with students or others in the early stages of career exploration.

The Strong, which focuses on interests, may be supplemented with instruments that ask clients to evaluate their abilities to succeed in different types of activities. Two instruments—the **Skills Confidence Inventory** (SCI) and the **Expanded Skills Confidence Inventory** (E-SCI)—have been developed specifically for this purpose (Betz, Borgen, et al., 1996; Betz et al., 2003). The SCI, discussed in Chapter 11, contains six scales that match the six Holland interest scales used on the Strong. The E-SCI contains 17 scales that parallel many of the Basic Interest scales found on the Strong. Research shows scores from either the SCI or E-SCI significantly enhance the validity of Strong scores in predicting occupational criteria (Donnay & Borgen, 1999; Jenkins, 2013; Rottinghaus, Betz, & Borgen, 2003). Both types of measures (interests and self-rated skills) should be taken into account in considering career options.

Campbell Interest and Skill Survey

David Campbell, who is known for his work in updating and revising early forms of the Strong (previously titled the Strong–Campbell Interest Inventory), created the **Campbell Interest and Skill Survey** (CISS) subsequent to his work on the Strong (D. P. Campbell, 2002). The CISS is one of several inventories in an integrated battery of psychological surveys called the **Campbell Development Surveys** (D. P. Campbell, 1993). The CISS is similar to the Strong in that it includes both general and occupational interest scales; it differs by its inclusion of a set of self-report skill scales to match each of the interest scales (D. P. Campbell, Hyne, & Nilsen, 1992).

The CISS provides interest and skill scores for seven Orientation scales, 29 Basic scales, 60 Occupational scales, and three Special scales (Academic Focus, Extraversion, and Variety). The seven Orientation scales are similar to the six Holland scales on the Strong. The Strong Realistic scale has been subdivided into Producing and Adventuring scales to create the seventh Orientation scale. The Basic scales on the CISS have much in common with the Basic scales on the Strong.

In contrast with the Strong, the CISS uses unisex Occupational scales instead of separate scales for men and women. These scales were formed by comparing the interests and skills of a combined sample of men and women in the occupation with a general reference sample of men and women. The proportions of men and women in the general reference sample were adjusted for each occupation to match the proportions of men and women in the occupational sample as a means of controlling for gender differences.

Reliability studies conducted with employed adults indicate that the CISS results are internally consistent (general scales) and stable over a 3-month time period (all scales). In regard to validity, people in the occupation score substantially higher on the interest and skill scales for that occupation than do people in general. On the average, people in the occupational criterion group used in creating an occupational scale scored about 2 *SD* higher (18 to 20 points) on the Occupational scale than did people in the general reference sample (D. P. Campbell et al., 1992). These results compare favorably with those reported for the Strong.

Validity studies indicate that the CISS interest scales effectively differentiate among students in different academic majors (Hansen & Neuman, 1999; Pendergrass, Hansen, Neuman, & Nutter, 2003; Severy, 2013). About 65% to 75% of the students in these studies were engaged in college majors compatible with their interest scores. Scores on the skill and interest scales for the same activities or occupations are interpreted in terms of the following four categories: (a) *Pursue:* high interest, high skill; (b) *Explore:* high skill, lower interest; (c) *Develop:* high interest, lower skill; and (d) *Avoid:* low interest, low skill. For example, individuals with a high score on the Attorney skill scale but a relatively low score on the Attorney interest scale are encouraged to explore this occupation with the thought that their interests in it might be enhanced or that they might find a niche in the occupational field that they would enjoy.

In addition to the CISS, other instruments in the Campbell Development Surveys include the **Campbell Organizational Survey**, **Campbell Leadership Index**, **Campbell–Hallam Team Development Survey**, and **Campbell Community Survey** (D. P. Campbell, 1993). These instruments, which possess many characteristics in common to aid interpretation, can help counselors in their work with teams, organizations, and communities in addition to individuals. An example of the use of the CISS in counseling is presented in Case Example 12.2.

Case Example 12.2

Tess

When Tess first came to the counseling center as a 31-year-old returning adult student, she had just graduated from college with a degree in business administration. At that time, she was actively involved in a job search. She wanted to learn more about herself and how her interests and skills related to a variety of occupations and leisure activities. The counselor assigned the CISS to help her in this process.

Her scores on the CISS report summary are shown in Figure 12.2. She produced a valid profile as shown by the Procedural Checks scale scores on the bottom of the second page of the report summary. Her response percentages for the interest and skill items were normally distributed, her responses to pairs of similar items were consistent in all but one case, and she omitted no items.

She obtained high scores (*T* score of 55 or higher) on all seven Orientation skill scales but on only two (Organizing and Analyzing) of the Orientation interest scales. As indicated on the profile, she was encouraged to pursue Organizing and Analyzing occupations and to explore occupations in the other fields.

Tess showed high interests and self-rated skills on the Leadership, Advertising/Marketing, Financial Services, Counseling, and Mathematics Basic scales—all areas that can be related to her major in business administration. She also obtained high interest and skill scores on the Art/Design, Mechanical Crafts, Woodworking, Plants/Gardens, and Animal Care scales, which can be looked on as possible leisure-time pursuits as well as career alternatives.

Tess obtained a large number of high scores on both the Occupational interest and skill scales (see second page of report summary), especially in the Organizing and Analyzing areas. She felt encouraged by the test results. She planned to investigate the following occupations in greater detail, all of which she was advised to pursue on the CISS report: financial planner, corporate trainer, bank manager, CEO/president, and restaurant manager. All of these occupations were consistent with her major in business administration.

In a follow-up interview conducted 4 years later, Tess reported that shortly after completing counseling, she obtained a job as a program manager that involved both organizing and influencing skills and interests. She disliked the influencing (public speaking) aspect of that job and left it after 6 months. She then obtained a job as a bookkeeper for a public agency, from which she was soon promoted to chief financial officer and assistant director. She thrived in this work, which matched her interests and skills on the Financial Services, Mathematics, and Leadership scales. The CISS helped Tess to identify a career field that proved to be satisfying and fulfilling for her.

• • •

Kuder Career Search With Person Match

G. Frederic Kuder contributed greatly to the field of interest measurement by developing three different types of interest inventories over a lifetime of work. First, he created the Kuder Preference Record–Vocational (KPR-V) in 1939, an instrument that was widely used in counseling settings for many years (Zytowski, 1992; Zytowski & Austin, 2001). The KPR-V, which measured interests in broad domains such as art and science, was revised several times and eventually replaced in 1963 by the **Kuder General Interest Survey** (KGIS), a simplified version of the KPR-V with a sixth-grade reading level. Second, he constructed the **Kuder Occupational Interest Survey** (KOIS), Form D, in 1956 to measure interests with occupational scales in a manner similar to the Strong. This instrument evolved into the KOIS, Form DD, which used improved test construction procedures and added college major scales. Finally, as a third type of inventory, he developed the **Kuder Career Search** (KCS) With Person Match, a truly innovative inventory that compares an individual's interests with those of specific people in various occupations (Kelly, 2002b; Zytowski, 1992).

The Kuder Career Search is also referred to formally as the **Kuder Career Assessment Instrument** and is part of Kuder's Career Planning System (Gibbons, 2013). The system also includes the **Kuder Skills Assessment** (KSA) and the revised **Super's Work Values Inventory** (discussed later in this chapter). The Kuder Career Planning System provides multiple levels of assessment to cater to different age groups, such as Kuder Galaxy

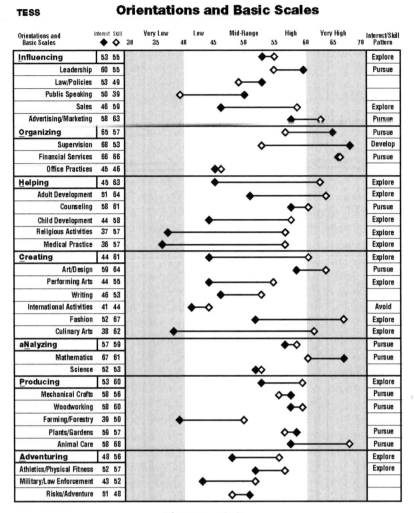

Figure 12.2
Campbell Interest and Skill Survey (CISS) Report Summary
for Tess, a 31-Year-Old Recent College Graduate (*Continued on next page*)

(Prekindergarten–5), Kuder Navigator (Grades 6–12), and Kuder Journey (postsecondary students and adults).

Kuder's first two interest inventories have both become somewhat dated and less useful for counselors (Kelly, 2002b; Pope, 2002). The broad interest scales used on the KGIS can also be found on the KCS, so that the latter instrument can essentially serve as a replacement for the KGIS as well as provide the Person Match information when desired. For these reasons, only the KCS with Person Match is discussed in detail here.

The KCS contains 32 forced-choice triads; each triad includes three activities, such as "Build birdhouses," "Write articles about birds," and "Draw sketches of birds," which clients rank in order according to their preferences. The use of forced-choice items makes it possible to control for response styles such as acquiescence (marking "like" to most items) and deviation (making extreme responses to most items). The forced-choice item format affects the interpretation of the results. The scores must be interpreted in regard to each other. A high score indicates that the person likes that type of activity more than other activities compared with members of the norm group, but it does not indicate the absolute magnitude of the interest.

TESS
Female
Age 31

Occupational Scales

DATE SCORED: 2/06/97
White
College Graduate

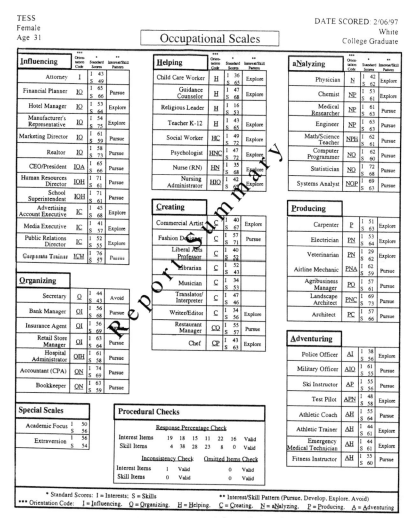

Influencing

Occupation	Orientation Code	Standard Scores	Interest/Skill Pattern
Attorney	I	I 43 / S 49	
Financial Planner	IO	I 65 / S 66	Pursue
Hotel Manager	IO	I 53 / S 64	Explore
Manufacturer's Representative	IO	I 54 / S 75	Explore
Marketing Director	IO	I 61 / S 59	Pursue
Realtor	IO	I 58 / S 73	Pursue
CEO/President	IOA	I 65 / S 66	Pursue
Human Resources Director	IOH	I 71 / S 61	Pursue
School Superintendent	IOH	I 71 / S 61	Pursue
Advertising Account Executive	IC	I 45 / S 68	Explore
Media Executive	IC	I 41 / S 57	Explore
Public Relations Director	IC	I 52 / S 55	Explore
Corporate Trainer	ICH	I 76 / S 57	Pursue

Organizing

Occupation	Orientation Code	Standard Scores	Interest/Skill Pattern
Secretary	O	I 44 / S 43	Avoid
Bank Manager	OI	I 56 / S 68	Pursue
Insurance Agent	OI	I 56 / S 69	Pursue
Retail Store Manager	OI	I 63 / S 64	Pursue
Hospital Administrator	OIH	I 61 / S 58	Pursue
Accountant (CPA)	ON	I 74 / S 69	Pursue
Bookkeeper	ON	I 63 / S 59	Pursue

Helping

Occupation	Orientation Code	Standard Scores	Interest/Skill Pattern
Child Care Worker	H	I 36 / S 65	Explore
Guidance Counselor	H	I 47 / S 68	Explore
Religious Leader	H	I 16 / S 53	
Teacher K-12	H	I 43 / S 65	Explore
Social Worker	HC	I 49 / S 72	Explore
Psychologist	HNC	I 47 / S 72	Explore
Nurse (RN)	HN	I 35 / S 67	Explore
Nursing Administrator	HIO	I 42 / S 64	Explore

Creating

Occupation	Orientation Code	Standard Scores	Interest/Skill Pattern
Commercial Artist	C	I 40 / S 67	Explore
Fashion Designer	C	I 57 / S 71	Pursue
Liberal Arts Professor	C	I 40 / S 52	
Librarian	C	I 52 / S 43	
Musician	C	I 34 / S 53	
Translator/Interpreter	C	I 47 / S 46	
Writer/Editor	C	I 34 / S 56	Explore
Restaurant Manager	CO	I 55 / S 57	Pursue
Chef	CP	I 43 / S 63	Explore

aNalyzing

Occupation	Orientation Code	Standard Scores	Interest/Skill Pattern
Physician	N	I 42 / S 62	Explore
Chemist	NP	I 53 / S 61	Explore
Medical Researcher	NP	I 61 / S 63	Pursue
Engineer	NP	I 63 / S 63	Pursue
Math/Science Teacher	NPH	I 62 / S 61	Pursue
Computer Programmer	NQ	I 62 / S 60	Pursue
Statistician	NQ	I 72 / S 68	Pursue
Systems Analyst	NOP	I 69 / S 63	Pursue

Producing

Occupation	Orientation Code	Standard Scores	Interest/Skill Pattern
Carpenter	P	I 51 / S 63	Explore
Electrician	PN	I 53 / S 64	Explore
Veterinarian	PN	I 29 / S 62	Explore
Airline Mechanic	PNA	I 62 / S 59	Pursue
Agribusiness Manager	PO	I 57 / S 61	Pursue
Landscape Architect	PNC	I 69 / S 73	Pursue
Architect	PC	I 57 / S 66	Pursue

Adventuring

Occupation	Orientation Code	Standard Scores	Interest/Skill Pattern
Police Officer	AI	I 38 / S 56	Explore
Military Officer	AIO	I 61 / S 55	Pursue
Ski Instructor	AP	I 55 / S 56	Pursue
Test Pilot	APN	I 48 / S 58	Explore
Athletic Coach	AH	I 55 / S 64	Pursue
Athletic Trainer	AH	I 44 / S 61	Explore
Emergency Medical Technician	AH	I 44 / S 61	Explore
Fitness Instructor	AH	I 55 / S 60	Pursue

Special Scales

	Standard Scores
Academic Focus	I 50 / S 56
Extraversion	I 56 / S 54

Procedural Checks

Response Percentage Check

Interest Items	19	18	15	11	22	16	Valid
Skill Items	4	38	28	23	8	0	Valid

Inconsistency Check		Omitted Items Check	
Interest Items	1 Valid	0	Valid
Skill Items	0 Valid	0	Valid

* Standard Scores: I = Interests; S = Skills   ** Interest/Skill Pattern (Pursue, Develop, Explore, Avoid)
*** Orientation Code: I = Influencing, O = Organizing, H = Helping, C = Creating, N = aNalyzing, P = Producing, A = Adventuring

Figure 12.2 (*Continued*)
**Campbell Interest and Skill Survey (CISS) Report Summary
for Tess, a 31-Year-Old Recent College Graduate**

Clients receive scores on six Career Cluster scales similar to the six Holland categories used on other interest inventories and on 10 Activity Preference scales similar to the 10 broad interest scales that appeared on the KGIS. The relationships among the Holland categories, Career Cluster scales, and the Activity Preference scales are indicated below:

Holland Category	Career Cluster Scale	Activity Preference Scale
Realistic	Outdoor/Mechanical	Nature, Mechanical
Investigative	Science/Technical	Science/Technical
Artistic	Arts/Communication	Performing Arts, Communications
Social	Social/Personal Service	Human Services
Enterprising	Sales/Management	Sales, Management
Conventional	Business Operations	Computations, Office Detail

A single grand norm group consisting of both males and females from sixth grade through adults is used to obtain percentile scores for the Career Cluster scales and the Activity Preference scales. Some sex differences have been found on the scales; however, Zytowski (2006) noted that such differences do not significantly affect the score interpretations because of the emphasis on rank order of scores within the individual.

The KCS has been designed to help clients identify and explore various career possibilities. Clients are provided with detailed descriptions of the type of work pursued by individuals with their same interests. This process helps clients to realize their multipotentiality, as shown by the wide range of occupations typically represented by the individual descriptions that they receive (Gibbons, 2013).

The KSA is a 90-item inventory that asks clients to rate their skills in six types of activities (Kuder, Inc., n.d.). These six activities match the six interest areas measured on the Kuder Career Search. Each item includes four response options ranging from "I don't think I could ever learn to do this task" to "I can already do this task." As with the KCS, this instrument may be used with individuals ranging from middle school age through adults. By using the KSA, counselors are able to take into account a client's perception of his or her abilities as well as interests in different type of activities.

Self-Directed Search

The **Self-Directed Search** (SDS), now in its fifth edition, was originally developed by Holland in the 1950s. Thus, it is based on Holland's theory of vocational choice. Holland's theory examines the congruence between person and environment and assumes that people will be most satisfied and successful if they live and work in an environment that is compatible with their interests and skills. The same six categories used to describe an individual's personality type (Realistic, Investigative, Artistic, Social, Enterprising, Conventional) are also used to describe occupational environments, so that comparisons between an individual's characteristics and an occupation's attributes can easily be made by means of the SDS.

The SDS can be self-administered, self-scored, and self-interpreted. Furthermore, the SDS contains six test components: the *Assessment Report,* the *Occupations Finder,* the *You and Your Career* booklet, *Educational Opportunities Finder, Leisure Activities Finder,* and the *SDS Professional Manual.* Clients can also be directed to take the SDS at http://www.self-directed-search.com and receive an Interactive Report and Client Interpretive Report by e-mail.

Although it is often classified as an interest inventory, the SDS is actually an inventory of both interests and abilities. Holland referred to it as a career counseling simulation. It consists of five sections: (a) Occupational Daydreams, in which a client expresses interests and an Aspirations Summary Code is provided; (b) Activities, which has the client rate whether he or she likes or dislikes various activities; (c) Competencies, in which a client describes his or her skills using a yes/no format; (d) Occupations, which gauges a client's attitudes toward a set of occupations using a yes/no format; and (e) Self-Estimates, which measures a client's self-efficacy related to specific tasks.

Many of the codes that Holland and his colleagues have assigned to different occupations are based primarily on judgments of job analysts. These codes may differ from the codes assigned by authors of interest inventories based on actual test scores. For example, food service manager is coded as an ESR (Enterprising–Social–Realistic) occupation in the *Occupations Finder,* whereas it is coded as a CES (Conventional–Enterprising–Social) occupation for both men and women on the Strong. In most cases, the codes based on the two types of systems agree. When they disagree, codes derived by means of actual data should be given greater weight.

The SDS uses the client's raw scores in determining Holland codes. Holland has been criticized for this approach in that it reinforces gender stereotypes. With the use of raw scores, men are more likely to obtain high scores on the Realistic, Investigative, and Enterprising scales, and women are more likely to score high on the Social, Artistic, and Conventional scales than they would if scores based on separate-sex norms were used. Holland defended his approach as reflecting the real world, namely, that men and women are in fact attracted to different types of activities (Holland, Fritzsche, & Powell, 1994).

Holland has recommended that the SDS be supplemented with the My Vocational Situation (MVS) inventory, which measures aspects of vocational identity not measured by the SDS (see Chapter 11). Clients with a clear vocational identity probably need relatively little assistance from counselors. The SDS by itself may be sufficient for such clients. Clients who score low on the Vocational Identity scale (indicating difficulties in self-perception) are more likely to need individual counseling or other interventions, such as career seminars or volunteer experiences, in addition to the SDS. In a similar manner, clients who show a need for occupational information or who face external barriers to their career development, such as lack of financial support, parental disapproval of career choice, or lack of ability to complete a training program, probably could profit from individual counseling. Case Example 12.3 illustrates the use of the SDS in counseling.

Case Example 12.3
Lisa

Lisa, a college sophomore, completed both the SDS and the MVS to help her in career exploration after she was dropped from her academic program for poor grades. She had been majoring in biology, with plans to become a dentist, but had lost interest in this career goal some time ago. She planned to reconsider her career plans during the next 3 to 4 months and then reapply to the university the following semester. According to the SDS, her Holland code was ESI (Enterprising–Social–Investigative). In discussing these results, she indicated that she wished to consider the possibility of pursuing a career in business with an emphasis on the environment, a career choice suggested by her SDS scores. The MVS indicated that she lacked occupational information. She planned to take advantage of the time that she would not be in college to explore this type of career direction by talking with people in the field, reading relevant materials, and obtaining volunteer or paid employment in a related field.

• • •

Career Decision-Making System–Revised

The **Career Decision-Making System–Revised** (CDM-R), by O'Shea and Feller (2012), offers a broad, simplified approach to career planning based on self-assessments that requires relatively little testing time (20 to 40 minutes altogether). Students rate themselves in terms of interests, career choices, school subjects, work values, abilities, and educational plans. Most emphasis is placed on an individual's interests, which are scored in terms of the six Holland interest categories.

The CDM-R is available in two versions: Level 1 (Grades 7 through 10) and Level 2 (high school students and adults). For both versions, students score their own answer sheets by simply counting the number of responses in each of the six interest categories. Raw scores (instead of standardized scores) are used in the same manner as with the SDS. In a long-term follow-up study of high school students who completed the original CDM in the 10th grade, Harrington (2006) found that most of them (61% of the boys and 52% of the girls) were employed in an occupation compatible with their Holland code (two highest scores) 20 years later.

Results from the CDM-R are used to suggest career clusters to students that they may wish to investigate. The CDM-R is accompanied by an extensive manual and helpful interpretive materials. This comprehensive, low-cost assessment package has received favorable reviews from guidance experts, especially as a means of stimulating career exploration (J. C. Campbell & Perry, 2013).

Jackson Vocational Interest Survey

The **Jackson Vocational Interest Survey** (JVIS), originally published in 1977 and revised in 1999, is designed for counselors to use in educational and career planning with high school students, college students, and other adults. A new set of norms, based on a sample of 3,500 adults and secondary school students, and new reliability analyses and interpretive materials were provided in 1999 (Jackson & Verhoeve, 2000).

Respondents must choose between 289 pairs of items that measure interests in different types of job-related activities. The items have been paired to control for response bias. Most people can complete the JVIS in 40 minutes to 1 hour. Similar to the Strong, the JVIS includes administrative indices, General Occupational Theme scales, Basic Interest scales, Occupational scores, and a Nonoccupational scale (Academic Satisfaction). It differs from the Strong by including measures of academic interests and by its emphasis on occupational clusters instead of specific occupations. Scores are provided for a total of 17 academic major clusters, such as Performing Arts and Environmental Resource Management, and for 32 occupational clusters, such as Agriculturalists and Health Service Workers.

The JVIS differs from most other interest inventories by including items that measure interests in different types of work environments (work style items) as well as different types of work activities (work role items). Of the 34 Basic Interest scales, eight reflect work style preferences. The work style scales, such as Independence and Job Security, are similar to the types of scales often included on values inventories.

The measures of occupational and academic major interests are unique in that these measures are derived from the scores on the Basic Interest scales. Scores for each of the 17 academic major and 32 occupational clusters are reported as correlation coefficients that show the degree of similarity between an individual's basic interest profile and the average basic interest profiles of people in different majors and occupations. In this manner, Jackson was able to make use of vast amounts of archival data accumulated for the Strong.

Tip Sheet
Interpreting Interest Inventories

- ✓ Check to make certain that the client has answered all or nearly all of the items and to ensure that the client understood and followed the directions. Total response and infrequent response indices should be helpful for this purpose. Check all validity indices, such as the typicality index on the Strong.
- ✓ Ask clients about their reactions to the inventory before interpreting the results. If possible, allow clients time to inspect their profile and to formulate questions before discussing the results with them.
- ✓ Note the percentage distribution of *like, indifferent,* and *dislike* responses for interest inventories with this type of response format. Remember that high scores on general or basic interest scales are based on likes, whereas low scores on these scales are based on dislikes. If a client marks an unusually high or low percentage of either *likes* or *dislikes,* be sure to interpret scores relatively; that is, give greatest consideration to the highest scores, regardless of their absolute level.
- ✓ Interpret the general (homogeneous) scales first. Help the client to determine his or her Holland code. Use the basic interest scales when available to clarify the meaning of the Holland codes, which can vary significantly for an individual from one inter-

est inventory to another (Savickas & Taber, 2006). Use the Holland code together with the basic interest scales as a framework for interpreting the occupational scales.

✓ When available, use separate-sex norms in interpreting scores on the interest scales. The separate-sex norms take into account the differences in the socialization process for men and women, which can affect the validity of the scales.

✓ Interpret the occupational scores as measuring similarity of interest patterns compared with those of people in the occupation. Emphasize that the scores reflect interests rather than abilities. The scores can be used to help predict job satisfaction but not job success.

✓ Do not overinterpret small differences in scores between scales. If *T* scores fall within 8 to 10 points of each other, do not consider them to be significantly different from each other for most scales.

✓ Refer to *dislike* as well as *like* responses in interpreting high scores on occupational scales. A client can obtain high scores for some occupational scales simply by sharing the same dislikes that people in the occupation possess.

✓ Use information from self-rated ability tests to take into account the client's confidence in pursuing different types of activities. Special attention may need to be devoted to those situations in which the client's interests and self-rated abilities disagree with one another.

✓ Use information from personality scales, such as the PSSs on the Strong or the Special Scales on the CISS, to introduce personality factors into career planning that can help to enhance the predictive validity of the occupational scales.

✓ Relate the scores to other information concerning the client, such as stated interests, work experience, academic background, and career plans. Help the client integrate the assessment data and generate hypotheses that may be helpful in interpreting the data and in suggesting directions for further career exploration.

✓ Bring into consideration occupations that are not on the profile by using Holland's occupational classification system. Use the O*NET database on the Internet to identify occupations related to the client's interest pattern (U.S. Department of Labor, ETA, n.d.).

✓ When feasible, use the interest inventory together with other assessment procedures—such as personality assessments or career readiness assessments (see Chapter 11)—in order to obtain a more complete picture of the client's situation.

✓ Ask clients to identify four or five occupations or two or three career-related questions suggested by the interest inventory that they would like to investigate. Suggest sources of occupational and educational information, including the *Occupational Outlook Handbook*, O*NET OnLine, career pamphlets, informational interviews, and volunteer work.

✓ Schedule a follow-up interview with clients to help them review their progress and address issues that they may have identified during the career exploration process.

Values Inventories

Assessment procedures for both work and personal values are discussed in this section. **Work values** are a subset of personal values that describe different motivations for working. **Personal values** include a broader range of motivations that pertain to school, family, community, leisure, and work. Research indicates that the structures of both work values and personal values are similar across different cultures (S. H. Schwartz, 2012; S. H. Schwartz et al., 2012). S. H. Schwartz et al. (2012) identified 19 more narrow values that originate from four higher order values (openness to change, self-enhancement, conservation, and self-transcendence) and 10 basic values. The 19 values are: self-direction—thought, self-direction—action, stimulation, hedonism, achievement, power—dominance, power—resources, face, security—personal, security—societal, conformity—rules, conformity—interpersonal, tradition, humility, benevolence—dependability, benevolence—caring, universalism—concern, universalism—nature, and universalism—tolerance. These values categories—or those that might parallel them—are used in various values inventories described here.

Table 12.3 provides sample items for the values inventories discussed briefly in this section. Inventories can be used as stand-alone instruments or as part of a larger, more comprehensive career-planning program. Values inventories are most likely to be used independently when you want to help a client focus on what is most important to that client in his or her work or personal situation.

Table 12.3
Measures of Work and Personal Values

Career Assessment	Sample Items
Work Values Inventories	
Work Importance Profiler	On my ideal job, it is important that . . .
	I make use of my abilities.
	I could try out my own ideas.
	My coworkers are easy to get along with.
	Rank these statements in order from 1 (*most important*) through 5 (*least important*):
	I could be busy all the time
	I could do things for other people.
Work Values Inventory–Revised	Achieve a feeling of success from a job well done
	Have good interactions with fellow workers
	Can try out new ideas
Career Orientation and Evaluation Survey	I value activities or jobs which (I) . . .
	Work on my own without direction.
	Work under careful supervision.
Values Scale	It is important for me to make life more beautiful.
	It is important for me to use my strength.
Personal Values Inventories	
Rokeach Value Survey	Taking care of loved ones
	Self-esteem
	A prosperous life
Schwartz Value Survey	Social power (control over other, dominance)
	Success (achieving goals)
	Daring (seeking adventure, risk)
Study of Values	If you were a university professor and had the necessary ability, would you prefer to teach (a) poetry; (b) chemistry or physics?
Salience Inventory	I have spent or do spend time working.
	It is or will be more important to me to be good in working.
Quality of Life Inventory	Health
	Philosophy of life
	Home

Inventories of Work Values

Work values inventories assess values that pertain primarily to work situations. They measure objectives that can be satisfied in the work itself (intrinsic values) or through work as a means to an end (extrinsic values). Intrinsic values include creativity, mental challenge, and achievement. Extrinsic values include prestige, income, and working conditions. Both types of values need to be taken into consideration in career planning. All of the values inventories discussed here assess values related to worker satisfaction.

O*NET Work Importance Profiler

The **Work Importance Profiler** (WIP) was briefly mentioned in Chapter 11 as part of the O*NET system. The WIP is a computer-based instrument that also has an equivalent paper-and-pencil version, known as the **Work Importance Locator** (WIL-P&P). The WIP, which can be downloaded from the O*NET website, has the advantage of being free of charge. Both instruments provide rankings on six core values—achievement, independence, recognition, relationships, support, and working conditions. Individuals rank these items in comparison with each other as a means of determining which values are most important for them. The number of statements (items) per category ranges from two to six. The computer analyzes the individual's responses and presents the results by first listing the top two values in red and then the remaining four values in black. No scores are given, but the values are listed in order of importance for each individual.

Preliminary research has shown that test–retest profiles are moderately stable for college students over short time periods (U.S. Department of Labor, ETA, n.d.). The top one or two values probably will not change substantially over short time periods, although the stability of other values is less certain, especially for the WIL-P&P. Administration of the WIP and WIL-P&P to the same students yields profiles that show relatively high agreement with each other. Both instruments produce results that are moderately correlated with results on the Minnesota Importance Questionnaire, their parent instrument. The correlations are somewhat suppressed by the ipsative nature of the questionnaire, the use of fewer items in a simplified response format (for the WIL-P&P), and changes in the wording of some of the items. Additional research is needed to establish the validities of the WIP and WIL-P&P each in its own right.

The WIP or the WIL-P&P can be helpful in counseling when used together with the other O*NET instruments for career exploration under the guidance of a skilled counselor (Del Corso, 2013). The work value ratings for all of the occupations are included in the O*NET database. Counselors or clients can check occupations directly, or they can enter particular values one at a time to find occupations in which those values rank highest.

Work Values Inventory–Revised

The **Work Values Inventory–Revised** (WVI), which was originally developed by Donald Super (1970) for career development research and counseling, has been revised (C. H. Robinson & Betz, 2008). It is often used with the Kuder Career Planning Program.

In the revised form, clients rate the relative importance in their work situation of 12 values or goals on the following scales: Creativity, Mental Challenge, Achievement, Independence, Prestige, Income, Security, Work Environment, Supervision, Co-Workers, Lifestyle, and Variety. Three (Altruism, Esthetics, and Management) of the original 15 scales, all of which overlapped with interest measures, have been dropped. The 12 remaining scales (some of which have been renamed) originally had three items but were all increased in length to six items, each with five response options ranging from *not important at all* to *crucial*. The revised version uses a combined norm group of 7th- through 12th-grade boys and girls for converting raw scores to percentile scores.

The emphasis in interpretation is placed on the rank of an individual's scores, that is, what is relatively most important for that individual compared with his or her other values. Clients are reminded that some values are associated with an occupation (e.g., business management occupations often have a higher income), whereas other values may be satisfied by a particular position within an occupation (e.g., a salesperson who works independently).

Career Orientation Placement and Evaluation Survey

The **Career Orientation Placement and Evaluation Survey** (COPES) is one of three instruments used in the Career Occupational Preference System (see Chapter 11). It measures work values on eight bipolar scales (EdITS, n.d.; Knapp-Lee, 1996): Investigative versus Accepting, Practical versus Carefree, Independence versus Conformity, Leadership versus Supportive, Orderliness versus Flexibility, Recognition versus Privacy, Aesthetic versus Realistic, and Social versus Reserved. Each bipolar scale consists of 16 pairs of items that represent the opposite ends of the scale. For each item pair, clients must choose which activity or type of work they value more. For example, "work on my own without direction" versus "work under careful supervision" is an item pair scored on the Independence versus Conformity scale.

The COPES has been designed so that it may be used with the COPSystem Interest Inventory and CAPS. Based on a review of the career literature, the scale authors have identified the three most relevant values for each of the 14 occupational clusters used within this system. For example, outdoor careers are matched with Practical, Independence, and Privacy values.

Studies indicate that the eight COPES scales measure values that are relatively homogeneous and independent of each other. Students in different occupational groups obtain COPES scores according to expectations. Longitudinal data indicate that the COPES scores successfully predict future job or college program placement (Bullock-Yowell & Osborne, 2013; Knapp-Lee, 1996).

Values Scale

Donald Super and Dorothy Nevill collaborated with vocational psychologists from several different countries as part of the Work Importance Study to construct both the **Values Scale** (VS) and the Salience Inventory (see below; Nevill & Super, 1986a, 1986b). The VS builds on the research conducted by Super on the WVI. It contains 21 scales, which represent the 15 work values originally measured by the WVI, plus six additional values measured on the following scales: Physical Activity, Physical Prowess, Risk, Advancement, Personal Development, and Cultural Identity.

Each VS scale contains five items with four response options ranging from 1 (*of little or no importance*) to 4 (*very important*). For each scale (except Working Conditions), at least two of the five items pertain to nonwork situations, whereas two others pertain to work. Most people complete the inventory in 30 to 45 minutes. The VS, which is intended for people age 13 and older, requires an eighth-grade reading level. It can be easily scored by hand in a few minutes.

Studies of the VS with cross-national samples indicate that five factors (or orientations) account for most of the variance in test scores (Nevill & Super, 1986b). The five factors, together with the scales that best represent them, include the following: (a) Utilitarian Orientation (Economics, Advancement, Prestige, Authority, Achievement), (b) Orientation Toward Self-Actualization (Ability, Personal Development, Altruism), (c) Individualist Orientation (Lifestyle, Autonomy), (d) Social Orientation (Social Interaction, Social Relations), and (e) Adventurous Orientation (Risk). These five factors can be used to help organize and explain the information obtained from the 21 scales. The Utilitarian and Individualist orientations primarily assess extrinsic values that can be satisfied by the outcomes of work, whereas Orientation Toward Self-Actualization, Social Orientation, and Adventurous Orientation measure intrinsic values that can be satisfied by participation in the work itself.

From a psychometric point of view, questions have been raised regarding the reliability estimates of the scale scores, the representativeness of the norms, and the lack of predictive validity studies (Green, 1998). Despite its limitations, the VS can be helpful in counseling for focusing on the importance of values in life and career planning (Nevill & Kruse, 1996). At this point, the VS can best be used for intraindividual comparisons; that is, to help clients determine the relative strength of their values compared with each other. The VS has been designed for use with other measures of career development, including the Adult Career Concerns Inventory and the Career Development Inventory (see Chapter 11), as well as the Strong Interest Inventory, as described in the C-DAC model (Super et al., 1992).

Inventories of Personal Values

Inventories of personal values can be used to evaluate what goals or objectives an individual considers to be important in a variety of situations beyond work itself. Some of these instruments, such as the Rokeach Value Survey (RVS) and the Schwartz Value Survey (SVS), are broad measures of values that have been used primarily for research purposes; however, counselors may find their comprehensive coverage of different types of values to be helpful in some counseling situations. Other instruments, including the Study of Values (SOV), Salience Inventory (SI), and Quality of Life Questionnaire (QOLI), have been specifically validated for use in counseling situations to predict criteria such as educational and occupational membership or life satisfaction. All five of these inventories are discussed below, together with outcome expectation questionnaires, which consider the degree to which particular values may be realized in different situations.

Rokeach Value Survey

The **Rokeach Value Survey** (RVS) is a short inventory that consists of two sets of 18 words or phrases that measure instrumental and terminal values (Rokeach, 1973). Instrumental values, such as obedience, forgiveness, and imagination, represent "modes of conduct." Terminal values, such as beauty, adventure, and friendship, represent the "end-states of existence." Respondents must rank each of the two sets of 18 items in order of their preferences for the different values (Cieciuch, Schwartz, & Davidov, 2015).

Although the inventory is designed for individuals age 11 and older, its results tend to be unreliable for younger individuals, especially those who lack the ability to handle verbal abstractions. Brookhart (1995) recommended that the use of the RVS be limited to "literate adults who are used to dealing with abstractions" (p. 879). Although the RVS has been used primarily for research purposes, Sanford (1995) noted that it can be "useful for examining an individual's value system and for determining if change has occurred within [it]" (p. 880). Because of limited norms, the results should be interpreted simply by comparing the ranks of the different values for an individual with each other (i.e., in an ipsative fashion), not by comparison with a norm group.

Schwartz Value Survey

The **Schwartz Value Survey** (SVS) is a 57-item instrument that is based in part on Rokeach's original work. S. H. Schwartz's (1994) goal was to develop a broad measure of basic values that would be applicable in most human cultures. He identified 10 basic values that can be arranged in a circular fashion (a circumplex) with two bipolar dimensions running through it at right angles: Self-Transcendence versus Self-Enhancement and Openness to Change versus Conservation. The SVS structure of values has been tested and confirmed in more than 60 countries (Cieciuch et al., 2015).

The values are arranged on the circumplex so that those close together have the most in common and those across from each other have the least in common. The two values of Tradition and Conformity are both diametrically opposed to Stimulation (excitement, novelty); however, Tradition, which indicates an adherence to cultural and religious customs and ideas, is even further removed from Stimulation than is Conformity, which shows a tendency to agree with family and friends more than with the culture as a whole. Values that tend to be more popular in general, such as Benevolence (concern for the welfare of others) and Universalism (understanding, appreciation), are shown by larger sizes in the circumplex.

Men and women show moderate differences in values across most cultures. Men score higher on the Power, Stimulation, Hedonism, Achievement, and Self-Direction values scales; women score higher on the Benevolence and Universalism values scales. Sex differences are not as great as age and cultural differences in most studies. Cultural differences are especially large in regard to Tradition, Conformity, Security, and Hedonism values scales (S. H. Schwartz, 2012).

Research indicates that values as measured by the SVS overlap somewhat with interests; however, most of the relationships are modest. Studies involving the SVS and the Self-Directed Search show the following positive relationships, which conform to expectations (Sagiv, 2002):

- Conventional interests—Conformity, Security, and Tradition values;
- Enterprising interests—Power and Achievement values;
- Social interests—Benevolence values;
- Artistic interests—Self-Direction and Universalism values;
- Investigative interests—Self-Direction and Universalism values; and
- Realistic interests—no significant relationships.

In counseling, these relationships were stronger for individuals who had made a career decision than for those who were undecided, suggesting that decided individuals may have been experiencing less conflict in their decision making.

Instead of the SVS, counselors may use the **Portrait Values Questionnaire** (PVQ-5X) The PVQ-5X includes three items each for 19 narrowed values scales (Cieciuch, Davidov, Vecchione, Beierlein, & Schwartz, 2014). The tool asks responders to indicate to what degree values portrayed by different individuals compare with their own. The PVQ-5X is reported to measure personal values across several countries better than previous editions (Cieciuch et al., 2014).

Study of Values

The **Study of Values** (SOV, 4th edition) is a measure of six personal values that has been updated with the rewriting of 15 of its original 45 items (Kopelman, Rovenpor, & Guan, 2003). The six values are Theoretical, Economic, Aesthetic, Social, Political, and Religious. For this edition, items that used sexist language (all male pronouns), dated examples (e.g., Amundsen, Byrd), and limited religious references (all Christian) were revised to make them more relevant and acceptable. The items ask people to choose among different values in terms of their preferences in particular situations, such as which individual (Aristotle or Abraham Lincoln) they feel has made the greatest contribution to society. Studies indicate that the updated version (SOV-U) compares favorably with the original version in terms of its psychometric properties.

There is no test manual or scoring instructions for the instrument (Shurts, 2013). Because of the measure's ipsative nature, emphasis should be placed on intraindividual comparisons in interpreting the test results. Research indicates that the SOV-U predicts external criteria, such as graduate field of study, more accurately than the RVS (Instrumental and Terminal versions) and the SVS (Shurts, 2013), presumably because of its use of behavioral items instead of items that ask about abstract values. Individuals may not be aware of their values until they are forced to choose among them in lifelike situations. The SOV-U is reprinted in Kopelman et al.'s (2003) article and may be used with permission of its authors.

Salience Inventory

The **Salience Inventory** (SI) measures the importance of different life roles for individuals in the context of Super's "lifespace, life span" model of career development (Nevill & Super, 1986a). Five life roles—studying, working, community service, home, and leisure activities—are assessed from three perspectives: participation, commitment, and value expectations. The five Participation scales measure the extent of a person's actual behavior in each of the five roles. The five Commitment scales assess the client's emotional attachment to each role. Finally, the five Value Expectations scales measure the degree to which a client expects that his or her values will be fulfilled in each of the five roles.

The instrument, which includes 170 items rated on a 4-point scale, requires about 30 to 45 minutes to complete. It can be hand scored easily without the use of templates. The SI scales have yielded high coefficients of internal consistency for student and adult samples; however, test–retest coefficients for college students have been somewhat low. A client's test scores can be expected to change somewhat over short time periods. Validity studies indicate that the SI differentiates among different occupational and cultural groups in expected directions. Individuals vary in the relative importance they place on the different roles on the basis of such factors as age, gender, and culture.

The SI provides information for counseling purposes that is not readily available from other instruments. It can help clarify the client's readiness to engage in career planning by indicating the relative significance of career in the client's life. It can be used to identify and explore role conflicts within clients or between clients and their environment. For example, discrepancies between Commitment or Value Expectations and Participation scale scores may suggest important topics for consideration.

When used in combination with the VS (or other measure of work values), the SI can help identify outlets for values not realized in one's career. Because the SI has been developed for use in multicultural settings, it can be particularly valuable in counseling students from different cultural backgrounds (Nevill & Calvert, 1996).

Quality of Life Inventory

The **Quality of Life Inventory** (QOLI) is a short, 32-item instrument that can be used to rate the importance of 16 different aspects of life, such as learning, helping, and health (Frisch, 1994). Individuals also rate the degree to which they are satisfied with each of these aspects of their lives. Total Quality of Life scores can be obtained by multiplying the Importance scale ratings by the Satisfaction scale ratings for each of the 16 areas and then adding these figures together. National norms have been supplemented by clinical norms drawn from various mental health settings (L. Carlson, 2013; Frisch et al., 2005).

Longitudinal research shows that the QOLI predicts academic retention 1 to 3 years in advance and that it is a sensitive indicator of treatment-related changes (Frisch et al., 2005). In general, it can serve as a vehicle for discussing values with clients. It has the advantages of being brief, comprehensive, easy to administer and score, and based on a quality-of-life model that can be used to interpret scores and suggest possible interventions (L. Carlson, 2013).

Activity 12.1
Selecting Measures of Work and Personal Values

Select one of the assessments discussed in this section. Use assessment sources discussed earlier in the text, as well as *A Counselor's Guide to Career Assessment Instruments* (C. T. Wood & Hays, 2013), to collect psychometric information on the assessment. Reflect on the following questions:

- What is the psychometric evidence (e.g., reliability, validity, standardization sample, scoring information) for the assessment? How strong is this evidence?
- How would you use this instrument in your practice?
- What are some of the advantages and disadvantages of the assessment?
- What are some multicultural and social justice considerations for using values inventories in counseling?

Present the information to the larger group.

Tip Sheet
Use of Values Inventories in Counseling

✓ Use a measure of values when a client wishes to clarify work or life goals and objectives. Integrate measures of values with measures of interests in attempting to understand client motivation for work or other activities.

✓ Use the scales or factors from a values inventory to provide a meaningful structure by which clients can consider their values. A structure of this sort enables the client to consider the nature of values expressed in various activities.

✓ Ask clients to estimate their own profile. Ask them to separate those needs that are most important for them from those that are least important. This approach will teach clients to apply a values structure to their own situation.

✓ Try to estimate the client's profile. This type of exercise helps the counselor to become more familiar with both the values inventory and the client. The counselor is forced to organize his or her thinking about the client's values in a systematic fashion.

✓ Compare the client's and the counselor's estimates with the actual profile from the values inventory. If they do not match, try to determine the reasons for the discrepancies. Clarify the meaning of both estimated and measured values.

✓ To what extent do the values scores agree with the client's experiences? Clients should report satisfaction with previous occupations and activities that provide rewards that agree with their needs and values.

✓ Ask clients to interpret individual items in regard to their situation. What do the items mean to them, particularly those items that they may be most concerned about?

✓ Look at the relationship between values scores and values that rank highest for different occupations as listed in the O*NET database to obtain a list of occupations that provide rewards appropriate to clients' values (U.S. Department of Labor, ETA, n.d.).

✓ Consider work values within a larger context of life values and life planning. Help clients to consider a range of values that may be expressed within a variety of roles and situations.

✓ Take into account the possible influence of cultural values, such as collectivism versus individualism, linear versus circular time orientation, and person–nature relationship, on career choice and development.

✓ Use the results from values inventories to stimulate self-exploration. The results should be used in conjunction with other data that take into account interests, abilities, previous experiences, and opportunities.

✓ Keep in mind that values can change. As basic needs (such as survival, safety, and belonging) are satisfied, higher order needs (such as esteem and self-actualization) become more important (Maslow, 1987). Counselors may need to help clients review their values as their situation changes.

Values Clarification Exercises

Values can be assessed either by a values inventory or by values clarification exercises. **Values clarification exercises** are strategies that enable clients to identify and to make comparisons among their values. Compared with values inventories, values clarification exercises require clients to engage in self-assessment at a deeper level that takes into account actual behavior as well as preferences. The exercises ask clients to review their beliefs and behaviors in response to different situations. They encourage clients to assume a more active role in exploring and expressing their values. These exercises possess all of the advantages of qualitative assessment procedures, including more active participation on the part of the client and a more holistic approach (Kirschenbaum, 2013).

Values clarification exercises have been used in regard to a wide variety of issues, including substance abuse, career transitions, grieving, and diversity training. For example, a typical values clarification exercise invites clients to list 15 to 20 things they love to do. For each activity, they are then asked to consider such matters as how long it has been since they participated in the activity, whether it is something that they do with others or alone, how much the activity costs, how important that activity is compared with other activities, how much planning the activity requires, and whether this is a new activity for them. The exercise requires clients to analyze their activities in terms of the values expressed. A value is considered to be fully developed when it meets the following six criteria: It has been (a) chosen freely (b) from among alternatives (c) after careful consideration of the consequences, (d) prized and (e) publicly affirmed, and (f) acted on repeatedly (Raths, Harmin, & Simon, 1978).

Most career-planning workbooks (see Chapter 11) contain several values clarification exercises. The workbooks help clients to integrate information derived from the values clarification exercises with other information about themselves and with occupational information. Different types of exercises include the values auction, values card sort, and guided fantasy. Other values clarification assessments include the use of stories in which work values are embedded (Krumboltz, Blando, Kim, & Reikowski, 1994) and the use of the Repertory Grid to help clients create their own values categories for making comparisons among occupations (Zytowski, 1994). Brott (2015) described several activities, including the life line, the life-space genogram, and life roles analysis, that counselors can use with clients to help clarify life roles and construct meaningful life stories. Knowdell constructed a **Career Values Card Sort** (CVCS) that requires clients to sort a total of 41 value-label cards into five categories ranging from "most valued" to "never valued" (Training Systems, Inc., 2016).

The **Life Values Inventory** combines qualitative and quantitative assessment of an individual's values (Crace & Brown, 1992). It is particularly helpful for identifying and addressing both intrarole conflicts (when values held by the individual conflict with values espoused in the workplace) and interrole conflicts (when values held by the individual conflict with his or her values expressed in another role outside of work). The inventory's scales provide a structure for analyzing the types of values demonstrated in an individual's life experiences or career choice. Clients repeat the quantitative section of the inventory after performing the qualitative exercises as a means of reviewing the priority of their values. This same technique can be used with other combinations of values inventories and values clarification exercises.

Kinnier (1995) noted that values clarification exercises have come under attack for the superficial and irrelevant manner in which they have been applied at times. He argued that values clarification can be most meaningful when it is applied to specific values conflicts, such as the relative importance that an individual places on family versus career commitment. He described a number of strategies (both rational and intuitive), such as problem solving, cognitive restructuring, life review, incubation ("sleeping on it"), and the "two-chair technique," that can be used for this purpose. He designed an assessment instrument—the **Values Conflict Resolution Assessment** (VCRA)—that can be used to identify a values conflict, guide its resolution, and evaluate the desirability of the resolution (Kinnier, 1987). VCRA scores correlated positively with self-reports of conflict resolution and self-esteem for a sample of graduate students.

Chapter Summary

In this chapter, several frequently used interest and values inventories were reviewed. Interest inventories offer multiple uses that assist academic and career planning. Two types of scales—general/basic interest scales and occupational scales—may be useful in counseling if there is an interest in assessing specific interests with or without comparison to a population. Six popular interest inventories were presented in the chapter.

The Strong is one of the most extensively researched interest inventories and has evidence of psychometric integrity and cross-cultural validity. The major sections of the Strong include administrative indices, GOT, BIS, OSs, and PSSs. The CISS, based on David Campbell's previous work on the Strong, provides interest and skill scores for seven Orientation scales, 29 Basic scales, 60 Occupational scales, and three Special scales (Academic Focus, Extraversion, and Variety). The CISS possesses elements similar to those of the Strong. The Kuder Career Search With Person Match, part of the Kuder Career Planning Program, provides a Career Cluster Scale and an Activity Preference Scale that correspond with Holland's categories.

The SDS uses Holland's six categories to describe both an individual's personality type as well as occupational environments; hence, comparisons can be made between the individual's characteristics and an occupation's attributes. The SDS provides a self-administering, self-scoring, and self-interpreting measure of occupational preferences that helps clients to organize their thinking about careers and guide their career exploration. This instrument appears to be used more often than any other instrument for career-planning purposes. The CDM-R offers a simplified assessment of individual factors important in career planning that can be especially helpful in stimulating career exploration, and the JVIS provides a comprehensive view of an individual's preferences for work environments as well as work activities. Counselors should use all of the scales on an interest inventory in combination to understand a client's profile. The administrative scales, especially response patterns, should be reviewed. Scores on the general scales should be used to help interpret scores on the occupational scales. Scores on special (personality) scales and on parallel measures of self-rated abilities should be used to further clarify the interpretation of the interest scores and to enhance their predictive validity. The chapter provides Tip Sheets for selecting and interpreting interest inventories depending on test and counseling purpose.

Values refer to a person's objectives or goals in work or other settings. Counselors usually assess clients' values by means of values inventories or values clarification exercises. Several work and personal values inventories were presented in this chapter. The WIP and WIL-P&P can be used to compare client values expressed in different occupations by means of the O*NET database. The revised version of the WVI provides a relatively pure measure of work values with 12 six-item scales.

The COPES assesses work values by means of eight bipolar scales. The VS provides a broad measure of work and personal values based on research conducted in cross-national settings. The RVS and SVS both measure personal values that can be used to assess motivational priorities in a variety of situations. The SVS assesses values by means of a two-dimensional circumplex that has applicability in most cultures. The SOV, one of the first psychological instruments to be used in career counseling, has been updated and shown to be effective in discriminating among students in different occupational fields. Both the SI and the QOLI can be used to assess personal values that affect life satisfaction. These inventories enable individuals to compare the relative importance of different life roles or aspects of their life and to determine to what degree their values are being met in their activities.

Values clarification exercises require clients to identify and compare their values with their behaviors. Thus, these exercises can be particularly valuable in stimulating exploration and development of clients' values.

Review Questions

1. What are some of the specific purposes of interest inventories? How might these purposes differ by population?
2. How do the popular interest inventories presented in this chapter compare? When might you use particular inventories?
3. What are some key strategies for selecting interest inventories? Interpreting interest inventories?
4. How do the popular values inventories presented in this chapter compare? When might you use particular inventories?
5. What are examples of values clarification exercises? What are some of the benefits and challenges associated with them?

Resources for Further Learning

Publications

Harrington, T., & Long, J. (2013). The history of interest inventories and career assessments in career counseling. *The Career Development Quarterly, 61*, 83–92. doi:10.1002/j.2161-0045.2013.00039.x

Kirschenbaum, H. (2013). *Values clarification in counseling and psychotherapy: Practical strategies for individual and group settings.* New York, NY: Oxford University Press.

Kuder, Inc. (2009). *Kuder Career Planning System technical brief.* Adel, IA: Author.

Web Resources

Campbell Interest and Skill Survey (CISS)
   http://www.pearsonclinical.com/talent/products/100000323/campbell-interest-and-skill-survey-ciss.html
      This website directly links to information about this assessment.
Career Decision-Making System–Revised (CDM-R)
   http://www.pearsonclinical.com/talent/products/100000512/harrington-oshea-career-decision-making-systemrevised-cdm-r.html
      This website directly links to information about this assessment.
Knowdell Career Assessment Instruments
   http://www.careernetwork.org/Career_Assessments.cfm
      This website directly links to information about the Knowdell Career Values Card Sort.
Kuder Assessments
   http://www.kuder.com/our-unique-approach/research-based-assessments/assessment-summaries/
      This website directly links to information about these assessments.
Self-Directed Search (SDS), 5th Edition
   http://www4.parinc.com/Products/Product.aspx?ProductID=SDS-R-5
      This website directly links to information about this assessment.
Strong Interest Inventory
   https://www.cpp.com/products/strong/index.aspx
      This website directly links to information about this assessment.

Chapter 13

Assessment of Personality

The term *personality* is often used to cover a very broad concept. When applied to psychological assessment instruments, however, it is used more narrowly to describe those instruments designed to assess personal, emotional, and social traits and behaviors, as distinguished from instruments that measure aptitudes, achievements, and interests. This chapter outlines popular personality assessments that counselors encounter across a variety of settings. Both structured and unstructured personality assessments are discussed. The chapter concludes with a brief description of health and lifestyle inventories.

Test Your Knowledge

Select the most appropriate choice for each item.

_____ 1. Which of the following is an example of a projective personality assessment?
   a. Tennessee Self-Concept Scale
   b. Personality Assessment Inventory
   c. Lifestyle Assessment Questionnaire
   d. Thematic Apperception Test

_____ 2. Which of the following personality assessments has been labeled as the most widely researched test of adult psychopathology?
   a. Myers–Briggs Type Indicator
   b. Minnesota Multiphasic Personality Inventory–2
   c. Sixteen Personality Factor Questionnaire
   d. Millon Clinical Multiaxial Inventory–III

_____ 3. The following personality assessment tends to measure positive aspects of personality:
   a. California Personality Inventory
   b. Myers–Briggs Type Indicator
   c. Millon Index of Personality Styles–Revised
   d. All of the above

☐ T ☐ F 4. The House–Tree–Person assessment has an extensive research base to detect psychopathology.

☐ T ☐ F 5. The Big Five personality factors included on the NEO PI-R are Neuroticism, Extraversion, Openness, Agreeableness, and Conscientiousness.

Introduction to Personality Assessment

Personality assessments typically are categorized as structured or unstructured. **Structured personality assessments**, also referred to as **objective assessments**, are standardized self-report measures that often use some forced-choice response format (e.g., multiple choice, true/false). Structured assessment data indicate personality traits, types, and so on. **Unstructured personality assessments**, or **projective assessments**, involve a counselor presenting unstructured tasks to the examinee, whose responses to these tasks are expected to reflect needs, experiences, inner states, and thought processes. This expectation is known as the **projective hypothesis**—that responses to ambiguous stimuli reflect a person's basic personality. Individuals often reveal more about themselves in their interpretation of a situation than they do about the situation itself, especially if the situation is ambiguous. In sum, structured assessments are typically used to test hypotheses and examine psychopathology and behavioral problems, whereas unstructured assessments are typically used to generate hypotheses and examine intrapsychic dynamics.

Four methods have been used to construct objective personality inventories (Kline, 2015; Sherman, 2009): (a) logical content, (b) theoretical, (c) criterion group, and (d) factor analysis. In the **logical content method**, a test developer identifies statements that seem to be related to the content of the characteristic being assessed. The content scales of the Minnesota Multiphasic Personality Inventory–2 (MMPI-2) use this method. The principal limitation of this approach is that it assumes the validity of each item—that individuals are capable of evaluating their own characteristics and that their answers can be taken at face value. If a client checks an item related to "not getting along with parents," this approach assumes that the client is having parental difficulties.

In the **theoretical method**, items are developed to measure constructs represented by a particular theory of personality. After the items have been grouped into scales, a construct validity approach is taken to determine whether the inventory results are consistent with the theory. Two examples of this approach are Jackson's Personality Research Form (PRF), based on Murray's (1938) theory of needs, and the Myers–Briggs Type Indicator (MBTI), based on Jung's (1960) theory of personality types.

Two methods make use of empirical (data-based) strategies to develop personality inventories. The **criterion group method** begins with a sample with known characteristics, such as a group of individuals diagnosed with schizophrenia. An item pool is then administered to individuals in the known sample and to a control group (usually a "normal" population). The items that distinguish the known sample from the control group are then placed in a scale in a manner similar to the method used to construct the Occupational scales on the Strong Interest Inventory. Typically, these items are then used on another similar sample (a process called *cross-validation*) to determine whether the scale continues to distinguish between the two groups. This method can also be used with groups that present contrasts on a particular trait. For example, members of fraternities and sororities are asked to judge the five most and the five least sociable individuals in their group, and then items that distinguish between these two groups are used in the development of a sociability scale. The MMPI-2 clinical scales and the majority of the scales on the California Psychological Inventory (CPI) are based on the criterion group method of inventory construction.

The **factor-analytic method** is the second method using an empirical strategy in test development. In this method, a statistical procedure is used to examine the intercorrelations between all of the items on the inventory. This technique, which can effectively be completed only on a computer, groups items into factors until a substantial proportion of the variability between the items has been accounted for by the dimensions that have resulted. An example of this approach is Cattell's Sixteen Personality Factor Questionnaire (16 PF), which resulted from a factor analysis of 171 terms that describe human traits and that, in turn, had been developed from a list of thousands of adjectives that in one way or another describe humans. Items that appear on particular dimensions resulting from a factor analysis are combined to form homogeneous scales.

Researchers using factor-analytic techniques across a number of personality inventories have synthesized personality traits into five major dimensions nicknamed the *Big Five*. These five factors are as follows: (a) Neuroticism—insecure versus self-confident, (b) Extraversion—outgoing versus shy, (c) Openness—imaginative versus concrete, (d) Agreeableness—empathic versus hostile, and (e) Conscientiousness—well organized versus impulsive. The NEO Personality Inventory–Revised (NEO PI-R) was developed specifically to assess these Big Five factors. The four dimensions of the MBTI are related to each of the last four of these factors but not to neuroticism. The MMPI-2, in contrast, contains numerous items related to neuroticism and fewer relating to the remaining four factors. Although there has been considerable agreement regarding the existences of these five general dimensions, there has been disagreement regarding the actual number of personality dimensions. There is also disagreement regarding some of the labels that have been given to these dimensions as well as disagreement regarding some of the specific personality characteristics and behaviors deemed to be associated with certain of these dimensions (Eysenck & Eysenck, 2013; Shedler & Westen, 2004; Zillig, Hemenover, & Dienstbier, 2002).

Popular Structured Personality Assessments

This section presents several popular structured personality assessments. It is important to remember as you review each assessment that, given their self-report nature, they can typically be distorted in a negative direction if individuals are motivated to present a poor image or in a positive direction if, for example, they are applying for a desired job or perhaps just wish to make a good impression in general. Several inventories contain validity or social desirability scales to detect such distortion.

Minnesota Multiphasic Personality Inventories

Three inventories are discussed in this section. The **Minnesota Multiphasic Personality Inventory–2** (MMPI-2), the oldest of these measures, is well researched and frequently used to assess personality (Pearson Assessments, 2016c). Second, the **Minnesota Multiphasic Personality Inventory–2–Restructured Form** (MMPI-2-RF) was published in 2008 as an alternative to the MMPI-2 based on updated clinical scales (Pearson Assessments, 2016d; Tellegen & Ben-Porath, 2008). Finally, the adolescent forms of the MMPI are the **Minnesota Multiphasic Personality Inventory–Adolescent** (MMPI-A) and the **Minnesota Multiphasic Personality Inventory–Adolescent–Restructured Form** (MMPI-A-RF). The MMPI-A, first published in 1992, is one of the most frequently used inventories for young people (Pearson Assessments, 2016f). The MMPI-A-RF, published in 2016, mirrors the MMPI-2-RF and contains several adolescent-specific subscales (Pearson Assessments, 2016e).

Minnesota Multiphasic Personality Inventory–2

The purpose of the MMPI-2 is to evaluate individuals for mental disorders and aid counselors and other helping professionals in treatment planning (Pearson Assessments, 2016c). In addition to clinical scales that are useful in assessing salient mental health issues, the MMPI-2 also contains several validity scales that enable the counselor to assess the client's attitude toward the testing process. Most of the clinical scales consist of items that significantly differentiate between people in a particular psychiatric diagnostic category (e.g., depression) and people in the general reference group (often referred to as "the Minnesota normals"). For example, the Depression scale (Scale 2) contains 60 items that people with depression endorsed significantly more (or less) often than did the

Table 13.1
Minnesota Multiphasic Personality Inventory–2 (MMPI-2) Clinical Scales

Scale and Description	Interpretation[a]
Hypochondriasis (1): symptoms of preoccupation with the body and fear of illness or disease	Extremely high scores ($T > 80$) indicate bizarre somatic concerns, and moderately high scores ($T = 60$–80) may correspond with vague complaints associated typically with somatoform disorders, anxiety disorders, and mood disorders. If high scores are accompanied by high scores for Scale 3 and Scale 8, the possibility of a conversion disorder and somatic delusions, respectively, should be considered.
Depression (2): symptoms of hopelessness or general dissatisfaction, psychomotor retardation, and lack of interest in activities	High scores (especially $T > 70$) indicate clinical depression, and moderately high scores illustrate low morale and lack of involvement. Other symptoms of high scorers indicate physical complaints, fatigue, indecisiveness, or lack of self-confidence.
Hysteria (3): dysfunctional reactions to stressful situations, with items assessing denial of physical health and specific complaints of a psychological or emotional nature	Elevated scores ($T > 80$) indicate individuals who avoid stressful situations by developing physical symptoms that do not correspond easily to well-known organic disorder patterns. High scorers tend to lack insight into causes of their physical symptoms.
Psychopathic Deviate (4): psychopathic symptoms such as lying, stealing, sexual promiscuity, and excessive drinking—a "measure of rebelliousness" (Graham, 2005b, p. 134)	Extremely high scores ($T > 75$) indicate asocial, antisocial, and often criminal behaviors. High scores typically correspond with hostile and immature behavior and significant family and legal problems.
Masculinity–Femininity (5): symptoms that measure "sexual inversion" or lack of the presence of traditional gender norms for each respective sex	High scores ($T > 60$) indicate a lack of stereotypically masculine interests for men and masculine interests for women. Low scores indicate extreme masculinity for men and stereotypically feminine interests for women.
Paranoia (6): paranoid symptoms such as feelings of persecution, grandiosity, excessive sensitivity, and rigidity of opinions	High scores ($T > 70$) indicate psychosis and a frequent diagnosis of paranoid disorders or schizophrenia. Scores between 60 and 70 indicate sensitivity and overreaction to others' opinions. It is possible to score high ($T > 65$) without endorsing the psychotic items on the scale.
Psychasthenia (7): symptoms closely associated with obsessive–compulsive disorder	High scorers tend to be anxious and irritated, with ritualistic behaviors and obsessive thoughts. High scores also tend to indicate rigidity and neatness and individuals who are shy and sensitive.
Schizophrenia (8): disturbances of thinking, mood, and behavior most often associated with schizophrenia	T scores ranging from 75 to 90 suggest the possibility of a psychotic disorder such as schizophrenia or a schizoid lifestyle. Extreme scores ($T > 90$) do not usually indicate a psychotic disturbance but rather a cry for help.
Hypomania (9): symptoms that include elevated mood, irritability, flight of ideas, accelerated speech, and some depression	Extreme scores ($T > 80$) may suggest a bipolar (manic) disorder.
Social Introversion (0): withdrawal from social situations	High scores indicate insecurity and discomfort in social situations and tasks. Low scores typically correspond with sociability and extraversion.

Note. Information is from Graham (2005a, 2005b).
[a]High scores are usually considered T scores above 65 and low scores those below 40, although these cutoffs are somewhat arbitrary and clinical judgment should be exercised. Low scores can be associated with the absence of symptoms or, for clinical populations, some negative characteristics. However, there is little basis for evaluating low scores as indicative of problems and negative characteristics for nonclinical populations (Graham, 2005a). Given the limited information on interpreting low scores, high scores are primarily interpreted.

Minnesota normals. Table 13.1 highlights the 10 clinical scales of the MMPI-2 and how high and low scores may be interpreted. Please refer to Chapter 5 to review a description of the 10 MMPI-2 validity scales.

Subsequent research has indicated that the MMPI-2 scales cannot be used to classify individuals into psychiatric categories with a high degree of accuracy. Instead, the scales are most useful in providing descriptions of personality and as a source of inference regarding a person's behavior. Because of the large amount of research that has been conducted with the MMPI, the scales convey a wealth of information about an individual's personality that transcends the original purpose of the scales. For this reason, the original names for the scales have been replaced by the scale numbers for most purposes (e.g., Scale 7 instead of *Pt* or Psychasthenia).

A normative sample (1,462 women and 1,138 men) was selected so that it would be representative of the adult U.S. population in terms of age, relationship status, race/ethnicity, and geography. With the new norms, the cutoff score used to detect psychological problems dropped from 70 on the MMPI to 65 on the MMPI-2. Research indicates that a *T* score of 65 provides optimal separation between clinical groups and the standardization sample (Butcher, Graham, Ben-Porath, Tellegen, & Dahlstrom, 2001; Tarescavage et al., 2013). The scores on the MMPI-2 have also been adjusted so that the distribution of the profile scores will be the same for the eight clinical scales (Scales 1, 2, 3, 4, 6, 7, 8, and 9) used to assess psychopathology. For example, a *T* score of 65 equals the 92nd percentile (based on the restandardization sample) for each of these scales.

The MMPI-2 scales should be interpreted in conjunction with the other scales on the profile, not in isolation. Counselors should be acquainted with the vast literature pertaining to the MMPI-2 if they work with clients who are mentally disturbed; however, they cannot expect to become proficient in its use without specialized training and extensive clinical experience.

Counselors should note critical items that the client has checked as well as scale scores. For example, if the client marked true to Item 506, "I have recently considered killing myself," or Item 524, "No one knows it but I have tried to kill myself," the counselor should review these items with the client. Clients might not bring these topics up on their own initiative. They may assume that the counselor already knows this information from their responses to these items on the MMPI-2.

Several critical item lists have been developed. For example, the Koss–Butcher critical item set contains 78 items related to six crisis areas. These items typically differentiate normal from psychiatric samples. Most computer-based MMPI-2 scoring programs will flag critical items checked by the clients. This information can also be obtained by means of hand scoring. The critical item lists provide a simple and straightforward means for counselors to discuss MMPI-2 results with clients and to identify topics that may need additional inquiry.

A number of additional scales have been created for the MMPI-2 that can be used to help interpret the clinical scales. Most of the clinical scales have been divided into subscales that can help clarify the meaning of scores on the scales (Graham, 2011). The Depression scale, for example, has been divided into the following subscales: Subjective Depression, Psychomotor Retardation, Physical Malfunctioning, Mental Dullness, and Brooding.

In addition to the subscales, 15 content scales devised by Butcher, Graham, Williams, and Ben-Porath (1990) can also be used to clarify the meaning of the MMPI-2 clinical scales. In contrast with the clinical scales, which were developed by empirical means, the content scales were constructed by logical analysis of the item content on the MMPI-2. The scales were refined by statistical procedures to ensure homogeneity of item content. Scales developed in this fashion are easier to interpret than empirical scales. The content scales also assess aspects of personality not measured by the standard scales, including Type A (hard-driving) behavior, work interference, family problems, and negative treatment indicators.

The Restructured Clinical (*RC*) scales (nine in all) were added to the MMPI-2 to provide relatively pure measures of the psychopathological factors measured by the clinical scales (Graham, 2011; Tellegen et al., 2003). The first *RC* scale, Demoralization, measures a broad factor of general complaint or malaise that runs throughout the eight clinical scales that assess psychopathology (Scales 5 and 0 were excluded because they are not measures of psychopathology). Each of the remaining eight *RC* scales was designed to assess the primary dimension of the clinical scale with which it was matched. For example, the *RC* scale Somatic Complaints is matched with Scale 1 (Hypochondriasis). Because of their purity of content, the *RC* scales can be easily interpreted by themselves and can be used to help interpret the original scales. Although based on fewer items, the *RC* scales produce results that are as reliable and valid as the original scales (Shkalim, 2015; Simms, Casillas, Clark, Watson, & Doebbelling, 2005).

In addition to the scales discussed thus far, many other scales have been constructed from the MMPI item pool for various purposes. Popular supplementary scales include *A* (Anxiety), *R* (Repression), and *Es* (Ego Strength). The *A* and *R* scales represent the two main factors derived from factor analyses of the clinical scales. As such, they offer a quick summary, or overview, of the MMPI-2 results. Scale *A* provides a measure of anxiety or general maladjustment; Scale *R* shows the client's tendency to repress or deny psychological difficulties. The *Es* scale is based on items that distinguish between clients with psychological problems who responded to therapy and those who did not. In contrast with most of the scores on the MMPI-2, high scores on the *Es* scale should be interpreted favorably. The use of the MMPI-2 in a counseling situation is illustrated in Case Example 13.1.

Case Example 13.1

Gracie

Gracie, a 19-year-old college sophomore, requested counseling because of low self-esteem, relationship difficulties, family conflict, and eating concerns. She marked 5 (*very much*) to the following items on the Inventory of Common Problems:

- Feeling irritable, tense, or nervous;
- Feeling fearful;
- Feeling lonely or isolated; and
- Eating, appetite, or weight problems.

She also completed the Beck Depression Inventory as part of the initial contact session, for which she received a raw score of 32, indicating "severe depression." The counselor asked Gracie to complete the MMPI-2 during her next visit to the counseling center to assess more thoroughly the nature and the level of her psychological problems. She obtained the profile shown in Figure 13.1.

The scores on the seven validity scales indicate self-criticism and a possible plea for help. Her low *L* and *K* scores indicate that she is describing herself in a negative fashion. The elevated *F* scores suggest self-criticism together with moderately severe psychopathology. Among the clinical scales, she obtained elevated scores on Scales 2, 6, 7, and 0. Her highest two scores are on Scales 7 and 2. According to Graham (2011), individuals with this code type (27 or 72) "tend to be anxious, nervous, tense, high-strung, and jumpy. They worry excessively, and they are vulnerable to real and imagined threat. They tend to anticipate problems before they occur and to overreact to minor stress. Somatic symptoms are common" (p. 96). Because of their acute discomfort, they are likely to respond well to psychotherapy. They are most likely to receive a psychiatric diagnosis of anxiety disorder, depressive disorder, or obsessive–compulsive disorder.

Gracie's elevated scores on Scales 6 and 0 indicate possible difficulties in interpersonal relationships. Scores between 66 and 75 on Scale 6 can possibly

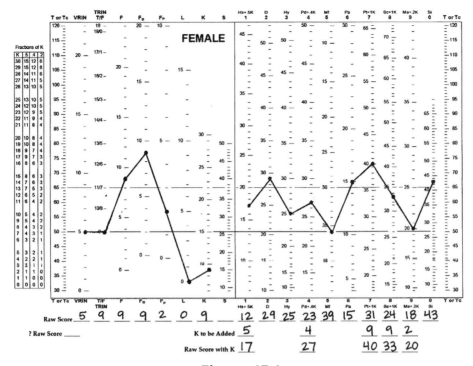

Figure 13.1
MMPI-2 Profile for Counseling Center Client

Note. Profile excerpted from *MMPI-2 (Minnesota Multiphasic Personality Inventory–2) Manual for Administration, Scoring, and Interpretation,* Revised Edition. Copyright © 2001 by the Regents of the University of Minnesota. Used by permission of the the University of Minnesota Press. All rights reserved. "MMPI" and "Minnesota Multiphasic Personality Inventory" are trademarks owned by the Regents of the University of Minnesota. Reprinted with permission.

be interpreted as follows: angry and resentful, displaces blame and criticisms, hostile and suspicious, rigid and stubborn, and misinterprets social situations (Butcher et al., 2001; Graham, 2011). Similarly, scores between 66 and 75 on Scale 0 suggest behavior that is introverted, shy, lacking self-confidence, moody, submissive, and rigid (Butcher et al., 2001).

The counselor provided counseling to Gracie to help her deal with her immediate situation. At the same time, she made arrangements to refer Gracie to a psychiatrist for a more complete assessment of some of the psychological problems suggested by the MMPI-2 and other assessment procedures.

• • •

Minnesota Multiphasic Personality Inventory–2–Restructured Form

The MMPI-2-RF is a psychometrically sound alternative to the MMPI-2 and is composed of only 338 items (as compared to 567 items). The instrument takes only 35 to 50 minutes to administer. The technical manual states that the scale data are applicable to a range of settings, including mental health settings, substance abuse agencies, legal institutions, personal injury and disability evaluations, and employment evaluations (Pearson Assessments, 2016d). The MMPI-2-RF was developed using the MMPI-2 normative sample and includes 51 scales, including a Response Bias Scale.

Minnesota Multiphasic Personality Inventory–Adolescent

Prior to the construction of the MMPI-A in 1992, adolescents were frequently administered the adult version of the MMPI despite the difficulties in adapting this version for adolescents.

The adolescent version of the MMPI is similar to the adult version in that it retains the same clinical scales as the old MMPI and also includes a new set of content scales (Butcher, Williams, & Fowler, 2000; Pearson Assessments, 2016f). As with the MMPI-2, the MMPI-A clinical scales and content scales both contain a number of subscales that can be used to help explain the meaning of the scale scores. The 1992 manual was supplemented in 2006 with an additional manual (see Pearson Assessments, 2016f).

The MMPI-A differs from the MMPI-2 in regard to its norms, its item content, and the nature of some of its scales. The MMPI-A provides separate-sex norms for adolescents ages 14 through 18 years. (The test authors recommend that the MMPI-2 be used with 18-year-olds who have moved away from their parental home.) The MMPI-A contains 89 fewer items than the MMPI-2 to help encourage cooperation by clients. Most of the omitted items are items that were not scored on any of the clinical scales or are items that were found on either Scales 5 and 0 (both exceptionally long scales on the MMPI-2) or the Fears content scale (which has been dropped from the MMPI-A). The MMPI-A includes a number of items from the original MMPI that have been rewritten to pertain to adolescents as well as a number of new items that deal specifically with adolescent circumstances (such as school, peers, teachers, and parents).

Whereas 11 of the 15 content scales on the MMPI-A are similar to those found on the MMPI-2, four of the scales—School Problems, Low Aspirations, Alienation, and Conduct Disorder—have been designed specifically to address issues common to adolescents. The F validity scale, which often produced high scores for adolescents on the MMPI, has been redesigned for the MMPI-A by including only those items answered infrequently (20% of the time or less) by adolescents. The MMPI-A also includes a new supplementary scale, the Immaturity scale, not found on the MMPI-2.

Scores on the clinical and content scales yield adequate test–retest reliability and internal consistency coefficients when used with adolescents. Both sets of scales have proved to be effective in predicting adolescent behavior and personality characteristics, especially when used in combination (Forbey & Ben-Porath, 2003). Much of the validity for the MMPI-A can be inferred from validity established for the MMPI because of the comparability of the instruments. As with the MMPI-2, T scores of 65 or greater suggest possible psychopathology. Scores between 60 and 65 should be viewed as indicating possible psychological problems.

Minnesota Multiphasic Inventory–Adolescent–Restructured Form
The MMPI-A-RF was published in 2016 and is the most updated personality assessment for use with adolescents (Pearson Assessments, 2016e). The MMPI-A-RF is a 241-item tool that contains 48 empirically validated scales relevant for use with adolescents in a variety of settings. Similar to the MMPI-A, it was developed for use with individuals ages 14 to 18 years. It can be delivered in paper-and-pencil, web-based, and computer-based formats.

Millon Clinical Multiaxial Inventory–IV

The **Millon Clinical Multiaxial Inventory–IV** (MCMI-IV), published in 2015, provides an attractive alternative to the MMPI-2 for diagnosing psychopathology. First, it is considerably shorter than the MMPI-2 (containing only 195 items), with most individuals completing the MCMI-IV in 25 to 30 minutes. Second, it is more closely tied to the *DSM-5* so that psychiatric classifications can be made more easily. Finally, it is more closely related to psychological theory, which can serve as a basis for interpreting test results (Pearson Assessments, 2016b).

The MCMI-IV conceptualizes personality style on a continuum of three levels of functioning: normal, adaptive functioning; abnormal, moderately maladaptive attributes; and clinical disorder. It is composed of 15 personality disorder scales and 10 clinical syndrome scales. The goal of the MCMI-IV is to guide the therapist toward areas within the client needing the most therapeutic attention (Pearson Assessments, 2016b).

The MCMI-IV was normed for individuals ages 18 and older, with norms representative of the current inpatient and outpatient clinical settings. It has been validated in terms of its effectiveness in differentiating individuals with particular psychiatric diagnoses from other psychiatric patients. This is a more rigorous criterion than differentiating these same types of individuals from a "normal" population, such as that originally used with the MMPI. The technique used with the MCMI-IV has proved to be more accurate in identifying the psychiatric diagnoses of patients in subsequent studies than has the technique used with the MMPI.

For adolescents ages 13 to 19, counselors should use the **Millon Adolescent Clinical Inventory** (MACI), published in 1993 (Millon & Davis, 1993). The MACI contains 27 scales and three clinically relevant categories based on four norm groups (i.e., 13- to 15-year-old males, 13- to 15-year-old females, 16- to 19-year-old males, 16- to 19-year-old females). The MACI contains 160 items and takes approximately 20 to 25 minutes to complete (Pearson Assessments, 2016a).

Millon Index of Personality Styles–Revised

The **Millon Index of Personality Styles–Revised** (MIPS-R), an inventory first developed in 1994 and revised in 2003, is designed to assess personality styles for adults within the normal range (Millon, 2003). It is intended for various counseling situations involving relationships, career placement, or problems in daily living. It consists of 180 true/false items yielding 24 scales and four validity indices. The scales are grouped into three dimensions of normal personality: (a) motivating styles, which assess a person's emotional style in dealing with his or her environment; (b) thinking styles, which examine a person's mode of cognitive processing; and (c) behaving styles, which assess a person's way of interrelating with others. The inventory is useful for counseling and helping professionals, including those in family and career settings. Millon has also authored the **Millon Adolescent Personality Inventory**, which can be used to assess the personality of adolescents who have at least a sixth-grade reading level (Millon & Davis, 1993).

Personality Assessment Inventory

The **Personality Assessment Inventory** (PAI) was designed to provide information on "relevant clinical variables" for individuals 18 years of age and older (Morey, 1991, 2003). Content areas for the PAI were selected on the basis of current diagnostic schemes and treatment planning. It consists of 344 items (selected from an original item pool of 2,200 items) that are scored on 22 scales. Final items for the PAI were selected on the basis of expert ratings, statistical analysis, and related criteria in a 10-stage process (PAR, Inc., n.d.).

The 22 full scales on the PAI include four types of scales, as follows: (a) *Validity Scales:* Inconsistency (ICN), Infrequency (INF), Negative Impression (NIM), Positive Impression (PIM); (b) *Clinical Scales:* Somatic Complaints (SOM), Anxiety (ANX), Anxiety-Related Disorders (ARD), Depression (DEP), Mania (MAN), Paranoia (PAR), Schizophrenia (SCZ), Borderline Features (BOR), Antisocial Features (ANT), Alcohol Problems (ALC), Drug Problems (DRG); (c) *Treatment Scales:* Aggression (AGG), Suicidal Ideation (SUI), Stress (STR), Nonsupport (NON), Treatment Rejection (RXR); and (d) *Interpersonal Scales:* Domination (DOM), Warmth (WRM). The clinical scales, which resemble many of the MMPI clinical scales, can be subdivided into three broad categories of disorders: (a) neurotic spectrum scales (SOM, ANX, ARD, DEP), (b) psychotic spectrum scales (MAN, PAR, SCZ), and (c) behavior disorder scales (BOR, ANT, ALC, DRG). The treatment scales focus on issues important in treatment but not necessarily apparent from the clinical scales. The interpersonal scales measure two critical bipolar dimensions in interpersonal relations: domination versus submission (DOM) and friendliness versus hostility (WRM). Information is also provided on the client's answers to 27 critical items, which were selected because of their potential seriousness and low endorsement rates.

Because of the heterogeneous nature of the clinical scales, nine have been divided into subscales. For example, the ANX scale includes Cognitive, Affective, and Physiological subscales, and the ARD scale includes Obsessive–Compulsive, Phobias, and Traumatic Stress subscales. The treatment scale for aggression has also been divided into three sub-scales: Aggressive Attitude, Verbal Aggression, and Physical Aggression.

The PAI has a fourth-grade reading level and requires about 50 minutes to complete. The item response format provides four alternatives: *false—not at all true, slightly true, mainly true,* or *very true.* All of the scales can be easily hand scored without the use of a template in 10 minutes or less. In contrast with the MMPI-2, none of the full scales contain overlapping items.

The PAI has been normed on a sample of 1,000 community-dwelling adults selected to match the characteristics of the U.S. population in terms of sex, race, and age. In addition to adult norms, comprehensive norms have also been established for college students and clinical populations.

The full scales exhibit adequate test–retest reliabilities over short time periods and relatively high internal consistency coefficients for samples of college students and community-dwelling adults. The PAI shows substantial convergent and discriminant validity based on its correlations with scales from other psychological measures. The PAI is an appealing instrument because of its ease of scoring and interpretation. It has been carefully constructed and appears to be psychometrically sound. Other PAI versions exist: the **Personality Assessment Inventory–Adolescent** (PAI-A), **Personality Assessment Inventory European Spanish with Norms**, and **Personality Assessment Screener** (PAS). The PAS can be particularly useful as a screening device to distinguish between those clients free from psychopathology and those in need of follow-up evaluation with the full PAI (PAR, Inc., n.d.).

Myers–Briggs Type Indicator

Work on the **Myers–Briggs Type Indicator** (MBTI) began in the 1920s by Katherine Briggs when she developed a system of psychological types by conceptualizing her observations and readings (I. B. Myers, McCaulley, Quenk, & Hammer, 1998). Upon finding much similarity between her conclusions and those of Carl Jung, who was working at the same time, she began using his theory. Together with her daughter, Isabel Myers, she developed an inventory now known as the Myers–Briggs Type Indicator. The inventory, in its several forms, was slow in gaining acceptance but is now reported to be the most widely used personality inventory in the world.

The MBTI is based on Jung's concepts that different types of people have differences in perception and judgment. Each of the several forms of the MBTI (in both self-scored and computer-scored formats) is scored on eight scales (four pairs) that yield four bipolar dimensions. More sophisticated item response theory methods were used for the item development and scoring weights in the latest versions—the 93-item Form M and the more recent 144-item MBTI Step II (Form Q). Jung's theory proposes that apparently random variations in human behavior can be systematically accounted for by the manner in which individuals prefer to use their capacities for perception and judgment. The MBTI is a self-reporting instrument designed to identify these preferences.

The first of the four dimensions involves the preference for extraversion versus introversion (E-I). Extraverts prefer to direct their energy to the outer world of people and things, whereas introverts tend to focus energy on the inner world of ideas.

The second dimension measures personal preference for mode of perceiving and is labeled the sensing–intuition (S-N) dimension. Sensing individuals prefer to rely on one or more of the five senses as their primary mode of perceiving. Intuitive people, in contrast, rely primarily on indirect perception by the way of the mind, incorporating ideas or associations that are related to perceptions coming from the outside.

The third MBTI dimension is designed to measure an individual's preference for judging data obtained through sensing or intuition by means of either thinking or feeling (T-F). A thinking orientation signifies a preference for drawing conclusions using an objective, impersonal, logical approach. A feeling-oriented individual is much more likely to base decisions on personal or social rationales that take into account the subjective feelings of others.

The fourth dimension measures a person's preference for either a judging or perceiving (J-P) orientation for dealing with the external world. Although individuals must use both perception and judgment in their daily lives, most find one of these orientations to be more comfortable than the other and use it more often, in the same way that a right-handed person favors the use of the right hand. People with a judgment orientation are anxious to use either the thinking or feeling mode to arrive at a decision or conclusion as quickly as possible, whereas those with a perceptive orientation are more comfortable continuing to collect information through either a sensing or intuitive process and delaying judgment as long as possible. This fourth dimension was not defined by Jung but represents an additional concept of Briggs and Myers.

Although the four dimensions of the MBTI are theoretically independent, significant correlations in the vicinity of .30 have been found between the S-N and J-P scales. This finding tends to support Jung's theory, which included only the first three dimensions. Other than the relationship between these two sets of scales, the remaining scales are statistically independent of each other.

A person's MBTI personality type is summarized in four letters that indicate the direction of the person's preference on each of the four dimensions. All possible combinations of the four paired scales result in 16 different personality types. Thus, an ENTJ is an extravert with a preference for intuition and thinking who generally has a judging attitude in his or her orientation toward the outer world. An ISFP type indicates an introvert with a preference toward sensing and feeling who has a perceptive orientation toward the outer world. The manual provides a summary of the processes, characteristics, and traits of each of the 16 types.

In computing personality type, scores resulting from forced-choice items are obtained for each of the opposite preferences and then subtracted to obtain the particular type. A large difference between the two scores indicates a clear preference and yields a higher score on that type, whereas a smaller difference yields a low score, indicating a preference on that type that is considered less strong and less clear. Even though the difference is small (the scoring formula eliminates ties), one or the other letter is included in the four-letter code type. These preferences are presumed to interact in complex, nonlinear ways to produce the 16 types. There is, however, little support for these 16 personality types as separate entities or clusters. Another major criticism of the MBTI is that the variables assessed are assumed to result in dichotomies, although there is little psychological or empirical evidence of such dichotomies or bimodal distributions. Instead, the variables can best be represented as continuous bipolar distributions that fall along the normal curve (T. Hall, 2014; Pittenger, 2005). An additional component of MBTI theory involves dominant and auxiliary functions that are controversial and lack substantial research.

Although an individual's type is supposed to remain relatively constant over a lifetime, norms on several MBTI dimensions change substantially between adolescence and adulthood as well as during the adult years (Cummings, 1995). Internal consistency studies of the MBTI Form M have generally yielded correlation coefficients exceeding .90. In terms of the four letter types, test–retest reliability data tend to be somewhat discouraging in that an individual's four-letter MBTI type has only about a 50–50 chance of being identical on retesting. On the average, 75% of the people completing the instrument will retain three of the four dichotomous type preferences on retesting.

One of the reasons the MBTI is attractive to many individuals is that there are no good or bad scores or good or bad combinations of types. Because both polarities can be viewed as strengths, this nonjudgmental quality facilitates interpreting results to clients. A score indicates a preference to use certain functions or behavioral preferences, although most individuals have the capacity to make use of the opposite preference as well. Each preference includes some strengths, joys, and positive characteristics, and each has its problems and blind spots. In the interpretive materials in the manual, as well as in a number of other publications, the strengths, weaknesses, abilities, needs, values, interests, and other characteristics are provided for scores on each of the scales as well as for the 16 types.

The MBTI is used in a number of counseling situations. It is often used to explore relationships between couples and among family members (discussed in Chapter 14). In work situations, counselors use the MBTI to develop teamwork and an understanding of relationships; in vocational counseling, they use it to examine the effects of each of the four preferences in work situations. For example, introverts like a work situation that provides quiet or concentration and may have problems communicating, whereas extraverts like variety in action and are usually able to communicate freely. People with strong thinking preferences are interested in fairness and logic and may not be sensitive to other people's feelings. Feeling types tend to be very aware of other people's feelings and find it difficult to tell people unpleasant things. Thus, preferences and strengths on the MBTI can be discussed in terms of occupational functions and work environments, although solid validity data for such use still need to be obtained. Readers are encouraged to visit publishers' websites for resources on interpreting and applying MBTI types in various settings (see "Resources for Further Learning").

In addition, the manual lists the types of people found in various occupations—information compiled from a vast data pool of people in different occupations who have completed the MBTI. People with certain MBTI types are found in substantially higher proportions in certain occupations. All types may enter all types of occupations, but certain types choose particular occupations far more often than they do others. For example, although all types are represented among psychologists, 85% of psychologists are intuitive types and only 15% are sensing types, but, like the general population, they are evenly split on the introvert–extravert dimension. Thus, the MBTI can be useful in career counseling.

Individuals who are intuitive, feeling, and perceptive seem to be more likely to seek counseling than individuals with other MBTI types (Mendelsohn & Kirk, 1962; Vilas, 1988). Counselors often share these preferences. A few counselors administer the MBTI before counseling has begun so that they can use the results, along with the knowledge of their own type, in structuring the counseling process for a particular client. Counselors who make use of this personality inventory should be aware not only of its strengths and usefulness in various settings but also of its various weaknesses, including ipsative scoring and lack of criterion-related validity studies in certain settings.

The MBTI should not be used to label or narrowly categorize people. Also, people should not feel limited by their personality type. Although most people have a preferred personality style that they can learn to use to their advantage, they can also learn to express the less dominant aspects of their personality when appropriate. Counselors can teach clients to become more flexible in the manner in which they respond to different situations.

An alternative to the MBTI is the **Keirsey Temperament Sorter II** (KTS-II; Keirsey, 2006), which was designed for personnel, consulting, and training settings (Zachar, 2005). It contains 70 questions similar to MBTI items and classifies individuals into four temperaments similar to MBTI personality types (Quinn, Lewis, & Fischer, 1992; Tucker & Gillespie, 1993). These temperaments, each of which consists of four MBTI letter codes, are titled Guardians, Artisans, Idealists, and Rationalists. The KTS-II yields an individual's four-letter MBTI type in addition to the Keirsey temperaments. Individuals may take the KTS-II online and obtain their four-letter code for free, or they can pay a fee to have it completely scored.

California Psychological Inventory

The **California Psychological Inventory** (CPI 434)—and its shorter version, the CPI 260—was developed to measure constructs that individuals typically use to describe themselves and groups around them (Chope, 2013; Gough & Bradley, 2002). It is a popular inventory because it assesses an individual's strengths and positive personality attributes. Although the MMPI was used as a basis for development of this inventory (over one third of the CPI items), the CPI is designed to measure everyday traits that its author, Harrison Gough, called "folk concepts"—traits such as sociability, tolerance, and responsibility, terms that people use every day and across cultures to classify and predict each other's behavior (Chope, 2013; Donnay & Elliott, 2003). The 1995 version of the CPI (3rd edition), containing 434 items and 30 scales, was normed on standardization samples of 3,000 men and 3,000 women. The CPI, 3rd edition, was restandardized in such a way that the scales on the earlier and 1995 forms can be considered interchangeable. It takes 45–60 minutes to complete. The CPI has been used in organizational training and evaluation, and the CPI 260 has been specifically developed for managerial assessment and leadership training, offering a coaching report as part of its results report.

The CPI items deal with typical behavior patterns and attitudes with less objectionable content than the MMPI. Thus, the scales are designed to assess positive personality characteristics and to aid in the understanding of "normal" individuals' interpersonal behavior.

The CPI contains 20 folk-concept scales that are organized into four separate clusters or classes (see Figure 13.2):

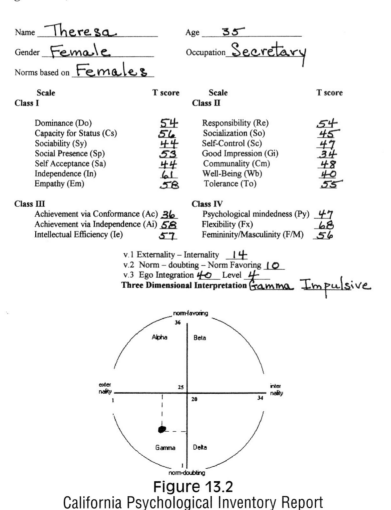

Figure 13.2
California Psychological Inventory Report

1. Class I is designed to assess interpersonal adequacy of poise, self-assurance, and ascendancy and contains seven scales, titled Dominance, Capacity for Status, Sociability, Social Presence, Self-Acceptance, Independence, and Empathy;
2. Class II contains measures of socialization, responsibility, and character with seven scales, titled Responsibility, Socialization, Self-Control, Good Impression, Communality, Well-Being, and Tolerance;
3. Class III contains scales measuring intellectual and academic themes useful in educational counseling. The three scales in this cluster are titled Achievement via Conformance, Achievement via Independence, and Intellectual Efficiency.
4. Class IV contains a mixed group of three scales that do not fit well together or are not highly related to scales in the other three clusters. They include Psychological Mindedness, Flexibility, and Femininity–Masculinity.

Of the 20 CPI scales, 13 were developed by the criterion group method, four (Social Presence, Self-Acceptance, Self-Control, and Flexibility) by internal consistency analysis, and three (Good Impression, Communality, and Well-Being) by a combination of these two methods (Chope, 2013; Gough & Bradley, 2002).

Three of the scales are validity scales developed to detect faking or other test-taking attitudes. "Faking bad" is detected by T scores of 35 or less on the Well-Being, Communality, or Good Impression scales. Low scores on the Well-Being scale reflect endorsement of items representing various physical and psychological complaints. Scores on the Communality scale are based on a frequency count of popular responses, with low scores ($T = 29$ or less for men, 24 or less for women) suggesting that the inventory has been taken in a random or idiosyncratic fashion (Groth-Marnat & Wright, 2016). When a "fake bad" profile is obtained, the counselor should ask why the individual feels a need to create an impression of serious problems. The person might in fact have very serious problems or might be malingering for some reason, or the low score might represent a cry for help. The Good Impression scale is based on responses by normal individuals asked to "fake good" to identify persons who are overly concerned about making a good impression. "Faking good" is suggested by a Good Impression T score of 65 or more, with this score as the highest on the profile. Generally, most other scales will also show scores in the positive direction, which makes it difficult to differentiate between an individual with an excellent level of adjustment and one who is faking good. Here, an individual's history can usually help the counselor to differentiate between faking good and superior adjustment.

Standard scores (T scores) are reported with a mean of 50 and a standard deviation of 10 (see Figure 13.2; Donnay & Elliott, 2003; Gough, 2000). High scores (T scores of 60 or above) tend to indicate psychological health, and lower scores (40 or below) tend to indicate psychological inadequacy or distress (except for the Femininity–Masculinity scale). Different profiles reflecting different gender norms are used to plot scores for men and women. Results can be obtained on a profile report, a narrative report, or a configural analysis report.

Norms in the current version are based on the 6,000 men and women who represent heterogeneous samples from high school and college students, teachers, business executives, prison executives, psychiatric patients, and prison inmates. Fifty percent are high school students, and 17% are college undergraduates. The manual (Gough & Bradley, 2002) contains many specialized norm groups—a total of 52 for males and 42 for females—that counselors should consider using with clients who match the characteristics of the norm group (Chope, 2013). Reliability coefficients for some scales show substantial reliability, whereas for others, coefficients are more moderate. Median alpha coefficients for the 20 folk concept scales were .72 for men and .73 for women. Test–retest reliabilities ran relatively high, from .51 to .84 after a 1-year period. The many validity studies conducted with the CPI, usually exploring either predictive or concurrent validity, have yielded validity indices that have varied widely among the scales and among different types of validity criteria, typically predicted behavior.

On the basis of factor-analytic work, Gough developed three vector scales to measure broad aspects of personality structure. Because a number of the 20 scales on the CPI show considerable overlap, the three dimensions (vectors) can be used to facilitate understanding and interpretation of the 20-scale profile. The three vectors are described generally as (a) internality versus externality, (b) norm favoring versus norm questioning, and (c) self-doubting vulnerability versus self-actualization (ego integration). These factors have been placed in an interpretive three-dimensional model (see Figure 13.2). The first two vectors measure personality type, whereas the third vector measures levels of personality adjustment.

- *Vector 1:* High scorers tend to be viewed as reticent, modest, shy, reserved, moderate, and reluctant to initiate or take decisive social action. Low scorers are talkative, outgoing, confident, and poised.
- *Vector 2:* High scorers are viewed as well organized, conscientious, conventional, dependable, and controlled. Low scorers are seen as rebellious, restless, self-indulgent, and pleasure seeking.
- *Vector 3:* High scorers are described as optimistic, mature, insightful, and free of neurotic trends and conflicts and as having a wide range of interests. Low scorers are seen as dissatisfied, unsure of themselves, and uncomfortable with uncertainty and complexity and as having constricted interests.

The intersection of Vectors 1 and 2 form four quadrants or lifestyles. Personality characteristics can be inferred from membership in one of these four quadrants: Alphas are ambitious, productive, and socially competent; Betas are responsible, reserved, and conforming; Gammas are restless, rebellious, and pleasure seeking; and Deltas are withdrawn, reflective, and detached. These four lifestyles are related both to going to college and to college majors (Gough, 2000). Among almost 3,500 high school graduates in 16 cities, the college-going rate for Alphas, who were most likely to major in engineering or business, was 61%; for Gammas, who were most likely to major in the social sciences, it was 40%; for Betas, who were most likely to major in teaching or nursing, it was 39%; and for Deltas, who were most likely to seek out the humanities or music, it was only 27%.

In addition to the 20 folk-concept scales, there are 13 special purpose or research scales: Management Potential, Work Orientation, Creative Temperament, Baucom's Unipolar Masculinity scale, Baucom's Unipolar Femininity scale, Leventhal's Anxiety scale, C. Dicken's scale for Social Desirability, C. Dicken's scale for Acquiescence, Leadership, Amicability, Law Enforcement Orientation, Tough-Mindedness, and Narcissism (Gough, 1999). A 33-item Depression scale has been constructed to identify depressive symptomatology (Jay & John, 2004).

The CPI has been shown to be useful in predicting success in a number of educational and vocational areas. Achievers in both high school and college have been shown to obtain relatively high scores on the Achievement via Conformance, Achievement via Independence, Responsibility, and Socialization scales. Studies making use of CPI scale scores have been shown to predict school and college performance beyond that using IQ scores or scholastic assessment test scores alone. Other scores (on the Achievement via Conformance, Capacity for Status, Sociability, Good Impression, and Intellectual Efficiency scales) have been shown to be related to achievement in different types of vocational and professional training programs. The Dominance scale has proved to be effective in differentiating leaders from nonleaders. The CPI has not been shown to be effective for clinical assessment because it was not designed for that purpose, although extreme scores can provide useful information about an individual's maladjustment. An individual's general level of adjustment or maladjustment is indicated by the overall level of the profile, but the scales do not yield much information related to a specific diagnosis. Juvenile delinquents and criminals tend to have low scores on the Responsibility and Socialization scales. Solitary delinquents tend to obtain low scores on the Intellectual Efficiency and Flexibility scales, whereas social delinquents tend to obtain high scores on the Sociability, Social Presence, and Self-Acceptance scales.

When interpreting the CPI results, the three validity scales (Good Impression, Communality, and Well-Being) should be inspected first. If the CPI results are valid, the three vector scales should then be reviewed to provide a broad overview of the results—including classification into one of the four lifestyles and the level of self-realization. After that, the profile for the 20 individual scales should be examined.

In analyzing the CPI profile, the counselor should begin by paying attention to the overall height of the profile. Higher scores represent psychologically healthy responses, and these should be compared not only with the standard scores on the profile but also, where possible, with an appropriate norm group. The mean on most of the scales, for example, is higher for college students than for high school students. Next, the counselor should pay attention to the highest scores (T score of 60 or above) and the lowest scores (40 or below) on the profile. The next step in examining the profile is to attend to the height of the scores within each of the four classes. The class in which the scores tend to run the highest and those in which they tend to run the lowest should be examined and interpreted. Continuing to examine the profile, the counselor should interpret and discuss both the highest and lowest scales within each class. Finally, the counselor should pay attention to the remaining scales on the profile to be described and interpreted. With this method, the most important aspects of the profile are discussed first and receive the most emphasis and are less likely to become lost by the client in the detailed interpretation that follows. Finally, all of the data, including scale interactions where appropriate, are integrated with other client information in the overall interpretation.

The manner in which the elevation of the scales can be interpreted is seen in Table 13.2 for the Dominance scale of the CPI (Gough, 2000; Groth-Marnat & Wright, 2016). Similar information for all the CPI scales can be found in these sources. Because of the care with which the CPI was originally constructed and has since been revised, along with the many hundreds of studies using this instrument, the CPI has become one of the best and most popular personality inventories available. Because the majority of the scales were empirically constructed and scale scores can be compared with different norm groups, the counselor can make use of the instrument in assessing and comparing the strength of clients' various personality characteristics, and clients can use the interpretation to assess their own strengths and weaknesses in comparison with normative samples.

Computer-based profile interpretation is also available. A limitation of the CPI is that few studies have examined the meaning of elevations on more than one scale, in contrast to the considerable research that has been conducted on two and three high-point codes of the MMPI. Case Example 13.2 provides a sample CPI interpretation.

Table 13.2
Sample Interpretive Descriptions for the
California Psychological Inventory Dominance Scale

Very High (T = above 65): Highly assertive; frequently seeks power and leadership positions in a direct manner; is confident, ambitious, and dominant; may be overbearing.

High (T = 60–65): Reasonably dominant and assertive, likely to take charge of situations, confident, optimistic, task oriented.

Moderately High (T = 55–60): Generally self-confident, can assume leadership roles when called upon.

Average (T = 45–55): Neither strongly dominant nor inhibited, not characterized by strongly assertive or unusually nonassertive behavior.

Moderately Low (T = 40–55): Likely to be hesitant to take the initiative, generally uncomfortable in leadership positions, may have difficulty making direct requests.

Low (T = 35–40): Likely to appear dependent, generally prefers a nonassertive participant role, may resist change and be seen as lacking in self-confidence.

Very Low (T = below 35): Likely to be socially withdrawn, appears shy and insecure, tends to avoid tension and pressure situations, usually seen as submissive and inhibited.

Case Example 13.2

Theresa

The CPI profile of scores for Theresa, a 35-year-old divorced administrative assistant, is shown in Figure 13.2. She sought counseling because of a general dissatisfaction with her current situation. She is not happy with her job; she has had three serious relationships with men since her divorce, none of which has developed into marriage; and she is often in conflict with her 15-year-old daughter. After graduation from high school, she attended college sporadically for 2 years, earning fewer than 40 credits and a GPA of 1.6. She attributes her poor record to a lack of goals, a lack of interest in liberal arts subjects, and to "too much partying."

The validity scales from Theresa's CPI profile show a tendency to present herself in a negative fashion (Good Impression = 34). Her personality type, Gamma, suggests self-confidence and social competence together with restlessness, pleasure seeking, and nonconforming beliefs and behaviors. At Level 4 (out of seven levels) on Vector 3 (Ego Integration), she shows average integration and realization of potential. As a Gamma at this level, she may feel somewhat alienated from society. At a higher level, she might be seen as creative or progressive; at a lower level, she might be viewed as antisocial.

In general, the scores on Theresa's profile fall near the midpoint, which corresponds with her Level 4 score on Vector 3. Her two high scores (*T* score of 60 or above) indicate that she is "self-sufficient, resourceful, detached" (Independence scale) and that she "likes change and variety"; that she is "easily bored by routine life and everyday experience"; and that she "may be impatient, and even erratic" (Flexibility scale; Gough & Bradley, 2002, pp. 12–13). Her three low scores (*T* score of 40 or below) indicate that she "insists on being herself, even if this causes friction or problems" (Good Impression scale); that she is "concerned about health and personal problems; worried about the future" (Well-Being scale); and that she "has difficulty in doing best work in situations with strict rules and expectations" (Achievement via Conformance scale; Gough & Bradley, 2002, pp. 12–13). Theresa used the information from the CPI together with other information to gain a better understanding of herself and her situation.

• • •

Sixteen Personality Factor Questionnaire

The **Sixteen Personality Factor Questionnaire** (16 PF, 5th edition) is a personality inventory developed through the factor-analytic technique by Raymond B. Cattell and others (H. E. P. Cattell & Schuerger, 2003; Karson, Karson, & O'Dell, 1997; Russell & Karol, 1993). On the basis of the commonsense theory that if a human trait exists, a word in the language would have been developed to describe it, Cattell began from a list of all adjectives that could be applied to humans from an unabridged dictionary and produced a list of 4,500 trait names. These were combined to reduce the list to 171 terms that seemed to cover all of the human characteristics on the longer list. He then asked college students to rate their acquaintances on these terms and, through factor analysis, arrived at 16 primary factors that were developed into the 16 scales. Additional scores are now also obtained on five global factors—Extraversion, Anxiety, Tough-Mindedness, Independence, and Self-Control (note resemblance to the Big Five)—as well as on a number of additional derived scales.

The adult edition now contains 185 items. High and low scores on each of the scales represent opposite characteristics. Thus, the scales are labeled Practical versus Imaginative,

Trusting versus Suspicious, Concrete versus Abstract, Shy versus Socially Bold, and Relaxed versus Tense. Separate-sex and combined-sex norms are available for adults, college students, and high school juniors and seniors. Scores are given in terms of stens—standard scores with a mean of 5.5 and a standard deviation of 2.0. Scores below 4 (10th percentile) are considered low, and scores above 7 (90th percentile) are considered high. Because the scales are bipolar, both high and low scores can be interpreted as representing a particular characteristic (H. E. P. Cattell & Schuerger, 2003). Several sets of equivalent forms of the inventory have been developed. In addition, the adult level has been extended downward to develop a form for high school students ages 12 to 18 (the **High School Personality Questionnaire**) and another one for use with children ages 8 to 12 (the **Children's Personality Questionnaire**).

Three different validity scales have been developed, one to detect random responding, one to detect faking-good responses (called the Motivational Distortion scale), and a third to predict attempts to give a bad impression (called the Faking Bad scale). Additional adaptations and computer-generated interpretations of the 16 PF have been published and promoted for use in marriage counseling, career counseling, job proficiency, and the assessment of managers.

The following steps constitute a suggested strategy for interpreting the 16 PF. After considering client information and the context of the assessment, the counselor should first inspect the three validity scales to determine whether the results are trustworthy. Second, the counselor should interpret global scores and their patterns and evaluate overall adjustment level (Craig, 1999). Third, the counselor should interpret very high or very low primary factor scores. Fourth, the counselor should interpret patterns (interrelationships) of primary factor scores, paying attention to any inconsistencies among the primary scores within the global factors that may affect the interpretation of the global scores (Schuerger, 2000). Another approach in using the 16 PF is to compare the client's overall profile with typical profiles of certain groups using available computer programs.

The 16 PF is based on a large amount of research both in the construction of the instrument and in the examination of its reliability and validity. Test–retest reliability coefficients over short periods tend to range from .60 to .85. The reliability coefficients are somewhat low because the scales are made up of relatively few items (10 to 13 items per scale). A wide variety of validity data is available, including the prediction of academic grades and mean profiles for many groups such as delinquents, neurotics, and workers in a variety of different occupations.

NEO Personality Inventory–Revised

The **NEO Personality Inventory–Revised** (NEO PI-R) was developed to assess the Big Five personality factors previously mentioned (Costa & McCrae, 1992). It consists of five 48-item scales answered on a 5-point agree–disagree continuum. Scores are obtained on each of the five domains of Neuroticism (high scores: poor adjustment and emotional distress; low scores: self-confident, free of neurotic conflicts), Extraversion (high scores: sociable, energetic; low scores: reserved, even-paced), Openness (high scores: imaginative, curious; low scores: practical, traditional), Agreeableness (high scores: sympathetic, dependent; low scores: egocentric, antagonistic), and Conscientiousness (high scores: organized, self-controlled; low scores: easygoing, disorganized) as well as on 30 facet subscales. Each of the five global dimensions is composed of six subscales of eight items, each designed to measure facets of the global dimension. The Neuroticism domain includes facets such as anxiety, hostility, and depression, whereas the Conscientiousness domain includes facets such as competence, order, and self-discipline. Except for the Neuroticism scale, higher scores are indicative of positive characteristics, but on two of the scales (Agreeableness and Conscientiousness), very high scores can indicate a lack of balance in the individual's personality structure.

Reliability coefficients ranging from .8 to .9 are reported for the global dimensions, with the facet scales ranging from .6 to .8. Separate profile sheets are provided with differing norms for males, females, and college students. The inventory is easy to administer and hand score, although computer administration, scoring, and interpretation are available. Concurrent validity studies (primarily with other personality measures) have yielded moderate to strong correlations in expected directions.

The NEO PI was originally developed on populations available from two large studies of aging adults indicating that the inventory can be used throughout the full range of adult ages. Because it was developed primarily with adults, different norms must be used with adolescents and college-age adults because they tend to achieve particularly high scores on certain of the inventory's five dimensions. In addition to the individual form (Form S), an additional form (Form R) is available; it has the same items but is designed to be completed on an individual by another rater—someone who knows the individual well, such as a spouse or peer. The scores representing an individual's self-perception and another's perception can then be compared. Correlations that range from .5 to .7, which are typically obtained between individual and partner or peer ratings, can be interpreted as evidence of the validity of the instrument.

A form for use in employment and career counseling settings where the Neuroticism factor is not relevant is the NEO-4. It can provide feedback in nonthreatening terms appropriate for both group and individual sessions. Again, two forms are provided: self-reports (Form S) and ratings by another individual (Form R). A shortened version, the **NEO Five-Inventory**, which yields scores only on the five domains, is also available.

A rapidly increasing number of research studies using the NEO PI-R have been conducted, and it has emerged as one of the better inventories available for the assessment of normal adult personality. In addition, when administered to clinical samples, NEO PI-R scores have been shown to add incremental predictive validity to MMPI-2 results (Costa & Widiger, 2002). It increased diagnostic classification an additional 7% to 23% beyond that obtained with 28 MMPI-2 scores. The NEO PI-R may have the potential to bridge the gap between general personality and psychopathological instruments (Piedmont, 2013).

Coopersmith Self-Esteem Inventories

Stanley Coopersmith, who devoted a large part of his career to the study of factors related to self-esteem, defined self-esteem as "the evaluation a person makes and customarily maintains with regard to him- or herself" (Coopersmith, 1993, p. 5). He reasoned that people who have confidence in their abilities will be more persistent and more successful in their activities than those who perceive themselves negatively. He looked on self-esteem as a global construct that affects a person's evaluation of his or her abilities in many areas. Because of the importance of self-esteem to the individual, in terms both of school or work performance and of personal satisfaction, Coopersmith believed that counselors and teachers in particular should be aware of deficits in children's self-esteem and that they should be aware of methods for helping to improve self-esteem.

He developed three forms of the **Coopersmith Inventory** (so named to avoid influencing responses) to measure self-esteem. The longest and most thoroughly developed form is the School Form (Form A). This form, which contains 58 items and six scales, was designed for students ages 8 to 15. An abbreviated version of this form, the School Short Form (B), was constructed from the first 25 items in the School Form for use when time is limited. (The School Form requires about 10 to 15 minutes for most students, whereas the School Short Form can usually be answered in about 5 minutes.) The Adult Form (C), which also contains 25 items, was adapted from the School Short Form. All items, such as "I'm a lot of fun to be with," are answered "like me" or "unlike me."

The School Form provides six scores: a total self-esteem score; four scores derived from subscales that measure self-esteem in regard to peers, parents, school, and personal interests; and a score based on a Lie scale that checks for defensiveness. The School Short From and the Adult Form yield only one score: the total self-esteem score. Measures of internal consistency show acceptable reliabilities for both the subscores and the total scores (Lane, White, & Henson, 2002). Studies based on the School Form show significant relationships between self-esteem and school performance (C. Peterson & Austin, 1985; Sewell, 1985).

As a check on the individual's self-report on the inventory, Coopersmith and Gilberts (1982) developed the **Behavioral Academic Self-Esteem** (BASE) rating scale for teachers to use in evaluating a student's performance in 16 situations. The scale contains items similar to "this child likes to work on new tasks" and "this child readily states his/her opinion." Teachers rate students on a 5-point scale based on the frequency with which they perform the behavior indicated. The BASE provides outside information to check the accuracy of a student's self-perception; however, it should be remembered that teacher ratings only infer student self-esteem and should be used only along with student responses (Marsh, 1985). Counselors can profit from both types of information in helping clients to enhance their self-esteem.

Tennessee Self-Concept Scale

The **Tennessee Self-Concept Scale** (2nd edition), a famous measure of self-concept, is a 90-item instrument that yields a total of 14 scales for counseling purposes. The scales assess self-concept in terms of identity, feelings, and behavior (PAR, Inc., 2012b). Items are answered on a 5-point scale ranging from *completely false* to *completely true*. Nine different measures of self-concept have been derived for areas such as identity, physical self, moral/ethical self, self-satisfaction, and social self. In addition, there are two summary scores and four validity scales. The second edition was standardized on a nationwide sample of 3,000 individuals ages 7 to 90. There is a child form for ages 7 to 14 and a young person–adult form for ages 13 and older. The first 20 items on either version can be administered as a short form when only a quick summary is needed. A similar instrument designed especially for younger children is the **Piers–Harris Children's Self-Concept Scale**, an 80-item instrument designed for children in Grades 3 through 12 and written at a third-grade level (Piers & Harris, 1996).

Popular Unstructured Personality Assessments

Whereas the previous section addressed several popular structured personality assessments, this section briefly describes popular unstructured or **projective assessments**. Because there is an infinite variety of possible responses to ambiguous stimuli, no particular conclusion can be drawn from any single response. Responses may be classified, however, and from a number of responses, general impressions and inferences regarding a person's personality may be derived. Projective assessments are individually administered and can require an extensive amount of time within a counseling session. The administration and scoring of most projective instruments require considerable training and experience on the part of the examiner. Interpretations have generally drawn on psychoanalytic theory.

Projective assessments are considered valuable clinical options among helping professionals (Piotrowski, 2015a, 2015b). As noted in Chapter 1, Piotrowski (2015b) found that human figure drawings, sentence completion exercises, and the Thematic Apperception Test were cited as among the top 15 most frequently used among practitioners. However, C. H. Peterson et al. (2014) noted minimal use of projective assessments across a variety of counseling specialties. Regardless of the frequency of their use, projective assessments will remain part of counseling practice in some form.

Lindzey (1959) classified projective techniques into five categories: (a) association to inkblots or words, (b) story construction or sequences, (c) sentence or story completion, (d) picture arrangement/selection or verbal choices, and (e) drawing or play techniques. Thus, a variety of ambiguous stimuli have been used for assessment purposes, such as inkblots, pictures, and incomplete sentences. In this section, several popular projective assessments are discussed in relation to many of Lindzey's categories: the Rorschach Inkblot Test (*association*); the Thematic Apperception Test, Children's Apperception Test, Thompson Thematic Apperception Test, and TEMAS (*story construction*); the Rotter Incomplete Sentences Blank (*sentence completion*); and the Draw-A-Person Test and House–Tree–Person (*drawing expression*).

Rorschach Inkblot Test

The most widely used projective test has been the **Rorschach Inkblot Test** (Cordón, 2005; Goldfried, Stricker, & Weiner, 1971; Ulett, 1994). In fact, there is an organization dedicated to the tool, the International Society of the Rorschach and Projective Methods, with its own journal, *Rorschachiana*. The tool was developed in 1921 by Hermann Rorschach, a Swiss psychiatrist. He placed ink on a piece of paper and folded the paper to form inkblots then asked people to say what images the inkblots suggested to them and used the responses to assess personality. A series of 10 inkblots have become the standardized stimuli, some of them in gray and several with combinations of colors. Several different methods of administration, along with various systems to score the responses, have been developed. Responses are classified and scored according to set criteria, such as the location of the response on the inkblot, the feature that determined the response, and the content of the response. Figure 13.3 provides an example of an inkblot similar to one used on the Rorschach.

Exner's (1993, 2001) Comprehensive System (CS) has emerged as the most popular scoring scheme and has been shown to have considerable interscorer reliability. Each response given to each inkblot is scored for (a) location (which part or whole of blot), (b) determinant (which feature or color), (c) content (e.g., clouds, geography, anatomy), and (d) popularity (common or original). Numbers and ratios of responses in different categories are related to the interpretation given to the test protocol. The Exner system has been shown to have considerable validity in identifying certain personality characteristics. It has been criticized, however, for problems with clinical sample norms and its tendency to make normal individuals appear as if they suffer from severe psychopathology (Garb, Wood, Lilienfeld, & Nezworski, 2005; Mihura, Meyer, Dumitrascu, & Bombel, 2013).

Although the Rorschach is difficult to evaluate because of its complexity, a meta-analysis of validity studies conducted with the Rorschach indicated that it showed more success than the MMPI in predicting objective criterion variables. The MMPI has been shown to be more effective in predicting psychiatric diagnoses and self-report criteria (Hiller, Rosenthal, Bornstein, Barry, & Brunell-Neuleib, 1999). The Rorschach continues its popularity in many clinical settings (Groth-Marnat & Wright, 2016).

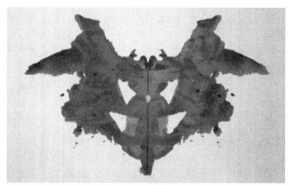

Figure 13.3
Rorschach Test Image

Note. From Hermann Rorschach, Rorschach Test. In the public domain.

Thematic Apperception Test and Additional Story Construction Assessments

The **Thematic Apperception Test** (TAT) was developed by Christina Morgan and Henry Murray based on Murray's theory of needs (*apperception* means to perceive in terms of past perceptions; Murray, 1943). It consists of 30 black-and-white picture cards, most containing one or more human figures, and one completely blank card. Twenty of the 30 cards are presented in a test administration, the selection of the 20 depending on the age and sex of the examinee. The examinee is asked to make up a story about each picture and to include what is currently happening in the picture, what led up to that situation, how the people in the story feel, and how the story ends. If examinees fail to include any of these elements, they are asked to fill in the information after the initial story has been completed. They are expected to identify with the hero in their story and project their needs, attitudes, and feelings on this character (Groth-Marnat & Wright, 2016).

When the entire test is administered, it is usually broken down into two sessions on two different days, with 10 cards administered at each session. The cards that illustrate more threatening material are usually included in the second session. Many of those who administer the TAT do not use all 20 cards but select 8 to 12 of them and use them (in the sequences noted by numbers on the back) in a single session. The TAT is usually not scored in any objective fashion, but the frequency of various themes, the intensity and duration of the stories, and the outcomes are taken into account. It is assumed that the hero in the story is the person with whom the examinee identifies. The assumption in interpreting the results is that examinees reveal their conflicts, experiences, needs, and strivings in their storytelling responses. A number of more objective scoring systems have been developed for the TAT to assess such concepts as achievement, ego development, or gender identity (Teglasi, 2010), but most are complex and do not provide the overall qualitative view of the individual usually sought by those using this instrument.

Instead of administering the entire TAT, counselors often select a few cards for use in an early interview. The cards can be used as a method of initially gaining rapport and as a method of encouraging the client to open up and talk during the counseling session. At the same time, the storytelling responses can yield considerable insight into the needs and personality of the client.

The **Children's Apperception Test** (CAT) consists of 10 pictures and is designed for use with children ages 3 to 10. Typically, a version using animals in human social settings is used (CAT-A) as it is believed that children can better identify with animals than humans. There is no psychometric information for the CAT.

The **Thompson TAT** (T-TAT) and the **TEMAS** (Spanish for *themes* and acronym for "tell me a story") are intended to represent adaptations of the TAT for diverse populations. The T-TAT was developed by redrawing 21 original TAT pictures using African American figures (C. Thompson, 1949). The TEMAS consists of 23 pictures of Latinos in urban settings (Groth-Marnat & Wright, 2016; Teglasi, 2010). A scoring key is provided, although the TEMAS yields questionable reliabilities across cognitive, ego, and affective functions.

Rotter Incomplete Sentences Blank

In the sentence completion technique, a person is asked to complete a number of sentence fragments that are related to possible conflicts or emotions. The most popular sentence completion test is the **Rotter Incomplete Sentences Blank** (2nd edition; Rotter, Lah, & Rafferty, 1992), which consists of 40 sentence fragments. Most of the sentence fragments are written in the first person, such as "My mother . . ." or "What bothers me most is . . .." There are three forms: one for high school, one for college, and one for adults. It is expected that attitudes, traits, and emotions will be expressed in the responses. Responses are compared with sample answers in the manual (Rotter et al., 1992) and scored on a continuum from

6 to 0, from unhealthy or maladjusted through neutral to healthy or positive responses (higher scores suggest greater maladjustment). Thus, a single overall adjustment score is produced that makes this particular form useful as a gross screening instrument.

Because sentence fragments are easy to construct, counselors often develop their own incomplete sentence instruments to deal with various types of conflicts and problems presented by clients. Sample sentence stems might include "I get worried when . . ." or "I think my future. . . ." Thus, one counselor-constructed incomplete sentence instrument will deal with problems and conflicts revolving around educational/vocational decision making, another might deal with family conflicts, another with interpersonal conflicts, and yet another with school difficulties.

Draw-A-Person

The **Draw-A-Person Test** (DAP) was developed by Machover (1949) and is still used as a clinical assessment tool. It was developed from Goodenough's (1926) Draw-A-Man task, which was used to assess intelligence. Counselors can administer the DAP by presenting a child or adolescent with a blank piece of paper and a pencil with eraser and requesting he or she "draw a person." Then, counselors may ask the client to draw another person of the opposite sex. Machover believed that psychodynamically based impulses would be differentially projected upon female and male persons. The manual contains interpretations for various body parts as well as general orientation of the figure(s). The DAP has been heavily critiqued for its lack of psychometric merit, and counselors are encouraged to use the projective assessment as a means for evaluating behavioral or emotional problems within the context of the clinical interview.

House–Tree–Person

The **House–Tree–Person** (HTP) projective drawing technique evolved from the earlier "draw-a-person" method of attempting to assess a child's level of cognitive maturity. It is one of the more widely used projective techniques because it often yields considerable clinical information and is easy to use (Buck, 1992). The individual simply draws a house, a tree, and a person, usually on three separate sheets of paper. Then the individual is asked to describe, define, and interpret each of the drawings. Characteristics of the drawings are scored, and interpretive concepts are applied to the characteristics and the responses. Interpretive guidelines are available, but they lack independent validation and any extensive research base (Groth-Marnat & Wright, 2016). The HTP tends to be used primarily as a way of interactively engaging a client to determine therapeutic interventions. Table 13.3 provides a sample of interpretations for H-T-P elements.

Activity 13.1
Evaluating Projective Assessments

Select one of the assessments discussed in this section. Use assessment sources discussed earlier in the text to collect psychometric information on the assessment. Reflect on the following questions:

- What is the psychometric evidence (e.g., reliability, validity, standardization sample, scoring information) for the assessment? How strong is this evidence?
- How would you use this instrument in your practice?
- What are some of the advantages and disadvantages of the assessment?
- What are some multicultural considerations with the assessment?

Present the information to the larger group.

Table 13.3
Selected House–Tree–Person Interpretations

Element	Interpretation
House: **home atmosphere, intrafamilial relationships**	
Rear of house drawn	Withdrawal, oppositional tendencies, possible paranoid tendencies
Close appearance	Interpersonal warmth
Very small house	Rejection of the home and home life, withdrawal
Multiple chimneys	Overconcern with sex, may represent compensation for sexual inadequacy
Absence of door	Feelings of isolation, possible psychosis
Small windows	Lack of interest in people, psychological inaccessibility
Tree: **experience of one's environment**	
Dead trees	Depression, guilt, potential suicidality, withdrawal
Very large trees	Possible aggressive tendencies, overcompensation
Broken or cut-off branches	Feelings of trauma and/or impotency
Excessive branches	Possible obsessive–compulsive or manic tendencies
Faintly drawn trunks	Inadequate ego strength, indecision, anxiety
Person: **interpersonal relationships**	
Folded arms	Suspiciousness and/or hostility
Buttons	Dependency
Very small eyes	Introversion, self-absorption, or regressive tendencies
Long feet	Need for security
Large ears	Hypersensitivity to criticism, paranoid tendencies
Omitted mouth	Guilt, depression, possible psychosomatic problems

Note. Information is from Buck (1992) and Ogdon (2001).

Health and Lifestyle Inventories

Researchers have recognized the importance that psychosocial factors play in individuals' efforts to recover from injury or illness as well as in their overall lifestyle satisfaction, and this recognition has led to the development of several so-called *biopsychosocial* inventories. Such inventories assess the psychosocial issues that encourage or inhibit the recovery of individuals from injury or illness. These measures can be particularly useful to rehabilitation counselors and other mental health professionals. Other inventories assess the overall physical and psychological wellness of clients.

The **Battery for Health Improvement 2** (BHI-2; Bruns & Disorbio, 2003) is designed to identify relevant factors that may interfere with health improvement or injury recovery. Its 217 items yield 16 scales plus two validity scales. There are three Affective scales (e.g., Depression, Anxiety), four Physical Symptom scales (e.g., Somatic Complaints, Pain Complaints), five Character Scales (e.g., Substance Abuse), and four Psychosocial scales (e.g., Family Dysfunction). The instrument was normed on a sample of 527 patients in actual treatment for physical rehabilitation and chronic pain as well as an additional 725 community individuals. Scale score reliabilities range from .74 to .92 for internal consistency and from .88 to .98 for test–retest (Fernandez, 2001). There is a shorter 63-item form, the **Brief Battery for Health Improvement 2** (BBHI-2), developed to help practitioners quickly evaluate psychosocial factors commonly seen in medical patients. It was derived from the longer form using the same norm groups.

The **Coping with Health Injuries and Problems** inventory (CHIP; Endler, Parker, & Summerfeldt, 1998) can be used both to examine the psychological strategies a client is using to cope with physical health problems and to suggest more effective ones. It was normed on more than 2,500 adult and university students, including almost 400 who were seeking medical treatment.

The **Wellness Evaluation of Lifestyle** (WEL) is a 131-item inventory that deals with lifestyle behaviors, perceptions, and attitudes (J. E. Myers, Luecht, & Sweeney, 2004). It is designed to assess five lifestyle tasks (e.g., Self-Regulation, Work and Leisure, Love) and 14 dimensions of wellness (e.g., sense of control, exercise, intellectual stimulation; Cox, 2003). Two briefer forms have been developed using factor analysis techniques—a 73-item five-factor WEL (5FWel) and a 56-item four-factor WEL (4-Wel; Abrahams & Balkin, 2006).

The **Lifestyle Assessment Questionnaire** is published by the National Wellness Institute of Stevens Point, Wisconsin. It contains 227 questions dealing with the assessment of lifestyles in six areas. The instrument is not well developed in terms of reliability and validity studies but can be useful in reviewing current behavior and planning future lifestyle activities.

Chapter Summary

This chapter presented several popular structured and unstructured personality assessments that counselors may find useful in evaluating personality characteristics for further diagnosis and treatment planning. Structured or objective assessments are typically used to test hypotheses and examine psychopathology and behavioral problems, whereas unstructured or projective assessments are typically used to generate hypotheses about personality using ambiguous stimuli. In this chapter, various methods for developing objective assessments were described: logical content, theoretical, criterion group, and factor analysis. To interpret results of a personality inventory competently, counselors must understand both the personality characteristics being assessed and the approach used to develop the various inventory scales. In addition, administering, scoring, and interpreting both structured and unstructured personality assessments often require additional specialized training.

Popular structured personality assessments include the Minnesota Multiphasic Personality Inventories (MMPI-2, MMPI-2-RF, MMPI-A), the MCMI-III, MIPS-R, PAI, MBTI, CPI, 16 PF, NEO PI-R, Coopersmith Self-Esteem Inventory, and the Tennessee Self-Concept Scale. Popular unstructured or projective personality assessments include the Rorschach Inkblot Test, TAT, CAT, TEMAS, Rotter Incomplete Sentences Blank, DAP, and HTP. For both practical and psychometric reasons, projective instruments such as the Rorschach Inkblot Test and the TAT are seldom used by counselors. Condensed or adapted versions of projective tests such as the TAT and Rotter Incomplete Sentences Blank are sometimes used by counselors as rapport-building techniques that may also yield insight into the client's personality.

This chapter also discussed health and lifestyle inventories. Biopsychosocial factors affecting health and lifestyles can be assessed using several recently developed inventories, such as the BHI-2, CHIP, WEL, and the Lifestyle Assessment Questionnaire.

Review Questions

1. Pretend you are interested in developing a personality measure to assess motivation to change. How could you use each of the four methods of objective test construction (logical content, theoretical, criterion group, factor analytic) to develop your assessment?
2. Several structured personality assessments discussed in this chapter addressed "normal" or positive personality characteristics. How was personality conceptualized by these instruments?
3. What are some of the strengths and limitations of structured personality assessments?
4. What are some of the strengths and limitations of unstructured personality assessments?
5. How can counselors use health and wellness inventories in their practice?

Resources for Further Learning

Publications

Burns, R. C. (1987). *Kinetic house-tree-person drawings: K-H-T-P: An interpretative manual.* New York, NY: Brunner-Routledge.

Graham, J. R. (2011). *Assessing personality and psychopathology* (5th ed.). New York, NY: Oxford University Press.

Rose, T., Maloney, M. P., & Kaser-Boyd, N. (2000). *Essentials of Rorschach assessment.* New York, NY: Wiley.

Teglasi, H. (2010). *Essentials of TAT and other storytelling assessments* (2nd ed.). New York, NY: Wiley.

Web Resources

16 PF Fifth Edition
http://www.pearsonclinical.com/psychology/products/100000483/16pf-fifth-edition.html
This website links to information about this assessment.

California Psychological Inventory (CPI)
https://www.cpp.com/products/cpi/index.aspx
This website links to information about this assessment.

International Society of the Rorschach and Projective Methods
http://www.rorschach.com
This association provides information about the latest use of the Rorschach and other unstructured personality assessments.

Keirsey Temperament Sorter II
http://keirsey.com/
This website links to information about this assessment.

Millon Inventories
http://www.pearsonclinical.com/psychology/products/100000509/millon-inventories.html#tab-details
This website links to information about these assessments.

Minnesota Multiphasic Personality Inventory (MMPI) scales
http://www.pearsonclinical.com/services/solr/search/.api?requestFrom=quickSearch&siteContext=ani.clinicalassessment.us.clinicalassessment&barsearch=psychology&searchText=MMPI&searcSubmit.x=0&searcSubmit.y=0&searcSubmit=submit
This website links to information about these assessments.

MMPI-2, MMPI-A, and Minnesota Reports: Research and Clinical Applications
http://mmpi.umn.edu/
This website provides research and recommendations related to the MMPI-2 assessment.

Myers & Briggs Foundation
http://www.myersbriggs.org/my-mbti-personality-type/mbti-basics/
This website links to information about the MBTI.

NEO Personality Inventory–Revised (NEO PI-R)
http://www4.parinc.com/Products/Product.aspx?ProductID=NEO-PI-R
This website links to information about this assessment.

Personality Assessment Inventory (PAI)
http://www4.parinc.com/Products/Product.aspx?ProductID=PAI
This website links to information about this assessment.

Wellness Evaluation of Lifestyle
    http://www.mindgarden.com/159-wellness-evaluation-of-lifestyle
        This website links to information about this assessment.

Chapter 14

Assessment of
Interpersonal Relationships

This chapter discusses various assessment tools that may be used to examine interpersonal relationships, specifically those within couples and families. First, instruments for couples and family counseling, particularly related to relationship satisfaction and quality of engagement, are presented. Guidelines for assessing intimate partner violence and child abuse are then discussed. Third, a brief description of genograms is provided. The chapter concludes with a brief discussion of assessments used to gauge other types of interpersonal relationships.

Test Your Knowledge

Select the most appropriate choice for each item.

_____ 1. Which of the following relationship inventories has not been normed with couples not identifying as heterosexual?
  a. Marital Satisfaction Inventory–Revised
  b. Couple's Precounseling Inventory
  c. Derogatis Sexual Functioning Inventory
  d. Dyadic Adjustment Scale

_____ 2. The highest child abuse victimization rate per 1,000 children occurs for which racial/ethnic group?
  a. Whites
  b. African Americans
  c. Latinos
  d. Native Americans

_____ 3. Which of the following is commonly included on a genogram?
  a. Marriages
  b. Births
  c. Interactional patterns
  d. All of the above

❏ T ❏ F 4. There are several relationship inventories with strong psychometric evidence available to counselors.

❏ T ❏ F 5. Very few intimate partner violence assessments solicit information about a client's available support systems or needs.

Inventories for Couples and Family Counseling

Snyder, Heyman, Haynes, Carlson, and Balderama-Durbin (2015) pointed out that the assessment of couples differs from individual assessment in a number of ways: (a) It focuses on the relationships and interactions between two or more persons, (b) it can provide the opportunity to directly observe interpersonal communication, and (c) it may involve attempting to maintain a supportive alliance while assessing antagonistic partners. Many of these differences can also be seen with family assessment. Snyder et al. also believed that when counseling individuals, assessment of couple functioning should be a standard practice; in a similar manner, when counseling couples, partners should be assessed individually for serious emotional or behavioral problems.

Although a number of instruments have been designed specifically for relationship counseling, relatively few of these instruments are used as a part of the counseling process. The 10 relationship inventories most likely to be used in counseling are briefly discussed in this chapter. Most of the other instruments lack substantial amounts of psychometric data. They have also almost always been developed with White, middle-class couples. Many of these instruments, which can be considered experimental at this point, are primarily used in research studies in this field.

It is important to note that many types of assessments may be useful in couples and family counseling beyond the relationship inventories presented in this section. Depending on the established counseling goals or selected interventions, informal assessments such as observation and interview protocols, self-monitoring methods, and genograms (described later in the chapter) can be particularly helpful in providing a comprehensive picture of a client's presenting problem or the effectiveness of an intervention from multiple perspectives.

Myers–Briggs Type Indicator

The **MBTI** (see Chapter 13) is used to help couples understand their differences in the four dimensions measured by the MBTI and therefore to help them use these differences constructively. Data accumulated by the Center for Applications of Psychological Type indicate that people are only slightly more likely to partner with individuals of similar than of opposite types (I. B. Myers et al., 1998). The proportion of couples alike in three or all four dimensions is only slightly higher than would be expected from a random assortment of types. The MBTI thus can be used to assist couples in understanding their differences and similarities.

When couples differ on the thinking–feeling dimension, feeling partners may find their significant other cold, unemotional, and insensitive, whereas the thinking spouse can become irritated with the seeming lack of logic of feeling types. Counselors can help thinking types to improve relationships by openly showing appreciation and by refraining from comments that sound like personal criticism. They can encourage feeling types to state wishes clearly, so the thinking partner does not have to guess their wishes. One spouse may be an extravert who needs considerable external stimulation, whereas the other may be an introvert who needs sufficient time alone. This situation becomes a problem when the introverted partner expends a good deal of energy in extraverted work all day and has little energy left for sociability in the evening. The extraverted partner, in contrast, may work in a more solitary setting and look forward to an evening of social stimulation and activity. Problems arising from judging–perceiving differences can be found when planning, order, and organization are important to the judging partner whereas freedom and spontaneity are important to the perceptive partner, who also has a great deal more tolerance for ambiguity.

In using the MBTI with couples, counselors sometimes ask couples to guess the types of their partners after describing the types briefly. It is also possible to have partners answer the MBTI twice, once for themselves and once as they believe their partner will respond. In either case, the accuracy of partners' type descriptions can be discussed, which can be useful to the couple as they see how such differences affect their relationship.

Flamez, Hicks, and Clark (2015) indicated that the MBTI is particularly useful for helping couples and family members to communicate more effectively as they understand their dimension preferences. Thus, the MBTI can also be helpful in family counseling for discussing issues such as difficulties in communication, differences in child-rearing styles, and dissimilarities in attitudes toward other family members. For example, a counselor can help an orderly, practical, sensing–judging parent to see that it is easier for him or her to raise a sensing–judging child, who desires structure and organization, than it is for that parent to raise an independent, intuitive–perceptive child, who rebels against structure and order.

Taylor–Johnson Temperament Analysis

The **Taylor–Johnson Temperament Analysis** (TJTA) could be a particularly useful tool as part of premarital counseling (Flamez et al., 2015). It consists of 180 items equally divided among nine bipolar scales measuring 18 traits related to interpersonal relationships and personal adjustment (e.g., Nervous–Composed, Depressive–Lighthearted, Responsive–Inhibited, Dominant–Submissive, and Self-Disciplined–Impulsive; R. H. Johnson, Taylor, Morrison, Morrison, & Romoser, 2007). The TJTA can be used in individual and group settings, and there is a form available for use with adolescents and individuals with lower reading levels. Norms are available for four groups (i.e., adolescent, young adult, general adult, and senior adult). The manual was updated in 2012 (Psychological Publications, 2015). Furthermore, the TJTA can be administered online and is available in six languages (English, Spanish, French, Korean, German, and Chinese).

Although the TJTA is a self-report questionnaire, a unique feature of this instrument is the criss-cross procedure in which one person records his or her impressions of another person. This use can be valuable in family counseling involving parent–adolescent interaction, in situations involving sibling conflict, or in premarital or couples counseling.

Marital Satisfaction Inventory–Revised

The **Marital Satisfaction Inventory–Revised** (MSI-R) is a 280-item self-report inventory designed to assess couples' interactions and the extent of couples' distress (Snyder, 1997). Scores are obtained on 13 subscales (e.g., Affective Communication, Problem-Solving Communication, Disagreement About Finances, Sexual Dissatisfaction, Conflict Over Child-Rearing) and a Global Distress scale, which measures general unhappiness and uncertain commitment in the partnership. A Social Desirability scale (conventionalization) and an Inconsistency scale are included as a check on the response set of the test taker, and an Aggression scale has been added. The scales contain nine to 19 true/false items per scale. In the revised version, items were changed to be appropriate for both traditional and nontraditional couples, and the inventory was restandardized on a larger and more representative sample of couples.

The MSI-R is intended to be used in couples counseling, with both partners taking the inventory and the results being displayed on a single profile that indicates areas of agreement and disagreement. It is typically administered during the initial contact with the counselor or agency so that results are available for the ensuing counseling sessions. The MSI-R provides useful information for counselors by providing a picture of the couple's overall relationship distress, the general quality of their communication, and the differences between their perceptions of aspects of their relationship. In addition to the paper-and-pencil instrument, there is a computerized version that generates a test report and an interpretation. Validity studies of the MSI-R scales generally show reasonable correlations with other measures of relationship satisfaction. The MSI-R significantly differentiates between various criterion groups experiencing relationship dissatisfaction. The manual (Snyder, 1997) for the MSI-R reports internal consistency coefficients and test–retest reliability coefficients in the .80 to .95 range. The MSI-R is available in Spanish.

Derogatis Sexual Functioning Inventory

It may be useful to evaluate sexual functioning, including sexual satisfaction, in individual and couples counseling. When exploring sexual functioning, counselors may want to explore variables and factors associated with sexual satisfaction in more than 40 years of research (del Mar Sánchez-Fuentes, Santos-Iglesias, & Sierra, 2014). These include physical and psychological health status; information regarding intimate relationships and history of sexual responses; factors associated with social support and family relationships; and cultural beliefs and values, such as religious affiliation.

One popular assessment tool for measuring sexual functioning is the **Derogatis Sexual Functioning Inventory** (DSFI). The DSFI yields 12 scores and consists of 10 scales with titles such as Information, Experience, Psychological Symptoms, Gender Role Definition, and Sexual Satisfaction (Derogatis, 1979). A total score and the client's evaluation of current functioning are also included. The Information subscale consists of 26 true/false items measuring the amount of a client's accurate sexual information. The Experience subscale lists 24 sexual behaviors ranging from kissing on the lips to oral–genital sex. The Sexual Drive subscale measures the frequency of various sexual behaviors, and the Attitude subscale measures the diversity of liberal and conservative attitudes.

The entire inventory can be expected to take 45 minutes to 1 hour to complete and was designed to assess individual rather than couple sexual functioning. The DSFI primarily measures current functioning, although the Sexual Experience and the Sexual Fantasy subscales ask the client to report lifetime experiences. Because the DSFI is one of the most studied instruments in sexual research, several different types of norms are available for the instrument. Certain subscales, such as Sexual Information, Sexual Desire, and Gender Roles, have produced relatively low internal consistency coefficients (below .70). Others tend to be more adequate, falling in the .80 to .92 range (L. Berman, Berman, Zicak, & Marley, 2002). The instrument can provide counselors with considerable information regarding sexual functioning. A computer-administered version is also available that yields extensive interpretive information.

Available in 10 languages, the DSFI was normed on 230 individuals who participated in continuing education courses; the sample, however, was primarily White and middle class, so caution should be exercised when using the tool with diverse individuals and couples.

PREPARE and ENRICH

PREPARE and **ENRICH** are two instruments designed to assess relationship strengths and challenges with attention to communication patterns, family dynamics, and significant stressors (Olson, Olson, & Larson, 2012). As part of a comprehensive couples counseling program that has been offered approximately 30 years, partners within a couple complete a 30- to 45-minute survey as part of premarital counseling (i.e., PREPARE) or once married (ENRICH). Then facilitators or counselors can interpret the findings with the couple and set relationship goals. The 125-item survey is scored on 12 relationship scales (e.g., communication, conflict resolution, roles, sexuality, finances, spiritual beliefs), five SCOPE (Social, Change, Organized, Pleasing, Emotionally Steady) personality scales, four couple and family scales, four relationship dynamic scales, and several customizable scales.

Couples Precounseling Inventory

The **Couples Precounseling Inventory** (CPCI) is a revision of the original inventory (Stuart & Jacobson, 1987). Norms are based on a small representative sample (60 couples) that included nonmarried heterosexual and gay couples. The purpose of the instrument is for use in planning and evaluating relationship therapy based on a social learning model. From a 16-page form, scores are obtained in 12 areas of relationships on scales such as Communication Assessment, Conflict Management, Sexual Interaction, Child Management, Relationship Change Goals, General Happiness With the Relationship, and Goals of Counseling. The authors reported high levels of internal consistency reliabilities (from .85 to .91). In taking the instrument, couples describe current interaction patterns rather than personality characteristics. Items tend to emphasize positive characteristics, and, if taken with some seriousness by the couple, the instrument can be educational and therapeutic. The CPCI is based on social learning theory and is designed to examine relationship characteristics and motivations that can be useful in suggesting avenues of treatment if the relationship is to survive (T. Patterson, 2011).

Family Environment Scale

The **Family Environment Scale** (FES, 3rd ed.) is one of a number of social climate scales developed by Moos and his associates (Moos & Moos, 1994a). It consists of three forms that assess the client's perception of the family as it is (the Real Form), as he or she would prefer it to be (the Ideal Form), and as he or she would expect it to react to new situations (the Expectation Form). The three 90-item inventories yield standard scores for 10 scales with titles such as Cohesion, Intellectual–Cultural Orientation, Active Recreational Orientation, Moral–Religious Emphasis, Expressiveness, and Control. Any of the three forms can be used alone or in combination with various family members to allow the counselor to explore differences between spouses' perceptions and between parents' and children's perceptions as a means of identifying family treatment issues. There is also a children's pictorial version (CVFES).

The 10 scales are grouped into three underlying domains: the family relationship domain, the personal growth domain, and the system maintenance change domain. The assumption behind all of the social climate scales is that environments—and in this case, families—have unique personalities that can be measured in the same way as individual personalities can. Norms are based on a group of 1,432 nondistressed and 788 distressed families. The items on the FES are statements about family environments originally obtained through structured interviews with family members. The items have been criticized for possessing a middle-class bias and for not taking into consideration today's varying family patterns (Mancini, 2001). Validity evidence is based primarily on the difference in mean scores between nondistressed and distressed families. The FES is available in multiple languages, including Spanish and Chinese.

Family Assessment Measure–III

The **Family Assessment Measure–III** (FAM-III) is a diagnostic tool for counseling that assesses family structure and strengths and challenges. It consists of three interrelated forms: a 50-item General Scale that examines general family functioning, a 42-item Dyadic Relationship Scale that examines how a family member perceives his or her relationship with another family member, and a 42-item Self-Rating Scale on which each individual rates his or her own functioning within the family (Skinner, Steinhauer, & Santa-Barbara, 1995). The FAM-III yields scores on seven scales—such as Role Performance, Affective Expression, and Communication—and two validity scales. It is available in paper-and-pencil and computer formats, in several languages, and in a brief screening version (Brief FAM). Administration, scoring, and interpretation of three forms for multiple family members can be very time-consuming, although computer administration can shorten the process (Manages, 2001).

Sternberg's Triangular Love Scale

Sternberg's **Triangular Love Scale** (STLS) is a 45-item scale that measures the three components of romantic relationships identified by Sternberg (1998): intimacy, passion, and commitment. Devising scales to measure these separate components, however, has been difficult (Myers & Shurts, 2002). According to Sternberg, all three components must be assessed in evaluating the quality of a romantic relationship.

Dyadic Adjustment Scale

The **Dyadic Adjustment Scale** (Spanier, 2001) is a 32-item scale that measures the quality of interpersonal adjustment. Couples rate the extent to which they agree with their partner as well as how often they engage in various activities. The instrument takes 5–10 minutes to complete and contains four subscales (Dyadic Consensus, Dyadic Satisfaction, Dyadic Cohesion, Affectional Expression). Although there is general support for the instrument in terms of reliability and validity, norms are dated (i.e., 1976) and involve 218 married White couples in Pennsylvania.

Case Example 14.1

Robin and Juanita

Robin and Juanita have been partnered for 5 years and decide to enter counseling to work on some communication difficulties they are having within the past 6 months. Specifically, they report avoiding each other during stressful situations or arguing over "small things." During the first session, they report that 2 years ago they adopted a child, Harrison, who is now 15 years old. They report several stressors within the past year, including Juanita's job loss and her family's lack of acceptance of her relationship as well as Harrison's behavioral and academic problems. Although they identify several stressors, they also emphasize they want to remain committed to each other.

- How might you approach counseling with Robin and Juanita?
- What are some of the major issues you want to explore?
- What are some multicultural considerations in the assessment process?
- What relationship inventories might be useful in your work with them? How might you use them?

• • •

Assessment of Intimate Partner Violence

Intimate partner violence (IPV) is actual or threatened physical, emotional, or sexual abuse against a partner by the other partner in a romantic relationship, such as a dating relationship, marriage, civil union, or other form of partnership. There are three major types of IPV: physical abuse (e.g., hitting, choking, pushing, throwing objects at partner), emotional abuse (e.g., isolating from family and friends, name-calling, jealousy, stalking), and sexual abuse (e.g., threatened or actual rape, sexual humiliation). Approximately 30% of women experience IPV over their lifetimes (Black et al., 2011), and from 61% to more than 80% of adolescents ages 13 to 17 report experiencing incidents of emotional abuse (Cyr, McDuff, & Wright, 2006; Holt & Espelage, 2005). The consequences for dating violence can involve acute injuries, substance abuse, eating disorders, sexual impulsivity and unplanned pregnancy, depression and suicidality, interpersonal problems, academic and occupational problems, and dissociative symptoms, to name a few. In fact, 81% of women experiencing IPV report symptoms of posttraumatic stress disorder (Black et al., 2011). These consequences are more pronounced for individuals of oppressed statuses (e.g., women of color, lesbian or bisexual women) because the resources available to them are more limited (D. G. Hays & Emelianchik, 2009; D. G. Hays, Snow, & Pusateri, 2015).

The effects of IPV for both survivors and perpetrators are long-lasting, and violent behaviors and notions of what constitutes a relationship have been found to pervade across relationships and generations. Thus, it important that counselors continually conduct a thorough assessment of IPV with clients beginning in early adolescence. Table 14.1 provides a list of the major IPV assessments available to counselors and other professionals.

As counselors work with individuals and couples affected by IPV, they should be aware that research shows that helping professionals show a heterosexual bias when evaluating the severity of IPV. For example, therapists often place equal blame for violence in same-sex relationships compared to male-to-female violence in heterosexual relationships (Blasko, Winek, & Bieschke, 2007). This bias is exacerbated by the notion that there may be a lack of understanding of IPV among couples and families of diverse backgrounds (including sexually diverse backgrounds), limited community support for nontraditional couples, and an underreporting of the incidence and prevalence of IPV among diverse populations.

Although there are several IPV assessments available today, it is important for counselors to understand their major components and the limitations associated with item content and the general assessment process. D. G. Hays and Emelianchik (2009) conducted a content analysis of 38 IPV assessments and identified seven themes and related limitations:

1. *Relationship context* refers to the specific type and depth of relationship. The majority of tools assess adult (44.7%) or, specifically, female adult (34.2%) IPV within a current relationship (68.4%). Thus, there are limited assessment tools available for adolescents and young adults, and there are few instruments that measure IPV from previous relationships—information that could be used to detect patterns of abuse.
2. *Forms of abuse* involves the three main types of abuse: physical, emotional, and sexual. Most assessments address emotional abuse (89.5%) and physical abuse (84.2%), although over half do not assess attempted or completed sexual abuse (55.2%). Furthermore, most instruments only focus on overt forms of abuse (84.2%).
3. *Imminent risk indicators* refers to immediate life-threatening acts or feelings (e.g., physical threat, suicidal ideation). Most assessments do not measure imminent risk indicators beyond threat of weapon (31.6%), use of weapon (23.7%), suicidal ideation for the survivor (21.1%), or immediate fear (21.1%). Although these indicators are important for counselors to make decisions on medical and legal assistance, other safety concerns are not being addressed.
4. *Family dynamics* includes the processes within the IPV survivor's current family system and/or family of origin. Unfortunately, most IPV assessments do not measure IPV in current family systems (65.8%) or families of origin (84.2%). Given the intergenerational and systemic influences of IPV, this is an important area to consider.
5. *Degree of support* refers to available resources and support systems for the IPV survivor. Most assessments (73.7%) do not include items that solicit information about the IPV survivor's need for assistance. It is important for prevention and intervention that IPV survivors are evaluated for available resources and support systems.
6. *Assessment structure* involves the assessment administration method (e.g., paper and pencil, computerized, clinical interview), test format (e.g., Likert scale, open-ended question), and scoring protocol (e.g., use of a criterion score or scoring method). The majority of assessments only allow for a forced-choice format (92.1%) with no scoring method (44.7%) or criterion score (36.8%). This structure can limit the counselor's ability to explore and make meaning of IPV assessment results.
7. *Psychometric information* includes the reliability and validity properties of an assessment, if available. Many tools lack reliability (68.4%) or validity (57.9%) evidence.

Along with these seven themes and related limitations, D. G. Hays and Emelianchik (2009) noted some global limitations of many of today's IPV assessments. These limitations

Table 14.1
Interpersonal Violence Assessments Used in Public and Mental Health Settings

Assessment Tool	Source
Abuse Assessment Screen	McFarlane et al. (1992)
American Medical Association Screening Questions	American Medical Association (1992)
Assessment of Immediate Safety Screening Questions	Family Violence Prevention Fund (2002)
Attitudes About Aggression in Dating Situations Scale	Slep et al. (2001)
Bartlett Regional Hospital Domestic Violence Assessment	Bartlett Regional Hospital (n.d.)
Childhood Maltreatment Interview Schedule– Short Form	Briere (1992)
Childhood Trauma Questionnaire	D. P. Bernstein et al. (1994)
Composite Abuse Scale	Hegarty et al. (2005)
Computer-Based IPV Questionnaire	K. V. Rhodes et al. (2002)
Conflict in Adolescent Dating Relationships Inventory	D. A. Wolfe et al. (2001)
Conflict Tactics Scale–Revised	Straus et al. (1996)
Danger Assessment Instrument	J. C. Campbell et al. (2009)
Dating Violence Questionnaire	Prospero (2006)
Domestic Violence Inventory	Behavior Data Systems (n.d.)
Domestic Violence Screening for Pediatric Settings	Siegel et al. (1999)
Domestic Violence Screening/Documentation Form	Family Violence Prevention Fund (1996)
Emergency Department Domestic Violence Screening Questions	Morrison et al. (2000)
HITS (Hurts, Insults, Threatens, and Screams)	Sherin et al. (1998)
Index of Spouse Abuse	Hudson & McIntosh (1981)
Intimate Partner Violence Strategy Index	Goodman et al. (2003)
Justification of Jealous and Coercive Tactics Scale	Slep et al. (2001)
Lesbian Partner Abuse Scale	McClennen et al. (2002)
Measure of Wife Abuse	Rodenburg & Fantuzzo (1993)
Minnesota Tool	McCollum (2007)
Ongoing Abuse Screen	S. J. Weiss et al. (2003)
Ongoing Violence Assessment Tool	S. J. Weiss et al. (2003)
Partner Violence Screen	Feldhaus et al. (1997)
Propensity for Abusiveness Scale	Clift et al. (2005)
RADAR[a]	Jaeger (2004)
SAVE[b]	L. Stevens (2003)
Severity of Violence Against Women Scale	Marshall (1992)
Sexual and Physical Abuse History Questionnaire	Leserman et al. (1995)
Sexual Experiences Survey	Koss & Oros (1982)
Sexual Relationship Power Scale	Pulerwitz et al. (2000)
Suggested Screening Questions	Family Violence Prevention Fund (2002)
Teen Screen for Dating Violence	Emelianchik-Key & Hays (2017)
Texas Rape Scale	Young & Thiessen (1992)
Timeline Follow-Back Spousal Violence Interview	Fals-Stewart et al. (2003)
Universal Violence Prevention Screening Protocol	Dutton et al. (1996)
Universal Violence Prevention Screening Protocol– Adapted	Heron et al. (2003)
Victimization Assessment Tool	Hoff & Rosenbaum (1994)
Violence Initiative Screening Questions	Webster et al. (1998)
Woman Abuse Screening Tool	J. B. Brown et al. (2000)
Women's Experience With Battering Scale	Smith et al. (1995)
Work/School Abuse Scale	Riger et al. (2001)

Note. IPV = intimate partner violence.
[a]R = routinely screen female patients, A = ask direct questions, D = document your findings, A = assess patient safety, R = respond, review options, and refer. [b]S = screening, A = asking, V = validating, E = evaluation.

include the following: IPV assessments may not provide equal attention to all IPV forms within an assessment itself; there is a lack of attention to degree of severity of abuse; they do not generally acknowledge frequency of abuse; tools do not adequately screen for IPV; there are problems with item formats, such as vague responses or double-barreled questions; and assessments contain cultural bias. Without careful attention, counselors may mistakenly equate scores for individuals who either have experienced different types, levels of severity, and frequency of IPV or have interpreted item content differently because of cultural issues or the assessment's structure. To help minimize some of the limitations of IPV assessments, counselors may want to engage in strategies listed in the following Tip Sheet (D. G. Hays & Emelianchik, 2009, p. 151).

Tip Sheet
Effective IPV Assessment Practices

✓ Prior to any assessment, seek individual-specific definitions of IPV, which will allow you to better interpret any assessment results.

✓ Use a variety of assessment tools, including paper-and-pencil tests, interviews with individuals and their support systems, and any records or documents you may access.

✓ Assess IPV beyond individuals' current relationships.

✓ Review all forms of abuse and provide specific, concrete examples for individuals to ensure their understanding that a specific act is an example of IPV.

✓ Ask about IPV offender acts to accurately gauge risk level.

✓ Offer a comprehensive list of resources regardless of whether individuals request them.

✓ For tools that offer no criterion score or scoring directions in general, collaborate with individuals to determine what could indicate IPV for that tool.

✓ Offer IPV assessments to individuals in multiple settings, particularly for those clients who do not have accessible resources.

✓ Evaluate any IPV assessment thoroughly before using a tool in practice. This evaluation involves looking at both the content and process of appraisal.

✓ Focus on time frame systematically. Evaluate individuals' IPV experiences for any time period as well as within the past 12 months, 6 months, 1 month, and 1 week.

✓ Discuss any IPV across every relationship and look for patterns.

✓ Appraise family violence: witnessing IPV in childhood, experiencing child abuse, undergoing violence in adolescent and college dating relationships, and experiencing IPV in current family systems.

✓ Be sure to ask about available support systems that IPV survivors have.

✓ Engage in assessment practices that offer multiple item formats.

✓ Ensure that assessment tools are culturally appropriate and that specific characteristics about a tool do not differentially affect certain groups.

✓ Combine effective assessment practices with preventive measures, such as psychoeducational and other screenings.

Activity 14.1
Selecting an IPV Assessment

Select an IPV assessment from the list in Table 14.1 and investigate its characteristics. Discuss the following in small groups:

- the tool's purpose and structure,
- item content,
- limitations, and
- its use with counseling various populations.

Assessment of Child Abuse

In addition to domestic violence associated with those in intimate partner relationships, counselors are likely to encounter clients who may be experiencing child abuse. Although definitions and categories of child abuse vary by state, following are some common characteristics and categories. **Physical abuse** refers to intentional infliction of physical injury, such as bruises, broken bones, head injuries, burns, and disfigurement. **Sexual abuse** includes exposing or involving children in age-inappropriate sexual content or behaviors such as fondling, intercourse, or pornography. **Psychological abuse** refers to verbal attacks and threats, and **neglect** includes engaging in acts or omissions that deprive a child of basic medical, educational, mental health, and other needs.

Child abuse has immediate and long-term effects on children, and C. B. Horton and Cruise (1997) noted the following immediate affective, behavioral, and cognitive consequences of which counselors should be aware: internalizing symptoms, such as low self-esteem, anger, hypervigilance, fear, depression, or withdrawal; externalizing symptoms, such as aggression toward siblings and peers as well as self-injurious behaviors; cognitive distortions, such as negative self-perceptions and excessive perceptions of the world as dangerous; and preoccupation with sexuality or sexual behavior and knowledge that are inconsistent with the child's age, which could indicate child sexual abuse. Long-term effects that occur in adulthood—which may be seen both in children who do and who do not display immediate effects—may include depression, suicidal ideation, generalized anxiety, self-destructive behaviors (e.g., eating disorders, substance abuse, sexual impulsivity), difficult interpersonal behaviors, dissociation from relationships or overwhelming situations, antisocial behaviors and aggression, and mental health disorders such as posttraumatic stress disorder, acute stress disorder, or dissociative disorders (C. B. Horton & Cruise, 1997). Many of these long-term effects of child abuse are similar to symptoms found in IPV cases, which is not surprising given that there is often an intergenerational link between child abuse and IPV (D. G. Hays, Green, Orr, & Flowers, 2007).

The U.S. Department of Health and Human Services (USDHHS) published a report on child maltreatment and noted the following data in 2010 for 45 reporting states with a population of 75 million children (USDHHS, 2011):

- There were 3.3 million referrals involving maltreatment of 5.9 million children, with over 2.6 million of these cases actually screened.
- Approximately 436,000 (22%) of referrals screened indicated substantiated reports of child abuse.
- With respect to reporting sources, 32.5% of the 2010 reports came from those working with children in clinical and educational settings.
- For unique cases (i.e., those with a singular type of abuse), 78% of the cases related to neglect, 17.6% to physical abuse, and 9.2% to sexual abuse.
- The child fatality rate was 2.07 deaths per 100,000 children; nearly 80% of these involved children under age 4.
- Victimization rates by child's gender were approximately equal (48.5% male, 51.2% female).
- Victimization rates by child's race/ethnicity for three groups reported were 44.8% White, 21.9% African American, and 21.4% Latino; however, African American, Native American, and multiracial populations had highest rates per 1,000 children (14.6%, 11.0%, and 12.7%, respectively).
- The majority of abusers were parents (81.2%, with 84.2% of these involving biological parents); for unique cases (i.e., those involving abuse from one gender), 53.6% of perpetrators were female and 45.2% were male.

Although these statistics are alarming, many child abuse cases go unreported. It is therefore important for counselors to properly assess child abuse and refer as appropriate.

C. B. Horton and Cruise (1997) provided guidelines for counselors for assessing child maltreatment among children and adult survivors. First, counselors are to be aware of the current abuse literature. This requirement includes being aware of common symptoms as well as legal and ethical considerations. Second, counselors should assess mediating factors in addition to common symptoms to intentionally assess abuse as an *experience* versus a *diagnosis*. These mediating factors include abuse factors such as age of onset, duration and intensity, and frequency; cognitive factors such as guilt and feelings of powerlessness; and other factors such as duration that abuse remained a secret, to whom the child or adult survivor disclosed the abuse, ongoing support, preabuse relationships with significant others and parents, and resiliency. The third guideline refers to taking an ecological approach to assessment, involving significant others in the individual's life as appropriate; this includes assessment of functioning and relationships before and after the abuse. Fourth, counselors should carefully select assessments with sound psychometric properties as relevant. Counselors are to use multiple assessment tools. Table 14.2 provides select child abuse assessment tools that counselors may want to use throughout the assessment process; some of these measures relate directly to assessing abuse whereas others refer to evaluating specific symptomatology (e.g., anxiety, depression). Finally, counselors should treat assessment as an ongoing process, including identifying initially symptoms and mediating factors, developing a diagnosis or treatment plan, and involving assessment as part of the termination process.

Genograms

A **genogram** is a map that provides a graphic representation of a family structure and is usually associated with Bowen's family system theory. A genogram has the potential to demonstrate origins of presenting problems, as it is assumed that family patterns tend to repeat themselves (Goldenberg & Goldenberg, 2013; McGoldrick, Gerson, & Petry,

Table 14.2
Child Abuse Assessment Tools

Assessment Tool	Source
Beck Depression Inventory–II	Beck et al. (2003)
Child Behavior Checklist	Achenbach & Edelbrock (1983)
Child Dissociative Checklist	Putnam et al. (1993)
Child Sexual Behavior Checklist	T. C. Johnson (1990)
Child Sexual Behavior Inventory	Friedrich (1997)
Childhood PTSD Interview	Fletcher (1991a)
Children's Depression Inventory	Kovacs (2003)
Children's Impact of Traumatic Events Scale	V. V. Wolfe et al. (1991)
Dissociative Experiences Survey	E. M. Bernstein & Putnam (1986)
Parent Report of Child's Reaction to Stress	Fletcher (1991b)
Revised Children's Manifest Anxiety Scale, 2nd edition	C. R. Reynolds & Richmond (2008)
Teacher Report Form	Achenbach & Edelbrock (1983)
Trauma Assessment Interview	Hindman (1989)
Trauma Symptom Checklist for Children	Briere (1996)
Trauma Symptom Inventory	Briere (1995)
When Bad Things Happen	Fletcher (1992)
Youth Self Report	Achenbach & Edelbrock (1983)
Projective Tests: storytelling cards, pictures, and sentence completion tasks	Various

Note. Information is from Horton and Cruise (1997). PTSD = posttraumatic stress disorder.

2008). This visual tool is useful in counseling interventions to understand an individual, couple, or family in relation to a broader family structure and its sociocultural context. As counselors develop a genogram with clients, they can generate hypotheses about family functioning for further evaluation (Petry & McGoldrick, 2005).

A genogram involves the collection of demographic information for approximately three generations of a family and organizes the information into a kind of family tree. Family should be broadly defined to include members that have played a major role in family life for a client. Members might include those of a nuclear family, extended family, or other kinship not necessarily related by blood or traditional marriage definitions.

The genogram should contain the names, ages, and gender of all family members, along with information about major events such as births, deaths, marriages and partnerships, divorces, adoptions, and conflicts. As the information is collected, it allows family relationship problems to be seen in the context of the developmental cycle for the whole family in addition to the situation of the individual who is presenting the problem. By examining the relational structure—including family composition, sibling constellations, and unusual family configurations—the counselor can hypothesize certain roles or relationships that can then be checked by eliciting further information. Repetitive patterns of functioning and relationships often occur across generations, and by recognizing these patterns, counselors can help family members to alter them.

How are data collected for the genogram? McGoldrick et al. (2008) used the metaphor of casting a net wider and wider to ascertain basic information, patterns, and indicators of family dysfunction: Gather data ranging from the presenting problem to the larger context of the problem, from the immediate household to the extended family and social systems, from the present family situation and events to historical occurrences, and from basic facts about the family to more sensitive information (e.g., abuse, mental illness) and hypothesized family patterns. In drawing a genogram, some counselors obtain the basic information to structure the genogram and then go back and question each individual about it and their relationships with other family members, both within and across generations. Others obtain this information as each individual is placed on the genogram. Some counselors obtain only a basic genogram illustrating the general family structure; others, through the use of figures, abbreviations, and symbols, develop a genogram that contains a great deal of organized data, including educational and occupational patterns, about the generations of a family system (McGoldrick, Gerson, & Shellenberger, 1999). In the case of a multihome stepfamily, the genogram can show (on a very large sheet of paper) all the members who are genetically, emotionally, and legally connected within three or more generations.

Some of the common symbols used to denote family structure and interaction patterns are provided in Figure 14.1. A sample basic genogram for the couple Joseph and Paula is shown in Figure 14.2. Software is available to assist you in developing genograms (see "Resources for Further Learning" at the end of the chapter).

The construction of a genogram is a cooperative task between the counselor and the client. Clients readily become interested and involved in the construction of a genogram; they enjoy the process and usually reveal much significant information about various relatives and their relationships with them. Although genograms seem deceptively simple, the construction of one provides much insight into both the family constellation and the individual's interpersonal relationships within the family system. Even from reticent clients, both the quantity and the emotional depth of the data produced are often superior to the data obtained through the typical interview process and are more easily obtained as well. The genogram can easily be adapted for counseling clients from diverse backgrounds on a variety of issues. The Tip Sheet provides guidelines for constructing and interpreting genograms.

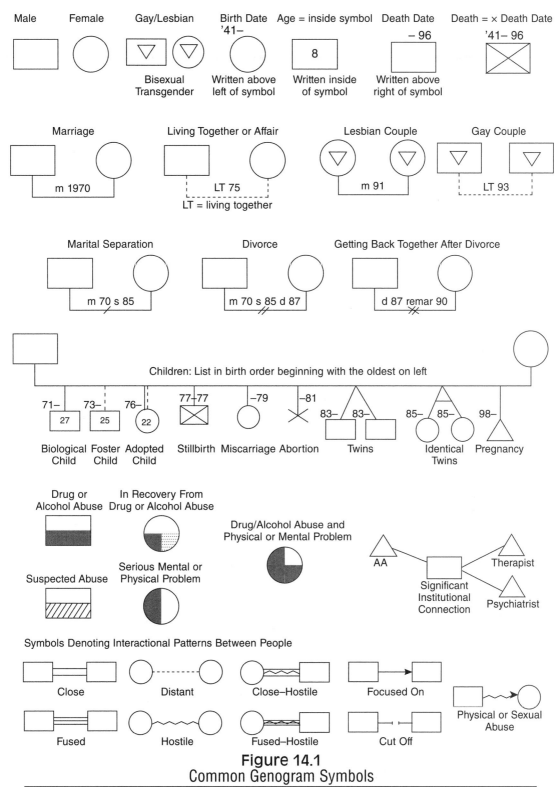

Figure 14.1
Common Genogram Symbols

Note. From "Genograms in Assessment and Therapy" (p. 368), by S. S. Petry and M. McGoldrick, *Psychologists' Desk Reference*, second edition, by G. P. Koocher, J. C. Norcross, & S. S. Hill, III (Eds.), 2005, New York, NY: Oxford University Press. Reprinted with permission of Oxford University Press, Inc.

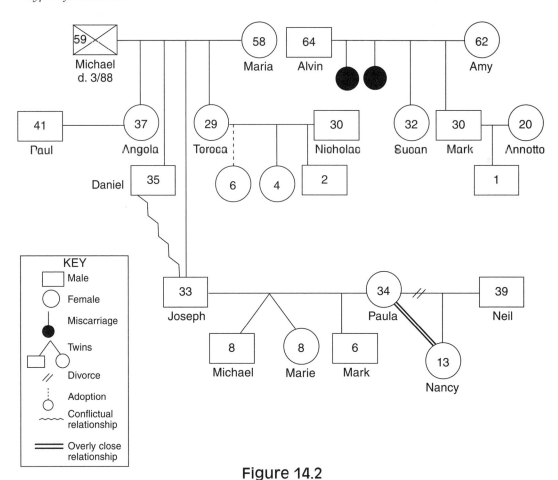

Figure 14.2
Genogram of Joseph and Paula

Tip Sheet
Genograms

✓ Use a broad definition of family when constructing a genogram to assess more comprehensively the diverse compositions of families today.

✓ Begin constructing the genogram in the first session and revise as appropriate.

✓ Minimize client resistance to the genogram development process. Collaborate with clients throughout the counseling relationship and remind them of the purpose of specific questions as you collect data (i.e., to better understand the individual and how contextual information might contribute to that understanding).

✓ Consider collecting all data first before developing the genogram to discern what information is most salient to include in the display. You will only be able to include major categories of current and historical information.

✓ Gather information from the index person (client) about a presenting problem and integrate basic family information and what impact the problem has on the current household. Cast a wider net to collect information on recent family changes and events, interaction patterns, extended family and kinship networks, and sociocultural context.

✓ Collect data from each side of the family separately. Ask about age, gender, ethnicity, migration patterns, occupation, treatment history, cultural traditions toward problems, current cultural values, individual functioning around issues of substance abuse, mental and physical health, and employment, to name a few. As you collect data, review for discrepancies or ways that events, roles, and dynamics mask or prevent family problems.

✓ Once the genogram is completed, look for family reactions to changes and untimely events. Also, scan data for repeated symptoms, relationships or functioning patterns across generations, and coincidences of dates (e.g., how one problem/event relates to another problem/event by date).

✓ Although popular, the technique has been subjected to only a few studies of reliability, and there is little validity evidence. Counselors should therefore consider such interpretations as only hypotheses and use caution in drawing conclusions from genograms without other confirming evidence.

Additional Interpersonal Assessment Inventories

Contemporary theories of interpersonal functioning assert that an individual's behavior can be understood only in relation to transactions with others and not for the individual in isolation. In the generally accepted model of interpersonal theory, each interaction represents a combination of two basic dimensions of interpersonal behavior: control (dominance vs. submission) and affiliation (friendliness vs. hostility; VanDenberg, Schmidt, & Kiesler, 1992). In any interaction (including client and counselor), individuals continually negotiate these two relationship issues: how friendly or hostile they will be and how much in control they will be in their relationship. This approach uses a circular rather than a linear model; behavior is viewed not solely by situational factors or psychic motivation but instead within a group of two or more people exerting mutual influence. These two dimensions are incorporated into a model called the **interpersonal circle**, or circumplex. It is organized around the horizontal and vertical axes representing affiliation and control (Tracey & Schneider, 1995).

Among the inventories designed to assess interpersonal interactions are the **Checklist of Interpersonal Transactions** (CLOIT), a 96-item interpersonal behavior inventory, and the **Checklist of Psychotherapy Transactions**, a parallel version of the CLOIT for rating clients and counselors. Both of these measures were developed by Kiesler (1987). Other promising measures of interpersonal functioning include the **Interpersonal Compass** (Fico & Hogan, 2000) and the **Impact Message Inventory** (Kiesler, Schmidt, & Wagner, 1997).

The **Interpersonal Adjective Scales** (IAS), a self-report instrument that assesses the two primary interpersonal dimensions of dominance and nurturance, builds on experience gained with previously developed interpersonal assessment inventories (Wiggins, 1993). The IAS yields scores on eight interpersonal variables that are ordered along the two primary axes of the interpersonal circumplex. It is designed to provide information about how an individual typically behaves in different interpersonal situations. The instrument consists of 64 adjectives that describe interpersonal interactions; respondents use an 8-point Likert scale to rate how accurately each word describes them as individuals. Responses yield octant scores, which are then plotted on the circumplex. The rationale for the circumplex is that personality structure is not made up of independent dimensions but a blending of dimensions (R. S. Adams & Tracey, 2004). The titles of the eight interpersonal octants are shown on the circumplex profile in Figure 14.3. Based on scores shown in this example, this individual would be described as coldhearted, aloof, introverted, unassured, and submissive.

In interpreting the results of the circumplex profile, counselors should use all of the information provided on the profile and not focus solely on the highest segment score or scores. By paying attention to only one or two octants, the counselor may miss considerable information regarding the client's interpersonal behavior, and hence the advantage of the circumplex model is lost (Pincus & Gurtman, 2003). Because interpersonal transactions include those between the client and counselor, the counselor's perception of client

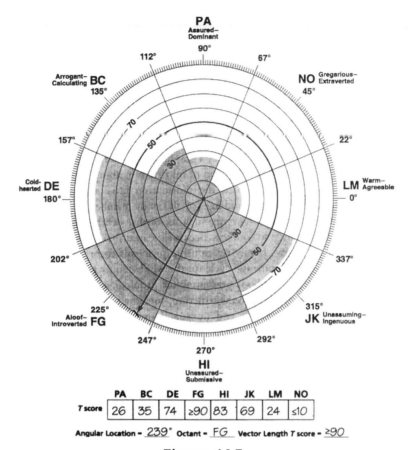

Figure 14.3

Interpersonal Adjective Scales Profile of Extreme Depression in a Former Bank Manager

interactions should be compared with those of the client's self-report represented by the circumplex profile. Counselors can examine the components of a client's interpersonal functioning and identify topics that will be more or less anxiety provoking to a client. Many client difficulties can be viewed as maladaptive transactional patterns. Clients can be helped to understand the predominantly automatic and unaware manner in which they communicate to others through their verbal and nonverbal behavior. Individuals often use a narrow range of interpersonal responses that may not be appropriate to the situation.

The **Thomas–Kilman Conflict Mode Instrument** is the inventory most often used in situations calling for conflict resolution (Thomas & Kilman, 1974). Individuals respond to 30 pairs of forced-choice statements to determine their preferred style or mode of handling conflict: competing, avoiding, compromising, collaborating, or accommodating. The inventory is quick and easy to take, score, and graph. Reliability indices, both internal consistency and test–retest, range from only .4 to .7 (R. Johnson, 1989). According to a study that compared MBTI types with conflict resolution styles, thinking types preferred collaboration, and introverts preferred conflict avoidance (A. K. Johnson, 1997). Results can lead to a discussion about how conflict affects personal and group relations and can suggest a practical approach to conflict resolution.

Chapter Summary

Counselors can expect to assess couples and families as they conceptualize presenting and underlying issues and develop and implement treatment goals. This chapter included a review of ten of the most frequently cited relationship inventories used with couples and families: MBTI, TJTA, MSI-R, DSFI, PREPARE and ENRICH, CPCI, FES, FAM-III, Sternberg's Love Scales, and the Dyadic Adjustment Scale. Although many of these inventories have limited psychometric data available, they still can be useful in clinical settings. However, counselors are to be cautious when administering and interpreting results with diverse or nontraditional couples and families.

Counselors are likely to encounter IPV among some couples with whom they work. This chapter provided a comprehensive list of major IPV assessments and outlined key strategies to assess for IPV with all clients, especially women. These strategies reference both informal and formal assessment procedures. Another counseling concern related to couples and families is child abuse, and assessment of its various forms is an ethical mandate for counselors. The chapter outlined immediate and long-term effects of child abuse to illustrate areas for assessment; these effects relate to affective, behavioral, and cognitive effects. Several assessments used to examine the existence of symptoms were presented in the chapter.

The last two sections of the chapter pertained to genograms and other interpersonal assessments. Through the cooperative construction of a multigenerational graphic family structure—the genogram—insight into family constellations and interpersonal relationships within the family can be revealed to both the counselor and the client. The chapter displayed common genogram symbols as well as a sample genogram. Finally, interpersonal assessment instruments usually evaluate an individual's interaction with others in terms of two dimensions: control (dominance vs. submission) and affiliation (friendliness vs. hostility).

Review Questions

1. What are some of the common elements of the nine relationship inventories included in this chapter?
2. What are the major themes identified in IPV assessments? What are their limitations?
3. What strategies can counselors use to effectively assess for IPV?
4. What are some of the specific immediate and long-term effects of child abuse counselors should assess for in children and adult survivors of child abuse?
5. How are genograms used in counseling?

Resources for Further Learning

Publications

McGoldrick, M., Gerson, R., & Petry, S. S. (2008). *Genograms: Assessment and intervention* (3rd ed.). New York, NY: Norton.

Thomlison, B. (2015). *Family assessment handbook: An introductory practice guide to family assessment* (4th ed.). Boston, MA: Cengage.

Web Resources

The following are links to popular genogram software:
Genogram Analytics 6.0
   http://www.genogramanalytics.com
Genogram-Maker Millennium Version 3.0
   http://www.genogram.org
GenoPro 2016
   http://www.genopro.com
Relativity
   http://www.interpersonaluniverse.net
SmartDraw
   http://www.smartdraw.com/specials/genogram.htm

Section V

The Assessment Report and Future Trends

Chapter 15

Communication of Assessment Results

Counselors are constantly required to communicate assessment results both to clients and to others, including parents, agencies, and other professionals. This chapter provides a description of the final phase of the assessment process—communication of findings—and outlines key strategies for engaging in this phase with clients and others. Five steps for communicating results in an assessment interview are also outlined. The chapter concludes with a description of assessment report components.

Test Your Knowledge

Respond to the following items by selecting T for "True" or F for "False":

❑ T ❑ F 1. Clients are likely to remember to use findings when they are allowed to actively participate in the interpretation of findings.

❑ T ❑ F 2. It is common during the assessment interview to discuss extensively the psychometric properties of assessments using specific statistical terminology.

❑ T ❑ F 3. Counselors are to wait until the end of the assessment interview to gauge clients' reactions so as not to disturb the flow of an interview.

❑ T ❑ F 4. A case conference is typically used when assessment data need to be shared with others, such as school personnel and parents.

❑ T ❑ F 5. The assessment report is a formalized method for communicating assessment results with the client and others.

Communication of Findings

Communication of findings can be considered the last phase of the assessment process, although the assessment process can certainly cycle if additional assessment data are needed (see Figure 2.1 in Chapter 2). As you may recall, Chapter 2 provided strategies for effective assessment selection, administration, and scoring, and Chapter 6 highlighted test interpretation considerations. This chapter describes how to communicate or report assessment results, and it will be important in this last phase for you to review guidelines from previous chapters along with those presented in this one. In addition to reviewing earlier phases of the assessment process, you will also want to revisit the ethical standards and guidelines discussed in Chapter 3, which often include sections on reporting assessment results.

Communicating assessment results is a balance of art and science: Counselors provide comprehensive information to clients about specific assessments and their implications while fostering a therapeutic relationship so that clients and others are engaged in the assessment process and ultimately apply results in a meaningful way. Assessments are often used to diagnose and predict; communication must lead to the desired understanding and results. It must be remembered that a huge number of factors are involved in producing assessment data. These factors include clients' inherited characteristics; their educational, cultural, family, and other experiences; their experiences with other assessments, particularly psychological tests; their motivation; their test anxiety; the physical and psychological conditions under which they took the test; and the lack of consistency in the assessment itself.

As mentioned in Chapter 2, communication of assessment results can occur both during and after test interpretation. A golden rule is that the more counselors communicate about findings throughout the assessment process itself, the more likely clients will remember the assessment results and apply them to treatment. In preparing for the assessment communication process, counselors are to adhere to the general guidelines presented in the following Tip Sheet.

Tip Sheet
Communicating Assessment Results

✓ Use only tests that you have personally scored and interpreted for yourself. Whenever possible, self-administer the assessment to maximize familiarity. Know the reasons a particular test was administered, what was expected from its interpretation, and the validity of the test for the purpose for which it was used.

✓ Remember that an assessment procedure is generally an anxiety-producing experience for most people and usually involves a discussion of personal information; thus, clients may feel vulnerable or exposed in the process.

✓ Know and understand the test manual as this information is imperative for communicating assessment data to clients. By using the information from the manual, the counselor can relate the validity and other psychometric properties of the assessment to the purpose for which the test was used. The manual is also likely to contain information regarding the limits to which the test can be used and suggestions for interpreting the results.

✓ Review the purposes for which the client took the assessment and its strengths and limitations. It is also helpful to go over with the client the questions that the client wanted answered by means of the assessment process.

✓ Explain the procedure by which the assessment is scored or evaluated and explain percentile ranks or standard scores if they are to be included in the interpretation.

✓ Where possible, present results in terms of probabilities, which can be understood by clients in the same way as a weather report, rather than certainties or specific predictions. Keep in mind standard errors of measurement and the intervals they represent as applicable.

✓ Emphasize during the process that a client's understanding is most important. Where appropriate, encourage clients to make their own interpretations. It is the client's understanding of the results, not the counselor's, that is ultimately important, because it is the client who will use, misuse, or ignore the results.

✓ Fully integrate assessment data in relation to all other available information about the client.

✓ Ensure that the client understands the interpretation of the test information and encourage him or her to express reactions to the information. Remember that clients prefer an interactive interpretation over one that is simply delivered.

✓ Adjust the pace of interpretations to clients' ability and understanding. Have clients summarize often to make sure the results are being understood. If necessary, additional information or alternative methods of interpretation can be used.

✓ Examine any relevant information or background characteristics, such as sex or disabilities, along with any apparent discrepancies or inconsistencies that appear.

✓ Discuss both strengths and opportunities revealed by the assessment results.

✓ Adjust interactional style to match eye contact, use of personal space, and rate of speech to client's cultural norms.

✓ Listen attentively to what the client says and be alert for unexpressed or nonverbal emotional reactions, especially when the test results are not what are expected or desired.

The Assessment Interpretation Interview

The assessment interview—whether formal or informal, and whether it occurs in a single counseling session or is ongoing as part of the counseling process—is the forum in which counselors and clients review assessment data in the context of other known information and plan interventions. G. A. Miller (1982), in a seminal article on interpreting test results with clients, identified five steps of the assessment communication process that are useful for the assessment interview. Each is highlighted below, with specific strategies you may find useful. Remember, these steps and related strategies can relate to any type of assessment, whether it might include more formal measures, such as standardized tests or protocols, or more informal, qualitative assessments, such as projective techniques or card sorts. Case Example 15.1 demonstrates briefly what an interview may look like for a counselor educator communicating test results to a student from a statistics test given on measurement concepts and raw score transformation.

Check in With the Client

The first step involves discussing with the client how he or she felt on the day the assessment was administered as well as how the client perceived the assessment itself (G. A. Miller, 1982). Counselors can ask about comfort, anxiety, or apprehensiveness regarding the assessment process in general and feelings associated with specific assessments. This step may yield information about the client's attitudes toward the particular assessments and provide information about the usefulness of some of the results. As you solicit the client's attitudes and feelings, stress to the client that he or she can ask questions and make comments; stress that you, as a counselor, are particularly interested in the reactions and thoughts regarding the interpretation.

Provide Structure for the Interpretation

The second step refers to the counselor repeating the purpose of the assessment process and reviewing the manner in which scores will be presented (G. A. Miller, 1982). It is important to present the purpose of a test in useful and understandable terms, avoiding psychological jargon. Do not begin discussing the results of any assessment without reminding the client which assessment is being discussed and for what purpose. Refresh his or her memory about it by saying, for example, "Remember the test where you checked whether the two sets of names and numbers were exactly the same or were different? That was a test designed to measure clerical aptitude or ability." If a copy of the assessment itself is available, it would probably help to show the client.

Review the Results

The third step includes the counselor and client examining the actual assessment, with the counselor presenting the scores or other assessment data to the client (G. A. Miller, 1982).

Where possible, use a graphic representation of the results in addition to a verbal explanation. Remember to turn test profiles so that a client can read them directly. If anyone is going to have to read the profile upside down, it should be counselors, who are familiar with profile sheets, rather than clients. It is probably better to position chairs so that you and your client can go over the results together from similar angles. Complicated profile sheets should be grouped and summarized; in this way, a number of scores can be more easily assimilated by the client. Show confidence in the client's ability to understand and make use of the information; however, do not assume that most clients have the ability to easily integrate information from several complex sources.

The results should be explained simply, without the use of elaborate statistics. Whenever possible, use the types of norms that are most relevant to clients. When such norms are not directly appropriate, present this information to clients and ensure the results make it clear.

Be prepared with a brief, clear description of what the results mean and what the results do not mean. For example, "These are some of the activities you indicated you liked, and these are some that you said you did not like. Your interests seem to be more like those of people in social service fields and unlike those of most people in mechanical and technical occupations." Be sure to clarify the differences between interests and aptitudes or between abilities and personality characteristics.

Avoid overidentifying with the assessment results. Discuss a client's rejection of low test scores. The primary concern is what the results mean to the client, not what they mean to the counselor. Low performance scores should be expressed honestly but with perspective and in regard to the presenting question. They should not be ignored or attributed to inadequate measures or chance.

Integrate the Results

The fourth step involves integrating the assessment results with other client information. Emphasize the importance of adding the assessment data to other information that the client has (G. A. Miller, 1982). For example, scholastic aptitude scores should be related to school grades. It should be remembered that the usual purpose of a scholastic aptitude test is to predict academic course grades. When such grades are available, emphasis should be placed on actual grades rather than on test results that merely predict those grades.

A client may not readily apply specific assessment findings to other information he or she has about his or her abilities, attitudes, mental health symptoms, career interests and values, and so on. Process questions might include the following: How does this information relate to other information you have about yourself? Do the results seem to correspond well to other sources of evidence? In what ways might other pieces of information be more useful?

Discuss the test results in the context of other information, particularly relating the results to past, present, and future behavior. Relate past information and current results to current decisions and to future long-range plans rather than treating each of these subjects separately.

Plan for the Future

The final step is planning with the client how assessment results will be applied (G. A. Miller, 1982). Emphasize the usefulness of the findings for the client's decision making rather than for the information it provides to the counselor. For example, in reviewing achievement assessment findings, you might say the following: "With this set of scores, you can see how you compare with other college-bound students regarding your ability to learn academic subject matter" rather than "These results confirm my belief that you have the ability to do well in most colleges." Encourage clients to make their own plans rather than simply agreeing with the counselor's suggestions.

Even though the immediate goal may be to help clients to make a particular decision, clients also gain the opportunity to understand themselves better. Ultimately, the self-knowledge acquired in counseling and assessment will enable individuals to pursue more effective and satisfying lives and to make wiser and more realistic plans.

Toward the end of the interview, have the client summarize the results of the entire interview rather than attempting to do this for them. Allow enough time to discuss this summarization and to discuss discrepancies or misunderstandings. Attempt to end on a positive note, even if some portions of the interview yielded information that the client was not happy to receive. If clients received discouraging information about educational, vocational, or other types of plans, try to broaden the scope of alternatives that might be considered. Emphasis should be placed not only on narrowing the focus of future plans but also on broadening them.

Case Example 15.1

Dr. Parks and Kenneth

Dr. Parks, a counselor educator teaching an assessment course to master's-level trainees, discusses with a student, Kenneth, a recent test on basic measurement concepts and raw score transformation procedures. To begin, she reminds Kenneth that he took the test last Tuesday and asks him how he was feeling that day of the exam. In addition, she asks how he felt about the test itself and whether there were any environmental or situational factors that influenced his performance on the exam. She also checks in to see what Kenneth remembered about the structure and format of the exam (Step 1).

Then, Dr. Parks reviews the purpose of the exam, which was to assess content knowledge specific to measurement principles, such as levels of measurement, measures of central tendency and variability, how to organize and display raw scores within data distributions, and how to convert raw scores into derived scores. She asks Kenneth to reflect on the degree to which he perceived the exam met that purpose. She then explains how the exam score will be presented and includes scoring procedures. That is, she describes the exam as representing 20% of the final course grade and containing 80 items. Dr. Parks further outlines how many items represent various formats (e.g., multiple choice, true/false, short answer, matching) and how these were weighted (Step 2).

Dr. Parks reviews the exam itself, using Kenneth's actual exam as a visual aid during this process. Kenneth answered 75 of the 80 items correctly, with his score representing 18.75% of a possible 20%. The following descriptive statistics were presented as part of the score review:

Mean:	17.92
Median:	18.43
Mode:	16.00
Standard deviation:	1.36
Skewness:	−0.55
Kurtosis:	1.59
Percentiles:	16.22 (25th), 18.43 (50th), and 19.24 (75th)

Dr. Parks avoids statistical jargon as she explains to Kenneth how his raw score compares with the data distributions (i.e., scores from his classmates).

She highlights that his score was slightly above the average, particularly when extremely high and low scores were not considered. Furthermore, she notes that his and his classmates' scores were slightly centered around the arithmetic average, the mean—creating a more peaked distribution—whereas the overall score distribution was slightly below the middlemost score—creating a negatively skewed picture. She then reviews that 25% of his classmates received a 16.22 or lower, 50% received a 18.43% or lower, and 75% received a 19.24 or lower. After her explanation, Dr. Parks asks Kenneth to summarize how his score relates to the overall score distribution. She reviews the specific items he answered incorrectly and reviews material as appropriate. Finally, she asks Kenneth how he feels about the results and what those results mean to him (Step 3).

Dr. Parks then integrates the test results with other sources of evidence related to Kenneth's knowledge of measurement concepts and raw score transformation specifically, as well as general assessment knowledge. As part of this comparative process, Dr. Parks has Kenneth reflect on his overall strengths and areas of growth (Step 4). As a final step, Dr. Parks assists Kenneth with planning how he would increase his knowledge related to incorrect items as well as expand his understanding of information in which he had excelled. They discuss ways that he could continue to do well in the course as well as ways he could apply the learning to counseling settings (Step 5).

• • •

Activity 15.1
Assessment Interview Practice

Get into pairs and have one participant administer a brief assessment tool featured in this text to the other member of the pair. This assessment might be a mental health screening tool, a substance abuse assessment, a personality test, or a career measure, to name a few. It is helpful to select something that is easy to score or interpret for the purposes of the activity. This individual should conduct an interview with the individual who was administered the assessment. Repeat the above process with reversed roles in order to allow both individuals a chance both to administer the measure and to experience the assessment interview. Reflect on the following:

- What are your reactions to each of G. A. Miller's (1982) steps?
- What strengths do you notice about your ability to conduct the assessment interview?
- What are areas of growth for you?
- How did you attend to cultural and developmental considerations during the interview?
- What might you do differently in future interviews?

The Case Conference

In addition to the assessment interview with individual clients, counselors often meet with other professionals and people interested in a client's welfare to discuss assessment results and their implications for treatment. When beginning the case conference, counselors are to make certain that all present are introduced, because they may not all be familiar with each other's roles, particularly if family members and helping professionals or school personnel are in the meeting together.

Counselors are to structure the session by briefly outlining how they will proceed and the contributions each stakeholder will be making. Throughout the conversation, encourage feedback, discussion, and questions. It is important that you recognize and accept the fact that, as the possessor of assessment information, you may be perceived by others as "the enemy" or perhaps the messenger with the bad news. Point out that the main concern of all present is the welfare of the client and that all are trying to help the client and thus have a common goal.

Counselors are to begin by covering the history that has led up to the meeting and the context in which it is taking place. Summarize previous meetings or interviews as applicable. To be effective, you must be well informed on the issue that is being assessed, such as attention-deficit/hyperactivity disorder or schizophrenia, not just on the assessment itself.

As you present assessment data, draw useful nontest information from those present. For example, a teacher sees a child in relation to many other children, and parents know much about the child's leisure-time interests and nonschool activities. If the client is present, pay particular attention to him or her. It is easy for the others present to become involved in their conversations and ignore the client.

In presenting information to parents, many professionals recommend the "bad news sandwich" approach: First give some positive information, then convey any negative information, and finally end on a positive note. When the purpose of the conference is to convey a diagnosis of a child's disorder or disability, it is especially important also to focus on some of the child's abilities, not just his or her disabilities.

When finishing, summarize the assessment information and any conclusions that have been reached in the meeting. Encourage and allow time for final questions and discussion.

Recognize that receiving a diagnosis of a serious disorder can cause strong feelings of loss, guilt, or frustration and that additional sessions may be useful because you, as a counselor, can help those who are affected work through these issues.

The Assessment Report

Counselors often need to summarize assessment results in a written report. Because such reports are often the only product of the assessment process that others see and because they are likely to have significant consequences for the examinee, they must be carefully prepared to be meaningful, readable, and well organized (Groth-Marnat & Wright, 2016; Kvall, Choca, Groth-Marnat, & Davis, 2011). The impact of the freedom of information legislation (including the Health Insurance and Portability Act [HIPAA]; American Psychological Association, 2013) means that a written report is now more likely to eventually be read by the client or their parents. It should be written with this in mind and include both a client's strengths and weaknesses in language that is likely to facilitate the client's growth.

In writing a report, counselors must have some understanding of what is necessary to include and a conceptualization of the client or person about whom the report is being written. The focus of the report and the way it is to be used are the first considerations in determining its content, including the reasons for referral and whether the report will be primarily oriented toward an objective summary of assessment results or an overall description of the individual being examined. Occasionally, the report is to provide baseline information for evaluating progress after interventions have been implemented (Lichtenberger, Mather, Kaufman, & Kaufman, 2012). The purpose of the report should be clearly stated. Often, there is a large amount of information available, and the report writer must decide what information should be included and what should be excluded.

Counselors should first decide the principal ideas that should be communicated and what other types of information play an auxiliary role. One of the ways of emphasizing material is by the order in which it is presented, with the most important information first. Another way is through the adjectives and adverbs used in describing the person and his or her behavior. It can also be done through illustrations, using a vivid example to point out critical information. Another mode is through repetition. Obviously, repetition needs to be handled skillfully to avoid repeating the same material more often than necessary.

Repeating information in the summary or conclusion is another way of adding emphasis. The psychological test results themselves can often be used as a framework to describe the client—for example, the Big Five factors from the NEO Personality Inventory, the interpersonal circumplex from the Interpersonal Adjective Scales, or the Holland hexagon.

Problems that should be avoided include (a) poor organization, in which the results are not integrated as a whole; (b) use of psychological jargon that will not be understood; (c) use of terms that do not have clearly understood definitions; and (d) lack of integration between the test results and information based on other data, such as observations or the client's history. Under the Administrative Simplification section of HIPAA, counselors seeking insurance reimbursement for psychological testing must learn and report the proper Current Procedural Terminology codes that are used to uniformly document why clients were seen and what was done for them.

In writing reports of psychological and educational assessments, counselors should be aware of the implications of test scores. All of the factors that have contributed to the scores should be considered when reporting predictions and recommendations. Counselors know very well that Miller Analogies Test (MAT) or Graduate Record Examination (GRE) scores account for only a small fraction of the variance in predicting which students, for example, will become skillful counselors. Therefore, test results should always include a statement about the validity of the entire testing situation. Counselors should include in their report social, ethnic, racial, and cultural variables that may affect intelligence, achievement, or personality test scores. Counselors should interpret cross-cultural test scores with caution and, when necessary, include a disclaimer for limitations in the report.

Writing a report is often much easier if an overall case conceptualization is developed first. Reports often include the general theoretical framework that is followed by the counselor. When psychoanalytic theory is the primary theory followed by a counselor, a great deal of emphasis is often placed on early childhood experiences. Those who follow Rogerian theory probably pay particular attention to the person's self-concept. The Gestalt theorist looks specifically at current relationships, and the behavioral counselor will be interested in personal and environmental factors that reinforce particular behaviors. Counselors may not feel they have a particular theory of behavior, but in the case report, their general theory of personality often emerges because it influences what they perceive from the interviews and test results and, therefore, what they report.

In reporting results, it is a good idea to stay away from assessment jargon. It is also important to avoid the extremes of focusing either too much or too little on the test results themselves. It is possible to report extensive test results without relating them to the individual and the individual's situation and future plans and, thus, not offer much in the way of conclusions or practical suggestions. It is also possible to depart too much from the test results and downplay them, particularly if the test information does not come out as expected or if it is not likely to be seen in positive terms by the client.

Counselors should also remember that it is better to write a report immediately after counseling and testing rather than letting a considerable period of time go by. Counselors enjoy working with people much more than writing reports, so it is easy to put these aside. Timeliness becomes particularly important when a number of clients are seen each day. It is important to at least write down the information that will be needed to write a report, even if it is not possible to write the final report immediately. In writing a report, the counselor should say what needs to be said, making clear statements and clear recommendations. Conversely, where results must be considered inconclusive, this also needs to be reported and not ignored.

Components of an Assessment Report

Although the assessment report components often vary by clinical setting, this section of the chapter includes some basic components of an assessment report. Reports can be primarily geared toward test data or can be broad to include several aspects of client history and presenting issues. Components of a more comprehensive report are included in this section for Elise (client). In addition to specific examples of each component, Appendix B offers a sample assessment report.

Brief Description of Client

This initial section of the report includes basic demographic information about the client, including name, age or date of birth, gender, and race/ethnicity, to name a few. Depending on the report format, it could also potentially include contact information, occupation, or year in school as applicable. Also included is information about the counselor who performed the assessment and wrote the report and perhaps dates of the evaluation and/or report.

Demographic Information

Client Name:	Elise Johnson
Gender:	Female
Age:	34 years
Race/Ethnicity:	White, non-Hispanic
Evaluation Date:	9/24/17
Report Date:	9/30/17
Counselor Name:	Mark Sallinger

Reason for Counseling or Referral

The next piece of information is the reason that the person is seeking counseling, the problem he or she presents, or the reason the person was referred for testing. A brief description of a client and a brief description of the nature of the problem and the reason for undertaking the evaluation give a general focus for the report.

Reason for Referral

Elise was referred to the Cherry Tree Counseling Center based on her partner's concerns with depression, decreased attendance at work and graduate school, and recent intoxication in her job. The client reported she was willing to attend counseling and noted she had experienced these symptoms for the past 3 months.

Relevant Background Information

Next to be included might be some additional descriptive data and some of the information available from the referral source. The background information should be relevant to the purpose of the assessment, should be related to the overall purpose of the report, and should be as succinct as possible. It is usually helpful to include the client's educational background, occupation, family background, health status, and current life situation. The report should also include other aspects of personal history that are related to the reason for assessment and that help to place the problem or reason for assessment in its proper context.

Background and History

Elise is currently enrolled full-time at Lafayette University as a second-year graduate student in curriculum and instruction. She returned to graduate school after approximately 10 years working full-time as an elementary school teacher. She currently works part-time at Eagle Elementary as a substitute teacher. She reports enjoying her job and graduate program, although she states her enjoyment has decreased the last few months.

She notes that she has a 2.8 grade point average this semester, although her cumulative grade point average is 3.8. She reports missing the last three weeks of school because of an inability to "get out of bed every morning" as well as crying spells and feelings of hopelessness. She states that she wishes "she could disappear." She denies previous depression symptoms or problems with work or school. She notes that she has been drinking more frequently (i.e., two glasses of wine per day for the past 2 months) and was suspended from her job this month. Prior to her suspension at work, she did not show up for work occasionally. Her partner confirms these behaviors.

Elise has been partnered for 8 years and reports being "relatively happy" in the relationship. She describes her partner as supportive. She has no children. With respect to family history, she is the oldest of three children, with parents who divorced when she was in college. She notes that her father lives with depression. She notes that she has a good relationship with her parents and siblings, although she admits to not communicating as often with them anymore.

Elise denies any current or previous medical issues. She denies previous substance abuse problems.

Evaluation Procedures

Evaluation procedures should be briefly described, giving the rationale for assessment, the names of the assessments used, and why the particular assessments were selected.

> Elise's evaluation included an intake interview, mental status examination, and suicide risk assessment (i.e., SAD PERSONS scale) to gauge her overall symptoms and clinically relevant history. In addition, she was administered the Beck Depression Inventory (BDI-II) and the Alcohol Use Disorders Identification Test (AUDIT) to assess more specifically for depression and substance abuse symptoms.

Behavioral Observations

Specific behaviors that were observed during the interviews and assessments can be included in this section. The way the client approached the assessment, any problems that arose, and any other factors that might bring into question the validity of any of the assessments used should be mentioned. Only relevant observations should be included. This section is likely to be very brief if the behaviors were normal and much lengthier if behaviors were unusual.

> Elise presented for the initial counseling session on time with her partner, who remained in the waiting room of the counseling center for the majority of the 50-minute session. She was cooperative with the majority of the assessments used yet questioned why she needed to take the AUDIT. She completed the BDI-II in 5 minutes and the AUDIT within 30 seconds.

Assessment Results and Their Interpretation

Next are a report of the assessment results, an overall interpretation, and diagnostic impressions. The description of the assessment results does not necessarily need to include actual test scores (as applicable), but they should be included if the report is for other professionals who are knowledgeable about testing. The most important part of this section is the interpretation of the results. Here, all of the assessment data are integrated, along with the behavioral observations and relevant background information. A discussion of the client's strengths and weaknesses is included. A statement regarding the client's future prospects in relation to the reason for the testing often needs to be included. This statement would include both favorable and unfavorable predictions.

> Mental Status Examination: Elise presented to counseling as cooperative and attentive with an appropriate activity level. She appeared her stated age, maintained minimal eye contact, and was slightly disheveled. She presented with anxious mood and flat affect. Her speech and thought patterns appeared normal; she was oriented to time, place, and person. She denied suicidal ideation and other self-harming thoughts and behaviors. Elise demonstrated insight into problems with good impulse control.

SAD PERSONS Scale: Elise scored a 2, corresponding to the following risk factors: presence of depression; and ethanol abuse. This indicates a low risk for suicide.

BDI-II: Elise's score of 22 indicates mild depression.

AUDIT: Elise received 9 points, exceeding the cutoff score of 8.

Based on assessment data, Elise presents with a major depressive disorder. Ongoing examination of alcohol use symptoms is needed to rule out a substance abuse disorder. Her strengths include a willingness to seek assistance through counseling and the presence of a support system. Potential minimization of alcohol use may be a challenge and should be further monitored. She demonstrates a favorable prognosis with ongoing clinical and personal support.

Recommendations

The primary reason for assessment and the subsequent case report is usually to make recommendations. Particularly if the case is a referral, recommendations can include further testing or activities that the client or others should undertake in relation to the problem. Recommendations should relate to the problem and to the general purpose of the assessment and report. They should be as practical and specific as possible.

> It is recommended that Elise continue counseling weekly until there is a decrease in depression and alcohol use symptoms as well as regular attendance at work and school. Alcohol education and advice on alcohol use are warranted based on AUDIT findings. It is recommended that Elise be readministered the BDI-II and AUDIT within two weeks to check for changes in levels of depression and alcohol use.

Brief Concluding Summary

A summary paragraph should succinctly restate the most important findings and conclusions.

> Elise presented to counseling at the request of her partner for depression and substance abuse symptoms that seem related to decreased occupational and academic functioning. Elise's scores on the SAD PERSONS Scale, BDI-II, and AUDIT are consistent with information presented during the intake interview and mental status examination. It is recommended that she continue counseling and receive periodic assessment for symptoms.

Chapter Summary

Communicating assessment findings is often considered the final phase of the assessment process, although this process recycles through the counseling relationship. This chapter presented several general guidelines for communicating results to clients as well as others such as in a case conference. Five steps for communicating assessment findings during the assessment interview were presented, which involve checking in with the client throughout the interview, collaborating on interpreting assessment findings, and providing the appropriate amount of structure and content to allow for positive use of assessment data in the future.

The assessment report, one of the more formal methods for communicating assessment findings, includes several components, such as demographic information, referral information, the client's background and history, assessment results, the client's strengths and challenges, recommendations, and a general summary. Depending on the clinical setting and report purpose, assessment reports may appear quite different.

Review Questions

1. What are the five steps of the assessment communication process discussed in this chapter?

2. What are some key strategies for an effective case conference?
3. What are things to avoid during the assessment communication process (i.e., assessment interview, case conference, assessment report)?
4. How can the assessment report be used in counseling?
5. What types of information should be included in the major components of an assessment report discussed in this chapter?

Resources for Further Learning

Groth-Marnat, G., & Davis, A. (2013). *Psychological report writing assistant.* New York, NY: Wiley.

Lichtenberger, E. O., Mather, N., Kaufman, N. L., & Kaufman, A. S. (2012). *Essentials of assessment report writing.* Hoboken, NJ: Wiley.

Chapter 16

Future Trends in Counseling Assessment

I begin this chapter by reflecting back on how the function of assessment has evolved, and then I present data to provide a picture of the changing cultural characteristics of the client presenting for assessment. Then, globalization and the consequent need to challenge current assumptions in the counseling and assessment process are discussed. The impact of technological advances and the continued sophistication of assessment practices are then outlined. Next, future considerations in educational and clinical settings are presented. The case for more coordinated assessment systems and greater partnership with the health community is then articulated Finally, the notion of relevance—in terms of assessment findings and the profession itself—is argued at the end of the chapter.

Test Your Knowledge

Respond to the following items by selecting T for "True" or F for "False":

❑ T ❑ F 1. It is expected that the proportion of the U.S. population ages 18 years and younger will increase most substantially, warranting additional assessment tools for this age cohort.

❑ T ❑ F 2. Technological advances will give counselors the ability to provide more real-time and individualized assessment data.

❑ T ❑ F 3. Greater attention will be placed on the process of learning (i.e., metacognition) in assessment.

❑ T ❑ F 4. Changes in educational accountability are likely to restrict advances in assessment.

❑ T ❑ F 5. Counselors will need to continually advocate with private health insurers for the utility of assessment as a reimbursable option for clients.

The Assessment Process: Looking Back to Look Ahead

Counseling and other related disciplines, particularly over the past 150 years or more, have developed and adapted assessments to meet the changing needs of U.S. society. As discussed in Chapter 1, the late 1800s and the 1900s represented a period of diverse mental tests used to detect individual characteristics in terms of ability, personality, and/or intelligence. These tests were administered to individuals and groups, and over time these tools were used to make decisions related to educational placement, college admissions, military screening, and career selection, to name a few.

With changing demographics and greater use of assessments across multiple settings, helping professionals began to consider how culture might intersect with the assessment process. For example, in the late 1960s and 1970s, those in the measurement community began to look at ways to minimize assessment bias in educational testing that disproportionately affected racial/ethnic minorities, English-language learners, those with disabilities, and females (R. E. Bennett, 2014). Furthermore, Malgady (2011) noted that few assessments had been developed with culturally diverse clientele. As counselors and members of other professions increasingly attend to the role of bias in assessment (see American Educational Research Association, American Psychological Association, & National Council on Measurement in Education, 2014), the ways in which we develop and use assessments will continue to change.

A common thread across this text is that assessment serves to engage the client in decision making while promoting knowledge, awareness, and skills for both the counselor and client. Through this engagement, counselors use assessments to identify areas of challenge or opportunity; articulate diagnoses; hold individuals or stakeholders accountable; screen for career and other opportunities; guide high-stakes decisions; allocate resources in academic or mental health settings; and predict outcomes such as workforce retention, suicidality, or graduation rates, to name a few functions. As the future unfolds, these roles of assessment are not expected to change substantially. It is necessary that the assessment process remain tied to treatment and outcomes, no matter the setting. Furthermore, assessment should be intentional and collaborative, use multiple methods, and not be done just for the sake of collecting information.

Despite the multiple uses of assessment—and the benefits of the assessment process in general for counselors and clients—there is a downward trend in usage that counselors will need to continue to address. Specifically, the overall amount of time spent performing assessment has decreased (Groth-Marnat, 2000; Youngstrom, 2013), and less attention has been paid to some forms of assessment as well as the assessment process in general (Youngstrom, 2013). Factors likely related to this trend include limited attention to assessment in training programs, the erosion of health care reimbursement for assessment for counselors and other helping professionals, the depletion of time and personnel resources in counseling settings, professionals' limited knowledge of the assessment process, and insufficient advocacy for and promotion of the utility of assessment in the counseling process to external stakeholders. These factors are interdependent, and some are discussed more fully in the sections that follow.

As we look back at the way assessments and the assessment process have evolved in counseling and related professions, it becomes clear that, looking ahead, counselors, no matter the extent to which they believe they will "do assessment," will have to attend to trends in assessment usage as part of sustaining their professional identity and livelihood. Some settings of assessment, such as schools and forensics, may be less affected; however, counselors across settings need to be mindful of the continual need for professional advocacy (i.e., ensuring that others know that counselors both value assessment as well as know how to engage well in the assessment process).

336

Changing Client Demographics and Assessment Practice

Counselors will continue to conduct assessment procedures with clients across settings, although the demographics of those clients will continue to shift and diversify. The increased diversification of the U.S. population is largely reflective of aging trends, higher birth rates for some racial and ethnic minority groups, and immigration trends. In addition, expanding economic gaps disproportionately affect racial and ethnic minorities and women. Collectively, these changes require continual reflection on whether particular assessments and the assessment process are equitably beneficial to a diverse clientele. Furthermore, counselors will need to "leave their offices" to engage in socially just assessment procedures, procedures that may be quite different from the case consultations and assessment reporting of today.

In terms of demographic trends, the current racial makeup of the United States is 77.28% White, 13.21% Black/African descent, and 5.46% Asian descent, with all other races (e.g., Native American, Alaska Native, Native Hawaiian, multiracial) making up 4.05% of the population. In addition to these racial classifications, about 17.66% of the U.S. population identifies as Latino/a when asked about ethnicity alone (U.S. Census Bureau, 2014). By 2060, individuals who are White non-Hispanic will make up less than half the population (43.6%), with the number of individuals of Latino/a and Asian descent increasing. Furthermore, the overall foreign-born population will increase from its current rate of 13% to 19% of the estimated U.S. population by 2060 (Colby & Ortman, 2015).

Changing age demographics will also impact the assessment process. The U.S. population is living longer. For example, individuals 65 to 84 years old are expected to constitute 18.82% of the U.S. population by 2060 (compared to the 2020 projected proportion of 14.86%); the percentage of those 85 years and older is projected to grow from 2.01% in 2020 to 4.73% by 2060. An increasingly aging population sparks new health and illness considerations with direct implications for assessment in counseling. For example, assessments and assessment processes will need to be developed and/or refined to address concerns of the geriatric population, such as organic disorders, cognitive degenerative disorders, substance abuse, psychopathology, and grief and loss.

Socioeconomic status will also remain a significant influence on assessment practices, particularly for those living in poverty and holding multiple oppressed statuses. The 2013 poverty rate was 15.8%; female heads of households represented the largest portion of those living in poverty (i.e., 32.5%). Poverty rates are disproportionately related to race/ethnicity, as African Americans and Latinos have rates of 27.2% and 25.3%, respectively, compared to 9.6% among Whites (DeNavas-Walt, Proctor, & Smith, 2013). Research indicates negative treatment outcomes for those living in poverty or having a lower socioeconomic status. Some of the risk factors and mental health consequences include food insecurity, insufficient educational opportunities, inadequate employment opportunities, lack of safe and affordable housing options, and limited access to health care and health insurance (Newton & Erford, in press).

This growing diversity, along with the demographics of race/ethnicity, age, and socio-economic status, will only amplify the disproportionate experiences culturally diverse individuals have in counseling. More specifically, D. G. Hays and McLeod (2018) high-lighted the fact that a perceived or actual lack of access to counseling (and thus assessment) services is linked to poorer clinical outcomes, such as suicide, hospitalization, and maladaptive social and occupational functioning. Furthermore, they noted multiple structural and attitudinal factors that influence the help-seeking behaviors of cultur-ally diverse individuals, whether these individuals seek or remain in counseling. Some of these factors include (a) the potential conflict between the "culture" of counseling and common cultural norms of diverse populations; (b) discrimination experiences that may occur within counseling; (c) stigma and cultural mistrust of the counselor and counseling process; (d) barriers associated with geography, socioeconomic status, and language; and (e) the insufficient knowledge base of counselors related to the relationship between culture and mental health. In sum, individuals have intersecting cultural identities that interact with counseling; therefore, the assessment process will continue to grow more complex to facilitate a positive counseling and assessment experience.

Thus, counselors will undoubtedly continue to refine their practice based on these changes in diversity as well as current factors that play a role in how culturally diverse clientele experience counseling. As attention to social justice will increase to ensure positive counseling and assessment outcomes, counselors will be challenged to demonstrate equity, harmony, participation, and access (Crethar, Rivera, & Nash, 2008) in their practice. Attending to social justice practices in counseling settings will involve the following: investigating the effects of systematic forms of inequity and oppression, empowering individuals through building knowledge and raising community awareness to change oppressive systems and structures, interacting with culturally diverse clientele with an open and inquiring stance to provide space for new cultural learning and client voice, and exploring one's role in perpetuating cultural privilege and oppression and how that impacts current or prospective clients.

As outlined in Chapter 4, cultural concerns are prominent in personality, career, ability, and intelligence assessment. As the United States continues to become increasingly diverse, the current utility of assessment content and type will become less relevant; counselors are to be prepared to make significant changes in how they integrate assessment into their practice. For example, with changing demographics and greater attention to diversity within U.S. society, career opportunities will continue to expand for women and members of other minority statuses (e.g., racial/ethnic minorities; lesbian, gay, bisexual, transgender, and queer individuals; persons with disabilities). Counselors are to make adjustments to their practice to reflect these changes.

Related to assessment changes and with regard for the immigration trends discussed earlier in this section, the issue of language will be increasingly prominent in assessment settings. Counselors will need to be well versed in test translation and adaptation procedures. Resources are included at the end of this chapter to help inform your knowledge about test translation and adaptation. In the next section, I discuss a related topic to changing demographics: the role of globalization and how indigenous ways of knowing may be incorporated into the assessment process.

Globalization and Problematizing Counseling and Assessment

Globalization impacts and will continue to impact U.S. society in general and counseling and assessment practice more specifically. **Globalization** is defined as the continual process of interaction and integration among various societies and cultures (Lorelle, Byrd, & Crockett, 2012). It will continue to lead to a changing workforce; increasing international competition among global economies; and the development of innovative ways to approach various social, political, educational, and economic challenges. With these challenges, counselors will have an opportunity to exchange information with members of other professions to improve outcomes for an increasingly diverse clientele.

Specific to counseling and the United States, globalization involves counselors interacting internationally to learn and share knowledge about counseling with the general population as well as international scholars. Globalization also relates to the influx of immigrants arriving annually with diverse cultural backgrounds, experiences, ideas about mental health, and expressions of wellness and mental illness. Collectively, these considerations warrant an increasingly reflective approach to counseling here in the United States as well as around the world.

Counseling practice—and practices of similar professions—vary from nation to nation, and, as immigration trends disproportionately impact different regions of the United States, I would argue that counseling practice will continue to adapt for different parts of this country too. This variability will require the globalized counselor to be more aware of other nations as well as information within his or her community about immigration patterns and the reasons why various immigrants may have immigrated to a community. Thus, assessment practices will need to change.

As part of learning about new cultures within and outside the United States, counselors are to consider how various mental health constructs are conceptualized. For example, how are depression, career development, psychopathology, intelligence, and wellness defined in international communities? How are these definitions different from those in the United States? How does this impact the assessment process? There may be opportunities to introduce new criteria or definitions for mental health and distress that serve to improve treatment for a particular community or subpopulation. As counselors spread the profession of counseling to other parts of the world, however, they must also be cognizant of the negative impact of introducing information that may conflict with existing values and norms in international communities.

In developing or revising assessments and the assessment process, as well as working within a more globalized society, counselors need to problematize what they know about the profession. In the previous section, I presented some of the factors noted in the literature that relate to how culturally diverse individuals experience help seeking; these factors certainly will need to be considered with international communities here in the United States and throughout the world. The process of **problematizing** refers to questioning the familiar, what is assumed about effective counseling and assessment practices. Thus, counselors are to challenge their thinking about how constructs are defined, what mental health and mental illness look like in different cultures, what criteria constitute which diagnoses, and how counseling should be done to be most effective for a given population, to name a few areas for problematizing. This process will lead to changes in assessment, including new constructs to be named and items to be developed for those constructs; new methods for collecting data for decision making and client self-awareness; and innovative ways of selecting, administering, interpreting, and reporting assessment tools and their findings. Perhaps in the future, we may not use assessments as they are traditionally used.

As counselors problematize what they have come to know as traditional knowledge of the practice of counseling and assessment, they will be motivated to integrate more indigenous ways of knowing into their work. Kovach (2009) noted "four R's" of indigenous ways of knowing: (a) **relational accountability/responsibility**, or the awareness that ways of knowing are based on the relationships between all life forms; (b) **respect**, or the notion that humility, active involvement, and shared knowledge should be valued; (c) **reciprocity**, or the give-and-take of shared power between an individual and an indigenous group; and (d) **rights and regulations**, or development and adherence to indigenous protocols to achieve jointly created goals. Integrating indigenous ways of knowing—found across the globe—should involve promoting these ways of knowing and protecting them from harmful influence.

Technological Advances

The nature of what we come to know and how we engage with others is ever changing, particularly because of technological advances. Technology can assist in the assessment process by facilitating learning and engagement, supporting multiple levels of complexity in assessment, and making information readily accessible and personally meaningful. In the future, counselors can expect clients to interact more with the assessment process.

Although we can anticipate how some technological aids will be useful for the assessment process, there are some we cannot imagine yet. No matter the aid, there will be a continued push to try and systematize an assessment process with multiple data collection points by the client, counselor, and other relevant individuals. Furthermore, outside data sources, such as medical or school records and interviews, are likely to be included. The assessment process will be heavily contextualized to the individual and the purpose of the assessment; this will allow for an interactive and engaging assessment experience, which ultimately will motivate the client to remain in counseling as long as is appropriate.

With increased technology, we can expect greater accuracy and efficiency in getting information from assessments and thus making decisions faster. In essence, data will be available in real time. Clients will be able to use mobile technology between sessions, interact in virtual environments with avatars and other systems, and complete more refined assessments on computers or tablets or the next technological advancement. There will be increased use of biofeedback, neuroimaging, and other physiological measures to evaluate personality, intelligence, and ability. Furthermore, counselors will be able to assess things like spatial orientation and interpersonal interactions, which have typically been evaluated with traditional assessment tools and modalities.

Technology will also bring greater attention to areas such as forensics and neuropsychology and how physiological, behavioral, cognitive, and affective functions interact within an individual. Moreover, it is expected that the number of forensic and neuropsychological evaluations connected to legal proceedings will likely increase. Counselors are encouraged to engage more in these areas.

Technological advances in assessment, however, will bring additional considerations related to laws and ethics. Current guidelines will need to be revised to address new concerns with privacy and confidentiality. Counselors will need to balance their ability and desire to collect data because there are more sophisticated technologies for doing so with a perspective of parsimony to avoid using too much or the wrong technology in counseling. Furthermore, the efficiency of data collection and retrieval will lead to new questions concerning how to address data interpretation and reporting.

Increased Sophistication of Assessment Practice

Although technological advances will certainly have implications for assessment design and administration, this section describes more specific anticipated changes related to more refined and sophisticated assessment practices. We can improve client outcomes by improving assessment practices, and we can improve these practices by attending to and broadening how and when we administer and interpret assessments and to what constructs we attend. In this section, I describe the expected increase in the use of formative assessments, the assessment of learning and other metacognitive processes, procedures that foster ecological validity, the evaluation of nonpathology, and the use of qualitative assessments.

The use of **formative assessment**, or measuring constructs of interest at various points to inform ongoing treatment and other forms of decision making, will continue to increase in counseling in a variety of settings. Given greater attention to the planning and evaluation of counseling interventions, counselors are to make better use of assessment within a counseling session itself, between sessions, and across several counseling sessions. As part of formative assessment, counselors will use multiple sources of evidence to make decisions and foster client self-awareness. As technology continues to become more sophisticated, counselors will be able to import assessment data from multiple sources into a central data storage system that can provide individualized, contextualized findings and recommendations.

Whether counselors are engaging in formative or summative assessment, it may be useful to understand not just what is learned but *how* it is learned—or more clearly, what metacognitive changes are occurring for test takers as they are being administered an assessment (Landgraf, 2014; Pellegrino, 2004). As R. E. Bennett (2014) noted, current assessments do not evaluate how knowledge is constructed, organized, and integrated with other knowledge, nor do assessments evaluate complex learning and/or problem-solving processes. Thus, assessing these processes can require different criteria for test development and thus different considerations: ". . . at specific standards of learning, there exist different integrations of knowledge, different forms of skill, differences in access to knowledge, and differences in the efficiency of performance" (Glaser, 1991, as cited in Pellegrino, 2004, p. 8). **Dynamic testing** was discussed in Chapter 4 of this text as one method of obtaining data about a client's ability to learn from immediate instruction and feedback loops (Stevenson et al., 2016). This form of assessment will continue to become more useful in ability and intelligence testing to gauge the learning process.

Counselors will need to embed assessment directly into the contexts in which clients live and work, whether that is a home, a classroom, a community, a workplace, or another setting. Integration can take the form of having clients self-administer tools in a natural setting, involving stakeholders that have a relationship to those clients, or developing items that directly relate to the environment or situation clients may be encountering. Thus, it is necessary to move beyond traditional item formats and use more realistic problems and examples readily available to clients by varying contexts. When assessment is infused into context, results become more meaningful and actionable, which improves their ecological validity. Although the term **ecological validity** is most often tied to research, the practice of ensuring that the assessment experience approximates real-life experience can also be considered evidence of ecological validity.

Assessment tools that focus on nonpathology and client strengths, such as wellness, resilience, and self-esteem, are expected to expand and could be particularly useful for counseling culturally diverse clients. In addition, strengths-based tools can inform treatment planning and prognosis, maximizing positive client outcomes. Although the work is a bit dated, Groth-Marnat (2000) highlighted several available assessments that may be infrequently used, such as the Vineland Social Maturity Scale, Strong Interest Inventory, Sixteen Personality Factor Questionnaire, and California Psychological Inventory.

In addition to more attention being paid to strengths-based assessments, the use of qualitative assessments as stand-alone or supplemental tools will increase. Qualitative assessments have not received a great amount of attention in counseling research (McMahon & Watson, 2015), although this is expected to change, given their potential utility in addressing cultural context. Qualitative assessments can include, for example, tools that solicit narratives from clients about their experiences, symptoms, or strengths; they can be administered through traditional methods, interviews, or arts-based methods. Greater attention must be paid to exploring, when relevant, the meanings behind assessment scores through assessment inquiry, as attending only to a score masks clinically significant information (Groth-Marnat, 2000). However, we must be cautious because sometimes quantitative scores, although appearing unremarkable, can be accurate and meaningful in themselves.

The Continuation and Adaptability of Educational Accountability

There will be continued increased public demand for educational accountability, and counselors of the future will need to be aware of the most up-to-date accountability legislation as well as support their educational partners with its implementation. The Every Student Succeeds Act (ESSA), signed into law in 2015, provides more flexibility than its predecessor, the No Child Left Behind Act of 2001, in how educational achievement gaps can be identified and addressed. With ESSA, the assumption is that high-quality standards and assessments are preferred to improve individual outcomes. ESSA refers to evaluating Common Core standards in a particular state's schools, which were developed as part of the U.S. Department of Education's Race to the Top Assessment Program (U.S. Department of Education, 2010). ESSA also articulates that schools are to use multiple measures to evaluate student learning, moving away from a sole focus on standardized testing (Office of the Press Secretary, 2015).

According to the Office of the Press Secretary (2015), ESSA helps to maximize educational opportunity for all students in the following ways:

- Holding all students to high academic standards that prepare them for success in college and careers.
- Ensuring accountability by guaranteeing that when students fall behind, states redirect resources into what works to help them and their schools improve, with a particular focus on the very lowest-performing schools, high schools with high dropout rates, and schools with achievement gaps.
- Empowering state and local decision-makers to develop their own strong systems for school improvement based upon evidence, rather than imposing cookie-cutter federal solutions like the No Child Left Behind Act did.
- Reducing the often onerous burden of testing on students and teachers, making sure that tests don't crowd out teaching and learning, without sacrificing clear, annual information parents and educators need to make sure our children are learning.
- Providing more children access to high-quality preschool.
- Establishing new resources for proven strategies that will spur reform and drive opportunity and better outcomes for America's students.

Thus, these objectives are intended to address several educational reform principles: ensuring that students are college and career ready, providing flexibility to school districts to allocate resources and increase targeted interventions within schools with the greatest gaps and/or disadvantage, closing the achievement gap, increasing opportunities for students to attend preschool, administering professional development workshops to school personnel to improve student outcomes, and offering wrap-around services to disadvantaged communities.

You are already aware that ability tests are often associated with high-stakes testing and are used to gauge learning outcomes and learning potential. With current and anticipated changes in educational accountability, greater attention will be given to the process of learning, described briefly in the previous section. Pellegrino (2004) noted, "The educational assessment community is becoming increasingly aware of the need to embed more valid and complex assessments into the fabric of instruction" (p. 9). Furthermore, the Gordon Commission on the Future of Assessment in Education has called for innovative assessment of the process and outcome of teaching and learning as it is occurring in the classroom or other learning settings. The goal is to have children learn how to learn, to not only consume knowledge but to create new knowledge and challenge existing knowledge (Gordon Commission on the Future of Assessment in Education, 2013). Furthermore, the Commission advocates for greater contextualization of assessment to determine what contributes to individual performance in which particular context in education.

Counselors, particularly those working in school settings, will need to be prepared to incorporate into their work with their students more process-oriented data concerning educational ability (American School Counselor Association, 2012). The increased flexibility in assessment and intervention as it pertains to educational accountability—in conjunction with an expansive look at the process of learning and instruction itself—will undoubtedly create more opportunities for counselors and other professionals to collaborate to maximize student educational and psychosocial outcomes.

Assessment and Managed Care

The Patient Protection and Affordable Care Act, commonly known as the Affordable Care Act, was signed into law in 2010. The intention of the Affordable Care Act is to provide health care coverage to all Americans while providing consumer protections from private health insurance companies and limiting long-term health care expenses. Although it is expected to be revised in the future, the Affordable Care Act currently mandates coverage of preventive health services such as depression, substance use, and HIV screenings; smoking cessation interventions; domestic and interpersonal violence screening and counseling; cervical cancer screenings; obesity screening and counseling; and behavioral assessments (American Counseling Association, 2012). With these health services now covered, counselors will increasingly be required in multiple settings, showcasing their assessment skills as well as interventions based on those assessment data. New checklists and other forms of assessment will be used more frequently.

For those individuals who continue to use private health insurance, counselors will have to continually demonstrate how the benefits of assessment outweigh its costs to insurance companies (Youngstrom, 2013). This challenge, however, is not new to counselors and other mental health professionals: About two decades ago, scholars (e.g., Groth-Marnat, 2000; Piotrowski, 1999; Stout & Cook, 1999) speculated that managed care companies would devalue psychological assessment services, given the costs in terms of both time and expense. Thus, assessment may not be available as a covered insurance benefit, even if it is clinically beneficial. Not receiving assessment services when they are warranted can further create problems in treatment planning; in essence, clients may not receive services if they are not evaluated for them. Counselors are to consider adding assessment services into a monthly premium, as a proportion of clients may require standardized services that may not be covered by private insurance. In sum, ongoing advocacy with managed care companies—articulating what counselors do, how assessment can benefit individuals and in what ways, and how ultimately assessment and counseling services yield cost savings to managed care companies—will remain paramount.

Building Assessment Systems

The aforementioned factors in this chapter (i.e., client demographics and the assessment process, globalization, technology, assessment logistics, considerations of educational accountability and managed care) will undoubtedly create a need for more complex assessment systems. Think of assessment as one large box of puzzle pieces, with the future allowing us to be in possession of more and more pieces. How do we connect these pieces to inform a more complete picture for decision making? Can we have a more coordinated system in which individuals from multiple professions and stakeholders talk to one another to efficiently and effectively assist a client?

Recall from Chapter 1 that no single test can do it all—and the findings from a single test represent just one sampling of behavior at one time. Counselors will need to devise assessment systems that bring together assessment tools in synergistic ways. More complex assessment systems can bring together multiple data sources, including traditional assessment; client self-monitoring; data from social media; naturalistic data; stakeholder observations and ratings; biofeedback; medical, academic, and public records; and simulation and other virtual reality feedback, to name a few. Assessment systems will become more flexible and creative.

Assessment systems should be developed in a manner that guides treatment planning and allows for monitoring in the most efficient and accurate way. As one example of an assessment system, Youngstrom (2013) offered 12 steps to what he coined **evidence-based assessment**:

1. Identify most common diagnoses in a setting.
2. Know the base rates.
3. Evaluate relevant risk and moderating factors.
4. Synthesize broad instruments into revised probability estimates.
5. Add narrow and incremental assessments to clarify diagnoses.
6. Interpret cross-informant data patterns.
7. Finalize diagnoses by adding necessary intensive assessment methods.
8. Complete assessment for treatment planning and goal setting.
9. Measure the change process using formative assessment methods (e.g., therapy assignments, visit check-ins, life charts).
10. Chart progress and outcome at multiple points of treatment.
11. Monitor maintenance and relapse.
12. Solicit feedback about the effectiveness of treatment and integrate clients' preferences.

Although Youngstrom had a nomothetic orientation to decision making, these steps can be altered to allow for more contextualized findings and predictions.

Building Partnerships With Health Professions

As you can surmise from the chapter, counselors have a long future in assessment, although the practice of assessment will certainly change as that future unfolds. One of the ways in which counselors can proactively protect their role in the practice of assessment overall is to collaborate more with members of other professions. It is important to consider settings that may have once seemed atypical for counselor engagement in assessment activities. Specifically, having a collaborative versus competitive mindset when considering working with other disciplines is essential. These partnerships can help to demonstrate the value of clinical assessment and the inclusion of counselors in a more holistic team approach.

It is increasingly becoming necessary to partner with medical professionals in today's world, particularly given the aforementioned changes in individual health care coverage. Counselors may consider serving as consultants or working in diverse health care settings, such as hospitals and physicians' offices, nursing homes, and dentist offices. In fact, counselors can serve these professions well by, for example, offering initial and follow-up assessment services, assisting professionals in sharing and coping with the findings of various physical and psychological assessments, helping patients and their families cope with an acute or chronic medical disorder, providing patients with resources to address medically necessary lifestyle changes, or intervening in psychosomatic illnesses. Many of these services could occur through individual or group counseling, psychoeducational workshops, or professional team meetings with patients and/or their families (Stout & Cook, 1999).

Part of increasing engagement with other disciplines will require counselors to clearly articulate their professional identity and the benefits of formal assessment services as well as ongoing counseling services for individuals. Counselors are to be especially mindful of which clinical interventions and related assessments are most appropriate for which medical conditions. Depending on the nature of an individual's medical concerns, assessment and counseling services may be useful before, during, and/or after medical interventions. Just as counselors need to periodically educate managed care companies about the value of their assessment services, they need to share the benefits (e.g., decreased costs, decreased inpatient stays, less intensive treatment) with those in the medical community.

Although counselors are to be knowledgeable about their profession and share this expertise with the medical community, they should also become educated about the work being done in the medical community across a variety of medical professions. Furthermore, they will need to be accessible to clients who are being seen by medical professionals. It is not always prudent to expect physicians and other health care providers to refer clients across town, and counselors should consider practicing onsite for part of their practice to better serve individuals while increasing their clientele.

Assessment as Relevant and Actionable

Relevance is not only an anticipated future trend but a necessity for the survival of the profession. In the end, there will need to be greater access to knowledge about the assessment process, greater access to the assessment process itself, and seamless collaboration among several professions to benefit clients and communities.

The ability to report assessment findings in a relevant way to practitioners, policymakers, and community members is becoming increasingly relevant, as there will be more attention to public policy and community assessment. Assessment systems will need to be developed to ensure that findings from formative and summative data are actionable, relevant, and accessible (R. E. Bennett, 2014). Therefore, there will be a continued need for meaningful results that lead to clinical and educational decision making that improves outcomes for clients and their communities. Thus, the assessment report will require greater attention to context: information about community factors as well as the client's cultural, social, physical, and psychological backgrounds. Adding context may involve bringing in multiple sources of data like in a larger assessment system.

This notion of relevance relates to Messick's (1995) concept of **consequential validity** as a component of assessment design. It refers to the applied consequences of assessment. Consequences can be positive, leading to policy development, or negative, leading to inaccurate interpretation for clients and other stakeholders. The establishment of consequential validity requires sound research during assessment development. Researchers need to be very careful to base their research on theories, use culturally appropriate measures, and then revise theories as the data indicate.

Furthermore, counseling and assessment constructs are complex, with complex solutions. We as counselors need to work with colleagues across disciplines to expand ways of thinking about assessment and the constructs we are trying to measure and treat to improve client well-being. What can we learn from our colleagues in mental health, schools, medical communities, business, public health, and so on?

In addition to working with other disciplines, we need to promote the benefits of assessment and its integral role in counseling as a whole, the counseling relationship, treatment planning, and interventions. The Association for Assessment and Research in Counseling (AARC; formerly the Association for Assessment in Counseling and Education) is an essential division for counselors and counselor trainees to engage with, as shifts continue to occur in client demographics, the practice of counseling and assessment, and subsequent professional identity. Part of ensuring that assessment is relevant in the future is strengthening the profession itself. Scholars in education (e.g., R. E. Bennett, 2014; Gordon Commission on the Future of Assessment in Education, 2013) have noted that principles of good teaching and learning should guide assessment design. Similarly, the best and most innovative practices in counseling should guide assessment design. AARC and its resources (e.g., *Standards for Multicultural Assessment* [Association for Assessment in Counseling and Education, 2012]; annual conferences) will be at the forefront of those changes. Furthermore, new resources and standards will become available for counselors, particularly from that division.

The Next Frontier in Counseling and Assessment Research

To maximize the benefits of the assessment process and develop innovative ways to address the needs of the future, we have to improve research related to assessment and the counseling profession itself. The fact is that most of the widely used assessments have little to no empirical evidence to support their construction or effectiveness in treatment outcomes (Youngstrom, 2013), and there is limited evidence of an understanding of common counseling constructs and interventions in counseling scholarship.

Furthermore, those conducting counseling research, those conducting assessments, and those training future counselors are not always aligned in their perspectives of best practice. As discussed in Chapter 1, research indicates a discrepancy between what tools are being used to conduct research and what tools practitioners are using with clients (Hogan & Rengert, 2008). Also, it seems that some tools that are frequently used in practice are not frequently taught in counselor education programs (Neukrug et al., 2013). This trend will undoubtedly continue as long as counselors in research, higher education, and practice settings are not collaborating on the future of counseling in general and assessment more specifically.

The nexus of counseling practice, research, training, and external influences (e.g., technological advances, partnership opportunities, educational accountability, shifting demographics) affords great opportunities for research in counseling and assessment. The following Tip Sheet provides considerations for conducting counseling and assessment research that helps support future trends in counseling assessment.

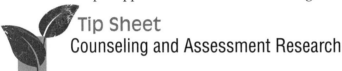

Tip Sheet
Counseling and Assessment Research

✓ Be cognizant of the concept of consequential validity (Messick, 1995) and the applied consequences that assessment has for research and practice.

✓ Broaden your research approach and work with multiple disciplines to better inform assessment practice. Work with colleagues across disciplines and professional associations to expand site access, new samples, and partnerships.

✓ Share research findings beyond academia to build relationships among universities, communities, and policymakers.

✓ Reflect on how your intersecting cultural identities impact all stages of the research process.

✓ Evaluate whether communities or subpopulations are disproportionately affected by some phenomena. This may be a nice starting point for new inquiry.

✓ Gain knowledge of past psychological and health research with minority populations.

✓ Expand research to look at how intersectionality impacts help-seeking attitudes, the counseling process and outcomes, and so on.

✓ Increase focus and respect for international counseling topics and research processes and designs.

✓ Use a diverse and collaborative team of researchers from both within and outside of a community of focus. A diverse team can help to provide growth for its members, provide alternative explanations, challenge stereotypic thinking, and promote critical thinking.

✓ Examine ways in which you can partner with a community of interest at various points of the research process.

✓ Consider ways that community members can assist you in making sure that research findings are accessible to various stakeholders and audiences.

✓ Understand participants' cultural histories, traditions of communities, and the sociopolitical climate of the research setting.

✓ Attend to how you treat gatekeepers/knowledge brokers before, during, and after the research process.

✓ Communicate openly about any problems that arise within research partnerships to allow those partnerships to be more flexible and solution oriented. With increased involvement, there is increased laterality in those partnerships (K. Adams & Faulkhead, 2012).

✓ Rely on multiple data methods and sources.

✓ Make questionnaires available in various formats.

✓ Consider ways to develop and/or use indigenous measures and tools.

✓ Report data in formal reports, as part of conversations to communities or other groups, or as community exhibitions that involve researchers and research participants.

✓ With increased attention to public policy, you need to write in a manner that is accessible to practitioners, policymakers, communities, and stakeholders.

✓ State explicit outcomes of a study without making leaps. Sample outcomes might be advancing knowledge; testing a community-based or targeted intervention; or describing a process for sustaining or translating research findings, interventions, or outcomes within a community.

✓ Consider cultural hypotheses as possible explanations for findings (American Psychological Association, 2013).

✓ Report on the sample's cultural, ethnic, and racial characteristics as well as cultural limitations and generalizability (American Psychological Association, 2013).

✓ Describe the study population in terms of how it defines a community.

✓ Provide context in terms of external data as relevant. For example, if presenting a small sample, show how similar trends are present in other groups using epidemiological data (Swank & Lambie, 2016).

✓ Outline how the setting for your study or intervention is relevant to the community.

✓ Explicitly describe roles of community members and community leaders in each stage of a project, from design to implementation to analysis.

✓ Outline the degree to which findings were shared/negotiated with the community.

✓ Outline the degree to which findings are generalizable to and replicable with regard to other communities, settings, circumstances, or policymakers.

✓ Emphasize in training programs and national associations that research topics and questions should be considered from different paradigms.

✓ Consider explicit ways to incorporate the AARC *Standards for Multicultural Assessment* (AARC, 2012) and the AARC *Standards for Multicultural Research* (O'Hara et al., 2016).

Chapter Summary

This chapter outlined several anticipated future trends in counseling assessment. The future of assessment in counseling can be projected from historical trends in terms of changing foci and functions of assessment, the degree to which the counseling process in general has catered to an increasingly diverse population, and changing assessment usage patterns. This chapter highlighted an upward trend in racial/ethnic diversity and immigration rates, an increasingly aging population, and a stable pattern of individuals facing financial barriers—particularly those who are female and racial/ethnic minorities. These changing demographics, coupled with a more globalized world, call attention to the need to problematize practice in counseling and assessment as well as the need to work innovatively within educational and clinical settings and with other professions. In addition, continued refinement in assessment format, structure, and delivery will be required as technological advances provide a greater opportunity for developing more complex assessment systems that can be more contextualized and efficient. The future of counseling and assessment is bright, and there are multiple opportunities to expand our professional identity as well as the quality of the research we produce in counseling in general and assessment more specifically.

Review Questions

1. How might shifts in demographics impact assessment delivery?
2. In what ways is globalization related to the assessment process?
3. What are the four R's of indigenous ways of knowing, and how might these be integrated into the assessment process?
4. What are expected technological advances, and how will they influence the assessment process?
5. In what ways are assessment tools and processes expected to become more sophisticated?
6. What role do changes in educational accountability and managed care have in how counselors will practice assessment? What partnerships need to be built and why?
7. How can counselors make assessment findings more relevant to various stakeholders?

Resources for Further Learning

Publications

Arnold, B. R., & Smith, J. L. (2013). Methodologies for test translation and cultural equivalence. In F. A. Paniagua & A. M. Yamada (Eds.), *Handbook of multicultural mental health* (pp. 243–262). New York, NY: Academic Press.

Hambleton, R. K., Merenda, P. F., & Spielberger, C. D. (Eds.). (2004). *Adapting educational and psychological tests for cross-cultural assessment.* New York, NY: Psychology Press.

Youngstrom, E. A. (2013). Future directions in psychological assessment: Combining evidence-based medicine innovations with psychology's historical strengths to enhance utility. *Journal of Clinical Child & Adolescent Psychology, 42,* 139–159. doi:10.1080/15374416.2012.736358

Web Resources

Association for Assessment and Research in Counseling
http://www.aarc-counseling.org
This official website of the AARC provides the latest information and resources on assessment practices in counseling.

Gordon Commission on the Future of Assessment in Education
http://gordoncommission.org/
This website provides several reports and resources related to educational assessment.

International Test Commission (ITC), ITC Guidelines for Translating and Adapting Tests
https://www.intestcom.org/files/guideline_test_adaptation.pdf
This website links you to the most updated guidelines for adapting tests for culturally diverse clientele.

Appendix A

Statistical Formulas

Pearson Product–Moment Correlation Coefficient

$$r_{xy} = \frac{n\sum XY - \sum X \sum}{\sqrt{[n\sum X^2 - (\sum X)^2 - [n\sum Y^2 - (\sum Y)^2]}}$$

r_{xy} = correlation between X and Y variables
n = sample size
XY = product of each score for variable X times each score for variable Y
X^2 = an individual's score on variable X squared
Y^2 = an individual's score on variable Y squared

Spearman–Brown

$$r_t = \frac{2r_h}{1 + r_h}$$

r_t = correlated Pearson correlation coefficient
r_h = Pearson correlation coefficient

Coefficient Alpha

$$r = \left[\frac{n}{n-1}\right]\left[\frac{SD^2 - \sum SD_i^2}{SD^2}\right]$$

n = number of items
SD^2 = variance
$\sum SD_i^2$ = sum of variances for all items

Kuder–Richardson

$$KR_{20} = \left[\frac{n}{n-1}\right]\left[\frac{SD^2 - \sum pq}{SD^2}\right]$$

n = number of items
SD^2 = variance
p = number of correct (true) items
q = number of incorrect (false) items

Standard Deviation

$$s = \sqrt{\frac{SS}{N-1}}$$

SS = sums of squared deviation scores. (Deviation scores are calculated by subtracting each individual score from the mean.)
N = sample size

Appendix B

Sample Assessment Report

Name: Jane Doe
Address: 123 Some Street
Phone: 555-555-5555
E-mail: jd@email.com
Interviewer: Ione N. Paiva

Date of Birth: 02-13-1979
Sex: Female
Race/Ethnicity: White
Date of Interview: 04-23-2017
Report Date: 04-30-2017

Reason for Referral

Jane, a 33-year-old partnered female, presented for counseling for anxiety symptoms. She noted a previous diagnosis of bipolar I disorder when she was in college. She stated that she has had at least three depressive episodes per year lasting 1 to 2 weeks at most and manic episodes once a month lasting approximately 3 days. She said that her last manic episode occurred approximately 3 weeks ago. She is no longer taking medication to treat her bipolar I disorder. She noted stress and depressive symptoms surrounding school and other challenges that led her to feel unmotivated, lose interest in activities she used to enjoy, and experience low self-esteem. She also noted anxiety and stress surrounding her job and her relationship with her mother. She noted that she has issues "standing her ground" with her mother, and her mother still expects Jane to "do as she says" without taking into consideration Jane's needs.

Background and History

Family Background

Jane was born in Germany, where her father was stationed as a Navy officer. She noted significant family issues, such as her father's infidelity. Her parents divorced, and her mother later married a man who was verbally, sexually, and emotionally abusive to her mother. Jane noted that she was not a witness to this behavior; however, the aftermath left her mother very rigid and overprotective. Jane noted a positive relationship with her stepfather's daughter that continues today. Her mother was not at home most evenings because of work; however, Jane noted that she had a very structured schedule and she feels her mother set this schedule for Jane to protect her. Jane stated that her mother never remarried after divorcing Jane's

351

stepfather, and her mother became emotionally volatile and developed a drinking problem. Jane noted that, as a result, she felt she had to be careful around her mother so she would not upset her. Jane noted that her mother's drinking was a major source of stress. According to Jane, her mother was diagnosed with bipolar I disorder and began taking lithium but later stopped taking the medication because of insurance reasons. Jane noted that she rarely saw her father, but when she would see him he would often make degrading comments regarding her appearance. She said that she often felt self-conscious around him, and she noted that he makes similar comments to her husband, which upsets her.

Jane has been partnered for approximately 10 years, and Jane stated that she is very happy in her marriage and has been with her partner since they were freshmen in high school. Jane noted one major relationship issue with regard to legal trouble involving her partner, and she discovered he had been lying about his drinking and drug use. She stated that she discovered after he had been thrown in jail for theft that he had been using drugs and stealing. He has also failed drug tests while on probation. She noted that, after his incarceration, she forgave him, and their relationship has been better, although she stated that she has some residual trust issues because of his lying about his drug use. She sees the experience as positive because she does not feel he would have changed if it had not been for his incarceration.

Medical/Counseling History

Jane was diagnosed with bipolar I disorder in 1999. She spent 5 years receiving medication management and outpatient therapy one to two times per month. Although she is no longer on medication, at the time of her diagnosis she was administered Wellbutrin XR 150 mg QD. During the time of her diagnosis, she experienced significant thoughts of suicide; self-esteem issues; and significant issues with family and her husband, who was her boyfriend at the time. She indicated she has not contemplated suicide in 13 years and is not currently receiving psychiatric treatment or counseling.

Substance Use and Abuse

Jane indicated no history of substance abuse and drinks approximately twice per week. She noted that social situations bring significant anxiety, and she drinks to relax.

Educational and Vocational History

Jane is a college graduate and currently pursuing a master's degree in counseling at Lakeview University. She has worked in many jobs in the helping profession and is currently working at the local community services board as a case management supervisor. She noted concerns regarding job security and burnout in her current position.

Other Pertinent Information

Jane described herself as introverted. She has a small social group and likes to spend time with her friends individually.

Evaluation Procedures

Jane completed the following assessments:

Beck Depression Inventory (BDI-II)
16 Personality Factor Questionnaire (16-PF)
Sentence Completion Test
Substance Abuse Subtle Screening Inventory–4 (SASSI-4)

Behavioral Observations

Jane presented alone for counseling on time. She appeared cooperative and maintained eye contact. She presented with anxious mood and affect. She fidgeted with her hands during the initial part of the counseling session. She was oriented to time, place, and person. She denied suicidal ideation.

Assessment Results

BDI-II

Jane yielded a score of 4 on the BDI-II, which indicates minimal or no depression. Jane rated herself as having minimally significant changes in areas of self-criticalness, crying, agitation, and irritability.

16-PF

Significant Profile Factor	Score	Rating
High Anxiety	8	High
Abstract	8	High
Apprehensive	8	High
Self-Reliant	8	High
Self-Controlled	7	High-average
Emotional and Social Adjustment[1]	4	Low-average
Differential	3	Low
Serious	3	Low
Emotional Expressivity*	3	Low
Grounded	2	Very low

Jane yielded scores that indicate high levels of anxiety, abstract thinking, apprehensiveness, and self-reliance. These high scores indicate that Jane is a very intelligent and abstract thinker who is self-sufficient and resourceful. She is also highly apprehensive and prone to self-doubt and worrying. Her high score on Apprehensive may be an indication of insecurity and guilt proneness. Her Self-Controlled score indicates that she is in control of her behavior and can inhibit her urges. Her low scores on the profile factors Differential, Serious, and Grounded indicate that she is dominant, assertive, enthusiastic, expressive, abstract, and idea oriented.

Sentence Completion Test

Jane's responses on the Sentence Completion Test indicate a high need for control in her life and a tendency to be self-critical and critical of others. Her responses indicate a tendency to be introverted and a desire to have time for herself. She also shows issues with her close family members and her need for them to see her as an adult. She sees herself as very funny and as a supportive person. She sees her parents as flawed and indicated that she is afraid to speak about her relationship with her mother with people, especially her mother. She described her mother as rigid and her father as insecure and indicated that she is afraid of becoming like her mother. Jane is optimistic about her future and likes helping

---

[1]These scores are predictions based on empirical research conducted by the test developers. The scores are noted because of Jane's significant lows on the factors Emotional and Social Adjustment and Emotional Expressivity. These scores should be used in conjunction with her global and profile scores and are only predictions of Jane's adjustment in these areas.

people. Pressure often brings her anxiety, and she indicated that her job often puts her under pressure that causes her to have anxiety. Her responses indicate that uncontrollable life changes, such as her husband possibly losing a job, also cause her anxiety. She is happy with her marriage and indicated that friends are important and that she highly values those relationships.

SASSI-4

Jane yielded scores on the SASSI-4 indicating a low probability of having a substance dependence disorder. Although Jane yielded no significant indications of substance dependence, she did elicit moderately significant scores on the Defensiveness and Family vs. Control Subjects subscales. These results indicate defensiveness as a possible personality trait and a tendency to put others' needs before her own. Jane's score on the Family vs. Control Subjects subscale also indicates that she has family with a history of substance abuse issues.

Diagnosis

Client presents with bipolar I disorder (296.45), with no developmental or medical concerns. Contextual concerns include parent–child relational problems and stressful relationships with coworkers.

Recommendations

It is recommended that Jane attend counseling weekly and consult with a physician for medication management of her mood symptoms.

Summary

Jane was a pleasant and willing participant in the completion of this report. She was well groomed and did not indicate any deception in any of the assessments administered. She did not indicate significant depressive symptoms. As Jane indicated, she does experience depressive episodes at various times throughout the year. There was no indication that she was having a manic episode at the time the BDI-II was administered that may have caused the results to be unusually low. Her minimally significant areas indicate that she is currently more self-critical, and she cries more than she used to. She is also more irritable and restless than usual.

Jane's results on the 16-PF indicate that she has clinically significant levels of anxiety and low-average levels of social and emotional adjustment. These findings may be related to her background and history, which should be explored in counseling. She is highly self-reliant, which she indicated in her interview, and has difficulty expressing her emotions to others. She noted a comfort in social isolation and a discomfort in social interaction, as indicated by her responses on the Sentence Completion Test and in the interview. She gives much support to others, especially her mother, while often pushing aside her own self-care. She shows resentment toward her parents and, as indicated by her interview and Sentence Completion Test, noted that they show a lack of respect toward her. Results from the Sentence Completion Test indicate highly self-critical thoughts toward herself and others. This same pattern is seen in her relationship with her parents, whom she described as rigid and judgmental themselves. Pressure and instability within her and her husband's job environment brings Jane anxiety. Anxiety and irritability can cause Jane to isolate, as evidenced by our interview and the Sentence Completion Test. The Sentence Completion Test also indicates a sense of optimism for Jane and a generally positive attitude despite her life circumstances. She is happy with her marriage and loves animals.

Jane's scores on the SASSI-4 and her interview indicate no substance abuse history. The results do indicate close relationships with those who have substance abuse issues, such as her husband and mother. The results from the SASSI-4 also support her indications that she often puts others' needs before her own. Although Jane indicated in her interview that she does not need many relationships with others and often enjoys being alone, there is an indication that she is guarded in addition to being introverted. The results from the SAS-SI-4 indicate a defensiveness within Jane, and this may contribute to her social isolation.

Jane's current issues with monthly manic episodes, occasional depressive episodes, and past diagnosis of bipolar I disorder support a diagnosis of bipolar I disorder. She is coping well, especially given that she is no longer on medication, and I rate her Global Assessment of Functioning at 65 when not having a bipolar episode and 57 when having a bipolar episode due to the frequency of episodes and the potential dangers associated with untreated bipolar disorder. I would recommend that Jane seek counseling with regard to her anxiety and noted stressors. I would also strongly recommend that Jane seek medication management for her mood symptoms.

Regards,

Ione N. Paiva

Test Your Knowledge
Answer Key

Chapter 1
1. F; 2. F; 3. T; 4. T; 5. F

Chapter 2
1. d; 2. e; 3. a; 4. b; 5. c

Chapter 3
1. c; 2. F; 3. T; 4. T; 5. d

Chapter 4
1. F; 2. T; 3. T; 4. F; 5. T

Chapter 5
1. T; 2. T; 3. F; 4. T; 5. F

Chapter 6
1. b; 2. c; 3. b; 4. d; 5. c

Chapter 7
1. a; 2. d; 3. c; 4. a; 5. a

Chapter 8
1. d; 2. a; 3. b; 4. F; 5. T

Chapter 9
1. c; 2. b; 3. b; 4. F 5. T

Chapter 10
1. b; 2. b; 3. a; 4. d; 5. T

Chapter 11
1. b; 2. a; 3. d; 4. a; 5. T

Chapter 12
1. b; 2. b; 3. T; 4. T; 5. F

Chapter 13
1. d; 2. b; 3. b; 4. F; 5. T

Chapter 14
1. d; 2. b; 3. d; 4. F; 5. T

Chapter 15
1. T; 2. F; 3. F; 4. T; 5. T

Chapter 16
1. F; 2. T; 3. T; 4. F; 5. T

References

Abidin, R. R. (2012). *Parenting Stress Index, fourth edition—Manual.* Odessa, FL: Psychological Assessment Resources.

Abrahams, S., & Balkin, R. S. (2006). A review of the Five Factor Wellness Inventory. *Association for Assessment in Counseling and Education Newsnotes, 46,* 2–3.

Achenbach, T. M., & Edelbrock, C. S. (1983). *The Achenbach Child Behavior Checklist.* Burlington, VT: Psychiatric Associates.

Achenbach, T. M., Rescorla, L. A., McConaughey, S. H., Pecora, P. J., Wetherbee, K. M., & Ruffle, T. M. (2003). *Achenbach System of Empirically Based Assessment (ASEBA).* Burlington, VT: Research Center for Children, Youth, and Families.

ACT, Inc. (2009a). *The ACT Interest Inventory and the World-of-Work Map.* Retrieved from http://www.act.org/uniact/index.html

ACT, Inc. (2009b). *ACT Interest Inventory technical manual.* Retrieved from http://www.act.org/content/dam/act/unsecured/documents/ACTInterestInventoryTechnicalManual.pdf

ACT, Inc. (2016a). *The ACT.* Retrieved from http://www.act.org/

ACT, Inc. (2016b). *ACT Asset.* Retrieved from https://www.act.org/content/act/en/products-and-services/act-asset.html

ACT, Inc. (2016c). *ACT Explore.* Retrieved from http://www.act.org/content/act/en/products-and-services/act-explore.html

ACT, Inc. (2016d). *Explore®, PLAN®, and the ACT.* Retrieved from https://forms.act.org/planstudent/tests/epas.html

ACT, Inc. (2016e). *WorkKeys.* Retrieved from http://www.act.org/workkeys/index.html

Adams, K., & Faulkhead, S. (2012). This is not a guide to indigenous research partnerships: But it could help. *Information, Communication & Society, 15,* 1016–1036.

Adams, R. S., & Tracey, T. J. G. (2004). Three versions of the Interpersonal Adjective Scales and their fit to the circumplex model. *Assessment, 11,* 263–270.

Ahmadi, S., Moloodi, R., Zarbaksh, M., & Ghaderi, A. (2014). Psychometric properties of the Eating Attitude Test-26 for female Iranian students. *Eating and Weight Disorders, 19,* 183–189. doi:10.1007/s40519-014-0106-7

Albanese, M. A. (2003). Mini-Mental State Examination. In B. S. Plake, J. C. Impara, & R. A. Spies (Eds.), *The fifteenth mental measurements yearbook* (pp. 589–590). Lincoln, NE: Buros Institute of Mental Measurements.

Albion, M. J., & Fogarty, G. J. (2002). Factors influencing career decision making in adolescents and adults. *Journal of Career Assessment, 10,* 91–126.

Alcántara, C., & Gone, J. (2014). Multicultural issues in the clinical interview and diagnostic process. In F. T. L. Leong, L. Comas-Díaz, G. C. Nagayama Hall, V. C. McLoyd, & J. E. Trimble (Eds.), *APA handbook of multicultural psychology: Vol. 2. Applications and training* (pp. 153–163). Washington, DC: American Psychological Association.

Alcohol Research Group. (n.d.). *Rapid Alcohol Problems Screen (RAPS) can help clinicians assess patients.* Retrieved from http://arg.org/news/rapid-alcohol-problems-screen-raps-can-help-clinicians assess-patients/

Alexander, A. (1999). *The functions of self-injury and its link to traumatic events in college students* (Doctoral dissertation). Available from UMI Dissertation Services. (UMI No. 9932285)

Allen, M. J., & Yen, W. M. (2002). *Introduction to measurement theory.* Long Grove, IL: Waveland Press.

Allport, G. W., & Vernon, P. E. (1931). A test of personal values. *Journal of Abnormal and Social Psychology, 26,* 231–248.

Alt, M., Arizmendi, G. D., Beal, C. R., & Hurtado, J. S. (2012). The effect of test translation on the performance of second grade English learners on the KeyMath-3. *Psychology in the Schools, 50,* 27–36. doi:10.1002/pits.21656

Alvarez-Rayón, G., Mancilla-Díaz, J. M., Vázquez-Arévalo, R., Unikel-Santoncini, C., Caballero-Romo, A., & Mercado-Corona, D. (2004). Validity of the Eating Attitudes Test: A study of Mexican eating disorders patients. *Eating and Weight Disorders, 9,* 243–248.

American Academy of Pediatrics. (2000). Diagnosis and evaluation of the child with attention-deficit/hyperactivity disorder. *Pediatrics, 105,* 1158–1170.

American Association for Geriatric Psychiatry, Alzheimer's Association, & American Geriatrics Society. (1997). Consensus statement: Diagnosis and treatment of Alzheimer disease and related disorders. *Journal of the American Medical Association, 278,* 1363–1371.

American Association of Suicidology. (2017). *Facts and statistics: National suicide statistics.* Retrieved from http://www.suicidology.org/resources/facts-statistics

American Association on Intellectual and Developmental Disabilities. (2013). *Supports Intensity Scale*®. Retrieved from https://aaidd.org/sis#.WJzNMxCIR-c

American College Testing Program. (1999). *Using the ACT in advising and course placement 1999–2000.* Iowa City, IA: Author.

American Counseling Association. (2003). *Standards for qualifications of test users.* Retrieved from http://aarc-counseling.org/assets/cms/uploads/files/standards.pdf

American Counseling Association. (2012). *The Affordable Care Act: What counselors should know.* Retrieved from http://www.counseling.org/PublicPolicy/PDF/What_counselors_should_know-the_Affordable_Care_Act_12-12.pdf

American Counseling Association. (2014). *ACA code of ethics.* Alexandria, VA: Author.

American Counseling Association. (n.d.). *The American Counseling Association (ACA) position statement on high stakes testing.* Retrieved from http://aarc-counseling.org/assets/cms/uploads/files/High_Stakes.pdf

American Dental Association. (2016). *Dental Admission Test (DAT).* Retrieved from http://www.ada.org/en/education-careers/dental-admission-test/

American Educational Research Association, American Psychological Association, & National Council on Measurement in Education. (2014). *Standards for educational and psychological testing.* Washington, DC: American Educational Research Association.

American Guidance Service. (2005). *KABC-II sampler.* Circle Pines, MN: Author.

American Medical Association. (1992). *Diagnosis and treatment guidelines on domestic violence.* Chicago, IL: Author.

American Psychiatric Association. (2000). *Diagnostic and statistical manual of mental disorders* (4th ed., text rev.). Washington, DC: Author.

American Psychiatric Association. (2003). *Practice guideline for the assessment and treatment of patients with suicidal behaviors.* Retrieved from https://psychiatryonline.org/pb/assets/raw/sitewide/practice_guidelines/guidelines/suicide.pdf

American Psychiatric Association. (2013). *Diagnostic and statistical manual of mental disorders* (5th ed.). Arlington, VA: Author.

American Psychological Association. (2013). *HIPAA: What you need to know now.* Retrieved from http://www.apapracticecentral.org/business/hipaa/hippa-privacy-primer.pdf

American School Counselor Association. (2012). *The ASCA national model: A framework for school counseling programs* (3rd ed.). Alexandria, VA: Author.

Anderson, J. O. (2010). Review of the TerraNova, Third Edition. In R. Spies, J. F. Carlson, & K. F. Geisinger (Eds.), *The eighteenth mental measurements yearbook* (pp. 608–611). Lincoln, NE: Buros Institute.

Anderson, N., Schlueter, J. E., Carlson, J. F., & Geisinger, K. F. (2016). *Tests in print* (9th ed.). Lincoln, NE: Buros Center for Testing.

Armstrong, P. I., Fouad, N. A., Rounds, J., & Hubert, L. (2010). Quantifying and interpreting group differences in interest profiles. *Journal of Career Assessment, 18,* 115–132.

Armstrong, P. I., & Vogel, D. L. (2009). Interpreting the interest–efficacy association from a RIASEC perspective. *Journal of Counseling Psychology, 56,* 392–407. doi:10.1037/a0016407

Association for Assessment and Research in Counseling. (2012). *Standards for multicultural assessment: Fourth revision, 2012.* Retrieved from aarc-counseling.org/assets/cms/uploads/files/AACE-AMCD.pdf

Association for Assessment in Counseling and Education. (2012). *Standards for multicultural assessment: Fourth revision, 2012.* Retrieved from http://aarc-counseling.org/assets/cms/uploads/files/AACE-AMCD.pdf

Association for Assessment in Counseling and Education & American Mental Health Counselors Association. (2010). *Standards for assessment in mental health counseling.* Retrieved from http://aarc-counseling.org/assets/cms/uploads/files/AACE-AMHCA.pdf

Association for Assessment in Counseling and Education & American Rehabilitation Counseling Association. (2003). *Pre-employment testing and the ADA.* Retrieved from http://aarc-counseling.org/assets/cms/uploads/files/employ(1).pdf

Association for Assessment in Counseling and Education & International Association of Addictions and Offender Counselors. (2010). *Standards for assessment in substance abuse counseling.* Retrieved from http://aarc-counseling.org/assets/cms/uploads/files/AACE-IAAOC.pdf

Association for Assessment in Counseling and Education & International Association of Marriage and Family Counselors. (2010). *Marriage, couple and family counseling assessment competencies.* Retrieved from http://aarc-counseling.org/assets/cms/uploads/files/AACE-IAMFC.pdf

Association for Assessment in Counseling and Education & National Career Development Association. (2010). *Career counselor assessment and evaluation competencies.* Retrieved from http://aarc-counseling.org/resources

Association of American Medical Colleges. (2016). *About the MCAT® exam.* Retrieved from https://students-residents.aamc.org/applying-medical-school/taking-mcat-exam/about-mcat-exam/

Atlas, J. (2014). Test review of the Children's Depression Inventory, 2nd Edition. In J. F. Carlson, K. F. Geisinger, & J. L. Jonson (Eds.), *The nineteenth mental measurements yearbook* (pp. 670–673). Lincoln, NE: University of Nebraska Press.

Attkisson, C. (2013). *Client Satisfaction Questionnaire CSQ-8.* Mill Valley, CA: Tamalpais Matrix Systems.

Babor, T. F., Higgins-Biddle, J. C., Saunders, J. B., & Monteiro, M. G. (2001). *The Alcohol Use Disorders Identification Test: Guidelines for use in primary care* (2nd ed.). Retrieved from whqlibdoc.who.int/hq/2001/WHO_MSD_MSB_01.6a.pdf

Bailey, D. C., Larson, L. M., Borgen, F. H., & Gasser, C. E. (2008). Changing of the guard: Interpretive continuity of the 2005 Strong Interest Inventory. *Journal of Career Assessment, 16,* 135–155.

Bain, S. K., & Allin, J. D. (2005). Review of the Stanford–Binet Intelligence Scales, Fifth Edition. *Journal of Psychoeducational Assessment, 23,* 87–95.

Baker, H. E. (2002). Reducing adolescent career indecision: The ASVAB Career Exploration Program. *The Career Development Quarterly, 50,* 359–370.

Baker, R. W., & Trzepacz, P. T. (2005). Mental status examination. In G. P. Koocher, J. C. Norcross, & S. S. Hill, III (Eds.), *Psychologists' desk reference* (2nd ed., pp. 7–12). Oxford, UK: Oxford University Press.

Ball, L. C., Cribbie, R. A., & Steele, J. R. (2013). Beyond gender differences: Using tests of equivalence to evaluate gender similarities. *Psychology of Women Quarterly, 37,* 147–154. doi:10.1177/0361684313480483

Bandura, A. (1986). *Social foundations of thought and action.* Englewood Cliffs, NJ: Prentice Hall.

Bandura, A. (1997). *Self-efficacy: The exercise of self-control.* New York, NY: Freeman.

Bardos, A. N. (2004). *Information package for BASI.* Minneapolis, MN: Pearson Assessments.

Barkley, R. A., & Murphy, K. R. (2006). *Attention-deficit hyperactivity disorder: A clinical workbook* (3rd ed.). New York, NY: Guilford Press.

Barrocas, A. L., Hankin, B. L., Young, J. F., & Abela, J. R. Z. (2012). Rates of nonsuicidal self-injury in youth: Age, sex, and behavioral methods in a community sample. *Pediatrics, 130,* 39–45. doi:10.1542/peds.2011-2094

Barrons Educational Series. (2015). *Profiles of American colleges* (32nd ed.). Hauppauge, NY: Author.

Bartlett Regional Hospital. (n.d.). *Bartlett Regional Hospital Domestic Violence Assessment.* Retrieved from www.hospitalsoup.com/public/dvassess.pdf

Bartling, H. C., & Hood, A. B. (1981). An 11-year follow-up of measured interest and vocational choice. *Journal of Counseling Psychology, 28,* 27–35.

Batshaw, M. L., Roizen, N. J., & Lotrecchiano, G. R. (2013). *Children with disabilities* (7th ed.). Baltimore, MD: Brookes.

Battle, C., Imber, S., Hoen-Saric, R., Stone, A., Nash, E., & Frank, J. (1966). Target complaints as criteria of improvement. *American Journal of Psychotherapy, 20,* 184–192.

Bault, M. W. (2012, July). *Americans with disabilities: 2010* (P70-131). Retrieved from the U.S. Census Bureau website: www.census.gov/prod/2012pubs/p70-131.pdf

Beatty, A. S. (2013). *A critical review of empirical and rational strategies for item selection and keying for biographical data inventories.* Retrieved from the University of Minnesota Digital Conservancy website: http://hdl.handle.net/11299/162418

Beck, A. T., & Steer, R. A. (1993). *Beck Anxiety Inventory manual.* San Antonio, TX: Psychological Corporation.

Beck, A. T., Steer, R. A., & Brown, G. K. (2003). *Beck Depression Inventory–II manual.* San Antonio, TX: Psychological Corporation.

Behavior Data Systems. (n.d.). *Domestic Violence Inventory research.* Retrieved from http://bds-research.com/Assessments/DVI/DVI.html

Bellah, C. G. (2005). Review of the Beta III. In R. A. Spies & B. S. Plake (Eds.), *The sixteenth mental measurements yearbook* (pp. 142–144). Lincoln, NE: Buros Institute of Mental Measurements.

Bennett, E. D., & Hastings, P. B. (2009). Key legal issues in assessment. In American Counseling Association (Ed.), *The ACA encyclopedia of counseling* (pp. 36–38). Alexandria, VA: American Counseling Association.

Bennett, G. K., Seashore, H. G., & Wesman, A. G. (1990). *Differential Aptitude Tests* (5th ed.). San Antonio, TX: Psychological Corporation.

Bennett, R. E. (2014). Preparing for the future: What educational assessment must do. *Teachers College Record, 116*(11), Article ID 17623.

Bennett, R. E., Rock, D. A., Kaplan, B. A., & Jirele, T. (1988). Psychometric characteristics. In W. W. Williamham, M. Ragosta, R. Bennett, H. Braun, D. A. Rock, & D. E. Powers (Eds.), *Testing handicapped people* (pp. 83–97). Needham Heights, MA: Allyn & Bacon.

Berens, D., & Erford, B. T. (2018). Disability, ableism, and ageism. In D. G. Hays & B. T. Erford (Eds.), *Developing multicultural counseling competency: A systems approach* (3rd ed., pp. 224–254). Boston, MA: Pearson.

Berg-Cross, L., & Zoppetti, L. (1991). Person-in-culture interview. *Journal of College Student Psychotherapy, 5*(4), 5–21. doi:10.1300/J035v05n04_02

Berman, A. L., & Silverman, M. M. (2014). Suicide risk assessment and risk formulation part II: Suicide risk formulation and the determination of levels of risk. *Suicide and Life-Threatening Behavior, 44*, 432–443. doi:10.1111/sltb/12067

Berman, L., Berman, J., Zicak, M. C., & Marley, C. (2002). Outcome measurement in sexual disorders. In W. W. IsHak, T. Burt, & L. I. Sederer (Eds.), *Outcome measurement in psychiatry: A critical review* (pp. 273–289). Washington, DC: American Psychiatric.

Berman, N. C., Stark, A., Cooperman, A., Wilhelm, S., & Cohen, I. G. (2015). Effect of patient and therapist factors on suicide risk assessment. *Death Studies, 39*, 433–441. doi:10.1080/07481187.2014.958630

Bernstein, D. P., Fink, L., Handelsman, L., Foote, J., Lovejoy, M., Wenzel, K., . . . Ruggiero, J. (1994). Initial reliability and validity of a new retrospective measure of child abuse and neglect. *American Academy of Child and Adolescent Psychiatry, 151*, 1132–1136.

Bernstein, E. M., & Putnam, F. (1986). Development, reliability, and validity of a dissociation scale. *Journal of Nervous and Mental Disorders, 174*, 727–735.

Betz, N. E., Borgen, F. H., & Harmon, L. W. (1996). *Skills Confidence Inventory applications and technical guide*. Palo Alto, CA: Consulting Psychologists Press.

Betz, N. E., Borgen, F. H., Rottinghaus, P., Paulsen, A., Halper, C. R., & Harmon, L. W. (2003). The Expanded Skills Confidence Inventory: Measuring basic dimensions of vocational activity. *Journal of Vocational Behavior, 62*, 76–100.

Betz, N. E., Hammond, M., & Multon, K. (2005). Reliability and validity of response continua for the Career Decision Self-Efficacy Scale. *Journal of Career Assessment, 13*, 131–149. doi:10.1177/1069072704273123

Betz, N. E., Klein, K. L., & Taylor, K. M. (1996). Evaluation of a short form of the Career Decision-Making Self-Efficacy Scale. *Journal of Career Assessment, 4*, 47–57.

Betz, N. E., & Luzzo, D. A. (1996). Career assessment and the Career Decision-Making Self-Efficacy Scale. *Journal of Career Assessment, 4*, 413–428.

Betz, N. E., & Rottinghaus, P. J. (2006). Current research on parallel measures of interests and confidence for basic dimensions of vocational activity. *Journal of Career Assessment, 14*, 56–76.

Betz, N. E., & Taylor, K. M. (1994). *Manual for the Career Decision-Making Self-Efficacy Scale*. Columbus: The Ohio State University, Department of Psychology.

Bieling, P. J., Antony, M. M., & Swinson, R. P. (1998). The State–Trait Anxiety Inventory, trait version: Structure and content re-examined. *Behaviour Research & Therapy, 36*, 777–788.

Blacher, J. H., Murray-Ward, M., & Uellendahl, G. E. (2005). School counselors and student assessment. *Professional School Counseling, 8*, 337–343.

Black, M. C., Basile, K. C., Breiding, M. J., Smith, S. G., Walters, M. L., Merrick, M. T., . . . Stevens, M. R. (2011). *The National Intimate Partner and Sexual Violence Survey (NISVS): 2010 summary report*. Atlanta, GA: National Center for Injury Prevention and Control.

Blando, J. (2011). *Counseling older adults*. New York, NY: Routledge.

Blasko, K. A., Winek, J. L., & Bieschke, K. J. (2007). Therapists' prototypical assessment of domestic violence situations. *Journal of Marital and Family Therapy, 33*, 258–269. doi:10.1111/j.1152-0606.2007.00020.x

Bodenmann, G. (2008). *Dyadisches coping inventar: Testmanual* [Dyadic Coping Inventory: Test manual]. Bern, Switzerland: Huber.

Bohn, M. J., Babor, T. F., & Kranzler, H. R. (1995). The Alcohol Use Disorders Identification Test (AUDIT): Validation of a screening instrument for use in medical settings. *Journal of Studies in Alcohol, 56,* 423–432.

Bolles, R. N. (2017). *What color is your parachute? 2017: A practical manual for job-hunters and career-changers.* Berkeley, CA: Ten Speed Press.

Borgen, F., & Grutter, J. (2005). *Where do I go next? Using your Strong results to manage your career* (Rev. ed.). Mountain View, CA: Consulting Psychologists Press.

Boswell, D. L., White, J. K., Sims, W. D., Harrist, R. S., & Romans, J. S. C. (2013). Reliability and validity of the Outcome Questionnaire-45.2. *Psychological Reports: Mental & Physical Health, 112,* 689–693.

Bourdeau, B., & Thomas, V. (2003). Counseling gifted clients and their families: Comparing clients' and counselors' perspectives. *Journal of Secondary Gifted Education, 14,* 114–126.

Bowers, J., & Hatch, P. A. (2005). *The ASCA national model: A framework for school counseling programs* (2nd ed.). Alexandria, VA: American School Counselor Association.

Brannigan, G. C., & Decker, S. L. (2003). *Bender Visual Motor Gestalt Test* (2nd ed.). Itasca, IL: Riverside.

Brannon, L., Feist, J., & Updegraff, J. (2013). *Health psychology: An introduction to behavior and health* (8th ed.). Belmont, CA: Wadsworth.

Brener, N. D., Kann, L., Shanklin, S., Kinchen, S., Eaton, D. K., Hawkins, J., & Flint, K. H. (2013). Methodology of the Youth Risk Behavior Surveillance System—2013. *MMWR Recommendations Report, 62,* 1–20.

Briere, J. (1992). *Child abuse trauma: Theory and treatment of the lasting effects.* Newbury Park, CA: Sage.

Briere, J. (1995). *Professional manual for the Trauma Symptom Inventory.* Odessa, FL: Psychological Assessment Resources.

Briere, J. (1996). *Professional manual for the Trauma Symptom Checklist for Children.* Odessa, FL: Psychological Assessment Resources.

Brodey, B. B., McMullin, D., Kaminer, Y., Winters, K. C., Mosshart, E., Rosen, C. S., & Brodey, I. S. (2008). Psychometric characteristics of the Teen Addiction Severity Index-2 (T-ASI-2). *Substance Abuse, 29,* 19–32.

Brookhart, S. M. (1995). Review of the Rokeach Value Survey. In J. C. Conoley & J. C. Impara (Eds.), *The twelfth mental measurements yearbook* (pp. 878–879). Lincoln, NE: Buros Institute of Mental Measurements.

Brott, P. (2015). Qualitative career assessment processes. In M. McMahon & M. Watson (Eds.), *Career assessment: Qualitative approaches* (pp. 31–39). Rotterdam, the Netherlands: Sense.

Brown, G. P., & Clark, D. A. (2014). *Assessment in cognitive therapy.* New York, NY: Guilford Press.

Brown, J. B., Lent, B., Schmidt, G., & Sas, G. (2000). Application of the Woman Abuse Screening Tool (WAST) and WAST-Short in the family practice setting. *Journal of Family Practice, 49,* 896–903.

Brown, M. B. (2000). Diagnosis and treatment of children and adolescents with attention-deficit/hyperactivity disorder. *Journal of Counseling & Development, 78,* 195–203.

Brown, R. P., & Day, E. (2006). The difference isn't black and white: Stereotype threat and the race gap on Raven's Progressive Matrices. *Journal of Applied Psychology, 91,* 979–985. doi:10.1037/0021-9010.91.4.979

Brown, T. E. (1996). *The Brown Attention-Deficit Disorder Scales.* San Antonio, TX: Psychological Corporation.

Brown-Chidsey, R., & Steege, M. W. (2010). *Response to intervention: Principles and strategies for effective practice* (2nd ed.). New York, NY: Guilford Press.

Bruns, D., & Disorbio, P. B. (2003). *Battery for Health Improvement 2 (BHI 2) manual.* Minneapolis, MN: NCS Pearson.

Bubenzer, D., Zimpfer, D., & Mahrle, C. (1990). Standardized individual appraisal in agency and private practice: A survey. *Journal of Mental Health Counseling, 12,* 51–66.

Buck, J. N. (1992). *House–Tree–Person Projective Drawing Technique H-T-P: Manual and interpretive guide.* Los Angeles, CA: Western Psychological Services.

Budman, S. H. (2000). Behavioral health care dot.com and beyond: Computer-mediated communications in mental health and substance abuse treatment. *American Psychologist, 55,* 1290–1300.

Bullock, E. E., & Madson, M. B. (2009). COPSystem: Career guidance program (COPS) (CAPS) (COPES). In E. Whitfield, R. Feller, & C. T. Wood (Eds.), *A counselor's guide to career assessment instruments* (5th ed., pp. 119–126). Broken Arrow, OK: National Career Development Association.

Bullock-Yowell, E., & Osborne L. K. (2013). COPSystem career guidance program: Career Occupational Preference System Interest Inventory, Career Ability Placement Survey, and Career Orientation Placement and Evaluation Survey. In C. T. Wood & D. G. Hays (Eds.), *A counselor's guide to career assessment instruments* (6th ed., pp. 177–182). Broken Arrow, OK: National Career Development Association.

Burgemeister, B. B., Blum, L. H., & Lorge, I. (1972). *Columbia Mental Maturity Scale* (3rd ed.). New York, NY: Harcourt Brace Jovanovich.

Butcher, J. (2013). Computerized personality assessment. In J. Graham, J. Naglieri, & I. Weiner (Eds.), *Handbook of psychology: Vol. 10. Assessment psychology* (pp. 165–191). Hoboken, NJ: Wiley.

Butcher, J. N., Cabiya, J., Lucio, E., & Garrido, M. (2007). *Assessing Hispanic clients using the MMPI-2 and MMPI-A.* Washington, DC: American Psychological Association.

Butcher, J. N., Graham, J. R., Ben-Porath, Y. S., Tellegen, A., & Dahlstrom, W. G. (2001). *MMPI-2 manual for administration, scoring, and interpretation* (Rev. ed.). Minneapolis: University of Minnesota Press.

Butcher, J. N., Graham, J. R., Williams, C. L., & Ben-Porath, Y. (1990). *Development and use of the MMPI-2 content scales.* Minneapolis: University of Minnesota Press.

Butcher, J. N., Williams, C. L., & Fowler, R. D. (2000). *Essentials of MMPI-2 and MMPI-A interpretation* (2nd ed.). Minneapolis: University of Minnesota Press.

Calvert, R., & Kellett, S. (2014). Cognitive analytic therapy: A review of the outcome evidence base for treatment. *Psychology and Psychotherapy: Theory, Research, and Practice, 87,* 253–277. doi:10.1111/papt.12020

Camara, W. J., Nathan, J. S., & Puente, A. E. (2000). Psychological test usage: Implications in professional psychology. *Professional Psychology: Research and Practice, 31,* 141–154.

Camp, D. C. (2000). Career decision-making difficulties in high school students: A study of reliability and validity of the Career Decision Difficulties Questionnaire. *Dissertation Abstracts International: Section A. Humanities and Social Sciences, 61*(1), 893.

Campbell, D. P. (1993). A new integrated battery of psychological surveys. *Journal of Counseling & Development, 71,* 575–587.

Campbell, D. P. (2002). The history and development of the Campbell Interest and Skill Survey. *Journal of Career Assessment, 10,* 150–168.

Campbell, D. P., Hyne, S. A., & Nilsen, D. L. (1992). *Manual for the Campbell Interest and Skill Survey.* Minneapolis, MN: National Computer Systems.

Campbell, J. C., & Perry, Q. A. (2013). Harrington-O'Shea Career Decision Making System-Revised. In C. T. Wood & D. G. Hays (Eds.), *A counselor's guide to career assessment instruments* (6th ed., pp. 251–254). Broken Arrow, OK: National Career Development Association.

Campbell, J. C., Webster, D., & Glass, N. (2009). The Danger Assessment: Validation of the lethality risk assessment instrument for intimate partner femicide. *Journal of Interpersonal Violence, 24,* 4653–4674.

Canals, J., Carbajo, G., & Fernández-Ballart, J. (2002). Discriminant validity of the Eating Attitudes Test according to American Psychiatric Association and World Health Organization criteria of eating disorders. *Psychological Reports, 91,* 1052–1056.

Canfield, A. A., & Canfield, J. S. (1988). *Canfield Learning Styles Inventory.* Los Angeles, CA: Western Psychological Services.

Canivez, G. L. (2010). Review of the Wechsler Adult Intelligence Scale–Fourth Edition. In R. Spies, J. F. Carlson, & K. F. Geisinger (Eds.), *The eighteenth mental measurements yearbook* (pp. 684–688). Lincoln, NE: University of Nebraska Press.

Carlson, J. F., Geisinger, K. F., & Jonson, J. L. (Eds.) (2014). *The nineteenth mental measurements yearbook.* Lincoln, NE: University of Nebraska Press.

Carlson, L. (2013). Quality of Life Inventory. In C. T. Wood & D. G. Hays (Eds.), *A counselor's guide to career assessment instruments* (6th ed., pp. 359–362). Broken Arrow, OK: National Career Development Association.

Carney, R. N. (2005). Review of the Stanford Achievement Test, Tenth Edition. In R. A. Spies & B. S. Plake (Eds.), *The sixteenth mental measurements yearbook* (pp. 969–972). Lincoln, NE: Buros Institute of Mental Measurements.

Carson, J. (2014). Mental testing in the early twentieth century: Internationalizing the mental testing story. *History of Psychology, 17,* 249–255.

Case, J. C., & Blackwell, T. L. (2008). Test review. *Rehabilitation Counseling Bulletin, 51,* 122–126.

Cattell, H. E. P., & Schuerger, J. M. (2003). *Essentials of 16PF assessment.* Hoboken, NJ: Wiley.

Cattell, R. B. (1973). *Measuring intelligence with the Culture Fair Test.* Champaign, IL: Institute for Personality and Ability Testing.

Centers for Disease Control and Prevention. (2015a). *WISQARS™ tutorials: Fatal injury reports.* Retrieved from https://www.cdc.gov/injury/wisqars/fatal_help/reports.html

Centers for Disease Control and Prevention. (2015b). *Suicide: Facts at a glance.* Retrieved from https://www.cdc.gov/violenceprevention/pdf/suicide-datasheet-a.pdf

Centers for Disease Control and Prevention. (2015c). *What is excessive alcohol use?* Retrieved from http://www.cdc.gov/alcohol/pdfs/excessive_alcohol_use.pdf

Chambless, D. L., & Hollon, S. D. (2012). Treatment validity for intervention studies. In H. Cooper, P. M. Camic, D. L. Long, A. T. Panter, D. Rindskopf, & K. J. Sher (Eds.), *APA handbook of research methods in psychology: Vol. 2. Research designs: Quantitative, qualitative, neuropsychological, and biological* (pp. 529–552). Washington, DC: American Psychological Association.

Chang, E. D., D'Zurilla, T. J., & Sanna, L. J. (2004). *Social problem solving: Theory, research, and training.* Washington, DC: American Psychological Association.

Charter, R. A., & Feldt, L. S. (2002). The importance of reliability as it relates to true score confidence intervals. *Measurement and Evaluation in Counseling and Development, 35,* 104–112.

Chartrand, J. M., Robbins, S. B., & Morrill, W. H. (1997). *Career Factors Inventory.* Palo Alto, CA: Consulting Psychologists Press.

Chernin, J., Holden, J. M., & Chandler, C. (1997). Bias in psychological assessment: Heterosexism. *Measurement and Evaluation in Counseling and Development, 30,* 68–76.

Cherpitel, C. J. (2000). A brief screening instrument for problem drinking in the emergency room: The RAPS4. *Journal of Studies on Alcohol, 61,* 447–449.

Cherpitel, C. J. (2002). Screening for alcohol problems in the U.S. general population: Comparison of the CAGE, RAPS4, and RAPS4-QF by gender, ethnicity, and service utilization. *Alcoholism, Clinical and Experimental Research, 26,* 1686–1691.

Chope, R. C. (2013). California Psychological Inventory, third edition. In C. T. Wood & D. G. Hays (Eds.), *A counselor's guide to career assessment instruments* (6th ed., pp. 367–371). Broken Arrow, OK: National Career Development Association.

Christensen, A., & Sullaway, M. (1984). *Relationship issues questionnaire.* Unpublished questionnaire, University of California, Los Angeles.

Chu, C., Klein, K. M., Buchman-Schmitt, J. M., Horn, M. A., Hagan, C. R., & Joiner, T. E. (2015). Routinized assessment of suicide risk in clinical practice: An empirically informed update. *Journal of Clinical Psychology, 71,* 1186–1200. doi:10.1002/jclp.22210

Cicchetti, D. V. (1994). Guidelines, criteria, and rules of thumb for evaluating normed and standardized assessment interests in psychology. *Psychological Assessment, 6,* 284–290.

Cieciuch, J., Davidov, E., Vecchione, M., Beierlein, C., & Schwartz, S. H. (2014). The cross-national invariance properties of a new scale to measure 19 basic human values: A test across eight countries. *Journal of Cross-Cultural Psychology, 45,* 764–776. doi:10.1177/0022022114527348

Cieciuch, J., Schwartz, S. H., & Davidov, E. (2015). Social psychology of values. In J. D. Wright (Ed.), *International encyclopedia of the social and behavioral sciences* (2nd ed., pp. 41–46). Oxford, UK: Elsevier.

Clausen, L., Rosenvinge, J. H., Friborg, O., & Rokkedal, K. (2011). Validating the Eating Disorder Inventory-3 (EDI-3): A comparison between 561 female eating disorders patients and 878 females from the general population. *Journal of Psychopathology and Behavioral Assessment, 33,* 101–110.

Clawson, T. W. (1997). Control of psychological testing: The threat and a response. *Journal of Counseling & Development, 76,* 90–94.

Clift, R. J. W., Thomas, L. A., & Dutton, D. G. (2005). Two-year reliability of the Propensity for Abusiveness Scale. *Journal of Family Violence, 20,* 231–234.

Climie, E. A., & Rostad, K. (2011). Wechsler Adult Intelligence Scale. *Journal of Psychoeducational Assessment, 29,* 581–586.

Cochran, S. D., Sullivan, J. G., & Mays, V. M. (2003). Prevalence of mental disorders, psychological distress, and mental health service use among lesbian, gay, and bisexual adults in the United States. *Journal of Consulting and Clinical Psychology, 71,* 53–61.

Cohen, G. L., & Sherman, D. K. (2005). Stereotype threat and the social and scientific context of the race achievement gap. *American Psychologist, 60,* 270–271.

Cohen, J. S., Edmunds, J. M., Brodman, D. M., Benjamin, C. L., & Kendall, P. C. (2013). Using self-monitoring: Implementation of collaborative empiricism in cognitive-behavioral therapy. *Cognitive and Behavioral Practice, 20,* 419–428. doi:10.1016/j.cbpra.2012.06.002

Cohen, P. J., Glaser, B. A., & Calhoun, G. B. (2005). Examining readiness for change: A preliminary evaluation of the University of Rhode Island Change Assessment with incarcerated adolescents. *Measurement and Evaluation in Counseling and Development, 38,* 45–62.

Colangelo, N., & Wood, S. M. (2015). Counseling the gifted: Past, present, and future directions. *Journal of Counseling & Development, 93,* 133–142.

Colby, S. L., & Ortman, J. M. (2015). *Projections of the size and composition of the U.S. population: 2014 to 2060.* Retrieved from the U.S. Census Bureau website: http://www.census.gov/content/dam/Census/library/publications/2015/demo/p25-1143.pdf?

College Board. (2016a). *AP students.* Retrieved from https://apstudent.collegeboard.org/home

College Board. (2016b). *CLEP.* Retrieved from https://clep.collegeboard.org

College Board. (2016c). *Equivalence tables.* Retrieved from http://research.collegeboard.org/programs/sat/data/equivalence

College Board. (2016d). *SAT suite of assessments.* Retrieved from https://info.assessmentportal.collegeboard.org/sat-suite/

College Board. (2017). *The college handbook 2017.* New York, NY: Author.

Conn, S. R., & Rieke, M. L. (1994). *The 16PF fifth edition technical manual.* Champaign, IL: Institute for Personality and Ability Testing.

Conners, C. K. (1997). *Conners' Rating Scales–Revised.* North Tonawanda, NY: Multi-Health Systems.

Conners, C. K., Erhardt, D., & Sparrow, E. (1998). *Conners' Adult ADHD Rating Scales.* North Tonawanda, NY: Multi-Health Systems.

Coopersmith, S. (1993). *Self-Esteem Inventories (SEI).* Palo Alto, CA: Consulting Psychologists Press.

Coopersmith, S., & Gilberts, R. (1982). *Professional manual: Behavioral Academic Self-Esteem (BASE), a rating scale.* Palo Alto, CA: Consulting Psychologists Press.

Cordón, L. A. (2005). *Popular psychology: An encyclopedia.* Westport, CT: Greenwood Press.

Correll, S. J. (2001). Gender and the career choice process: The role of biased self-assessments. *American Journal of Sociology, 106,* 1691–1730.

Costa, P. T., Jr., & McCrae, R. (1992). *NEO-PI-R professional manual.* Odessa, FL: Psychological Assessment Resources.

Costa, P. T., Jr., & Widiger, T. A. (Eds.). (2002). *Personality disorders and the five-factor model of personality* (2nd ed.). Washington, DC: American Psychological Association.

Costantino, G. (1987). *TEMAS (Tell-Me-A-Story) picture cards.* Flushing, NY: TEMAS Test.

Costantino, G., Dana, R. H., & Malgady, R. G. (2007). *TEMAS (Tell-Me-A-Story) assessment in multicultural societies.* Mahwah, NJ: Erlbaum.

Coughlin, S. S., & Sher, L. (2013). *Suicidal behavior and neurological illnesses.* Retrieved from http://www.ncbi.nlm.nih.gov/pmc/articles/PMC3910083/

Cox, A. A. (2003). The Wellness Evaluation of Lifestyle. In B. S. Plake, J. C. Impara, & R. A. Spies (Eds.), *The fifteenth mental measurements yearbook* (pp. 1005–1007). Lincoln, NE: Buros Institute of Mental Measurements.

Crace, R. K., & Brown, D. (1992). *The Life Values Inventory.* Minneapolis, MN: National Computer Systems.

Craig, R. J. (1999). *Interpreting personality tests.* New York, NY: Wiley.

Craigen, L. M., Healey, A. C., Walley, C. T., Byrd, R., & Schuster, J. (2010). Assessment and self-injury: Implications for counselors. *Measurement and Evaluation in Counseling and Development, 43,* 3–15.

Craigen, L. M., & Milliken, T. (2010). The self-injury experiences of young adult women: Implications for counseling. *Journal of Humanistic Counseling, Education and Development, 49,* 112–126.

Crethar, H. C., Rivera, E. T., & Nash, S. (2008). In search of common threads: Linking multicultural, feminist, and social justice counseling paradigms. *Journal of Counseling & Development, 86,* 269–278.

Crites, J. O. (1978). *Career Maturity Inventory: Theory and research handbook* (2nd ed.). Monterey, CA: CTB/McGraw-Hill.

Crites, J. O. (1993). *Career Mastery Inventory sourcebook.* Boulder, CO: Crites Career Consultants.

Crocker, L. (2005). Teaching for the test: How and why test preparation is appropriate. In R. P. Phelps (Ed.), *Defending standardized testing* (pp. 159–174). Mahwah, NJ: Erlbaum.

Cross, T. L., & Coleman, L. J. (2014). School-based conception of giftedness. *Journal for the Education of the Gifted, 37,* 94–103.

CTB/Macmillan/McGraw-Hill. (1993). *Test of Cognitive Skills test coordinator's handbook and guide to interpretation.* Monterey, CA: Author.

Cummings, W. H. (1995). Age group differences and estimated frequencies of the Myers–Briggs Type Indicator preferences. *Measurement and Evaluation in Counseling and Development, 2,* 69–77.

Cyr, M., McDuff, P., & Wright, J. (2006). Prevalence and predictors of dating violence among adolescent female victims of child sexual abuse. *Journal of Interpersonal Violence, 21,* 1000–1017. doi:10.1177/0886260506290201

D'Costa, A. (2013). Career Factors Inventory. In C. T. Wood & D. G. Hays (Eds.), *A counselor's guide to career assessment instruments* (6th ed., pp. 325–328). Broken Arrow, OK: National Career Development Association.

Dagley, J. C., & Salter, S. K. (2004). Practice and research in career counseling and development—2003. *The Career Development Quarterly, 53*, 98–157.

Dana, R. H. (2011). Comprehensive assessment for a multicultural society. In R. G. Malgady (Ed.), *Cultural competence in assessment and intervention with ethnic minorities: Some perspectives from psychology, social work and education* (pp. 3–23). Oak Park, IL: Bentham Science.

Darcy, M., & Tracey, T. J. G. (2003). Integrating abilities and interests in career choice: Maximal versus typical assessment. *Journal of Career Assessment, 11*, 219–237.

Data Recognition Corporation/CTB. (2016). *TABE Tests of Adult Basic Education*. Retrieved from http://www.ctb.com/ctb.com/control/productFamilyViewAction?productFam ilyId=608&p=products

Day, S. X., & Rounds, J. (1998). Universality of vocational interest structure among racial and ethnic minorities. *American Psychologist, 53*, 728–736.

de la Cruz, L. F., Simonoff, E., McGough, J. J., Halperin, J. M., Arnold, E., & Stringaris, A. (2015). Treatment of children with attention-deficit/hyperactivity disorder (ADHD) and irritability: Results from the multimodal treatment study of children with ADHD (MTA). *Journal of the American Academy of Child & Adolescent Psychiatry, 54*, 62–70. doi:10.1016/j.jaac.2014.10.006

Debra P. v. Turlington, 644 F.2d 397 (5th Cir. 1981), 730 F.2d 1405 (11th Cir. 1984).

Dejong, P., & Berg, I. S. (2012). *Interviewing for solutions* (3rd ed.). Belmont, CA: Thomson Brooks/Cole.

Del Corso, J. (2013). O*NET Work Importance Profiler and Work Importance Locator. In C. T. Wood & D. G. Hays (Eds.), *A counselor's guide to career assessment instruments* (6th ed., pp. 269–274). Broken Arrow, OK: National Career Development Association.

del Mar Sánchez-Fuentes, M., Santos-Iglesias, P., & Sierra, J. C. (2014). A systematic review of sexual satisfaction. *International Journal of Clinical and Health Psychology, 14*, 67–75.

DeNavas-Walt, C., Proctor, B. D., & Smith, J. C. (2013). *Income, poverty, and health insurance coverage in the United States: 2012*. Retrieved from https://www.census.gov/ prod/2013pubs/p60-245.pdf

Denis, C. M., Cacciola, J. S., & Alterman, A. I. (2013). Addiction Severity Index (ASI) summary scores: Comparison of the recent status scores of the ASI-6 and the composite scores of the ASI-5. *Journal of Substance Abuse Treatment, 45*, 444–450. doi:10.106/j.jsat.2013.06.003

Denis, C., Fatséas, M., Beltran, V., Serre, F., Alexandre, J. M., Debrabant, R., . . . Auriacombe, M. (2016). Usefulness and validity of the modified Addiction Severity Index: A focus on alcohol, drugs, tobacco, and gambling. *Substance Abuse, 37*, 168–175.

DePaola, S. J. (2003). Clinical Assessment Scales for the Elderly. In B. S. Plake, J. C. Impara, & R. A. Spies (Eds.), *The fifteenth mental measurements yearbook* (pp. 190–193). Lincoln, NE: Buros Institute of Mental Measurements.

Derogatis, L. R. (1979). *Sexual Functioning Inventory manual*. Riderwood, MD: Clinical Psychometric Research.

Derogatis, L. R. (1993). *BSI: Administration, scoring, and procedures for the Brief Symptom Inventory* (3rd ed.). Minneapolis, MN: National Computer Systems.

Derogatis, L. R. (1994). *Administration, scoring, and procedures manual for the SCL-90-R*. Minneapolis, MN: National Computer Systems.

Derogatis, L. R. (2000). *BSI-18: Administration, scoring and procedures manual*. Minneapolis, MN: National Computer Systems.

Derogatis, L. R., & Fitzpatrick, M. (2004). The SCL-90-R, the Brief Symptom Inventory (BSI), and the BSI-18. In M. E. Maruish (Ed.), *The use of psychological testing for treatment planning and outcomes assessment: Vol. 3. Instruments for adults* (3rd ed., pp. 1–41). Mahwah, NJ: Erlbaum.

Derogatis, L. R., & Unger, R. (2010). Symptom checklist-90-Revised. In I. B. Weiner & W. E. Craighead (Eds.), *The Corsini encyclopedia of psychology* (Vol. 4, pp. 1743–1744). Hoboken, NJ: Wiley.

Dickinson, J., & Tokar, D. M. (2004). Structural and discriminant validity of the Career Factors Inventory. *Journal of Vocational Behavior, 65,* 239–254.

DiPerna, J. C. (2005). Review of the Cognitive Abilities Test Form 6. In R. A. Spies & B. S. Plake (Eds.), *The sixteenth mental measurements yearbook* (pp. 228–231). Lincoln, NE: Buros Institute of Mental Measurements.

Dollaghan, C. (2013). *Client-centered communication and patient decision aids.* Retrieved from http://cred.pubs.asha.org/article.aspx?articleid=2441858

Donnay, D. A. C., & Borgen, F. H. (1996). Validity, structure, and content of the 1994 Strong Interest Inventory. *Journal of Counseling Psychology, 43,* 275–291.

Donnay, D. A. C., & Borgen, F. H. (1999). The incremental validity of vocational self-efficacy: An examination of interest, self-efficacy, and occupation. *Journal of Counseling Psychology, 46,* 432–447.

Donnay, D. A. C., & Elliott, T. E. (2003). The California Psychological Inventory. In L. E. Beutler & G. Groth-Marnat (Eds.), *Integrative assessment of adult personality* (pp. 227–261). New York, NY: Guilford Press.

Donnay, D. A. C., Morris, M. L., Schaubhut, N. A., & Thompson, R. C. (2005). *Strong Interest Inventory manual: Research, development, and strategies for interpretation.* Mountain View, CA: Consulting Psychologists Press.

Donoso, O. A., Hernandez, B., & Horin, E. V. (2010). Use of psychological tests within vocational rehabilitation. *Journal of Vocational Rehabilitation, 32,* 191–200.

Dougherty, E. H., & Schinka, J. A. (1988). *Mental Status Checklist for Adolescents.* Lutz, FL: Psychological Assessment Resources.

Dougherty, E. H., & Schinka, J. A. (1989). *Mental Status Checklist for Children.* Lutz, FL: Psychological Assessment Resources.

Duffy, M., Giordano, V. A., Farrell, J. B., Paneque, O. M., & Crump, G. B. (2008). No Child Left Behind: Values and research issues in high-stakes assessments. *Counseling and Values, 53,* 53–66.

Duncan, B. L., Miller, S. D., Sparks, J. A., Claud, D. A., Reynolds, L. R., Brown, J., & Johnson, L. D. (2003). The Session Rating Scale: Preliminary psychometric properties of a "working" alliance measure. *Journal of Brief Therapy, 3,* 3–12.

Dunn, L. M., & Dunn, L. M. (2007). *The Peabody Picture Vocabulary Test–Fourth edition: Examiner's manual.* San Antonio, TX: Pearson.

Dunn, R., Dunn, K., & Price, G. E. (1987). *Manual for the Learning Style Inventory (LSI).* Lawrence, KS: Price Systems.

DuPaul, G. J., Power, T. J., Anastopoulos, A. D., & Reid, R. (1998). *ADHD Rating Scale–IV: Checklists, norms, and clinical interpretation.* New York, NY: Guilford Press.

Dutton, M. A., Mitchell, B., & Haywood, Y. (1996). The emergency department as a violence prevention center. *Journal of American Medical Women's Association, 51,* 92–96.

Dykeman, C. (2013). Childhood Career Development Scale. In C. T. Wood & D. G. Hays (Eds.), *A counselor's guide to career assessment instruments* (6th ed., pp. 343–346). Broken Arrow, OK: National Career Development Association.

EdITS. (n.d.). *The COPSystem career measurement package.* Retrieved from http://www.edits.net/products/career-guidance/copsystem-career-measurement.html

Educational Testing Service. (2016a). *About the TOEFL® test.* Retrieved from http://www.ets.org/toefl/institutions/about/

Educational Testing Service. (2016b). *The GRE® tests.* Retrieved from http:///www.ets.org/gre

Eggerth, D. E., Bowles, S. M., Tunick, R. H., & Andrew, M. E. (2005). Convergent validity of O*NET Holland code classifications. *Journal of Career Assessment, 13,* 150–168.

Eisen, S. V., Normand, S., Belanger, A. J., Spiro, A., & Esch, D. (2004). The Revised Behavior and Symptom Identification Scale (BASIS-R): Reliability and validity. *Medical Care, 42,* 1230–1241.

Ekstrom, R. B., Elmore, P. B., Schafer, W. D., Trotter, T. V., & Webster, B. (2004). A survey of assessment and evaluation activities of school counselors. *Professional School Counseling, 8,* 24–30.

Elliott, S. N., McKevitt, B. C., & Kettler, R. J. (2002). Testing accommodations research and decision making: The case of "good" scores being highly valued but difficult to achieve for all students. *Measurement and Evaluation in Counseling and Development, 35,* 153–166.

Emelianchik-Key, K., & Hays, D. G. (2017). *Initial development and validation of the Teen Screen for Dating Violence.* Manuscript submitted for publication.

Endler, N. S., Parker, J. D. A., & Summerfeldt, L. S. (1998). Coping with health problems: Developing a reliable and valid multidimensional measure. *Psychological Assessment, 10,* 195–205.

Erford, B. T., Hays, D. G., & Crockett, S. (2014). *Mastering the National Counselor Examination and the Counselor Preparation Comprehensive Examination* (2nd ed.). Boston, MA: Pearson.

Essig, G. N., & Kelly, K. R. (2015). Comparison of the effectiveness of two assessment feedback models in reducing career indecision. *Journal of Career Assessment, 21,* 519–536. doi:10.1177/1069072712475283

Evans, W. N. (1998). Assessment and diagnosis of the substance use disorders (SUDs). *Journal of Counseling & Development, 76,* 325–333.

Ewing, J. A. (1984). Detecting alcoholism: The CAGE Questionnaire. *Journal of the American Medical Association, 252,* 1905–1907.

Exner, J. E. (1993). *The Rorschach: A comprehensive system: Vol. 1. Basic foundations* (3rd ed.). New York, NY: Wiley.

Exner, J. E. (2001). *A Rorschach workbook for the comprehensive system* (5th ed.). Odessa, FL: Psychological Assessment Resources.

Eyde, L. D., Robertson, G. J., & Krug, S. E. (2010). *Responsible test use: Case studies for assessing human behavior* (2nd ed.). Washington, DC: American Psychological Association.

Eysenck, H. J., & Eysenck, S. B. (2013). *Personality structure and measurement.* New York, NY: Routledge.

Fair Access Coalition on Testing. (n.d.). *The National Fair Access Coalition on Testing mission.* Retrieved from http://www.fairaccess.org

Fals-Stewart, W., Birchler, G. R., & Kelley, M. L. (2003). The Timeline Followback Spousal Violence Interview to assess physical aggression between intimate partners: Reliability and validity. *Journal of Family Violence, 18,* 131–142.

Fals-Stewart, W., O'Farrell, T. J., Feitas, T. T., McFarlin, S. K., & Rutigliano, P. (2000). The Timeline Followback reports of psychoactive substance use by drug-abusing patients: Psychometric properties. *Journal of Consulting and Clinical Psychology, 68,* 134–144.

Family Violence Prevention Fund. (1996). *Health alert: Strengthening the healthcare system's response to domestic violence.* San Francisco, CA: Author.

Family Violence Prevention Fund. (2002). *National consensus guidelines on identifying and responding to domestic violence and victimization in health care settings.* San Francisco, CA: Author.

Feldhaus, K., Kozoil-McLain, J., Amsbury, H., Norton, I., Lowenstein, S., & Abbott J. (1997). Accuracy of 3 brief screening questions for detecting partner violence in the emergency department. *Journal of the American Medical Association, 277,* 1357–1361.

Fernandez, E. (2001). Review of the Battery for Health Improvement 2. In B. S. Plake & J. C. Impara (Eds.), *The fourteenth mental measurements yearbook* (pp. 119–121). Lincoln, NE: Buros Institute of Mental Measurements.

Fico, J. M., & Hogan, R. (2000). *Interpersonal Compass manual.* Tulsa, OK: Hogan Assessment Systems.

Finn, S. E., & Tonsager, M. E. (1992). Therapeutic effects of providing MMPI-2 test feedback to college students awaiting therapy. *Psychological Assessment, 4,* 278–287.

Flamez, B., Hicks, J. F., & Clark, A. (2015). Effectively using research and assessment in couples and family therapy. In D. Capuzzi & M. D. Stauffer (Eds.), *Foundations of couples, marriage, and family counseling* (pp. 71–100). New York, NY: Wiley.

Flanagan, D. P. (2008). The Cattell-Horn-Carroll theory of cognitive abilities. In St. John's University (Ed.), *Encyclopedia of special education* (pp. 368–382). New York, NY: Wiley.

Fletcher, K. E. (1991a). *Childhood PTSD interview.* Worcester: University of Massachusetts Medical Center.

Fletcher, K. E. (1991b). *Parent report of the Child's Reaction to Stress.* Worcester: University of Massachusetts Medical Center.

Fletcher, K. E. (1992). *When bad things happen.* Worcester: University of Massachusetts Medical Center.

Flores, L. Y., Berkel, L. A., Nilsson, J. E., Ojeda, L., Jordan, S. E., Lynn, G. L., & Leal, V. M. (2006). Racial/ethnic minority vocational research: A content and trend analysis across 36 years. *The Career Development Quarterly, 55,* 2–21.

Floyd, R. G., Shands, E. I., Alfonso, V. C., Phillips, J. F., Autry, B. K., Mosteller, J. A., . . . Irby, S. (2015). A systematic review and psychometric evaluation of adaptive behavior scales and recommendation for practice. *Journal of Applied School Psychology, 31,* 83–113. doi:10.1080/15377903.2014.979384

Foa, E. B., Riggs, D. S., Dancu, C. V., & Rothbaum, B. O. (1993). Reliability and validity of a brief instrument for assessing post-traumatic stress disorder. *Journal of Traumatic Stress, 6,* 459–473.

Folstein, M. F., Folstein, S. E., McHugh, P. R., & Fanjiang, G. (2001). *Mini-Mental State Examination user's guide.* Odessa, FL: Psychological Assessment Resources.

Forbey, J. D., & Ben-Porath, Y. S. (2003). Incremental validity of the MMPI-A content scales in a residential treatment facility. *Assessment, 10,* 191–202.

Ford, D. Y., Grantham, T. C., & Whiting, G. W. (2008). Culturally and linguistically diverse students in gifted education: Recruitment and retention issues. *Exceptional Children, 74,* 289–306.

Ford, M. R., & Widiger, T. A. (1989). Sex bias in the diagnosis of histrionic and antisocial personality disorders. *Journal of Consulting and Clinical Psychology, 57,* 301–305.

Fortin, N. M., Oreopoulos, P., & Phipps, S. (2015). Leaving boys behind: Gender disparities in high academic achievement. *Journal of Human Resources, 50,* 549–579. doi:10.3368/jhr.50.3.549

Fouad, N. A., Harmon, L. W., & Borgen, F. H. (1997). Structure of interests in employed male and female members of U.S. racial-ethnic minority and nonminority groups. *Journal of Counseling Psychology, 44,* 339–345.

Fouad, N. A., & Mohler, C. J. (2004). Cultural validity of Holland's theory and the Strong Interest Inventory for five racial/ethnic groups. *Journal of Career Assessment, 12,* 423–439.

Fowler, J. C. (2012). Suicide risk assessment in clinical practice: Pragmatic guidelines for imperfect assessments. *Psychotherapy, 49,* 81–90. doi:10.1037/a0026148

Frauenhoffer, D., Ross, M. J., Gfeller, J., Searight, H. R., & Piotrowski, C. (1998). Psychological test usage among licensed mental health practitioners: A multidisciplinary survey. *Journal of Psychological Practice, 4,* 28–33.

French, J. W. (1962). Effective anxiety on verbal and mathematical examination scores. *Educational and Psychological Measurement, 22,* 553–564.

Friedrich, W. N. (1997). *Child Sexual Behavior Inventory.* Lutz, FL: Psychological Assessment Resources.

Frisch, M. B. (1994). *Manual and treatment guide for the Quality of Life Inventory.* Minneapolis, MN: National Computer Systems.

Frisch, M. B., Clark, M. P., Rouse, S. V., Rudd, M. D., Paweleck, J. K., Greenstone, A., & Kopplin, D. A. (2005). Predictive and treatment validity of life satisfaction and the Quality of Life Inventory. *Assessment, 12,* 66–78.

Furnham, A., & Mansi, A. (2014). The self-assessment of the Cattell-Horn-Carroll broad stratum abilities. *Learning and Individual Differences, 32,* 233–237. doi:10.1016/j.lindif.2014.03.014

Galton, F. (1883). *Inquiries into human faculty and its development.* London, UK: Macmillan.

Garb, H. N., Wood, J. M., Lilienfeld, S. O., & Nezworski, M. T. (2005). Roots of the Rorschach controversy. *Clinical Psychology Review, 25,* 97–118.

Gardner, H. (2006). *Multiple intelligences: New horizons.* New York, NY: Basic Books.

Garner, D. M. (2005). Eating Disorders Inventory–3. In *Catalog of selected professional testing resources* (p. 13). Lutz, FL: Psychological Assessment Resources.

Garner, D. M., & Garfinkel, P. E. (1979). The Eating Attitudes Test: An index of the symptoms of anorexia nervosa. *Psychological Medicine, 9,* 273–279.

Garrett, M. T., Garrett, J. T., Portman, T. A. A., Grayshield, L., Rivera, E. T., Williams, C., & Parrish, M. (2018). Counseling individuals and families of Native American descent. In D. G. Hays & B. T. Erford (Eds.), *Developing multicultural counseling competence: A systems approach* (3rd ed., pp. 394–430). Boston, MA: Pearson.

Garrett, M. T., & Pichette, E. F. (2000). Red as an apple: Native American acculturation and counseling with or without reservation. *Journal of Counseling & Development, 78,* 3–13.

Gati, I., Kraus, M., & Osipow, S. H. (1996). A taxonomy of difficulties in career decision making. *Journal of Counseling Psychology, 43,* 510–526.

Gati, I., & Saka, N. (2001). High school students' career-related decision-making difficulties. *Journal of Counseling & Development, 79,* 331–440.

Geiger, I. (2007). A cultural assessment framework and interview protocol. In L. A. Suzuki & J. G. Ponterotto (Eds.), *Handbook of multicultural assessment: Clinical, psychological, and educational applications* (pp. 132–161). Hoboken, NJ: Wiley.

Gibbons, M. M. (2013). Kuder Career Planning System: Kuder Career Interest Assessment, Kuder Skills Confidence Assessment, and Kuder Work Values Assessment. In C. T. Wood & D. G. Hays (Eds.), *A counselor's guide to career assessment instruments* (6th ed., pp. 208–210). Broken Arrow, OK: National Career Development Association.

Gibson, J., Booth, R., Davenport, J., Keogh, K., & Owens, T. (2014). Dialectical behavior therapy-informed skills training for deliberate self-harm: A controlled trial with 3-month follow-up data. *Behaviour Research and Therapy, 60,* 8–14. doi:10.1016/j.brat.2014.06.007

Glosoff, H. L., Benshoff, J. M., Hosie, T. W., & Maki, D. R. (1995). The 1994 ACA model legislation for licensed professional counselors. *Journal of Counseling & Development, 73,* 209–220.

Glynn, L. H., & Moyers, T. B. (2010). Chasing change talk: The clinician's role in evoking client language about change. *Journal of Substance Abuse Treatment, 39,* 65–70.

Goddard, H. H. (1917). Mental tests and the immigrant. *Journal of Delinquency, 2,* 243–277.

Goldenberg, H., & Godenberg, I. (2013). *Family therapy: An overview* (8th ed.). Belmont, CA: Brooks/Cole.

Goldfried, M. R., Stricker, G., & Weiner, I. R. (1971). *Rorschach handbook of clinical and research applications.* Englewood Cliffs, NJ: Prentice Hall.

Good, M. J. D., James, C., Good, B. J., & Becker, A. E. (2003). The culture of medicine and racial, ethnic, and class disparities in health care. In B. D. Smedley, A. Y. Stith, & A. R. Nelson (Eds.), *Unequal treatment: Confronting racial and ethnic disparities in health care* (pp. 594–625). Washington, DC: National Academies Press.

Goodenough, F. (1926). *Measurement of intelligence by drawings.* New York, NY: World Book.

Goodman, L., Dutton M. A., Weinfurt, K., & Cook, S. (2003). The Intimate Partner Violence Strategies Index. *Violence Against Women, 9,* 163–186.

Gordon Commission on the Future of Assessment in Education. (2013). *To assess, to teach, to learn: A vision for the future of assessment.* Retrieved from http://gordoncommission.org/rsc/pdfs/gordon_commission_technical_report.pdf

Goslin, D. A. (1963). *The search for ability.* New York, NY: Russell Sage Foundation.

Gottfredson, G. D., & Holland, J. L. (1996). *Dictionary of Holland occupational codes* (3rd ed.). Odessa, FL: Psychological Assessment Resources.

Gough, H. G. (1999). *CPI: Introduction to Form 434*. Palo Alto, CA: Consulting Psychologists Press.

Gough, H. G. (2000). The California Psychological Inventory. In C. E. Watkins & V. L. Campbell (Eds.), *Testing and assessment in counseling practice* (pp. 45–71). Mahwah, NJ: Erlbaum.

Gough, H. G., & Bradley, P. (2002). *CPI manual* (3rd ed.). Mountain View, CA: Consulting Psychologists Press.

Graduate Management Admission Council. (2016). *The GMAT exam*. Retrieved from http://www.mba.com/us/the-gmat-exam.aspx

Graham, J. R. (2005a). Characteristics of high and low scores on the MMPI-2 clinical scales. In G. P. Koocher, J. C. Norcross, & S. S. Hill, III (Eds.), *Psychologists' desk reference* (2nd ed., pp. 141–149). New York, NY: Oxford University Press.

Graham, J. R. (2005b). Clinical scales of the MMPI-2. In G. P. Koocher, J. C. Norcross, & S. S. Hill, III (Eds.), *Psychologists' desk reference* (2nd ed., pp. 132–136). New York, NY: Oxford University Press.

Graham, J. R. (2011). *Assessing personality and psychopathology* (5th ed.). New York, NY: Oxford University Press.

Gratz, K. L. (2001). Measurement of deliberate self-harm: Preliminary data on the Deliberate Self-Harm Inventory. *Journal of Psychopathology and Behavioral Assessment, 23*, 253–263.

Gray-Little, B., & Kaplan, D. A. (1998). Interpretation of psychological tests in clinical and forensic evaluations. In J. Sandoval, C. L. Frisby, K. F. Geisinger, J. D. Scheuneman, & J. R. Grenier (Eds.), *Test interpretation and diversity* (pp. 141–178). Washington, DC: American Psychological Association.

Green, K. E. (1998). Review of the Values Scale, Second Edition. In J. C. Impara & B. S. Plake (Eds.), *The thirteenth mental measurements yearbook* (pp. 1112–1114). Lincoln, NE: Buros Institute of Mental Measurements.

Greene, R. L., Albaugh, B., Robin, R. W., & Caldwell, A. (2003). Use of the MMPI-II in American Indians: II. Empirical correlates. *Psychological Assessment, 15*, 360–369.

Greenfield, T. K., & Attkisson, C. C. (2004). The UCSF Client Satisfaction Scales: II. The Service Satisfaction Scale–30. In M. E. Maruish (Ed.), *The use of psychological testing for treatment planning and outcomes assessment: Vol. 3. Instruments for adults* (3rd ed., pp. 813–837). Mahwah, NJ: Erlbaum.

Gregory, R. J. (2013). *Psychological testing: History, principles, and applications* (7th ed.). Boston, MA: Pearson.

Greiff, S., Holt, D. V., & Funke, J. (2013). Perspectives on problem solving in educational assessment: Analytical, interactive, and collaborative problem solving. *Journal of Problem Solving, 5*, 71–91.

Grice, J. W. (2004). Bridging the idiographic–nomothetic divide in ratings of self and others on the Big Five. *Journal of Personality, 72*, 203–241.

Griffith, A. L., Cohen, G. R., & Ehrenberg, R. G. (2015). *Explaining racial differences in post-college aspirations: Evidence from the NLSF*. Retrieved from https://www.ilr.cornell.edu/sites/ilr.cornell.edu/files/cheri_wp166_0.pdf

Groth-Marnat, G. (2000). Visions of clinical assessment: Then, now, and a brief history of the future. *Journal of Clinical Psychology, 56*, 349–365.

Groth-Marnat, G., & Wright, A. J. (2016). *Handbook of psychological assessment* (6th ed.). New York, NY: Wiley.

Gual, A., Segura, L., Contel, M., Heather, N., & Colom, J. (2002). AUDIT-3 and AUDIT-4: Effectiveness of two short forms of the Alcohol Use Disorders Identification Test. *Alcohol and Alcoholism, 37*, 591–596. doi:10.1093/alcalc/37.6.591

Guilford, J. P. (1959). *Personality*. New York, NY: McGraw-Hill.

Guion, R. M. (2011). *Assessment, measurement, and prediction for personnel decisions* (2nd ed.). New York, NY: Routledge.

Gushue, G. V. (2004). Race, color-blind racial attitudes, and judgments about mental health: A shining standards perspective. *Journal of Counseling Psychology, 51*, 398–407.

Hall, M. E., & Rayman, J. R. (2002). Review of Career Beliefs Inventory. In J. T. Kapes & E. A. Whitfield (Eds.), *A counselor's guide to career assessment instruments* (4th ed., pp. 316–322). Alexandria, VA: National Career Development Association.

Hall, T. (2014). *A study of code inspection performance and personality traits* (Unpublished doctoral dissertation). University of Guelph, Ontario, Canada.

Halpern, D. F. (2013). *Sex differences in cognitive abilities* (4th ed.). New York, NY: Taylor & Francis.

Hambleton, R. K. (2005). Review of the WMS–3rd edition abbreviated. In R. A. Spies & B. S. Plake (Eds.), *The sixteenth mental measurements yearbook* (pp. 1097–1099). Lincoln, NE: Buros Institute of Mental Measurements.

Hansen, J. C., & Dik, B. J. (2005). Evidence of 12-year predictive and concurrent validity for SII Occupational Scale scores. *Journal of Vocational Behavior, 67*, 365–378.

Hansen, J. C., & Neuman, J. L. (1999). Evidence of concurrent prediction of the Campbell Interest and Skill Survey (CISS) for college major selection. *Journal of Career Assessment, 7*, 239–247.

Harmon, L. W., Hansen, J. C., Borgen, F. H., & Hammer, A. L. (1994). *Strong Interest Inventory applications and technical guide.* Stanford, CA: Stanford University Press.

Harrington, T. F. (2006). A 20-year follow-up of the Harrington–O'Shea Career Decision-Making System. *Measurement and Evaluation in Counseling and Development, 38*, 198–202.

Harrington, T., & Long, J. (2013). The history of interest inventories and career assessments in career counseling. *The Career Development Quarterly, 61*, 83–92. doi:10.1002/j.2161-0045.2013.00039.x

Harwell, M. R. (2005). Review of the Metropolitan Achievement Tests, Eighth Edition. In R. A. Spies & B. S. Plake (Eds.), *The sixteenth mental measurements yearbook* (pp. 609–612). Lincoln, NE: Buros Institute of Mental Measurements.

Hawton, K., Casañas i Comabella, C., Haw, C., & Saunders, K. (2013). Risk factors for suicide in individuals with depression: A systematic review. *Journal of Affective Disorders, 147*, 17–28. doi:10.1016/j.jad.2013.01.004

Hays, D. G., & Emelianchik, K. (2009). A content analysis of intimate partner violence assessments. *Measurement and Evaluation in Counseling and Development, 42*, 139–153.

Hays, D. G., Green, E., Orr, J. J., & Flowers, L. (2007). Advocacy counseling for female survivors of partner abuse: Implications for counselor education. *Counselor Education and Supervision, 46*, 186–198.

Hays, D. G., & McLeod, A. L. (2018). The culturally competent counselor. In D. G. Hays & B. T. Erford (Eds.), *Developing multicultural counseling competence: A systems approach* (3rd ed., pp. 2–36). Boston, MA: Pearson.

Hays, D. G., McLeod, A. L., & Prosek, E. A. (2009). Diagnostic variance among counselors and counselor trainees. *Measurement and Evaluation in Counseling and Development, 42*, 3–14.

Hays, D. G., Prosek, E. A., & McLeod, A. L. (2010). A mixed methodological analysis of the role of culture in clinical decision-making. *Journal of Counseling & Development, 88*, 114–121.

Hays, D. G., Snow, K. C., & Pusateri, C. G. (2015). Violence, abuse, and trauma in family therapy. In D. Capuzzi & M. D. Stauffer (Eds.), *Foundations of couples, marriage, and family counseling* (pp. 419–447). New York, NY: Wiley.

Hays, R. D., Merz, J. D., & Nicholas, R. (1995). Response burden, reliability, and validity of the CAGE, Short MAST, and AUDIT alcohol screening measures. *Behavioral Research Methods, Instruments & Computers, 27*, 277–280.

Heck, E. J. (1991). Developing a screening questionnaire for problem drinking in college students. *Journal of American College Health, 39*, 227–234.

Hegarty, K., Bush, R., & Sheehan, M. (2005). The Composite Abuse Scale: Further development and assessment of reliability and validity of a multidimensional partner abuse measure in clinical settings. *Violence and Victims, 20,* 529–547.

Helzer, J. E., Badger, G. J., Rose, G. L., Mongeon, J. A., & Searles, J. S. (2002). Decline in alcohol consumption during two years of daily reporting. *Journal of Studies on Alcohol, 63,* 551–557.

Hemphill, J. F. (2003). Interpreting the magnitudes of correlation coefficients. *American Psychologist, 58,* 78–79.

Henfield, M. S. (2013). School counseling for gifted Black males. *Gifted Child Today, 36,* 57–61.

Henfield, M. S., Owens, D., & Moore, J. L. (2008). Influences on young gifted African Americans' school success: Implications for elementary school counselors. *Elementary School Journal, 108,* 392–406.

Heron, S., Thompson, M. P., Jackson, E., & Kaslow, N. (2003). Do responses to an intimate partner violence screen predict scores on a comprehensive measure of intimate partner violence in low-income Black women? *Annals of Emergency Medicine, 42,* 483–491.

Herr, E. (2013). Trends in the history of vocational guidance. *The Career Development Quarterly, 61,* 277–282. doi:10.1002/j.2161-0045.2013.00056.x

Herr, E., Cramer, S. H., & Niles, S. G. (2004). *Career guidance and counseling through the lifespan: Systematic approaches* (6th ed.). Boston, MA: Pearson.

Hiller, J. B., Rosenthal, R., Bornstein, R. F., Barry, D. R., & Brunell-Neuleib, T. (1999). A comparative meta-analysis of Rorschach and MMPI validity. *Psychological Assessment, 11,* 278–296.

Hindman, J. (1989). *Just before dawn: Trauma assessment and treatment of sexual victimization.* Ontario, OR: Alexandria Association.

Hirschi, A., Herrmann, A., & Keller, A. C. (2015). Career adaptivity, adaptability, and adapting: A conceptual and empirical investigation. *Journal of Vocational Behavior, 87,* 1–10.

Hirschi, A., & Valero, D. (2015). Career adaptability profiles and their relationship to adaptivity and adapting. *Journal of Vocational Behavior, 88,* 220–229.

Hodgson, R. J., & Rachman, S. (1977). Obsessional–compulsive complaints. *Behaviour Research and Therapy, 15,* 389–395.

Hoff, L. A., & Rosenbaum, L. (1994). A victimization assessment tool: Instrument development and clinical implications. *Journal of Advanced Nursing, 20,* 627–634.

Hoffman, J. A., & Weiss, B. (1986). A new system for conceptualizing college students' problems: Types of crises and the Inventory of Common Problems. *Journal of American College Health, 34,* 259–266.

Hogan, T. P. (2005). A list of 50 widely used psychological tests. In J. P. Koocher, J. C. Norcross, & S. S. Hill (Eds.), *Psychologist's desk reference* (2nd ed., pp. 101–104). New York, NY: Oxford University Pres.

Hogan, T. P., & Rengert, C. (2008). Test usage in published research and the practice of counseling: A comparative review. *Measurement and Evaluation in Counseling and Development, 41,* 51–56.

Holland, J. L. (1997). *Making vocational choices: A theory of vocational personalities and work environments* (3rd ed.). Lutz, FL: Psychological Assessment Resources.

Holland, J. L., Daiger, D. C., & Power, P. G. (1980). *My Vocational Situation.* Palo Alto, CA: Consulting Psychologists Press.

Holland, J. L., Fritzsche, B. A., & Powell, A. B. (1994). *The Self-Directed Search technical manual.* Odessa, FL: Psychological Assessment Resources.

Holland, J. L., & Gottfredson, G. D. (1994). *CASI: Career Attitudes and Strategies Inventory.* Odessa, FL: Psychological Assessment Resources.

Holmes, T. H., & Rahe, R. H. (1967). The Social Adjustment Rating Scale. *Journal of Psychosomatic Research, 11,* 213–218.

Holt, M. K., & Espelage, D. L. (2005). Social support as a moderator between dating violence victimization and depression/anxiety among African American and Caucasian adolescents. *School Psychology Review, 34,* 309–328.

Holroyd, S., & Clayton, A. H. (2000). Measuring depression in the elderly: Which scale is best. *Medscape Mental Health, 5*(5), 1–8.

Horn, J. L., Wanberg, K. W., & Foster, F. M. (1986). *Alcohol Use Inventory.* Minneapolis, MN: National Computer Systems.

Horton, A. M., Jr. (1999). Test review: Wechsler Memory Scale III. *Archives of Clinical Neuropsychology, 14,* 473–477.

Horton, C. B., & Cruise, T. K. (1997). Clinical assessment of child victims and adult survivors of child maltreatment. *Journal of Counseling & Development, 76,* 94–104.

Horvath, A. O., & Greenberg, L. (1989). Development and validation of the Working Alliance Inventory. *Journal of Counseling Psychology, 36,* 223–232.

Howard, J. (2001). Graphic representations as tools for decision making. *Social Education, 65,* 220–223.

Hudson, W. W., & McIntosh, S. R. (1981). The assessment of spouse abuse: Two quantifiable dimensions. *Journal of Marriage and Family, 43,* 873–885, 888.

Hunsley, J., & Meyer, G. J. (2003). The incremental validity of psychological testing and assessment: Conceptual, methodological, and statistical issues. *Psychological Assessment, 15,* 446–455.

Hurley, E., & Murphy, R. (2015). The development of a new method of idiographic measurement for dynamic assessment intervention. *Journal of Pedagogy, 6,* 43–60.

Hutton, J. B., Dubes, R., & Muir, S. (1992). Assessment practices of school psychologists: Ten years later. *School Psychology Review, 21,* 271–284.

Impara, J. C., & Plake, B. S. (1995). Comparing counselors', school administrators', and teachers' knowledge in student assessment. *Measurement and Evaluation in Counseling and Development, 28,* 78–87.

International Bureau of Weights and Measures. (2012). *International vocabulary of metrology: Basic and general concepts and associated terms* (3rd ed.). Retrieved from http://www.bipm.org/

International Test Commission. (2014). ITC guidelines on quality control in scoring, test analysis, and reporting of test scores. *International Journal of Testing, 14,* 195–217. doi: 10.1080/15305058.2014.918040

Iwata, B. A., Pace, G. M., & Kissel, R. C. (1990). The Self-Injury Trauma (SIT) Scale: A method for quantifying surface tissue damage caused by self-injurious behavior. *Journal of Applied Behavior Analysis, 23,* 99–110.

Jackson, D. N. (1998). *Multidimensional Aptitude Battery–II manual.* Port Huron, MI: Sigma Assessment Systems.

Jackson, D. N., & Verhoeve, M. (2000). *Jackson Vocational Interest Survey manual* (2nd ed., Rev.). Port Huron, MI: Sigma Assessment Systems.

Jaeger, J. R. (2004). *RADAR for Men (teaching protocol).* Philadelphia, PA: Institute for Safe Families.

Jay, M., & John, O. P. (2004). A depressive symptom scale for the California Psychological Inventory: Construct validation of the CPI-D. *Psychological Assessment, 16,* 299–309.

Jenkins, J. A. (2013). Strong Interest Inventory (SII) and Skills Confidence Inventory (SCI). In C. T. Wood & D. G. Hays (Eds.), *A counselor's guide to career assessment instruments* (6th ed., pp. 279–284). Broken Arrow, OK: National Career Development Association.

Johnson, A. K. (1997). Conflict-handling intentions and the MBTI: A construct validation study. *Journal of Psychological Types, 43,* 29–39.

Johnson, J. A., D'Amato, R. C., & Harrison, M. L. (2005). Review of the Stanford–Binet Intelligence Scales, Fifth Edition. In R. A. Spies & B. S. Plake (Eds.), *The sixteenth mental measurements yearbook* (pp. 976–979). Lincoln, NE: Buros Institute of Mental Measurements.

Johnson, R. (1989). Review of the Thomas–Kilmann Conflict Mode Instrument. In J. C. Conoley & J. L. Kramer (Eds.), *The tenth mental measurements yearbook* (pp. 868–869). Lincoln, NE: Buros Institute of Mental Measurements.

Johnson, R. H., Taylor, R. M., Morrison, L. P., Morrison, W. L., & Romoser, R. C. (2007). *Taylor–Johnson Temperament Analysis*®. Simi Valley, CA: Psychological Publications.

Johnson, T. C. (1990). *Child Sexual Behavior Checklist–Revised.* Unpublished manuscript.

Joint Committee on Testing Practices. (1999). *Rights and responsibilities of test takers: Guidelines and expectations.* Retrieved from http://www.apa.org/science/programs/testing/rights.aspx

Joint Committee on Testing Practices. (2004). *Code of fair testing practices in education.* Retrieved from http://www.apa.org/science/programs/testing/fair-testing.pdf

Juhnke, G. A. (1996). The Adapted–SAD PERSONS: A suicide assessment scale designed for use with children. *Elementary School Guidance and Counseling, 30,* 252–258.

Juhnke, G. A., Vacc, N. A., & Curtis, R. C. (2003). Assessment instruments used by addictions counselors. *Journal of Addictions & Offender Counseling, 23,* 66–72.

Jung, C. G. (1910). The association method. *American Journal of Psychology, 31,* 219–269.

Jung, C. G. (1960). *The structure and dynamics of the psyche.* New York, NY: Bollingan Foundation.

Kagee, A. (2005). Review of Adult Manifest Anxiety Scale. In R. A. Spies & B. S. Plake (Eds.), *The sixteenth mental measurements yearbook* (pp. 29–31). Lincoln, NE: Buros Institute of Mental Measurements.

Kane, M. T. (2013). Validating the interpretations and uses of test scores. *Journal of Educational Measurement, 50,* 1–73.

Kann, L., Kinchen, S., Shanklin, S. L., Flint, K. H., Hawkins, J., Harris, W. A., . . . Zaza, S. (2014). *Youth Risk Behavior Surveillance—United States, 2013.* Retrieved from http://www.cdc.gov/mmwr/preview/mmwrhtml/ss6304a1.htm

Karlsen, B., & Gardner, F. E. (1986). *Adult Basic Learning Examination* (2nd ed.). San Antonio, TX: Psychological Corporation.

Karson, M., Karson, S., & O'Dell, J. (1997). *16PF interpretation in clinical practice: A guide to the fifth edition.* Champaign, IL: Performance Assessment Network.

Kaufman, A. S., & Kaufman, N. L. (1993). *Manual: Kaufman Adolescent and Adult Intelligence Test.* Circle Pines, MN: American Guidance Service.

Kaufman, A. S., & Kaufman, N. L. (2002). *Kaufman Brief Intelligence Test II manual.* Circle Pines, MN: American Guidance Service.

Kaufman, A. S., & Kaufman, N. L. (2003). *K-TEA-II.* Circle Pines, MN: American Guidance Service.

Kaufman, A. S., Lichtenberger, E. O., Fletcher-Janzen, E., & Kaufman, N. L. (2005). *Essentials of KABCII assessment.* Hoboken, NJ: Wiley.

Keirsey, D. M. (2006). *Keirsey Temperament Sorter II (KTS-II).* Retrieved from http://www.keirsey.com

Kelly, K. R. (2002a). Mapping the domain of career decision problems. *Journal of Vocational Behavior, 61,* 302–326.

Kelly, K. R. (2002b). Review of Kuder Occupational Interest Survey Form DD (KOIS-DD) and Kuder Career Search with Person Match (KCS). In J. T. Kapes & E. A. Whitfield (Eds.), *A counselor's guide to career assessment instruments* (4th ed., pp. 263–275). Tulsa, OK: National Career Development Association.

Kennedy, M. L., Faust, D., Willis, W. G., & Piotrowski, C. (1994). Social–emotional assessment practices in school psychology. *Journal of Psychological Assessment, 12,* 228–240.

Kenrick, D. T., & Funder, D. C. (1988). Profiting from controversy: Lessons from the person–situation debate. *American Psychologist, 43,* 23–34.

Kerr, B., & Gagliardi, C. (2003). Measuring creativity in research and practice. In S. J. Lopez & C. R. Snyder (Eds.), *Positive psychological assessment* (pp. 155–169). Washington, DC: American Psychological Association.

Kessler, R. C., Berglund, P., Demler, O., Jin, R., & Walters, E. E. (2005). Lifetime prevalence and age-of-onset distributions of *DSM-IV* disorders in the National Comorbidity Survey Replication. *Archives of General Psychiatry, 62,* 593–602.

Kessler, R. C., Chiu, W. T., Demler, O., & Walters, E. E. (2005). Prevalence, severity, and comorbidity of 12-month *DSM-IV* disorders in the National Comorbidity Survey Replication. *Archives of General Psychiatry, 62,* 617–627.

Kessler, R. C., Demler, O., Frank, R. G., Olfson, M., Pincus, H. A., Walters, E. E., . . . Zaslavsky, A. M. (2005). Prevalence and treatment of mental disorders, 1990 to 2003. *New England Journal of Medicine, 352,* 2515–2523.

Kettler, R. J., Niebling, B. C., Mroch, A. A., Feldman, E. S., Newell, M. L., Elliott, S. N., . . . Bolt, D. M. (2005). Effects of testing accommodations on math and reading scores: An experimental analysis of the performance of students with and without disabilities. *Assessment for Effective Intervention, 31,* 37–48. doi:10.1177/073724770503100104

Kiesler, D. J. (1987). *Checklist of Psychotherapy Transactions–Revised (CLOPT-R) and Checklist of Interpersonal Transactions–Revised (CLOIT-R).* Richmond, VA: Virginia Commonwealth University Press.

Kiesler, D. J., Schmidt, J. A., & Wagner, C. C. (1997). A circumplex inventory of impact messages: An operational bridge between emotion and interpersonal behavior. In R. Plutchik & H. R. Conte (Eds.), *Circumplex models of personality and emotions* (pp. 221–224). Washington, DC: American Psychological Association.

Kinnier, R. T. (1987). Development of a values conflict resolution assessment. *Journal of Counseling Psychology, 34,* 31–37.

Kinnier, R. T. (1995). A reconceptualization of values clarification: Values conflict resolution. *Journal of Counseling & Development, 74,* 18–24.

Kinnier, R. T., & Gorin, J. (2013). O*NET Ability Profiler. In C. T. Wood & D. G. Hays (Eds.), *A counselor's guide to career assessment instruments* (6th ed., pp. 141–145). Broken Arrow, OK: National Career Development Association.

Kiresuk, T. J., Smith, A., & Cardillo, J. E. (2014). *Goal attainment scaling: Applications, theory, and measurement.* New York, NY: Taylor & Francis.

Kirschenbaum, H. (2013). *Values clarification in counseling and psychotherapy: Practical strategies for individual and group settings.* New York, NY: Oxford University Press.

Kitchens, J. M. (1994). Does this patient have an alcohol problem? *Journal of the American Medical Association, 272,* 1782–1787.

Klieger, D. M., Cline, F. A., Holtzman, S. L., Minsky, J. L., & Lorenz, F. (2014). New perspectives on the validity of the GRE® General Test for predicting graduate school grades. *ETS Research Report Series, 2014*(2), 1–62. doi:10.1002/ets2.12026

Kline, P. (2015). *A handbook of test construction: Introduction to psychometric design.* New York, NY: Routledge.

Knapp, L., Knapp, R. R., & Knapp-Lee, L. (1992). *Career Ability Placement Survey technical manual.* San Diego, CA: Educational and Industrial Testing Service.

Knapp-Lee, L. J. (1996). Use of the COPES, a measure of work values, in career assessment. *Journal of Career Assessment, 4,* 429–443.

Knapp-Lee, L. (2000). A complete career guidance program: The COPSystem. In C. E. Watkins, Jr., & V. L. Campbell (Eds.), *Testing and assessment in counseling practice* (2nd ed., pp. 295–338). Mahwah, NJ: Erlbaum.

Kobak, K. A., & Reynolds, W. M. (2004). The Hamilton Depression Inventory. In M. E. Maruish (Ed.), *The use of psychological testing for treatment planning and outcomes assessment: Vol. 3. Instruments for adults* (3rd ed., pp. 327–362). Mahwah, NJ: Erlbaum.

Kohar, R. (2016). *Basic discrete mathematics: Logic, set theory and probability.* Hackensack, NJ: World Scientific.

Kolb, D. A. (1985). *Learning Style Inventory.* Boston, MA: McBer.

Konold, T. R., & Abidin, R. R. (2001). Parenting alliance: A multifactor perspective. *Assessment, 8,* 47–65.

Kopelman, R. E., Rovenpor, J. L., & Guan, M. (2003). The study of values: Construction of the fourth edition. *Journal of Vocational Behavior, 62,* 203–220.

Korotitsch, W. J., & Nelson-Gray, N. O. (1999). An overview of self-monitoring research in assessment and treatment. *Psychological Assessment, 11,* 415–425.

Koss, M. P., & Oros, C. J. (1982). Sexual Experiences Survey: A research instrument investigating sexual aggression and victimization. *Journal of Counseling and Clinical Psychology, 50,* 455–457.

Kovach, M. (2009). *Indigenous methodologies: Characteristics, conversations, and contexts.* Toronto, Ontario, Canada: University of Toronto Press.

Kovacs, M. (2003). *CDI technical manual update.* North Tonawanda, NY: Multi-Health Systems.

Kovacs, M. (2015). *Children's Depression Inventory 2.* North Tonawanda, NY: Multi-Health Systems.

Kraepelin, E. (1892). *Uber die beeinflussung einfacher psychischer vorgagne durch einige arzneimittel* [About the influence of some medicines on mental health]. Jena, Germany: Fischer.

Kraus, D. R., Seligman, D. A., & Jordan, J. R. (2005). Validation of a behavioral health treatment outcome and assessment tool designed for naturalistic settings: The Treatment Outcome Package. *Journal of Clinical Psychology, 61,* 285–314.

Krenek, M., Lyons, R., & Simpson, T. L. (2016). Degree of correspondence between daily monitoring and retrospective recall of alcohol use among men and women with comorbid AUD and PTSD. *American Journal on Addictions, 25,* 145–151. doi:10.1111/ajad.12342

Kress, V., Dixon, A., & Shannonhouse, S. (2018). Multicultural diagnosis and conceptualization. In D. G. Hays & B. T. Erford (Eds.), *Developing multicultural counseling competency: A systems approach* (3rd ed., pp. 558–590). Boston, MA: Pearson.

Krumboltz, J. D. (1988). *Career Beliefs Inventory manual.* Menlo Park, CA: Mind Garden.

Krumboltz, J. D. (1991). *Manual for the Career Beliefs Inventory.* Palo Alto, CA: Consulting Psychologists Press.

Krumboltz, J. D., Blando, J. A., Kim, H., & Reikowski, D. J. (1994). Embedding work values in stories. *Journal of Counseling & Development, 73,* 57–62.

Kuder, G. F. (1934). *Kuder Preference Record–Vocational.* Chicago, IL: Science Research Associates.

Kuder, G. F. (1966). The Occupational Interest Survey. *Personnel and Guidance Journal, 45,* 72–77.

Kuder, G. F., & Diamond, E. E. (1979). *Occupational Interest Survey: General manual* (2nd ed.). Chicago, IL: Science Research Associates.

Kuder, Inc. (n.d.). *Technical briefs.* Retrieved from http://www.kuder.com/our-unique-approach/research-based-assessments/assessment-summaries/

Kuncel, N. R., Hezlett, S. A., & Ones, D. S. (2004). Academic performance, career potential, creativity, and job performance: Can one construct predict them all? *Journal of Personality and Social Psychology, 86,* 148–161.

Kush, J. C. (2005). Review of the Stanford–Binet Intelligence Scales. In B. S. Plake & R. Spies (Eds.), *The sixteenth mental measurements yearbook* (pp. 979–984). Lincoln, NE: Buros Institute.

Kvall, S., Choca, J., Groth-Marnat, G., & Davis, A. (2011). The integrated psychological report. In T. M. Harwood, L. E. Beutler, & G. Groth-Marnat (Eds.), *Integrative assessment of adult personality* (3rd ed., pp. 413–444). New York, NY: Guilford Press.

LaBrie, J. W., Pedersen, E. R., Earleywine, M., & Olsen, H. (2006). Reducing heavy drinking in college males with the decisional balance: Analyzing an element of motivational interviewing. *Addictive Behaviors, 31,* 254–263.

Lachar, D., Bailley, S. E., Rhoades, H. M., Espadas, A., Aponte, M., Cowan, K. A. . . . Wassef, A. (2001). New subscales for an anchored version of the brief psychiatric rating scale: Construction, reliability, and validity in acute psychiatric admissions. *Psychological Assessment, 13*, 384–395. doi:10.1037/1040-3590.13.3.384

Lai, S. A., & Berkeley, S. B. (2012). High-stakes test accommodations research and practice. *Learning Disability Quarterly, 35*, 158–169. doi:10.1177/0731948711433874

Lakin, J. M. (2013). Sex differences in reasoning abilities: Surprising evidence that male–female ratios in the tails of the quantitative reasoning distribution have increased. *Intelligence, 41*, 263–274. doi:10.1016/j.intell.2013.04.004

Lambert, M. J. (2012). Helping clinicians to use and learn from research-based systems: The OQ-Analyst. *Psychotherapy, 49*, 109–114. doi:10.1037/a0027110

Lambert, M. J., Morton, J. S., Hatfield, D., Harmon, C., Hamilton, S., Reid, R. C., . . . Burlingame, G. M. (2004). *Outcome questionnaire 45.2*. Salt Lake City, UT: OQ Measures.

Landgraf, K. (2014). Foreword: Special issue on the future of educational assessment. *Teachers College Record, 116*(11), 1–3.

Lane, G. G., White, A. E., & Henson, R. K. (2002). Expanding reliability methods with KR-21 estimates: An RG study of the Coopersmith Self-Esteem Inventory. *Educational and Psychological Measurement, 62*, 685–711.

Larson, L. M., Bonitz, V. S., & Pesch, K. M. (2013). Assessing key vocational constructs. In W. B. Walsh, M. L. Savickas, & P. J. Hartung (Eds.), *Handbook of vocational psychology: Theory research and practice* (pp. 219–248). New York, NY: Routledge.

Last, A., Miles, R., Wills, L., Brownhill, L., & Ford, T. (2012). Reliability and sensitivity to change of the Family Life Questionnaire in a clinical population. *Child and Adolescent Mental Health, 17*, 121–125.

Law School Admission Council. (2016). *Law School Admission Test (LSAT)*. Retrieved from http://www.lsac.org/jd/lsat/about-the-lsat

Lawyer, S. R., & Smitherman, T. A. (2004). Trends in anxiety assessment. *Journal of Psychopathology and Behavioral Assessment, 26*, 101–108.

Lazowksi, L. E., Miller, F. G., Boye, M. W., & Miller, G. A. (1998). Efficacy of the Substance Abuse Subtle Screening Inventory–3 (SASSI-3) in identifying substance dependence disorders in clinical settings. *Journal of Personality Assessment, 71*, 114–128.

LeardMann, C. A., Powell, T. M., Smith, T. C., Bell, M. R., Smith, B., Boyko, E. J., . . . Hoge, C. W. (2013). Risk factors associated with suicide in current and former U.S. military personnel. *Journal of the American Medical Association, 310*, 496–506. doi:10.1001/jama.2013.65164

Lent, R. W., Brown, S. D., & Hackett, G. (1994). Toward a unifying social cognitive theory of career and academic interest, choice, and performance. *Journal of Vocational Behavior, 45*, 79–122.

Leong, F. (2014). *Career development and vocational behavior of racial and ethnic minorities*. New York, NY: Routledge.

Leong, F. T., & Flores, L. Y. (2013). Multicultural perspectives in vocational psychology. In W. B. Walsh, M. L. Savickas, & P. T. Hartung (Eds.), *Handbook of vocational psychology: Theory, research and practice* (pp. 53–80). New York, NY: Routledge.

Leserman, J., Drossman, D., & Zhiming, L. (1995). The reliability and validity of a sexual and physical abuse history questionnaire in female patients with gastrointestinal disorders. *Behavioral Medicine, 21*, 141–150.

Levin, M. E., Lillis, J., Seeley, J., Hayes, S., Pistorello, J., & Biglan, A. (2012). Exploring the relationship between experiential avoidance, alcohol use disorders, and alcohol-related problems among first-year college students. *Journal of American College Health, 60*, 443–448.

Lichtenberger, E. O., & Kaufman, A. S. (1998). Assessment Battery for Children (K-ABC). In R. J. Samuda, R. Feuerstein, A. S. Kaufman, J. E. Lewis, R. J. Sternberg, & Associates (Eds.), *Advances in cross-cultural assessment* (pp. 56–99). Thousand Oaks, CA: Sage.

Lichtenberger, E. O., Mather, N., Kaufman, N. L., & Kaufman, A. S. (2012). *Essentials of assessment report writing*. Hoboken, NJ: Wiley.

Lindzey, G. (1959). On the classification of projective techniques. *Psychological Bulletin, 56*, 158–168.

Linehan, M. M., Comtois, K. A., Brown, Z. M., Heard, H. L., & Wagner, A. (2006). Suicide Attempt Self-Injury Interview (SASSI): Development, reliability, and validity of a scale to assess suicide attempts and intentional self-injury. *Psychological Assessment, 18*, 303–312.

Lopez, M. N., Charter, R. A., Mostafavi, B., Nibut, L. P., & Smith, W. E. (2005). Psychometric properties of the Folstein Mini-Mental State Examination. *Assessment, 12*, 137–144.

Lorelle, S., Byrd, R., & Crockett, S. (2012). Globalization and counseling: Professional issues for counselors. *The Professional Counselor, 2*, 115–123. doi:10.15241/sll.2.2.115

Low, K. D., Yoon, M., Roberts, B. W., & Rounds, J. (2012). The stability of vocational interests from early adolescence to middle adulthood: A quantitative review of longitudinal studies. *Psychological Bulletin, 131*, 713–737. doi:10.1037/0033-2909.131.5.713

Luria, A. R. (1980). *Higher cortical functions in man* (2nd ed.). New York, NY: Basic Books.

Luu, L. P., Inman, A. G., & Alvarez, A. N. (2018). Individuals and families of Asian descent. In D. G. Hays & B. T. Erford (Eds.), *Developing multicultural competence: A systems approach* (3rd ed., pp. 320–362). Boston, MA: Pearson.

Luzzo, D. A. (2008). *Making career decisions that count: A practical guide* (3rd ed.). Upper Saddle River, NJ: Prentice Hall.

Machover, K. (1949). *Personality projection in the drawing of a human figure*. Springfield, IL: Charles C Thomas.

Madaus, G., & Russell, M. (2010–2011). Paradoxes of high-stakes testing. *Journal of Education, 190*, 21–30.

Malgady, R. G. (2011). Assessment bias in psychological measurement of ethnic minorities. In R. G. Malgady (Ed.), *Cultural competence in assessment and intervention with ethnic minorities: Some perspectives from psychology, social work and education* (pp. 24–27). Oak Park, IL: Bentham Science.

Mallen, M. J., Vogel, D. L., Rochlen, A. B., & Day, S. X. (2005). Online counseling: Reviewing the literature from a counseling psychology framework. *The Counseling Psychologist, 33*, 819–871.

Manages, K. J. (2001). Review of the Family Assessment Measure III. In B. S. Plake & J. C. Impara (Eds.), *The fourteenth mental measurements yearbook* (pp. 480–482). Lincoln, NE: Buros Institute of Mental Measurements.

Mancini, J. A. (2001). Review of the Family Environment Scale (Third Edition). In B. S. Plake & J. C. Impara (Eds.), *The fourteenth mental measurements yearbook* (pp. 482–484). Lincoln, NE: Buros Institute of Mental Measurement.

Marks, I. M., & Mathews, A. M. (1978). Brief standard self-rating for phobic patients. *Behavior Research and Therapy, 17*, 263–267.

Marlatt, G. A., & Miller, W. R. (1984). *Comprehensive Drinking Profile*. Odessa, FL: Psychological Assessment Resources.

Marotta, S. A., & Watts, R. E. (2007). An introduction to the best practices section in the *Journal of Counseling & Development*. *Journal of Counseling & Development, 85*, 491–503.

Marsh, H. W. (1985). Behavioral Academic Self-Esteem (BASE). In J. W. Mitchell (Ed.), *The ninth mental measurements yearbook* (pp. 169–170). Lincoln, NE: Buros Institute of Mental Measurement.

Marsh, H. W., & Hau, K.-T. (2003). Big-fish-little-pond effect on academic self-concept. *American Psychologist, 58*, 364–376.

Marsh, H. W., & Seaton, M. (2013). Academic self-concept. In J. Hattie & E. M. Anderman (Eds.), *International guide to student achievement* (pp. 62–63). New York, NY: Routledge.

Marshall, L. (1992). Development of the Severity of Violence Against Women Scales. *Journal of Family Violence, 7*, 103–121.

Martins, R. K., & McNeil, D. W. (2009). Review of motivational interviewing in promoting health behaviors. *Clinical Psychology Review, 29*, 283–293. doi:10.1016/j.cpr.2009.02.001

Maslow, A. H. (1987). *Motivation and personality* (3rd ed.). New York, NY: Harper & Row.

Mau, W. (2001). Assessing career decision-making difficulties: A cross-cultural study. *Journal of Career Assessment, 9*, 353–364.

Mau, W. (2004). Cultural dimensions of career decision-making difficulties. *The Career Development Quarterly, 53*, 67–77.

McAllister, M. (2003). Multiple meanings of self-harm: A critical review. *International Journal of Mental Health Nursing, 12*, 177–185.

McCarney, S. B., & Anderson, P. D. (1996). *Adult Attention Deficit Disorders Evaluation Scale.* Columbia, MO: Hawthorne Educational Services.

McClennen, J. C., Summers, A. B., & Daley, J. G. (2002). The Lesbian Partner Abuse Scale. *Research on Social Work Practice, 12*, 277–292.

McCollum, D. (2007). Minnesota tool. In K. C. Basile, M. F. Hertz, & S. E. Back (Eds.), *Intimate partner violence and sexual violence victimization assessment instruments for use in healthcare settings* (pp. 44–45). Retrieved from https://www.cdc.gov/violenceprevention/pdf/ipv/ipvandsvscreening.pdf

McCrimmon, A. W., & Smith, A. D. (2012). Test review: Wechsler Abbreviated Scale of Intelligence-Second Edition. *Journal of Psychoeducational Assessment, 31*, 337–341. doi:10.1177/0734282912467756

McDaniel, J. W. (2013). *Physical disability and human behavior* (2nd ed.). New York, NY: Pergamon Press.

McDivitt, P. J. (2002). Review of Career Maturity Inventory (CMI). In J. T. Kapes & E. A. Whitfield (Eds.), *A counselor's guide to career assessment instruments* (4th ed., pp. 336–342). Tulsa, OK: National Career Development Association.

McDougal, J. L., Bardos, A. N., & Meier, S. T. (2012). *Behavior Intervention Monitoring Assessment System.* Toronto, Ontario, Canada: Multi-Health Systems.

McFarlane, J., Parker, B., Soeken, K., & Bullock, L. (1992). Assessing for abuse during pregnancy: Severity and frequency of injuries and associated entry into prenatal care. *Journal of the American Medical Association, 267*, 3176–3178.

McGlothlin, J. (2008). *Developing clinical skills in suicide assessment, prevention, and treatment.* Alexandria, VA: American Counseling Association.

McGoldrick, M., Gerson, R., & Petry, S. S. (2008). *Genograms: Assessment and intervention* (3rd ed.). New York, NY: Norton.

McGoldrick, M., Gerson, R., & Shellenberger, S. (1999). *Genograms: Assessment and interpretation* (2nd ed.). New York, NY: Norton.

McIlveen, P., Burton, L. J., & Beccaria, G. (2013). A short form of the Career Futures Inventory. *Journal of Career Assessment, 21*, 127–138. doi:10.1177/1069072712450493

McIntosh, D. E., & Dixon, F. A. (2005). Use of intelligence tests in the identification of giftedness. In D. P. Flanagan & P. L. Harrison (Eds.), *Contemporary intellectual assessment* (pp. 545–556). New York, NY: Guilford Press.

McLellan, A. T., Kushner, H., Metzger, D., Peters, R., Smith, I., Grissom, G., . . . Argeriou, M. (1992). The fifth edition of the Addiction Severity Index: Reliability and validity in three centers. *Journal of Nervous and Mental Disease, 173*, 412–423.

McMahon, M., & Patton, W. (2015). Incorporating career assessment and career counseling. In M. McMahon & M. Watson (Eds.), *Career assessment: Qualitative approaches* (pp. 49–58). Rotterdam, The Netherlands: Sense.

McMahon, M., & Watson, M. (2012). Telling stories of career assessment. *Journal of Career Assessment, 20*, 440–451. doi:10/1177/1069072712448999

McMahon, M., & Watson, M. (Eds.). (2015). *Career assessment: Qualitative approaches.* Rotterdam, The Netherlands: Sense.

Meier, S. T. (2015). *Incorporating progress monitoring and outcome assessment into counseling and psychotherapy: A primer.* New York, NY: Oxford University Press.

Mendelsohn, G. A., & Kirk, B. A. (1962). Personality differences not used. *Journal of Counseling Psychology, 9,* 341–346.

Merikangas, K. R., He, J., Burstein, M., Swanson, S. A., Avenevoli, S., Cui, L., . . . Swendsen, J. (2010). Lifetime prevalence of mental disorders in U.S. adolescents: Results from the National Comorbidity Study–Adolescent Supplement (NCS-A). *Journal of the American Academy of Child and Adolescent Psychiatry, 10,* 980–989.

Messick, S. (1995). Validity of psychological assessment: Validation of inferences from persons' responses and performances as scientific inquiry into score meaning. *American Psychologist, 50,* 741–749.

Meyers, L. (2006, December). Asian-American mental health. *Monitor on Psychology, 37,* 44–46.

Michael, W. B., Michael, J. J., & Zimmerman, W. S. (1988). *Study Attitudes and Methods Survey, manual of instructions and interpretations.* San Diego, CA: EdITS.

Michell, J. B. (1997). Quantitative science and the definition of measurement in psychology. *British Journal of Psychology, 88,* 355–383.

Mihura, J. L., Meyer, G. J., Dumitrascu, N., & Bombel, G. (2013). The validity of individual Rorschach variables: Systematic reviews and meta-analyses of the comprehensive system. *Psychological Bulletin, 139,* 548–605. doi:10.1037/a0029406

Miller, D. J., Spengler, E. S., & Spengler, P. M. (2015). A meta-analysis of confidence and judgment accuracy in clinical decision making. *Journal of Counseling Psychology, 62,* 553–567. doi:10.1037/cou0000105

Miller, G. A. (1982). Deriving meaning from standardized tests: Interpreting test results to clients. *Measurement and Evaluation in Guidance, 15,* 87–94.

Miller, S. D., Duncan, B. L., Brown, J., Sparks, J. A., & Claud, D. A. (2003). The Outcome Rating Scale: A preliminary study of the reliability, validity, and feasibility of a brief visual analog measure. *Journal of Brief Therapy, 2,* 91–100.

Miller, W. R., & Moyers, T. B. (2005). Motivational interviewing. In G. P. Koocher, J. C. Norcross, & S. S. Hill, III (Eds.), *Psychologists' desk reference* (2nd ed., pp. 267–271). Oxford, UK: Oxford University Press.

Miller, W. R., & Muñoz, R. F. (2005). *Controlling your drinking: Tools to make moderation work for you.* New York, NY: Guilford Press.

Miller, W. R., & Rollnick, S. (2013). *Motivational interviewing: Helping people change.* New York, NY: Guilford Press.

Millon, T. (2003). *MIPS Revised manual.* Minneapolis, MN: Pearson Assessments.

Millon, T., & Davis, R. D. (1993). The Millon Adolescent Personality Inventory and the Millon Adolescent Clinical Inventory. *Journal of Counseling & Development, 71,* 570–574.

Miner, J. (1922). An aid to the analysis of vocational interest. *Journal of Educational Research, 5,* 311–323.

Mintz, L. B., & O'Halloran, M. S. (2000). The Eating Attitudes Test: Validation with *DSM-IV* eating disorder criteria. *Journal of Personality Assessment, 74,* 489–503.

Mintz, L. B., O'Halloran, M. S., Mulholland, A. M., & Schneider, P. A. (1997). Questionnaire for Eating Disorder Diagnoses: Reliability and validity of operationalizing *DSM-IV* criteria into a self-report format. *Journal of Counseling Psychology, 44,* 63–79.

Mitchell, A. J. (2013). The Mini-Mental State Examination (MMSE): An update on its diagnostic validity for cognitive disorders. In A. J. Larner (Ed.), *Cognitive screening instruments* (pp. 15–46). New York, NY: Springer.

Montalto, M. (2014). The ethical implications of using technology in psychological testing and treatment. *Ethical Human Psychology and Psychiatry, 16,* 127–136.

Moos, R. H., & Moos, B. S. (1994a). *Family Environment Scale manual: Development, application and research.* Palo Alto, CA: Consulting Psychologists Press.

Moos, R. H., & Moos, B. S. (1994b). *Life Stressors and Social Resources Inventory–Adult form.* Odessa, FL: Psychological Assessment Resources.

Moos, R. H., & Moos, B. S. (1994c). *Life Stressors and Social Resources Inventory–Youth form.* Odessa, FL: Psychological Assessment Resources.

Moreland, K. L., Eyde, L. D., Robertson, G. J., Primoff, E. S., & Most, R. B. (1995). Assessment of test user qualifications: A research-based measurement procedure. *American Psychologist, 50,* 14–23.

Morey, L. (1991). *Personality Assessment Inventory: Professional manual.* Odessa, FL: Psychological Assessment Resources.

Morey, L. C. (2003). *Essentials of PAI assessment.* Hoboken, NJ: Wiley.

Morris, M., Chartrand, J., & Donnay, D. (2002). *Instrument development: Reliability and validity of the Strong Interest Explorer.* Palo Alto, CA: Consulting Psychologists Press.

Morrison, L., Allan, R., & Grunfeld, A. (2000). Improving the emergency department detection rate of domestic violence using direct questioning. *Journal of Emergency Medicine, 19,* 117–124.

Mueller, G., Schumacher, P., Wetzlmair, J., & Pallauf, M. (2016). Screening questionnaires to identify problem drinking in the primary care setting: A systematic review. *Journal of Public Health, 24,* 9–19. doi:10.1007/s10389-015 0691-3

Mulder, R. T. (2012). Cultural aspects of personality. In R. A. Widiger (Ed.), *The Oxford handbook of personality disorders* (pp. 260–274). New York, NY: Oxford University Press.

Murray, H. A. (1938). *Explorations in personality.* New York, NY: Oxford University Press.

Murray, H. A. (1943). *Thematic Apperception Test manual.* Cambridge, MA: Harvard University Press.

Myers, I. B., McCaulley, M. H., Quenk, N. L., & Hammer, A. L. (1998). *MBTI manual: A guide to the development and use of the Myers–Briggs Type Indicator* (3rd ed.). Palo Alto, CA: Consulting Psychologists Press.

Myers, J. E., Luecht, R. M., & Sweeney, T. J. (2004). The factor structure of wellness: Reexamining theoretical and empirical models underlying the Wellness Evaluation of Lifestyle (WEL) and the five-factor model. *Measurement and Evaluation in Counseling and Development, 36,* 194–208.

Myers, J. E., & Shurts, W. M. (2002). Measuring positive emotionality: A review of instruments assessing love. *Measurement and Evaluation in Counseling and Development, 34,* 238–254.

Na, S. D., & Burns, T. G. (2016). Wechsler Intelligence Scale for Children–V: Test review. *Applied Neuropsychology: Child, 5,* 156–160. doi:10/1080/21622965.2015.1015337

Naglieri, J. A. (1996). *Naglieri Nonverbal Ability Test–Multilevel form.* San Antonio, TX: Psychological Corporation.

Naglieri, J. A. (2000). *Naglieri Nonverbal Ability Test: Individual administration.* San Antonio, TX: Psychological Corporation.

Naglieri, J. A. (2005). *The Cognitive Assessment System.* Odessa, FL: Psychological Assessment Resources.

Naglieri, J. A., Das, J. P., & Goldstein, S. (2012). Planning, attention, simultaneous, successive: A cognitive-processing based theory of intelligence. In D. P. Flanagan & P. L. Harrison (Eds.), *Contemporary intellectual assessment: Theories, tests, and issues* (3rd ed., pp. 526–552). New York, NY: Guilford Press.

Naglieri, J. A., & Ford, D. Y. (2015). Misconceptions about the Naglieri Nonverbal Ability Test: A commentary of concerns and disagreement. *Roeper Review, 37,* 234–240. doi:10.1 080/02783193.2015.1077497

Nasab, M. F., Abdul Kadir, R., & Hassan, S. A. (2015). Psychometric evaluation of the career decision scale with Iranian undergraduate students. *Journal of Counseling & Development, 93,* 344–351.

National Alliance on Mental Illness. (2015). *Mental health facts: Multicultural.* Retrieved from https://www.nami.org/NAMI/media/NAMI-Media/Infographics/Multicultural MHFacts10-23-15.pdf

National Alliance on Mental Illness. (2016). *Mental health facts: Children & teens.* Retrieved from https://www.nami.org/NAMI/media/NAMI-Media/Infographics/Children-MH-Facts-NAMI.pdf

National Board for Certified Counselors. (2012). *National Board for Certified Counselors (NBCC) code of ethics.* Retrieved from www.nbcc.org/Assets/Ethics/nbcc-codeofethics.pdf

National Commission on Excellence in Education. (1983). *A nation at risk: The imperative for educational reform.* Washington, DC: Author.

National Council on Measurement in Education. (2012). *Testing and data integrity in the administration of statewide student assessment programs.* Madison, WI: Author.

National Institute of Mental Health. (2012). *Suicide.* Retrieved from https://www.nimh.nih.gov/health/statistics/suicide/index.shtml

National Institute of Mental Health. (n.d.). *Statistics.* Retrieved from http://www.nimh.nih.gov/health/statistics/index.shtml

National Institute on Alcohol Abuse and Alcoholism. (2005). *Helping patients who drink too much.* Retrieved from http://pubs.niaaa.nih.gov/publications/Practitioner/CliniciansGuide2005/clinicians_guide.htm

Naugle, K. A. (2009). Counseling and testing: What counselors need to know about state laws on assessment and testing. *Measurement and Evaluation in Counseling and Development, 42,* 31–45.

Neisser, V., Boodoo, G., Bouchardt, T. J., Boykin, A. W., Brody, N., Ceci, S. J., . . . Urbina, S. (1996). Intelligence: Knowns and unknowns. *American Psychologist, 51,* 77–101.

Neukrug, E. S., Peterson, C. H., Bonner, M. W., & Lomas, G. I. (2013). A national survey of assessment instruments taught by counselor educators. *Counselor Education and Supervision, 52,* 207–220.

Nevill, D. D., & Calvert, P. D. (1996). Career assessment and the Salience Inventory. *Journal of Career Assessment, 4,* 312–399.

Nevill, D. D., & Kruse, S. J. (1996). Career assessment and the Values Scale. *Journal of Career Assessment, 4,* 383–397.

Nevill, D. D., & Super, D. E. (1986a). *Manual for the Salience Inventory.* Palo Alto, CA: Consulting Psychologists Press.

Nevill, D. D., & Super, D. E. (1986b). *Manual for the Values Scale.* Palo Alto, CA: Consulting Psychologists Press.

Newton, K. S., & Erford, B. T. (2018). Social class and classism. In D. G. Hays & B. T. Erford (Eds.), *Developing multicultural counseling competence: A systems approach* (3rd ed., pp. 188–223). Boston, MA: Pearson.

Nezu, A. M., Nezu, C. M., & D'Zurilla, T. J. (2012). *Problem-solving therapy: A treatment manual.* New York, NY: Springer.

Nickerson, R. S., Perkins, D. N., & Smith, E. E. (2014). *The teaching of thinking.* New York, NY: Routledge.

Niles, S. G., & Harris-Bowlsbey, J. (2017). *Career development interventions* (5th ed.). Boston, MA: Pearson.

Niv, N., Kaplan, Z., Mitrani, E., & Shiang, J. (1998). Validity study of the EDI-2 in Israeli population. *Israel Journal of Psychiatry and Related Sciences, 35,* 287–292.

No Child Left Behind Act of 2001, Pub. L. No. 107-110, 20 U.S.C. §§ 6301 *et seq.* (2002).

Noble, J., Davenport, M., Schiel, J., & Pommerich, M. (1999). *High school academic and noncognitive variables related to the ACT scores of racial/ethnic groups.* Iowa City, IA: American College Testing Program.

Nock, M. K., & Banjai, M. R. (2007). Prediction of suicide ideation and attempts among adolescents using a brief performance-based test. *Journal of Consulting and Clinical Psychology, 75,* 705–715.

Nock, M. K., Holmber, E. B., Photos, V. I., & Michel, B. D. (2007). Self-Injurious Thoughts and Behaviors Interview: Development, reliability and validity in an adolescent sample. *Psychological Assessment, 19,* 309–317.

Nock, M. K., Kessler, R. C., & Franklin, J. C. (2016). Risk factors for suicide ideation differ from those for the transition to suicide attempt: The importance of creativity, rigor, and urgency in suicide research. *Clinical Psychology: Science and Practice, 23,* 31–34. doi:10.1111/cpsp/12133

Noel-Levitz. (2016). *College Student Inventory™.* Retrieved from https://www.noellevitz. com/student-retention-solutions/retention-management-system-plus/college-student-inventory

Norman, G. J., Hawkley, L. C., Luhmann, M., Cacioppo, J. T., & Berntson, G. G. (2012). Social neuroscience and the modern synthesis of social and biological levels of analysis. In D. D. Franks & J. H. Turner (Eds.), *Handbook of neuroscience* (pp. 67–81). New York, NY: Springer.

O'Hara, C., Clark, M., Hays, D. G., McDonald, P., Chang, C. Y., Crockett, S. A., . . . Wester, K. L. (2016). AARC Standards for Multicultural Research. *Counseling Outcome Research and Evaluation, 7,* 67–72. doi:10.1177/2150137816657389

O'Shea, A. J., & Feller, R. (2012). *Career Decision-Making® System–Revised (CDM®-R).* Retrieved from http://www.pearsonassessments.com/HAIWEB/Cultures/en-us/ Productdetail.htm?Pid=PAa12633&Mode=summary

Office of the Press Secretary. (2015). *Fact sheet: Congress acts to fix No Child Left Behind.* Retrieved from https://www.whitehouse.gov/the-press-office/2015/12/03/fact-sheet-congress-acts-fix-no-child-left-behind

Ogdon, D. P. (2001). *Psychodiagnostics and personality assessment* (3rd ed.). Los Angeles, CA: Western Psychological Services.

Okazaki, S., Kallivayalil, D., & Sue, S. (2002). Clinical personality assessment with Asian Americans. In J. N. Butcher (Ed.), *Clinical personality assessment: Practical approaches* (pp. 135–153). New York, NY: Oxford University Press.

Okocha, A. (1998). Using qualitative appraisal strategies in career counseling. *Journal of Employment Counseling, 35,* 151–160.

Olson, D. H., Olson, A. K., & Larson, P. J. (2012). PREPARE-ENRICH program: Overview and new discoveries about couples. *Journal of Family & Community Ministries, 25,* 30–44.

Oltmanns, T. F., Friedman, J. N. W., Fiedler, E. R., & Turkheimer, E. (2004). Perceptions of people with personality disorders based on thin slices of behavior. *Journal of Research in Psychology, 38,* 216–229.

Ortiz, S. O., Ochoa, S. H., & Dynda, A. M. (2012). Testing with culturally and linguistically diverse populations. In D. P. Flanagan & P. L. Harrison (Eds.), *Contemporary intellectual assessment: Theories, tests, and issues* (3rd ed., pp. 526–622). New York, NY: Guilford Press.

Ortman, J. M., Velkoff, V. A., & Hogan, H. (2014, May). *An aging nation: The older population in the United States* (P25-1140). Retrieved from the U.S. Census Bureau website: www. census.gov/prod/2014pubs/p25-1140.pdf

Osborn, D. S. (2013). WorkKeys assessments. In C. T. Wood & D. G. Hays (Eds.), *A counselor's guide to career assessment instruments* (6th ed., pp. 157–162). Broken Arrow, OK: National Career Development Association.

Osborn, D. S., Kronholz, J. F., Finklea, J. T., & Cantonis, A. M. (2014). Technology-savvy career counseling. *Canadian Psychology, 55,* 258–265. doi:10.1037/a0038160

Osipow, S. H. (1987). *Manual for the Career Decision Scale* (rev. ed.). Odessa, FL: Psychological Assessment Resources.

Osipow, S. H., & Winer, J. L. (1996). The use of the Career Decision Scale in career assessment. *Journal of Career Assessment, 4,* 117–130.

Oswald, F. L., Schmitt, N., Kim, B. H., Ramsay, L. J., & Gillespie, M. A. (2004). Developing a biodata measure and situational judgment inventory as predictors of college student performance. *Journal of Applied Psychology, 89,* 187–207.

Overall, J. E., & Gorham, D. R. (1988). The Brief Psychiatric Rating Scale (BPRS): Recent developments in ascertainment and scaling. *Psychopharmacology Bulletin, 24,* 97–99.

Paniagua, F. A. (2014). *Assessing and treating culturally diverse clients: A practical guide* (4th ed.). Thousand Oaks, CA: Sage.

PAR, Inc. (2012a). *State–Trait Anger Expression Inventory-2.* Lutz, FL: Author.

PAR, Inc. (2012b). *Tennessee Self-Concept Scale, 2nd edition (TSCS:2).* Retrieved from http://www4.parinc.com/Products/Product.aspx?ProductID=TSCS-2

PAR, Inc. (n.d.). *Personality Assessment Inventory™ (PAI®).* Retrieved from http://www4.parinc.com/Products/Product.aspx?ProductID=PAI

Parsons, F. (1909). *Choosing a vocation.* Boston, MA: Houghton Mifflin.

Patterson, T. (2011). Cognitive-behavioral couple therapy: Multiple couple illustrations and comparisons. In D. K. Carson & M. Casado-Kehoe (Eds.), *Case studies in couples therapy: Theory-based approaches* (pp. 109–120). New York, NY: Routledge.

Patterson, W. M., Dohn, H. H., Bird, J., & Patterson, G. A. (1983). Evaluation of suicidal patients: The SAD PERSONS Scale. *Psychosomatics, 24,* 343–349.

Pearson Assessments. (2012). *Otis-Lennon School Ability Test®, Eighth Edition (OLSAT 8®).* Retrieved from http://www.pearsonassessments.com/learningassessments/products/100000003/otis-lennon-school-ability-test-eighth-edition-olsat-8-olsat-8.html

Pearson Assessments. (2016a). *Millon® Adolescent Clinical Inventory (MACI®).* Retrieved from http://www.pearsonclinical.com/psychology/products/100000667/millon-adolescent-clinical-inventory-maci.html?origsearchtext=MACI

Pearson Assessments. (2016b). *The Millon® Clinical Multiaxial Inventory–IV (MCMI®-IV).* Retrieved from http://www.pearsonclinical.com/psychology/products/100001362/millonsupsup-clinical-multiaxial-inventoryiv-mcmi-iv.html

Pearson Assessments. (2016c). *Minnesota Multiphasic Personality Inventory®–2 (MMPI®-2).* Retrieved from http://www.pearsonclinical.com/psychology/products/100000461/minnesota-multiphasic-personality-inventory-2-mmpi-2.html

Pearson Assessments. (2016d). *Minnesota Multiphasic Personality Inventory–2–Restructured Form® (MMPI-2-RF®).* Retrieved from http://www.pearsonclinical.com/psychology/products/100000631/minnesota-multiphasic-personality-inventory-2-rf-mmpi-2-rf.html

Pearson Assessments. (2016e). *Minnesota Multiphasic Personality Inventory®–Adolescent (MMPI®-A).* Retrieved from http://www.pearsonclinical.com/psychology/products/100000465/minnesota-multiphasic-personality-inventory-adolescent-mmpi-a.html

Pearson Assessments. (2016f). *Minnesota Multiphasic Personality Inventory–Adolescent–Restructured Form™ (MMPI-A-RF™).* Retrieved from http://www.pearsonclinical.com/psychology/products/100001762/minnesota-multiphasic-personality-inventoryadolescent-restructured-form-mmpi-a-rf.html

Pellegrino, J. W. (2004). *The evolution of educational assessment: Considering the past and imagining the future.* Retrieved from www.ets.org/Media/Research/pdf/PICANG6.pdf

Pendergrass, L. A., Hansen, J. C., Neuman, J. L., & Nutter, K. J. (2003). Examination of the concurrent validity of scores from the CISS for student–athlete college major selection: A brief report. *Measurement and Evaluation in Counseling and Development, 35,* 212–217.

Perrone, K. M., Gordon, P. A., Fitch, J. C., & Civiletto, C. L. (2003). The Adult Career Concerns Inventory: Development of a short form. *Journal of Employment Counseling, 40,* 172–180.

Peterson, C., & Austin, J. T. (1985). Review of Coopersmith Self-Esteem Inventories. In J. V. Mitchell, Jr. (Ed.), *The ninth mental measurements yearbook* (pp. 396–397). Lincoln, NE: Buros Institute of Mental Measurements.

Peterson, C. H., Lomas, G. I., Neukrug, E. S., & Bonner, M. W. (2014). Assessment use by counselors in the United States: Implications for policy and practice. *Journal of Counseling & Development, 92,* 90–98.

Peterson, G. W. (1998). Using a vocational card sort as an assessment of occupational knowledge. *Journal of Career Assessment, 6,* 49–67.

Peterson, J. S. (2015). School counselors and gifted kids: Respecting both cognitive and affective. *Journal of Counseling & Development, 93,* 153–162.

Petry, S. S., & McGoldrick, M. (2005). Genograms in assessment and therapy. In G. P. Koocher, J. C. Norcross, & S. S. Hill, III (Eds.), *Psychologists' desk reference* (2nd ed., pp. 366–373). New York, NY: Oxford University Press.

Piedmont, R. L. (2013). *The revised NEO Personality Inventory: Clinical and research applications.* New York, NY: Springer.

Piers, E. B., & Harris, D. B. (1996). *Piers–Harris Children's Self-Concept Scale, Revised manual.* Los Angeles, CA: Western Psychological Services.

Pietrzak, D. (2013). The Career Development Inventory. In C. T. Wood & D. G. Hays (Eds.), *A counselor's guide to career assessment instruments* (6th ed., pp. 319–323). Broken Arrow, OK: National Career Development Association.

Pincus, A. L., & Gurtman, M. B. (2003). Interpersonal assessment. In J. S. Wiggins (Ed.), *Paradigms of personality assessment* (pp. 246–261). New York, NY: Guilford Press.

Piotrowski, C. (1999). Assessment practices in the era of managed care: Current status and future directions. *Journal of Clinical Psychology, 55,* 787–796.

Piotrowski, C. (2007). Forensic psychological testing as a function of affiliation and organizational setting. *Organization Development Journal, 25,* 94–98

Piotrowski, C. (2015a). On the decline of projective techniques in professional psychology training. *North American Journal of Psychology, 17,* 259–265.

Piotrowski, C. (2015b). Projective techniques usage worldwide: A review of applied settings 1995-2015. *Journal of the Indian Academy of Applied Psychology, 41,* 9–19.

Pittenger, D. J. (2005). Cautionary comments regarding the Myers–Briggs Type Indicator. *Counseling Psychology Journal: Practice and Research, 57,* 210–221.

Plake, B. S., & Parker, C. S. (1982). The development and validation of a revised version of the Mathematics Anxiety Rating Scale. *Educational and Psychological Measurement, 42,* 551–557.

Podar, I., Hannus, A., & Allik, J. (1999). Personality and affectivity characteristics associated with eating disorders: A comparison of eating disordered, weight-preoccupied, and normal samples. *Journal of Personality Assessment, 73,* 133–147.

Polanczyk, G. V., Willcutt, E. G., Salum, G. A., Kieling, C., & Rohde, L. A. (2014). ADHD prevalence estimates across three decades: A updated systematic review and meta-regression analysis. *International Journal of Epidemiology, 43,* 434–442. doi:10.1093/ije/dyt261

Polanski, P. J., & Hinkle, J. S. (2000). The Mental Status Examination: Its use by professional counselors. *Journal of Counseling & Development, 78,* 357–364.

Pollak, J., Levy, S., & Breitholtz, T. (1999). Screening for medical and neurodevelopmental disorders for the professional counselor. *Journal of Counseling & Development, 77,* 350–358.

Ponterotto, J. G., Rivera, L., & Sueyoshi, L. A. (2000). The Career-in-Culture Interview: A semi-structured protocol for the cross-cultural intake interview. *The Career Development Quarterly, 49,* 85–96.

Pope, M. (2002). Review of Kuder General Interest Survey Form E (KGIS-Form E). In J. T. Kapes & E. A. Whitfield (Eds.), *A counselor's guide to career assessment instruments* (4th ed., pp. 257–268). Tulsa, OK: National Career Development Association.

Powell, A. L. (2013). Computer anxiety: Comparison of research from the 1990s and 2000s. *Computers in Human Behavior, 29,* 2337–2381.

Powell, J. E., & McInness, E. (1994). Alcohol use among older hospital patients: Findings from an Australian study. *Drug and Alcohol Review, 13,* 5–12.

Presti, A. L., Pace, F., Mondo, M., Nota, L., Casarubia, P., Ferrari, L., & Betz, N. E. (2013). An examination of the structure of the Career Decision Self-Efficacy Scale (short form) among Italian high school students. *Journal of Career Assessment, 21,* 337–347. doi:10.1177/1069072712471506

Prieto, L. R., McNeill, B. W., Walls, R. G., & Gomez, S. P. (2001). Chicanas/os and mental health services: An overview of utilization, counselor preference, and assessment issues. *The Counseling Psychologist, 29,* 18–54.

PRO-ED. (2012). *Career Interests, Preferences, and Strengths Inventory.* Retrieved from http:// http://www.proedinc.com/customer/productView.aspx?ID=8367

Prochaska, J. O., DiClemente, C. C., & Norcross, J. C. (1992). In search of how people change: Applications to addictive behaviors. *American Psychologist, 47,* 1102–1114.

Prochaska, J. O., Norcross, J. C., & DiClemente, C. C. (2013). Applying the stages of change. *Psychotherapy in Australia, 19*(2), 10–15.

Prospero, M. (2006). The role perceptions in dating violence among young adolescents. *Journal of Interpersonal Violence, 21,* 470–484.

Psychological Corporation. (1997). *WAIS-III WMS-III technical manual.* San Antonio, TX: Author.

Psychological Publications. (2015). *Taylor Johnson Temperament Analysis® (T-JTA®).* Retrieved from https://www.tjta.com/asp/index.asp

Pulerwitz, J., Gortmaker, S., & DeJong, W. (2000). Measuring sexual relationship power in HIV/STD research. *Sex Roles, 42,* 637–660.

Putnam, F. W., Helmer, K., & Trickett, P. K. (1993). Development, reliability, and validity of a child dissociation scale. *Child Abuse & Neglect, 17,* 731–741.

Quinn, M. T., Lewis, R. J., & Fischer, K. L. (1992). A cross-correlation of the Myers–Briggs and Keirsey instruments. *Journal of College Student Development, 33,* 279–280.

Randahl, G. J., Hansen, J. C., & Haverkamp, B. E. (1993). Instrumental behaviors following test administration and interpretation: Exploration validity of the Strong Interest Inventory. *Journal of Counseling & Development, 71,* 435–439.

Raths, L., Harmin, M., & Simon, S. (1978). *Values and teaching: Working with values in the classroom* (2nd ed.). Columbus, OH: Merrill.

Ratts, M. J., Singh, A. A., Nassar-McMillan, S., Butler, S. K., & McCullough, J. R. (2016). Multicultural and social justice counseling competencies: Guidelines for the counseling profession. *Journal of Multicultural Counseling and Development, 44,* 28–48.

Raven, J. C., Court, J. H., & Raven, J. (1993). *Manual for Raven's Progressive Matrices and Vocabulary Scales.* San Antonio, TX: Psychological Corporation.

Rayman, J. R. (1976). Sex and the Single Interest Inventory: The empirical validation of sex-balanced interest inventory items. *Journal of Counseling Psychology, 23,* 239–246.

Reardon, R. C., Lenz, J. G., Sampson, J. P., & Peterson, G. W. (2012). *Career development and planning: A comprehensive approach* (4th ed.). New York, NY: Custom.

Rector, N. A. (2012). Cognitive behavioral approaches to anxiety and depression comorbidity: Introduction to the special section. *International Journal of Cognitive Therapy, 5,* 113–117.

Reeves, T. D., & Marbach-Ad, G. (2015). Contemporary test validity in theory and practice: A primer for discipline-based education researchers. *CBE Life Sciences Education, 15,* 1–9. doi:10.1187/cbe.15-08-0183

Renzulli, J. S., & Smith, L. H. (1978). *Learning Styles Inventory: A measure of student preference for instructional techniques.* Mansfield Center, CT: Creative Learning Press.

Resing, W. C. M., Tunteler, E., De Jong, F., & Bosma, T. (2009). Dynamic testing in indigenous and ethnic minority children. *Learning and Individual Differences, 19,* 445–450. doi:10.1016/j.lindif.2009.03.006

Reynolds, C. R., & Bigler, E. D. (2000). *CASE/CASE–SF professional manual.* Odessa, FL: Psychological Assessment Resources.

Reynolds, C. R., & Kamphaus, R. W. (2005). *BASC-2: Behavior Assessment System for Children–Second edition.* Circle Pines, MN: American Guidance Service.

Reynolds, C. R., & Richmond, B. O. (2008). *Revised Children's Manifest Anxiety Scale* (2nd ed.). Los Angeles, CA: Western Psychological Services.

Reynolds, C. R., Richmond, B. O., & Lowe, P. A. (2003). *Adult Manifest Anxiety Scale.* Los Angeles, CA: Western Psychological Services.

Reynolds, W. M. (1999). *Professional manual for Multidimensional Anxiety Questionnaire.* Odessa, FL: Psychological Assessment Resources.

Reynolds, W. M., & Kobak, K. A. (1995). *Professional manual for Hamilton Depression Inventory: A self report version of the Hamilton Depression Rating Scale.* Odessa, FL: Psychological Assessment Resources.

Rhodes, K. V., Lauderdale, D. S., He, T., Howes, D. S., & Levinson, W. (2002). "Between me and the computer": Increased detection of intimate partner violence using a computer questionnaire. *Annals of Emergency Medicine, 40,* 476–484.

Rhodes, R. L. (2010). Multicultural school neuropsychology. In D. C. Miller (Ed.), *Best practices in school neuropsychology: Guidelines for effective practice, assessment, and evidence-based intervention* (pp. 61–77). New York, NY: Wiley.

Rice, K. G., Suh, H., & Ege, E. (2014). Further evaluation of the Outcome Questionnaire–45.2. *Measurement and Evaluation in Counseling and Development, 47,* 102–117. doi:10.1177/0748175614522268

Richardson, J. T. E. (2003). Howard Andrew Knox and the origins of performance testing on Ellis Island, 1912–1916. *History of Psychology, 6,* 143–170.

Richardson, J. T. E. (2011). *Howard Andrew Knox: Pioneer of intelligence testing at Ellis Island.* New York, NY: Columbia University Press.

Ridley, C. R., Li, L. C., & Hill, C. L. (1998). Multicultural assessment: Reexamination, reconceptualization, and practical application. *The Counseling Psychologist, 26,* 827–910.

Riger, S., Ahrens, C., & Blickenstaff, A. (2001). Measuring interference with employment and education reported by women with abusive partners: Preliminary data. In D. O'Leary & R. Maiuro (Eds.), *Psychological abuse in violent domestic relations* (pp. 119–133). New York, NY: Springer.

Robinson, C. H., & Betz, N. E. (2008). A psychometric evaluation of Super's Work Values Inventory–Revised. *Journal of Career Assessment, 16,* 456–463. doi:10.1177/1069072708318903

Robinson, G. (2015, December 18). *Every Student Succeeds Act (ESSA) of 2015: Gains and challenges* [web log post]. Retrieved from https://www.aei.org/publication/every-student-succeeds-act-essa-of-2015-gains-and-challenges/

Rodenburg, F. A., & Fantuzzo, J. W. (1993). The measure of wife abuse: Steps toward the development of a comprehensive assessment technique. *Journal of Family Violence, 8,* 203–228.

Rodgers, B. G. (2005). Review of the Cognitive Abilities Test Form 6. In R. A. Spies & B. S. Plake (Eds.), *The sixteenth mental measurements yearbook* (pp. 232–234). Lincoln, NE: Buros Institute of Mental Measurements.

Rodriguez, A. M., Salar, N. V., Carretero, C. M., Gimeno, E. C., & Collado, E. R. (2015). Eating disorders and diet management in contact sports: EAT-26 questionnaire does not seem appropriate to evaluate eating disorders in sports. *Nutrición Hospitalaria, 32,* 1708–1714.

Rogers, J. R., Alexander, R. A., & Subich, L. M. (1994). Development and psychometric analysis of the Suicide Assessment Checklist. *Journal of Mental Health Counseling, 16,* 352–368.

Rogers, J. R., Lewis, M. M., & Subich, L. M. (2002). Validity of the Suicide Assessment Checklist in an emergency crisis center. *Journal of Counseling & Development, 80,* 493–502.

Roid, G. H. (2003). *Stanford–Binet Intelligence Scales, Fifth Edition, examiner's manual.* Itasca, IL: Riverside Press.

Roivainen, E., Veijola, J., & Miettunen, J. (2015). Careless responses in survey data and the validity of a screening instrument. *Nordic Psychology.* Advance online publication. doi: 10.1080/19012276.2015.1071202

Rokeach, M. (1973). *The nature of human values.* New York, NY: Free Press.

Rosenthal, R. (1990). How are we doing in soft psychology? *American Psychologist, 45,* 775–776.

Rosnow, R. L., & Rosenthal, R. (1988). Focused tests of significance and effect size estimation in counseling psychology. *Journal of Counseling Psychology, 35,* 203–208.

Ross, H. E., Gavin, D. R., & Skinner, H. A. (1990). Diagnostic validity of the MAST and the Alcohol Dependence Scale in the assessment of *DSM-III* alcohol problems. *Journal of Studies on Alcohol, 51,* 506–513.

Rotter, J. B., Lah, M. I., & Rafferty, J. E. (1992). *Manual for the Rotter Incomplete Sentence Blank, second edition.* San Antonio, TX: Psychological Corporation.

Rottinghaus, P. J., Betz, N. E., & Borgen, F. H. (2003). Validity of parallel measures of vocational interests and confidence. *Journal of Career Assessment, 11,* 355–378.

Rottinghaus, P. J., Day, S. X., & Borgen, F. H. (2005). The Career Futures Inventory: A measure of career related adaptability and optimism. *Journal of Career Assessment, 13,* 3–24.

Rowland, C. M., Quinn, E. D., & Steiner, S. A. (2015). Beyond legal crafting high-quality IEPs for children with complex communication needs. *Communication Disorders Quarterly, 37,* 53–62. doi:10.1177/1525740114551632

Rubinstein, J. (2004). Test preparation: What makes it effective? In J. E. Wall & G. R. Walz (Eds.), *Measuring up: Assessment issues for teachers, counselors, and administrators* (pp. 397–415). Greensboro, NC: CAPS Press.

Russell, M., & Karol, D. (1993). *16-PF, fifth edition, administrator's manual.* Champaign, IL: Institute for Personality and Ability Testing.

Sackett, P. R., Borneman, M. J., & Connelly, B. S. (2008). High-stakes testing in higher education and employment: Appraising the evidence for validity and fairness. *American Psychologist, 63,* 215–227.

Sackett, S. A., & Hansen, J. C. (1995). Vocational outcomes of college freshmen with flat profiles on the Strong Interest Inventory. *Measurement and Evaluation in Counseling and Development, 28,* 9–24.

Sacks, S. (2008). Brief overview of screening and assessment of co-occurring disorders. *International Journal of Mental Health and Addiction, 6,* 7–19.

Sagiv, L. (2002). Vocational interests and basic values. *Journal of Career Assessment, 10,* 233–257.

Sampson, J. P., & Makela, J. P. (2014). Ethical issues associated with information and communication technology in counseling and guidance. *International Journal for Educational and Vocational Guidance, 14,* 135–148. doi:10.1007/s10775-013-9258-7

Sampson, J. P., Jr., Peterson, G. W., Lenz, J. G., Reardon, R. C., & Saunders, D. E. (1996). *Career Thoughts Inventory: Professional manual.* Odessa, FL: Psychological Assessment Resources.

Sanchez, E. I. (2013). *Differential effects of using ACT College Readiness Assessment scores and high school GPA to predict first-year college GPA among racial/ethnic, gender, and income groups.* Retrieved from http://files.eric.ed.gov/fulltext/ED555597.pdf

Sanford, E. E. (1995). Review of the Rokeach Value Survey. In J. C. Conoley & J. C. Impara (Eds.), *The twelfth mental measurements yearbook* (pp. 879–880). Lincoln, NE: Buros Institute of Mental Measurements.

Sansone, R. A., Wiederman, M. W., & Sansone, L. A. (1998). The Self-Harm Inventory (SHI): Development of a scale for identifying self-destructive behaviors and borderline personality disorder. *Journal of Clinical Psychology, 54,* 973–983.

Sapp, M. (2013). *Test anxiety: Applied research, assessment, and treatment interventions.* Lanham, MD: University Press of America.

Sarason, I. G. (Ed.). (1980). *Test anxiety: Theory, research, and applications.* Hillsdale, NJ: Erlbaum.

Sarason, I. G., Johnson, J. H., & Siegel, J. M. (1978). Assessing the impact of life changes: Development of the Life Experiences Survey. *Journal of Consulting and Clinical Psychology, 46,* 932–946.

SASSI Institute. (2016). *The Substance Abuse Subtle Screening Inventory–4.* Springville, IN: Author.

Satcher, D. (2000). Mental health: A report of the Surgeon General—Executive summary. *Professional Psychology: Research and Practice, 31,* 5–13.

Sattler, J. M. (2005). *Assessment of children: Behavioral and clinical applications.* La Mesa, CA: Sattler.

Saunders, S. M., & Wojcik, J. V. (2004). The reliability and validity of a brief self-report questionnaire to screen for mental health problems: The Health Dynamics Inventory. *Journal of Clinical Psychology in Medical Settings, 11,* 233–241.

Savickas, M. L. (1997). Career adaptability: An integrative construct for life-span, life-space theory. *The Career Development Quarterly, 45,* 247–259.

Savickas, M. L. (1998). Career style assessment and counseling. In T. Sweeney (Ed.), *Adlerian counseling: A practitioner's approach* (4th ed., pp. 329–359). Philadelphia, PA: Accelerated Development.

Savickas, M. L., Briddick, W. C., & Watkins, C. E. (2002). The relation of career maturity to personality type and social adjustment. *Journal of Career Assessment, 10,* 24–41.

Savickas, M. L., & Hartung, P. J. (1996). The Career Development Inventory in review: Psychometric and research findings. *Journal of Career Assessment, 4,* 171–188.

Savickas, M. L., & Taber, B. J. (2006). Individual differences in RIASEC profile similarity across five interest inventories. *Measurement and Evaluation in Counseling and Development, 38,* 203–210.

Scarpati, S. (2013). Current perspectives in the assessment of the handicapped. In R. K. Hambleton & J. N. Zaal (Eds.), *Advances in educational and psychological testing: Theory and applications* (pp. 251–276). New York, NY: Springer.

Scheiber, C. (2016). Does the KABC-II display ethnic bias in the prediction of reading, math, and writing in elementary school through high school? *Assessment.* Advance online publication. doi:10.1177/1073191115624545.

Schinka, J. A. (1988). *Mental Status Checklist for Adults.* Lutz, FL: Psychological Assessment Resources.

Schmidt, F. L., & Hunter, J. L. (2014). *Methods of meta-analysis: Correcting error and bias in research findings.* Thousand Oaks, CA: Sage.

Schmidt, M., Perels, F., & Schmitz, B. (2010). How to perform idiographic and a combination of idiographic and nomothetic approaches: A comparison of time series analyses and hierarchical linear modeling. *Journal of Psychology, 218,* 166–174.

Schoemaker, C., Verbraak, M., Breteler, R., & vanderStaak, C. (1997). The discriminant validity of the Eating Disorder Inventory–2. *British Journal of Clinical Psychology, 36,* 627–629.

Schuerger, J. M. (2000). The Sixteen Personality Factor Questionnaire (16PF). In C. E. Watkins, Jr., & V. L. Campbell (Eds.), *Testing and assessment in counseling and practice* (2nd ed., pp. 73–110). Mahwah, NJ: Erlbaum.

Schultheiss, D. E. P., & Stead, G. B. (2004). Childhood Career Development Scale: Scale construction and psychometric properties. *Journal of Career Assessment, 12,* 113–134.

Schwartz, R. C., & Blankenship, D. M. (2014). Racial disparities in psychotic disorder diagnosis: A review of empirical literature. *World Journal of Psychiatry, 4,* 133–140. doi:10.5498/wjp.v4.i4.133

Schwartz, S. H. (1994). Are there universal aspects in the structure and contents of human values? *Journal of Social Issues, 50,* 19–45.

Schwartz, S. H. (2012). *An overview of the Schwartz theory of basic values.* Retrieved from http://scholarworks.gvsu.edu/orpc/vol2/iss1/11/

Schwartz, S. H., Cieciuch, J., Vecchione, M., Davidov, E., Fischer, R., Beierlein, C., . . . Konty, M. (2012). Refining the theory of basic individual values. *Journal of Personality and Social Psychology, 103,* 663–668. doi:10.1037/a0029393

Scogin, F., & Crowther, M. R. (2003). Integrative personality assessment with older adults and ethnic minority clients. In L. E. Beutler & G. Groth-Marnat (Eds.), *Integrative assessment of adult personality* (2nd ed., pp. 338–355). New York, NY: Guilford Press.

Searles, J. S., Helzer, J. E., Rose, G. L., & Badger, G. J. (2002). Concurrent and retrospective reports of alcohol consumption across 30, 90 and 366 days: Interactive voice response compared with the Timeline Follow Back. *Journal of Studies on Alcohol, 63,* 352–362.

Segura-Garcia, C., Aloi, M., Rania, M., Ciambrone, P., Palmieri, A., Pugliese, V., . . . De Fazio, P. (2015). Ability of the EDI-2 and EDI-3 to correctly identify patients and subjects at risk for eating disorders. *Eating Behaviors, 19,* 20–23. doi:10.1016/j.eatbeh.2015.06.010

Selzer, M. L. (1971). The Michigan Alcoholism Screening Test: The quest for a new diagnostic instrument. *American Journal of Psychiatry, 127,* 1653–1658.

Selzer, M. L., Vinokur, A., & van Rooijen, L. (1975). A self-administered short Michigan Alcoholism Screening Test (SMAST). *Journal of Studies on Alcohol, 36,* 117–126.

Severy, L. (2013). Campbell Interest and Skills Survey. In C. T. Wood & D. G. Hays (Eds.), *A counselor's guide to career assessment instruments* (6th ed., pp. 226–231). Broken Arrow, OK: National Career Development Association.

Sewell, T. E. (1985). Review of Coopersmith Self-Esteem Inventories. In J. V. Mitchell, Jr. (Ed.), *The ninth mental measurements yearbook* (pp. 397–398). Lincoln, NE: Buros Institute of Mental Measurements.

Shedler, J., & Westen, D. (2004). Dimensions of personality pathology: An alternative to the five-factor model. *American Journal of Psychiatry, 161,* 1743–1754.

Sherin, K. M., Sinacore, J. M., Li, X. Q., Zitter, R. E., & Shakil, A. (1998). HITS: A short domestic violence screening tool for use in a family practice setting. *Family Medicine, 30,* 508–512.

Sherman, N. E. (2009). Personality tests. In American Counseling Association (Ed.), *The ACA encyclopedia of counseling* (pp. 398–399). Alexandria, VA: American Counseling Association.

Shkalim, E. (2015). Psychometric evaluation of the MMPI-2/MMPI-2-RF Restructured Clinical Scales in an Israeli sample. *Assessment, 22,* 607–618. doi:10.1177/1073191114555884

Shurts, M. (2013). Study of Values, fourth edition. In C. T. Wood & Hays, D. G. (Eds.), *A counselor's guide to career assessment instruments* (6th ed., pp. 285–289). Broken Arrow, OK: National Career Development Association.

Siegel, R. M., Hill, T. D., Henderson, V. A., & Boat, B. W. (1999). Screening for domestic violence in the community and pediatric settings. *Pediatrics, 104,* 874–877.

Simms, L. J., Casillas, A., Clark, L. A., Watson, D., & Doebbeling, B. N. (2005). Psychometric evaluation of the Restructured Clinical Scales of the MMPI-2. *Psychological Assessment, 17,* 345–358.

Skinner, H. A., Steinhauer, P. D., & Santa-Barbara, J. (1995). *The Family Assessment Measure.* North Tonawanda, NY: Multi-Health Systems.

Slep, A. M. S., Cascardi, M., Avery-Leaf, S., & O'Leary, K. D. (2001). Two new measures of attitudes about the acceptability of teen dating aggression. *Psychological Assessment, 13,* 306–318.

Smith, P. H., Tessaro, I., & Earp, J. A. (1995). Women's experience with battering: A conceptualization from qualitative research. *Women's Health Issues, 5,* 173–182.

Snyder, D. K. (1997). *Marriage Satisfaction Inventory manual.* Los Angeles, CA: Western Psychological Services.

Snyder, D. K., Heyman, R., Haynes, S. N., Carlson, C. I., & Balderama-Durbin, C. (2015). *Couple and family assessment.* Washington, DC: American Psychological Association.

Sobell, L. C., Agrawal, S., Annis, H., Ayala-Velazquez, H., Echeverria, L., Leo, G. I., . . . Zióikowski, M. (2001). Cross cultural evaluation of two drinking assessment instruments: Alcohol Timeline Follow Back and Inventory of Drinking Situations. *Substance Use & Misuse, 36,* 313–331.

Sobell, L. C., & Sobell, M. B. (1996). *Timeline Follow-Back user's guide: A calendar method for assessing alcohol and drug use.* Toronto, Ontario, Canada: Addiction Research Foundation.

Soberay, A. D., Grimsley, P., Faragher, M. J., Barbash, M., & Berger, B. (2014). Stages of change, clinical presentation, retention, and treatment outcomes in treatment-seeking outpatient problem gambling clients. *Psychology of Addictive Behaviors, 28,* 414–419. doi:10.1037/a0035455

Spanier, G. B. (1976). Measuring dyadic adjustment: New scales for assessing the quality of marriage and similar dyads. *Journal of Marriage and Family, 38*(1), 15–28.

Spanier, G. (2001). *DAS™ Dyadic Adjustment Scale.* Retrieved from https://ecom.mhs.com/(S(xuyshm45fy1x1345lxujn02o))/product.aspx?gr=cli&prod=das&id=overview#description

Sparrow, S. S., Cicchetti, D. V., & Balla, D. A. (2006). *Vineland Adaptive Behavior Scales, Second Edition: Survey form manual.* Circle Pines, MN: American Guidance Service.

Spearman, C. (1923). *The nature of intelligence and the principles of cognition.* London, UK: Macmillan.

Spencer, S. J., Logel, C., & Davies, P. G. (2016). Stereotype threat. *Annual Review of Psychology, 67,* 415–437. doi:10.1146/annurev-psych-073115-103235

Spielberger, C. D. (1999). *State–Trait Anger Expression Inventory–2.* Odessa, FL: Psychological Assessment Resources.

Spielberger, C. D., Edwards, C. D., Montuori, J., & Lushene, R. (2013). *State–Trait Anxiety Inventory for Children: The most widely used self-report measure of anxiety.* Palo Alto, CA: Consulting Psychologist Press.

Spielberger, C. D., Gorsuch, R. L., Lushene, R., Vagg, P. R., & Jacobs, G. A. (1983). *Manual for State–Trait Anxiety Inventory.* Palo Alto, CA: Consulting Psychologists Press.

Spitzer, R. L., Kroenke, K., Williams, J. B. W., & the Patient Health Questionnaire Primary Care Study Group. (1999). Validation and utility of a self-report version of PRIME-MD. *Journal of the American Medical Association, 282,* 1737–1744.

Stanley, B., & Brown, G. K. (2012). Safety planning intervention: A brief intervention to mitigate suicide risk. *Cognitive and Behavioral Practice, 19,* 256–264.

Steele, C. M., & Aronson, J. (1995). Stereotype threat and the intellectual test performance of African Americans. *Journal of Personality and Social Psychology, 69,* 797–811.

Steele, C. M., Spencer, S. J., & Aronson, J. (2002). Contending with group image: The psychology of stereotype and social identity threat. *Advances in Experimental Social Psychology, 34,* 379–440.

Stehouwer, R. S., & Stehouwer, J. D. (2005). Review of Beck Depression Inventory–II. In D. J. Keyser (Ed.), *Test critiques: Vol. XI* (pp. 13–20). Austin, TX: PRO-ED.

Stein, S. (2003). Review of Multidimensional Anxiety Questionnaire. In B. S. Plake, J. C. Impara, & R. A. Spies (Eds.), *The fifteenth mental measurements yearbook* (pp. 599–601). Lincoln, NE: Buros Institute of Mental Measurements.

Sternberg, R. J. (1985). *Beyond IQ: A triarchic theory of intelligence.* Cambridge, MA: Cambridge University Press.

Sternberg, R. J. (1994). *Encyclopedia of human intelligence.* New York, NY: Macmillan.

Sternberg, R. J. (1998). *Cupid's arrow: The course of love through time.* New York, NY: Cambridge University Press.

Sternberg, R. J. (2004). Culture and intelligence. *American Psychologist, 59,* 325–338.

Sternberg, R. J., Kaufman, J. C., & Grigorenko, E. L. (2008). *Applied intelligence.* New York, NY: Cambridge University Press.

Stevens, L. (2003). *SAVE.* New York: New York State Coalition Against Sexual Assault.

Stevens, S. S. (1946, June 7). On the theory of scales of measurement. *Science, 103,* 677–680.

Stevenson, C. E. (2012). *Puzzling with potential: Dynamic testing of analogical reasoning in children.* Retrieved from https://openaccess.leidenuniv.nl/bitstream/handle/1887/19813/07.pdf

Stevenson, C. E., Bergwerff, C. E., Heiser, R. H., & Resing, W. C. M. (2014). Working memory and dynamic measures of analogical reasoning as predictors of children's math and reading achievement. *Infant and Child Development, 23,* 51–66.

Stevenson, C. E., Heiser, W. J., & Resing, W. C. M. (2016). Dynamic testing: Assessing cognitive potential of children with culturally diverse backgrounds. *Learning and Individual Differences, 47,* 27–36. doi:10.1016/j.lindif.2015.12.025

Stevenson, C. E., Hickendorff, M. H., Resing, W. C. M., Heiser, W. H., & De Boeck, P. A. L. (2013). Explanatory item response modeling of children's change on a dynamic test of analogical reasoning. *Intelligence, 41,* 157–168.

Stice, E., Fisher, M., & Martinez, E. (2004). Eating Disorder Diagnostic Scale: Additional evidence of reliability and validity. *Psychological Assessment, 16,* 60–71.

Storgaard, H., Nielsen, S. D., & Gluud, C. (1994). The validity of the Michigan Alcoholism Screening Test (MAST). *Alcohol & Alcoholism, 29,* 493–502.

Stout, C. E., & Cook, L. P. (1999). New areas for psychological assessment in general health care settings: What to do today to prepare for tomorrow. *Journal of Clinical Psychology, 55,* 97–112.

Straus, M. A., Hamby, S. L., Boney-McCoy, S., & Sugarman, D. B. (1996). The revised Conflict Tactics Scales (CTS2): Development and preliminary psychometric data. *Journal of Family Issues, 17,* 283–316.

Strong, E. K., Jr. (1927). *Vocational interest blank.* Stanford, CA: Stanford University Press.

Stuart, R. B., & Jacobson, B. (1987). *Couple's Precounseling Inventory, Revised edition.* Champaign, IL: Research Press.

Su, R., & Rounds, J. (2015). All STEM fields are not created equal: People and things interests explain gender disparities across STEM fields. *Frontiers in Psychology, 6,* 1–20. doi:10.3389/fpsyg.2015.00189

Substance Abuse and Mental Health Services Administration. (2014). *Results from the 2013 National Survey on Drug Use and Health: Mental health findings* (NSDUH Series H-49, HHS Pub. No. [SMA] 14-4887). Rockville, MD: Author.

Substance Abuse and Mental Health Services Administration. (2015a). *Behavioral health trends in the United States: Results from the 2014 National Survey on Drug Use and Health.* Retrieved from http://www.samhsa.gov/data/sites/default/files/NSDUH-FRR1-2014/NSDUH-FRR1-2014.pdf

Substance Abuse and Mental Health Services Administration. (2015b). *Cultural competence.* Retrieved from https://www.samhsa.gov/capt/applying-strategic-prevention/cultural-competence

Sue, D. W., Arredondo, P., & McDavis, R. J. (1992). Multicultural counseling competencies and standards: A call to the profession. *Journal of Counseling & Development, 70,* 477–486.

Suhr, J. (2015). *Psychological assessment: A problem-solving approach.* New York, NY: Guilford Press.

Sullivan, E. M., Annest, J. L., Luo, F., Simon, T. R., & Dahlberg, L. L. (2013). *Suicide among adults aged 35-36 years—United States, 1999-2010.* Retrieved from http://www.cdc.gov/mmwr/preview/mmwrhtml/mm6217a1.htm

Super, D. E. (1970). *Manual for the Work Values Inventory.* Boston, MA: Houghton-Mifflin.

Super, D. E., Osborne, W. L., Walsh, D., Brown, S. D., & Niles, S. G. (1992). Developmental career assessment and counseling: The C-DAC model. *Journal of Counseling & Development, 71,* 74–80.

Super, D. E., Thompson, A. S., & Lindeman, R. H. (1988). *Adult Career Concerns Inventory: Manual for research and exploratory use in counseling.* Palo Alto, CA: Consulting Psychologists Press.

Swank, J. M., & Lambie, G. W. (2016). Development of the Research Competencies Scale. *Measurement and Evaluation in Counseling and Development, 49,* 91–108.

Swanson, J. L., & D'Achiardi, C. (2005). Beyond interests, needs/values, and abilities: Assessing other important career constructs over the life span. In S. D. Brown & R. W. Lent (Eds.), *Career development and counseling: Putting theory and research to work* (pp. 353–381). Hoboken, NJ: Wiley.

Taber, B. J., Hartung, P. J., Briddick, H., Briddick, W. C., & Rehfuss, M. C. (2011). Career style interview: A contextualized approach to career counseling. *The Career Development Quarterly, 59,* 274–287.

Tandler, N., Mosch, A., Wolf, A., & Borkenau, P. (2015). Effects of personality disorders on self-other agreement and favorableness in personality descriptions. *Journal of Personality Disorders, 29*, 1–18.

Tarescavage, A. M., Marek, R. J., Finn, J. A., Hicks, A., Rapier, J. L., & Ben-Porath, Y. S. (2013). Minnesota Multiphasic Personality Inventory-2-Restructured Form (MMPI-2-RF) normative elevation rates: Comparisons with epidemiological prevalence rates. *The Clinical Neuropsychologist, 27*, 1106–1120. doi:10.1080/13854046.2013.832386

Tassé, M. J., Schalock, R. L., Balboni, G., Bersani, H., Jr., Borthwick-Duffy, S. A., Spreat, S., . . . Zhang, D. (2012). The construct of adaptive behavior: Its conceptualization, measurement, and use in the field of intellectual disability. *American Journal on Intellectual and Developmental Disabilities, 117*, 291–303. doi:10.1352/1944-7558-117.4.291

Teglasi, H. (2010). *Essentials of TAT and other storytelling assessments* (2nd ed.). New York, NY: Wiley.

Teitelbaum, L., & Mullen, B. (2000). The validity of the MAST in psychiatric settings: A meta-analytic investigation. *Journal of Studies on Alcohol, 61*, 254–261.

Tellegen, A., & Ben-Porath, Y. S. (2008). *Minnesota Multiphasic Personality Inventory–2 Restructured form.* Minneapolis: University of Minnesota Press.

Tellegen, A., Ben-Porath, Y. S., McNulty, J. L., Arbisi, P. A., Graham, J. R., & Kaemmer, B. (2003). *The MMPI-2 Restructured Clinical (RC) scales: Development, validation, and interpretation.* Minneapolis: University of Minnesota Press.

Thomas, K. W., & Kilman, R. H. (1974). *Thomas–Kilman Conflict Mode Instrument.* Palo Alto, CA: Consulting Psychologists Press.

Thompson, A. S., Lindeman, R. H., Super, D. E., Jordaan, J. P., & Myers, R. A. (1981). *Career Development Inventory: Vol. 1. User's manual.* Palo Alto, CA: Consulting Psychologists Press.

Thompson, C. (1949). The Thompson modification of the Thematic Apperception Test. *Journal of Projective Techniques, 13*, 469–478.

Thorndike, E. L. (1923). *Education: A first book.* New York, NY: Macmillan. (Original work published 1912)

Thorndike, R. (1985). Reliability. *Journal of Counseling & Development, 63*, 528–530.

Thurstone, L. L. (1973). *The nature of intelligence.* London, UK: Routledge. (Original work published 1924)

Thurstone, L. L., & Thurstone, T. (1930). A neurotic inventory. *Journal of Social Psychology, 1*, 3–30.

Tidemalm, D., Haglund, A., Karanti, A., Landén, M., & Runeson, B. (2007). Attempted suicide in bipolar disorder: Risk factors in a cohort of 6086 patients. *PLoS ONE, 9*(4), 1–9.

Toporek, R. J., & Pope-Davis, D. B. (2001). Comparison of vocational identity factor structures among African American and White American college students. *Journal of Career Assessment, 9*, 135–151.

Torrance, E. P. (1974). *Torrance Tests of Creative Thinking: Norms and technical manual.* Bensenville, IL: Scholastic Test Services.

Tracey, T. J., Allen, J., & Robbins, S. B. (2012). Moderation of the relation between person–environment congruence and academic success: Environmental constraint, personal flexibility and method. *Journal of Vocational Behavior, 80*, 38–49. doi:10.1016/j.jvb.2011.03.005

Tracey, T. J., & Robbins, S. B. (2006). The interest–major congruence and college success relation: A longitudinal study. *Journal of Vocational Behavior, 69*, 64–89. doi:10.1016/j.jvb.2005.11.003

Tracey, T. J. G., & Schneider, P. L. (1995). An evaluation of the circular structure of the Checklist of Interpersonal Transactions and the Checklist of Psychotherapy Transactions. *Journal of Counseling Psychology, 42*, 496–507.

Training Systems, Inc. (2016). *Knowdell career assessment instruments.* Retrieved from http://www.careernetwork.org/Career_Assessments.cfm

Trimble, J. E., King, J., LaFromboise, T. B., Bigfoot, D. S., & Norman, D. (2013). American Indian and Alaska Native mental health perspectives. In R. Parekh (Ed.), *The Massachusetts General Hospital textbook on diversity and cultural sensitivity in mental health* (pp. 119–138). New York, NY: Springer.

Tryon, G. S., & Winograd, G. (2011). Goal consensus and collaboration. *Psychotherapy, 48,* 50–57.

Tucker, I. F., & Gillespie, B. V. (1993). Correlations among three measures of personality type. *Perceptual and Motor Skills, 77,* 650.

Turner, S. M., Beidel, D. C., & Dancu, C. V. (1996). *Social Phobia and Anxiety Inventory.* North Tonawanda, NY: Multi-Health Systems.

Tyler, L. E. (1984). Testing the test: What tests don't measure. *Journal of Counseling & Development, 63,* 48–50.

Uehara, M., & Sakakibara, H. (2015). Prevalence of eating disorders assessed using Eating Attitudes Test-26 and their relevant factors in Japanese working women. *Japanese Journal of Hygiene, 70,* 54–61. doi:10.1265/jjh.70.54

Ulett, G. (1994). *Rorschach introductory guide.* Los Angeles, CA: Western Psychological Services.

U.S. Census Bureau. (2014). *Percent distribution of the projected population by Hispanic origin and race for the United States: 2015 to 2060* (NP2014-T11). Retrieved from https://www.census.gov/population/projections/data/national/2014/summarytables.html

U.S. Department of Defense. (2005). *ASVAB counselor manual.* North Chicago, IL: U.S. Military Entrance Processing Command.

U.S. Department of Education. (2010). *Race to the Top assessment program: Application for new grants.* Washington, DC: Author.

U.S. Department of Education. (2015). *Every Student Succeeds Act (ESSA).* Retrieved from https://www.ed.gov/ESSA

U.S. Department of Health and Human Services. (2011). *Child maltreatment 2010.* Retrieved from https://www.acf.hhs.gov/cb/resource/child-maltreatment-2010

U.S. Department of Labor, Employment and Training Administration. (n.d.). *O*NET OnLine.* Retrieved from http://www.onetonline.org/

Valpar. (2016). *SIGI³.* Retrieved from http://sigi3.org/

Van Brunt, B. (2009a). Mental status examination. In American Counseling Association (Ed.), *The ACA encyclopedia of counseling* (pp. 332–334). Alexandria, VA: American Counseling Association.

Van Brunt, B. (2009b). Validity scales. In American Counseling Association (Ed.), *The ACA encyclopedia of counseling* (pp. 558–559). Alexandria, VA: American Counseling Association.

VanDenberg, T. F., Schmidt, J. A., & Kiesler, D. J. (1992). Interpersonal assessment in counseling and psychotherapy. *Journal of Counseling & Development, 71,* 84–90.

Velasquez, R. J., Maness, P. J., & Anderson, U. (2002). Culturally competent assessment of Latino clients: The MMPI-2. In J. N. Butcher (Ed.), *Clinical personality assessment: Practical approaches* (pp. 154–170). New York, NY: Oxford University Press.

Vilas, R. C. (1988). *Counseling outcome as related to MBTI client type, counselor type and counselor–client type similarity* (Unpublished doctoral dissertation). University of Iowa, Iowa City.

Villalba, J. (2018). Individuals and families of Latin descent. In D. G. Hays & B. T. Erford (Eds.), *Developing multicultural competence: A systems approach* (3rd ed., pp. 363–393). Boston, MA: Pearson.

Vocational Research Institute. (2011). *CareerScope® V10 comprehensive career assessment.* Retrieved from http://www.vri.org/products/careerscope-v10/benefits

Vocopher. (n.d.). *Vocopher.* Retrieved from http://www.vocopher.com

Vogeltanz-Holm, N., Lilienthal, K., Kulig, A., & Wilsnack, S. C. (2013). Alcohol use in women. In M. V. Spiers & P. A. Geller (Eds.), *Women's health psychology* (pp. 91–122). Hoboken, NJ: Wiley.

von der Embse, N., Barterian, J., & Segool, N. (2013). Test anxiety interventions for children and adolescents: A systematic review of treatment studies from 2000-2010. *Psychology in the Schools, 50,* 57–71.

Vonk, M. E., & Thyer, B. A. (1999). Evaluating the effectiveness of short-term treatment at a university counseling center. *Journal of Clinical Psychology, 55,* 1095–1106.

Voyer, D., & Voyer, S. D. (2014). Gender differences in scholastic achievement: A meta-analysis. *Psychological Bulletin, 140,* 1174–1204. doi:10.1037/a0036620

Wadsworth, M. E., & Markman, H. J. (2012). Where's the action? Understanding what works and why in relationship education. *Behavior Therapy, 43,* 99–112.

Wakefield, J. C. (2016). Diagnostic issues and controversies in *DSM-5:* Return of the false positives problem. *Annual Review of Clinical Psychology, 12,* 105–132.

Watkins, C. E., Jr., Campbell, V. L., & Nieberding, R. (1994). The practice of vocational assessments by counseling psychologists. *The Counseling Psychologist, 22,* 115–128.

Watkins, C. E., Jr., Campbell, V. L., Nieberding, R., & Hallmark, R. (1995). Contemporary practice of psychological assessment by clinical psychologists. *Professional Psychology: Research & Practice, 24,* 54–60.

Watson, J. (2013). Career Decision Self-Efficacy Scale and Career Decision Self-Efficacy Scale–Short Form. In C. T. Wood & D. G. Hays (Eds.), *A counselor's guide to career assessment instruments* (6th ed., pp. 315–318). Broken Arrow, OK: National Career Development Association.

Webster, J., Stratigos, M. A., & Grimes, K. M. (1998). *Dating Violence Initiative screening questions.* Queensland, Australia: Queensland Government.

Wechsler, D. (1944). *The measurement of adult intelligence* (3rd ed.). Baltimore, MD: Williams & Wilkins.

Wechsler, D. (1949). *Manual for the Wechsler Intelligence Scale for Children.* New York, NY: Psychological Corporation.

Wechsler, D. (1955). *Manual for the Wechsler Adult Intelligence Scale.* New York, NY: Psychological Corporation.

Wechsler, D. (1981). *WAIS-R manual: Wechsler Adult Intelligence Scale–Revised manual.* San Antonio, TX: Psychological Corporation.

Wechsler, D. (1991). *WISC-III: Wechsler Intelligence Scale for Children: Manual.* San Antonio, TX: Psychological Corporation.

Wechsler, D. (1997). *Wechsler Adult Intelligence Scale–Third edition: Administration and scoring manual.* San Antonio, TX: Psychological Corporation.

Wechsler, D. (1999). *Wechsler Abbreviated Scale of Intelligence manual.* San Antonio, TX: Psychological Corporation.

Wechsler, D. (2003). *Wechsler Intelligence Scale for Children–Fourth edition: Administration and scoring manual.* San Antonio, TX: Psychological Corporation.

Wechsler, D. (2008). *Wechsler Adult Intelligence Scale–Fourth edition.* San Antonio, TX: Psychological Corporation.

Wechsler, D. (2009). *WIAT-III examiner's manual.* San Antonio, TX: Psychological Corporation.

Weiss, L. G., Keith, T. Z., Zhu, J., & Chen, H. (2013). WAIS-IV and clinical validation of the four- and five-factor interpretative approaches. *Journal of Psychoeducational Assessment, 31,* 94–113. doi:10.1177/0734282913478030

Weiss, S. J., Ernst, A. A., Cham, E., & Nick, T. G. (2003). Development of a screening tool for ongoing intimate partner violence. *Violence and Victims, 18,* 131–141.

Werts, C. E., & Watley, D. J. (1969). A student's dilemma: Big fish–little pond or little fish–big pond. *Journal of Counseling Psychology, 16,* 14–19.

Wiggins, J. S. (1993). *Interpersonal Adjective Scales professional manual.* Odessa, FL: Psychological Assessment Resources.

Wilkinson, G. S. (1993). *Wide Range Achievement Test* (3rd ed.). Lutz, FL: Psychological Assessment Resources.

Wilkinson, G. S., & Robertson, G. J. (2005). *WRAT4 manual.* Lutz, FL: Psychological Assessment Resources.

Williams, N. (2014). The CAGE questionnaire. *Occupational Medicine, 64,* 473–474. doi:10.1093/occmed/kqu058

Williams, R. L. (2013). Overview of the Flynn effect. *Intelligence, 41,* 753–764.

Wilson, M. S., & Reschly, D. J. (1996). Assessment in school psychology training and practice. *School Psychology Review, 25,* 9–23.

Wolfe, D. A., Scott, K., Reitzel-Jaffe, D., Wekerle, C., Grasley, C., & Straatman, A. L. (2001). Development and validation of the Conflict in Adolescent Dating Relationships Inventory. *Psychological Assessment, 13,* 277–293.

Wolfe, V. V., Gentile, C., Michienzi, T., Sas, L., & Wolfe, D. A. (1991). The Children's Impact of Traumatic Events Scale: A measure of post-sexual-abuse PTSD symptoms. *Behavior Assessment, 13,* 359–383.

Wonderlic, E. F. (2005). *Wonderlic Personnel Test and Scholastic Level Exam.* Libertyville, IL: Author.

Wood, C. T., & Hays, D. G. (Eds.). (2013). *A counselor's guide to career assessment instruments* (6th ed.). Broken Arrow, OK: National Career Development Association.

Wray, T. B., Braciszewski, J. M., Zywiak, W. H., & Stout, R. L. (2015). Examining the reliability of alcohol/drug use and HIV-risk behaviors using Timeline Follow-Back in a pilot sample. *Journal of Substance Abuse, 21,* 294–297.

Xu, H., & Tracey, T. J. (2016). Stability and change in interests: A longitudinal examination of grades 7 through college. *Journal of Vocational Behavior, 93,* 129–138. doi:10.1016/j.jvb.2016.02.002

Yell, M. L., Drasgow, E., & Ford, L. (2000). The Individuals with Disabilities Education Act Amendments of 1997: Implications for school-based teams. In C. F. Telzrow & M. Tankersley (Eds.), *IDEA Amendments of 1997: Practice guidelines for school-based teams* (pp. 1–27). Bethesda, MD: National Association of School Psychologists.

Yesavage, J. A., Brink, T. I., Rose, T. L., Lum, O., Huang, V., Adey, M., & Leirer, V. O. (1983). Development and validation of a geriatric depression screening scale: A preliminary report. *Journal of Psychiatric Research, 17,* 37–49.

Young, R. K., & Thiessen, D. (1992). The Texas Rape Scale. *Ethology & Sociobiology, 13,* 19–33.

Youngstrom, E. A. (2013). Future directions in psychological assessment: Combining evidence-based medicine innovations with psychology's historical strengths to enhance utility. *Journal of Clinical Child & Adolescent Psychology, 42,* 139–159. doi:10.1080/15374416.2012.736358

Zachar, P. (2005). Review of the Keirsey Temperament Sorter II (KTSII). In R. A. Spies & B. S. Plake (Eds.), *The sixteenth mental measurements yearbook* (pp. 529–531). Lincoln, NE: Buros Institute of Mental Measurements.

Zachary, R. A. (1986). *Shipley Institute of Living Scale: Revised manual.* Los Angeles, CA: Western Psychological Services.

Zafar, B. (2013). College major choice and the gender gap. *Journal of Human Resources, 48,* 545–595. doi:10.3368/jhr.48.3.545

Zanello, A., Berthoud, L., Ventura, J., & Merlo, M. C. G. (2013). The Brief Psychiatric Rating Scale (Version 4.0) factorial structure and its sensitivity in the treatment of outpatients with unipolar depression. *Psychiatry Research, 210,* 626–633. doi:10.1016/j.psychres.2013.07.001

Zhang, L. F., & Sternberg, R. J. (2001). Thinking styles across cultures: Their relationships with student learning. In R. J. Sternberg & L. F. Zhang (Eds.), *Perspectives on thinking, learning and cognitive styles* (pp. 197–226). Mahwah, NJ: Erlbaum.

Zhou, C. S., & Hansen, J. C. (2009). Test adaptation and test translation. In American Counseling Association (Ed.), *The ACA encyclopedia of counseling* (pp. 541–542). Alexandria, VA: American Counseling Association.

Zierau, F., Hardt, F., Henriksen, J. H., Holm, S. S., Jorring, S., Melsen, T., & Becker, U. (2005). Validation of a self-administered modified CAGE test (CAGE-C) in a somatic hospital ward: Comparison with biochemical markers. *Scandinavian Journal of Clinical & Laboratory Investigation, 65,* 615–622.

Zillig, L. M. P., Hemenover, S. H., & Dienstbier, R. A. (2002). What do we assess when we assess a Big 5 trait? A content analysis of the affective, behavioral, and cognitive processes represented in Big 5 personality inventories. *Personality and Social Psychology Bulletin, 28,* 847–858. doi:10.1177/014616720228901

Zimet, G. D., Dahlem, N. W., Zimet, S. G., & Farley, G. K. (1988). The Multidimensional Scale of Perceived Social Support. *Journal of Personality Assessment, 52,* 30–41.

Zimmerman, M., Martinez, J. H., Young, D., Chelminski, I., & Dalrymple, K. (2013). Severity classification on the Hamilton Depression Rating Scale. *Journal of Affective Disorders, 150,* 384 388. doi:10.1016/j.jad.2013.04.028

Zimmerman, M., & Mattia, J. I. (1999). The reliability and validity of a screening questionnaire for 13 *DSM-IV* Axis I disorders (the Psychiatric Diagnostic Screening Questionnaire) in psychiatric outpatients. *Journal of Clinical Psychiatry, 60,* 677–683.

Zytowski, D. G. (1985). *Manual supplement: Kuder DD Occupational Interest Survey.* Chicago, IL: Science Research Associates.

Zytowski, D. G. (1992). Three generations: The continuing evolution of Frederic Kuder's interest inventories. *Journal of Counseling & Development, 71,* 245–248.

Zytowski, D. G. (1994). A super contribution to vocational theory: Work values. *The Career Development Quarterly, 43,* 25–31.

Zytowski, D. G. (2006). *Technical manual for Kuder Career Search with Person Match.* Retrieved from https://www.kuder.com/research/technical-briefs/

Zytowski, D. G., & Austin, J. T. (2001). Frederic Kuder (1903–2000). *American Psychologist, 56,* 1170.

Subject Index

Figures and tables are indicated by f and t following the page number.

A

AAMFT (American Association for Marriage and Family Therapy), 53
AARC (Association for Assessment and Research in Counseling) (*formerly* Association for Assessment in Counseling and Education (AACE)), 48, 53, 222–223, 345
Ability assessments, 203–220. *See also specific names of assessments*
  achievement tests, 211–215
    for adults, 214
    college-level, 213–214
    defined, 204
    high-stakes testing, 52, 215–216, 216*t*, 342
    in schools, 211–213
  aptitude tests, 205–209
    college admissions and, 207–209
    defined, 22, 204
    dynamic testing and, 87–88, 341
    gender differences in, 79
    for higher education, 205–206
    racial and ethnic differences in, 81–82
    socioeconomic status and, 81–82
    validity of, 206–207
  case study, 208
  defined, 5
  graduate admissions tests, 12, 104, 111, 112, 130, 209–210
  guidelines for, 218
  history of, 12
  overview, 203–204
  professional school tests, 106, 110–111, 210–211
  study habits inventories, 217–218
Ability Profiler, 238

ABLE (Adult Basic Learning Examination), 214
Abuse. *See also* Substance abuse assessments
  of children, 312–313, 313*t*
  defined, 312
  intimate partner violence, 308–311, 310*t*
ACA. *See* American Counseling Association
ACA Code of Ethics, 48, 49*t*
Academic assessments. *See* Ability assessments
ACA Position Statement on High Stakes Testing, 48, 52
ACCI (Adult Career Concerns Inventory), 227
Acculturation, 75–77
Accuracy of assessments. *See* Validity
Achenbach System of Empirically Based Assessment, 181
Achievement tests, 211–215. *See also specific names of tests*
  for adults, 214
  college-level, 213–214
  defined, 22, 204
  high-stakes testing, 52, 215–216, 216*t*, 342
  in schools, 211–213
ACT (American College Testing)
  career assessments and, 234–237
  components and layout of, 206
  reliability of, 106
  school counselor use of, 17
  standard scores for, 130
  validity of, 206–207
Action stage of assessment, 32
ADA (Americans with Disabilities Act of 1990), 53, 89
Addiction assessments. *See* Substance abuse assessments
Addiction Severity Index (ASI), 166
ADHD (attention-deficit/hyperactivity disorder) assessments, 181–182

Administrative indexes of Strong Interest Inventory, 249
Adolescents. *See* Children and adolescents
Adult achievement tests, 214
Adult Attention Deficit Disorders Evaluation Scale, 181
Adult Basic Learning Examination (ABLE), 214
Adult Career Concerns Inventory (ACCI), 227
Adult Manifest Anxiety Scales, 174
Advanced Placement (AP) programs, 213
AERA (American Educational Research Association), 49
Affective characteristics, 22
Affordable Care Act of 2010, 343
African Americans
    aptitude tests and, 82
    career assessments and, 82–83
    personality assessments and, 83
    suicide risk and, 151
    test sophistication and, 75–76
Aging populations. *See* Elderly and aging populations
Agoraphobia, 173
Alcohol abuse, defined, 162
Alcohol abuse or dependence assessments, 161–170
    Addiction Severity Index (ASI), 166
    Alcohol Use Disorders Identification Test (AUDIT), 41, 166, 167f
    Alcohol Use Inventory (AUI), 168
    CAGE questionnaire, 163
    Comprehensive Drinking Profile (CDP), 166–167
    criteria for, 162–163
    Michigan Alcoholism Screening Test (MAST), 164–165, 164f
    motivational interviewing (MI), 169
    Rapid Alcohol Problems Screen (RAPS), 163
    self-monitoring methods, 168–169
    Substance Abuse Subtle Screening Inventory (4th ed.; SASSI-4), 101, 165–166
    Timeline Follow-Back (TLFB), 167–168
Alcohol dependence, defined, 162
Alcohol Use Disorders Identification Test (AUDIT), 41, 166, 167f
Alcohol Use Inventory (AUI), 168
Alternate-form reliability, 105–106, 106f
American Academy of Pediatrics, 181
American Association for Marriage and Family Therapy (AAMFT), 53
American College Testing. *See* ACT
American Counseling Association (ACA)
    on high-stakes testing, 48, 52
    on qualifications for licensure testing, 57
American Educational Research Association (AERA), 49
American Indians. *See* Native Americans
American Mental Health Counselors Association (AMHCA), 53
American Psychological Association (APA), 49
American Rehabilitation Counseling Association (ARCA), 53

American School Counselor Association (ASCA), 17, 52
Americans with Disabilities Act of 1990 (ADA), 53, 89
Anchoring, 139
Anger assessments, 174–175
AnimaLogica, 88, 88f
Anorexia nervosa, 178–179
Anxiety
    anxiety disorders, prevalence of, 160
    defined, 173
    test-taking and, 62–63
Anxiety and fear assessments, 172–174
    Beck Anxiety Inventory (BAI), 17, 41, 174
    Multidimensional Anxiety Questionnaire (MAQ), 174
    Social Phobia and Anxiety Inventory (SPAI), 174
    State-Trait Anxiety Inventory (STAI), 173–174
APA (American Psychological Association), 49
Apperception, 296
AP (advanced placement) programs, 213
Aptitude tests, 205–209. *See also specific names of tests*
    college admissions and, 207–209
    defined, 22, 204
    dynamic testing and, 87–88, 341
    gender differences in, 79
    for higher education, 205–206
    racial and ethnic differences in, 81–82
    socioeconomic status and, 81–82
    validity of, 206–207
Armed Forces Qualification Test, 235
Armed Services Vocational Aptitude Battery (ASVAB), 14, 17, 235–236
Army Alpha and Beta intelligence assessments, 12, 13f, 196
ASCA (American School Counselor Association), 17, 52
ASI (Addiction Severity Index), 166
Asian Americans
    career assessment and, 83, 228
    demographic changes and, 337
    ethnic differences among, 81
    personality assessments and, 83, 84
    suicide risk and, 151
    test sophistication and, 76
Assessment (journal), 34
Assessments, 3–46. *See also specific types and names of assessments*
    categories of, 5
    construction and development of, 114–115, 276–277
    cultural considerations. *See* Multicultural assessments
    data interpretation. *See* Psychometrics; Raw score calculations
    defined, 4–5, 57
    ethical concerns. *See* Ethical, legal, and professional considerations
    future trends, 343–344
    history of, 9–15, 10t
    idiographic vs. nomothethic approach, 22
    initial. *See* Initial assessments

locating, 35
methods of, 27–31
    behavioral observations, 30
    biographical measures, 30–31
    group vs. individual, 28
    interviews, 30
    physiological measures, 31
    projective, 30
    rating scales, 29–30, 43–44*t*, 44–45
    speed vs. power tests, 28–29
    standardized vs. nonstandardized, 28
overview, 3–4
principles of, 24–25
problem-solving steps and, 6–8, 7*t*
process of, 31–46, 31*f*
    administration of tests, 35–36
    case study, 39
    evaluation of progress and outcomes,
        39–45, 40*t*, 41 42*f*, 43–44*t*
    future trends in, 336. *See also* Future
        trends in assessments
    guidelines for, 38
    interpretation of findings, 36–38
    selection of tests, 32–35
    stages of, 31–32
purpose of, 6–9
research studies and, 20–21, 20*t*
results. *See* Communication of assessment
    results
selection considerations for, 21–23
sources of information for, 34
trends in. *See* Future trends in assessments
used by counselors, 15–21, 16*t*, 18*t*
ASSET Student Success System, 206
Assimilation model, 76
Association for Assessment and Research in
    Counseling (AARC) (*formerly* Association for
    Assessment in Counseling and Education
    (AACE)), 48, 53, 222–223, 345
ASVAB (Armed Services Vocational Aptitude
    Battery), 14, 17, 235–236
Attention-deficit/hyperactivity disorder
    (ADHD) assessments, 181–182
Attribution bias, 24, 139
AUDIT (Alcohol Use Disorders Identification
    Test), 41, 166, 167*f*
AUI (Alcohol Use Inventory), 168
Availability bias, 139

B

BAC (blood alcohol concentration) tables, 170
Bad news sandwich approach, 329
Bar graphs, 122, 123*f*
Barkley Screening Checklist for ADHD, 181
Base rates, 111
Basic Achievement Skills Inventory (BASI),
    214
Basic Interest Scales (BISs), 80, 248–250
Battery for Health Improvement 2 (BHI-2), 298
BBHI-2 (Brief Battery for Health Improvement 2),
    298

Beck Anxiety Inventory (BAI), 17, 41, 174
Beck Depression Inventory–II (BDI–II), 17, 171
Behavioral Academic Self-Esteem (BASE) rating
    scale, 294
Behavioral level of counseling relationships, 71,
    74
Behavioral observations, 30
Behavior Assessment System for Children,
    181
Bell-shaped curves, 124, 124*f*, 125
Beta III intelligence test, 196
BHI-2 (Battery for Health Improvement 2), 298
Bias. *See also* Multicultural assessments
    attribution bias, 24
    cultural bias in assessment, 25, 69–71, 336
    in *DSM*, 157
    gender bias, 79–80
    in interviews, 139
    types of, 72–73*t*
Biculturalism model, 76
Big Three measures of career counseling, 17
Big Five personality factors, 277, 292
Big-Fish-Little-Pond Effect, 209
Binet-Simon scale, 11
Biodata, 30–31
Biographical measures, 30–31
Biopsychosocial inventories, 298
Bipolar disorder, 149, 160, 170. *See also*
    Depression assessments
BISs (Basic Interest Scales), 80, 248–250
Blood alcohol concentration (BAC) tables,
    170
Boston Vocational Bureau, 14
Bowen's family system theory, 313
Brief Battery for Health Improvement 2 (BBHI-2),
    298
Brief Psychiatric Rating Scale (BPRS), 145
Brief Symptom Inventory (BSI), 144
Brown Adult ADHD Rating Scales, 181
Bulimia nervosa, 178–179
Buros Institute, 34

C

CACAM (culturally appropriate career
    assessment model), 223
CACREP (Council for the Accreditation of
    Counseling and Related Educational
    Programs), 57
CAGE questionnaire, 163
Calculations. *See* Psychometrics; Raw score
    calculations
California Achievement Tests–5, 197
California Psychological Inventory (CPI), 276,
    287–291, 287*f*, 290*t*, 341
California Test of Mental Maturity-Short Form,
    197
Campbell Development Surveys, 255–256
Campbell Interest and Skill Survey (CISS),
    255–257, 258–259*f*
Card sorts, 223, 248, 271
Career adaptability, 224

Career and life-planning assessments, 221–243.
See also Interest inventories; Values inventories
  case study, 227–228
  for children, 231, 235
  comprehensive programs for, 233–241
    guidelines for use of, 240–241
    nonstandardized, 233–234
    standardized, 234–241
  computer-based, 233
  defined, 5
  gender differences in, 79–80, 228
  genograms for, 224
  history of, 14
  measures of career readiness, 224–233, 225–226t
    Adult Career Concerns Inventory (ACCI), 227
    Career Attitudes and Strategies Inventory (CASI), 227
    Career Beliefs Inventory (CBI), 227
    Career Decision-Making Difficulties Questionnaire (CDDQ), 228
    Career Decision-Making Self-Efficacy Scale (CDMSE), 229
    Career Decision Scale (CDS), 228
    Career Development Inventory, 229
    Career Factors Inventory, 229–230
    Career Futures Inventory, 230
    Career Mastery Inventory (CMAS), 230
    Career Maturity Inventory–Revised (CMI-R), 230–231
    Career Thoughts Inventory (CTI), 231
    Childhood Career Development Scale (CDDS), 231
    guidelines for use of, 232–233
    My Vocational Situation (MVS), 231
    Skills Confidence Inventory (SCI), 232
  multicultural considerations in, 222–223, 228, 232–233
  overview, 221–224
  qualitative techniques for, 223, 224, 233
  racial and ethnic differences in, 82–83
  standards for, 52–53
  uses of, 223
Career Attitudes and Strategies Inventory (CASI), 227
Career Beliefs Inventory (CBI), 227
Career Counselor Assessment and Evaluation Competencies (AARC & NCDA), 48, 53
Career counselors, 17
Career Decision-Making Difficulties Questionnaire (CDDQ), 228
Career Decision-Making Self-Efficacy Scale (CDMSE), 229
Career Decision-Making System–Revised (CDM-R), 261–262
Career Decision Scale (CDS), 228
Career Development and Planning: A Comprehensive Approach (Reardon et al.), 234
Career Development Inventory, 229
The Career Development Quarterly (journal), 34
Career Exploration Scores, 235

Career Factors Inventory, 229–230
Career Futures Inventory, 230
Career-in-Culture Interview, 138
Career Interest Inventory (CII), 235
Career Interests, Preferences, and Strengths Inventory (CIPSI; PRO-ED), 233
Career Mastery Inventory (CMAS), 230
Career maturity, 224, 229, 230–231
Career Maturity Inventory–Revised (CMI-R), 230–231
Career Occupational Preference System (COP-System), 239–240, 266
Career Orientation Placement and Evaluation Survey (COPES), 266
Career Planning Guide (ACT), 234
Career Planning Survey (CPS), 234–235
Career readiness measures. *See* Career and life-planning assessments
CareerScope Version 10 (Vocational Research Institute), 233
Career Style Interview, 223–224
Career Thoughts Inventory (CTI), 231
Career Values Card Sort (CVCS), 271
Carnegie Interest Inventory, 14
CASE (Clinical Assessment Scales for the Elderly), 92
Case conferences, 328–329
CASI (Career Attitudes and Strategies Inventory), 227
CAT (Children's Apperception Test), 296
Categorical assessments, 155
Categorical variables, 6
Cattell–Horn–Carroll theory of cognitive ability, 189–190
Cattell's Culture-Fair Intelligence Test, 84–85, 85f
Cattell's Sixteen Personality Factor Questionnaire (16 PF), 276–277, 291–292, 341
CBI (Career Beliefs Inventory), 227
CDC (Centers for Disease Control and Prevention), 147, 151
CDDQ (Career Decision-Making Difficulties Questionnaire), 228
CDDS (Childhood Career Development Scale), 231
CDI 2 (Children's Depression Inventory 2), 172
CDM-R (Career Decision-Making System–Revised), 261–262
CDMSE (Career Decision-Making Self-Efficacy Scale), 229
CDP (Comprehensive Drinking Profile), 166–167
CDS (Career Decision Scale), 228
CEEB. *See* College Entrance Examination Board
Center for Applications of Psychological Type, 304
Centers for Disease Control and Prevention (CDC), 147, 151
Central tendency errors, 29
Central tendency measures, 122–123
Checklist of Interpersonal Transactions (CLOIT), 317
Checklist of Psychotherapy Transactions, 317

Childhood Career Development Scale (CDDS), 231

Children and adolescents. *See also* Ability assessments; Schools
    abuse assessments for, 312–313, 313t
    ADHD assessment and, 181–182
    career assessments for, 231, 235
    giftedness and creativity in, 199–200
    intelligence assessments for, 193–195, 197, 199–200
    mental health assessments for, 139, 172–174, 181–182
    personality assessments for, 277, 281–283, 292, 296
    prevalence of mental disorders in, 160, 170–171
    progress monitoring of, 40
    substance abuse assessments for, 166
    substance/alcohol abuse and, 161–162

Children's Apperception Test (CAT), 296
Children's Depression Inventory 2 (CDI 2), 172
Children's Personality Questionnaire, 292
CHIP (Coping with Health Injuries and Problems inventory), 298
Choosing a Vocation (Parsons), 246
CII (Career Interest Inventory), 235
CIPSI; PRO-ED (Career Interests, Preferences, and Strengths Inventory), 233
Circumplex model of interpersonal relationships, 317–318, 318f
CISS (Campbell Interest and Skill Survey), 255–257, 258–259f
CLEP (College-Level Examination Program), 213

Clients
    defined, 4
    demographic changes and, 337–338. *See also* Racial and ethnic differences
    self-report scales, 42–44, 43t. *See also* Progress monitoring and outcome assessments
    welfare issues and, 58–60

Client satisfaction forms, 42
Client worldview, 68–69
Clinical Assessment Scales for the Elderly (CASE), 92
Clinical decision making, 74
CLOIT (Checklist of Interpersonal Transactions), 317
Closed system of scales, 246
CMAS (Career Mastery Inventory), 230
CMI-R (Career Maturity Inventory–Revised), 230–231
CMMS (Columbia Mental Maturity Scale), 87
Coaching for tests, 63–64
Code of Fair Testing Practices in Education (JCTP), 51–52
Coefficient alpha, 107, 349
Coefficient of determination, 103
Cognitive Abilities Test, Form 6 (CogAT-6), 197
Cognitive abilities theory of intelligence, 189–190
Cognitive Assessment System, 195
Cognitive disabilities, 91–92

Cognitive variables, 22
College admissions and assessments, 207–209, 213–214. *See also* Schools
College Entrance Examination Board (CEEB), 12, 129–130, 205, 213
The College Handbook (College Board), 208
College-Level Examination Program (CLEP), 213
College Student Inventory, 217
Columbia Mental Maturity Scale (CMMS), 87
Common Core standards. *See* Every Student Succeeds Act of 2015
Communication of assessment results, 323–334
    case conferences and, 328–329
    case study, 327–328
    components of reports, 330–331
    guidelines for use of, 324–325
    interpretation interview and, 325–328
    interpretation of results, 332–333
    overview, 36–37, 323–324
    sample assessment report, 351–355
    written assessment reports, 329–333
Community-oriented needs assessments, 160–161
Componential intelligence, 190
Comprehensive career assessment programs, 233–241
    guidelines for use of, 240–241
    nonstandardized, 233–234
    standardized, 234–241
Comprehensive Drinking Profile (CDP), 166–167
Computer-based assessments
    benefits of, 35, 60–61
    career and life planning, 233
    confidentiality and, 59
    ethical considerations and, 60–61
    limitations of, 35, 61
    for personality inventories, 279, 290
    scoring and, 37
    technological advances, 339–340
Conceptual level of counseling relationships, 71
Concurrent validity, 110
Confidentiality, 58–60
Confirmatory bias, 24
Confounding variables, 6
Conners' Rating Scales, 17, 181
Consequential validity, 345
Consistency of results. *See* Reliability
Construct irrelevant variance, 109
Construct underrepresentation, 109
Construct validity, 113
Contemplation stage of assessment, 32
Content bias, 71
Content validity, 109–110, 113
Contextual intelligence, 190
Continuous variables, 6
Convergent validity, 113
Coopersmith Inventory, 293–294
COPES (Career Orientation Placement and Evaluation Survey), 266
Coping with Health Injuries and Problems inventory (CHIP), 298
COPSystem (Career Occupational Preference System), 239–240, 266

Correlation coefficients
  Pearson product-moment, 102, 103*f*, 106, 349
  reliability and, 102–104, 103*f*, 106
  Spearman-Brown, 106, 349
  validity and, 110, 111
Council for the Accreditation of Counseling and
  Related Educational Programs (CACREP), 57
Counseling and advocacy interventions
  domain, 68
Counseling and testing centers, 14
Counseling Outcome Research and Evaluation
  (journal), 34
Counselors
  assessments used by, 15–21, 16*t*, 18*t*
  career, 17
  client diversity and, 337–338
  competence of, 57–58
  discrimination by, 74–75, 337
  globalization and problematizing and, 338–339
  health insurance and, 343
  medical professional partnerships and,
    344–345
  mental health, 17
  multicultural competence and, 68–69
  relevant and actionable assessment, 345
  research and, 20–21, 20*t*, 345–347
  school, 17, 18*t*, 60, 89–90, 342
A Counselor's Guide to Career Assessment Instruments
  (National Career Development Association),
  226
Couples and family counseling assessments,
  304–308
  Couples Precounseling Inventory (CPCI),
    306–307
  Derogatis Sexual Functioning Inventory
    (DSFI), 306
  Dyadic Adjustment Scale, 308
  Family Assessment Measure–III (FAM–III),
    307
  Family Environment Scale (FES), 307
  Marital Satisfaction Inventory–Revised
    (MSI-R), 305–306
  Myers–Briggs Type Indicator (MBTI),
    304–305
  PREPARE and ENRICH, 306
  Sternberg's Triangular Love Scale (STLS),
    307–308
  Taylor-Johnson Temperament Analysis
    (TJTA), 305
Couples Precounseling Inventory (CPCI),
  306–307
CPI. *See* California Psychological Inventory
CPS (Career Planning Survey), 234–235
Creativity assessments, 199–200
Criterion group method of assessment construction,
  276
Criterion-referenced scores and tests, 5, 120
Criterion-related validity, 110–112
Cronbach's alpha reliability coefficient, 107
Cross-validation, 276
Crystallized intelligence, 11, 189–190
CTI (Career Thoughts Inventory), 231
Cultural Assessment Interview Protocol, 76–77

Cultural bias, 69–71
Cultural level of counseling relationships, 74
Culturally appropriate career assessment model
  (CACAM), 223
Culture-fair tests, 84–87. *See also* Multicultural
  assessments
  AnimaLogica, 88, 88*f*
  Columbia Mental Maturity Scale (CMMS),
    87
  Culture Fair Intelligence Test, 84–85, 85*f*
  Draw-A-Person Test (DAP), 87, 297
  Naglieri Nonverbal Ability Test (NNAT),
    86–87
  Raven's Progressive Matrices, 85–86, 86*f*
  Tell-Me-A-Story (TEMAS), 87
  Wechsler Nonverbal Scale of Ability
    (WNV), 87
Culture-free tests, 84
Cutoff scores, 112
CVCS (Career Values Card Sort), 271

D

DAP (Draw-A-Person Test), 15, 87, 297
Das Naglieri Cognitive Assessment System, 195
Data interpretation. *See* Psychometrics; Raw
  score calculations
Decay, 29
Decisional balance method, 169
Decision-tree assessment approach, 153
Deliberate Self-Harm Inventory, 175
Demographic trends, 337–338
Dental Admission Test (DAT), 210–211
Department of. *See specific name of department*
Dependability of results. *See* Reliability
Dependent variables, 6
Depression assessments
  Beck Depression Inventory–II (BDI–II), 17,
    171
  Children's Depression Inventory 2 (CDI 2),
    172
  CPI scale, 289
  Geriatric Depression Scale (GDS), 172
  Hamilton Depression Inventory (HDI), 172
  MMPI scale, 104, 112, 277–279
  suicide risk assessments and, 111, 112, 149
Derived scores, 120, 126
Derogatis Psychiatric Rating Scale, 144
Derogatis Sexual Functioning Inventory (DSFI),
  306
Developmental domains, 68
Developmental norms, 126–127
Deviation IQ scores, 130–131, 188
Diagnostic and Statistical Manual of Mental Disorders
  (5th ed.; *DSM-5*)
  on ADHD assessment, 181
  on alcohol dependence, 162
  bias and, 157
  on eating disorders, 178–179
  guidelines for use, 156–157
  initial assessments and, 154–157
  revisions in, 154, 155

Diagnostic overshadowing, 139
Diagnostic variance, 156
Dictionary of Holland Occupational Codes
    (Gottfredson & Holland), 254
Differential Aptitude Tests, 17, 235
Dimensional assessments, 155
Disabilities and assessment
    accommodations for, 89–90
    bias and, 336
    cognitive disabilities, 91–92
    hearing disabilities, 91
    standards for, 53
    visual disabilities, 90–91
Discriminant validity, 113
Discrimination. *See also* Multicultural assessments
    in career assessments, 223
    by counselors, 74–75, 337
Diversity. *See* Multicultural assessments
Domestic violence, 308–311, 310*t*
Draw-A-Person Test (DAP), 15, 87, 297
Drift, 29
Drug abuse. *See* Substance abuse assessments
DSFI (Derogatis Sexual Functioning Inventory),
    306
DSM. See Diagnostic and Statistical Manual of
    Mental Disorders
Dual diagnoses, 169
Dyadic Adjustment Scale, 308
Dynamic testing, 87–88, 88*f*, 341

E

Eating Attitudes Test (EAT), 179
Eating disorder assessments, 178–180
Eating Disorders Inventory–3 (EDI-3), 41, 180
Ecological validity, 341
Education. *See* Ability assessments; Schools
Educational Testing Service (ETS), 12, 205,
    213–214
Education Department, U.S., 342
Education of All Handicapped Children Act of
    1975, 89
Elderly and aging populations
    Clinical Assessment Scales for the Elderly
        (CASE), 92
    demographic changes and, 337
    mental health assessments for, 172, 174
    Mini-Mental State Examination (MMSE),
        92–93, 93*f*, 139
    suicide rates in, 147
    Wechsler Memory Scale (WMS), 93–94
Employment. *See* Career and life-planning
    assessments
Errors of central tendency, 29
Error variance, 102
E-SCI (Expanded Skills Confidence Inventory),
    255
ESSA. *See* Every Student Succeeds Act of 2015
Ethical, legal, and professional considerations,
    47–65
    case study, 60
    client welfare issues, 58–60

coaching, 63–64
computer-based assessments and, 60–61
confidentiality, 58, 59
in counseling process, 61–62
counselor competence and, 57–58
court decisions affecting, 54–56, 55–56*t*
guidelines for evaluating assessments,
    49–54
    ACA Code of Ethics, 48, 49*t*
    Joint Committee on Testing Practices,
        50–52
    NBCC Code of Ethics, 48
    Standards for Educational and Psychological
        Testing, 4, 49–50, 57, 102, 108, 109
informed consent, 59–60
overview, 47
practice effects, 63, 105–106
test anxiety, 62–63
Ethnic differences. *See* Racial and ethnic
    differences
ETS (Educational Testing Service), 12, 205,
    213–214
Evaluation objective in career assessment, 223
Every Student Succeeds Act of 2015 (ESSA), 90,
    215–216, 341–342
Evidence-based assessment, 343–344
Exclusion criteria for mental disorders, 156
Exner's Comprehensive System for ink blot
    scoring, 295
Expanded Skills Confidence Inventory (E-SCI),
    255
Expectancy effects, 36
Experiential intelligence, 190
EXPLORE program, 206
Exploring Careers: The ASVAB Career Exploration
    Guide (Defense Department), 236
Extraneous variables, 6
Extrinsic values, 265

F

Face validity, 109
Factor analyses, 113
Factor-analytic method of assessment construction,
    276–277
Fair Access Coalition on Testing (FACT), 58
Fairness in assessments, 69–71
Faking on assessments, 14, 113, 288, 292
False positives and negatives, 112, 112*t*
Family Assessment Measure–III (FAM–III), 307
Family counseling. *See* Couples and family
    counseling assessments
Family Educational Rights and Privacy Act of
    1974 (FERPA), 59
Family Environment Scale (FES), 307
Family system theory, 313
Fear assessments. *See* Anxiety and fear
    assessments
Fear Questionnaire, 174
Feedback-enhanced therapy, 40
Feedback loops, 39, 40, 88
Find Your Interests (FYI) inventory, 236

Fluid intelligence, 11, 189–190
Flynn effect, 199
Folk concepts, 287–288
Formative assessment, 340
Frequency distributions, 120–121, 121t, 125
Frequency polygons, 122, 122f
Full circle feedback, 21
Future trends in assessments, 335–348
    building assessment systems, 343–344
    consequential validity, 345
    demographic trends, 337–338
    dynamic testing, 341
    ecological validity, 341
    educational accountability, 341–342
    formative assessment, 340
    globalization, 338–339
    immigration patterns, 338–339
    managed care, 343
    overview, 335
    partnerships with health professions, 344–345
    problematizing counseling, 339
    relevant and actionable assessment, 345
    research trends and tips, 345–347
    sophistication increases, 340–341
    technological advances, 339–340
    themes in the discipline, 336

G

"g" (factor theory of intelligence), 188–189, 189f
Gardner's multiple intelligences theory, 190
GDS (Geriatric Depression Scale), 172
Gender differences, 78–80, 336
    in aptitude tests, 79
    in career assessment, 79–80, 228
    in personality assessments, 83, 84
    on Strong Interest Inventory, 80, 248–250
General Aptitude Test Battery (GATB), 111, 130, 238
Generalizability theory, 104
General Occupational Themes (GOTs) scale, 249–250
Genograms
    for career and life planning, 224
    construction of, 314, 316–317
    defined, 313
    for interpersonal relationship assessment, 313–317, 315–316f
Geriatric Depression Scale (GDS), 172
Giftedness assessments, 199–200
Globalization, 338–339
Global Severity Index (GSI), 143
Goodenough-Harris Drawing Test, 87
Gordon Commission on the Future of Assessment in Education, 342
GOTs (General Occupational Themes) scale, 249–250
Grade equivalents, 126–127
Graduate admissions tests, 12, 104, 111, 112, 130, 209–210
Graduate Management Admission Test (GMAT), 210–211

GRE (Graduate Record Examination), 12, 104, 111, 112, 130, 209–210
Group intelligence assessments, 196–198
    history of, 11–12, 196
    Multidimensional Aptitude Battery–II (MAB–II), 198
    school administered, 197
        Cognitive Abilities Test, Form 6, 197
        Otis–Lennon School Ability Test (8th ed.; OLSAT8), 197
        Test of Cognitive Skills, 197
        Shipley Institute of Living Scale–Revised, 198
        Wonderlic Personnel Test and Scholastic Level Exam, 198
GSI (Global Severity Index), 143

H

Halo effects, 29
Hamilton Depression Inventory (HDI), 172
Health and Human Services Department, U.S., 312
Health and lifestyle inventories, 298–299
Health Dynamics Inventory, 139
Health insurance, 343
Hearing disabilities, 91
Heterogeneous scales, 246, 284
Higher education assessments, 205–209. *See also* Ability assessments; Schools
High School Personality Questionnaire, 292
High-stakes testing, 52, 215–216, 216t, 342
Histograms, 121, 121f
Holland's personality types, 249–250, 249f, 259
Holland's theory of vocational choice, 260–261
Homogeneous scales, 246, 249, 262, 266, 277
House–Tree–Person (HTP) test, 15, 297, 298t

I

IAAOC (International Association of Addictions and Offender Counseling), 53
IAS (Interpersonal Adjective Scales), 317
ICP (Inventory of Common Problems), 141–143, 142f
IDEIA (Individuals With Disabilities Education Improvement Act) of 2004, 90
Idiographic assessment, 22
IELI (Iowa Early Learning Inventory), 212
IEPs (Individualized Education Programs), 89–90
Immigration patterns, 338–339
Imminent risk, 147–148
Impact Message Inventory, 317
Impulse control and conduct disorders, 160
Inclusion criteria for mental disorders, 156
Incremental validity, 111
Independent variables, 6
Indians. *See* Native Americans
Indigenous ways of knowing. *See* Native Americans; Racial and ethnic differences

Individual error, 102
Individual intelligence assessments, 190–196
    advantages and disadvantages of, 195–196
    Das Naglieri Cognitive Assessment System, 195
    history of, 9–11, 12*f*
    Kaufman batteries, 194–195
    Peabody Picture Vocabulary Test (4th ed.; PPVT-IV), 195
    Stanford-Binet, 11, 130, 191–192
    Wechsler scales, 130, 132, 192–194
    Wide Range Intelligence Test, 195
    Woodcock–Johnson Tests of Cognitive Abilities (WJ IV), 195
Individualized Education Programs (IEPs), 89–90
Individuals with Disabilities Education Improvement Act of 2004 (IDEIA), 90
Informed consent, 59–60
Initial assessments, 137–158
    case study, 143, 154
    DSM and, 154–157
    guidelines for, 145–146
    intake interviews and, 138–139
    mental status examinations (MSEs) and, 139, 140–141*t*
    overview, 137
    screening inventories and, 139, 141–145
        Brief Psychiatric Rating Scale (BPRS), 145
        Brief Symptom Inventory (BSI), 144
        Derogatis Psychiatric Rating Scale, 144
        Inventory of Common Problems (ICP), 141–143, 142*f*
        for mental disorders, 145
        Outcome Questionnaire 45.2 (OQ-45.2), 144–145
        overall accuracy of, 141
        Symptom Check List-90–Analogue (SCL-90-Analogue), 144
        Symptom Check List-90–Revised (SCL-90-R), 143–144
    for suicide risk, 147–154
        decision-tree approach, 153
        depression and, 111, 112
        factors affecting, 148–151
        rates of suicide, 147, 151
        risk levels, 147–148
        SAD PERSONS Scale, 152
        safety planning, 153–154
        substance abuse and, 148
        Suicide Assessment Checklist (SAC), 152
        suicide plan evaluation, 148–149
Intake interviews, 138–139
Integration model, 76
Integrative Structured Interview (ISI), 224
Intelligence
    componential, 190
    contextual, 190
    crystallized, 11, 189–190
    definitions of, 188
    experiential, 190
    fluid, 11, 189–190

    theories of, 187–190, 194
        cognitive abilities, 190
        "g" factor, 188–189, 189*f*
        multiple, 190
        neuropsychological, 194
        primary mental abilities, 189
        triarchic, 190
Intelligence assessments, 187–201
    for children, 193–195, 197, 199–200
    defined, 5
    giftedness and creativity and, 199–200
    for groups, 196–198
        history of, 11–12, 196
        Multidimensional Aptitude Battery–II (MAB–II), 198
        school administered, 197
        Shipley Institute of Living Scale–Revised, 198
        Wonderlic Personnel Test and Scholastic Level Exam, 198
    history of, 9–12, 12*f*, 188, 196
    for individuals, 9–11, 190–196
        advantages and disadvantages of, 195–196
        Das Naglieri Cognitive Assessment System, 195
        Kaufman batteries, 194–195
        Peabody Picture Vocabulary Test (4th ed.; PPVT-IV), 195
        Stanford-Binet, 11, 130, 191–192
        Wechsler scales, 130, 132, 192–194
        Wide Range Intelligence Test, 195
        Woodcock-Johnson Tests of Cognitive Abilities (WJ IV), 195
    interpreting results of, 199
    overview, 187
    standard scores for, 130–131
Intelligence Quotient (IQ), 11, 130–131, 188, 199
Interest inventories, 245–273. *See also* Values inventories
    Campbell Interest and Skill Survey (CISS), 255–257, 258–259*f*
    Career Decision-Making System–Revised (CDM-R), 261–262
    case studies, 251*t*, 253–255, 256–257, 258–259*f*, 261
    defined, 245
    guidelines for selection of, 247–248
    interpreting, 262–263
    Jackson Vocational Interest Survey (JVIS), 262
    Kuder Career Search (KCS) With Person Match, 257–260, 265
    overview, 246, 247*t*
    Self-Directed Search (SDS), 260–261
    Strong Interest Inventory, 248–255, 251*t*. *See also* Strong Interest Inventory
Interest Profiler, 238
Interitem reliability, 106–107, 107*f*
Internal reliability, 106–107
International Association of Addictions and Offender Counseling (IAAOC), 53
International student testing, 213–214

Internet-based assessments. *See* Computer-based assessments
Interpersonal Adjective Scales (IAS), 317
Interpersonal circle model, 317–318, 318*f*
Interpersonal Compass, 317
Interpersonal relationship assessments, 303–319
　case study, 308
　for child abuse, 312–313, 313*t*
　circumplex model and, 317–318, 318*f*
　for couples and family counseling, 304–308
　　Couples Precounseling Inventory
　　　(CPCI), 306–307
　　Derogatis Sexual Functioning Inventory
　　　(DSFI), 306
　　Dyadic Adjustment Scale, 308
　　Family Assessment Measure–III
　　　(FAM–III), 307
　　Family Environment Scale (FES), 307
　　Marital Satisfaction Inventory–Revised
　　　(MSI-R), 305–306
　　Myers–Briggs Type Indicator (MBTI),
　　　304–305
　　PREPARE and ENRICH, 306
　　Sternberg's Triangular Love Scale
　　　(STLS), 307–308
　　Taylor–Johnson Temperament Analysis
　　　(TJTA), 305
　genograms and, 313–317, 315–316*f*
　for intimate partner violence, 308–311, 310*t*
　overview, 303
　standards for, 53
Interquartile ranges, 123
Interrater reliability, 107–108
Interval scales, 101
Interviews
　defined, 30
　intake, 138–139
　life career assessment, 224
　motivational, 169
　results interpretation, 325–328
Intimate partner violence (IPV), 308–311, 310*t*
Intrinsic values, 265
Invalidity, 109
Inventory of Common Problems (ICP), 141–143,
　142*f*
Inventory of Work-Relevant Abilities, 234
Involuntary responses, 22
Iowa Early Learning Inventory (IELI), 212
Iowa Tests of Basic Skills (ITBS), 197, 211
Iowa Tests of Educational Development (ITED),
　104, 130, 197, 206, 211
IPV (intimate partner violence), 308–311, 310*t*
IQ. *See* Intelligence Quotient
ISI (Integrative Structured Interview), 224
Item response theory, 115, 132

J

Jackson Vocational Interest Survey (JVIS), 262
Jobs. *See* Career and life-planning assessments
Joint Committee on Testing Practices (JCTP), 48,
　50–52

Journal of Career Assessment, 34
Journal of Counseling & Development, 20, 34
Journal of Counseling Psychology, 20, 34
Journal of Mental Health Counseling, 20
Journal of Personality Assessment, 34
Jung's theory of personality types, 284, 285
JVIS (Jackson Vocational Interest Survey), 262

K

Kaufman Adolescent and Adult Intelligence
　Test (KAIT), 194–195
Kaufman Assessment Battery for Children
　(KABC–II), 194
Kaufman Brief Intelligence Test, 195
Kaufman Test of Educational Achievement-
　Normative Update (K-TEA–II), 214
Keirsey Temperament Sorter II (KTS–II), 286
Koss–Butcher critical item set, 279
Kuder Career Planning System, 257–258
Kuder Career Search (KCS) With Person Match,
　257–260, 265
Kuder General Interest Survey (KGIS), 91, 257
Kuder Occupational Interest Survey (KOIS), 257
Kuder Preference Record, 14
Kuder–Richardson (KR) Formula, 107, 350
Kuder Skills Assessment (KSA), 257, 260
Kurtosis, 125

L

Labor Department, U.S., 237, 238
Latinos/Latinas
　career assessment and, 83
　demographic changes and, 337
　ethnic differences among, 81
　personality assessments and, 83–84
　suicide risk and, 151
Law School Admission Test (LSAT), 12, 210–211
Learning and Study Strategies Inventory
　(LASSI), 217
Learning Style Inventory, 217–218
Legal considerations. *See* Ethical, legal, and
　professional considerations
Leniency errors, 29
Leptokurtosis, 125
LGBTQ (lesbian, gay, bisexual, transgender, and
　questioning) population, 160, 309, 338
Licensure boards, 57
Life career assessment interview, 224
Life Career Rainbow, 224
Life Experiences Survey, 150
Life line tools, 224
Life-planning assessments. *See* Career and life-
　planning assessments
Life Stressors and Social Resources Inventory,
　150
Lifestyle Assessment Questionnaire, 299
Lifestyle inventories, 298–299
Life Values Inventory, 271
Likert scales, 100–101

Logical content method of assessment construction, 276

LSAT (Law School Admission Test), 12, 210–211

M

MAB–II (Multidimensional Aptitude Battery–II), 198

MACI (Millon Adolescent Clinical Inventory), 283

Maintenance stage of assessment, 32

Major depressive disorder. *See* Depression assessments

Making Career Decisions That Count: A Practical Guide (Luzzo), 234

Managed care, 343

MAP (multicultural assessment process) model, 223

MAQ (Multidimensional Anxiety Questionnaire), 174

Marginalization model, 76

Marginalized populations, 68, 87–88, 160

Marital Satisfaction Inventory–Revised (MSI-R), 305–306

Marriage, Couple and Family Counseling Assessment Competencies (AARC & AAMFT), 48, 53

Marriage counseling. *See* Couples and family counseling assessments

MAST (Michigan Alcoholism Screening Test), 164–165, 164*f*

MAT (Miller Analogies Test), 210

Mathematics Anxiety Rating Scale–Revised, 174

Maudsley Obsessional-Compulsive Inventory, 174

MBTI. *See* Myers-Briggs Type Indicator

MCAT (Medical College Admission Test), 106, 111, 210–211

MCMI–IV (Millon Clinical Multiaxial Inventory–IV), 282–283

Mean, 122

Measurement and Evaluation in Counseling and Development (journal), 34

Measurement error, 102

Measurements, defined, 5–6. *See also* Psychometrics; Raw score calculations

Measures of central tendency, 122–123

Measures of variability, 123

Median, 122, 125

Medical College Admission Test (MCAT), 106, 111, 210–211

Medication effects, 94, 138, 149–150

Mental age, 11

Mental health assessments, 159–184

for anger, 174–175

for anxiety and fear, 172–174

Beck Anxiety Inventory (BAI), 17, 41, 174

Multidimensional Anxiety Questionnaire (MAQ), 174

Social Phobia and Anxiety Inventory (SPAI), 174

State-Trait Anxiety Inventory (STAI), 173–174

for attention-deficit/hyperactivity disorder (ADHD), 181–182

case study, 179–180

for children, 139, 172–174, 181–182

for depression

Beck Depression Inventory–II (BDI–II), 17, 171

Children's Depression Inventory 2 (CDI 2), 172

CPI scale, 289

Geriatric Depression Scale (GDS), 172

Hamilton Depression Inventory (HDI), 172

MMPI scale, 104, 112, 277–279

suicide risk assessments and, 111, 112, 149

for eating disorders, 41, 178–180

for elderly populations, 172, 174

in LGBTQ population, 160

multicultural considerations in, 75

overview, 159–161, 161*t*

procedures for using, 182–183

screening inventories and, 145

for self-injury, 175–178, 176*t*

standards for, 53

Mental health counselors, 17

Mental Measurements Yearbook (*MMY*, Buros Institute), 34

Mental self-government, 218

Mental Status Checklist, 139

Mental status examinations (MSEs), 139, 140–141*t*

Mental testing, 10. *See also* Intelligence assessments

Mesokurtosis, 125

Meta-analyses techniques, 111

Metropolitan Achievement Tests, 197, 212

MI (Motivational Interviewing), 169

Michigan Alcoholism Screening Test (MAST), 164–165, 164*f*

Military career assessments, 235–236

Military Entrance Score, 235

Miller Analogies Test (MAT), 210

Millon Adolescent Clinical Inventory (MACI), 283

Millon Adolescent Personality Inventory, 283

Millon Clinical Multiaxial Inventory–IV (MCMI–IV), 282–283

Millon Index of Personality Styles–Revised (MIPS-R), 283

Mini-Mental State Examination (MMSE), 17, 92–93, 93*f*, 139

Minnesota Importance Questionnaire, 265

Minnesota Multiphasic Inventory–Adolescent–Restructured Form (MMPI-A-RF), 282

Minnesota Multiphasic Personality Inventory–2 (MMPI-2), 14, 15, 83–84, 112–114, 276–282, 278*t*

Minnesota Multiphasic Personality Inventory–2 Restructured Form (MMPI-2-RF), 277, 281

Minnesota Multiphasic Personality Inventory–Adolescent (MMPI-A), 277, 281–282

Minorities. *See* Racial and ethnic differences

MMY (*Mental Measurements Yearbook*, Buros Institute), 34

Mode, 123

Monitoring objective in career assessment, 223

Mood disorders, 160, 170. *See also* Depression assessments

Motivational characteristics, 22
Motivational Distortion scale, 292
Motivational Interviewing (MI), 169
MSEs (mental status examinations), 139, 140–141*t*
MSI-R (Marital Satisfaction Inventory–Revised), 305–306
Multicultural and Social Justice Counseling Competencies (MSJCC), 68–69
Multicultural assessment process (MAP) model, 223
Multicultural assessments, 67–96. *See also* Culture-fair tests
    career assessment and, 222–223, 228, 232–233
    case study, 78
    counseling competency and, 68–69
    defined, 68
    disability and
        accommodations for, 89–90
        assessment bias, 336
        cognitive disabilities, 91–92
        hearing disabilities, 91
        standards for, 53
        visual disabilities, 90–91
    dynamic testing, 87–88
    elderly and aging populations and
        Clinical Assessment Scales for the Elderly (CASE), 92
        mental health assessments for, 172, 174
        Mini-Mental State Examination (MMSE), 92–93, 93*f*, 139
        suicide rates in, 147
        Wechsler Memory Scale (WMS), 93–94
    factors affecting, 74–78
        acculturation, 75–77
        client motivation and test sophistication, 75–76
        counselor discrimination, 74–75
        cultural acceptance of counseling, 71, 74
        language, 77–78
        mental disorder rates, 75
    fairness and cultural bias in, 25, 69–71, 336
    gender differences, 78–80, 336
        in aptitude tests, 79
        in career assessment, 79–80, 228
        in personality assessments, 83, 84
        on Strong Interest Inventory, 80, 248–250
    guidelines for, 94–95
    overview, 67
    personality assessments and, 296
    racial and ethnic differences
        in aptitude tests, 81–82
        in career assessments, 82–83
        in diagnostic decisions, 156
        in mental health treatment, 160
        in outcomes, 40, 337–338
        in personality assessments, 83–84
        in suicide rates, 151
    socioeconomic status and, 81–82
    standards for, 52

Multidimensional Anxiety Questionnaire (MAQ), 174
Multidimensional Aptitude Battery–II (MAB–II), 198
Multidimensional Scale of Perceived Social Support, 151
Multiple intelligences theory, 190
Myers–Briggs Type Indicator (MBTI), 17, 113, 276, 284–286, 304–305
My Vocational Situation (MVS), 231

N

Naglieri Nonverbal Ability Test (NNAT), 86–87
National Board for Certified Counselors (NBCC), 48
National Career Development Association (NCDA), 53
National Council on Measurement in Education (NCME), 49
National Institute on Alcohol Abuse and Alcoholism, 162
National Merit Scholarship Qualifying Test (NMSQT), 205
National Wellness Institute, 299
Native Americans
    acculturation and, 76
    assessment challenges and, 81
    demographic changes and, 337
    ethnic differences among, 81
    personality assessments and, 84
    suicide risk and, 151
NBCC Code of Ethics, 48
NCDA (National Career Development Association), 53
NCLB. *See* No Child Left Behind Act of 2001
NCME (National Council on Measurement in Education), 49
Neglect, 312
NEO Five Factor Inventory, 293
NEO Personality Inventory–Revised (NEO PI-R), 84, 277, 292–293
Neuropsychology
    technological advances and, 340
    theory of intelligence, 194
New SAT. *See* SAT (Scholastic Aptitude Test)
Next Generation Iowa Assessments, 212
NMSQT (National Merit Scholarship Qualifying Test), 205
NNAT (Naglieri Nonverbal Ability Test), 86–87
No Child Left Behind Act of 2001 (NCLB), 52, 215, 341, 342
Noel-Levitz Retention Management System, 217
Nominal scales, 100
Nomothetic assessment, 22
Nonstandardized assessments, 28, 233–234
Nonverbal behaviors, 138
Normal curves, 124–125, 124*f*
Norm-referenced scores and tests, 5, 120, 126
Norms, 126–127

O

Objective personality assessments, 277–294
  California Psychological Inventory (CPI), 276, 287–291, 287f, 290t, 341
  Coopersmith self-esteem inventories, 293–294
  defined, 276
  Million inventories, 282–283
  Minnesota Multiphasic Personality Inventories, 14, 83–84, 112–114, 276–282, 278t
  Myers–Briggs Type Indicator (MBTI), 17, 276, 284–286
  NEO Personality Inventory–Revised (NEO PI-R), 84, 277, 292–293
  overview, 276–277
  Personality Assessment Inventory (PAI), 283–284
  Sixteen Personality Factor Questionnaire (16 PF), 276–277, 291–292, 341
  Tennessee Self-Concept Scale, 294
Occupational Information Network (O*NET), 237–239, 254, 255, 265
Occupational Outlook Handbook (Labor Department), 263
Occupational planning. *See* Career and life-planning assessments
Occupational Scales (OSs), 80, 250–252
Occupational trees, 224
O-data (peer data), 21
Open system of scales, 246
Ordinal scales, 100–101
Origin of Species (Darwin), 9
Otis–Lennon School Ability Test (8th ed.; OLSAT8), 197
Outcome assessments. *See* Progress monitoring and outcome assessments
Outcome Questionnaire 45.2 (OQ-45.2), 144–145
Outcome variables, 6
Overall accuracy, 141

P

Parallel-form reliability, 105–106, 106f
PAS (Personality Assessment Screener), 284
PASS model of intelligence, 194
Patient Health Questionnaire (PHQ), 145
Patient Protection and Affordable Care Act of 2010, 343
PDSQ (Psychiatric Diagnostic Screen Questionnaire), 145
Peabody Picture Vocabulary Test (4th ed.; PPVT-IV), 195
Pearson product-moment correlation coefficient, 102, 103f, 106, 349
Percentile ranks, 127–128
Personality Assessment Inventory (PAI), 283–284
Personality assessments, 275–301
  case studies, 280–281, 281f, 291
  for children, 277, 281–283, 292, 296
  computer-based, 279, 290
  defined, 5

  gender differences in, 83, 84
  health and lifestyle inventories, 298–299
  history of, 14–15
  multicultural considerations in, 296
  objective (structured), 277–294
    California Psychological Inventory (CPI), 276, 287–291, 287f, 290t, 341
    Coopersmith self-esteem inventories, 293–294
    defined, 276
    Million inventories, 282–283
    Minnesota Multiphasic Personality Inventories, 14, 83–84, 112, 113–114, 276–282, 278t
    Myers–Briggs Type Indicator (MBTI), 17, 276, 284–286
    NEO Personality Inventory–Revised (NEO PI-R), 84, 277, 292–293
    Personality Assessment Inventory (PAI), 283–284
    Sixteen Personality Factor Questionnaire (16 PF), 276–277, 291–292, 341
    Tennessee Self-Concept Scale, 294
  overview, 275–277
  projective (unstructured), 294–298
    defined, 30, 276
    Draw–A–Person Test (DAP), 15, 87, 297
    House–Tree–Person (HTP) test, 15, 297, 298t
    Rorschach Inkblot Test, 15, 295, 295f
    Rotter Incomplete Sentences Blank, 296–297
    Tell-Me-A-Story (TEMAS), 87
    Thematic Apperception Test (TAT), 15, 296
  racial and ethnic differences in, 83–84
Personality Assessment Screener (PAS), 284
Personality Research Form (PRF), 276
Personal Style Scales (PSSs), 253
Personal values inventories, 263, 264t, 267–269
  Quality of Life Inventory (QOLI), 269
  Rokeach Value Survey (RVS), 267
  Salience Inventory (SI), 269
  Schwartz Value Survey (SVS), 267–268
  Study of Values (SOV), 268–269
Person-in-Culture Interview, 138
Person Match, 257, 258
PHQ (Patient Health Questionnaire), 145
Physical abuse, 312
Physiological measures of assessment, 31
Piers–Harris Children's Self-Concept Scale, 294
PLAN Program, 206
Platykurtosis, 125
Portrait Values Questionnaire (PVQ), 268
Position Statement on High Stakes Testing (ACA), 52
Positive Symptom Distress Index (PSDI), 143
Positive Symptom Total (PST), 143
Posttraumatic Stress Disorder Symptom Scale, 174
Power tests, 28–29
PPVT-IV (Peabody Picture Vocabulary Test, 4th ed.), 195

Practice effects, 63, 105–106

Praxis, 12

Precontemplation stage of assessment, 32

Prediction objective in career assessment, 223

Predictive validity, 110–111

Pre-Employment Testing and the ADA (AARC & ARCA), 53

Preliminary SAT/National Merit Scholarship Qualifying Test (PSAT/NMSQT), 205

Preparation stage of assessment, 32

PREPARE and ENRICH, 306

PRF (Personality Research Form), 276

Primary mental abilities theory of intelligence, 189

Privacy of information, 58–60

Problematizing, 338–339

Problem-solving steps, 6–8, 7t

Professional considerations. *See* Ethical, legal, and professional considerations

Professional School Counseling (journal), 20

Professional school tests, 106, 110–111, 210–211

Profiles of American Colleges (Barrons Educational Series), 208

Progress monitoring and outcome assessments
    assessment tools, 41–45, 43–44t
    client self-reporting, 42–44
    defined, 39
    examples of progress monitoring, 41–42f
    overview, 39–41
    reflection questions, 40, 40t

Projective hypotheses, 276

Projective personality assessments, 276, 294–298
    defined, 30, 276
    Draw–A–Person Test (DAP), 15, 87, 297
    House–Tree–Person (HTP) test, 15, 297, 298t
    Rorschach Inkblot Test, 15, 295, 295f
    Rotter Incomplete Sentences Blank, 296–297
    Tell-Me-A-Story (TEMAS), 87
    Thematic Apperception Test (TAT), 15, 296

Prospective assessments, 22

PSAT/NMSQT (Preliminary SAT/National Merit Scholarship Qualifying Test), 205

PSDI (Positive Symptom Distress Index), 143

PSSs (Personal Style Scales), 253

PST (Positive Symptom Total), 143

Psychiatric assessments. *See* Mental health assessments

Psychiatric Diagnostic Screen Questionnaire (PDSQ), 145

Psychological abuse, 312

Psychological Assessment (journal), 34

Psychometrics, 99–117. *See also* Raw score calculations
    defined, 6
    guidelines for, 115–116
    reliability, 101–108
        correlation coefficients and, 102–104, 103f, 106
        defined, 101
        measurement error and, 102
        types of, 104–108, 105t
    scales of measurement, 99–101, 100t
    validity, 108–114
        base rates and, 111

correlation coefficients and, 110, 111
    defined, 108
    scales, 113–114
    threats to, 109
    types of, 109–114, 110t

Pub. L. 94-142, 89

Publishers of tests, 34, 56–57

PVQ (Portrait Values Questionnaire), 268

Q

Qualitative assessment techniques, 23, 28, 223, 224, 233, 341

Qualitative variables, 6

Quality of Life Inventory (QOLI), 269

Quantitative assessment techniques, 23

Quantitative variables, 6

R

Race to the Top Assessment Program (U.S. Education Department), 342

Racial and ethnic differences
    in aptitude tests, 81–82
    in career assessments, 82–83
    demographic trends for the future, 337–338
    in diagnostic decisions, 156
    in mental health treatment, 160
    in outcomes, 40, 337–338
    in personality assessments, 83–84
    in suicide rates, 151

Range of restriction error, 29

Ranges, 123

Rank-order scales, 29

Ranks, 127–128

Rapid Alcohol Problems Screen (RAPS), 163

Rating scales, 29–30, 43–44t, 44–45

Ratio IQ scores, 130–131, 188

Ratio scales, 101

Raven's Progressive Matrices, 85–86, 86f

Raw score calculations, 119–133. *See also* Psychometrics
    central tendency measures, 122–123
    data distribution characteristics, 124–125
    guidelines for, 132–133
    norms and ranks, 126–128
    organization of, 120–121
    overview, 120–122, 120t
    standard error of measurement, 131–132
    standard scores, 128–131
        CEEB scores, 129–130
        deviation IQ scores, 130–131, 188
        stanines, 131
        T scores, 129, 130t
        z scores, 128–129
    variability measures, 123

RC (Restructured Clinical) scales, 279–280

Reciprocity, 339

Reflection questions, 40, 40t

Regression effect, 25

Rehabilitation Act of 1973, 89

Relational accountability/responsibility, 339
Reliability, 101–108
    correlation coefficients and, 102–104, 103*f*, 106
    defined, 101
    measurement error and, 102
    types of, 104–108, 105*t*
Reports of assessment results, 329–333, 351–355
Respect, 339
Response bias, 71
Response sets, 71, 113–114
Response to intervention (RTI), 40
Response variables, 6
Responsibilities of Users of Standardized Tests (RUST Statement, AARC), 48, 52
Responsible Test Use: Case Studies for Assessing Human Behavior (JCTP), 50, 51*t*
Restriction of range, 110
Restructured Clinical (RC) scales, 279–280
Results. *See* Communication of assessment results
Retrospective assessments, 22
Rights and regulations to adhere to indigenous protocols, 339
Rights and Responsibilities of Test Takers: Guidelines and Expectations (JCTP), 51
Rokeach Value Survey (RVS), 267
Rorschach Inkblot Test, 15, 295, 295*f*
Rosenthal effect, 36
Rotter Incomplete Sentences Blank, 296–297
RTI (response to intervention), 40

S

SAC (Suicide Assessment Checklist), 152
SAD PERSONS Scale, 152
SAFE-T (Suicide Assessment Five-Step Evaluation and Triage), 153
Salience Inventory (SI), 269
SAMHSA (Substance Abuse and Mental Health Services Administration), 153, 160–161
SAMS (Study Attitudes and Methods Survey), 217
SASSI-4 (Substance Abuse Subtle Screening Inventory; 4th ed.), 101, 165–166
SAT (Scholastic Aptitude Test)
    components and layout of, 205
    history of, 12
    school counselor use of, 17
    standard scores for, 129–130
    validity of, 206–207
SB5 (Stanford-Binet Intelligence Scale; 5th ed.), 11, 130, 191–192
Scales of measurement, 99–101, 100*t*
Scatterplot diagrams, 102, 103*f*
Scholastic Level Exam, 198
Schools. *See also* Ability assessments
    achievement tests in, 211–213
    college admissions and assessments, 207–209, 213–214
    counselors in, 17, 18*t*, 60, 89–90, 342
    educational accountability and, 341–342

graduate admissions tests, 12, 104, 111, 112, 130, 209–210
high-stakes testing and, 52, 215–216, 216*t*, 342
intelligence assessments administered in, 197
professional school tests, 106, 110–111, 210–211
study habits inventories and, 217–218
Schwartz Value Survey (SVS), 267–268
SCI (Skills Confidence Inventory), 232, 255
SCL-90-Analogue (Symptom Check List-90–Analogue), 144
SCL-90-R (Symptom Check List-90–Revised), 143–144
Scoring procedures, 37
Screening inventories, 139, 141–145
    Brief Psychiatric Rating Scale (BPRS), 145
    Brief Symptom Inventory (BSI), 144
    Derogatis Psychiatric Rating Scale, 144
    Inventory of Common Problems (ICP), 141–143, 142*f*
    for mental disorders, 145
    Outcome Questionnaire 45.2 (OQ-45.2), 144–145
    overall accuracy of, 141
    Symptom Check List-90–Analogue (SCL-90-Analogue), 144
    Symptom Check List-90–Revised (SCL-90-R), 143–144
S-data, 21
SDS (Self-Directed Search), 224
Self-assessment modules, 233
Self-awareness (counselors), 68
Self-concept assessments, 294
Self-Directed Search (SDS), 224, 260–261
Self-esteem assessments, 293–294
Self-Harm Inventory, 175
Self-Injurious Thoughts and Behaviors Interview, 175
Self-injury assessments, 175–178, 176*t*
Self-Injury Implicit Association Test, 175
Self-Injury Questionnaire, 175
Self-Injury Trauma Scale, 175
Self-monitoring assessments, 44, 168–169
Self-referenced scores and tests, 5, 120
Self-report scales, 42–44, 43*t*
SEM (standard error of measurement), 131–132
Semantic differential rating techniques, 29
Semistructured interviews, 30
Seniors. *See* Elderly and aging populations
Sensitivity, 112, 112*t*, 141
Sentence completion tests, 15
Separation model, 76
Sequin form board, 10–11
Sex differences. *See* Gender differences
Sexual abuse, 312
"S" factor theory of intelligence, 189
Shipley Institute of Living Scale–Revised, 198
SI (Salience Inventory), 269
SIGI³ (System of Integrated Guidance and Information-third edition), 233
SIS (Supports Intensity Scale), 92

Situational tests, 29–30
Sixteen Personality Factor Questionnaire
(16 PF), 276–277, 291–292, 341
Skewness, 125
Skills Confidence Inventory (SCI), 232, 255
Social climate scales, 307
Social justice, 145, 222–223, 338. *See also* Multicultural assessments
Social phobia, defined, 174
Social Phobia and Anxiety Inventory (SPAI), 174
Socioeconomic status
aptitude tests and, 81–82
in counseling and assessment, 337–338
SOV (Study of Values), 268–269
Spearman-Brown correlation coefficient, 106, 349
Specialty assessment standards, 52–53
Specificity, 112, 112*t*, 141
Speed tests, 28–29
Split-half reliability, 106, 107, 107*f*
Stability of results. *See* Reliability
STAI (State-Trait Anxiety Inventory), 173–174
STAIC (State-Trait Anxiety Inventory for Children), 173–174
Standard deviation, 123–125, 350
Standard error of measurement (SEM), 131–132
Standardized assessments. *See also* Achievement tests
for career planning, 234–241
Armed Services Vocational Aptitude Battery (ASVAB), 14, 235–236
Career Interest Inventory (CII), 235
Career Occupational Preference System (COPSystem), 239–240, 266
Career Planning Survey (CPS), 234–235
Differential Aptitude Tests, 235
Occupational Information Network (O*NET), 237–239, 254, 255, 265
WorkKeys system, 236–237
defined, 28
Standard nine, 131
Standard scores, 128–131
CEEB scores, 129–130
deviation IQ scores, 130–131, 188
stanines, 131
T scores, 129, 130*t*
z scores, 128–129
Standards for Assessment in Mental Health Counseling (AARC & AMHCA), 48, 53
Standards for Assessment in Substance Abuse Counseling (AARC & IAAOC), 48, 53
Standards for Educational and Psychological Testing (AERA, APA, & NCME)
on assessment definition, 4
competency and, 57
on disabilities and assessment, 90
fairness in testing, 69–71
overview, 49–50
on reliability, 102
on validity, 108, 109
Standards for Multicultural Assessment (AARC), 52, 222–223, 345
Standards for Qualifications of Test Users (ACA), 52

Stanford Achievement Test Series (10th ed.; Stanford 10), 12, 197, 212
Stanford-Binet Intelligence Scale (5th ed.; SB5), 11, 130, 191–192
Stanines, 131
State licensure boards, 57
State-Trait Anger Expression Inventory-2 (STAXI-2), 174–175
State-Trait Anxiety Inventory (STAI), 173–174
State-Trait Anxiety Inventory for Children (STAIC), 173–174
Statistical considerations. *See* Psychometrics; Raw score calculations
Stereotype threats, 36, 79. *See also* Multicultural assessments
Sternberg's Triangular Love Scale (STLS), 307–308
Sternberg's triarchic theory of intelligence, 190
Strong Interest Explorer, 255
Strong Interest Inventory
administrative indexes, 249
Basic Interest Scales (BISs), 80, 248–250
case study, 251*t*, 253–255
gender differences on, 80, 248–250
General Occupational Themes (GOTs) scale, 249–250
Occupational Scales (OSs), 80, 250–252
overview, 248
Personal Style Scales (PSSs), 253
reliability and validity of, 108–109, 113
Skills Confidence Inventory and, 232, 255
as strengths-based assessment, 341
visual disabilities and, 91
Strong Vocational Interest Blank, 14
Structured interviews, 30
Structured personality assessments. *See* Objective personality assessments
Study Attitudes and Methods Survey (SAMS), 217
Study habits inventories, 217–218
Study of Values (SOV), 268–269
Substance Abuse and Mental Health Services Administration (SAMHSA), 153, 160–161
Substance abuse assessments, 159–170
for alcohol abuse or dependence, 161–170
Addiction Severity Index (ASI), 166
Alcohol Use Disorders Identification Test (AUDIT), 41, 166, 167*f*
Alcohol Use Inventory (AUI), 168
CAGE questionnaire, 163
Comprehensive Drinking Profile (CDP), 166–167
criteria for, 162–163
Michigan Alcoholism Screening Test (MAST), 164–165, 164*f*
motivational interviewing (MI), 169
Rapid Alcohol Problems Screen (RAPS), 163
self-monitoring methods, 168–169
Substance Abuse Subtle Screening Inventory (4th ed.; SASSI-4), 101, 165–166
Timeline Follow-Back (TLFB), 167–168
case study, 165
for children, 166

overview, 159–161, 161*t*
procedures for using, 169–170
standards for, 53
suicide risk and, 149
Substance Abuse Subtle Screening Inventory (4th ed.; SASSI-4), 101, 165–166
Suicide Assessment Checklist (SAC), 152
Suicide Assessment Five-Step Evaluation and Triage (SAFE-T), 153
Suicide Attempt Self-Injury Interview, 175
Suicide risk assessments, 147–154
    decision-tree approach, 153
    depression and, 111, 112, 149
    factors affecting, 148–151
    rates of suicide, 147, 151
    risk levels, 147–148
    SAD PERSONS Scale, 152
    safety planning, 153–154
    substance abuse and, 149
    Suicide Assessment Checklist (SAC), 152
    suicide plan evaluation, 148–149
Sums of squares, 123
Super's Work Values Inventory, 257
Supports Intensity Scale (SIS), 92
SVS (Schwartz Value Survey), 267–268
Symptom Check List-90–Analogue (SCL-90-Analogue), 144
Symptom Check List-90–Revised (SCL-90-R), 143–144
System of Integrated Guidance and Information-third edition (SIGI³), 233

T

TABE (Tests of Adult Basic Education), 214
TAT (Thematic Apperception Test), 15, 296
Taylor–Johnson Temperament Analysis (TJTA), 305
Technological advances, 339–340
Technology-based assessments. *See* Computer-based assessments
Teens. *See* Children and adolescents
Tell-Me-A-Story (TEMAS), 87
TEMAS (Tell-Me-A-Story), 87
TEMAS assessment, 296
Temperamental characteristics, 22
Tennessee Self-Concept Scale, 294
Termination rates, 40
TerraNova Tests, 197, 212–213
Test Anxiety Scale, 174
Test Critiques (ProEd), 34
Testing condition error, 102
Test of Cognitive Skills, 197
Test of English as a Foreign Language (TOEFL), 12, 213–214
Test-retest reliability, 104–105, 105*f*
Tests. *See also* Assessments
    adaptation of, 78
    administration of, 35–36
    anxiety taking, 62–63
    defined, 5
    interpretation of, 36–38

publishers of, 34, 56–57
selection of, 32–35
sophistication of, 75–76
translation of, 78
Tests (ProEd), 34
Tests in Print (*TIP*, Buros Institute), 34
Tests of Adult Basic Education (TABE), 214
Thematic Apperception Test (TAT), 15, 296
Theoretical method of assessment construction, 276
Therapist Rating Form, 142, 143
Thinking Styles Inventory, 218
Thomas–Kilman Conflict Mode Instrument, 318
Thompson TAT (T-TAT), 296
360° feedback, 21
Timeline Follow-Back (TLFB), 167–168
TIP (*Tests in Print*, Buros Institute), 34
TJTA (Taylor-Johnson Temperament Analysis), 305
TOEFL (Test of English as a Foreign Language), 12, 213–214
Torrance Tests of Creativity, 200
Treatment failure, 39–40
Treatment validity, 113
Trends. *See* Future trends in assessments
Triarchic theory of intelligence, 190
T scores, 129, 130*t*

U

UNIACT Interest Inventory, 80, 206
University of Rhode Island Change Assessment (URICA), 32
Unstructured interviews, 30
Unstructured personality assessments. *See* Projective personality assessments
U.S. Employment Service, 111, 130

V

Validity, 108–114
    of aptitude tests, 206–207
    base rates and, 111
    correlation coefficients and, 110, 111
    defined, 108
    scales, 113–114
    threats to, 109
    types of, 109–114, 110*t*
Values clarification exercises, 271–272
Values Conflict Resolution Assessment (VCRA), 271–272
Values inventories, 245–273. *See also* Interest inventories
    defined, 245
    guidelines for use of, 270
    of personal values, 263, 264*t*, 267–269
        Quality of Life Inventory (QOLI), 269
        Rokeach Value Survey (RVS), 267
        Salience Inventory (SI), 269
        Schwartz Value Survey (SVS), 267–268
        Study of Values (SOV), 268–269
(Continued)

Values inventories *(Continued)*
    values clarification exercises, 271–272
    of work values, 264*t*, 265–267
        Career Orientation Placement and
            Evaluation Survey (COPES), 266
        Values Scale (VS), 266–267
        Work Importance Profiler (WIP),
            238–239, 265
        Work Values Inventory–Revised
            (WVI), 265–266
Values Scale (VS), 266–267
Variability measures, 123
Variables, defined, 6, 22
VCRA (Values Conflict Resolution Assessment),
    271–272
Vineland Adaptive Behavior Scales, 91–92
Vineland Social Maturity Scale, 341
Violence
    child abuse, 312–313, 313*t*
    intimate partner violence, 308–311, 310*t*
Visual disabilities, 90–91
Vocational guidance, 222. *See also* Career and
    life-planning assessments
Voluntary responses, 22
VS (Values Scale), 266–267

W

Wechsler Abbreviated Scale of Intelligence
    (WASI), 194
Wechsler Adult Intelligence Scale (WAIS), 15,
    17, 130, 132, 192–193
Wechsler Bellevue Intelligence Scale, 192, 193
Wechsler Individual Achievement Test (WIAT-
    III), 214–215
Wechsler Intelligence Scale for Children (WISC),
    17
Wechsler Intelligence Scale for Children (WISC-V),
    193
Wechsler Memory Scale (WMS), 93–94
Wechsler Nonverbal Scale of Ability (WNV), 87
Wechsler Preschool and Primary Scale of
    Intelligence (WPPSI-IV), 193–194
Welfare of clients, 58–60
Wellness Evaluation of Lifestyle (WEL), 299
Western Psychological Services, 56

What Color Is Your Parachute? (Bolles), 234
WHO (World Health Organization), 162
WIAT-III (Wechsler Individual Achievement
    Test), 214–215
Wide Range Achievement Test (4th ed.;
    WRAT4), 214
Wide Range Intelligence Test, 195
WISC (Wechsler Intelligence Scale for Children),
    17
WISC-V (Wechsler Intelligence Scale for
    Children), 193
WMS (Wechsler Memory Scale), 93–94
WNV (Wechsler Nonverbal Scale of Ability), 87
Wonderlic Personnel Test, 198
Woodcock–Johnson Tests of Cognitive Abilities
    (WJ IV), 17, 195
Woodworth Personal Data Sheet, 14
Workbooks for career assessment, 233–234, 271
Work Importance Locator (WIL-P&P), 265
Work Importance Profiler (WIP), 238–239, 265
Working Alliance Inventory, 42
WorkKeys system, 236–237
Work values inventories, 17, 264*t*, 265–267
    Career Orientation Placement and Evaluation
        Survey (COPES), 266
    Values Scale (VS), 266–267
    Work Importance Profiler (WIP), 238–239,
        265
    Work Values Inventory–Revised (WVI),
        265–266
Work Values Inventory–Revised (WVI), 265–266
World Health Organization (WHO), 162
World-of-Work Map, 206, 234–235
WPPSI-IV (Wechsler Preschool and Primary
    Scale of Intelligence), 193–194
WRAT4 (Wide Range Achievement Test, 4th ed.),
    214

Y

Youths. *See* Children and adolescents

Z

Z scores, 128–129

Name Index

A

Abdul Kadir, R., 228
Abela, J. R. Z., 175
Abidin, R. R., 19
Abrahams, S., 299
Achenbach, T. M., 181, 313
ACT, Inc., 80, 130, 206, 208, 210, 219, 234, 236, 237
Adams, K., 347
Adams, R. S., 317
ADHD Institute, 184
Aguilar, D. P., 18
Ahmadi, S., 179
Albanese, M. A., 93
Albaugh, B., 84
Albion, M. J., 228
Alcántara, C., 139, 158
Alcohol Research Group, 163
Alexander, A., 175, 176
Alexander, R. A., 152
Alfonso, V. C., 200
Allen, J., 253
Allen, M. J., 117, 132
Allik, J., 180
Allin, J. D., 191
Allport, G. W., 14
Alt, M., 77
Alterman, A. I., 166
Alvarez, A. N., 81
Alvarez-Rayón, G., 179
Alzheimer's Association, 93
American Academy of Pediatrics, 181
American Association for Geriatric Psychiatry, 93
American Association for Marriage and Family Therapy, 53
American Association of Suicidology, 149, 150, 158

American Association on Intellectual and Developmental Disabilities, 92
American College Testing Program, 63, 81, 206
American Counseling Association, 36, 48, 49, 50, 52, 57, 58, 59, 64, 343
American Dental Association, 210
American Educational Research Association, 4, 25, 36, 48, 49, 50, 57, 64, 69, 71, 90, 102, 104, 106, 108, 109, 113, 336
American Foundation for Suicide Prevention, 158
American Geriatrics Society, 93
American Guidance Service, 194
American Medical Association, 310
American Mental Health Counselors Association, 48, 53
American Psychiatric Association, 145, 148, 149, 158, 173, 174, 175, 178, 179, 181
American Psychological Association, 4, 12, 25, 36, 48, 49, 50, 51, 57, 64, 69, 71, 82, 90, 102, 104, 106, 108, 109, 113, 158, 329, 336, 347
American Rehabilitation Counseling Association, 48, 53
American School Counselor Association, 17, 18, 19, 52, 342
American Speech-Language-Hearing Association, 50
Amundsen, A., 268
Anastopolous, A. D., 181
Anderson, J. O., 213
Anderson, N., 34
Anderson, P. D., 181
Anderson, U., 83
Andrew, M. E., 238
Annest, J. L., 147
Antony, M. M., 173
Anxiety and Depression Association of America, 184
Arizmendi, G. D., 77

421

Armstrong, P. I., 247, 248
Arnold, B. R., 348
Aronson, J., 36
Arredondo, P., 52
Association for Assessment and Research in Counseling, 48, 52, 53, 96, 222–223, 345, 347, 348
Association for Assessment in Counseling and Education, 48, 52, 345
Association of American Medical Colleges, 210
Atlas, J., 172
Attkisson, C. C., 43
Austin, J. T., 257, 294

B

Babor, T. F., 162, 166, 167
Badger, G. J., 169
Bailey, D. C., 248
Bain, S. K., 191
Baker, H. E., 235, 236
Baker, R. W., 141
Balderama-Durbin, C., 304
Balkin, R. S., 299
Ball, L. C., 79
Balla, D. A., 91
Bandura, A., 229
Banjai, M. R., 175, 176
Barbash, M., 32
Barden, S. M., 19
Bardos, A. N., 214
Barkley, R. A., 181
Barram, R. A., 201
Barrocas, A. L., 175
Barrons Educational Series, 208
Barry, D. R., 295
Barterian, J., 62
Bartlett Regional Hospital, 310
Bartling, H. C., 252
Batshaw, M. L., 89, 91
Battle, C., 43
Bault, M. W., 89
Beal, C. R., 77
Beatty, A. S., 30, 31
Beccaria, G., 230
Beck, A. T., 171, 174, 313
Becker, A. E., 74
Behavior Data Systems, 310
Beidel, D. C., 174
Beierlein, C., 268
Bellah, C. G., 196
Benjamin, C. L., 44
Bennett, E. D., 56
Bennett, G. K., 235
Bennett, R. E., 91, 336, 341, 345
Ben-Porath, Y. S., 277, 279, 282
Benshoff, J. M., 57
Berens, D., 89, 91
Berg, I. S., 145
Berg-Cross, L., 138, 158
Berger, B., 32
Berglund, P., 170, 172, 173
Bergwerff, C. E., 88

Berkel, L. A., 242
Berkeley, S. B., 90
Berman, A. L., 147, 148, 149, 151
Berman, J., 306
Berman, L., 306
Berman, N. C., 148
Bernstein, D. P., 310
Bernstein, E. M., 313
Berntson, G. G., 31
Berthoud, L., 145
Betz, N. E., 229, 232, 247, 255, 265
Bieling, P. J., 173
Bieschke, K. J., 309
Bigfoot, D. S., 84
Bigler, E. D., 92
Binet, A., 10, 11, 187, 188
Bird, J., 152
Blacher, J. H., 17
Black, M. C., 308
Blackwell, T. L., 248
Blando, J. A., 94, 271
Blankenship, D. M., 74
Blasko, K. A., 309
Blum, L. H., 87
Bodenmann, G., 19
Bohn, M. J., 166
Bolles, R. N., 234, 242
Bombel, G., 295
Bonitz, V. S., 252
Bonner, M. W., 15, 16, 21
Booth, R., 144
Borgen, F. H., 20, 230, 232, 248, 250, 253, 254, 255
Borkenau, P., 21
Borneman, M. J., 63
Bornstein, R. F., 295
Bosma, T., 88, 96
Boston Vocational Bureau, 14
Boswell, D. L., 7
Bourdeau, B., 199
Bowers, J., 19
Bowles, S. M., 238
Boye, M. W., 166
Braciszewski, J. M., 168
Bradley, P., 287, 288, 291
Brannigan, G. C., 20
Brannon, L., 31
Breitholtz, T., 146
Brener, N. D., 151
Breteler, R., 180
Briddick, H., 224
Briddick, W. C., 224, 229
Briere, J., 310, 313
Briggs, K., 284, 285
Brodey, B. B., 166
Brodman, D. M., 44
Brookhart, S. M., 267
Brott, P., 23, 28, 223, 233, 271
Brown, D., 271
Brown, G. K., 153, 154, 171
Brown, G. P., 111
Brown, J. B., 310
Brown, M. B., 181
Brown, R. P., 87

Brown, S. D., 223, 229
Brown, T. E., 181
Brown, Z. M., 175
Brown-Chidsey, R., 40
Brunell-Neuleib, T., 295
Bruns, D., 298
Bubenzer, D., 15
Buck, J. N., 15, 297, 298
Budman, S. H., 166
Bullock, E. E., 240
Bullock-Yowell, E., 240, 266
Burgemeister, B. B., 87
Burns, R. C., 300
Burns, T. G., 193
Buros, O., 34
Buros Center for Testing, 10, 45
Buros Institute of Mental Measurements, 34
Burton, L. J., 230
Butcher, J. N., 61, 83, 84, 279, 281, 282
Butler, S. K., 68
Byrd, R., 175, 268, 338

C

Cabiya, J., 83
Cacciola, J. S., 166
Cacioppo, J. T., 31
Caldwell, A., 84
Calhoun, G. B., 32
Calvert, P. D., 269
Calvert, R., 144
Camara, W. J., 15
Camic, P. M., 117
Camp, D. C., 228
Campbell, D. P., 245, 255, 256, 259, 272
Campbell, J. C., 262, 310
Campbell, V. L., 15, 17
Canals, J., 179
Canfield, A. A., 217
Canfield, J. S., 217
Canivez, G. L., 192
Cantonis, A. M., 37
Carbajo, G., 179
Cardillo, J. E., 25
Carlson, C. I., 304
Carlson, J. F., 34
Carlson, L., 269
Carney, R. N., 212
Carretero, C. M., 179
Carroll, J. B., 190
Carson, J., 11, 25
Casañas i Comabella, C., 149
Case, J. C., 248
Casillas, A., 280
Cattell, H. E. P., 291, 292
Cattell, J., 9, 10
Cattell, R. B., 11, 78, 85, 95, 188, 189, 276–277, 291
Center for Applications of Psychological Type, 304
Centers for Disease Control and Prevention, 147, 148, 151, 162
Chambless, D. L., 113, 117
Chang, E. D., 6

Charter, R. A., 93, 132
Chartrand, J. M., 229, 255
Chelminski, I., 172
Chen, H., 192
Chernin, J., 73
Cherpitel, C. J., 163
Chiu, W. T., 24, 156, 173
Choca, J., 329
Chope, R. C., 287, 288
Christensen, A., 19
Chu, C., 153
Cicchetti, D. V., 91, 102, 112
Cieciuch, J., 267, 268
Civiletto, C. L., 227
Clark, A., 305
Clark, D. A., 111
Clark, K. E., 247
Clark, L. A., 280
Clausen, L., 180
Clawson, T. W., 57
Clayton, A. H., 172
Clift, R. J. W., 310
Climie, E. A., 192, 193
Cline, F. A., 210
Coalson, D. L., 201
Cochran, S. D., 74
Cohen, G. L., 82
Cohen, G. R., 82
Cohen, I. G., 148
Cohen, J. S., 44
Cohen, P. J., 32
Colangelo, N., 199, 200
Colby, S. L., 337
Coleman, L. J., 199
Collado, E. R., 179
College Board, 10, 63, 90, 129, 130, 205, 207, 208, 213, 220
College Entrance Examination Board, 10, 12, 63, 128, 129–130, 133, 213
Colom, J., 166
Comas-Díaz, L., 158
Comtois, K. A., 175
Conn, S. R., 20
Connelly, B. S., 63
Conners, C. K., 44, 181
Consulting Psychologists Press, 35
Contel, M., 166
Cook, L. P., 343, 344
Cooper, H., 117
Cooperman, A., 148
Coopersmith, S., 293, 294
Cordón, L. A., 295
Correll, S. J., 80
Costa, P. T., Jr., 292, 293
Costantino, G., 87
Coughlin, S. S., 150
Council for Accreditation of Counseling and Related Educational Programs, 57
Court, J. H., 85
Cox, A. A., 299
Crace, R. K., 271
Craig, R. J., 292
Craigen, L. M., 175, 176, 178

Cramer, S. H., 17
Crethar, H. C., 338
Cribbie, R. A., 79
Crites, J. O., 229, 230
Crocker, L., 64
Crockett, S., 338
Cronbach, L. J., 106, 107
Cross, T. L., 199
Crowdery, K., 247
Crowther, M. R., 94
Cruise, T. K., 312
Crump, G. B., 216
CTB/Macmillan/McGraw-Hill, 197
Cummings, J., 184
Cummings, W. H., 285
Curtis, R. C., 165
Cyr, M., 308

D

D'Achiardi, C., 17
Dagley, J. C., 231
Dahlberg, L. L., 147
Dahlem, N. W., 151
Dahlstrom, W. G., 279
Daiger, D. C., 231
Dalrymple, K., 172
D'Amato, R. C., 192
Dana, R. H., 68, 87
Dancu, C. V., 174
Darcy, M., 253
Darwin, C., 9, 188
Das, J. P., 190
Data Recognition Corporation/CTB, 214
Davenport, J., 144
Davenport, M., 81
Davidov, E., 267, 268
Davies, P. G., 36
Davis, A., 329, 334
Davis, J., 247
Davis, R. D., 283
Day, E., 87
Day, S. X., 61, 230, 250
D'Costa, A. G., 230, 247
De Boeck, P. A. L., 88
Decker, S. L., 20, 201
De Jong, F., 88, 96
Dejong, P., 145
de la Cruz, L. F., 181
Del Corso, J., 265
del Mar Sánchez-Fuentes, M., 306
DeMars, C., 133
Demler, O., 24, 160, 170
DeNavas-Walt, C., 337
Denis, C. M., 166
DePaola, S. J., 92
Derogatis, L. R., 143, 144, 306
DeVellis, R. F., 117
Diamond, E. E., 14
Dicken, C., 289
Dickinson, J., 230
DiClemente, C. C., 32

Dienstbier, R. A., 277
Dik, B. J., 252
DiPerna, J. C., 197
Disorbio, P. B., 298
Dixon, A., 74
Dixon, F. A., 200
Doebbeling, B. N., 280
Dohn, H. H., 152
Doll, E., 92
Dullaghan, C., 7
Donnay, D. A. C., 248, 249, 250, 252, 253, 254, 255, 287, 288
Donoso, O. A., 15
Dougherty, E. H., 139
Drasgow, E., 89
Dubes, R., 15
DuBois, R., 25
Duffy, M., 216
Dumitrascu, N., 295
Duncan, B. L., 43
Dunn, K., 217
Dunn, L. M., 195
Dunn, R., 217
DuPaul, G. J., 181, 184
Dutton, M. A., 310
Dykeman, C., 231
Dynda, A. M., 84
D'Zurilla, T. J., 6

E

Earleywine, M., 169
Edelbrock, C. S., 313
EdITS (Educational and Industrial Testing Service), 239, 240, 266
Edmunds, J. M., 44
Educational Testing Service, 10, 12, 46, 205, 209, 210, 213, 214, 220, 247
Edwards, C. D., 173
Ege, E., 145
Eggerth, D. E., 238
Ehrenberg, R. G., 82
Eisen, S. V., 43
Ekstrom, R. B., 17, 18
Elliott, S. N., 90
Elliott, T. E., 287, 288
Elmore, P. B., 17, 18
Emelianchik-Key, K., 308, 309, 310, 311
Endler, N. S., 298
Erb, B., 182
Erford, B. T., 56, 73, 89, 91, 337
Erhardt, D., 181
Espadas, A., 43
Espelage, D. L., 308
Esquirol, J., 10, 188
Essig, G. N., 113
Evans, W. N., 164
Ewing, J. A., 163
Exner, J. E., 295
Eyde, L. D., 50, 51, 65
Eysenck, H. J., 277
Eysenck, S. B., 277

F

Fair Access Coalition on Testing, 58
Fals-Stewart, W., 168, 310
Family Violence Prevention Fund, 310
Fanjiang, G., 92
Fantuzzo, J. W., 310
Faragher, M. J., 32
Farley, G. K., 151
Farrell, J. B., 216
Faulkhead, S., 347
Faust, D., 15
Feist, J., 31
Feit, M. D., 184
Feitas, T. T., 168
Feldhaus, K., 310
Feldt, L. S., 132
Feller, R., 261
Fernandez, E., 298
Fernández-Ballart, J., 179
Fico, J. M., 317
Fiedler, E. R., 21
Fieldhaus, K., 310
Finklea, J. T., 37
Finn, S. E., 113
Fischer, K. L., 286
Fisher, C., 184
Fisher, M., 179
Fitch, J. C., 227
Fitzpatrick, M., 144
Flamez, B., 305
Flanagan, D. P., 190, 200
Fletcher, K. E., 313
Fletcher-Janzen, E., 194
Flores, L. Y., 223, 242, 250
Flowers, L., 312
Floyd, R. G., 92
Foa, E. B., 174
Fogarty, G. J., 228
Folstein, M. F., 92, 139
Folstein, S. E., 92
Forbey, J. D., 282
Ford, D. Y., 86, 87, 199
Ford, L., 89
Ford, M. R., 156
Forer, R., 247
Fortin, N. M., 79
Foster, F. M., 168
Fouad, N. A., 82–83, 248, 250
Fowler, J. C., 149, 150, 151, 152, 153
Fowler, R. D., 282
Franklin, J. C., 147
Frauenhoffer, D., 15
French, J. W., 62–63
Freyd, M., 247
Friborg, O., 180
Friedman, J. N. W., 21
Friedrich, W. N., 313
Frisch, M. B., 269
Fritzsche, B. A., 261
Funder, D. C., 29
Funke, J., 4

Furnham, A., 190

G

Gagliardi, C., 200
Galton, F., 9, 10, 14, 188
Garb, H. N., 295
Gardner, F. E., 214
Gardner, H., 188, 190, 200, 201
Garfinkel, P. E., 179
Garner, D. M., 41, 179, 180
Garrett, M. T., 76, 84
Garrido, M., 83
Garruto, J. M., 201
Gasser, C. E., 248
Gati, I., 228
Gavin, D. R., 165
Geiger, I., 76
Geisinger, K. F., 34
Gerson, R., 313–314, 319
Gfeller, J., 15
Ghaderi, A., 179
Gibbons, M. M., 257, 260
Gibson, J., 144
Gilberts, R., 294
Gillespie, B. V., 286
Gillespie, M. A., 31
Gimeno, E. C., 179
Giordano, V. A., 216
Glaser, B. A., 32, 341, 367
Glosoff, H. L., 57
Gluud, C., 165
Glynn, L. H., 169
Goddard, H. H., 10, 11
Goldenberg, H., 313–314
Goldenberg, I., 313–314
Goldfried, M. R., 295
Goldman, B. A., 45
Goldstein, S., 190
Gomez, S. P., 84
Gone, J., 139, 158
Good, B. J., 74
Good, M. J. D., 74
Goodenough, F., 87, 95, 297
Goodman, L., 310
Gordon, P. A., 227
Gordon Commission on the Future of Assessment
    in Education, 342, 345, 348
Gorham, D. R., 145
Gorin, J., 238
Gorsuch, R. L., 173
Goslin, D. A., 12
Gottfredson, G. D., 227, 254
Gough, H. G., 287, 288, 289, 290, 291
Graduate Management Admission Council, 210
Graham, J. R., 278, 279, 280, 281, 300
Grantham, T. C., 199
Gratz, K. L., 175, 176
Gray-Little, B., 83
Green, E., 312
Green, K. E., 267
Greenberg, L., 42

Greene, R. L., 84
Greenfield, T. K., 43
Greenlund, N. E., 219
Gregory, R. J., 6, 12, 14
Greiff, S., 4
Grice, J. W., 22
Griffith, A. L., 82
Grigorenko, E. L., 190
Grimsley, P., 32
Groth-Marnat, G., 83, 93, 288, 290, 295, 296, 297, 329, 334, 336, 341, 343
Grutter, J., 254
Gual, A., 166
Guan, M., 268
Guilford, J. P., 22
Guion, R. M., 7
Gurtman, M. B., 317
Gushue, G. V., 156

H

Hackett, G., 229
Haglund, A., 149
Hall, M. E., 227
Hall, T., 285
Hallmark, R., 15
Halpern, D. F., 79, 96
Hambleton, R. K., 94, 348
Hammer, A. L., 20, 284
Hammond, M., 229
Hankin, B. L., 175
Hannus, A., 180
Hansen, J. C., 20, 78, 113, 252, 256
Harmin, M., 271
Harmon, L. W., 20, 232, 250, 254
Harrington, T. F., 247, 261, 273
Harris, D. B., 294
Harris-Bowlsbey, J., 222
Harrison, M. L., 192
Hartung, P. J., 224, 229
Harwell, M. R., 212
Hase, T., 133
Hassan, S. A., 228
Hastings, P. B., 56
Hatch, P. A., 19
Hau, K.-T., 209
Haverkamp, B. E., 113
Haw, C., 149
Hawkley, L. C., 31
Hawton, K., 149
Haynes, S. N., 304
Hays, D. G., 17, 40, 45, 74, 76, 139, 156, 160, 226, 232, 242, 269, 308, 309, 310, 311, 312, 337
Hays, R. D., 166
Healey, A. C., 175
Heard, H. L., 175
Heather, N., 166
Heck, E. J., 163
Hegarty, K., 310
Heiser, R. H., 88
Heiser, W. H., 88
Heiser, W. J., 88

Helzer, J. E., 169
Hemenover, S. H., 277
Hemphill, J. F., 109
Henfield, M. S., 199
Henson, R. K., 294
Hernandez, B., 15
Heron, S., 310
Herr, E., 17, 222, 223
Herrmann, A., 223
Heyman, R., 304
Hezlett, S. A., 210
Hickendorff, M. H., 88
Hicks, J. F., 305
Higgins-Biddle, J. C., 162
Hill, C. L., 223, 242
Hill, S. S., 315
Hiller, J. B., 295
Hindman, J., 313
Hinkle, J. S., 139, 141
Hirschi, A., 223, 224
Hodgson, R. J., 174
Hoff, L. A., 310
Hoffman, J. A., 43, 141, 142
Hogan, H., 92
Hogan, R., 317
Hogan, T. P., 15, 20, 346
Holland, J. L., 80, 206, 227, 231, 238, 247, 248, 249, 251, 254, 255, 256, 260, 261, 263, 272, 330
Hollon, S. D., 113, 117
Holmber, E. B., 175
Holmes, T. H., 72
Holosko, M. J., 184
Holroyd, S., 172
Holt, D. V., 4
Holt, M. K., 308
Holtzman, S. L., 210
Hood, A. B., 252
Horin, E. V., 15
Horn, J. L., 168, 189
Horton, A. M., Jr., 94
Horton, C. B., 312, 313
Horvath, A. O., 42
Hosie, T. W., 57
Howard, J., 7
Hubert, L., 248
Hudson, W. W., 310
Hughes, I. F., 133
Hunsley, J., 111
Hunter, J. L., 109, 111
Hurley, E., 22
Hurtado, J. S., 77
Hutton, J. B., 15
Hyne, S. A., 256

I

Impara, J. C., 17
Inman, A. G., 81
International Association of Addictions and Offender Counselors, 48, 53
International Association of Marriage and Family Counselors, 48

International Bureau of Weights and Measures, 5
International Society of the Rorschach and Projective Methods, 300
International Test Commission, 38, 45, 96, 348
Iwata, B. A., 175, 176

J

Jackson, D. N., 198, 262, 276
Jacobs, G. A., 173
Jacobson, B., 306
Jaeger, J. R., 310
James, C., 74
Jay, M., 289
Jenkins, J. A., 232, 248, 255
Jin, R., 170
Jirele, T., 91
John, O. P., 289
Johnson, A. K., 318
Johnson, J. A., 192
Johnson, J. H., 150
Johnson, R., 318
Johnson, R. H., 305
Johnson, T. C., 313
Joint Committee on Testing Practices, 48, 50, 51, 52, 64
Jonson, J. L., 34
Jordaan, J. P., 229
Jordan, S. E., 242
Juhnke, G. A., 152, 165
Jung, C. G., 14, 15, 276, 284, 285

K

Kagee, A., 174
Kallivayalil, D., 84
Kamphaus, R. W., 181
Kane, M. T., 28
Kann, L., 147
Kaplan, B. A., 91
Kaplan, D. A., 83
Kaplan, Z., 180
Karanti, A., 149
Karlsen, B., 214
Karol, D., 291
Karson, M., 291
Karson, S., 291
Kaser-Boyd, N., 300
Kaufman, A. S., 81, 194, 195, 214, 329, 334
Kaufman, J. C., 190
Kaufman, N. L., 194, 195, 214, 329, 334
Keirsey, D. M., 286
Keith, T. Z., 192
Keller, A. C., 223
Kellett, S., 144
Kelly, K. R., 113, 230, 257, 258
Kendall, P. C., 44
Kennedy, M. L., 15
Kenrick, D. T., 29
Keogh, K., 144
Kerr, B., 200

Kessler, R. C., 24, 147, 156, 160, 170, 172, 173
Kettler, R. J., 90, 91
KeyTrain, 237
Kieling, C., 181
Kiesler, D. J., 317
Kilman, R. H., 318
Kim, B. H., 31
Kim, H., 271
King, J., 84
Kinnier, R. T., 238, 271, 272
Kiresuk, T. J., 7, 25, 44
Kirk, B. A., 286
Kirschenbaum, H., 271, 273
Kissel, R. C., 175
Kitchens, J. M., 163
Klein, K. L., 229
Klieger, D. M., 210
Kline, P., 276
Knapp, L., 240
Knapp, R. R., 240
Knapp-Lee, L. J., 239, 240, 266
Knowdell, R. L., 271
Knox, H. A., 11, 12
Kobak, K. A., 172
Kohar, R., 8
Kolb, D. A., 217
Konold, T. R., 19
Koocher, G. P., 315
Koons, P. B., 247
Kopelman, R. E., 268, 269
Korotitsch, W. J., 7
Koss, M. P., 310
Kovach, M., 339
Kovacs, M., 172, 313
Kraepelin, E., 14
Kranzler, H. R., 166
Kraus, D. R., 43
Kraus, M., 228
Krenek, M., 168, 169
Kress, V., 74, 75, 157
Kroenke, K., 145
Kronholz, J. F., 37
Krug, S. E., 50, 65
Krumboltz, J. D., 227, 271
Kruse, S. J., 267
Kuder, G. F., 14, 17, 247, 257, 258
Kuder, Inc., 260, 273
Kulig, A., 165
Kuncel, N. R., 210
Kush, J. C., 191
Kvall, S., 329

L

LaBrie, J. W., 169
Lachar, D., 43
LaFromboise, T. B., 84
Lah, M. I., 296
Lai, S. A., 90
Lakin, J. M., 79
Lambert, M. J., 39–40, 43, 144
Lambie, G. W., 347

Landén, M., 149
Landgraf, K., 341
Lane, G. G., 294
Larson, L. M., 248, 252
Larson, P. J., 306
Last, A., 44
Law School Admission Council, 210
Lawyer, S. R., 31
Lazowski, L. E., 166
Leal, V. M., 242
LeardMann, C. A., 149
Lee, E. A., 247
Lent, R. W., 229
Lenz, J. G., 231, 234, 242
Leong, F. T. L., 158, 233, 250
Leserman, J., 310
Levin, M. E., 25
Le Suer, B., 247
Levy, S., 146
Lewis, M. M., 152
Lewis, R. J., 286
Li, L. C., 223, 242
Lichtenberger, E. O., 81, 194, 329, 334
Lilienfeld, S. O., 295
Lilienthal, K., 165
Lindeman, R. H., 227, 229
Lindzey, G., 294, 295
Linehan, M. M., 175, 176
Logel, C., 36
Lomas, G. I., 15, 16, 21
Long, D. L., 117
Long, J., 247, 273
Lopez, M. N., 93
Lorelle, S., 338
Lorenz, F., 210
Lorge, I., 87
Lotrecchiano, G. R., 89
Low, K. D., 252
Lowe, P. A., 174
Lucio, E., 83
Luecht, R. M., 299
Luhmann, M., 31
Luo, F., 147
Luria, A. R., 194
Lushene, R., 173
Luu, L. P., 81, 84
Luzzo, D. A., 229, 234, 242
Lynn, G. L., 242
Lyons, R., 168

M

Machover, K., 297
Madaus, G., 215, 216
Madson, M. B., 240
Mahrle, C., 15
Makela, J. P., 37
Maki, D. R., 57
Malgady, R. G., 69, 87, 336
Mallen, M. J., 61
Maloney, M. P., 300
Manages, K. J., 307

Mancini, J. A., 307
Maness, P. J., 83
Mansi, A., 190
Manson, G., 247
Marbach-Ad, G., 108, 109
Markham, H. J., 19
Marks, I. M., 174
Marlatt, G. A., 166
Marley, C., 306
Marotta, S. A., 16
Marriage and Family Research Institute, 19
Marsh, H. W., 209, 294
Marshall, L., 310
Martinez, E., 179
Martinez, J. H., 172
Martins, R. K., 169
Maslow, A. H., 270
Mather, N., 329, 334
Mathews, A. M., 174
Mattia, J. I., 145
Mau, W., 228
Mays, V. M., 74
McAllister, M., 175
McCarney, S. B., 181
McCaulley, M. H., 284
McCollum, D., 310
McCrimmon, A. W., 194
McCullough, J. R., 68
McDaniel, J. W., 89, 90
McDavis, R. J., 52
McDivitt, P. J., 230
McDougal, J. L., 43
McDuff, P., 308
McFarlane, J., 310
McFarlin, S. K., 168
McGlothlin, J., 148, 149
McGoldrick, M., 313–314, 315, 319
McHugh, P. R., 92
McIlveen, P., 230
McInness, E., 166
McIntosh, D. E., 200
McIntosh, S. R., 310
McKevitt, B. C., 90
McLellan, A. T., 166
McLennen, J. C., 310
McLeod, A. L., 40, 74, 76, 139, 160, 337
McLoyd, V. C., 158
McMahon, M., 23, 28, 222, 223, 224, 233, 242, 341
McNeil, D. W., 169
McNeill, B. W., 84
McRae, R., 292
Meier, S. T., 39, 40, 41, 42, 45
Mendelsohn, G. A., 286
Merenda, P. F., 348
Merikangas, K. R., 172
Merlo, M. C. G., 145
Merz, J. D., 166
Messick, S., 108, 109, 345, 346
Meyer, G. J., 111, 295
Meyer, P., 117
Meyers, L., 84
Michael, J. J., 217
Michael, W. B., 217

Michel, B. D., 175
Michell, J. B., 5
Miettunen, J., 113
Mihura, J. L., 295
Miller, D. J., 139
Miller, F. G., 166
Miller, G. A., 166, 325, 326, 328
Miller, S. D., 43
Miller, W. R., 165, 166, 169, 170, 184
Milliken, T., 175
Millon, T., 283
Miner, J., 14, 247
Minsky, J. L., 210
Mintz, L. B., 179
Mitchell, A. J., 93
Mitchell, D. F., 45
Mitrani, E., 180
Mohler, C. J., 82–83, 250
Moloodi, R., 179
Mongeon, J. A., 168
Montalto, M., 61
Monteiro, M. G., 162
Montuori, J., 173
Moore, B., 247
Moore, J. L., 199
Moos, B. S., 150, 151, 307
Moos, R. H., 150, 151, 307
Moreland, K. L., 50, 51
Morey, L. C., 283
Morgan, C., 296
Morrill, W. H., 229
Morris, M. L., 248, 255
Morrison, L., 310
Morrison, L. P., 305
Morrison, W. L., 305
Mosch, A., 21
Most, R. B., 50, 51
Mostafavi, B., 93
Moyers, T. B., 169
Mueller, G., 165
Muir, S., 15
Mulder, R. T., 84
Mulholland, A. M., 179
Mullen, B., 165
Multi-Health Systems, 56
Multon, K. D., 229
Muñoz, R. F., 165, 170
Murphy, K. R., 181
Murphy, R., 22
Murray, H. A., 276, 296
Murray-Ward, M., 17
Myers, I. B., 284, 285, 304
Myers, J. E., 299, 308
Myers, R. A., 229
Myers & Briggs Foundation, 300

N

Na, S. D., 193
Nagayama Hall, G. C., 158
Naglieri, J. A., 86, 87, 95, 190, 195, 201
Nasab, M. F., 228

Nash, S., 338
Nassar-McMillan, S., 68
Nathan, J. S., 15
National Alliance on Mental Illness, 160
National Association of School Psychologists, 50
National Association of Test Directors, 50
National Board for Certified Counselors, 48, 58, 64
National Career Development Association, 48, 53, 242
National Commission on Excellence in Education, 216
National Council of Social Service, 158
National Council on Measurement in Education, 4, 25, 35–36, 48, 49, 50, 57, 64, 69, 71, 90, 102, 104, 106, 108, 109, 113, 336
National Eating Disorders Association, 184
National Institute of Mental Health, 148, 151, 160, 170
National Institute on Alcohol Abuse and Alcoholism, 162, 184
National Institute on Drug Abuse, 184
National Wellness Institute, 299
Naugle, K. A., 50, 56, 57
Neisser, V., 76, 79, 82
Nelson-Gray, N. O., 7
Neukrug, E. S., 15, 16, 21, 346
Neuman, J. L., 256
Nevill, D. D., 266, 267, 269
Newton, K. S., 337
Nezu, A. M., 6
Nezu, C. M., 6
Nezworski, M. T., 295
Nibut, L. P., 93
Nicholas, R., 166
Nickerson, R. S., 10, 14
Nieberding, R., 15, 17
Nielsen, S. D., 165
Niles, S. G., 17, 222, 223
Nilsen, D. L., 256
Nilsson, J. E., 242
Niv, N., 180
Noble, J., 81
Nock, M. K., 147, 148, 175, 176
Noel-Levitz, 217
Norcross, J. C., 32, 315
Norman, D., 84
Norman, G. J., 31
Nutter, K. J., 256

O

Ochoa, S. H., 84
O'Dell, J., 291
Odgers, J. G., 247
O'Farrell, T. J., 168
Ogdon, D. P., 298
O'Halloran, M. S., 179
O'Hara, C., 347
Ojeda, L., 242
Okazaki, S., 84
Okocha, A., 224, 242

Olsen, H., 169
Olson, A. K., 306
Olson, D. H., 306
Oltmanns, T. F., 21
Ones, D. S., 210
Oreopoulos, P., 79
Oros, C. J., 310
Orr, J. J., 312
Ortiz, S. O., 84, 87
Ortman, J. M., 92, 337
Osborn, D. S., 37, 237
Osborne, W. L., 223
Osborne L. K., 240, 266
O'Shea, A. J., 261
Osipow, S. H., 228
Oswald, F. L., 31
Overall, J. E., 145
Owens, D., 199
Owens, T., 144

P

Pace, G. M., 175
Pallauf, M., 165
Pandya, J. Z., 219
Paneque, O. M., 216
Paniagua, F. A., 69, 71, 73, 74, 75, 76, 77, 81, 82, 83, 94, 96, 348
Panter, A. T., 117
PAR, Inc., 175, 283, 284, 294
Parker, C. S., 174
Parker, J. D. A., 298
Parsons, F., 14, 222, 246
Patient Health Questionnaire Primary Care Study Group, 145
Patterson, G. A., 152
Patterson, T., 307
Patterson, W. M., 152
Patton, W., 23, 28, 223
Pearson Assessments, 35, 197, 210, 259, 277, 281, 282, 283
Pearson Education, Inc., 86
Pedersen, E. R., 169
Peery, A., 184
Pellegrino, J. W., 341, 342
Pendergrass, L. A., 256
Perels, F., 22
Perkins, Carl D., 55
Perkins, D. N., 10
Perrone, K. M., 227
Perry, Q. A., 262
Pesch, K. M., 252
Peterson, C., 294
Peterson, C. H., 15, 16, 17, 21, 56, 294
Peterson, G. W., 223, 231, 234, 242
Peterson, J. S., 199, 200, 201
Petry, S. S., 313–314, 315, 319
Phipps, S., 79
Photos, V. I., 175
Pichette, E. F., 76
Piedmont, R. L., 293

Piers, E. B., 294
Pietrzak, D., 229
Pincus, A. L., 317
Piotrowski, C., 15, 16, 294, 343
Pittenger, D. J., 285
Plake, B. S., 17, 174
Podar, I., 180
Polanczyk, G. V., 181
Polanski, P. J., 139, 141
Pollak, J., 146
Pommerich, M., 81
Ponterotto, J. G., 138
Pope, M., 258
Pope-Davis, D. B., 231
Powell, A. B., 261
Powell, A. L., 35
Powell, J. E., 166
Power, P. G., 231
Power, T. J., 181
Presti, A. L., 228
Price, G. E., 217
Prieto, L. R., 84
Primoff, E. S., 50, 51
Prochaska, J. O., 32
Proctor, B. D., 337
PRO-ED, 233
Prosek, E. A., 74, 139
Prospero, M., 310
Psychological Assessment Resources, 35, 249
Psychological Corporation, 94
Psychological Publications, 305
Puente, A. E., 15
Pulerwitz, J., 310
Pusateri, C. G., 308
Putnam, F. W., 313

Q

Quenk, N. L., 284
Quinn, E. D., 90
Quinn, M. T., 286

R

Rachman, S., 174
Rafferty, J. E., 296
Rahe, R. H., 72
Raiford, S. E., 201
Ramsay, L. J., 31
Randahl, G. J., 113
Raths, L., 271
Ratts, M. J., 68, 71, 222
Raven, J., 85
Raven, J. C., 85, 86, 95
Rayman, J. R., 80, 227
Reardon, R. C., 231, 234, 242
Rector, N. A., 24
Reeves, T. D., 108, 109

Rehfuss, M. C., 224
Reid, R., 181
Reikowski, D. J., 271
Rengert, C., 20, 346
Renzulli, J. S., 217
Reschly, D. J., 15
Resing, W. C. M., 88, 96
Reynolds, C. R., 92, 174, 181, 313
Reynolds, W. M., 172, 174
Rhodes, K. V., 310
Rhodes, R. L., 87
Rice, K. G., 145
Richardson, J. T. E., 11, 12
Richeson, B. K., 19
Richmond, B. O., 174, 313
Ridley, C. R., 223, 242
Rieke, M. L., 20
Riger, S., 310
Riggs, D. S., 174
Rindskopf, D., 117
Rivera, E. T., 338
Rivera, L., 138
Robbins, S. B., 229, 253
Roberts, B. W., 252
Robertson, G. J., 50, 51, 65, 214
Robin, R. W., 84
Robinson, C. H., 265
Robinson, G., 215, 216
Rochlen, A. B., 61
Rock, D. A., 91
Rodenburg, F. A., 310
Rodgers, B. G., 197
Rodriguez, A. M., 179
Rogers, J. R., 152
Rohde, L. A., 181
Roid, G. H., 192, 201
Roivainen, E., 113
Roizen, N. J., 89
Rokeach, M., 267
Rokkedal, K., 180
Rollnick, S., 169, 170, 184
Romoser, R. C., 305
Rorschach, H., 15, 295
Rose, G. L., 169
Rose, T., 300
Rosenbaum, L., 310
Rosenthal, R., 109, 111, 295
Rosenvinge, J. H., 180
Rosnow, R. L., 111
Ross, H. E., 165
Ross, M. J., 15
Rostad, K., 192, 193
Rothbaum, B. O., 174
Rotter, J. B., 296
Rottinghaus, P. J., 230, 247, 255
Rounds, J., 248, 250, 252
Rovenpor, J. L., 268
Rowland, C. M., 90
Rubinstein, J., 64
Runeson, B., 149
Russell, M., 215, 216, 291
Rutigliano, P., 168

S

Sackett, P. R., 63, 70, 82
Sackett, S. A., 252
Sacks, S., 141
Sagiv, L., 268
Saka, N., 228
Sakakibara, H., 179
Salar, N. V., 179
Salter, S. K., 231
Salum, G. A., 181
Sampson, J. P., Jr., 37, 231, 234, 242
Sanchez, E. I., 81
Sanford, E. E., 267
Sanna, L. J., 6
Sansone, L. A., 175
Sansone, R. A., 175, 176
Santa-Barbara, J., 307
Santos-Iglesias, P., 306
Sapp, M., 63, 65
Sarason, I. G., 150, 174
SASSI Institute, 101, 165, 166
Satcher, D., 156
Sattler, J. M., 92, 200
Saunders, D. E., 231
Saunders, J. B., 162
Saunders, K., 149
Saunders, S. M., 139
Savickas, M. L., 223, 224, 229, 263
Scarpati, S., 91
Schafer, W. D., 17, 18
Schaubhut, N. A., 248
Scheiber, C., 194
Schiel, J., 81
Schinka, J. A., 139
Schlueter, J. E., 34
Schmidt, F. L., 109, 111
Schmidt, J. A., 317
Schmidt, M., 22
Schmitt, N., 31
Schmitz, B., 22
Schneider, P. A., 179
Schneider, P. L., 317
Schoemaker, C., 180
Schrank, F. A., 201
Schuerger, J. M., 291, 292
Schultheiss, D. E. P., 231
Schumacher, P., 165
Schuster, J., 175
Schwartz, R. C., 74
Schwartz, S. H., 263, 267, 268
Scogin, F., 94
Searight, H. R., 15
Searles, J. S., 169
Seashore, H. G., 235
Seaton, M., 209
Segool, N., 62
Segura, L., 166
Segura-Garcia, C., 180
Selzer, M. L., 164, 165
Sequin, E., 10, 188

Severy, L., 256
Sewell, T. E., 294
Shannonhouse, S., 74
Shedler, J., 277
Shellenberger, S., 314
Sher, K. J., 117
Sher, L., 150
Sherin, K. M., 310
Sherman, D. K., 82
Sherman, N. E., 276
Shiang, J., 180
Shkalim, E., 280
Shurts, W. M., 308
Siegel, J. M., 150
Siegel, R. M., 310
Sierra, J. C., 306
Silverman, M. M., 147, 148, 149, 151
Simms, L. J., 280
Simon, S., 271
Simon, T., 10, 11, 188
Simon, T. R., 147
Simpson, T. L., 168
Singh, A. A., 68
Skinner, H. A., 165, 307
Slep, A. M. S., 310
Smith, A., 25
Smith, A. D., 194
Smith, E. E., 10
Smith, J. C., 337
Smith, J. L., 348
Smith, L. H., 217
Smith, P. H., 310
Smith, W. E., 93
Smitherman, T. A., 31
Snow, K. C., 308
Snyder, D. K., 304, 305, 306
Sobell, L. C., 167, 168
Sobell, M. B., 167
Soberay, A. D., 32
Spanier, G. B., 19, 308
Sparrow, E., 181
Sparrow, S. S., 91
Spearman, C., 11, 187–188, 189, 200
Spencer, S. J., 36, 79
Spengler, E. S., 139
Spengler, P. M., 139
Spielberger, C. D., 173, 174, 348
Spitzer, R. L., 145
Stanley, B., 153, 154
Stark, A., 148
Stead, G. B., 231
Steege, M. W., 40
Steele, C. M., 36
Steele, J. R., 79
Steer, R. A., 171, 174
Stehouwer, J. D., 171
Stehouwer, R. S., 171
Stein, S., 174
Steiner, S. A., 90
Steinhauer, P. D., 307
Sternberg, R. J., 84, 188, 190, 200, 218, 307, 308, 319
Stevens, L., 310

Stevens, S. S., 6
Stevenson, C. E., 88, 341
Stice, E., 179
Stoner, G., 184
Storgaard, H., 165
Stout, C. E., 343, 344
Stout, R. L., 168
Straus, M. A., 310
Stricker, G., 295
Strong, E. K., Jr., 14, 247, 248
Stuart, R. B., 306
Su, R., 250
Subich, L. M., 152
Substance Abuse and Mental Health Services Administration, 147, 151, 158, 160, 161, 170, 171
Sue, D. W., 52
Sue, S., 84
Sueyoshi, L. A., 138
Suh, H., 145
Suhr, J., 4
Sullaway, M., 19
Sullivan, E. M., 147
Sullivan, J. G., 74
Summerfeldt, L. S., 298
Super, D. E., 223, 224, 227, 229, 231, 265, 266, 267, 269
Swank, J. M., 347
Swanson, J. L., 17
Sweeney, T. J., 299
Swinson, R. P., 173

T

Taber, B. J., 224, 263
Tandler, N., 21
Tarescavage, A. M., 279
Tassé, M. J., 91
Taylor, C. S., 117
Taylor, K. M., 229
Taylor, R. M., 305
Teglasi, H., 296, 300
Teitelbaum, L., 165
Tellegen, A., 277, 279
Terman, L., 10, 11, 12, 188
Thiessen, D., 310
Thomas, K. W., 318
Thomas, V., 199
Thomlison, B., 319
Thompson, A. S., 227, 229
Thompson, C., 296
Thompson, R. C., 248
Thorndike, E. L., 12, 14
Thorndike, R., 103
Thorpe, L. P., 247
Thurstone, L. L., 14, 188, 189, 200, 247
Thurstone, T., 14
Thyer, B. A., 144
Tidemalm, D., 149
Tokar, D. M., 230
Tonsager, M. E., 113
Toporek, R. J., 231

Torrance, E. P., 200
Tracey, T. J. G., 248, 253, 317
Training Systems, Inc., 271
Trimble, J. E., 84, 158
Trotter, T. V., 17, 18
Tryon, G. S., 8
Trzepacz, P. T., 141
Tucker, I. F., 286
Tunick, R. H., 238
Tunteler, E., 88, 96
Turkheimer, E., 21
Turner, S. M., 174
Tyler, L. E., 8, 248

U

Uehara, M., 179
Uellendahl, G. E., 17
Ulett, G., 295
Unger, R., 143
Updegraff, J., 31
U.S. Census Bureau, 337
U.S. Department of Defense, 235, 236
U.S. Department of Education, 342
U.S. Department of Health and Human
   Services, 312
U.S. Department of Labor, 247
U.S. Department of Labor, Employment and
   Training Administration, 237, 238, 255, 263,
   265, 270
U.S. Department of Veterans Affairs, 17
U.S. Employment Service, 111, 130

V

Vacc, N. A., 165
Vagg, P. R., 173
Valero, D., 223, 224
Valpar, 233
Van Brunt, B., 113, 114, 141
VanDenberg, T. F., 317
vanderStaak, C., 180
van Rooijen, L., 164
Vecchione, M., 268
Veijola, J., 113
Velasquez, R. J., 83
Velkoff, V. A., 92
Ventura, J., 145
Verbraak, M., 180
Verhoeve, M., 262
Vernon, P. E., 14
Vilas, R. C., 286
Villalba, J., 81
Vineland Training School, 10, 11, 92
Vinokur, A., 164
Vocational Research Institute, 233
Vocopher, 225, 243
Vogel, D. L., 61, 247
Vogeltanz-Holm, N., 165
von der Embse, N., 62, 63
Vonk, M. E., 144

Voyer, D., 79
Voyer, S. D., 79

W

Wadsworth, M. E., 19
Wagner, A., 175
Wagner, C. C., 317
Wakefield, J. C., 155, 156, 158
Walley, C. T., 175
Walls, R. G., 84
Walsh, D., 223
Walters, E. E., 24, 170
Wanberg, K. W., 168
Watkins, C. E., Jr., 15, 16, 17, 229
Watley, D. J., 209
Watson, D., 280
Watson, J., 229
Watson, M., 222, 224, 233, 242, 341
Watts, R. E., 16
Waugh, C. K., 219
Webster, B., 17, 18
Webster, J., 310
Wechsler, D., 11, 20–21, 78, 87, 94, 188, 192, 194,
   214
Weiner, I. R., 295
Weisberg, H. F., 133
Weiss, B., 43, 141, 142
Weiss, L. G., 192, 193
Weiss, S. J., 310
Werts, C. E., 209
Wesman, A. G., 235
Westen, D., 277
Western Psychological Services, 56
Wetzlmair, J., 165
White, A. E., 294
White House Office of the Press Secretary, 342
Whiting, G. W., 199
Widiger, T. A., 156, 293
Wiederman, M. W., 175
Wiggins, J. S., 317
Wilhelm, S., 148
Wilkinson, G. S., 21, 214
Willcutt, E. G., 181
Williams, C. L., 279, 282
Williams, J. B. W., 145
Williams, N., 163
Williams, R. L., 199
Willis, W. G., 15
Wilsnack, S. C., 165
Wilson, M. S., 15
WIN Career Solutions, 237
Winefordner, D. W., 247
Winek, J. L., 309
Winer, J. L., 228
Winograd, G., 8
Wodarski, J. S., 184
Wojcik, J. V., 139
Wolf, A., 21
Wolfe, D. A., 310
Wolfe, V. V., 313
Wonderlic, E. F., 198

Wood, C. T., 17, 45, 226, 232, 242, 269
Wood, J. M., 295
Wood, S. M., 199, 200
World Health Organization, 158, 162, 166, 167
Wray, T. B., 168
Wright, A. J., 83, 93, 288, 290, 295, 296, 297, 329
Wright, J., 308
Wundt, W., 9, 10, 188

X

Xu, H., 248

Y

Yamada, A. M., 348
Yell, M. L., 89
Yen, W. M., 117, 132
Yerkes, R., 12
Yesavage, J. A., 172
Yoon, M., 252
Young, D., 172
Young, J. F., 175

Young, R. K., 310
Youngstrom, E. A., 336, 343, 344, 346, 348

Z

Zachar, P., 286
Zachary, R. A., 198
Zafar, B., 79
Zanello, A., 145
Zarbaksh, M., 179
Zhang, L. F., 218
Zhou, C. S., 78
Zhu, J., 192
Zicak, M. C., 306
Zierau, F., 163
Zillig, L. M. P., 277
Zimet, G. D., 151
Zimet, S. G., 151
Zimmerman, M., 145, 172
Zimmerman, W. S., 217
Zimpfer, D., 15
Zoppetti, L., 138, 158
Zytowski, D. G., 14, 257, 260, 271
Zywiak, W. H., 168